Deutsch: Na klar!

FIFTH EDITION

Deutsch: Na klar!

An Introductory German Course

Robert Di Donato
Miami University
Oxford, Ohio

Monica D. Clyde
St. Mary's College of California
Moraga, California

Jacqueline Vansant
University of Michigan, Dearborn

Contributing Writer
Lida Daves-Schneider

Boston   Burr Ridge, IL   Dubuque, IA   Madison, WI   New York   San Francisco   St Louis
Bangkok   Bogotá   Caracas   Kuala   Lupur   Lisbon   London   Madrid   Mexico City
Milan   Montreal   New Delhi   Santiago   Seoul   Singapore   Sydney   Taipei   Toronto

The McGraw·Hill Companies

McGraw Hill | **Higher Education**

DEUTSCH: NA KLAR! AN INTRODUCTORY GERMAN COURSE, FIFTH EDITION

Published by McGraw-Hill, an imprint of The McGraw-Hill Companies, Inc., 1221 Avenue of the Americas, New York, NY 10020. Copyright © 2008 by The McGraw-Hill Companies, Inc. All rights reserved. No part of this publication may be reproduced or distributed in any form or by any means, or stored in a database or retrieval system, without the prior written consent of The McGraw-Hill Companies, Inc., including, but not limited to, in any network or other electronic storage or transmission, or broadcast for distance learning.

Some ancillaries, including electronic and print components, may not be available to customers outside the United States.

This book is printed on acid-free paper.

1 2 3 4 5 6 7 8 9 0 DOW/ DOW 0 9 8 7

ISBN-13: 978-0-07-110157-8
MHID: 0-07-110157-8

ww.mhhe.com

Contents

Preface   xvii

Maps   xxviii

Einführung

Hallo! Guten Tag! Herzlich willkommen!   2

Wie schreibt man das?   3

Hallo!   Mach's gut!   5

Na, wie geht's?   7

So zählt man auf Deutsch.   8

Nützliche Ausdrücke im Sprachkurs   13

Sie können schon etwas Deutsch!   14

Kulturtipps

Forms of Address   3

Inquiring About Someone's Well-Being   8

Country Abbreviations   11

Wo spricht man Deutsch?   16

	Wörter im Kontext	Grammatik im Kontext

KAPITEL 1 **Das bin ich** 20	**THEMA 1** Persönliche Angaben 22
	THEMA 2 Sich erkundigen 25
	THEMA 3 Eigenschaften und Interessen 30
		Nouns, Gender, and Definite Articles 32
		Personal Pronouns 34
		The Verb: Infinitive and Present Tense 36
		    Use of the Present Tense 36
		    The Verb **sein** 40
		Word Order in Sentences 40
		Asking Questions 41
		    Word Questions 41
		    Yes/No Questions 42

KAPITEL 2 **Wie ich wohne** 50	**THEMA 1** Auf Wohnungssuche 52
	THEMA 2 Auf Möbelsuche im Kaufhaus 56
	THEMA 3 Was wir gern machen 58
		The Plural of Nouns 62
		The Nominative and Accusative Cases 64
		    The Definite Article: Nominative and Accusative 65
		    Weak Masculine Nouns 65
		    The **der**-Words **dieser** and **welcher** 67
		    The Indefinite Article: Nominative and Accusative 68
		    Nominative and Accusative Interrogative Pronouns 69
		The Verb **haben** 70
		Negation with **nicht** and the Negative Article **kein** 71
		Verbs with Stem-Vowel Changes 73
		Demonstrative Pronouns 74

KAPITEL 3 **Familie und Freunde** 82	**THEMA 1** Ein Familienstammbaum 84 **THEMA 2** Der Kalender: Die Wochentage und die Monate 88 **THEMA 3** Feste und Feiertage 89	Possessive Adjectives 93 Personal Pronouns in the Accusative Case 98 Prepositions with the Accusative Case 100 The Irregular Verbs **werden** and **wissen** 102 Using the Verbs **wissen** and **kennen** 103

Erstes Zwischenspiel
Persönlichkeiten: Drei Kurzbiographien: 110

Sprachtipps	Kulturtipps	Sprache im Kontext

Sprachtipps	Kulturtipps	Sprache im Kontext

Stating One's Height 23
The Particle **denn** 26
Ways to say **to study** 27
Saying You Like Doing
   Something 32
Using Infinitives as Nouns 38
The Question Word **woher** 46
	The **Einwohnermeldeamt** 24
	Foreigners in Germany 47
		Videoclips 45
		Lesen 45
		   „Dialog" von Nasrin
		     Siege 46
		Zu guter Letzt 47

Using **einen** with Direct
   Objects 53
Describing Things: Attributive
   Adjectives and Predicate
   Adjectives 55
Using **den** with Direct
   Objects 57
Recognizing Stem-Changing
   Verbs 58
Saying What You Like
   to Do: **gern** + Verb 59
Turning Down an Invitation 61
Gender-inclusive Nouns 63
The Prefix **un-** on Adjectives 66
	German Apartments 52
	The Euro 54
		Videoclips 75
		Lesen 76
		   „So wohne ich" 77
		Zu guter Letzt 78

Talking about Relationships with
   Possessive **-s** or **von** 85
Talking about Relatives Using
   Stief-, Halb-, or **Ur-** 86
Saying When Things Take Place:
   am and **im** 88
Using Ordinal Numbers 91
Stating Reasons: **nämlich** 92
	German Holidays and
	   Celebrations 91
	Celebrating Milestone
	   Birthdays 107
		Videoclips 105
		Lesen 105
		   „Wie feierst du deinen
		     großen Tag?" 106
		Zu guter Letzt 107

	Wörter im Kontext	Grammatik im Kontext

KAPITEL 4 **Mein Tag** 112	**THEMA 1** Die Uhrzeit 114 **THEMA 2** Pläne machen 118 **THEMA 3** Kino, Musik und Theater 121	Separable-Prefix Verbs 124 The Sentence Bracket 125 Modal Auxiliary Verbs 128 The Present Tense of Modals 129 The Imperative 133 Formal Imperative 134 Particles and **bitte** with the Imperative 134 Informal Imperative 135
KAPITEL 5 **Einkaufen** 144	**THEMA 1** Kleidungsstücke 146 **THEMA 2** Beim Einkaufen im Kaufhaus 149 **THEMA 3** Lebensmittel 152	The Dative Case 157 Personal Pronouns in the Dative 158 Articles and Possessive Adjectives in the Dative 160 The Dative Case for Indirect Objects 160 Position of Dative and Accusative Objects 161 Verbs with a Dative Object Only 162 Prepositions with the Dative Case 164 Interrogative Pronouns **wo,** **wohin,** and **woher** 166
KAPITEL 6 **Wir gehen aus** 174	**THEMA 1** Lokale 176 **THEMA 2** Die Speisekarte, bitte! 180 **THEMA 3** Im Restaurant 184	Two-Way Prepositions 186 Describing Location 189 Describing Placement 191 Expressing Time with Prepositions 193 Expressing Events in the Past 194 The Simple Past Tense of **sein** and **haben** 194 The Simple Past Tense of Modals 196
Zweites Zwischenspiel Begegnung mit der Kunst der Gegenwart; Konkrete Poesie 204		

Sprachtipps	Kulturtipps	Sprache im Kontext

Stating Official Time: The
Twenty-Four-Hour Clock 115
Saying What Time Something
Takes Place: **Um wie
viel Uhr?** 116
Saying *this morning, tomorrow,*
etc. 119
Saying When You Do Something
Regularly 119
Saying Where You're Going:
in 122
Making Generalizations: The
Indefinite Pronoun **man** 131

Die deutschen Theater 121

Videoclips 137
Lesen 138
„Immer das Gleiche" von
Christine Wuttke 139
Zu guter Letzt 140

Expressing What There Is:
es gibt 148
Giving Opinions about Clothing:
gefallen, passen, and
stehen 151
Dative Case + **zu** with
Adjectives 151
Using the Metric System 153
Putting Statements in Order
Using Connectors 154

German Sizes for Clothing 150
Geschäfte und Läden 153

Videoclips 167
Lesen 168
„Im Hutladen" von Karl
Valentin 169
Zu guter Letzt 170

Making Suggestions: **Lass uns
doch …** 178
Sitting Down: **sich setzen** 191
Saying What's Been Stated in
Print: **stehen** 192

Eating and Drinking
Establishments 177
Regional Culinary
Specialties 182
Calling the Server and Sharing
Tables 183
Paying the Bill 185

Videoclips 198
Lesen 198
„Die Soße" von Ekkehard
Müller 199
Zu guter Letzt 201

	Wörter im Kontext	Grammatik im Kontext

KAPITEL 7
Freizeit und
Sport   206
	THEMA 1
	Sportarten 208
	THEMA 2
	Hobbys und andere
	Vergnügungen 210
	THEMA 3
	Jahreszeiten und Wetter 212
		Connecting Ideas: Coordinating
		   Conjunctions 216
		     Expressing a Contrast: **aber**
		       vs. **sondern** 216
		Expressing Events in the Past:
		   The Present Perfect Tense 217
		     Weak Verbs 218
		     Strong Verbs 220
		     The Use of **haben** or **sein** as
		       Auxiliary 221
		     Mixed Verbs 223
		     Past Participles of Verbs with
		       Prefixes 223
		Expressing Comparisons: The
		   Comparative 225
		     Expressing Equality 227

KAPITEL 8
Wie man fit und
gesund bleibt   234
	THEMA 1
	Fit und gesund 236
	THEMA 2
	Der menschliche Körper 238
	THEMA 3
	Morgenroutine 242
		Connecting Sentences:
		   Subordinating
		   Conjunctions 244
		     Indirect Questions 245
		Reflexive Pronouns and
		   Verbs 248
		     Verbs with Accusative
		       Reflexive Pronouns 248
		     Verbs with Reflexive
		       Pronouns in the
		       Accusative or Dative 250
		     Expressing Reciprocity 252

KAPITEL 9
In der Stadt   260
	THEMA 1
	Unterkunft online buchen 262
	THEMA 2
	Im Hotel 265
	THEMA 3
	Ringsum die Stadt 267
		The Genitive Case 271
		   Proper Names in the
		     Genitive 271
		   Prepositions with the
		     Genitive 273
		Attributive Adjectives 274
		   Adjectives after a Definite
		     Article 275
		   Adjectives after an Indefinite
		     Article 278
		   Adjectives without a
		     Preceding Article 279
		   Adjectives Referring to Cities
		     and Regions 282

Drittes Zwischenspiel
Die Entwicklung der
Stadt   290

Sprachtipps	Kulturtipps	Sprache im Kontext
Saying How Often You Do Something 210	Temperature Conversion 215 Sport, Hobbys und Vereine 222	Videoclips 229 Lesen 229 „Vergnügungen" von Bertolt Brecht 231 Zu guter Letzt 231
Expressing How You're Feeling 241	German Health Spas 236 Arztbesuche 240 **Apotheken** vs. **Drogerien** 246 Der deutsche Frühstückstisch 254	Videoclips 252 Lesen 253 „Sage mir, was du isst ..." von Monika Hillemacher 255 Zu guter Letzt 257
Interpreting Abbreviations Concerning Lodging 263 Using Two or More Attributive Adjectives 275 Using Adjectives Ending in **-a** 280	Tourist i (*for information*) 264 Wittenberg 270	Videoclips 283 Lesen 283 „Die Gitarre des Herrn Hatunoglu" von Heinrich Hannover 284 Zu guter Letzt 287

Wörter im Kontext	Grammatik im Kontext

KAPITEL 10
Auf Reisen   292

THEMA 1
Ich möchte verreisen 294
THEMA 2
Eine Wandertour 297
THEMA 3
Eine Fahrkarte, bitte! 299

Expressing Comparisons: The
   Superlative 301
Attributive Adjectives in the
   Comparative 303
Attributive Adjectives in the
   Superlative 305
Adjectival Nouns 306
Narrating Events in the Past:
   The Simple Past Tense 308
      Weak Verbs 308
      Strong Verbs 310
      Mixed Verbs 311
The Conjunction **als** 311
The Past Perfect Tense 313

KAPITEL 11
Der Start in die Zukunft   322

THEMA 1
Meine Interessen, Wünsche und
Erwartungen 324
THEMA 2
Berufe 326
THEMA 3
Stellenangebote und
Bewerbungen 328

Future Tense 333
   Expressing Probability 335
Describing People or Things:
   Relative Clauses 335
     The Relative Pronoun 336
The Interrogative Pronoun **was
   für (ein)** 339
Negating Sentences 341
   Summary: The Position of
     nicht 341
   Negation: **noch nicht / noch
     kein(e); nicht
     mehr / kein(e) ... mehr** 341

Sprachtipps	Kulturtipps	Sprache im Kontext
Saying How Long Something Lasts: Compound Adjectives with **-stündig, -tägig, -wöchig,** and **-monatig** 297	Deutsche Urlaubszeit 296 Wissenswertes über Deutschland 305	Videoclips 313 Lesen 314 „The American Dream" von Bernd Maresch 316 Zu guter Letzt 319
	Das deutsche Schulsystem 332 Zivildienst 347	Videoclips 342 Lesen 343 „Karriere beim Film" 344 Zu guter Letzt 347

	Wörter im Kontext	Grammatik im Kontext

KAPITEL 12
Haus und Haushalt 350

THEMA 1
Finanzen der Studenten 352
THEMA 2
Unsere eigenen vier Wände 356
THEMA 3
Unser Zuhause 358

Verbs with Fixed
  Prepositions 361
    Prepositional Objects:
      da-Compounds 362
    Asking Questions:
      wo-Compounds 364
The Subjunctive 364
    Expressing Requests
      Politely 365
    Forms of the Present
      Subjunctive II 365
    The Use of **würde** with an
      Infinitive 367
    Expressing Wishes and
      Hypothetical
      Situations 368
    Talking about Contrary-
      to-Fact Conditions 370
The Past Subjunctive II 372

Viertes Zwischenspiel
Deutsche Einwanderung
nach Nordamerika 380

KAPITEL 13
Medien und Technik 382

THEMA 1
Medien 384
THEMA 2
Leben mit Technik 390

Infinitive Clauses with **zu** 393
The Verbs **brauchen** and
  scheinen 395
Infinitive Clauses with **um ... zu**
  and **ohne ... zu** 395
Indirect Discourse 397
    Subjunctive I: Present
      Tense 398
    Subjunctive I: Past Tense 400

KAPITEL 14
Die öffentliche Meinung 408

THEMA 1
Globale Probleme 410
THEMA 2
Umwelt 414

The Passive Voice 417
    Formation of the Passive
      Voice 417
    Expressing the Agent 419
    Expressing a General
      Activity 421
    The Passive with Modal
      Verbs 422
    Use of **man** as an Alternative
      to the Passive 424
The Present Participle 424

Sprachtipps	Kulturtipps	Sprache im Kontext

Sprachtipps	Kulturtipps	Sprache im Kontext
	Der Schweizer Franken 352	Videoclips 374
	Wie finanziert man das Studium? 353	Lesen 375
	Ladenschlussgesetz 368	„Fahrkarte bitte" von Helga M. Novak 376
		Zu guter Letzt 377
	Fernsehprogramme 388	Videoclips 402
		Lesen 402
		„Gute Freunde im Netz" von Kerstin Kohlenberg 404
		Zu guter Letzt 406
	Tempogrenzen auf der Autobahn 415	Videoclips 425
	Abfall und Giftstoffe 415	Lesen 426
	Umweltbewusstsein 422	„Was in der Zeitung steht" von Reinhard Mai 426
		Zu guter Letzt 429

Übergang: Gestern und heute

Kleine Chronik deutscher Geschichte 433

Beiträge zur deutschen Geschichte 438
„Wir leben im Verborgenen" von Ceja Stojka 439
„Briefe an Herbert Hoover" 441

Kulturtipps
Die Kaiser-Wilhelm-Gedächtniskirche 435
Berlin: Hauptstadt im Wandel 438
Frauen im Dritten Reich 439
Der Weg nach Europa 443

Zu guter Letzt 443

Videoclips 444

Appendix A   Hin und her: Part 2 A-1

Appendix B   Studienfächer A-12

Appendix C   Grammar Tables A-13
1. Personal Pronouns A-13
2. Definite Articles A-13
3. Indefinite Articles and the Negative Article **kein** A-13
4. Relative and Demonstrative Pronouns A-14
5. Principal Parts of Strong and Mixed Verbs A-14
6. Conjugation of Verbs A-16

Appendix D   Alternate Spelling and Capitalization A-20

Vocabularies A-21
German-English Vocabulary A-21
English-German Vocabulary A-57

Index A-71

Preface

Welcome to the Fifth Edition of *Deutsch: Na klar!* Those familiar with this textbook know that *Deutsch: Na klar!* offers a versatile, comprehensive, and colorful program for introductory German courses. The Fifth Edition provides an exciting, innovative package designed to suit a wide variety of approaches, methodologies, and classrooms, while still preserving many standard pedagogical features that instructors have come to trust since the publication of the first edition. Among the trusted and proven features of *Deutsch: Na klar!*, you will recognize the following:

- a rich array of authentic visual and textual materials with accompanying activities and exercises
- succinct grammar explanations
- a commitment to the balanced development of both receptive skills (listening and reading) and productive skills (speaking and writing)
- abundant communicative activities, as well as many form-focused activities and exercises
- the promotion of meaningful acquisition of vocabulary and structures with considerable regard to accuracy

As noted above, one of the trusted hallmarks of *Deutsch: Na klar!* is its unique approach to the use of authentic materials. Authentic materials motivate and interest students and allow them to see the immediate application of their newly acquired skills in authentic contexts. Thus, in *Deutsch: Na klar!*, authentic materials are used to illustrate vocabulary in context, communicative functions of grammatical structures, and cultural points. Moreover, realia-based activities are extremely effective in helping students develop receptive skills.

Vocabulary and grammar are presented in a functional framework so that students begin to associate forms with functions. Vocabulary is introduced in context through the use of visuals, dialogues, short narratives, or "built-in" activities to stimulate meaningful language. **Neue Wörter** boxes help students verify the meaning of words after they have encountered them in an initial presentation. Wherever useful, grammatical structures are contrasted with parallel structures in English. Vocabulary and grammar activities progress from controlled and form-focused to open-ended and interactive, and from receptive to productive.

A Textbook Audio Program is tied to several activities in every chapter. Indicated in the student text with a headphone icon, some of these listening comprehension activities are designed for global comprehension, while others have been designed to give students practice in noting specific details. In a similar fashion, students learn to skim for general information and scan for specific details when reading. In both listening and reading, students are encouraged to use background knowledge and context to aid comprehension.

The Fifth Edition integrates an enhanced interview-based video **(Videoclips)** and computer-based realia into the program. Taped on location in Berlin, these interviews with native speakers of German provide authentic input directly related to the chapter theme and functions. New footage from Bonn and Cologne has been added as visual support for the interviewees' statements. The comprehensible yet natural speech of the interviews, combined with the new images, provides students with a window into the lives and habits of today's German citizens, thus promoting both the development of communicative skills and cultural awareness. The Fifth Edition video also contains cultural snippets that complement and elaborate on the topics of the interviews.

The five Cs of the National Standards—Communication, Connections, Culture, Comparisons, and Communities—developed by ACTFL in collaboration with AATG, AATF, and AATSP (*Standards for Foreign Language Learning: Preparing for the 21st Century*) permeate the activities, exercises, readings, cultural and language tips, and video of *Deutsch: Na klar!* Each chapter provides opportunities for students to communicate in German in real-life situations for real purposes. Authentic materials and the new video, as well as the exercises based on them, stimulate students' thinking about their own language and culture in order to draw cross-cultural comparisons and connect their study of German language and culture with other disciplines. And finally, opportunities for students to reach out to German-speaking communities locally and globally are provided through Internet activities.

In summary, through its authentic materials, cultural features, readings, listening passages, activities, and innovative technology, *Deutsch: Na klar!* teaches skills that will help students to communicate successfully in the German-speaking world.

Organization of the Text

Deutsch: Na klar! consists of a preliminary chapter **(Einführung)**, fourteen regular chapters, and a closing chapter **(Übergang)**. Each of the fourteen regular chapters is developed around a major theme and has the following organization:

- Alles klar?
- Wörter im Kontext
  Themen 1, 2, (3)
- Grammatik im Kontext
- Sprache im Kontext
  Videoclips
  Lesen
  Zu guter Letzt
- Wortschatz
- Das kann ich nun!

Cultural collages **(Zwischenspiele)**, containing visuals and activities, appear after **Kapitel 3, 6, 9,** and **12** and give students the opportunity to review, consolidate, and apply what they have learned in previous chapters to cultural topics of German-speaking countries in new contexts.

A Guided Tour through Deutsch: Na klar!

Alles klar?

The chapter opener introduces students to the theme of the chapter through a guided two-part activity that involves a visual or an authentic text and a thematically related, global listening comprehension passage.

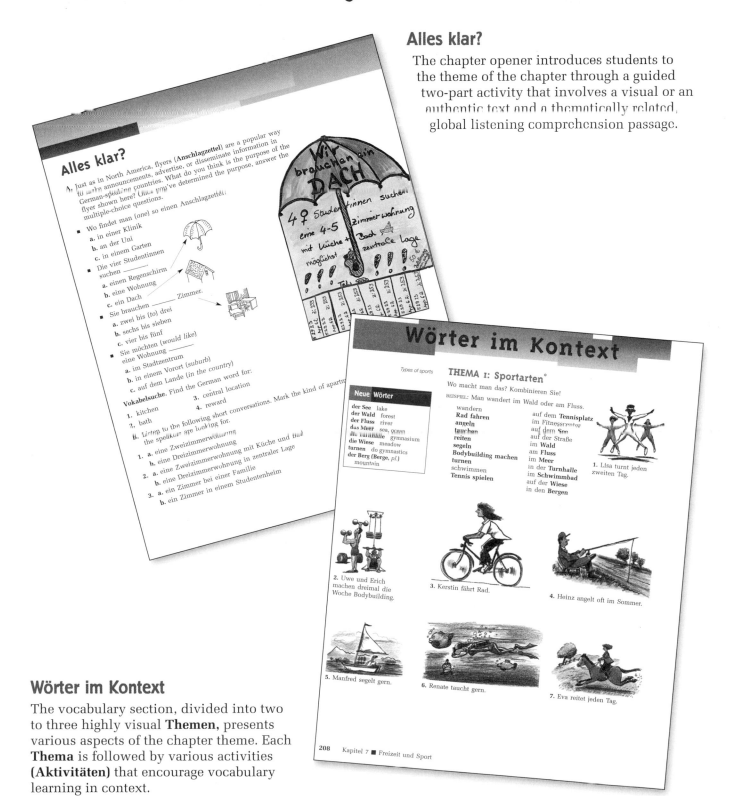

Alles klar?

A. Just as in North America, flyers (**Anschlagzettel**) are a popular way to make announcements, advertise, or disseminate information in German-speaking countries. What do you think is the purpose of the flyer shown here? Once you've determined the purpose, answer the multiple-choice questions.

- Wo findet man (*one*) so einen Anschlagzettel?
  - **a.** in einer Klinik
  - **b.** an der Uni
  - **c.** in einem Garten
- Die vier Studentinnen suchen
  - **a.** einen Regenschirm
  - **b.** eine Wohnung
  - **c.** ein Dach
- Sie brauchen _____ Zimmer.
  - **a.** zwei bis (*to*) drei
  - **b.** sechs bis sieben
  - **c.** vier bis fünf
- Sie möchten (*would like*) eine Wohnung
  - **a.** im Stadtzentrum
  - **b.** in einem Vorort (*suburb*)
  - **c.** auf dem Lande (*in the country*)

Vokabelsuche. Find the German word for:

1. kitchen
2. bath
3. central location
4. reward

B. Listen to the following short conversations. Mark the kind of apartment the speakers are looking for.

1. **a.** eine Zweizimmerwohnung
   b. eine Dreizimmerwohnung mit Küche und Bad
2. **a.** eine Zweizimmerwohnung in zentraler Lage
   b. eine Dreizimmerwohnung
3. **a.** ein Zimmer bei einer Familie
   b. ein Zimmer in einem Studentenheim

Wörter im Kontext

Types of sports

THEMA 1: Sportarten°

Wo macht man das? Kombinieren Sie!

BEISPIEL: Man wandert im Wald oder am Fluss.

Neue Wörter

der See	lake
der Wald	forest
der Fluss	river
das Meer	sea, ocean
die Turnhalle	gymnasium
die Wiese	meadow
turnen	do gymnastics
der Berg (Berge, *pl.*)	mountain

wandern
Rad fahren
angeln
tauchen
reiten
segeln
Bodybuilding machen
turnen
schwimmen
Tennis spielen

auf dem **Tennisplatz**
im **Fitnesscenter**
auf dem **See**
auf der **Straße**
im **Wald**
am **Fluss**
im **Meer**
in der **Turnhalle**
im **Schwimmbad**
auf der **Wiese**
in den **Bergen**

1. Lisa turnt jeden zweiten Tag.
2. Uwe und Erich machen dreimal die Woche Bodybuilding.
3. Kerstin fährt Rad.
4. Heinz angelt oft im Sommer.
5. Manfred segelt gern.
6. Renate taucht gern.
7. Eva reitet jeden Tag.

Wörter im Kontext

The vocabulary section, divided into two to three highly visual **Themen,** presents various aspects of the chapter theme. Each **Thema** is followed by various activities (**Aktivitäten**) that encourage vocabulary learning in context.

Grammatik im Kontext

Grammar is presented in succinct explanations with abundant charts and examples and, whenever possible, via authentic materials. Some grammar explanations expand on points that are previewed in **Sprachtipps**.

Verben mit trennbaren Präfixen

Separable-Prefix Verbs°

You are already familiar with sentences such as the following:

Susanne und Peter **kommen**
per Fahrrad **vorbei**.
Ich gehe heute tanzen.
Kommst du **mit**?

Susanne and Peter **are coming**
by on their bikes.
I am going dancing today. Will
you **come along**?

German, like English, has many two-part verbs that consist of a verb and a short complement that affects the meaning of the main verb. Examples of such two-part verbs in English are to come by, to come along, to call up, to get up.

Wüstenrot-Rendite°-Programm mit 470 Euro pro anno.

Jede Million fängt klein an.°

RENDITE PROGRAMM

Ich rufe an....

°yield on investment
²fängt ... an: begins
³simple

Sprache im Kontext

This culminating four-skills section is divided into three parts: **Videoclips,** featuring interviews with German speakers on topics presented in each chapter and reflecting the vocabulary and grammar presented; **Lesen,** an authentic reading passage with pre- and post-reading activities; and **Zu guter Letzt,** interactive, task-oriented culminating activities that provide open-ended oral and written practice on the chapter theme.

Videoclips

A. Watch the interviews with Sara and Ali as they talk about what they are studying, their hobbies, and how their friends would describe them. Write **S** if the phrase or word applies to **Sara** or **A** if it applies to **Ali.**

_____ Medienwissenschaft
_____ Mathematik
_____ Joggen
_____ Gitarre spielen
_____ Zeichnen
_____ Tanzen
_____ Fahrrad fahren

_____ Schwimmen
_____ spontan
_____ zurückhaltend (reserved)
_____ lustig
_____ fröhlich
_____ sehr aktiv

B. Who does what? Watch the interviews and match each person with a profession or job.

1. _____ Peter
2. _____ Oliver
3. _____ Alex
4. _____ Jasmin
5. _____ Frau Simon

a. ist Grafikdesigner
b. ist Pilot
c. ist Bankkauffrau
d. arbeitet bei KDW im Silbershop
e. ist Web-Designer

C. Watch the interviews again and jot down notes about things you have in common with the interviewees. If you have anything in common, then write a few sentences that describe the commonalities. Follow the model.

BEISPIEL: Ali studiert Mathematik. Ich studiere auch Mathematik. Saras Hobby ist Tanzen. Mein Hobby ist auch Tanzen ...

The Deutsch: Na klar! vocabulary system

Vocabulary is presented by means of authentic materials, illustrations, descriptive texts, dialogues, and built-in activities. Students must first "discover" the meaning of the new vocabulary, which is highlighted in the presentation, through contextual guessing. Less transparent new vocabulary is then reflected in the **Neue Wörter** lists, which students should use to verify their contextual guessing.

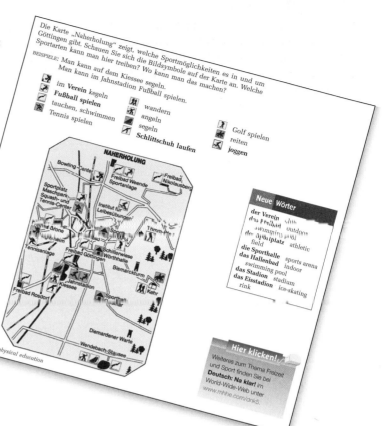

Analyse

Before doing **Aktivitäten** or **Übungen**, students develop receptive skills by examining authentic texts for specific vocabulary or grammatical structures.

Aktivitäten und Übungen

A broad range of activities and exercises allows for structured communicative practice of vocabulary and grammatical structures. Whereas some activities and exercises are tied to the audio program and provide receptive vocabulary and grammar practice, others develop productive skills.

Übung 7   Neu in Göttingen

You will now hear a conversation between Stefan and Birgit. As you listen, check off what Stefan already has and what he still needs for his new apartment. Not all items are mentioned; leave them blank.

	DAS HAT STEFAN	DAS BRAUCHT STEFAN
1. einen DVD-Spieler	☐	☐
2. eine Zimmerpflanze	☐	☐
3. eine Uhr		
4. einen Couchtisch	☐	☐
5. einen Computer	☐	☐
6. einen Schreibtisch	☐	☐
7. ein Bücherregal	☐	☐
8. eine Kaffeemaschine	☐	☐
9. einen Schlafsack (sleeping bag)	☐	☐
10. ein Bett	☐	☐
11. einen Sessel	☐	☐

Übung 8   Was sehen Sie?

Das ist eine typische Studentenbude.

Da ist ____.

Das Zimmer hat ____.

Hier klicken!

At relevant locations throughout the text, this feature directs students to the **Deutsch: Na klar!** Online Learning Center (www. mhhe.com/dnk5), which contains additional vocabulary, grammar, and cultural activities.

Hier klicken!

You'll find more about housing in German-speaking countries in **Deutsch: Na klar!** on the World Wide Web at www.mhhe.com/dnk5.

Icons

Icons identify pair or small-group activities, video activities, writing activities, information gap, listening comprehension, and activities requiring an extra sheet of paper.

Sprachtipp

Expressions and "grammar for communication" are provided to assist students in carrying out a given activity. These grammar points may be elaborated on in the same or a later chapter.

SPRACHTIPP

Das ist **ein** Balkon. Das ist **eine** Küche. Das ist **ein** Badezimmer.

When a masculine noun is used as a direct object, **ein** changes to **einen**; however, feminine **eine** and neuter **ein** do not change:

Mein Haus hat **einen** Balkon, **eine** Küche und **ein** Badezimmer.

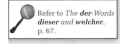
Refer to *The der-Words dieser* and *welcher*, p. 67.

Closer Look

At relevant locations throughout the **Wörter im Kontext** section, a magnifying glass alerts students where to find supporting grammar explanations that will enable them to complete the communicative activities with substantial attention to structural accuracy.

Kulturtipp

Often enhanced with photos or other visuals, this feature expands on the cultural information presented in the **Themen,** activities and exercises, and readings.

KULTURTIPP

In ihrer Freizeit treiben viele Deutsche gern Sport; besonders beliebt sind Fußball, Rad fahren, Schwimmen und Tennis. Andere bleiben lieber zu Hause und machen Gartenarbeit, pflegen (*take care of*) ihren Wagen, spielen mit ihren Haustieren, sammeln Briefmarken, lesen oder sehen fern. Viele Deutsche haben ein Hobby, das sie in einem Verein ausüben. In vielen Städten gibt es Gesangs- und Heimatvereine sowie (*as well as*) Vereine für Schützen (*marksmen*), Amateurfunker (*ham radio operators*) und Kegler.

Radfahren auf der Landstraße

Lesen

Zum Thema

A. Wie gesund essen Sie? Was betrifft Sie? Kreuzen Sie an.

1. Gesund essen ist mir wichtig. ☐
2. Ich esse regelmäßig drei Mahlzeiten am Tag. ☐
3. Ich habe nie Zeit zum Frühstücken. ☐
4. Ich habe oft keine Zeit zum Essen oder esse sehr schnell. ☐
5. Ich esse oft vor dem Fernseher. ☐
6. Ich esse gern und oft Fastfood. ☐
7. Ich esse möglichst viele Bioprodukte. ☐
8. Ich bin Vegetarier/Vegetarierin. ☐
9. Ich möchte abnehmen (*lose weight*). ☐
10. Ich möchte zunehmen (*gain weight*) ☐
11. Ich esse sehr gesund. ☐

Zum Thema

This section contains activities that prepare students to read the text. Students use their background knowledge or brainstorm about the topic to predict what will happen in the reading passage.

Auf den ersten Blick

In this activity, students skim the reading to get the gist or scan it for specific pieces of information in order to achieve a global understanding.

Auf den ersten Blick

A. Skim over the short texts below. Who are the respondents? What are their ages? What is the general topic?

B. Now scan the texts more closely, looking for words of the following types.
- words relating to family
- words related to places where a celebration is held
- compound nouns: locate five compound nouns in the texts, and determine their components and their English equivalents

C. The two most frequently used words in the texts are the verb **feiern** and the noun **Geburtstag**. How do they relate to the expression "deinen großen Tag" in the title? What is implied?

Zum Text

Here students read intensively, focusing on content, vocabulary, structures, and finally, implications and interpretation.

Zu guter Letzt

A new task-based culminating project toward the end of each chapter integrates skills and competencies learned in multimodal group or class activities.

Das kann ich nun!

Students check that they've learned the basic material presented by completing a short series of concise exercises at the close of each chapter.

WHAT'S NEW IN THE FIFTH EDITION?

Retaining the aspects that reviewers have praised and that have set *Deutsch: Na klar!* apart from other texts, while at the same time adding new features to keep it lively, contemporary, and up to date, has been our major goal during the revision process. Instructors have given us feedback on the previous edition and we have responded. We have revised many of the dialogues, optimized the grammar explanations for more balance across chapters, added more features to the vocabulary program, included new readings, and improved the video program. Major features appear in the visual *Guided Tour Through Deutsch: Na klar!*

The Fifth Edition has been improved in numerous ways:

- Expanded and improved **Neue Wörter** boxes make it easier for students to learn and use key chapter vocabulary.
- New and updated authentic materials keep the textbook current and interesting for students.
- New and exciting authentic readings in chapters 3, 6, 8, 10, 11, and 13 provide students with high-interest input that reinforces chapter themes and vocabulary.
- Revised and rebalanced grammar presentations streamline and clarify the grammatical points.
- New cross-references in the vocabulary sections provide quick links between communicative activities and supporting grammar explanations.
- A new task-based culminating activity in each chapter, called **Zu guter Letzt,** integrates skills and competencies learned in multimodal group or class projects.
- A new end-of-chapter skill-check called **Das kann ich nun!** uses a series of concise exercises to help students verify that they've learned the basic material in the chapter.
- Video interviews with native speakers have been enhanced with the addition of footage that visually supports the interviewees' statements.
- The **Übergang** chapter has been revised and updated to reflect recent developments in Germany and Europe.

SUPPLEMENTS

The following components of *Deutsch: Na klar!* Fifth Edition are designed to complement your instruction and to enhance your students' learning experience. Please contact your local McGraw-Hill sales representative for details concerning policies, prices, and availability of the supplementary materials, as some restrictions may apply. Available to students and instructors:

- The *Student Text* includes a grammar appendix and German-English/English-German end vocabularies.
- The *Textbook Audio Program* contains material tied to the listening activities in the main text. This audio material is available free of charge at the *Deutsch: Na klar!* Online Learning Center (www.mhhe.com/dnk5).
- The *Workbook,* by Jeanine Briggs, includes additional form-focused vocabulary and grammar exercises as well as abundant guided writing practice.
- The Quia™ online *Workbook* offers all the content of the print *Workbook* plus immediate feedback and a robust instructor gradebook feature.
- The *Laboratory Manual,* by Lida Daves Schneider and Michael Büsges, contains engaging listening comprehension activities and pronunciation practice. Available on audio CD and free of charge at the *Online Learning Center* (www.mhhe.com/dnk5), the *Laboratory Audio Program* includes an audioscript for instructors.
- The Quia™ online *Laboratory Manual* offers all the content of the print *Laboratory Manual,* integrated audio, plus immediate feedback and a robust instructor gradebook feature.
- New to the Fifth Edition of *Deutsch: Na klar!* is the online *ActivityPak.* The *ActivityPak* replaces the previous editions' *Interactive CD-ROM* and offers students a variety of fun and engaging interactive activities and media. The online *ActivityPak* includes Flash™-based activities that provide interactive review and practice of vocabulary and grammar, as well as the complete video program. This unified language learning experience is practical and convenient and eliminates the need for multiple components. The online *ActivityPak* is contained within and accessed via the *Deutsch: Na klar! Online Learning Center.* Please note that the *ActivityPak* content is a saleable supplement and is not provided free of charge.
- The *Deutsch: Na klar! Online Learning Center* (www.mhhe.com/dnk5) provides a variety of vocabulary and grammar self-quizzes as well as cultural activities and the complete *Laboratory Audio Program.* These quizzes, activities and the *Laboratory Audio Program* are available to students free of charge.

Available to instructors only:

- The *Annotated Instructor's Edition* of the main text includes marginal notes, answers, and an audioscript to the in-text listening comprehension activities.

- The combined *Instructor's Manual and Testing Program* provides theoretical background, practical guidance, and ideas for using **Deutsch: Na Klar!** It also contains tests and exams written by Jennifer Redmann (Kalamazoo College) and Pennylyn Dykstra-Pruim (Calvin College).

- The *Audioscript* found on the Online Learning Center, contains the material found on the *Laboratory Audio Program*.

- The *Video to accompany* **Deutsch: Na Klar!** contains a wide variety of interviews with native speakers of German, newly enhanced with images that support the content and make it more accessible to students.

ACKNOWLEDGMENTS

The publisher would like to thank these instructors who participated in surveys and reviews that were indispensable in the development of **Deutsch: Na klar!** Fifth Edition. The appearance of their names does not necessarily constitute their endorsement of the text or its methodology.

Scott Baker, University of Missouri, Kansas City
John Blair, University of West Georgia
Madelyn Burchill, Concordia College, Moorhead
Troy Byler, Indiana University, Bloomington
Muriel Cormican, University of West Georgia
Katy Fraser, Indiana University, Bloomington
Steve Grollman, Concordia College, Moorhead
Derek Hillard, Kansas State University
Ruth Kath, Luther College
Jurgen Koppensteiner, University of Northern Iowa
Douglas Lightfoot, University of Alabama, Tuscaloosa
Denise Meuser, Northwestern University
Susanne Rott, University of Illinois, Chicago
Frangina Spandau, Santa Barbara City College
Rudi Strahl, College of Dupage
Cynthia Trocchio, Kent State University, Kent
Meike Wernick-Heinrichs, Capilano College

We also wish to thank the instructors who participated in our Introductory German survey. Their input on trends in German language learning today significantly enriched this edition, and we are very grateful.

Zsuzsanna I. Abrams, University of Texas, Austin
Thomas Hendrik Aulbach, University of Florida
Ingetraut R. Baird, Anderson University
Karen Bell, Delta State University
Peter Böhm, Canisius College
Nancy Marie Borosch, Butler University
Kirsten M. Christensen, Pacific Lutheran University

Siegfried Christoph, University of Wisconsin, Parkside
T. Craig Christy, University of North Alabama
Irene B. Compton, Xavier University
Matthew Michael Conner, Texas State University
Michael Davidson-Schmich, University of Miami
Sharon Marie DiFino, University of Florida, Gainesville
Peter Ecke, University of Arizona
Anke Finger, University of Connecticut
Lidia Frazier, American River College
Helen Frink, Keene State College
Gordon Gamlin, Loyola Marymount University
Valentina Glajar, Texas State University, San Marcos
Lawrence F. Glatz, Metropolitan State College of Denver
Amelia J. Harris, The University of Virginia's College at Wise
Ursula Horstmann-Nash, Southern Oregon University
Constance E. Hubbard, Black Hills State University
Dorothea Kaufmann, Oberlin College
Jennifer Kelley-Thierman, University of Cincinnati
Martin Klebes, University of New Mexico
Richard Langston, The University of North Carolina at Chapel Hill
Edward T. Larkin
Caralinda Lee, St. Mary's College of California
Randall Lund, Brigham Young University
Alan D. Lytle, University of Arkansas at Little Rock
Marion Picker, Dickinson College
Hartmut Rastalsky, University of Michigan
Michael H. Rice, Mississippi State University
Claudette Roper, Mineral Area College
Eva-Marie Russo, Washington State University in St. Louis
Ebba W. Schoonover, University of Louisiana, Lafayette
David I. Smith, Calvin College
Elfriede Smith, Drew University
Sabine H. Smith, Kennesaw State University
Lorna Sopcak, Ripon College
Christian P. Stehr, Oregon State University
William E. Stuermann, North Greenville University
John Sundquist, Purdue University
John R. te Velde, Oklahoma State University
Finley M. Taylor, University of Central Florida
Walter G. Tschacher, Chapman University
Mary Upman, McDaniel College
Walter von Reinhart, University of Rhode Island
Jerry T. Wood, Glendale Community College
Amy D. Young, Fort Hays State University
Paul A. Youngman, The University of North Carolina, Charlotte

We would also like to thank the many people who worked on this book behind the scenes: Arden

Smith, who painstakingly compiled the German-English/English-German vocabularies, and Veronica Oliva, who secured reprint permissions for the realia and texts. The look of this Fifth Edition owes much to the creative talents of Carolyn Deacy and Anne Flanagan, who designed the interior of the book, and Susan Breitbard, who designed the cover. We would also like to acknowledge Wolfgang Horsch for his engaging line drawings and cartoons.

We would also particularly like to thank Michael Conner of Texas State University for the excellent annotations he wrote for the Instructor's Edition. His contribution of new teaching suggestions, activity extensions, alternative activities and other teaching ideas has significantly enriched the Instructor's Edition.

The authors wish to express gratitude to Monika Rähse Weber, University of Freiburg, Germany, and Caralinda Lee, Saint Mary's College of California. Over the past few years, both of them have shared suggestions and made many useful comments regarding work on the new edition. Thanks go as well to Bettina Lülsdorf, Annette (Emmi) Unkelbach, and Uta Kalwe for their special assistance in matters of German *Landeskunde.* Our deep gratitude goes to Paul Listen, our development editor, whose tireless efforts and welcome inspiration helped to shape the Fifth Edition and make this book what we wanted it to be. We also wish to acknowledge the editing, production, and art and design team at McGraw-Hill: Brett Coker, Richard DeVitto, Violeta Díaz, David Tietz, Sonia Brown, and Ayelet Arbel. Thanks also to Marie Deer for her wonderful copyediting and to Stacey Sawyer for her excellent proofreading, and to Nick Agnew, Rachel Dornan, and the rest of the McGraw-Hill marketing and sales staff, who have so actively promoted this book over the past four editions. Thanks to Techbooks for their careful composition of the book. Finally, we would like to express our gratitude to the McGraw-Hill foreign language editorial staff: Christa Harris, our sponsoring editor, whose guidance in the revision was invaluable; Bill Glass, our Publisher; and Emily G. Barrosse, our Editor in Chief. Special thanks are due to Thalia Dorwick, whose belief in the project made it a reality, and whose constant support helped bring it to completion, and Eirik Børve, whose vision made this book happen in the first place.

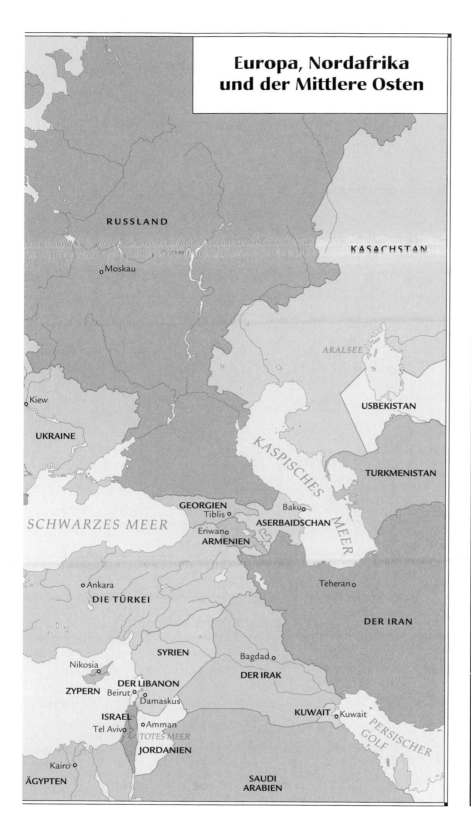

Europa, Nordafrika und der Mittlere Osten

RUSSLAND

KASACHSTAN

o Moskau

ARALSEE

Kiew

USBEKISTAN

UKRAINE

KASPISCHES MEER

TURKMENISTAN

GEORGIEN
Tiblis o   Baku o
SCHWARZES MEER   ASERBAIDSCHAN
Eriwan o
ARMENIEN

Teheran o

o Ankara
DIE TÜRKEI

DER IRAN

SYRIEN
Nikosia   Bagdad o
DER LIBANON   DER IRAK
ZYPERN   Beirut o o
Damaskus
ISRAEL   o Amman   KUWAIT o Kuwait
Tel Aviv o   PERSISCHER
TOTES MEER   GOLF
JORDANIEN
Kairo o
ÄGYPTEN   SAUDI
ARABIEN

EU-LÄNDER (2006)	EINWOHNER (2006)
	Millionen
Belgien	10,4
Dänemark	5,4
Deutschland	82,5
Estland	1,4
Finnland	5,2
Frankreich	59,9
Griechenland	11,0
Großbritannien	59,7
Irland	4,0
Italien	57,9
Lettland	2,3
Litauen	3,4
Luxemburg	0,5
Malta	0,4
die Niederlande	16,3
Österreich	8,1
Polen	38,2
Portugal	10,5
Schweden	9,0
die Slowakei	5,4
Slowenien	2,0
Spanien	42,3
Tschechien	10,2
Ungarn	10,1
Zypern	0,7
GESAMT	456,8

Österreich

Einwohner (2006): 8,1 Mio

TSCHECHIEN

DEUTSCHLAND

Gmünd
Horn
Krems
Donau
Linz
Melk · Sankt Pölten
WIEN
OBERÖSTERREICH
Wien
Amstetten
NIEDERÖSTERREICH
Baden
Gmunden
Salzburg
Bad Ischl
Eisenstadt
Wiener Neustadt
Hallstatt
Liezen
Mariazell
BURGENLAND
Bregenz
Kufstein · Sankt Johann in Tirol
Bischofshofen
Enns
STEIERMARK
Bruck an der Mur
Oberwart
VORARLBERG
Reutte
Wörgl
Zell am See
Feldkirch
Arlberg
Innsbruck
Kitzbühel
Inn
Bruck
SALZBURG
Radstadt
Mauterndorf
Sankt Georgen
Mur
Landeck
TIROL
Graz
Güssing
DIE
SCHWEIZ
SÜDTIROL
Osttirol
(zu Tirol)
Lienz
Spittal an der Drau
Feldkirchen
UNGARN
Meran
Drau
KÄRNTEN
Klagenfurt
Bozen
Villach
Wörther See
Bodensee
Neusiedler See

ITALIEN
SLOWENIEN

SCHAFFHAUSEN
Schaffhausen
DEUTSCHLAND
Rhein
BASEL
(STADT)
THURGAU
Kreuzlingen
Basel
Liestal
Rhein
Baden
Winterthur
Frauenfeld
Bodensee
FRANKREICH
BASEL
(LAND)
AARGAU
ZÜRICH
St. Gallen
St. Margrethen
Delemont
Aarau
Zürich
Herisau
APPENZEL
AUSSER-RHODEN
JURA
SOLOTHURN
Reuss
Zürichsee
Appenzell
INNER-RHODEN
Solothurn
LUZERN
Zug
Einsiedeln
Vaduz
ÖSTERREICH
JURA
Biel
Aare
ZUG
SCHWYZ
Glarus
LIECHTENSTEIN
NEUENBURG
Neuchâtel
BERN
Vierwaldstätter See
Luzern
Schwyz
GLARUS
Neuenburger See
BERNER
OBERLAND
Sarnen
Stans
Braunwald
Rhein
Chur
Bern
UNTERWALDEN
NIDW.
Altdorf
Davos
Fribourg
OBW.
Engelberg
Klosters
WAADT
Brienz
URI
GRAUBÜNDEN
FREIBURG
Thun
Brienzer See
Interlaken
Andermatt
Disentis
Rhein
Inn
Thuner See
Grindelwald
Lausanne
Jungfrau
St. Moritz
Jungfraujoch
Tessin
Montreux
Gstaad
Genfer See
Brig
TESSIN
Rotten
GENF
Sion
Bellinzona
Genf
WALLIS
Locarno
Rhône
Zermatt
Matterhorn
Lugano
Langensee
ITALIEN

Die Schweiz und Liechtenstein

Einwohner

Schweiz (2006): 7,5 Mio
Liechtenstein (2006): 34 000

NIDW = NIDWALDEN
OBW = OBWALDEN

Einführung

—Grüß dich! Geht's gut?
—Na klar!

In diesem Kapitel

- **Themen:** Greetings and farewells, getting acquainted, spelling in German, numbers, useful classroom expressions
- **Kultur:** Forms of address, inquiring about someone's well-being, postal codes and country abbreviations, German-speaking countries and their neighbors

Videoclips
Wer ist das?

Hallo! Guten Tag! Herzlich willkommen!*

Internationale Studenten

PROFESSOR: **Guten Tag! Herzlich willkommen! Mein Name ist** Pohle, Norbert Pohle. Und **wie ist Ihr Name?**

SABINE: Sabine Zimmermann.

PROFESSOR: Und Sie? **Wie heißen Sie?**

ANTONIO: **Ich heiße** Antonio Coletti.

ARI: Und **ich bin** Ari Pappas.

Auf einer Party

PETER: **Grüß dich.** Ich heiße Peter Sedlmeier.

KATARINA: Mein Name ist Katarina Steinmetz.

PETER: **Woher kommst du?**

KATARINA: **Aus** Dresden. Und du?

PETER: Aus Rosenheim.

---

*New, active vocabulary is shown in bold print.

HERR GROTE:	**Frau** Kühne, **das ist Herr** Michels aus Berlin. Frau Kühne kommt aus Potsdam.
HERR MICHELS:	**Freut mich.**
FRAU KÜHNE:	**Gleichfalls.**

Ein Treffen (meeting) *in Berlin*

```
STADT-
BIBLIOTHEK                          >00946850
GÖTTINGEN
                    Postfach 3842 · 37073 Göttingen
                    Gotmarstraße 8
Herr/Frau


    Weber, Melissa Alexandra

Benutzerausweis · Bitte bei jedem Besuch mitbringen
```

Aktivität 1 Wie ist der Name?

Introduce yourself to several people in your class.

s1: Mein Name ist _____.
s2: Ich heiße _____.

s1: Woher kommst du?
s2: Aus _____. Und du?

s1: Aus _____.

Aktivität 2 Darf ich vorstellen?°

May I introduce?

Introduce a classmate to another.

BEISPIEL: GINA: Paul, das ist Chris.
          PAUL: Tag, Chris.
          CHRIS: Hallo, Paul.

Wie schreibt man das?°

How is that spelled?

When you introduce yourself or give information about yourself, you may have to spell out words for clarification. In contrast to English, German follows fairly predictable spelling and pronunciation rules. You will gradually learn these rules throughout the course.

The German alphabet has the same twenty-six letters as the English alphabet, plus four other letters of its own. The four special German letters are written as follows. Note that the letter **ß** has no capital; **SS** is used instead.

Ä ä a-Umlaut: **Bär, Käse**

Ö ö o-Umlaut: **böse, hören**

Ü ü u-Umlaut: **müde, Süden**

ß sz („ess tsett"): **süß, Straße**

A pair of dots above a German vowel is called an "umlaut." Although this book refers to these vowels as **a-, o-,** or **u-umlaut,** they are actually distinct letters. When spelling words, speakers of German refer to them as they are pronounced. Listen carefully to these vowels on the laboratory audio recordings and in your instructor's pronunciation of them.

The alphabet house (**Buchstabenhaus**) below shows how German schoolchildren learn to write the letters of the alphabet. In addition to displaying individual letters, the **Buchstabenhaus** also practices such frequently used combinations as **ch, sch,** and the diphthongs.

Aktivität 3　Das ABC

Repeat the letters of the German alphabet after your instructor.

Aktivität 4　B-E-R-L-I-N: So schreibt man das!°

That is how you spell it!

Listen as your instructor spells some common German words. Write the words as you hear them.

Aktivität 5　Wie bitte?°

I beg your pardon?

Introduce yourself to another student and spell your name.

BEISPIEL: s1: Mein Name ist _____.
         s2: Wie bitte?
         s1: (*repeat your name; then spell it in German*)
         s2: Ah, so!

Aktivität 6　Buchstabieren Sie!°

Spell!

Think of three German words, names, products, or company names you already know or choose three items from the list below. Then close your book. Without saying the word, spell it in German (**auf Deutsch**) for a classmate, who writes it down and says the word back to you.

Frankfurt　　Autobahn　　Gesundheit
Delikatessen　　Hotel　　Volkswagen
Radio　　Einstein　　Kindergarten

Hallo! – Mach's gut!°

Take care!

How do people in German-speaking countries greet one another and say goodbye? Look at the following expressions and illustrations (pp. 5–6), and see whether you can guess which ones are greetings and which ones are goodbyes.

German speakers use various formal and informal hellos and good-byes, depending on the situation and the person with whom they are speaking.

Saying hello:

FORMAL	CASUAL	USE
guten Morgen	Morgen	*until about 10:00 A.M.*
guten Tag	Tag	*generally between 10:00 A.M. and early evening*
guten Abend	'n Abend*	*from about 5:00 P.M. on*
grüß Gott†	grüß Gott	*southern German and Austrian for* **guten Tag**
	grüß dich **hallo** **hi**	*greetings among young people any time*

Saying good-bye and good night:

FORMAL	CASUAL	USE
auf Wiedersehen	Wiederseh'n	*any time*
	mach's gut	*among young people, friends, and family*
	tschüss	*among young people, family*
gute Nacht	Nacht	*only when someone is going to bed at night*

---

*The 'n before **Abend** is short for **guten.**

†*Lit.* Greetings in the name of God.

Aktivität 7 Was sagt man?° *What does one say* What do you say?

What would people say in the following circumstances?

1. _____ your German instructor entering the classroom
2. _____ two students saying good-bye
3. _____ a person from Vienna greeting an acquaintance
4. _____ two students meeting at a café
5. _____ a mother as she turns off the lights in her child's room at night
6. _____ a student leaving a professor's office
7. _____ family members greeting one another in the morning

a. Gute Nacht!
b. Grüß dich! *I greet you (informal)*
c. Tschüss!
d. Mach's gut! *Do well*
e. Guten Tag! *Good day*
f. (Auf) Wiedersehen! *See you again*
g. (Guten) Morgen!
h. Grüß Gott!
i. Hallo!/Hi!
j. Guten Abend! *Good evening*

Aktivität 8 Minidialoge

Complete the following short dialogues with an appropriate greeting or leave-taking.

1. A: _____ _____! Ich heiße Stefan. Wie heißt du?
   B: Ich heiße Fusün.
2. C: _____ _____. Mein Name ist Eva Schrittmeier.
   D: Und mein Name ist Georg Stillweg. Woher kommen Sie?
   C: Aus Stuttgart.
3. E: Wiederseh'n und gute _____, Markus.
   F: _____, Johannes, mach's _____!

Na, wie geht's?°

So, how's it going?

German has several ways of asking *How are you?*

Wie geht es dir? ⎫
Wie geht's? ⎬ *a family member or friend*
                      (Ehen)
ᶠᵒʳᵐᵃˡ **Wie geht es Ihnen,** Herr Lindemann? *an acquaintance*

You can respond in a number of different ways.

Und der – And you?

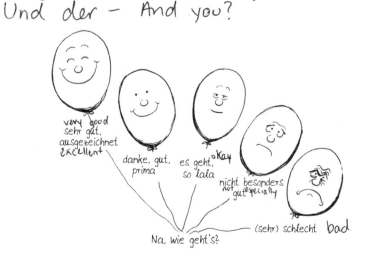

very good
sehr gut,
ausgezeichnet
excellent

danke, gut,
prima

es geht,
so lala

okay

nicht besonders
gut not specially

(sehr) schlecht bad

Na, wie geht's?

NA, WIE GEHT'S?

ICH WEISS NICHT! ICH FÜHLE MICH HEUTE MORGEN SO ZERSCHLAGEN![1]

[1]Ich ... *I don't know! I feel so beat this morning!*

KULTURTIPP

German speakers will ask someone **Na, wie geht's?**, **Geht's gut?**, or **Wie geht es Ihnen?** only if they already know the person well. When you ask a native German speaker, be prepared for a detailed answer, particularly if the person is not feeling well. **Hi** or **Hallo, wie geht's?** is sometimes used as a general greeting among young people even if they don't know each other.

Aktivität 9   Wie geht's?

Listen as three pairs of people greet each other and conduct brief conversations. Indicate whether the statements below match what you hear.

	JA	NEIN
DIALOG 1		
a. The conversation takes place in the morning.	☐	☐
b. The greetings are informal.	☐	☐
c. The man and the woman are both doing fine.	☐	☐
DIALOG 2		
a. The two speakers must be from southern Germany or Austria.	☐	☐
b. The speakers are close friends.	☐	☐
c. Both of them are doing fine.	☐	☐
DIALOG 3		
a. The two speakers know each other.	☐	☐
b. The man is feeling great.	☐	☐
c. They use a formal expression to say good-bye.	☐	☐

Aktivität 10   Und wie geht es dir?

Start a conversation chain by asking one classmate how he/she is.

BEISPIEL: s1: Na, Peter, wie geht's?
s2: So lala. Wie geht es dir, Kathy?
s3: Ausgezeichnet! Und wie geht's dir, …?

This is how you count in German.

So zählt man auf Deutsch.°

Eins,

zwei,

drei...

0 null	9 neun	18 achtzehn	90 neunzig
1 eins	10 zehn	19 neunzehn	100 (ein)hundert
2 zwei	11 elf	20 zwanzig	200 zweihundert
3 drei	12 zwölf	30 dreißig	300 dreihundert
4 vier	13 dreizehn	40 vierzig	1 000 (ein)tausend
5 fünf	14 vierzehn	50 fünfzig	2 000 zweitausend
6 sechs	15 fünfzehn	60 sechzig	3 000 dreitausend
7 sieben	16 sechzehn	70 siebzig	
8 acht	17 siebzehn	80 achtzig	

The numbers 21 through 99 are formed by combining the numbers 1–9 with 20–90.

21 einundzwanzig	24 vierundzwanzig	27 siebenundzwanzig
22 zweiundzwanzig	25 fünfundzwanzig	28 achtundzwanzig
23 dreiundzwanzig	26 sechsundzwanzig	29 neunundzwanzig

The numbers *one* and *seven* are written as follows:

German uses a period or a space where English uses a comma.

In German-speaking countries, telephone numbers generally have a varying number of digits and may be spoken as follows:

24 36 71

↓

zwei vier, drei sechs, sieben eins

[*or*]

vierundzwanzig, sechsunddreißig, einundsiebzig

Zwei,
Fünf,
Neun,
Eins,
Sechs,
Eins:

Telefonische
Anzeigenannahme[1]

BERLINER MORGENPOST
Berlins größte Abonnementzeitung

[1]Telefonische … *Submit your ad by phone*

Aktivität 11   Wichtige Telefonnummern°

You need the phone numbers for the following items and services. Write the phone numbers you hear in the appropriate space.

Telefon-Ansagen	☎		Theater und Konzerte	~~175~~ 11517
Polizei	110		Feuerwehr/ Rettungsleitstelle	112
Kinoprogramme	~~115~~ 11511		Wetter	~~185~~ 3853
Küchenrezepte	1167		Zahlenlotto	~~1162~~ 1162
Sport	~~1130~~ 1163		Zeit	1994

ANALYSE

Look over the examples of addresses (**Adressen**) from German-speaking countries. How do they differ from the way addresses are written in your country?

- Locate the name of the street (**Straße**) and the town (**Stadt**).
- Where is the house number (**Hausnummer**) placed? Where is the postal code (**Postleitzahl**) placed?
- Can you guess what the **A** before **9020 Klagenfurt** and the **CH** before **8050 Zürich-Oerlikon** represent?
- Now say each address out loud.

Universitätsstraße 65–67
A-9020 Klagenfurt

VERKEHRSMUSEUM DRESDEN
Augustusstraße 1, 01067 Dresden · Tel. 0351/ 86440 · Fax 0351/ 8644110
http://www.verkehrsmuseum.sachsen.de
e-mail: verkehrsmuseum@verkehrsmuseum.sachsen.de

Gebecke
Buchhandlung & Antiquariat
Bücher · Musikalien · Graphik
seit 1881
Pölkenstraße 3 · 06484 Quedlinburg ☎2698   www.antiquariat-gebecke.de

Ferienträume ?
Wir erfüllen sie !

TRAVELLER REISEN

Filiale Oerlikon
CH-8050 Zürich-Oerlikon, Ohmstrasse 14

Telefon 01- 312 10 14
Telex 823 221
Telegramm: Travellerag Zürich

Aktivität 12 Die Adresse und Telefonnummer, bitte!

You will hear three brief requests for addresses and telephone numbers. As you listen, mark the correct street numbers and jot down the postal codes and telephone numbers.

1. Professor Hausers Adresse ist …
   Gartenstraße   9   12   <u>19</u>   *8 2 0 6 7*
   _____ Ebenhausen/Isartal
   Die Telefonnummer ist _____. *41 34 76*

2. Die Adresse von Margas Fitnessstudio ist …
   Bautzner Straße   5   <u>15</u>   14   *010 93*
   _____ Dresden   ~~010 9~~
   Die Telefonnummer ist _____   *20*

3. Die Adresse von Autohaus Becker ist …
   Landstuhler Straße   <u>54</u>   44   45   *664 82*
   _____ Zweibrücken-Ixheim
   Die Telefonnummer ist _____.   *188 42*

Hier klicken!

You'll find more about the postal and country codes in **Deutsch: Na klar!** on the World Wide Web at www.mhhe.com/dnk5.

KULTURTIPP

When mail is sent between countries in Europe, international abbreviations are used for the country names. Refer to the map and provide the missing country names and country codes.

_____	B	**Rumänien**	____
Dänemark	____	**Russland**	____
_____	D		CH
Frankreich	____	**die Slowakei**	____
Griechenland	____		E
Großbritannien	____	**Tschechien**	____
Irland	____	**Ungarn**	____
Italien			
_____	FL		
_____	L		
die Niederlande	____		
_____	A		
Polen	____		
Portugal	____		

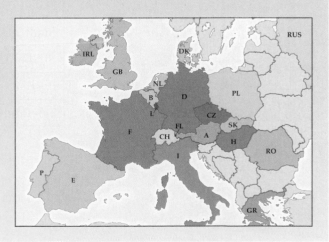

Volkswagen – da weiß man, was man hat.

Danke schön, Europa.

So zählt man auf Deutsch. **11**

Aktivität 13 Hin und her°: Wie ist die Postleitzahl?

This is the first of many activities in which you will exchange information with a partner. Here, one of you uses the chart below; the other turns to the corresponding chart in Appendix A. Take turns asking each other for the postal codes missing from your charts.

BEISPIEL: s1: Wie ist die Postleitzahl von Bitburg?
s2: D-54634. Wie ist die Postleitzahl von Salzburg?
s1: A-5020.

	Bitburg
A-5020	Salzburg
	Interlaken
D-94315	Straubing
	Merseburg
D-21614	Buxtehude
	Vaduz
D-99817	Eisenach

Aktivität 14 Ein Interview

Schritt 1: Jot down answers to the following questions.

Wie heißt du?   Woher kommst du?

Wie ist deine Telefonnummer?

Wie ist die Postleitzahl?   Wie ist deine Adresse?
Meine Adresse ist

Schritt 2: Use the questions in **Schritt 1** to interview a partner and fill in the information in the grid below.

Name	
Stadt	
Straße und Hausnummer	
Postleitzahl	
Telefonnummer	

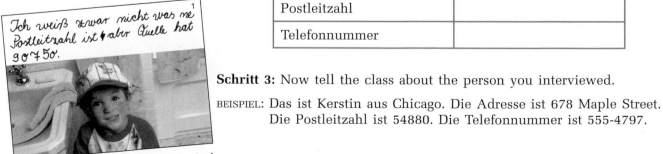

Ich weiß zwar nicht was ne Postleitzahl ist, aber Quelle hat 90750.

Schritt 3: Now tell the class about the person you interviewed.

BEISPIEL: Das ist Kerstin aus Chicago. Die Adresse ist 678 Maple Street. Die Postleitzahl ist 54880. Die Telefonnummer ist 555-4797.

1. Ich ... *I don't know what a* (**ne = eine**)

Nützliche Ausdrücke im Sprachkurs°

Useful expressions for the language course

IHR DEUTSCH**LEHRER** / IHRE DEUTSCH**LEHRERIN** SAGT:

Bitte ...	Please . . .
Hören Sie zu.	Listen.
Schreiben Sie.	Write.
Machen Sie die Bücher auf Seite _____ auf.	Open your books to page _____.
Lesen Sie.	Read.
Machen Sie die Bücher zu.	Close your books.
Setzen Sie sich.	Be seated.
Wiederholen Sie.	Repeat.
Haben Sie Fragen?	Do you have any questions?
[Ist] Alles klar?	Is everything clear?
Noch einmal, bitte!	Once more, please; could you say that again, please?

SIE SAGEN: *you say*

Langsamer, bitte!	Slower, please.
Wie bitte?	Pardon? What did you say?
Wie schreibt man _____?	How do you write _____?
Ich habe eine Frage.	I have a question.
Wie sagt man _____ auf Deutsch?	How do you say _____ in German?
Was bedeutet _____?	What does _____ mean?
Das weiß ich nicht.	I don't know.
Ich verstehe das nicht.	I don't understand.
Alles klar.	I get it.
Ja.	Yes.
Nein.	No.
Danke [schön].	Thank you.

Aktivität 15   Wie sagt man das auf Deutsch?

Match the English expressions to their German equivalents.

1. _____ I have a question.
2. _____ I don't understand.
3. _____ Is everything clear?
4. _____ Be seated.
5. _____ How do you write _____?
6. _____ Open your books.
7. _____ What does _____ mean?
8. _____ Pardon, what did you say?
9. _____ Open your books to page _____.
10. _____ Once more, please. / Could you say that again, please?

a. Alles klar?
b. Machen Sie die Bücher auf.
c. Was bedeutet _____?
d. Machen Sie die Bücher auf Seite _____ auf.
e. Setzen Sie sich.
f. Ich verstehe das nicht.
g. Noch einmal, bitte.
h. Wie schreibt man _____?
i. Wie bitte?
j. Ich habe eine Frage.

Sie können schon etwas Deutsch!°

Even if you have never studied German before, you will soon find that you know more German than you think. For example, look at the ad below taken from a German phone book's yellow pages (**gelbe Seiten**).

- What is this ad for?
- Which words are *identical* in English?
- Which words in the ad look *similar* to words you use in English?

Words such as **Motel, Hotel, Restaurant,** and **Sauna** are borrowed from other languages: **Motel** from American English, **Restaurant** and **Hotel** from French, and **Sauna** from Finnish. These words are used internationally.

Some words in the ad look similar to English words, for example **Biergarten.** You may already have seen the word **Biergarten** in English-language text. This word has been borrowed from German, along with some other German words commonly used in English, such as **Kindergarten** and **Delikatessen.** You recognize the words *beer* and *garden* in **Biergarten. Bier** and *beer,* **Garten** and *garden* have the same meaning in both languages. These words are cognates. Cognates are descended from the same word or form. Since English and German are both Germanic languages, they share many cognates. This common linguistic ancestry will help you a great deal in understanding German. Recognizing cognates is an important skill stressed throughout this textbook.

Cognates such as **Bier** and **Garten** are easy to recognize. Understanding other words takes more imaginative guessing: for instance, what do you think **Hallenbad** means? Other words in the ad probably look completely unfamiliar. The word **Ruf,** for instance, is not easily guessed. The meaning can be guessed from the context, however, and you already know a synonym for this word. What is it?

Now summarize what you have found out about "Zum Dorfkrug." Add any additional information you were able to extract from the ad by guessing.

Aktivität 16   Sie verstehen schon etwas Deutsch!°

You have learned that you can use visual and verbal cues to understand a considerable amount of written German. Now you will hear some short radio announcements and news headlines. Listen for cognates and other verbal clues as you try to understand the gist of what is being said. As you hear each item, write its number in front of the topic(s) to which it corresponds. Not all the following topics will be mentioned.

_____ Automobil	_____ Musik	_____ Sport
_____ Bank	_____ Politik	_____ Tanz
_____ Film	_____ Restaurant	_____ Theater
_____ Kinder		

Aktivität 17 Informationen finden

An important first step in reading is identifying the type of text you have in front of you. Look for verbal as well as visual clues. Look at the texts below. Write the letter of each text in front of the appropriate category in the list below (some categories will remain empty).

1. ____ ticket for an event
2. ____ short news item about crime
3. ____ concert announcement
4. ____ newspaper headline
5. ____ recipe
6. ____ section from a TV guide
7. ____ ad for a restaurant

CAFÉ KADENZ

Pfiffige Mischung aus Bistro, Café, Restaurant und Bar. Schlemmerfrühstück, großes Kaffeeangebot, kleine, leckere Gerichte, ausgesuchte Weine und Cocktails verlocken dazu, in einem Hauch von Wiener Caféhausatmosphäre zu genießen.

Täglich geöffnet
von 10.00 - 01.00 Uhr
Jüdenstr. 17 • 37073 Göttingen
Übrigens: Auch Sonntags geöffnet
Tel. 0551/ 4 72 08

a.

SYMPHONISCHES ORCHESTER BERLIN

Heute, 16 Uhr   **PHILHARMONIE**

Dirigent: **László Kovács**
Solist: **Boris Bloch**
Kodály: Tänze aus Galanta
Tschaikowsky: Konzert für Klavier und Orchester Nr. 2, G-Dur, op. 44
Rimsky-Korsakoff: „Scheherazade" Symphonische Suite aus „Tausend und eine Nacht"

b.

20.15 KABEL 1
FILM Lawrence von Arabien
Kairo, 1916: Im Auftrag seiner Regierung vereint der britische Offizier Thomas E. Lawrence (Peter O'Toole, l., mit Anthony Quinn) die Wüstenstämme Arabiens zu einer schlagkräftigen Armee und führt sie in den Aufstand gegen die Türken.

c.

Frankfurter wird Lotto-Millionär

Mit den sechs richtigen Zahlen 33, 29, 58, 12, 11 und 90 hat ein Frankfurter am Samstag im Lotto 2 000 000 Euro gewonnen.

d.

KABARETT
Leipziger Pfeffermühle

Kabarett Leipziger Pfeffermühle gGmbH
Thomaskirchhof 16 · 04109 Leipzig
Kartentelefon: 0341/9 60 31 96 · Fax: 0341/9 60 31 07
Internet: www.Kabarett-Leipziger-Pfeffermuehle.de
E-Mail: Kabarett.Pfeffermuehle@t-online.de

"Verkehrte Welt" mit Ute Loeck, Jan Gärtig, Marco Schiedt

Parkett Links / Reihe 05 / Sitz 05
Preisklasse 1 - 10.00 Euro
Mittwoch 10.08.2005 - 20:00 Uhr

e.

Sie können schon etwas Deutsch! **15**

Wo spricht man Deutsch? (*Where is German spoken?*) Naturally, German is spoken in Germany, but it is also spoken in many other countries. Which of the following countries have relatively large German-speaking populations?

- ☐ Argentinien
- ☐ Belgien
- ☐ Bosnien
- ☐ Brasilien
- ☐ Italien
- ☐ Jamaika

- ☐ Korea
- ☐ Liechtenstein
- ☐ Luxemburg
- ☐ die Mongolei
- ☐ Österreich
- ☐ Polen

- ☐ Rumänien
- ☐ Russland
- ☐ die Schweiz
- ☐ die Slowakei
- ☐ Tschechien
- ☐ Ungarn

German is the official language of Germany (**Deutschland**), Austria (**Österreich**), and Liechtenstein. It is one of four official languages of Switzerland (**die Schweiz**) and one of three official languages of Luxembourg and Belgium. German is also spoken in regions of France, Denmark, Italy, the Czech Republic, Poland, Rumania, Bosnia and Herzegovina, Hungary, Latvia, Lithuania, Estonia, Russia, Slovakia, and Ukraine. Altogether, between 120 and 140 million Europeans speak German as their first language—more than the number of people in Europe who speak English as their first language.

German is also spoken by many people as a first language in other countries such as Brazil, Argentina, Canada, and the United States (Pennsylvania Dutch). In Namibia, German is spoken by a sizable minority. It is estimated that outside Europe, an additional 20 million people speak German as their first language. Another 50 million speak German as a foreign language.

According to U.S. census figures from 2000, over 40 million U.S. citizens claim German descent. In Canada, the figure is approximately 2.7 million.

At present, approximately 20 million people worldwide are learning German in formal courses. Most of these people live in eastern Europe.

Videoclips

A. Michael, our moderator for the interviews throughout ***Deutsch: Na klar!,*** asks people their names in two different ways. Watch the video segment and complete the following questions.

1. Using the informal form, he asks Dennis: "_____ _____ du?"
2. Using the formal form, he asks Herr Borowsky: "_____ _____ Sie?"

B. Several people respond to the preceding questions in one of two ways. Watch and complete the following.

1. „Hallo! _____ Name _____ Dennis".
2. „Ich _____ Beatrice. Guten Morgen!"
3. „_____ _____ ist Kurt Borowsky".

C. Now concentrate on the segments with Peter, Jasmin, and Frau Simon. Complete their profiles.

Peter	„Guten Tag! _____ _____ ist Peter Junkel." „Ich _____ _____ Berlin-Spandau." „Die _____ ist Bechsteinweg Numero (*number*) 10 in _____ Berlin." „Meine Telefonnummer ist _____."
Jasmin	„_____ Tag! Mein _____ ist Jasmin Walter. _____ komme _____ Berlin. _____ _____ ist die Lietzenburgerstraße Numero 20 in _____ Berlin. Meine Telefonnummer ist _____."
Frau Simon	„Guten Tag, _____ _____ Malle Simon und wohne in _____ auf der Schönhauser Allee." „Meine Telefonnummer ist 030/_____."

D. Watch all the interviews again and listen for the following information. Select the correct response.

1. Oliver geht es …
   a. glänzend. **b.** sehr gut. **c.** so lala.

2. Jan wohnt …
   a. in Berlin. **b.** in Hamburg. **c.** in Hannover.

3. Harald kommt ursprünglich (*originally*) …
   a. aus Hannover. **b.** aus Berlin. **c.** aus Leipzig.

4. Nicolettas Adresse ist …
   a. Lietzenburgerstraße 13. **b.** Pappelallee 35. **c.** Schönhauser Allee 41.

5. Saras Postleitzahl ist …
   a. 10557 Berlin. **b.** 12203 Berlin. **c.** 10437 Berlin.

6. Herr Borowsky kommt …
   a. aus Hamburg. **b.** aus Düsseldorf. **c.** aus Berlin.

7. Michael fragt: „Wie heißt du?" Ali sagt: …
   a. „Mein Name ist Ali." **b.** „Ich bin der Ali." **c.** „Ich heiße Ali."

das **Wortschatz**
vocabulary

Zur Begrüßung / Greetings

grüß dich	hello, hi (*among friends and family*)
guten Abend	good evening
(guten) Morgen	good morning
(guten) Tag	hello, good day
hallo	hello (*among friends and family*)
herzlich willkommen	welcome
hi	hi

Beim Abschied / Saying Good-bye

(auf) Wiedersehen	good-bye
gute Nacht	good night
Mach's gut.	Take care, so long. (*informal*)
tschüss	so long, 'bye (*informal*)

Bekannt werden / Getting Acquainted

Frau; die **Frau**	Mrs., Ms.; woman
Herr; der **Herr**	Mr.; gentleman

der – masculine
die – feminine
das – neutral

der **Lehrer**/die **Lehrerin**	teacher
Das ist …	This is . . .
Wie heißt du?	What's your name? (*informal*)
Wie ist dein Name?	What's your name? (*informal*)
Wie heißen Sie?	What's your name? (*formal*)
Wie ist Ihr Name?	What's your name? (*formal*)
Woher kommst du?	Where are you from? (*informal*)
Woher kommen Sie?	Where are you from? (*formal*)
Ich bin …	I'm . . .
Ich heiße …	My name is . . .
Ich komme aus …	I'm from . . .
Mein Name ist …	My name is . . .
bitte	please; you're welcome
danke	thanks
danke schön	thank you very much
Freut mich.	Pleased to meet you.
gleichfalls	likewise
und	and

Auskunft erfragen / Asking for Information

ja	yes
na klar	absolutely, of course
nein	no
Wie heißt …	What is the name of . . .
die Stadt?	the town; city?
die Straße?	the street?
Wie ist …	What is . . .
deine/Ihre Telefonnummer?	your (*informal/formal*) telephone number?
die Adresse?	the address?
die Hausnummer?	the street address?
die Postleitzahl?	the postal code?

Nach dem Befinden fragen / Asking About Someone's Well-being

Geht's gut?	Are you doing well? (*informal*)
Na, wie geht's?	How are you? (*casual*)
Wie geht's?	How are you? (*informal*)
Wie geht's dir?	How are you? (*informal*)
Wie geht es Ihnen?	How are you? (*formal*)
ausgezeichnet	excellent
danke, gut	fine, thanks
nicht besonders gut	not particularly well
prima	great, super
schlecht	bad(ly), poor(ly)

sehr gut	very well; fine; good
so lala	OK, so-so

Im Deutschunterricht / In German Class

Alles klar.	I get it.
Das weiß ich nicht.	I don't know.
Ich habe eine Frage.	I have a question.
Ich verstehe das nicht.	I don't understand.
Langsamer, bitte.	Slower, please.
Was bedeutet ____?	What does ____ mean?
Wie bitte?	Pardon? What did you say?
Wie sagt man ____ auf Deutsch?	How do you say ____ in German?
Wie schreibt man ____?	How do you write ____?

Zahlen / Numbers

0 **null**	17 **siebzehn**
1 **eins**	18 **achtzehn**
2 **zwei**	19 **neunzehn**
3 **drei**	20 **zwanzig**
4 **vier**	30 **dreißig**
5 **fünf**	40 **vierzig**
6 **sechs**	50 **fünfzig**
7 **sieben**	60 **sechzig**
8 **acht**	70 **siebzig**
9 **neun**	80 **achtzig**
10 **zehn**	90 **neunzig**
11 **elf**	100 **(ein)hundert**
12 **zwölf**	200 **zweihundert**
13 **dreizehn**	300 **dreihundert**
14 **vierzehn**	1 000 **(ein)tausend**
15 **fünfzehn**	2 000 **zweitausend**
16 **sechzehn**	3 000 **dreitausend**

Deutschsprachige Länder und ihre Nachbarn / German-speaking Countries and Their Neighbors

Belgien	Belgium
Dänemark	Denmark
Deutschland	Germany
Frankreich	France
Italien	Italy
Liechtenstein	Liechtenstein
Luxemburg	Luxembourg
die **Niederlande** (*pl.*)	Netherlands
Österreich	Austria
Polen	Poland
die **Schweiz**	Switzerland
die **Slowakei**	Slovakia
Slowenien	Slovenia
Tschechien	Czech Republic
Ungarn	Hungary

DAS KANN ICH NUN!

Now that you have completed the **Einführung,** do the following in German to check what you have learned.

1. Formulate appropriate expressions to:
   a. Introduce yourself to a stranger.
   b. Introduce someone to another person.
   c. Greet a friend.
   d. Greet a stranger.
   e. Say good-bye to a friend.

2. Say the alphabet and spell your full name.

3. Ask a friend how he/she is doing and tell him/her how you are doing.

4. a. Give your phone number.
   b. Count from 1 to 100.

5. Formulate an appropriate statement or question for when . . .
   a. you don't understand something.
   b. you don't hear what someone has said.
   c. you want to know what something means.
   d. you want to know how to say something in German.

6. State five countries where German is spoken and give their official abbreviations.

Das bin ich

Was macht ihr hier?

In diesem Kapitel

- **Themen:** Personal information, characteristics, inquiring about others, hobbies and interests
- **Grammatik:** Nouns, gender, and definite articles; personal pronouns; infinitives and present tense; the verb **sein;** word order; asking questions; interrogatives; **denn**
- **Kultur: Einwohnermeldeamt,** foreigners in Germany
- **Lesen:** "Dialog" (Nasrin Siege)

Videoclips
Beruf, Studium und Hobbys

Alles klar?

A. One of the things you will learn to do in German is to give information about people in different contexts and situations. People give information about themselves in personal documents—documents they use in everyday life—as, for example, in personal IDs. Let's take a close look at one such ID.

Try to find the following information in the personal ID:

- What is the full name of the ID holder?
- When was he born?
- What is his nationality?
- Where does he live?
- What information is provided after the word **Größe?**
- What color are his eyes?
- What does the word **Unterschrift** refer to?

Vokabelsuche (*word search*). Find the German word for:

1. birthdate
2. nationality
3. color of eyes
4. height

Gegenwärtige Anschrift
Adresse:
Oldenburg
Am Teich 42

Größe
183 cm

Augenfarbe:
braun

PERSONALAUSWEIS
Nachname:
Emslander

Vorname:
Niels

Geburtstag:
24.05.85

Staatsangehörigkeit:
Deutsch

Gültig bis:
30.08.2010

Unterschrift:
Niels Emslander

B. You will now hear five speakers introduce themselves. As you listen, see whether you can hear what cities they are from.

1. Berlin   Leipzig   München
2. Rostock   Köln   Luzern
3. Wien   Jena   Mainz
4. Düsseldorf   Graz   Leipzig
5. Erfurt   Zürich   Frankfurt

Wörter im Kontext

THEMA 1: Persönliche Angaben°

Wer sind diese Leute? Scan the information, then create a profile of each person.

1. Mein Name ist Harald Lohmann. Ich **bin** am 23. Mai 1965 in Dessau **geboren** und **wohne jetzt** in Magdeburg. **Ich bin Hochschullehrer von Beruf.** Meine Adresse ist Bahnhofstraße 20. Ich bin 1,82 Meter **groß**.

2. Mein **Nachname** ist Lercher und mein **Vorname** Daniela. Ich bin am 7. Januar 1984 in Graz in Österreich geboren und wohne jetzt in Wien. Meine Adresse ist Mozartstraße 36. Ich bin 1,65 groß und bin Studentin.

3. Anton ist mein Vorname und Rütli mein Nachname. Ich komme aus der Schweiz. Ich bin am 14. September 1960 in Luzern geboren und wohne und **arbeite** in Luzern. Meine Adresse ist Schulstrasse 8. Ich bin Architekt von Beruf. Ich bin 1,79 groß.

Schreiben Sie Steckbriefe (*profiles*) von diesen Personen:

1. Vorname: Harald
   Nachname:
   Geburtstag:
   Geburtsort:
   Größe:
   Beruf:
   Wohnort:
   Straße und Hausnummer:
   Land:

2. Vorname:
   Nachname: Lercher
   Geburtstag:
   Geburtsort:
   Größe:
   Beruf:
   Wohnort:
   Straße und Hausnummer:
   Land:

Neue Wörter

bin ... geboren was born . . .
wohne (wohnen) live
ich bin ... von Beruf my profession is . . .
der Hochschullehrer university instructor
groß tall
arbeite (arbeiten) work

3. Vorname:
Nachname: Rütli
Geburtstag:
Geburtsort:
Größe:
Beruf:
Wohnort:
Straße und Hausnummer:
Land:

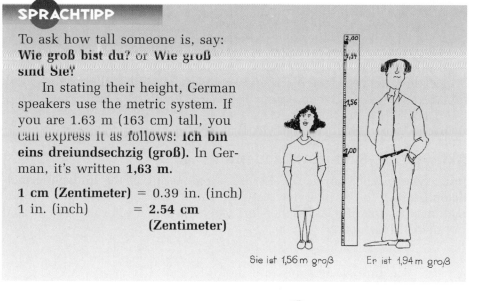

To ask how tall someone is, say:
Wie groß bist du? or **Wie groß sind Sie?**

In stating their height, German speakers use the metric system. If you are 1.63 m (163 cm) tall, you can express it as follows: **Ich bin eins dreiundsechzig (groß).** In German, it's written **1,63 m.**

1 cm (Zentimeter) = 0.39 in. (inch)
1 in. (inch)   = **2.54 cm (Zentimeter)**

Sie ist 1,56 m groß   Er ist 1,94 m groß

Aktivität 1   Interessante Personen

Listen to the following statements about the people in the profiles and say whether they are true (**das stimmt**) or false (**das stimmt nicht**).

	DAS STIMMT	DAS STIMMT NICHT
1. a.	☒	☐
b.	☒	☒
c.	☒	☐
d.	☐	☐
e.	☒	☐
f.	☒	☐
2. a.	☒	☒
b.	☐	☒
c.	☒	☐
d.	☒	☐
e.	☒	☒
3. a.	☒	☐
b.	☒	☐
c.	☒	☐
d.	☐	☒
e.	☐	☒

Jetzt sind Sie dran! (Now it's your turn!)

    Mein Nachname ist _____.

    Mein Vorname ist _____.

    Ich komme aus _____.

    Ich wohne in _____.

    Meine Adresse ist _____.

    Ich bin _____,_____ groß.

Hier klicken!

You'll find more about the **Einwohnermeldeamt** in **Deutsch: Na klar!** on the World Wide Web at www.mhhe.com/dnk5.

KULTURTIPP

Everyone who lives in Germany must register with the **Einwohnermeldeamt** (residents' registration office) within two weeks of moving to a new community. This applies to everyone, even students living in a community only temporarily. The **Einwohnermeldeamt** must also be notified when one moves from one place to another.

Aktivität 2 Eine neue Studentin

Julie, who recently arrived in Berlin, is registering at the **Einwohnermeldeamt.** Listen to the interview between the official and Julie. What information does the official ask her for? Check **ja** if the information is asked for, **nein** if it is not.

	JA	NEIN
BEISPIEL: Vor- und Nachname	☒	☐
1. Wohnort in den USA	☐	☐
2. Beruf	☐	☐
3. Geburtsort *place of birth*	☐	☐
4. Geburtstag	☐	☐
5. Telefonnummer	☐	☐
6. Straße und Hausnummer	☐	☐
7. Postleitzahl	☐	☐

Ask!

Aktivität 3 Fragen Sie!°

A. Unscramble the following to form questions for a short interview.

1. dein / wie / Name / ist /, bitte / ?
2. Adresse / ist / deine / wie / ?
3. deine / Telefonnummer / wie / ist / ?
4. Geburtsort / was / dein / ist / ?
5. groß / bist / wie / du / ?

B. Now use the questions to interview two people in your class.

C. Tell the class what you've found out.

- Das ist _____.
- (Tims/Elizabeths) Adresse ist _____.
- Seine/Ihre Telefonnummer ist _____.
- Er/Sie ist in _____ geboren.
- Er/Sie ist ___,_____ groß.

Aktivität 4 Wie groß bist du? Wie alt bist du?

Figure out your height in meters with the help of the conversion chart. Then exchange this information with one or two people in the class.

BEISPIEL: s1: Wie groß bist du?
s2: Ich bin 1,64 (eins vierundsechzig) groß.
s1: Wie alt bist du?
s2: Ich bin dreiundzwanzig.

THEMA 2: Sich erkundigen°

Inquiring

„Glücksrad Fortuna": eine Quizshow

213 cm	7 ft
210 cm	6 ft 10 in
205 cm	6 ft 8 in
200 cm	6 ft 6 in
195 cm	6 ft 4 in
190 cm	6 ft 2 in
185 cm	6 ft
180 cm	5 ft 10 in
175 cm	5 ft 8 in
170 cm	5 ft 6 in
165 cm	5 ft 4 in
160 cm	5 ft 2 in
155 cm	
153 cm	5 ft

ANSAGER: Guten Abend, meine Damen und Herren. Willkommen **heute** im Studio bei Glücksrad Fortuna. Und hier kommt Quizmaster Dieter Sielinsky.

HERR SIELINSKY: Guten Abend und herzlich willkommen. Und **wer** ist unsere Kandidatin? Wie ist Ihr Name, bitte?

FRAU LENTZ: Lentz, Gabi Lentz.

HERR SIELINSKY: Woher kommen Sie, Frau Lentz?

FRAU LENTZ: Aus München.

HERR SIELINSKY: Und **was machen** Sie denn in Berlin?

FRAU LENTZ: Ich **besuche Freunde** hier.

HERR SIELINSKY: Na, und **wie finden Sie** Berlin denn?

FRAU LENTZ: **Ganz toll,** faszinierend.

HERR SIELINSKY: Und was sind Sie von Beruf, Frau Lentz?

FRAU LENTZ: Ich bin Web-Designerin.

HERR SIELINSKY: Und haben Sie Hobbys?

FRAU LENTZ: **Aber natürlich!** Lesen, Reisen, Wandern, Kochen, und ich mache **Kreuzworträtsel.**

HERR SIELINSKY: So, na dann **viel Glück heute Abend.**

FRAU LENTZ: **Danke sehr.**

Neue Wörter

heute today
wer who
was what
machen are doing
besuche (besuchen) am visiting
Freunde friends
wie finden Sie …? how do you like . . . ?
ganz toll really great
aber but
natürlich of course
das Lesen reading
das Reisen traveling
das Wandern hiking
das Kochen cooking
das Kreuzworträtsel crossword puzzle
viel Glück good luck
heute Abend this evening
danke sehr thanks a lot

Neue Wörter

sag mal tell me
jetzt now
hier here
lerne (lernen) am learning
das Deutsch German
studiere (studieren) am studying; am majoring in
echt (*coll.*) really
die Universität university
bleibst (bleiben) are staying
nächstes Jahr next year

Ein Gespräch an der Uni

HELMUT: Grüß Gott! Helmut Sachs.

JULIE: Guten Tag! Ich heiße Julie Harrison.

HELMUT: Woher kommst du, Julie?

JULIE: Ich komme aus Cincinnati.

HELMUT: Ah, aus den USA! Cincinnati? Ist das im Mittelwesten?

JULIE: Ja, im Bundesstaat Ohio.

HELMUT: **Sag mal,** was machst du **jetzt hier?**

JULIE: Ich **lerne Deutsch** am Sprachinstitut. Und du?

HELMUT: Ich **studiere** Physik an der T.U.

JULIE: **Echt?** Was ist die T.U. denn?

HELMUT: Die Technische **Universität.** Und wie lange **bleibst** du hier in München?

JULIE: Zwei Semester. **Nächstes Jahr** bin ich wieder in Ohio.

HELMUT: Ach so.

ANALYSE

Look at the dialogues again and locate the following information.

Glücksrad Fortuna

- How does the quizmaster ask his guest what her name is?
- What phrase does the quizmaster use to ask Frau Lentz where she is from?
- What does the quizmaster ask to find out Frau Lentz's profession?
- What question does he ask to find out about her hobbies?
- What question does he ask to find out if Frau Lentz likes Berlin?
- What pronoun does the quizmaster use to address Frau Lentz?

Ein Gespräch an der Uni

- How do Helmut and Julie greet each other?
- How does Helmut ask Julie where she is from? How does this differ from the same question asked by the quizmaster?
- What phrase does Helmut use to ask Julie what she is doing in Munich?
- Helmut doesn't know where Cincinnati is. What does he ask Julie to get that information?
- What pronoun do Julie and Helmut use to address each other?

SPRACHTIPP

To convey strong curiosity or surprise, add the particle **denn** to your question.

Wo ist **denn** das?
Where is that?
(strong curiosity)

Arbeitest du **denn** heute?
Are you working today? (surprise)

Refer to *Personal Pronouns,* p. 34.

SPRACHTIPP

To say that you are studying at a university or to state your major, use the verb **studieren**.

> Ich **studiere** in München.
> Ich **studiere** Physik.

To say you are studying specific material, such as for a test, use **arbeiten** or **lernen**.

> Ich **lerne** heute Abend für eine Chemieprüfung.
> Ich **arbeite** auch für die Matheprüfung.

To say that you are learning or taking a language, use the verb **lernen**.

> Ich **lerne** Deutsch.

Aktivität 5   Steht das im Dialog?

Mark whether the statements below are correct or incorrect, based on the information found in the dialogues in **Thema 2**.

pg. 25

		DAS STIMMT	DAS STIMMT NICHT
1.	Der Quizmaster heißt Dieter Sielinsky.	☒	☐
2.	Gabi Lentz kommt aus Augsburg.	☐	☑
3.	Frau Lentz ist Professorin von Beruf.	☐	☑
4.	Tanzen ist ein Hobby von Frau Lentz.	☐	☐
5.	Frau Lentz findet Berlin zu groß. *to big*	☐	☐
6.	Julie kommt aus Cincinnati.	☑	☐
7.	Julie lernt Deutsch in München.	☐	☑
8.	Helmut studiert Mathematik.	☐	☑
9.	Julie bleibt zwei Jahre in München.	☐	☑

Aktivität 6   Was sagen diese Leute zueinander?°

What are these people saying to each other?

Determine whether the following phrases and questions would be used by two students addressing each other, by a professor and a student, or by both pairs of speakers.

		ZWEI STUDENTEN	PROFESSOR UND STUDENT
1.	Was studierst du? *What are you studying*	☒	☐
2.	Grüß dich! *Hello*	☒	☐
3.	Auf Wiedersehen. *See you again*	☐	☒
4.	Wie heißt du?	☒	☐
5.	Guten Tag!	☐	☒
6.	Wie heißen Sie?	☐	☒
7.	Was machst du hier?	☒	☐
8.	Was studieren Sie?	☐	☒
9.	Tschüss!	☒	☐
10.	Mach's gut! *Good luck*	☐	☐

Questions & Answers

Aktivität 7   Fragen und Antworten°

Match each question in the left-hand column with a possible answer from the right-hand column. More than one answer is possible for some.

1. _C, d_ Wie heißen Sie?
2. _h f_ Woher kommst du?
3. _a e_ Was machen Sie hier?
4. _b_ Wo ist das?
5. _g_ Wer ist das?

a. Ich studiere hier.
b. Das ist im Mittelwesten.
c. Mein Name ist Meier.
d. Ich heiße Keller.
e. Ich lerne Deutsch.
f. Ich komme aus Deutschland.
g. Das ist Peter.
h. Ich bin aus Kalifornien.

Aktivität 8   Kurzdialoge°

Listen to the brief conversational exchanges and indicate in each case whether the response to the first question or statement is logical (**logisch**) or illogical (**unlogisch**).

	LOGISCH	UNLOGISCH
1.	☑	☐
2.	☐	☐
3.	☐	☐
4.	☐	☐
5.	☐	☐
6.	☐	☐
7.	☐	☐
8.	☐	☐
9.	☐	☐
10.	☐	☐

Aktivität 9   Eine Konversation

Number the following sentences in order to form a short conversation between Herr Brinkmann and Frau Garcia, who are just getting acquainted. Then perform it with a partner.

— Ich besuche Freunde.

_1_ Guten Tag. Ich heiße Garcia.

— Wie finden Sie Hamburg?

— Ich finde Hamburg interessant.

Ach so!

— Wie bitte?

— Ich komme aus Florida.

— Brinkmann.

— Guten Tag. Mein Name ist Brinkmann.

— Woher kommen Sie?

— Und was machen Sie hier?

Aktivität 10　Was studierst du?

Schritt 1: Find your major in the following list. Then, by asking questions, try to find at least one other classmate who has the same major as you.

BEISPIEL: s1: Was studierst du?
　　　　　s2: Ich studiere Geschichte. Und du?
　　　　　s1: Ich studiere Informatik.

• Vorlesungsverzeichnis •

Betriebswirtschaft°　　　　　　　　　　　　*management*

Biologie

Chemie

Deutsch/Germanistik

Englisch/Anglistik

Französisch/Romanistik

Geschichte°　　　　　　　　　　　　　　　*history*

Informatik

Kunst°　　　　　　　　　　　　　　　　　*art*

Marketing

Maschinenbau°　　　　　　　　　　　　　*engineering*

Mathematik

Medienwissenschaft°　　　　　　　　　　*media studies*

Musik

Pädagogik

Philosophie

Physik

Politik

Psychologie

Soziologie

Spanisch/Romanistik

Volkswirtschaft°　　　　　　　　　　　　*economics*

Schritt 2: Now report back to the class. Does anyone have the same major as you?

BEISPIEL: Ich studiere Informatik. Candice und Ben studieren auch
　　　　　Informatik.

THEMA 3: Eigenschaften und Interessen°

Neue Wörter

bestimmt no doubt
nie never
langweilig boring
Was macht ihm / ihr Spaß?
What does he/she like to do?
diskutieren to discuss/discussing
vielleicht perhaps
immer always
ernst serious
ruhig quiet
Interessen interests
Musik hören listening to music
freundlich friendly
wirklich really
sympathisch likable
oft often
sportlich athletic
nicht not
die Zeitung newspaper
faul lazy
fleißig hardworking
lustig cheerful
nett nice
praktisch practical
treu loyal
Das macht mir Spaß. I like to do that.
Bücher books
gehen to go/going
Computerspiele spielen to play/playing computer games
essen to eat/eating
Fahrrad fahren to ride/riding a bicycle
Karten spielen to play/playing cards
SMS schicken to send/sending text messages
tanzen to dance/dancing

Hm ... Wie ist er? **Exzentrisch? Bestimmt nie langweilig. Und was macht ihm Spaß? Diskutieren vielleicht?**

Heißt er Rolf oder Florian? Ist er **immer** so **ernst** und **ruhig**? Und **Interessen?** Vielleicht Lesen und **Musik hören.**

Ist sie **freundlich**? Tolerant? Sie ist **wirklich sympathisch.** Und Hobbys? Na, vielleicht Kochen? **Oft** im Internet surfen?

Sie ist bestimmt **sportlich. Was macht ihr Spaß?** Wandern? Bestimmt **nicht Zeitung** lesen.

So bin ich! (*That's me!*) Check the characteristics that apply to you.

- ☐ chaotisch ~k~
- ☐ dynamisch ~dy~
- ☐ ernst
- ☐ exzentrisch
- ☐ **faul** lazy
- ☐ **fleißig** hard working
- ☐ freundlich friendly
- ☐ interessant inter
- ☐ konservativ conser
- ☐ langweilig - boring
- ☐ liberal
- ☐ **lustig** - funny
- ☐ **nett** - nice
- ☐ **praktisch** - practical
- ☐ progressiv
- ☐ **romantisch**
- ☐ ruhig - quiet
- ☐ sympathisch - nice
- ☐ tolerant
- ☐ **treu** - faithful ~true~

Das macht mir Spaß! Check off your interests and hobbies.

- ☐ **Bücher** lesen read books
- ☐ ins Café **gehen** go into
- ☐ **Computerspiele spielen**
- ☐ **Essen**
- ☐ **Fahrrad fahren** - ridding bike
- ☐ Fotografieren
- ☐ im Internet **surfen**
- ☐ **Karten spielen** - play hard
- ☐ Kochen - cook
- ☐ Musik -
- ☐ Reisen - travel
- ☐ **SMS schicken** text
- ☐ Sport
- ☐ **Tanzen** - to dance
- ☐ Telefonieren
- ☐ Wandern - take a hike
- ☐ Zeitung lesen read newspaper

Aktivität 11   Gegenteile

Refer to the list of characteristics in **Thema 3** and provide the opposite of the following adjectives.

1. lustig ≠ _____
2. faul ≠ _____
3. konservativ ≠ _____
4. langweilig ≠ _____
5. dynamisch ≠ _____

Aktivität 12   Interessen und Hobbys

Provide the name of the activity represented by each drawing.

1. _____

2. _____

3. _____

4. _____

5. _____

6. _____

One way to say that you like (doing) something is by using the following expression.

| Fotografieren **macht mir Spaß.** | *I like photography.* |
| **Was macht dir Spaß?** | *What do you like (to do)?* |

Aktivität 13 Ratespiel: Wie bin ich? Was macht mir Spaß?

Write down two adjectives that describe you and one of your interests. Do not write your name. Your instructor will collect and distribute everyone's list. Then each class member will read a description out loud, while the others try to guess who the writer is.

BEISPIEL: Ich bin dynamisch und exzentrisch. Im Internet surfen macht mir Spaß.

Important

Aktivität 14 Wichtig° oder nicht?

1. Make a list of three characteristics and three interests that you consider important in a friend.
2. Tally the results on the board.

    Which characteristic is most important for the class?

    Which interest is most frequently mentioned?

Grammatik im Kontext

Nomen, Genus und bestimmte Artikel

Nouns, Gender, and Definite Articles°

Nouns in German can be easily recognized in print or writing because they are capitalized.

German nouns are classified by grammatical gender as either masculine, feminine, or neuter. The definite articles **der, die,** and **das** (all meaning *the* in German) signal the gender of nouns.

MASCULINE: der	FEMININE: die	NEUTER: das
der Mann	die Frau	das Haus
der Beruf	die Adresse	das Buch
der Name	die Straße	das Semester

The grammatical gender of a noun that refers to a human being generally matches biological gender; that is, most words for males are masculine, and words for females are feminine. Aside from this, though, the grammatical gender of German nouns is largely unpredictable.

Even words borrowed from other languages have a grammatical gender in German, as you can see from the following newspaper headline.

Fußball ist der Hit

Since the gender of nouns is generally unpredictable, you should make it a habit to learn the definite article with each noun.

Sometimes gender is signaled by the ending of the noun. The suffix **-in,** for instance, signals a feminine noun.

der Amerikaner, die Amerikaner**in**

der Freund, die Freund**in**

der Professor, die Professor**in**

der Student, die Student**in**

Compound nouns (**Komposita**) are very common in German. They always take the gender of the final noun in the compound.

       second

der Biergarten   = das Bier + **der** Garten

das Telefonbuch = das Telefon + **das** Buch

die Telefonnummer = das Telefon + **die** Nummer

Übung 1 Was hören Sie?

Circle the definite article you hear in each of the following questions and statements.

1. (der) die (das)   5. der die das
2. der die das   6. der die das
3. der die das   7. der die das
4. der die das   8. der die das

Übung 2 Hier fehlen die Artikel.

Complete each sentence with the missing article—**der, die,** or **das.**

die Sprache – language

1. _Die_ Studentin aus Cincinnati lernt Deutsch am Sprachinstitut.
2. _Der_ Student studiert Physik an der T.U.
3. _Die_ Frau aus München findet Berlin ganz toll. *great*
4. Was ist _das_ Hobby von Frau Lentz?
5. _Die_ Adresse vom Hotel ist bestimmt im Telefonbuch. *certainly*
6. Wie heißt _das_ Land südlich von Österreich?
7. Fußballtrainer? _Der_ Beruf ist interessant, aber oft stressig.
8. _das_ Kreuzworträtsel ist sehr kompliziert.
9. _Der_ Freund von Ute studiert Informatik.
10. _die_ Zeitung aus München heißt *Süddeutsche Zeitung.*
    newspaper

Übung 3 Wörter bilden°

Creating words

Create compound nouns using the words supplied.

BEISPIEL: der Garten + das Haus = das Gartenhaus

das Bier	die Frau	das Haus	die Nummer
das Buch	der Garten	der Mann	das Telefon

Personal Pronouns°

A personal pronoun stands for a person or a noun.

Mein Name ist **Ebert. Ich** bin Architekt.
*My name is **Ebert. I** am an architect.*

Du bist immer so praktisch, **Gabi.**
*You are always so practical, **Gabi.***

Der Wagen ist toll. Ist **er** neu?
The car is fabulous. Is it new?

Ich bin rundum Spitze [1]
mit pan-ADRESS

[1]*Ich ... I am really sharp.
(I am great in every way.)*

	SINGULAR	PLURAL
1st person	ich *I*	wir *we*
2nd person	du *you (informal)* Sie *you (formal)*	y'all ihr *you (informal)* Sie *you (formal)*
3rd person	er *he; it* sie *she; it* es *it*	sie *they*

Note:

- The pronoun **ich** is not capitalized unless it is the first word in a sentence.

- German has three words to express *you:* **du, ihr,** and **Sie.** Use the familiar singular form **du** for a family member, close friend, fellow student, child, animal, or deity. If speaking to two or more of these, use the familiar plural form **ihr.** Use the formal form **Sie** (always capitalized) for one or more casual acquaintances, strangers, or anyone with whom you would use **Herr** or **Frau**.

- The third-person pronouns **er, sie** (*she*), and **es** reflect the grammatical gender of the noun or person for which they stand (the antecedent).

Mark und Anja sind Studenten.
Mark and Anja are students.

Er kommt aus Bonn und **sie** kommt aus Wien.
He comes from Bonn, and she comes from Vienna.

—Wie ist **der Film?**
—**Er** ist wirklich lustig.
How is the film?
It is really funny.

—Wo ist **die Zeitung?**
—**Sie** ist hier.
Where is the newspaper?
It is here.

—Wo ist **das Buch?**
—**Es** ist nicht hier.
Where is the book?
It is not here.

Übung 4 Du, ihr oder Sie?

Would you address the following people with **du, ihr,** or **Sie?**

1. Frau Lentz aus München
2. Ute und Felix, zwei gute Freunde
3. Sebastian, ein guter Freund
4. Herr Professor Rauschenbach
5. Herr und Frau Zwiebel aus Stuttgart
6. eine Studentin in der Mensa
7. ein Tourist aus Kanada
8. ein Vampir
9. Max, 10 Jahre alt

Übung 5 Herr und Frau Lentz

Working with a partner, take turns asking and answering questions, using a pronoun in each answer.

BEISPIEL: S1: Wie ist Frau Lentz?
    S2: <u>Sie</u> ist nett und freundlich.

1. Wo wohnen Herr und Frau Lentz?   _____ wohnen in München.
2. Was ist Frau Lentz von Beruf?   _____ ist Web-Designerin.
3. Was ist Herr Lentz von Beruf?   _____ ist Koch im Hofbräuhaus.
4. Wie groß ist Frau Lentz?   _____ ist 1,63 m groß.
5. Und wie groß ist Herr Lentz?   _____ ist 1,90 m groß.
6. Wie heißt Frau Lentz mit Vornamen?   _____ heißt Gabi.

Übung 6 Was meinst du?°

What do you think?

Ask a partner for his/her opinion. Create questions and answers with the words and phrases in the two columns, completing each blank with information of your choice. Follow the model.

BEISPIEL: S1: Wie ist der Film „Casablanca"?
    S2: Er ist ausgezeichnet.

FRAGE	ANTWORT
Wie ist der Film [*Titel*]?	freundlich / unfreundlich
... das Buch [*Titel*]?	ausgezeichnet
... das Wetter (*weather*) in [*Stadt*]?	gut / schlecht
... die Studentenzeitung hier?	interessant / uninteressant
... das Essen im Studentenwohnheim?	kompliziert
... das Kreuzworträtsel in der *New York Times*?	langweilig
... die Freundin von [*Name*]?	ernst / lustig
... der Freund von [*Name*]?	nicht besonders gut
... der _____kurs?* (z.B. Deutschkurs)	sympathisch / unsympathisch

---

*Refer to the list of subjects in **Aktivität 10, Was studierst du?,** earlier in this chapter.

The Verb: Infinitive and Present Tense°

In German, the basic form of the verb, the infinitive, consists of the verb stem plus the ending **-en** or, sometimes, just **-n.**

INFINITIVE	VERB STEM	ENDING
kommen	komm	**-en**
wandern	wander	**-n**

The present tense is formed by adding different endings to the verb stem. These endings vary according to the subject of the sentence.

Here are the present-tense forms of three common verbs.

	kommen	**finden**	**heißen**
ich	komm**e**	find**e**	heiß**e**
du	komm**st**	find**est**	heiß**t**
er sie } es	komm**t**	find**et**	heiß**t**
wir	komm**en**	find**en**	heiß**en**
ihr	komm**t**	find**et**	heiß**t**
sie/Sie	komm**en**	find**en**	heiß**en**

Note:

- German has four different endings to form the present tense: **-e, -(e)st, -(e)t,** and **-en.** English, in contrast, has only one ending, -(e)s, for the third-person singular (*comes, goes*).

- Verbs with stems ending in **-d** or **-t** (**finden, arbeiten**) add an **-e-** before the **-st** or **-t** ending (**du findest, er arbeitet**).

- Verbs with stems ending in **-ß, -s,** or **-z** (**heißen, reisen, tanzen**) add only a **-t** in the **du** form (**du heißt, reist, tanzt**).

Use of the Present Tense

The present tense in German may express either something happening at the moment or a recurring or habitual action.

Wolfgang spielt Karten.   *Wolfgang is playing cards.*
Antje arbeitet viel.   *Antje works a lot.*

It can also express a future action or occurrence, particularly with an expression of time.

Nächstes Jahr lerne ich   *Next year I'm going to learn*
  Spanisch.   *Spanish.*

German has only one form of the present tense, whereas English has three.

Hans **tanzt** wirklich gut.   { *Hans **dances** really well.*
                                *Hans **is dancing** really well.*
                                *Hans **does dance** really well.*

- Identify the different verb endings in the illustrations.
- What is the subject in each sentence?
  Is it in the singular or in the plural?
- What is the infinitive form of each verb?

Ich lese das Journal, weil ...

MARS – WIR KOMMEN!

Hat den Flamenco in Berlin mitgeprägt: Amparo de Triana – heute zu erleben auf dem Pfefferberg

Berlin tanzt Flamenco

Foto: Randy Kühn

Ob' fünf oder zehn Jahre alt: „Schule macht Spaß "

Fußgänger² findet 10 000 Euro auf der Straße

Hier kommt Ihr Glück!³

Informationen zum Gewinnsparen

¹Whether ²pedestrian ³happiness

conversation

Übung 7 Im Gespräch° mit Wolfgang und Gisela

Supply the missing verb endings.

„Ich heiße____[1] Wolfgang Ebert und studiere____[2] Mathematik in Zürich." Wolfgang kommt____[3] aus Deutschland, aber er studiert____[4] in der Schweiz. Er arbeitet____[5] viel. Wolfgangs Freundin heißt____[6] Gisela. Sie studiert____[7] auch Mathematik. Nächstes Jahr machen____[8] sie (Wolfgang und Gisela) ein Praktikum in Berlin.

Und Hobbys? Sport machen____[9] Gisela Spaß. Wolfgang findet____[10] Kochen interessant. Wolfgang und Gisela geh____[11] oft ins Café und diskutieren____[12] über Politik. Gisela sagt____[13]: „Wir mach____[14] auch oft Musik mit Freunden. Ich spiel____[15] Gitarre, und Wolfgang spiel____[16] Xylophon." Und heute Abend? „Heute Abend tanz____[17] wir Tango!"

Übung 8 Sabine und Michael in Österreich

Working with a partner, complete the following questions and answers by supplying the missing verb endings.

1. s1: Wie heißen____ du?
   s2: Ich heiße____ Sabine Keller.
2. s1: Woher kommst____ du?
   s2: Ich komme____ aus den USA.
3. s1: Was machen____ du im Internetcafé?
   s2: Na, ich surfe____ im Internet und spiel____ Videogames.
4. s1: Wie findest____ du das Essen in der Mensa?
   s2: Ich finde____ das Essen da gut.
5. s1: Woher komm____ Michael?
   s2: Er komm____ aus Kanada.
6. s1: Was mach____ ihr in Graz?
   s2: Wir lern____ Deutsch und wir studier____ hier.
7. s1: Wie find____ ihr die Professoren hier?
   s2: Wir find____ die Professoren sehr gut.
8. s1: Wie lange bleib____ ihr in Graz?
   s2: Ich bleib____ zwei Semester hier. Michael bleib____ ein Semester.

Übung 9   Kombinieren Sie.

Combine elements from the two columns to create as many different sentences as you can.

BEISPIEL: Wolfgang studiert Mathematik.

1. ich   *6* heißt Gisela
2. Wolfgang   studieren in Zürich
3. Wolfgang und Gisela   *6* tanzt wirklich gut
4. Wolfgangs Freundin   machen oft Musik
5. mein Freund und ich   findest Mathematik sehr interessant
6. ihr   machst ein Praktikum
7. wir   *2* studiert Mathematik
8. du   *1* wohne in Zürich

Übung 10   Kleine Szenen

Supply the missing verb endings and then role-play each scene.

Szene 1 (drei Personen)

A: Das ist Herr Witschewatsch. Er komm_t_ aus Rosenheim.

B: Ah, guten Tag, Herr Wischewas.

C: Nein, nein, ich heiß_e_ Witschewatsch.

B: Ach so, Sie heiß_en_ Wischewasch?

C: Nein, Wit-sche-wat-sch.

B: Oh, Entschuldigung (*excuse me*), ich hör_e_ nicht gut.

Szene 2 (zwei Personen)

A: Ich hör_e_, Sie komm_en_ aus Rosenheim?

B: Nein, nein, ich komm_e_ nicht aus Rosenheim. Ich komm_e_ aus Rüdesheim, Rüdesheim am Rhein.

A: Ach, meine Freundin Antje komm_t_ auch aus Rüdesheim.

Szene 3 (drei Personen)

A: Wie find_et_ ihr Andreas?

B: Ich find_e_ Andreas echt langweilig.

C: Ich auch.

A: Sabine find_t_ Andreas super.

C: Na, und er find_et_ Sabine total langweilig.

Szene 4 (zwei Personen)

A: Guten Morgen, meine Damen und Herren. Willkommen in Dresden. Heute besuch_en_ wir das Verkehrsmuseum (*transport museum*).

B: Das Verkehrsmuseum? Ich bleib_e_ im Hotel!

The Verb **sein**

The irregular verb **sein** is used to describe or identify someone or something.

> Marion **ist** Studentin.
> Sie **ist** sehr sympathisch.

¹eagle

sein			
ich	**bin**	wir	**sind**
du	**bist**	ihr	**seid**
er sie es	**ist**	sie	**sind**
Sie **sind**			

That's the way he is.

Übung 11   So ist er.°

Everyone is picking on Thomas. Complete the sentences with the appropriate form of **sein**.

1. Die Freundin von Thomas sagt: „Du _bist_ so konservativ, Thomas."
2. Thomas sagt: „Wie bitte? Das stimmt nicht. Ich _bin_ sehr progressiv."
3. Der Vater von Thomas sagt: „Thomas _ist_ so unpraktisch."
4. Die Mutter von Thomas sagt: „Wir _sind_ zu kritisch. Thomas _ist_ sehr intelligent und sensibel."
5. Der Chef von Thomas sagt zu Thomas: „Herr Berger, Sie _sind_ nicht sehr fleißig."
6. Thomas denkt: „Ihr _seid_ alle unfair. Ich _bin_ ein Genie (*genius*)!"

Wortstellung

Word Order° in Sentences

One of the most important rules of German word order is the fixed position of the conjugated verb (the verb with the personal ending).

First Element (Subject, Adverb, etc.)	Second Element (Verb)	Other Elements
Ich	studiere	Informatik in Deutschland.
Nächstes Jahr	mache	ich ein Praktikum.
Heute	besuchen	wir das Verkehrsmuseum.

Note:

- The conjugated verb is always the second element in a sentence.
- The subject of the sentence can either precede or follow the verb.

Übung 12 Leas Freund

Restate the information in each sentence by starting with the boldfaced word or words.

BEISPIEL: Leas Freund heißt **Stefan.**
Stefan heißt Leas Freund.

1. Stefan ist Musiker **von Beruf.**
2. Er wohnt **jetzt** in Berlin.
3. Er findet **Berlin** ganz fantastisch.
4. Er spielt **oft** im Jazzclub.
5. Stefans Hobby ist **Fahrrad fahren.**
6. Er arbeitet **nächstes Jahr** in Wien.

Übung 13 Wer macht was und wann?

Create two sentences for each group of words.

BEISPIEL: besuchen / das Museum / heute / wir →
Wir besuchen heute das Museum. [or]
Heute besuchen wir das Museum.

1. Karten / wir / spielen / heute Abend
2. bei McDonald's / Peter / arbeitet / jetzt
3. ich / oft / mache / Kreuzworträtsel
4. spielen / wir / vielleicht / Tennis mit Boris
5. ein Praktikum / Peter / nächstes Jahr / macht / in Dresden

Übung 14 Meine Pläne°

plans

Tell a partner two things you may do today and tomorrow (**morgen**). Tell the class about your partner's plans.

BEISPIEL: Heute spiele ich Karten. Morgen spiele ich Tennis. →
Heute spielt Bob Karten. Morgen spielt er Tennis.

Asking Questions°

Fragen stellen

There are two types of questions. We refer to them as *word questions* and *yes/no questions*.

Word Questions ⚔

Wann kommst du?	*When* are you coming?
Was machst du?	*What* are you doing?
Wer ist das?	*Who* is that?
Wie findest du Berlin?	*How* do you like Berlin?
Wo wohnst du?	*Where* do you live?
Woher sind Sie? from where	*Where* are you from?

[1]am ... *on the weekend*

Note:

- Word questions begin with an interrogative pronoun. They require specific information in the answer.
- The conjugated verb is the second element in a word question.

Kommst Du?

- German uses only one verb form to formulate a question, in contrast to English.

Wo **wohnst** du?   { *Where **do** you **live**?*
                      *Where **are** you **living**?* }

Yes/No Questions

Kommst du?   *Are you coming?*
Studiert Lea in Berlin?   *Is Lea studying in Berlin?*
Heißt der Professor Kuhn?   *Is the professor's name Kuhn?*

Note:

- A yes/no question begins with the conjugated verb and can be answered with either **ja** or **nein**.
- The verb is immediately followed by the subject.

Ich heiße Petra, bin 28 Jahre alt, 168 cm groß und arbeite in einem Ingenieurbüro.

Jürgen ist 25 Jahre alt, 185 cm groß, blond, sportlich-schlank, gut aussehend und sympathisch.

Übung 15   Zwei Menschen

Read the two personal ads and answer the questions.

1. Wie heißt der Mann?
2. Wie heißt die Frau?
3. Wie alt ist die Frau?
4. Wie alt ist der Mann?
5. Wie groß ist der Mann?
6. Wie groß ist die Frau?
7. Wie ist Jürgen? (drei Adjektive)
8. Was macht Petra?

Übung 16   Ergänzen Sie.

Complete each question with an appropriate interrogative pronoun: **wann, was, wer, wie, woher,** or **wo.**

1. _Wie_ heißt du?
2. _Woher_ kommst du?
3. _Was_ studierst du denn? What are you studying
4. _Wie_ findest du Heidelberg? How do you find ...
5. _Wo_ wohnst du denn?
6. _Wer_ studiert Mathematik in Zürich?
7. _Was_ machst du denn hier?
8. _Wann_ besuchst du das Verkehrsmuseum?

Übung 17   Formulieren Sie passende Fragen.

Formulate a word question for each answer.

BEISPIEL: ___*Woher kommst du*___? Ich komme aus Kanada.

1. _____? Ich heiße Peter.
2. _____? Ich wohne in Essen.
3. _____? Ich studiere da Medizin.

4. _____? Ich komme aus Süddeutschland.

5. _____? Nächstes Jahr mache ich ein Praktikum.

6. _____? Meine Familie wohnt in Nürnberg.

7. _____? Ich finde Hamburg sehr schön.

Übung 18 Ja und nein

What questions could trigger the following answers?

BEISPIEL: *Kommen Sie aus Hamburg* ? Ja, ich komme aus Hamburg.

1. _____? Nein, ich bin nicht Frau Schlegel; ich bin Frau Weber.

2. _____? Ja, wir wohnen in Köln.

3. _____? Ja, ich finde Köln sehr interessant.

4. _____? Nein, ich arbeite nicht bei der Telekom.

5. _____? Ja, Köln ist sehr groß.

6. _____? Ja, wir spielen oft Karten.

Übung 19 Zur information

Take a survey and then share some of the results in class.

Schritt 1: Write down five yes/no questions using verbs and other words from the lists below or others if you like. Use the pronoun **du** in each question.

BEISPIELE: Wohnst du im Studentenwohnheim?
Surfst du oft im Internet?

spielen	oft	Karten, Fußball
surfen	nie	im Internet
telefonieren	manchmal (*sometimes*)	Kreuzworträtsel
sein	heute Abend	chaotisch, fleißig, praktisch, exzentrisch
studieren	immer	Informatik, Biologie
tanzen	jetzt	in der Disko
wohnen	heute	im Studentenwohnheim
arbeiten		im Café
kochen		Musik
hören		

Schritt 2: Now move around the classroom asking and answering these questions to find classmates who do those things. Your responses to one another need not be complete sentences.

BEISPIEL: s1: Wohnst du im Studentenwohnheim?
s2: Ja. / Aber natürlich! / Na klar! / Nein.

Schritt 3: Now report back to the class on who does what.

BEISPIEL: Matt wohnt im Studentenwohnheim. Trudi surft oft im Internet. …

Übung 20 Wie bitte?

Schritt 1: Invent a fictitious person and fill in the blanks as if you were that person.

1. Ich heiße _____.

2. Ich komme aus _____.

3. Das ist in _____.

4. Ich studiere _____.

5. _____ macht Spaß.

6. Nächstes Jahr studiere ich in _____.

Schritt 2: Now take turns reading the statements to each other. Imagine you do not entirely understand what the other is saying and ask him or her to repeat it. Follow the model.

BEISPIEL: s1: Ich heiße Karl-Heinz Rüschenbaum.
s2: Wie bitte? Wie heißt du?
s1: Karl-Heinz Rüschenbaum.
s2: Ach so!
s1: Ich komme aus …
s2: Wie bitte? Woher kommst du?

Student life

Übung 21 Das Studentenleben°

Schritt 1: You will hear some information about a German university student. Compare what you hear with the statements below. If a statement is incorrect, find the correct answer from among the choices in parentheses.

	DAS STIMMT	DAS STIMMT NICHT
1. Die Studentin heißt Claudia. (_____ Katrin, _____ Karin)	☐	☐
2. Sie kommt aus Göttingen. (_____ Dresden, _____ Bremen)	☐	☐
3. Der Familienname ist Renner. (_____ Reuter, _____ Reiser)	☐	☐
4. Sie studiert jetzt in Tübingen. (_____ Göttingen, _____ Dresden)	☐	☐
5. Sie studiert Mathematik. (_____ Jura, _____ Informatik)	☐	☐
6. Sie wohnt bei einer Familie. (_____ im Studentenwohnheim, _____ allein)	☐	☐
7. Sie geht oft schwimmen. (_____ wandern, _____ Tennis spielen)	☐	☐
8. Sie geht oft ins Café. (_____ in die Disko, _____ ins Museum)	☐	☐

Schritt 2: Now formulate yes/no questions based on the statements given in **Schritt 1.** Ask another student in your class to verify the information.

BEISPIEL: s1: Heißt die Studentin Claudia?
s2: Nein, sie heißt Karin.

Sprache im Kontext

Videoclips

A. Watch the interviews with Sara and Ali as they talk about what they are studying, their hobbies, and how their friends would describe them. Write **S** if the phrase or word applies to **Sara** or **A** if it applies to **Ali.**

_____ Medienwissenschaft	_____ Schwimmen
Mathematik	spontan
_____ Joggen	_____ zurückhaltend (*reserved*)
_____ Gitarre spielen	_____ lustig
_____ Zeichnen	_____ fröhlich
_____ Tanzen	_____ sehr aktiv
_____ Fahrrad fahren	

B. Who does what? Watch the interviews and match each person with a profession or job.

1. _____ Peter   **a.** ist Grafikdesigner
2. _____ Oliver   **b.** ist Pilot
3. _____ Alex   **c.** ist Bankkauffrau
4. _____ Jasmin   **d.** arbeitet bei KDW im Silbershop
5. _____ Frau Simon   **e.** ist Web-Designer

C. Watch the interviews again and jot down notes about things you have in common with the interviewees. If you have anything in common, then write a few sentences that describe the commonalities. Follow the model.

BEISPIEL: Ali studiert Mathematik. Ich studiere auch Mathematik. Saras Hobby ist Tanzen. Mein Hobby ist auch Tanzen …

Lesen

Zum Thema°

Where do the students in your German class come from? Were all students in the class born in the same country? What nationalities and ethnic groups are represented? How many students can speak more than one language? How many students have bilingual parents?

About the topic

Auf den ersten Blick°

1. Look at the title and the text itself. What type of text is this? What led you to your conclusions?
2. Label the exchanges in the dialogue with *S1 (Speaker 1)* and *S2 (Speaker 2).*

At first glance

3. Skim the text for references to geographical locations and references to a person's appearance.

4. From the context, what do you think **reden** and **aussehen (siehst ... aus, sehe aus)** mean?

DIALOG

von Nasrin Siege

„Du redest so gut deutsch. Wo kommst du denn her?"

„Aus Hamburg."

„Wieso? Du siehst aber nicht so aus!"

„Wie sehe ich denn aus?"

5 „Na ja, so schwarzhaarig und dunkel ..."

„Na und?"

„Wo bist du denn geboren?"

„In Hamburg."

„Und dein Vater?"

10 „In Hamburg."

„Deine Mutter?"

„Im Iran."

„Da haben wir's!"

„Was denn?"

15 „Dass du keine° Deutsche bist!"   *not a*

„Wer sagt das?"

„Na ich!"

„Warum?"

About the text

Hier klicken!

You'll find information about the topic of foreigners in Germany in **Deutsch: Na klar!** on the World Wide Web at www.mhhe.com/dnk5.

Zum Text°

1. What does the text tell you about the birthplace, place of residence, citizenship of Speaker 2? What else can you determine about him or her?

2. Consider what you've learned about different forms of "you" in German. Speculate: How old are the two speakers? How well do they know each other? Where might this dialogue take place? How do you think it started?

3. Why is the nationality of Speaker 2 an issue for Speaker 1?

More than seven million foreigners make up roughly 9% of Germany's population and contribute to the country's economic growth. Most Germans and foreigners live in peaceful coexistence; however, incidents of discrimination and even violence against foreigners have occurred, especially following the economic difficulties in the wake of the unification of Germany in 1990. The German government strives to promote tolerance toward foreigners through media campaigns, and the governments of the German states try to integrate children of foreigners into the German school system.

Dein Christus ein Jude
Dein Auto ein Japaner
Deine Pizza italienisch
Deine Demokratie griechisch
Dein Kaffee brasilianisch
Dein Urlaub türkisch
Deine Zahlen arabisch
Deine Schrift Lateinisch
Und Dein Nachbar nur ein Ausländer?

Plakat gegen Rassismus und Ausländerfeindlichkeit (antiforeigner sentiments), *gesehen in einer Hamburger U-Bahn Station*

Zu guter Letzt

Einander kennen lernen

You are going to be working with other students in the class on various speaking and writing tasks in German. Some students you already know, others you don't. In this activity, you will interview three students you have not already met, tell someone else about one of them, and write a short profile of each of them.

Schritt 1: Before you ask the questions below, formulate them in German. Ask:

- his/her name _____
- where he/she comes from _____
- where he/she was born _____
- what he/she likes to do _____
- what he/she is studying _____
- how he/she likes the university here _____

Schritt 2: Now interview the three students and jot down their responses.

Schritt 3: Using your notes, tell another student about one of the persons you interviewed.

Schritt 4: Write a short profile of each student you interviewed, using complete sentences. Use the model below.

BEISPIEL: Eine Studentin heißt Stacey. Sie kommt aus …

Wortschatz

Eigenschaften — Characteristics

alt	old
ernst	serious
exzentrisch	eccentric
fantastisch	fantastic
faul	lazy
fleißig	hardworking, diligent
freundlich/unfreundlich	friendly/unfriendly
groß	tall
gut	good, well
Er tanzt gut.	He dances well.
interessant	interesting
kompliziert	complicated
konservativ	conservative
langweilig	boring
lustig	cheerful; fun-loving
nett	nice
praktisch/unpraktisch	practical/impractical
romantisch	romantic
ruhig	quiet
sportlich	athletic
stressig	stressful
sympathisch/ unsympathisch	likable/unlikable
toll! (*coll.*)	super!
ganz toll!	super! great!
treu	loyal

Substantive — Nouns

der **Amerikaner** / die **Amerikanerin**	American
der **Beruf**	profession, occupation
Was sind Sie von Beruf?	What do you do for a living?
das **Buch**	book
(das) **Deutsch**	German (language)
das **Essen**	food; eating
der **Freund** / die **Freundin**	friend
der **Geburtsort**	birthplace
der **Geburtstag**	birthday, date of birth
das **Hobby**	hobby
der **Hochschullehrer** / die **Hochschullehrerin**	university instructor
das **Interesse**	interest
das **Jahr**	year
nächstes Jahr	next year
der **Journalist** / die **Journalistin**	journalist

der **Mann**	man
die **Mensa**	student cafeteria
die **Musik**	music
der **Name**	name
der **Nachname**	family name, surname
der **Vorname**	first name, given name
das **Praktikum**	internship
ein Praktikum machen	to do an internship
der **Professor** / die **Professorin**	professor
das **Semester**	semester
der **Spaß**	fun
der **Student** / die **Studentin**	student
die **Universität**	university
der **Wohnort**	place of residence
die **Zeitung**	newspaper

Verben — Verbs

arbeiten	to work
besuchen	to visit
bleiben	to stay, remain
diskutieren	to discuss
essen	to eat
fahren	to drive, ride
Fahrrad fahren	to ride a bicycle
finden	to find
Wie findest du ...?	How do you like . . . ?; What do you think of . . . ?
gehen	to go
heißen	to be called, be named
hören	to listen, hear
kochen	to cook
kommen	to come
lernen	to learn, study
lesen	to read
machen	to do; to make
Kreuzworträtsel machen	to do crossword puzzles
reisen	to travel
sagen	to say, tell
sag mal	tell me
schicken	to send
sein	to be
spielen	to play
Computerspiele spielen	to play computer games
Karten spielen	to play cards
studieren	to study

surfen	to surf	**Sonstiges**	**Other**
tanzen	to dance	aber	but
telefonieren	to talk on the phone	auch	also
wandern	to hike	ich auch	me too
wohnen	to reside, live	bestimmt	no doubt; definitely
		danke sehr	thanks a lot

Personalpronomen — Personal Pronouns

ich	I	**Das macht Spaß.**	That's fun.
du	you (*informal sing.*)	echt (*coll.*)	really
er	he; it	ganz	quite, very, really
sie	she; it; they	heute	today
es	it	heute Abend	this evening
wir	we	hier	here
ihr	you (*informal pl.*)	ich bin geboren	I was born
Sie	you (*formal sing./pl.*)	immer	always
		jetzt	now

Interrogativ-pronomen — Interrogative Pronouns

		natürlich	of course, natural(ly)
wann	when	nicht	not
was	what	nie	never
wer	who	oft	often
wie	how	sehr	very
wo	where	viel	a lot, much
woher	from where	viel Glück!	good luck!
		viel Spaß!	have fun!
		vielleicht	maybe, perhaps
		wirklich	really

DAS KANN ICH NUN!

1. Sagen Sie, wie Sie heißen und wo Sie wohnen. Sagen Sie auch Ihre Telefonnummer, wie groß Sie sind, und wo Sie geboren sind.

2. Was studieren/lernen Sie an der Universität? Nennen Sie zwei Fächer.

3. Beschreiben Sie einen Freund / eine Freundin. Drei Adjektive bitte.

   Mein Freund heißt … Er ist …

   Meine Freundin heißt … Sie ist …

4. Haben Sie Hobbys? Nennen Sie zwei.

5. Ergänzen Sie diese Sätze:

   a. Der Film _____ interessant. **b.** Ich _____ Berlin toll. **c.** Woher _____ Sie? **d.** Fotografieren _____ mir Spaß.

6. Was sind die Artikel?

   a. _____ Semester **b.** _____ Name **c.** _____ Zeitung

7. Sagen Sie „Sie", „du", oder „ihr"?

   a. ein Freund: _____ **b.** Herr und Frau Lentz: _____ **c.** dein Bruder und deine Schwester: _____

8. Wie fragt man auf Deutsch?

   a. *When are you coming?* **b.** *Where do you live?* **c.** *Is Susan studying in Munich?* **d.** *Who is visiting Berlin next year?*

Wie ich wohne

Wie hoch ist die Miete? Hmm, ein Zimmer in einer WG?

Videoclips
So wohnen sie.

In diesem Kapitel

- **Themen:** Types of housing, furnishings, favorite activities
- **Grammatik:** Noun plurals; nominative and accusative case of definite and indefinite articles, nouns, and interrogative pronouns; **haben**; negation with **nicht** and **kein; dieser** and **welcher** verbs with stem-vowel changes; demonstrative pronouns; the adverb **gern**
- **Kultur:** Living arrangements, the euro
- **Lesen:** „So wohne ich"

Alles klar?

A. Just as in North America, flyers (**Anschlagzettel**) are a popular way to make announcements, advertise, or disseminate information in German-speaking countries. What do you think is the purpose of the flyer shown here? Once you've determined the purpose, answer the multiple-choice questions.

- Wo findet man (*one*) so einen Anschlagzettel?

  a. in einer Klinik

  b. an der Uni

  c. in einem Garten

- Die vier Studentinnen suchen _____.

  a. einen Regenschirm

  b. eine Wohnung

  c. ein Dach

- Sie brauchen _____ Zimmer.

  a. zwei bis (*to*) drei

  b. sechs bis sieben

  c. vier bis fünf

- Sie möchten (*would like*) eine Wohnung _____.

  a. im Stadtzentrum

  b. in einem Vorort (*suburb*)

  c. auf dem Lande (*in the country*)

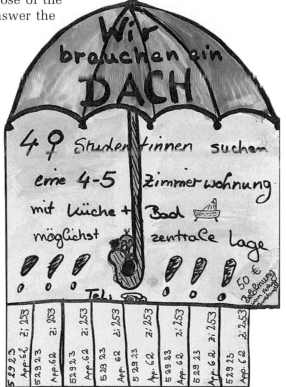

Vokabelsuche. Find the German word for:

1. kitchen
2. bath
3. central location
4. reward

B. Listen to the following short conversations. Mark the kind of apartment the speakers are looking for.

1. a. eine Zweizimmerwohnung

   b. eine Dreizimmerwohnung

2. a. eine Zweizimmerwohnung mit Küche und Bad

   b. eine Dreizimmerwohnung in zentraler Lage

3. a. ein Zimmer bei einer Familie

   b. ein Zimmer in einem Studentenheim

In German-speaking countries, the kitchen and bathroom are not counted as "rooms" when describing the number of rooms in an apartment. Thus, a **Zweizimmerwohnung** has one bedroom and a living room, while a **Dreizimmerwohnung** has two bedrooms and a living room. An **Appartement** is a studio, or efficiency apartment.

Apartments are expensive in German-speaking countries. Students either live in a **Studentenwohnheim,** a residence hall, or share living accommodations such as an apartment to cut expenses. Many students prefer living in a **Wohngemeinschaft (WG),** a co-op in which each student has a private room while kitchen and bath facilities are shared.

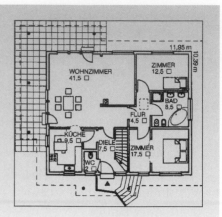

Wörter im Kontext

Was ist denn los? What's the matter?
suche (suchen) am looking for
dringend desperately
die Wohnung apartment
das Zimmer room
so teuer very expensive
nichts nothing
frei free, available
etwas something
da here; there
schönes (schön) beautiful
möbliertes (möbliert) furnished
der Nichtraucher (Nichtraucher, *pl.*) nonsmoker
hoch high
die Miete rent
nur only
recht quite
preiswert reasonable
das Geld money
weit von der Uni far from the university
Da hast du Recht. You're right.
gerade just, exactly
zentral gelegen centrally located
frage (fragen) ask
genau exactly

THEMA 1: Auf Wohnungssuche

*Ulla und Stefan treffen sich (meet) vor der Mensa der Uni Freiburg. Ulla hat ein großes **Problem.***

STEFAN: Tag, Ulla! Wie geht's?
ULLA: Ach, nicht besonders.
STEFAN: **Was ist denn los?**
ULLA: Ich **suche dringend** eine **Wohnung** oder ein **Zimmer.** Wohnungen sind aber alle **so teuer.**
STEFAN: Ist denn **nichts frei** im **Studentenwohnheim?**
ULLA: Hier in Freiburg? Bestimmt nicht!
STEFAN: Hier ist die Zeitung von heute. Ah, hier ist **etwas. Da,** schau mal: **schönes, möbliertes** Zimmer für **Nichtraucher.**
ULLA: Wie **hoch** ist die **Miete?**
STEFAN: **Nur** 250 Euro.
ULLA: Das ist **recht preiswert.** Ich habe nicht viel **Geld** für Miete. Wo ist das Zimmer?
STEFAN: In Gundelfingen.
ULLA: In Gundelfingen?! Das ist aber **weit von der Uni.**
STEFAN: Na, **da hast du Recht.** Preiswert ist es, aber Gundelfingen ist nicht **gerade zentral gelegen.**
ULLA: Naja, ich brauche dringend ein Zimmer. Ich **frage** mal, **genau** wie weit das bis zur Innenstadt ist.

Mark whether the following statements are correct (**das stimmt**) or incorrect (**das stimmt nicht**) based on the information in the dialogue.

	DAS STIMMT	DAS STIMMT NICHT
1. Stefan sucht ein Zimmer.	☐	☐
2. Im Studentenwohnheim ist nichts frei.	☐	☐
3. Stefan findet ein Zimmer für Nichtraucher.	☐	☐
4. Das Zimmer ist nicht möbliert.	☐	☐
5. Die Miete ist nicht sehr hoch.	☐	☐
6. Gundelfingen ist nicht zentral gelegen.	☐	☐

Wie wohnen Sie? Kreuzen Sie an.

☐ Appartement   ☐ **Wohngemeinschaft (WG)**
☐ Haus   ☐ Wohnung
☐ Studentenwohnheim   ☐ Zimmer

Ich wohne …

☐ allein (*alone*)   ☐ bei einer Familie
☐ bei den Eltern (*with my parents*)

Ich habe …

☐ einen **Mitbewohner** / eine **Mitbewohnerin**   ☐ einen Goldfisch
☐ einen Hund (*dog*)   ☐ ein **Handy**
☐ eine Katze   ☐ ein Telefon

Beschreiben Sie Ihre Wohnung / Ihr Zimmer / Ihr Haus!

Sie/Es hat …   Sie/Es ist …

☐ ein **Arbeitszimmer**   ☐ **groß**
☐ eine schöne Aussicht (*view*) ☐ **klein**
☐ ein **Badezimmer** / **Bad**   ☐ **dunkel**
☐ einen **Balkon**   ☐ **hell**
☐ ein **Esszimmer**   ☐ möbliert
☐ ein (zwei/drei) **Fenster**   ☐ **unmöbliert**
☐ eine **Garage**   ☐ preiswert
☐ einen **Garten**   ☐ teuer
☐ eine **Küche**   ☐ schön
☐ ein (zwei/drei) **Schlafzimmer** ☐ **hässlich**
☐ ein **Wohnzimmer**   ☐ zentral gelegen
☐ **Computeranschluss**   ☐ weit von der Uni
☐ eine **Terrasse**

Die Miete ist …

☐ hoch   ☐ **niedrig**

SPRACHTIPP

Das ist **ein** Balkon. Das ist **eine** Küche. Das ist **ein** Badezimmer.

When a masculine noun is used as a direct object, **ein** changes to **einen**; however, feminine **eine** and neuter **ein** do not change:

Mein Haus hat **einen** Balkon, **eine** Küche und **ein** Badezimmer.

Aktivität 1   Welches Zimmer ist das?

With which room do you associate the following?

1. wohnen: _____   5. lernen: _____
2. kochen: _____   6. essen: _____
3. baden: _____   7. schlafen: _____
4. Auto: _____

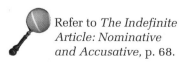
Refer to *The Indefinite Article: Nominative and Accusative*, p. 68.

Aktivität 2   Wir brauchen eine Wohnung / ein Zimmer.

Scan the five ads from people looking for housing. Label the ads from 1 to 5 in the order in which you hear them.

Freundl. junger 37-jähriger Englischlehrer su. 1 Zi. in WG um mit euch Deutsch zu sprechen und es besser zu lernen.
☎ 570 56 39

Freundlicher Schauspieler[4] aus Hamburg sucht Zi in WG vom 1. Mai bis 1. August in München.
☎ 637 88 78, ♂ Manfred

Musiker (24) sucht Zimmer oder Raum in WG zum 1.6. oder etwas früher. ☎ 040/439 84 20 Markus (rufe zurück[1]) PS.: Zahle[2] bis 250 Euro incl.[3]

Fotodesignerin, 22, sucht preiswertes Zimmer in junger WG, möglichst zentral zum 1.7.07.
☎ 0170 123 45 678, Nichtraucherin.

Architekturstudentin (25) sucht zum 1. od. 15.5. ruhiges Zim. bis 200 Euro incl. in WG ☎ 857 63 90 (oder 50 72 58)

[1]rufe ... *call back*   [2]*pay*
[3]incl. = inclusive *including utilities*   [4]*actor*

The euro (€) is used in the countries of the European Union, including Germany. The currency has seven denominations of bills and eight different coins. The front side of each coin is the same in all countries, but for the reverse side each nation can choose motifs particular to that country.

VORDERSEITEN

DEUTSCHE RÜCKSEITEN

2 €   1 €   50 Cent   20 Cent   10 Cent   5 Cent   2 Cent   1 Cent

10 €: 127 x 67 mm, rot

50 €: 140 x 77 mm, orange

Short History of the Euro

- January 1, 1999. The euro is born. The euro's exchange rate is established relative to other world currencies; however, people in Germany still used the **Deutsche Mark (D-Mark)** for everyday transactions.

- December 17, 2001. Starter kits are provided to banks for distribution to 53 million homes. The kits contain 20 marks worth of euros.

- January 1, 2002. The euro coins and bills make their debut. The euro replaces the **D-Mark** as legal tender in Germany.

- March 1, 2002. In January and February of 2002, people can still exchange D-Marks for euros at any bank. After March 1, only the **Bundesbank** will exchange the D-Mark.

- June 30, 2002. While the new euro postage stamps make their appearance on January 1, 2002, stamps in **D-Mark** and **Pfennig** remain in circulation until June 30, 2002.

Aktivität 3 Wer braucht eine Wohnung?

Schritt 1: Look over the five ads from **Aktivität 2** and complete the following:

1. Der junge Englischlehrer sucht ...
   a. eine Wohnung
   b. ein Zimmer in einer WG
   c. ein Appartement

2. Der Musiker braucht ein Zimmer ...
   a. zum 1. Juli
   b. zum 1. Juni
   c. zum 1. August

3. Der Schauspieler sucht ein Zimmer ...
   a. in München
   b. in Hamburg
   c. in Zürich

4. Die Fotodesignerin sucht ...
   a. ein Zimmer
   b. eine Wohnung
   c. eine Nichtraucherin

5. Für das Zimmer zahlt die Architekturstudentin ...
   a. bis 250 Euro
   b. bis 200 Euro
   c. bis 300 Euro

Schritt 2: Now look over the ads again and say as much as you can about each, giving more detailed information.

BEISPIEL: Ein Englischlehrer sucht ein Zimmer in einer WG.
    Er ist 37.
    Er ist freundlich und nett.

Aktivität 4 Eine Anzeige° schreiben   *ad*

Using the newspaper ads on the previous page as models, create a simple ad in the following format. Trade ads with another person, who will read yours to the class.

$$\left\{\begin{array}{l}\text{Student}\\\text{Studentin}\\\text{??}\end{array}\right\} \text{ sucht} \left\{\begin{array}{l}\text{großes}\\\text{kleines}\\\text{ruhiges}\\\text{helles}\\\text{möbliertes}\\\text{unmöbliertes}\\\text{??}\end{array}\right\} \text{Zimmer mit} \left\{\begin{array}{l}\text{Telefon}\\\text{Bad}\\\text{Küche}\\\text{Garten}\\\text{Computeranschluss}\end{array}\right\} \text{in} \left\{\begin{array}{l}\text{einer WG}\\\text{einem Haus}\\\text{zentraler Lage}\\\text{??}\end{array}\right\} \text{bis zu Euro} \text{—.}$$

THEMA 2: Auf Möbelsuche im Kaufhaus

das Bett

das Foto

der Kleiderschrank
€ 2.000

die Kommode
€ 600
€ 1500

die Lampe

der Wecker
€ 20
€ 325

der Nachttisch

das Poster

das Bücherregal

die Wand

die Verkäuferin

die Tür

€ 1575

der Computer

der Kunde

der Stuhl
€ 150

€ 850

€ 89

das Telefon

der Schreibtisch

das Regal

der Fernseher

der Sessel

die Zimmerpflanze

die Uhr

die Stereoanlage

€ 1400

das Radio

der CD-Spieler

das Sofa

der Videorecorder

€ 70

€ 350

der DVD-Spieler
€ 200

die Lampe

der Couchtisch

der Teppich

Welche Möbel haben Sie **schon** in Ihrem Zimmer / in Ihrer Wohnung?

Ich habe …

☐ einen **Fernseher** ☐ ein **Radio** ☐ einen **CD-Spieler**
☐ eine **Lampe** ☐ einen Computer ☐ ??

Ich brauche noch …

☐ einen **DVD-Spieler** ☐ einen **Tisch**
☐ ein **Bücherregal** ☐ ??

Was **kostet** das?

☐ **Dieser** DVD-Spieler kostet 200 Euro.
☐ **Diese** Lampe kostet 70 Euro
☐ **Dieses** Bett kostet 1500 Euro.
☐ ??

Neue Wörter

das Kaufhaus department
   store
welche which
die Möbel (*pl.*) furniture
schon already
der Tisch table
dieser, diese, dieses this

 Refer to *The der-Words dieser and welcher*, p. 67.

Aktivität 5   Ulla hat jetzt endlich° ein Zimmer.

finally

Listen as Ulla tells her friend Karin about the room she has just found. As you listen, check off the items that Ulla already has.

☐ ein Bett ☐ einen Sessel
☐ ein Bücherregal ☐ einen Stuhl
☐ eine Lampe ☐ ein Telefon
☐ einen Schreibtisch ☐ einen Tisch

SPRACHTIPP

When a masculine noun is used as a direct object, **der** changes to **den.** The articles **das** and **die** remain unchanged.

   Wie findest du **den** Computer?
   Wie findest du **das** Bett und **die** Lampe?

Refer to *The Definite Article: Nominative and Accusative*, p. 65.

Aktivität 6   Einkäufe°

Purchases

Neue Wörter

bequem comfortable
billig inexpensive, cheap

Schritt 1: Look at the department store displays at the beginning of **Thema 2** and give your opinion of the furniture and other items shown.

BEISPIEL: s1: Wie findest du den Computer?
               das Bett?
               die Lampe?
         s2: Sehr schön. Und wie findest du _____?

REAKTIONEN

   zu (*too*) …   teuer   praktisch
   sehr …   hässlich   (un)bequem
   nicht …   schön   billig
                  preiswert   toll

Schritt 2: Bring in several photos of pieces of furniture you have in your room, apartment, or house, or bring in several from magazines. Show them to a partner and, using the following model ask them to react.

BEISPIEL: s1: Wie findest du diesen Fernseher?
               dieses Radio?
               diese Lampe?
         s2: Nicht sehr preiswert. Und wie findest du _____?

Aktivität 7 Ein Gespräch im Kaufhaus

Listen as Ulla talks with a salesperson. Then answer the true/false questions and correct any false statements.

	DAS STIMMT	DAS STIMMT NICHT
1. Ulla braucht nur eine Lampe.	☐	☐
2. Ulla findet die italienische Lampe schön.	☐	☐
3. Die Lampe aus Italien ist nicht teuer.	☐	☐
4. Ulla kauft eine Lampe für 25 Euro.	☐	☐
5. Das Kaufhaus führt (*carries*) keine (*no*) Bücherregale.	☐	☐

THEMA 3: Was wir gern machen

 Refer to *Verbs with Stem-Vowel Changes,* p. 73.

Was machen diese **Leute** gern? Match each caption with the corresponding drawing.

1. _____ Dieser Herr **liest** gern.
2. _____ Diese Frau **isst** gern.
3. _____ Dieser **Mensch schläft** gern.
4. _____ Diese Frau **fährt** gern **Motorrad.**
5. _____ Dieser **Junge sieht** gern Videos.
6. _____ Dieser Mensch **läuft** gern.

a. Ernst Immermüd

b. Herr Wurm

c. Frau Renner

d. Frau Schlemmer

e. Uschi Schnell

f. Gerhard Glotze

Was machen Sie gern?

	JA	NEIN
Hören Sie gern Musik?	☐	☐
Essen Sie gern Sushi?	☐	☐
Fahren Sie gern **Auto**?	☐	☐
Kochen Sie gern?	☐	☐
Schreiben Sie gern E-Mails?	☐	☐
Schwimmen Sie gern?	☐	☐
Laufen Sie gern?	☐	☐
Sprechen Sie gern Deutsch?	☐	☐
Trinken Sie gern Cappuccino?	☐	☐
Schicken Sie gern SMS?	☐	☐

Neue Wörter

liest (lesen) reads
isst (essen) eats
der Mensch person
schläft (schlafen) sleeps
fährt (fahren) rides
der Junge boy
sieht (sehen) sees, watches
läuft (laufen) runs
schreiben write

SPRACHTIPP

In **Kapitel 1** you learned to express what you like to do, using the expression **Das macht mir Spaß.** Another common way to say you like to do something is to use the adverb **gern** with a conjugated verb.

Ich schwimme **gern**.	I like to swim.
Ich esse **gern** Fisch.	I like to eat fish.

If you want to say you dislike doing something, use **nicht gern.**

Ich schwimme **nicht gern**.	I don't like to swim.
Ich esse **nicht gern** Fisch.	I don't like to eat fish.

Note that **(nicht) gern** usually precedes direct objects.

Ich spiele **gern** Tennis.	I like to play tennis.
Frau Spitz hört **nicht gern** laute Musik.	Ms. Spitz does not like to listen to loud music.
Frau Heil nimmt **nicht gern** Medikamente.	Mrs. Heil doesn't like to take medicine.

Aktivität 8 Hin und her: Machen sie das gern?

Find out what the following people like to do or don't like to do by asking your partner.

BEISPIEL: s1: Was macht Denise gern?
        s2: Sie reist gern. Was macht Thomas nicht gern?
        s1: Er fährt nicht gern Auto.

	GERN	**NICHT GERN**
Thomas	arbeiten	Auto fahren
Denise		
Niko	Eis essen	Karten spielen
Anja		
Sie		
Ihr Partner / Ihre Partnerin		

- What activities are described in the ad and headline?
- Can you rephrase the following sentences using **(nicht) gern**?

1. Wandern macht mir Spaß.
2. Arbeiten macht mir keinen (*no*) Spaß.

Warum ich so gern in Hamburg arbeite

Von WOLFGANG JOOP, Hamburg

Ich lebe und arbeite in Hamburg.

Wandern Sie gerne?
Das Wandermagazin
– die große Zeitschrift nur fürs Wandern. Info (natürlich kosten-los) oder Leseexemplar (3 € in Briefmarken beifügen) anfordern:
Verlag Andrea Sänger
Moltkestr. 95/320,
53173 Bonn
Tel. 02 28/36 12 59

Two people from Berlin

Aktivität 9 Zwei Berliner°

Read the following questions and then scan the profiles of the two people from Berlin to find the answers to the questions.

1. Was trinkt Jasmin gern? Und Mehmet?
2. Was essen die beiden gern?
3. Was für (*what kind of*) Musik hören sie gern?
4. Was liest Mehmet gern?
5. Wer kocht gern?
6. Wer fährt gern einen Twingo?

Name: *Jasmin*
Alter: *23*
Lieblingsgetränk: *Rotwein*
Lieblingsessen: *Nudelgerichte*
Lieblingskleidung: *Jeans, Röcke*
Lieblingsmusik: *Klassische Musik, Jazz*
Lieblingsauto: *Renault Twingo*
Hobbys: *im Internet surfen, lesen, kochen, Sport*

Name: *Mehmet*
Alter: *30*
Lieblingsgetränk: *Tee*
Lieblingsessen: *Hackbraten*
Lieblingskleidung: *Jeans, Pullover*
Lieblingsmusik: *die Wise Guys*
Lieblingsauto: *BMW*
Hobbys: *Zeitung lesen, ins Kino gehen, wandern*

Ich esse
I eat

Aktivität 10 Wer macht was gern?

Schritt 1: Find out who likes to do the following things by asking different classmates the questions below. If they answer *yes,* have them sign their name in the blank to the right (or keep track by jotting down the people's names on a separate sheet).

BEISPIEL: s1: Siehst du gern Filme?
s2: Ja, ich sehe gern Filme.

1. Wanderst du gern?   _____
2. Hörst du gern laute Musik?   _____
3. Liest du gern?   _____
4. Surfst du gern im Internet?   _____
5. Isst du gern Brokkoli?   _____
6. Fährst du gern Motorrad?   _____

Schritt 2: Now ask three people in your class: **"Was machst du gern und was machst du nicht gern?"** Jot down their responses and report them to the class

BEISPIEL: Jeff reist gern, aber er tanzt nicht gern.
Sharon spielt gern Karten, aber sie kocht nicht gern.
Dave hört gern Musik, aber er arbeitet nicht gern.

SPRACHTIPP

In order to turn down an invitation, you could offer the following excuses.

s1: Wir gehen ins Konzert. Kommst du mit?	*We're going to the concert. Will you come along?*
s2: Nein, ich habe keine Zeit.	*No, I don't have the time.*
or	
s2: Nein, ich habe keine Lust.	*No, I don't feel like it.*
or	
s2: Nein, ich habe kein Geld.	*No, I don't have any money.*

Aktivität 11 Interaktion

You receive invitations from several people. Do you want to accept or reject the invitations?

BEISPIEL: s1: Wir gehen heute tanzen. Kommst du mit?
s2: Schön. Ich komme mit. Ich tanze sehr gern.
or
s2: Ich habe keine Lust.

EINLADUNG	REAKTION
Ich gehe / Wir gehen heute ... I go	Ja, schön.
in ein Rockkonzert.	Gut.
ins Kino (*to a movie*).	Tut mir leid (*I'm sorry*).
ins Theater.	Ich habe ...
schwimmen.	keine Zeit.
Tennis/Fußball spielen.	keine Lust. No interest
	kein Geld. No money

Grammatik im Kontext

Substantive im Plural

The Plural of Nouns°

German forms the plural of nouns in several different ways. The following chart shows the most common plural patterns and the notation of those patterns in the vocabulary lists of this book.

SINGULAR	PLURAL	TYPE OF CHANGE	NOTATION
das Zimmer die Mutter	die Zimmer die Mütter	*no change* *stem vowel is umlauted*	**-** **¨**
der Tag der Stuhl	die Tage die Stühle	*ending* **-e** *is added* *ending* **-e** *is added and stem vowel is umlauted*	**-e** **¨e**
das Buch	die Bücher	*ending* **-er** *is added and stem vowel is umlauted*	**¨er**
die Lampe die Frau die Studentin	die Lampen die Frauen die Studentinnen	*ending* **-n** *is added* *ending* **-en** *is added* *ending* **-nen** *is added*	**-n** **-en** **-nen**
das Radio	die Radios	*ending* **-s** *is added*	**-s**

Note:

- The definite article (*the*) in the plural is **die** for all nouns, regardless of gender.
- Nouns ending in **-er** or **-el** do not, with a few exceptions, change this ending in the plural.

SINGULAR	PLURAL
der Amerikan**er**	die Amerikan**er**
das Zimm**er**	die Zimm**er**
der Sess**el**	die Sess**el**

However, the stem vowel may change, as follows:

die M**u**tter	die M**ü**tter
der V**a**ter	die V**ä**ter

- Most feminine nouns (over 90%) form the plural by adding **-n** or **-en** to the singular.

SINGULAR	PLURAL
die Küche	die Küche**n**
die Arbeit	die Arbeit**en**

- Feminine nouns ending in -**in** form the plural by adding -**nen** to the singular.

SINGULAR	PLURAL
die Amerikaner**in**	die Amerikaner**innen**
die Mitbewohner**in**	die Mitbewohner**innen**

- Many masculine nouns form the plural by adding -**e**.

SINGULAR	PLURAL
der Tisch	die Tisch**e**
der Teppich	die Teppich**e**

- Nouns ending in vowel sounds and vowels other than -**e** usually form the plural by adding -**s**.

SINGULAR	PLURAL
das Handy	die Handy**s**
das Kino	die Kino**s**
das Sofa	die Sofa**s**

SPRACHTIPP

In order to use gender-inclusive language to refer to people, Germans frequently write forms such as **Student/in**, **Amerikaner/in**, or even **StudentIn**, **AmerikanerIn**, and for the plural of such nouns, **StudentInnen**, **AmerikanerInnen**.

Although most nouns follow a predictable pattern in forming the plural, many do not. Make it a habit to learn the plural formation with each new noun you learn.

Übung 1   Zimmer zu vermieten
Supply the plural forms.

1. Mathias und Susanne suchen zwei _____ oder _____ für eine WG im Zentrum von Leipzig. (Mitbewohnerin, Mitbewohner)

2. Die schöne, große Wohnung hat vier _____. (Zimmer)

3. Sie hat auch eine Küche, zwei _____ und einen Balkon. (Bad).

4. Preiswerte _____ in zentraler Lage sind rar. (Wohnung)

5. Die _____ sind sehr hoch. (Miete)

6. Sie sind viel zu hoch für viele _____ und _____ wie Mathias und Susanne. (Studentin, Student)

7. Mathias und Susanne suchen zwei _____ oder _____. (Nichtraucherin, Nichtraucher)

8. Ein Zimmer in der Wohnung ist sehr groß und hat zwei _____ zum Garten. (Fenster)

9. Da hört man die _____ auf der Straße nicht so. (Auto)

Übung 2 Wie viele?

List items in your classroom and students in your class.

BEISPIEL: Das Klassenzimmer hat 27 Stühle.

Das Klassenzimmer hat …

Fenster (-)	Student (-en)
Tür (-en)	Studentin (-nen)
Stuhl (ˉe)	Buch (ˉer)
Tisch (-e)	??

Übung 3 Im Studentenwohnheim

Choose suitable nouns from the box below to complete Kerstin's e-mail to Lea, making sure to put them in the plural.

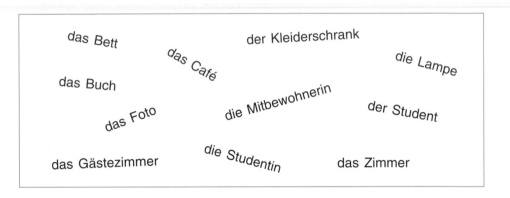

Kerstin hat jetzt ein Zimmer im Studentenwohnheim in Berlin. Das Wohnheim ist ganz neu und modern. Hier ist Kerstins E-Mail an eine Freundin.

Hallo, Lea! Na wie geht's? Ich hab' jetzt endlich ein Zimmer im Wohnheim. Gottseidank! Das Wohnheim hat 100 _____.[a] Es gibt einen Computerraum, einen Fitnessraum, einen Musikraum und zwei Bierkeller. Und wir haben auch fünf _____[b] für Besucher. Ich liebe die vielen _____[c] in der Stadt. Man sieht dort immer viele _____[d] und _____.[e] Sie trinken Kaffee und diskutieren über alles und nichts. Ich habe übrigens eine _____[f] auf meinem Zimmer. Sie kommt aus Stuttgart und ist sehr sympathisch. Das Zimmer hat zwei _____,[g] zwei _____,[h] und zwei _____[i] aber nur *einen* Schreibtisch und *einen* Stuhl! Und wir haben nur ein Regal für die _____.[j] Ich schicke dir drei _____[k] mit dieser E-Mail als Anhang (*attachment*). Du siehst, es geht mir ausgezeichnet. Tschüss, Kerstin

Kasus: der Nominativ und der Akkusativ

The Nominative and Accusative Cases°

In English, the subject and the direct object in a sentence are distinguished by their placement. The subject usually precedes the verb, whereas the direct object usually follows the verb.

In German, however, the subject and the object are not distinguished by their placement in the sentence. Instead, subjects and objects are indicated by grammatical cases. In this chapter you will learn about the nominative case (**der Nominativ**) for the subject of the sentence (as well as the predicate noun) and the accusative case (**der Akkusativ**) for the direct object and the object of certain prepositions.

German typically signals the case and the grammatical gender of a noun through different forms of the definite and indefinite articles that precede a noun.

The Definite Article°: Nominative and Accusative

Der bestimmte Artikel

You are already familiar with the nominative case. Those are the forms you used in **Kapitel 1.** Here are the nominative and the accusative case forms of the definite article (*the*).

NOMINATIVE	ACCUSATIVE
Der Stuhl kostet 70 Euro.	Ich kaufe **den** Stuhl.
The chair costs 70 Euro.	*I am going to buy the chair.*
Wo ist **die** Zeitung?	Ich brauche **die** Zeitung.
Where is the newspaper?	*I need the paper.*
Wie ist **das** Zimmer?	Ich miete **das** Zimmer.
How is the room?	*I am going to rent the room.*

	SINGULAR			PLURAL
	Masculine	*Feminine*	*Neuter*	*All Genders*
Nominative	der Stuhl	die Zeitung	das Zimmer	die Stühle
Accusative	**den** Stuhl	die Zeitung	das Zimmer	die Stühle

Note:

- Only the masculine definite article has a distinct accusative form: **den.**
- The plural has only one article for all three genders: **die.**

Weak Masculine Nouns°

Schwache Maskulina

A few common masculine nouns have a special accusative singular form. Five nouns of this type are shown in the following table.

NOMINATIVE	ACCUSATIVE
der **Mensch**	den Mensch**en**
der **Student**	den Student**en**
der **Herr**	den Herr**n**
der **Name**	den Name**n**
der **Kunde**	den Kunde**n**

Note:

- Weak masculine nouns, as they are called, are indicated in the vocabulary lists of this book by the notation (**-en** *masc.*) or (**-n** *masc.*).

In einer Studentenbude

Student room

Übung 4   Die Studentenbude°

What do you think of the things you see in this room?

BEISPIEL: Ich finde den Stuhl praktisch.

Ich finde ...

das Zimmer	nicht	praktisch
das Bücherregal	zu (*too*)	unpraktisch
der Stuhl	sehr	hässlich
die Schuhe		klein
der Sessel		modern
der Schreibtisch		unmodern
der Teppich		schön
der Student		bequem
die Bilder		unbequem
die Möbel		groß
der Nachttisch		sympathisch
		unsympathisch

SPRACHTIPP

Some adjectives can combine with the prefix **un-** to indicate the opposite meaning.

praktisch	**un**praktisch
practical	*impractical*

sympathisch	**un**sympathisch
likeable	*unlikeable*

Übung 5 Was kaufen Sie?

Sie haben 500 Euro. Was kaufen Sie?

BEISPIEL: Ich kaufe den Tisch für _____ Euro und ... .

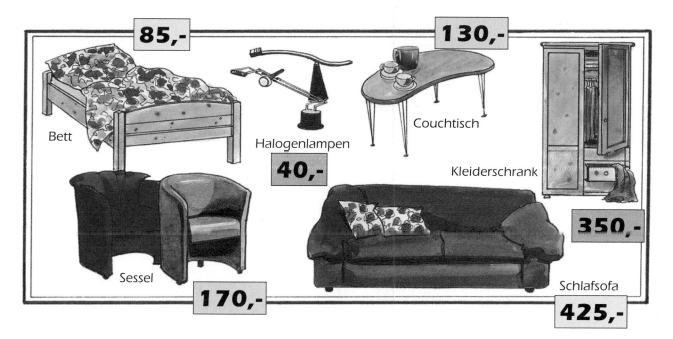

Bett — 85,-
Halogenlampen — 40,-
Couchtisch — 130,-
Kleiderschrank — 350,-
Sessel — 170,-
Schlafsofa — 425,-

The der-Words dieser and welcher

The word **dieser** (*this*) and the interrogative **welcher** (*which*) have the same endings as the definite article. For this reason they are frequently referred to as **der**-words.

Diese Wohnung ist zentral gelegen	*This apartment is centrally located.*
Dieser Schreibtisch kostet 400 Euro.	*This desk costs 400 Euros.*
Welchen Schreibtisch kaufst du?	*Which desk are you going to buy?*
Dieses Sofa ist nicht sehr bequem.	*This sofa is not very comfortable.*

All **der**-words follow the same pattern as the definite articles.

	MASCULINE	FEMININE	NEUTER	PLURAL
Nominative	dieser	diese	dieses	diese
	welcher	welche	welches	welche
Accusative	diesen	diese	dieses	diese
	welchen	welche	welches	welche

Note:

- Just as with the definite article, only the accusative masculine has an ending different from the nominative.

Übung 6   Im Geschäft

Insert the appropriate form of **dieser** or **welcher** in the following sentences.

1. Was kostet _____ Schreibtisch?
2. Ich finde _____ Schreibtisch zu groß.
3. _____ Schreibtisch ist zu groß?
4. _____ Sofa ist bequem?
5. _____ Lampe kostet 250 Euro.
6. _____ Studentin hat nicht viel Geld.
7. _____ Zimmer hat Computeranschluss?
8. _____ Zimmer sind möbliert?
9. _____ Studenten suchen eine Wohnung.

Der unbestimmte Artikel

The Indefinite Article°: Nominative and Accusative

Here are the nominative and accusative forms of the indefinite article (*a/an*).

NOMINATIVE

Das ist **ein** Stuhl.
That is a chair.

Das ist **eine** Zeitung.
That is a newspaper.

Das ist **ein** Zimmer.
That is a room.

ACCUSATIVE

Ich brauche **einen** Stuhl.
I need a chair.

Wo finde ich hier **eine** Zeitung?
Where do I find a newspaper here?

Ich brauche **ein** Zimmer.
I need a room.

SINGULAR			
	Masculine	*Feminine*	*Neuter*
Nominative	ein Stuhl	eine Zeitung	ein Zimmer
Accusative	**einen** Stuhl	eine Zeitung	ein Zimmer

Note:

- Only the masculine indefinite article has a distinct accusative form: **einen.**
- There is no plural indefinite article.

Nominative and Accusative Interrogative Pronouns°

To ask about the subject of a sentence, use **wer** (*who*) or **was** (*what*). To ask about the direct object, use **wen** (*whom*) or **was** (*what*).

Wer braucht Geld?	*Who needs money?*
Was ist ein Praktikum?	*What is an internship?*
Wen besucht Frau Martin?	*Whom is Mrs. Martin visiting?*
Was braucht der Mensch?	*What does a person need?*

Übung 7 Neu in Göttingen

You will now hear a conversation between Stefan and Birgit. As you listen, check off what Stefan already has and what he still needs for his new apartment. Not all items are mentioned; leave them blank.

	DAS HAT STEFAN	DAS BRAUCHT STEFAN
1. einen DVD-Spieler	☐	☐
2. eine Zimmerpflanze	☐	☐
3. eine Uhr	☐	☐
4. einen Couchtisch	☐	☐
5. einen Computer	☐	☐
6. einen Schreibtisch	☐	☐
7. ein Bücherregal	☐	☐
8. eine Kaffeemaschine	☐	☐
9. einen Schlafsack (*sleeping bag*)	☐	☐
10. ein Bett	☐	☐
11. einen Sessel	☐	☐

Übung 8 Was sehen Sie?

Das ist eine typische Studentenbude.

Da ist ＿＿＿.

Das Zimmer hat ＿＿＿.

Übung 9 Was brauchen Sie noch?

You are shopping for several items. Referring to the items and prices under **Thema 2: Auf Möbelsuche im Kaufhaus** in this chapter, create short conversational exchanges with a partner.

BEISPIEL: s1: Ich brauche eine Lampe.
s2: Hier haben wir Lampen.
s1: Was kostet die Lampe hier?
s2: 130 Euro.
s1: Das ist zu teuer. [*oder:*]
Das ist preiswert.

The Verb **haben**

The irregular verb **haben** (*to have*), like many other verbs, needs an accusative object (a direct object) to form a complete sentence.

Wir haben **eine Vorlesung** um zwei Uhr. *We have a lecture at two o'clock.*

Anja hat **einen Schreibtisch.** *Anja has a desk.*

haben			
ich	habe	wir	haben
du	**hast**	ihr	habt
er sie es	**hat**	sie	haben
Sie haben			

ANALYSE

Lesen Sie den Dialog.

Ein Gespräch zwischen zwei Studenten. Es ist 12 Uhr mittags.

JÜRGEN: Grüß dich, Petra. Hast du Hunger?

PETRA: Warum fragst du?

JÜRGEN: Ich geh' jetzt essen. Ich hab' Hunger. Kommst du mit?

PETRA: Na, gut. Da kommt übrigens Hans. Der hat bestimmt auch Hunger.

HANS: Habt ihr zwei vielleicht Hunger?

PETRA: Ja, und wie! Aber ich hab' nicht viel Zeit. Um zwei haben wir nämlich eine Vorlesung.

- Which forms of the verb **haben** can you find in the dialogue?
- The **ich**-form of **haben** appears without the ending **-e.** What could be the reason for this?

Übung 10 Hast du Hunger?

Complete the sentences with **haben** or **sein.**

Jürgen, Petra und Hans _____ª Studenten. Es _____ᵇ gerade
Mittagszeit. Jürgen _____ᶜ Hunger. Er fragt Petra: „_____ᵈ du Hunger?"
Hans _____ᵉ Petras Freund. Hans und Petra _____ᶠ um zwei eine
Vorlesung. Sie _____ᵍ nicht viel Zeit. Und Jürgen _____ʰ nicht viel
Geld (*money*). Er fragt Hans „_____ⁱ du etwas Geld?"

Übung 11 Was ich habe und was ich brauche

Schritt 1: Identify three items from **Übung 7** that you already have and
at least one item that you need. Tell your partner about these things in
German.

Schritt 2: Report to the class what your partner has and needs.

BEISPIEL: John hat einen Computer, einen Schreibtisch, und ein Bett. Er
braucht einen Sessel.

Negation° with nicht and the Negative Article kein

Verneinung

In **Kapitel 1** you learned to negate a simple statement by adding the word
nicht (*not*) before a predicate adjective.

Die Lampe ist **nicht** billig.   *The lamp is not cheap.*

You can also use **nicht** to negate an entire statement, or just an adverb.

Karin kauft die Lampe **nicht.**   *Karin is not buying the lamp.*

Ralf schreibt **nicht** besonders gut.   *Ralf doesn't write particularly well.*

One other important way to express negation is by using the negative article **kein** (*no, not a, not any*), which parallels the forms of **ein.**

—Ist das **eine** Zeitung?   *Is that a newspaper?*
—Das ist **keine** Zeitung!   *That isn't a newspaper!*

—Hast du **einen** Computer?   *Do you have a computer?*
—Nein, ich habe **keinen** Computer.   *No, I don't have a computer.*

—Hast du Geld?   *Do you have any money?*
—Nein, ich habe **kein** Geld.   *No, I do not have any money.*

—Sind das Studenten?   *Are those students?*
—Nein, das sind **keine** Studenten   *No, those are not students.*

[handwritten notes in margin:]
kein
Anything w/ a in front
use kein
der die das — the
eine / keine — a

Note:

- Use **kein** to negate a noun that is preceded by an indefinite article or
no article at all.

- Unlike **ein,** the negative article **kein** has plural forms.

	SINGULAR			PLURAL
	Masculine	*Feminine*	*Neuter*	*All Genders*
Nominative	kein Sessel	keine Lampe	kein Sofa	keine Stühle
Accusative	keinen Sessel	keine Lampe	kein Sofa	keine Stühle

Excuses, excuses!

Zwei Störche und ein Frosch

¹Die ... *That line never fails.*

Übung 12 Immer diese Ausreden!°

Everyone has a different excuse for turning down an invitation. Listen and check off the excuse given by each person.

1. Reinhard ...
   □ hat keine Zeit.
   □ hat keine Lust.
   □ hat kein Geld.

2. Erika ...
   □ hat keinen Freund.
   □ hat keine Zeit.
   □ hat keine Lust.

3. Frau Becker ...
   □ trinkt keinen Kaffee.
   □ hat keine Lust.
   □ hat keine Zeit.

4. Jens und Ulla ...
   □ haben kein Examen.
   □ haben keine Zeit.
   □ haben keinen Hunger.

5. Peter ...
   □ hat keine Lust.
   □ hat kein Geld.
   □ hat kein Auto.

Übung 13 Ein Frühstück°

Breakfast

Was ist hier komisch (*funny*)? In Grimm's fairy tale "The Frog Prince," a prince turned into a frog is transformed back into a prince by a beautiful princess. The cartoon on the left draws on this story for its comical effect. Circle the correct option in each statement.

1. Die zwei Störche (*storks*) suchen ein/kein Frühstück.

2. Der Frosch hat ein/kein Problem.

3. Störche essen gern / nicht gern Frösche zum Frühstück.

4. Der Frosch ist ein/kein Prinz.

5. Der Frosch ist sehr / nicht sehr intelligent.

6. Die Störche essen heute ein/kein Frühstück.

7. Ich finde den Cartoon komisch / nicht komisch.

Übung 14 Das stimmt nicht.

Complete each sentence with the appropriate form of **kein.**

BEISPIEL: Susanne sucht __kein__ Zimmer, sie sucht eine Wohnung.

1. Ein Zimmer suchen? Das macht __keinen__ Spaß.

2. Haben Sie eine Wohnung frei? —Nein, hier ist _____ Wohnung frei.

3. Brauchst du Geld? —Nein, ich brauche _____ Geld.

4. Ulla hat _____ Zimmer im Studentenwohnheim. Sie wohnt in einer WG.

5. Stefan wohnt bei seiner Familie. Da zahlt er __keine__ Miete.

6. Ist das Zimmer möbliert? —Es hat ein Bett, aber __keinen__ Schreibtisch.

7. Fährst du einen BMW? —Nein, ich habe __kein__ Auto.

Übung 15 Wer hat das nicht?

Find out what your fellow students do not have.

BEISPIEL: S1: Wer hat kein Handy? →
          S2: Sieben Studenten haben kein Handy.

Wer hat kein- ...?

Computer	Bett	Stühle
Stereoanlage	Zimmerpflanzen	Wecker
Schreibtisch	Radio	Nachttisch
Lampe	Auto	Videorecorder
Telefon	Motorrad	Handy
Sessel	Kommode	Poster (*pl.*)
Fernseher	Teppich	DVD-Spieler
Sofa	Regal	

Verbs with Stem-Vowel Changes°

Verben mit Wechsel des Stammvokals

A number of common verbs have vowel changes in some of the present tense forms.

to drive · sleep · run/walk · eat · see · read · take

	fahren	schlafen	laufen	essen	sehen	lesen	nehmen
ich	fahre	schlafe	laufe	esse	sehe	lese	nehme
du	**fährst**	**schläfst**	**läufst**	**isst**	**siehst**	**liest**	**nimmst**
er sie es	**fährt**	**schläft**	**läuft**	**isst**	**sieht**	**liest**	**nimmt**
wir	fahren	schlafen	laufen	essen	sehen	lesen	nehmen
ihr	fahrt	schlaft	lauft	esst	seht	lest	nehmt
sie/Sie	fahren	schlafen	laufen	essen	sehen	lesen	nehmen

Note:

- The vowel changes are in the second-person singular (**du**) and the third-person singular (**er, sie, es**).
- The verb **nehmen** (*to take*) has additional consonant changes: **du nimmst; er, sie, es nimmt.**

Verbs with vowel changes in the present tense will be indicated in the vocabulary sections of this book as follows: **schlafen (schläft).**

Übung 16 Kontraste

Mr. and Mrs. Wunderlich don't have a lot in common. Create a profile of each of them using the phrases provided.

BEISPIEL: Frau Wunderlich fährt gern Motorrad.
Herr Wunderlich fährt gern Auto.

fährt gern Motorrad/Auto

sieht gern Horrorfilme/Komödien

isst gern Sauerkraut/Fisch

liest jeden Tag Zeitung/nur das Horoskop

läuft jeden Tag im Park/macht keinen Sport

Übung 17 Was machen wir?

1. Ich _esse_ gern italienisch, Karin _ist_ gern chinesisch. (essen)
2. Klaus und Petra _e_____ heute im Restaurant. (essen) Petra _nimmt_ Fisch und Klaus _____ ein Wiener Schnitzel. (nehmen)
3. Hans braucht eine Lampe. Er _____ eine supermoderne Lampe im Kaufhaus. (sehen)
4. Ilse _____ gern Auto. Morgen _____ wir nach Berlin. (fahren)
5. Herr Renner _____ jeden Tag im Park. Dort _____ viele Jogger. (laufen)
6. —Was _____ du gern? —Ich _____ gern Zeitung. (lesen)

Übung 18 Was machen Sie gern, manchmal, nie, oft?

Tell a partner several things you do or don't like to do and how often: **gern, manchmal** (*sometimes*), **nie** (*never*), **oft.** Report to the class what you've learned.

BEISPIEL: s1: Ich esse gern, ich tanze manchmal, ich laufe nie.
s2: John isst gern, tanzt manchmal und läuft nie.

arbeiten   reisen   schwimmen

Auto/Motorrad fahren   tanzen

laufen

einen Hamburger/Sushi essen   Zeitung lesen

wandern   SMS schicken

schlafen

Spanisch sprechen

Karten/Tennis/Fußball spielen   telefonieren

Demonstrativpronomen

Demonstrative Pronouns°

ROBERT: Hat ⌐Thomas¬ Hunger?

KARIN: **Der** hat immer Hunger. [*Instead of*: Er hat immer Hunger.]

HERR HOLZ: Was kostet ⌐der Sessel¬ hier?

VERKÄUFER: **Der** kostet nur 150 Euro.

FRAU HOLZ: Gut, **den** nehmen wir.

ULLA: Wie findest du ⌐die Lampe¬?

ROBERT: **Die** finde ich prima.

In conversational German, demonstrative pronouns, identical to the definite articles, may be used instead of personal pronouns. Since demonstratives are more emphatic than personal pronouns, they are usually placed at the beginning of a sentence.

Übung 19   Fragen und Antworten

Answer, replacing the nouns or names with demonstrative pronouns.

BEISPIEL: Was macht Frau Schlemmer schon wieder? →
Die isst schon wieder.

1. Was macht Ernst Immermüd schon wieder?
   _____ schläft schon wieder.

2. Was macht Uschi Schnell schon wieder?
   _____ fährt schon wieder Motorrad.

3. Was kostet die Zeitung?
   _____ kostet zwei Euro.

4. Was kostet der Stuhl?
   _____ kostet 35 Euro.

5. Nimmst du den Stuhl?
   Ja, _____ nehme ich.

6. Liest du das Horoskop?
   Nein, _____ lese ich nie.

7. Wie findest du das Poster?
   _____ ist sehr schön.

8. Siehst du Thomas?
   Nein, _____ sehe ich nicht.

9. Wo studiert Lena?
   _____ studiert in Zürich.

Sprache im Kontext

Videoclips

A. Listen to what the following people say about where they live and complete the information.

1. Sabine hat eine _____. Sie hat vier _____, eine _____ und ein _____. Die Wohnung hat ungefähr _____ Quadratmeter. Wiebke und ihr Mann _____ gern.

2. Nicoletta wohnt in Berlin-Kreuzberg in einer _____. Es ist eine _____. Man kann eine Wohnung über die Mitwohnzentrale, über die _____, über _____ oder am Schwarzen Brett finden.

3. Claudia hat eine helle _____ im vierten Stock. Das Wohnzimmer hat eine _____, einen _____ Schreibtisch mit einem _____, verschiedene _____, einen _____ und Regale mit CDs. Die Wohnung war nicht _____.

4. Harald _____ in Berlin-Kreuzberg in einer alten Fabrik. Die Wohnung hat eine große Küche, zwei _____ und ein _____. Harald _____ gern vegetarisch und auch Fisch.

B. Watch the interviews with Sabina and Claudia. Listen as they say what they still need for their apartments. Who needs what?

C. Now describe your house, apartment, or room.

Lesen

Wie und wo wohnen junge Leute in Deutschland? In this section you will look at texts in which young people in Germany tell how they live.

Zum Thema

Wie wohnen Sie?

A. Take a few moments to complete the questionnaire; then interview a partner to see how he/she answered the questions.

Wo wohne ich?

1. Ich wohne _____.
   a. in einem Studentenwohnheim
   b. in einer Wohnung
   c. bei meinen Eltern
   d. in meinem eigenen (*own*) Haus
   e. privat in einem Zimmer
   f. ??

2. Ich teile (*share*) mein Zimmer / meine Wohnung / mein Haus mit _____.
   a. einer anderen Person
   b. zwei, drei, vier, ... Personen
   c. niemand anderem. Ich wohne allein.

3. Ich habe _____.
   a. eine Katze (*cat*)
   b. einen Hund (*dog*)
   c. einen Goldfisch
   d. andere Haustiere (eine Kobra, einen Hamster, ...)
   e. keine Haustiere

4. Ich wohne gern/nicht gern _____.
   a. in einer Großstadt
   b. in einer Kleinstadt
   c. auf dem Land

5. Als Student hat man hier _____ Probleme, eine Wohnung zu finden.
   a. keine
   b. manchmal
   c. große

6. Die Mieten sind hier _____.
   a. niedrig
   b. hoch

B. Report to the class what you found out about your partner.

Auf den ersten Blick

In the following passages students in Bonn, the former capital of the Federal Republic of Germany, and Rostock, a city in northeastern Germany, tell about their living arrangements. Skim through the texts, and for each one organize the vocabulary you recognize into the following categories.

PERSON	HOUSING	OBJECTS FOUND IN ROOM
BEISPIEL: Katja	Studentenwohnheim	Betten, Schreibtisch, Esstisch, Regale ...

SO WOHNE ICH

Name: Katja Meierhans
Wohnort: Rostock
Hauptfächer: Mathematik, Chemie

Während des Studiums wohne ich im Studentenwohnheim mit noch einer[1] Studentin auf einem
Zimmer; Gemeinschaftswaschräume[2] und WCs[3]
für den ganzen Flur[4] (22 Zimmer); im Raum
sind Betten, Schreibtisch, Esstisch, viele Regale,
viele Schränke. Ich bin zufrieden[5]. Zu Hause
(300 km von Rostock) wohne ich bei meinen
Eltern. Wir haben mein Zimmer zusammen aus-
gebaut[6], deshalb[7] ist es natürlich mehr nach
meinen Wünschen. Ich fahre gern nach Hause,
aber in Rostock bin ich unabhängiger[8].

Name: Christina Stiegen
Wohnort: Niederkassel (Rheidt)
Hauptfächer: Politologie, Italienisch

Ich wohne in einer Wohnung etwas außerhalb
von[9] Bonn. Die Wohnung hat 52m[2], zwei
Zimmer, Küche, Diele[10], Bad. Ich teile mir[11] die
Wohnung mit meinem Freund, der auch in
Bonn studiert. Es handelt sich um[12] eine
Dachwohnung[13].

Name: Jennifer Wolcott
Wohnort: Mönchengladbach
Hauptfächer: Englisch, Politische
Wissenschaften

Ich wohne in einem Zimmer (12m[2]) in einem
Studentenwohnheim. In dem Zimmer sind ein
Schreibtisch mit einer Schublade,[14] ein Bett, ein
Regal, ein Kleiderschrank und ein Waschbecken[15] mit Spiegel[16]. Ich habe einen Teppich[17]
hingelegt, Pflanzen auf die große Fensterbank[18]
gestellt, noch ein Regal (für meine vielen Bücher
und meine Stereoanlage). Außerdem habe ich
Bilder, Poster und Erinnerungen[19] an die weißen
Wände gehängt. Ich teile Bad/Toiletten und eine
große Küche mit zwanzig Studenten.

Name: Peter Kesternich
Wohnort: Euskirchen
Hauptfächer: Englisch, Geschichte

Ich wohne in einem Zimmer bei meinen Eltern.
Ich fahre jeden Morgen mit dem Zug[20] zur Uni
(ca. 50 Min.). Das ist für mich praktischer (und
billiger), als in Bonn ein Zimmer zu suchen.

---

[1]noch … one other [2]common washrooms [3]toilets [4]floor [5]content, satisfied [6]renovated [7]for that reason [8]more independent
[9]etwas … just outside of [10]front hall [11]teile … share [12]Es … It is [13]attic apartment [14]drawer [15]sink [16]mirror [17]carpet
[18]windowsill [19]mementos, souvenirs [20]train

Zum Text

A. Read the texts more thoroughly and look at the drawings here and on
the following page. Which description most closely matches which
drawing?

1.

2.

3.   4.

B. Look at the chart below and then scan the texts for specific information in order to complete it. If there is no information given for a particular category, leave that space blank.

NAME	WOHNORT	WIE ER/SIE WOHNT	WAS IM ZIMMER IST	WEITERE INFORMATIONEN

1. Using the information in the chart, construct sentences about the students. Have the rest of the class guess which person you are describing.

2. Using the information in the chart, describe one of the people by creating true and false statements. The rest of the class has to say whether your statements are true or false.

Zu guter Letzt

Wir suchen einen Mitbewohner / eine Mitbewohnerin.

In this chapter you have learned how to talk about student living situations and furnishings. In this project you will join others to interview a prospective roommate, choose a roommate, explain your choice, and report to the class.

Schritt 1: Work in groups of three or four. Imagine that you all live in a large apartment, house, or WG as roommates and that one of you is moving out. You are seeking a replacement for him/her. Create a flyer, in German, in which you describe what you have to offer. Feel free to consult and utilize the housing ads and flyers found in **Kapitel 2** as you create your own. You might start as follows:

Wir, drei Studentinnen, suchen eine Mitbewohnerin für unsere Wohnung. ...

Distribute your housing flyer to classmates and find at least two people who want to interview for the room.

Schritt 2: Interview each applicant. Use German to ask the questions. You will want to ask the applicant several questions, such as whether . . .

- he/she is a student
- he/she is also working
- he/she is a (non)smoker
- he/she has a pet (**einen Hund, eine Katze, einen Hamster**)
- owns a car, motorcycle, bicycle
- telephones frequently
- plays loud music (**laute Musik**)
- has a lot of visitors (**viel Besuch haben**)
- has a computer and will need a high-speed connection (**Computeranschluss**)
- he/she considers herself/himself chaotic and eccentric or quiet and serious

The applicant might have questions, as well, such as . . .

- how large the room is
- whether the room is furnished
- how much the rent is
- whether there is a telephone, a garage, a yard
- how many people live in the apartment

Schritt 3: After you have interviewed prospective roommates, compare notes about the different people you interviewed, and decide whom to invite to become your roommate.

Schritt 4: Report back to the class on whom you have chosen and why.

BEISPIEL: Wir vermieten (*rent*) das Zimmer an Jeanine. Sie ist sehr nett und sympathisch. Sie studiert Informatik. Sie ist Nichtraucherin und spielt keine laute Musik. ...

Wortschatz

Im Kaufhaus

At the Department Store

das **Bett, -en**	bed
der **CD-Spieler, -**	CD player
der **Computer, -**	computer
der **Computeranschluss, ⸚e**	computer connection
der **DVD-Spieler, -**	DVD player
der **Fernseher, -**	TV set
das **Foto, -s**	photograph
das **Handy, -s**	cell phone
der **Kleiderschrank, ⸚e**	clothes closet
die **Kommode, -n**	dresser
die **Lampe, -n**	lamp
die **Möbel** (*pl.*)	furniture
das **Poster, -**	poster
das **Radio, -s**	radio
das **Regal, -e**	shelf
das **Bücherregal, -e**	bookcase, bookshelf
der **Sessel, -**	armchair
das **Sofa, -s**	sofa
die **Stereoanlage, -n**	stereo
der **Stuhl, ⸚e**	chair
das **Telefon, -e**	telephone
der **Teppich, -e**	rug, carpet

der **Tisch**, -e	table
der **Couchtisch**, -e	coffee table
der **Nachttisch**, -e	nightstand
der **Schreibtisch**, -e	desk
die **Uhr**, -en	clock
der **Videorecorder**, -	video recorder, VCR
der **Wecker**, -	alarm clock

Das Haus — The House

das **Bad**, ¨er	bathroom
der **Balkon**, -e	balcony
das **Fenster**, -	window
die **Garage**, -n	garage
der **Garten**, ¨	garden; yard
das **Haus**, ¨er	house
die **Küche**, -n	kitchen
die **Terrasse**, -n	terrace, patio
die **Tür**, -en	door
die **Wand**, ¨e	wall
das **Zimmer**, -	room
das **Arbeitszimmer**, -	workroom, study
das **Badezimmer**, -	bathroom
das **Esszimmer**, -	dining room
das **Schlafzimmer**, -	bedroom
das **Wohnzimmer**, -	living room

Sonstige Substantive — Other Nouns

das **Auto**, -s	car
der **Euro**, -s	euro
das **Geld**	money
der **Junge** (-n *masc.*), -n	boy
das **Kaufhaus**, ¨er	department store
der **Kunde** (-n *masc.*), -n / die **Kundin**, -nen	customer
die **Leute** (*pl.*)	people
der **Mensch** (-en *masc.*), -en	person, human being
die **Miete**	rent
der **Mitbewohner**, - / die **Mitbewohnerin**, -nen	roommate, housemate
das **Motorrad**, ¨er	motorcycle
der **Nichtraucher**, - / die **Nichtraucherin**, -nen	nonsmoker
das **Problem**, -e	problem
das **Studentenwohnheim**, -e	dormitory
der **Tag**, -e	day
der **Verkäufer**, - / die **Verkäuferin**, -nen	salesperson
das **Video**, -s	video(tape)
die **Wohngemeinschaft**, -en (WG)	shared housing

die **Wohnung**, -en	apartment
die **Zeit**, -en	time
die **Zimmerpflanze**, -n	houseplant

Verben — Verbs

brauchen	to need
essen (isst)	to eat
fahren (fährt)	to drive, ride
fragen	to ask
haben (hat)	to have
Durst haben	to be thirsty
gern haben	to like (*a person or thing*)
Hunger haben	to be hungry
Lust haben	to feel like (*doing something*)
Recht haben	to be correct
Zeit haben	to have time
kaufen	to buy
kosten	to cost
laufen (läuft)	to run, jog
lesen (liest)	to read
nehmen (nimmt)	to take
schlafen (schläft)	to sleep
schreiben	to write
schwimmen	to swim
sehen (sieht)	to see
sprechen (spricht)	to speak
suchen	to look for
trinken	to drink

Adjektive und Adverbien — Adjectives and Adverbs

bequem	comfortable, comfortably
billig	inexpensive(ly), cheap(ly)
da	there
dringend	desperate(ly)
dunkel	dark
frei	free(ly)
genau	exact(ly)
gerade	just, exactly
gern	gladly
gern + *verb*	to like to do something
groß	big, large
hässlich	ugly
hell	bright(ly), light
hoch	high(ly)
klein	small
möbliert	furnished
unmöbliert	unfurnished
niedrig	low
noch	still; yet

nur	only		
preiswert	a bargain, inexpensive(ly)		
recht	quite, rather		
recht preiswert	quite inexpensive, reasonable		
schon	already		
schön	nice(ly), beautiful(ly)		
selten	rare(ly)		
so	so		
teuer	expensive(ly)		
viel/viele	much/many		
wieder	again		

Sonstiges / Other

dieser	this
etwas	something; somewhat, a little (*adverb*)
kein	no, none, not any
nichts	nothing
warum	why
Was ist denn los?	What's the matter?
weit (weg) von …	far (away) from . . .
welcher	which
zentral gelegen	centrally located

DAS KANN ICH NUN!

1. Sagen Sie:

   a. Wo und wie wohnen Sie? **b.** Wie hoch ist die Miete? **c.** Haben Sie Computeranschluss und ein Handy?

2. Nennen Sie vier Zimmer in einer Wohnung.

3. Nennen Sie fünf Möbelstücke in Ihrem Zimmer. Was haben Sie nicht? (Zwei Möbelstücke) Ich habe …

4. Was machen Sie gern? Nennen Sie drei Aktivitäten.

5. Nennen Sie die Artikel und Pluralformen von …

   a. Zimmer **b.** Buch **c.** Handy **d.** Küche **e.** Stuhl **f.** Mitbewohnerin **g.** Kunde

6. Wie sagt man das auf Deutsch?

   a. A salesperson offers you a desk at a price that she considers reasonable, but you find it too expensive. Express your opinion.
   b. You are telling someone who has invited you for coffee that you have no time.
   c. You are telling someone that Frau Renner likes to ride a motorcycle.

Familie und Freunde

Ein oder zwei gegrillte
Würstchen?

In diesem Kapitel

- **Themen:** Family members, days of the week, months, holidays, celebrations, ordinal numbers
- **Grammatik:** Possessive adjectives; personal pronouns in accusative case; prepositions with accusative; **werden, wissen,** and **kennen**
- **Kultur:** German holidays and celebrations
- **Lesen:** „Wie feierst du deinen großen Tag?"

Videoclips
Familien und Feste

Alles klar?

Families are important in every culture. We often define ourselves in terms of our family background. Even with the fast pace of modern life, family members take time to come together for important celebrations such as weddings, birthdays, and holidays.

A. Below you see a picture of Bernd Thalhofer's family with his relatives labeled. Your knowledge of cognates and contextual guessing will help you understand what these words mean. Look at the picture and identify the words for mother, father, sister, brother in law, and niece. Now, can you guess at what family celebration the picture was taken?

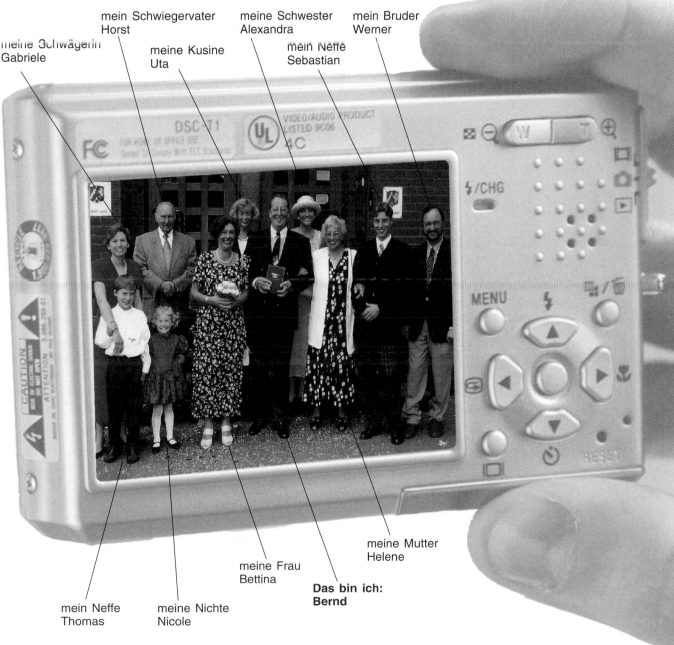

mein Schwiegervater Horst

meine Schwester Alexandra

mein Bruder Werner

meine Schwägerin Gabriele

meine Kusine Uta

mein Neffe Sebastian

meine Mutter Helene

meine Frau Bettina

Das bin ich: Bernd

mein Neffe Thomas

meine Nichte Nicole

B. Now listen as Bernd's sister, Alexandra, describes her family. As you listen, indicate whether the following statements are correct or incorrect.

	DAS STIMMT	DAS STIMMT NICHT
1. Das Foto zeigt Familie Thalhofer bei einer Geburtstagsfeier.	☐	☒
2. Familie Thalhofer wohnt in Leipzig.	☐	☐
3. Alexandra Thalhofer hat zwei Brüder.	☐	☐
4. Ihr Bruder Bernd und Bernds Frau, Bettina, sind Lehrer von Beruf.	☐	☐
5. Alexandra plant eine Reise nach Kanada.	☐	☐
6. Alexandras Bruder Werner hat zwei Kinder.	☐	☐
7. Alexandras Mutter ist nicht auf dem Foto.	☐	☐

Wörter im Kontext

A family tree

THEMA 1: Ein Familienstammbaum°

Bernd Thalhofers Familie

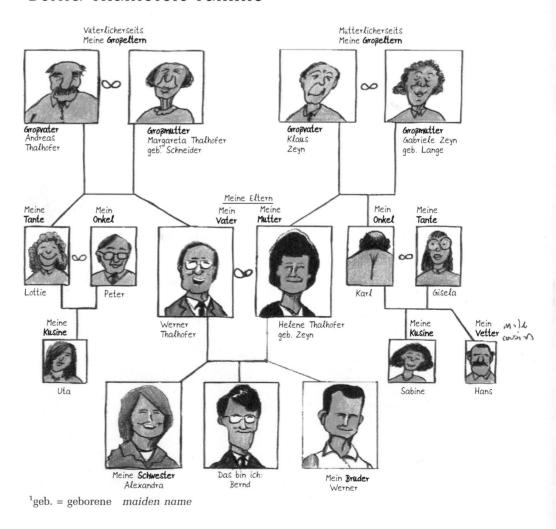

¹geb. = geborene *maiden name*

Wer ist wer? How is each relative related to you?

1. der Bruder
2. der **Enkel**
3. die **Enkelin**
4. die **Geschwister** (*pl.*)
5. die **Großeltern** (*pl.*)
6. die **Großmutter** (**Oma**)
7. der **Großvater** (**Opa**)
8. die Kusine
9. der **Neffe**
10. die **Nichte**
11. der Onkel
12. der **Schwager** *in law*
13. die **Schwägerin**
14. die Schwester
15. die Tante
16. der Vetter

a. Mein _neffe_: der **Sohn** meines (*of my*) Bruders oder meiner (*of my*) Schwester
b. Meine _schwester_ die **Tochter** meiner Eltern
c. Meine _Nichte_: die Tochter meines Bruders oder meiner Schwester
d. Meine _Tante_: die Schwester meines Vaters oder meiner Mutter
e. Mein _____: der Sohn meines Sohnes oder meiner Tochter
f. Mein _____: der **Mann** meiner Schwester
g. Meine _____: die Söhne und Töchter meiner Eltern
h. Meine _____: die Mutter meines Vaters oder meiner Mutter
i. Mein _____: der Bruder meines Vaters oder meiner Mutter
j. Mein _____: der Sohn meiner Eltern
k. Mein _____: der Sohn meines Onkels und meiner Tante
l. Meine _____: die Tochter meines Sohnes oder meiner Tochter
m. Meine _____: die **Frau** meines Bruders
n. Meine _____: die Eltern meiner Eltern
o. Meine _____: die Tochter meines Onkels und meiner Tante
p. Mein _____: der Vater meines Vaters oder meiner Mutter

Neue Wörter	
der Enkel	grandson
die Enkelin	granddaughter
die Geschwister (*pl.*)	siblings
die Oma	grandma
der Opa	grandpa
der Neffe	nephew
die Nichte	niece
der Schwager	brother-in-law
die Schwägerin	sister-in-law
der Sohn	son
die Tochter	daughter
der Mann	husband
die Frau	wife

SPRACHTIPP

As in English, to indicate that somebody is related to another person, add an **-s** to the person's name—though without an apostrophe.

Das ist Bernd **Thalhofers** Familie.
Bernds Eltern heißen Werner und Helene.

Another way to indicate relationships is with the preposition **von** (*of*).

Das ist die Familie **von** Bernd Thalhofer.
Die Eltern **von** Bernd heißen Werner und Helene.

The **von** construction is preferred if a name ends in an **-s** or **-z**.

Die Frau **von** Markus heißt Julia.
Die Eltern **von** Frau Lentz kommen aus München.

Aktivität 1 Wer ist das?

Unscramble the letters to find out which family member each item represents. The vocabulary at the top of the previous page will help you.

1. feeNf
2. eTtna
3. esKnui
4. treeVt
5. chNeti

6. klnOe
7. sewrStche
8. drerBu
9. tmßGorture
10. rVaet

Aktivität 2 Ein Interview

Schritt 1: Ask a person in your class about his/her family.

1. Wie heißen deine Eltern?
2. Wie viele Geschwister hast du?
3. Wie heißen deine Geschwister?
4. Wo wohnt deine Familie?
5. Wie alt sind deine Geschwister?
6. ??

Schritt 2: Report back to the class about your partner's family.

BEISPIEL: Jennys Familie wohnt in Toronto. Jenny hat fünf
Brüder und drei Schwestern. Ihre Brüder heißen Mark und
Stephen …

SPRACHTIPP

To indicate that someone is related only through one parent, compounds can be formed using **Stief-** (*step*) and **Halb-** (*half*). The German equivalent to English *great* is the prefix **Ur-**.

Maria ist meine **Stiefschwester.**	*Maria is my stepsister.*
Mein **Halbbruder** heißt Jens.	*My half-brother is named Jens.*
Wilhelmine ist meine **Urgroßmutter.**	*Wilhelmine is my great-grandmother.*

Aktivität 3 Generationen: Wer ist wer?

Schritt 1: Look closely at the family portrait on the next page and answer the questions.

1. Wie viele Generationen sind auf diesem Foto?
2. Wie heißen die Frauen mit Vornamen?
3. Wie heißen die zwei jüngsten (*youngest*) Frauen?
   Wie alt sind sie?
4. Wer ist die älteste (*oldest*) Frau? Wie alt ist sie?
5. Wer ist die Mutter von Susanne und Nicole?
6. Wer ist die Großmutter von Frauke?
7. Wer ist die Tochter von Pauline?

Landkinder: Tochter Susanne, 18; Großmutter Alma, 63; Tochter Nicole, 19; Urgroßmutter Pauline, 87; Mutter Frauke, 40

Schritt 2: Now fill in the missing information.

1. Susanne ist Fraukes _____.

2. Pauline ist Susannes und Nicoles _____ und Fraukes _____.

3. Alma ist Paulines _____ und Susannes und Nicoles _____.

4. _____ spielt gern Fußball. Sie ist Paulines Enkelin.

5. Alma hat zwei Enkelinnen, _____ und _____. Und wer ist das in der Mitte? Sie gehört (*belongs*) auch zur Familie.

Aktivität 4 Ein merkwürdiger° Stammbaum

peculiar

A very special family is celebrating its birthday. What is the name of the family?

1. Welche Namen kennen Sie, welche Namen kennen Sie nicht?

2. Wer fehlt (*is missing*) in diesem Stammbaum? Ich sehe keine/keinen _____.

3. Wer hat keinen Namen?

4. Das Insekt hier ist ein Käfer. Wie heißt „Käfer" auf Englisch?

5. Wissen Sie, wie alt der Großvater ungefähr (*roughly*) ist?

   a. über 100 Jahre

   b. ungefähr 60–70 Jahre

   c. ungefähr 10 Jahre

6. Wie heißt die „Käfer" Familie?

DER GROSSVATER.

DIE SCHWESTER KARMANN GHIA.   DER BRUDER KÄFER.

DER ONKEL ILTIS.   DIE TANTE GOLF.   DER NEFFE PASSAT.

DER VETTER POLO.   DIE COUSINE JETTA.   DER COUSIN SANTANA.   DER ENKELIN SCIROCCO.

Wir gratulieren der ganzen Familie.

THEMA 2: Der Kalender: Die Wochentage und die Monate

die Monate	
Januar	Juli
Februar	August
März	September
April	Oktober
Mai	November
Juni	Dezember

Oktober

Montag	Dienstag	Mittwoch	Donnerstag	Freitag	Samstag	Sonntag
4	5	6	7	1	2	3
11	12	13	14	8	9	10
18	19	20	21	15	16	17
25	26	27	28	22	23	24
			29	30	31	

Aktivität 5 Welcher Tag ist das?

Newspaper ads often abbreviate the days of the week. Can you identify which days of the week these abbreviations represent?

1. Mo _____
2. Fr _____
3. Do _____
4. So _____
5. Mi _____
6. Sa _____
7. Di _____

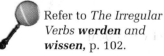

Refer to *The Irregular Verbs* **werden** *and* **wissen,** p. 102.

> **SPRACHTIPP**
>
> Use the following phrases to say the day or month when something takes place.
>
> —Wann wirst du 21?
> —Ich werde **am Samstag** 21.
>
> —Wann hast du Geburtstag?
> —Ich habe **im Dezember** Geburtstag.

time = um

Aktivität 6 Wie alt bist du?

Interview several classmates to learn their ages and birthdates.

BEISPIEL: s1: Wie alt bist du?
s2: Ich bin 23.
s1: Wann wirst du 24?
s2: Ich werde im August 24. Und du?

Aktivität 7   Eine Einladung° zum Geburtstag

invitation

Listen and take notes as Tom and Heike talk about an upcoming birthday party. Read the questions first before listening to the conversation.

1. Wer hat Geburtstag?
2. Wann ist der Geburtstag?
3. Wo ist die Party?
4. Wer kommt sonst noch (*else*)?
5. Kommt die Person am Telefon, oder nicht?

Aktivität 8   Hin und her: Verwandtschaften°

relationships

Ask a partner questions about Bernd's family. How is each person related to Bernd?

BEISPIEL: s1: Wie ist Gisela mit Bernd verwandt?
s2: Gisela ist Bernds Tante.
s1: Wie alt ist sie denn?
s2: Sie ist 53.
s1: Wann hat sie Geburtstag?
s2: Im Februar.

PERSON	VERWANDTSCHAFT	ALTER	GEBURTSTAG
Gisela			
Alexandra	Schwester	25	März
Christoph			
Andreas	Großvater	80	Juni
Sabine			

THEMA 3: Feste und Feiertage°

Celebrations and holidays

Geburtstagswünsche

Germans express birthday wishes in many ways. Here are some typical birthday wishes taken from German newspapers.

❤ **Heike**
wird heute
„21"
Herzlichen Glückwunsch

Lieber Vater und Opa!
Zu Deinem 85. Geburtstag gratulieren
*Hansi – Waltraud – Angela – Torsten
Birgit – Peter – Jan und Marco*

Ralf hat
Geburtstag!
Alles Gute!

Hallo Belinda!
Viel Glück und alles Gute
zum 18.
wünschen Mutti und Papa
und der ganze Clan.
W. W. B. U. S. U. J. D. M.
S. W. P. S. W. und Chris

Liebe Oma *Marie Sudhoff*
zu Deinem **80. Geburtstag** wünschen
Dir Deine Kinder, Enkel und Urenkel alles
Liebe und Gute.

Neue Wörter

wird (werden) turns, becomes
Herzlichen Glückwunsch (zum Geburtstag) Happy birthday!
gratulieren congratulate
Alles Gute! All the best!
wünschen wish

Feiertage in der Familie Thalhofer

Valentinstag ist relativ **neu** für viele Deutsche. Bernd und Alexandra **kennen** diesen Tag aus den USA. Muttertag ist für Frau Thalhofer nicht so **wichtig**, aber ihre Familie gibt ihr **oft** Blumen.

Dieses Jahr gibt es noch eine **Hochzeit** in Bernds Familie. Seine Kusine Sabine **heiratet** nämlich im September.

Die Familie **plant** ein großes **Familienfest** mit einem Abendessen in der Marxburg am Rhein. Bernds Großeltern feiern dieses Jahr ihre goldene Hochzeit, aber sie **wissen** noch nicht wo.

Bernd hat im April Geburtstag. Dieses Jahr **feiert** er mit seiner Frau Bettina bei Freunden in Berlin. Natürlich feiern sie auch bei den Eltern in Köln, und **es gibt** auch eine kleine **Party** und natürlich auch **Geschenke.**

Weihnachten hat eine lange **Tradition. Am Heiligen Abend** gibt es Geschenke und ein Familienessen. Auch am ersten Weihnachtstag (25. Dezember) feiert die Familie zusammen. Am zweiten Weihnachtstag (26. Dezember) besucht die Familie die Großeltern, Tanten und Onkel.

Silvester sind Thalhofers oft bei Freunden. **Um Mitternacht** gibt es dann oft ein kleines Feuerwerk im Garten. Manchmal bleiben sie aber auch zu Hause.

Neue Wörter

neu new
kennen know
wichtig important
die Hochzeit wedding
heiratet (heiraten) is getting married
plant (planen) is planning
das Familienfest family gathering
wissen know
feiert (feiern) celebrates
es gibt there is
das Geschenk (Geschenke, *pl.*) present
das Weihnachten Christmas
am Heiligen Abend on Christmas Eve
das Silvester New Year's Eve
um Mitternacht at midnight

To form most ordinal numbers (*first, second, third,* and so on) in German, add the suffix **-te** or **-ste** to the cardinal number. Note that the words for *first, third, seventh,* and *eighth* are exceptions to the rule.

eins	**erste**	neun	neun**te**
zwei	zwei**te**	zehn	zehn**te**
drei	**dritte**	elf	elf**te**
vier	vier**te**	zwölf	zwölf**te**
fünf	fünf**te**	dreizehn	dreizehn**te**
sechs	sechs**te**	. . .	. . .
sieben	sieb(en)**te**	zwanzig	zwanzig**ste**
acht	**achte**		

Ordinal numbers are normally used with the definite article.

Freitag ist **der erste** Oktober.

To talk about dates for special occasions, you can say:

Wann hast du Geburtstag? —**Am 18. (achtzehnten)** September.

Der erste Weihnachtstag ist **am 25. (fünfundzwanzigsten)** Dezember.

Note that ordinal numbers are written with a period: **der 4. Juli; am 4. Juli.**

Hier klicken!

You'll find more about holidays and festivals in German-speaking countries in **Deutsch: Na klar!** on the World Wide Web at www.mhhe.com/dnk5.

Legal holidays in German-speaking countries are largely religious holidays. The most important ones are Christmas (**Weihnachten**), New Year (**Neujahr**), and Easter (**Ostern**) and are celebrated for two days each. An important nonreligious holiday in Germany is the Day of German Unity (**Tag der deutschen Einheit**) on October 3.

There are a number of regional holidays as well. Mardi Gras (**Karneval** in the Rhineland and **Fasching** in southern Germany) is celebrated before Lent, in early spring. People get one day off work to participate in the merriment in and out of doors. Germans in northern and eastern regions do not celebrate Mardi Gras.

Germans go all out for family celebrations such as weddings and silver and golden wedding anniversaries.

Karneval in Köln

Aktivität 9 Feste und Feiertage

Match up the German holidays and celebrations with their English equivalents.

1. _____ Weihnachten
2. _____ Karneval
3. _____ Geburtstag
4. _____ Ostern
5. _____ Silvester
6. _____ Hochzeit
7. _____ der Heilige Abend
8. _____ Tag der deutschen Einheit

a. Mardi Gras
b. Christmas Eve
c. Easter
d. Labor Day
e. birthday
f. wedding
g. Memorial Day
h. German Unity Day
i. Christmas
j. New Year's Eve

Aktivität 10 Geburtstagsgrüße

Choose several of the following words and phrases to create birthday greetings for someone.

alles Gute   du wirst   ich gratuliere   liebe _____

herzlichen Glückwunsch   lieber _____   viel Glück

wir gratulieren   wünscht / wünschen dir   zum Geburtstag

zu deinem _____ Geburtstag   _____ wird _____

Aktivität 11 Eine Einladung zu einer Party

Invite someone to a party, using the expressions provided.

BEISPIEL: s1: Ich mache am Sonntag eine Party. Kommst du?
s2: Am Sonntag? Vielen Dank. Ich komme gern. [*oder*]
Vielen Dank. Leider kann ich nicht kommen.

OTHER EXCUSES

Es tut mir leid. / Ich bin leider nicht zu Hause. / Ich fahre nämlich nach _____. / Mein Vater / Meine Mutter usw. (*and so on*) hat nämlich auch Geburtstag.

Neue Wörter

Es tut mir leid. I'm sorry.
leider unfortunately
nämlich namely, that is to say
morgen tomorrow

SPRACHTIPP

When stating your reason for an action, use the adverb **nämlich.** Note that there is no exact equivalent of **nämlich** in English.

Ich kann nicht kommen. Ich fahre **nämlich** nach Hamburg.
I cannot come. The reason is, I am going to Hamburg.

Grammatik im Kontext

Possessive Adjectives°

Possessivartikel

Possessive adjectives (e.g., *my, your, his, our*) indicate ownership or belonging.

—Wie ist **Ihr** Name?　　　　　*What is your name?*
—**Mein** Name ist Schiller.　　　*My name is Schiller.*

Wie heißt **deine** Schwester?　　*What's your sister's name?*

Sandra, 8 Jahre: *Meine Mutter Martina, mein Bruder Kelvin, meine Schwester Andrea, mein Vater Uli und ich beim Fahrrad fahren*

Each possessive adjective corresponds to a personal pronoun.

der, die, das to conjugate

SINGULAR		PLURAL	
PERSONAL PRONOUN	**POSSESSIVE ADJECTIVE**	**PERSONAL PRONOUN**	**POSSESSIVE ADJECTIVE**
ich	**mein** *my*	wir	**unser** *our*
du	**dein** *your (informal)*	ihr	**euer** *your (informal)*
Sie	**Ihr** *your (formal)*	Sie	**Ihr** *your (formal)*
er	**sein** *his; its*		
sie	**ihr** *her; its*	sie	**ihr** *their*
es	**sein** *its*		

OLD – alt
Give – Geben
schon – already
dog – der hund
our – eule

sus – cute

Possessives—short for possessive adjectives—take the same endings as the indefinite article **ein.** They are sometimes called **ein**-words because their endings are the same as those of **ein.** Unlike **ein,** however, they also have plural forms. They agree in gender, case, and number with the nouns they modify.

The nominative and accusative forms of **mein** and **unser** illustrate the pattern for all possessives.

	SINGULAR			PLURAL
	Masculine	*Neuter*	*Feminine*	*All Genders*
Nominative	mein Freund unser Freund	mein Buch unser Buch	mein**e** Oma unser**e** Oma	mein**e** Eltern unser**e** Eltern
Accusative	mein**en** Freund unser**en** Freund	mein Buch unser Buch	mein**e** Oma unser**e** Oma	mein**e** Eltern unser**e** Eltern

Note:

- The masculine singular possessive adjective is the only one for which the accusative form differs from the nominative: **Mein** → **meinen, unser** → **unseren.**
- The formal possessive adjective **Ihr** (*your*) is capitalized, just like the formal personal pronoun **Sie** (*you*).
- The possessive adjective **euer** (*your*) drops the **e** of the stem when an ending is added: eu~~e~~re → **eure,** eu~~e~~ren → **euren.**

Everything plural is femine

An- und Verkauf von
Büchern und
Schallplatten

Vorsicht
Lesen gefährdet
eure Dummheit!

Modernes
Antiquariat
LeseZeichen
Hindenburgplatz 64
Tel. 43933

- Scan the Valentine's Day greetings taken from a German newspaper and identify all possessive adjectives.

- In each case, determine whether the possessives refer to a male or female individual or to several people. What is the gender of each name or noun?

Herzliche Grüße zum Valentinstag

Liebe Deule,
ich liebe Dich
Dein Rainer
GF100037

Für meine Lieben Helmut und Sandra
einen lieben Gruß und ein dickes Küsschen[1]
Eure Doris Ma GF100081

Hallo Maus!
Nun ist es doch schon das 4. Jahr!
In Liebe Deine Katze
GE90558

Guten Morgen, mein Tiger
Die Welt[2] ist wieder schön durch Dich.
Dein Stern von Rio GD81183

Lieber Andre!
Alles Liebe zum Valentinstag.
Dein Häschen
GF100036

Liebe Christina
Zum Valentinstag herzliche Grüße und alles Liebe und Gute wünscht
Dir Dein Vater
GC114748

[1]ein ... *a big kiss*
[2]*world*

Übung 1   Herzlichen Glückwunsch!

You will hear eight congratulatory messages taken from a radio program. Write out who receives the greetings (**der Empfänger**) and who sends them (**der Absender**). Include the possessive adjectives you hear, if any. Follow the example.

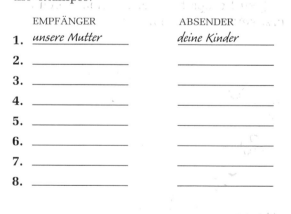

	EMPFÄNGER	ABSENDER
1.	*unsere Mutter*	*deine Kinder*
2.		
3.		
4.		
5.		
6.		
7.		
8.		

Übung 2 Unser Familienporträt

Dirk und Ute machen eine Website über ihre Familie.

Schritt 1: Complete each sentence with the correct form of **unser.**

1. Hier seht ihr _unser_ (das) Haus in Bonn.
2. Und das ist _unsere_ (die) Familie.
3. Da links ist _unsere_ (der) Sohn. Er heißt Dylan und ist 23 Jahre alt.
4. Und hier ist _unseren_ Tochter. Sie heißt Lena und ist 19.
5. Und hier seht ihr _unseren_ (der) Hund. Er heißt Rakete.

Schritt 2: Now restate the sentences from **Schritt 1** using the correct form of **mein.**

BEISPIEL: Hier seht ihr mein Haus in Bonn.

Übung 3 Suchen

Complete each sentence with the appropriate possessive adjective.

BEISPIEL: sie (Frau Müller): Wo ist _ihr_ Mann? Sie sucht _ihren_ Mann.

1. er (Herr Müller): Wo ist _seine_ Frau? Er sucht _seine_ Frau.
2. sie (Herr und Frau Müller): Wo sind _ihre_ Kinder? Sie suchen _ihre_ Kinder.
3. du: Wo ist _deine_ Schwester? Suchst du _deine_ Schwester?
4. ihr: Wo sind _eure_ Eltern? Ihr sucht _eure_ Eltern.
5. wir: Wo ist _____ Großvater? Wir suchen _unseren_ Großvater.
6. ich: Wo ist _mein_ Handy? Ich suche _____ Handy schon den ganzen Tag.

everyday life

Übung 4 Kleine Gespräche im Alltag°

Complete the minidialogues with appropriate possessive adjectives.

1. CLAUDIA: Hier ist _meine_ neue Telefonnummer.
   STEFAN: Gut, und _deine_ neue Adresse?
   CLAUDIA: _Meine_ neue Adresse ist Rosenbachweg 2.
2. LILO: Und dies hier ist _meinen_ Freund.
   HELGA: Wie heißt er denn?
   LILO: _Sein_ Name ist Max.
   HELGA: Max? Na, so was! So heißt nämlich _mein_ Hund.
3. HERR WEIDNER: Und was sind Sie von Beruf, Frau Rudolf?
   FRAU RUDOLF: Ich bin Automechanikerin.
   HERR WEIDNER: Und was ist _Ihr_ Mann von Beruf?
   FRAU RUDOLF: _Mein_ Mann ist Hausmann.
   HERR WEIDNER: Hausmann?
4. FRAU SANDERS: Ach, wie niedlich! Ist das _Ihre_ Tochter?
   FRAU KARSTEN: Ja, das ist _meine_ Tochter.
   FRAU SANDERS: Und ist das _Ihre_ Hund?
   FRAU KARSTEN: Ja, das ist _unser_ Hund. Das ist der Caesar.

5. INGE: Kennst du _meine_ Freund Klaus?

   ERNST: Ich kenne Klaus nicht, aber ich kenne _sein._ Schwester.

   INGE: Morgen besuchen wir _sein_ Eltern in Stuttgart.

6. KLAUS: Morgen fahren Inge und ich nach Stuttgart. Da wohnen _____ (her) Eltern.

   KURT: Wie fahrt ihr denn?

   KLAUS: Wir nehmen _mein_ (my) Auto.

   KURT: _Dein_ Auto?

   KLAUS: Na, klar. Warum denn nicht?

   KURT: _Dein_ Auto gehört ins Museum, nicht auf die Autobahn.

7. POLIZIST: Ist das _ihr_ Auto?

   FRAU KUNZE: Ja, leider ist das _mein_ Auto.

   POLIZIST: Hier ist Parkverbot.

Übung 5   Persönliche Angaben

Schritt 1: Complete a personal profile of yourself. Add one or two items of your own choice.

_____ Name ist _____.

_____ Adresse ist _____.

_____ Telefonnummer ist _____.

_____ Familie wohnt in _____.

_____ Mutter heißt _____.

_____ Vater heißt _____.

_____ Geschwister heißen _____.

_____ Auto/Motorrad/Fahrrad ist ein _____.

_____ Geburtstag ist im _____. (z.B. Juli)

_____ Lieblingsessen (_favorite food_) ist _____.

_____ Hobby ist _____.

_____ Freund/Freundin heißt _____.

??

Schritt 2: Exchange personal profiles with someone in your class and report about him/her to the class.

BEISPIEL: Das ist Sam Lee. Seine Telefonnummer ist 555–8762.
Sein Lieblingsessen ist Pizza. ...

Personal Pronouns in the Accusative Case°

You have already learned the personal pronouns for the nominative case. Here are the corresponding accusative forms.

SINGULAR			PLURAL		
NOMINATIVE	**ACCUSATIVE**		**NOMINATIVE**	**ACCUSATIVE**	
ich	**mich**	*me*	wir	**uns**	*us*
du	**dich**	*you (informal)*	ihr	**euch**	*you (informal)*
Sie	**Sie**	*you (formal)*	Sie	**Sie**	*you (formal)*
er	**ihn**	*him; it*			
sie	**sie**	*her; it*	sie	**sie**	*them*
es	**es**	*it*			

Note:

- The third-person singular pronouns **ihn, sie,** and **es** must agree in gender with the noun to which they refer.
- In the accusative case, **ihn** can mean *him* or *it,* and **sie** can mean *her* or *it* depending on the gender of the noun to which they refer.

—Kennst du **meinen Freund?**	*Do you know my friend?*
—Ja, ich kenne **ihn.**	*Yes, I know him.*
—Brauchst du **den Computer?**	*Do you need the computer?*
—Na klar brauche ich **ihn.**	*I absolutely do need it.*
—Hast du **meine Telefon-nummer?**	*Do you have my phone number?*
—Ich glaube, ich habe **sie.**	*I think I have it.*

ANALYSE

- Identify all personal pronouns in the ads and announcements and determine whether they are in the nominative or in the accusative case. Then provide the English meaning of each phrase.

Gourmets lieben ihn.

Mein Schatz,[1]
Ich liebe Dich.
Deine Jutta
I Love you
[1]mein ... my dear
GA140650

Wir sind da, wo Sie uns brauchen.

Ruth Brandt,
Unsere Omi ist das Liebste, was wir haben, das wollen wir heute einmal[2] sagen:
WIR LIEBEN DICH
Deine Kinder
Deine Enkelkinder

[1]das ... the dearest thing that [2]just

Übung 6 Wer kennt wen?

Supply the missing direct-object personal pronouns corresponding to the nominative pronouns provided.

BEISPIEL: Ich kenne _euch_ (ihr).

euch - ach

1. Ich kenne _dich_ (du).
2. Kennst du _mich_ (ich) denn nicht?
3. Du kennst ja meine Familie. Oder kennst du _sie_ (sie) nicht?
4. Wir kennen _euch_ (ihr) aber schon lange.
5. Hier kommt Herr Wunderlich. Kennst du _____ (er)?
6. Herr Wunderlich kennt _uns_ (wir).
7. Ich kenne die Stadt nicht so gut. Meine Freundin kennt _sie_ (sie) aber sehr gut.

Übung 7 Liebst° du das? Ja oder nein?

Love

Answer the following questions using a pronoun in your answer. The genders of unfamiliar words are provided in parentheses.

BEISPIEL: Liebst du Schweizer Käse? (der Käse) →
    Ja, ich liebe ihn.
  oder: Nein, ich liebe ihn nicht.

1. Liebst du deutsches Bier? (das Bier)
2. Liebst du den neuen BMW? (der BMW)
3. Liebst du Partys?
4. Liebst du Geld?
5. Liebst du Familienfeste?
6. Liebst du Hip-Hop-Musik? (die Musik)
7. Liebst du Jessica Simpson?
8. Liebst du Brad Pitt?

Übung 8 Im Café Kadenz

Several students are conversing at different tables at the Café Kadenz. Complete the blanks with appropriate personal pronouns in the nominative or the accusative case.

1. A: Wie findest _du_ den Professor Klinger?
   B: Also, ich finde _ihn_ unmöglich. _Er_ kommt nie pünktlich. Wir warten (*wait*) und warten, dann kommt _er_ endlich und hält seine Vorlesung, keine Diskussion, keine Fragen, nichts. _Er_ ist echt langweilig.
   A: Ich verstehe _____ nicht, Karin. Warum gehst du dann hin?
2. C: Machst du jetzt das Linguistik-Seminar?
   D: Ja, ich brauche _es_ für mein Hauptfach (*major*).
3. E: Und wie findest du deine Mitbewohner im Wohnheim?
   F: Ich finde _sie_ ganz prima. Da sind zwei Italienerinnen aus Venedig. _Sie_ sind wirklich nett. Ich verstehe _____ allerdings nicht immer.
4. G: Im Lumière läuft der Film „Paradies jetzt". Kennst du _ihn_?   *der film - it*
   H: Nein, aber die Filmkritiker finden _ihn_ ausgezeichnet.
5. I: Da kommt endlich unser Kaffee. Wie trinkst du _ihn_?
   J: Gewöhnlich trinke ich _ihn_ schwarz.
6. K: Meine Eltern besuchen _mich_ nächste Woche. Das ist immer stressig.
   L: Ja, ich verstehe _____ gut.

Übung 9 Wie findest du das?

With a partner, create five questions regarding student life. Then interview several people in your class.

BEISPIEL: s1: Wie findest du die Vorlesungen von Professor Ziegler?
s2: Ich finde sie ausgezeichnet. Und du?
s1: Ich finde sie zu lang.

Essen in der Mensa	ausgezeichnet
Kaffee in der Mensa	faul
Leben (*life*) an der Uni	sympathisch
Uni-Zeitung	langweilig
Studenten an der Uni	schlecht
Mitbewohner im Studentenheim	gut
Professor ____	freundlich
Film ____	interessant
Freund/Freundin	arrogant
??	??

Präpositionen mit dem Akkusativ

Prepositions with the Accusative Case°

You have already seen and used a number of German prepositions.

> Ich studiere Architektur **in** Berlin.
> Ich brauche eine Lampe **für** meinen Schreibtisch.

The use of prepositions, in English as well as in German, is highly idiomatic. An important difference, however, is that German prepositions require certain cases; that is, some prepositions are followed by nouns or pronouns in the accusative case, others by nouns or pronouns in other cases. In this chapter, we focus on prepositions that always require the accusative case.

Wir tun etwas **gegen** den Hunger.	*We are doing something against hunger.*
Es ist **gegen** fünf Uhr.	*It's around five o'clock.*
Herr Krause fährt **durch** die Stadt.	*Mr. Krause drives through town.*
Er braucht ein Geschenk **für** seine Tochter.	*He needs a gift for his daughter.*
Er geht **ohne** seine Frau einkaufen.	*He goes shopping without his wife.*
Die Geburtstagsfeier beginnt **um** sechs.	*The birthday party begins at six.*

Er sucht einen Parkplatz und fährt dreimal **um** den Marktplatz (**herum**).	He looks for a parking space and drives around the marketplace three times.

ACCUSATIVE PREPOSITIONS	
durch	through, across
für	for
gegen	against; around (*with time*)
ohne	without
um	at (*with time*)
um (... herum)	around (*a place*)

✗

Note:

- When the preposition **um** is used to indicate movement around something, the word **herum** is often added after the place.

  um die Stadt (**herum**)

- Three accusative prepositions often contract with the article **das**.

  durch das → **durchs** Zimmer

  für das → **fürs** Auto

  um das → **ums** Haus

Übung 10 Dieter braucht ein Geschenk

Choose the correct preposition.

1. Dieter braucht dringend ein Geburtstagsgeschenk _____ (um/für) seine Freundin Sonja.
2. Leider hat Sonja schon alles, aber _____ (ohne/durch) Geschenk geht es nicht.
3. Dieter gibt _____ (für/um) sieben Uhr abends eine kleine Party _____ (für/ohne) sie.
4. Sonja hat Partys gern, aber sie ist _____ (gegen/ohne) große Partys.
5. Dieter fährt also in die Stadt. Er fährt dreimal _____ (um/durch) den Marktplatz herum. Er sucht einen Parkplatz. Er findet nichts.
6. Er fährt und fährt _____ (um/durch) die Straßen.
7. Er sucht und sucht _____ (für/ohne) Erfolg (*success*). Was nun? ← what now
8. Er parkt schließlich illegal. Was tut er nicht alles _____ (ohne/für) Sonja.
9. Was macht Sonja Spaß? Kochen! Also ein Kochbuch _____ (durch/für) Vegetarier. (Sonja ist nämlich Vegetarierin.)
10. Im Buchladen geht Dieter _____ (für/um) den Tisch mit (*with*) Kochbüchern herum.
11. Es gibt tausend Kochbücher _____ (für/gegen) Vegetarier. Was tun?

Übung 11   Kleine Geschenke

Uwe is having difficulty choosing birthday gifts for friends and relatives. Express your gift recommendations based on the facts provided about everyone. Include a suitable adjective in your answer, such as **perfekt, passend** (*suitable*), **praktisch, originell, nett, gut,** or **schön.**

BEISPIEL: Seine Oma geht oft in die Stadt ins Café. →
Ich finde den Hut gut für seine Oma.

1. Seine Tante Ingrid lernt Kochen in Paris.
2. Seine Eltern reisen und fotografieren viel.
3. Sein Großvater wandert gern.
4. Sein Bruder Dirk schläft immer zu lange.
5. Seine Schwester Maria fährt nach Spanien.
6. Seine Freundin Sara trägt gern Schmuck (*jewelry*).
7. Seine Kusine Julia ist ein Fitnessfan.
8. Seine Mutter liest gern Detektivromane.
9. Sein Freund Marco ist etwas exzentrisch.

 der Wecker    das Buch    die Zehensocken    der Ring    der Hut

 Die Fitness-DVD   zwei Wanderstöcke   der Holzlöffel   die Sonnenbrille   das Fotoalbum

Unregelmäßige Verben

The Irregular Verbs° werden and wissen

Two common verbs that show irregularities in the present tense are **werden** (*to become*) and **wissen** (*to know*).

Heidewitzka, Herr Kapitän!
Der beste Opa der Welt wird 70!

Es gratulieren:
David
Inge
Ulf
Uwe
Sandra
Schira
Afra

Helmut
2.7. 2007

	werden	*wissen*
ich	werde	**weiß**
du	**wirst**	**weißt**
er sie es	**wird**	**weiß**
wir	werden	wissen
ihr	werdet	wisst
sie/Sie	werden	wissen

Übung 12　Kennen Sie eigentlich meine Familie?

Complete the sentences using the appropriate form of **werden.**

1. Ich _____ im September 16 Jahre alt.
2. Meine zwei Kusinen _____ am Samstag 13.
3. Mein kleiner Bruder Bernd _wird_ im November 11.
4. Meine kleine Schwester Sara _wird_ dieses Jahr 5 Jahre alt.
5. Mein Vater hat im Dezember Geburtstag. Er _wird_ 38 Jahre alt.
6. Mein Großvater fragt immer: „Wann _____ du 15?" Er vergisst (*forgets*), dass ich schon 15 bin!

Übung 13　Eine Umfrage: Wer wird wann wie alt?

Do a class poll.

1. Wer _____ dieses Jahr _____ Jahre alt?
2. Wie viele Leute _____ dieses Jahr 19?
3. Wann _____ du 50? 100? (Ich werde in 30 Jahren 50.)
4. Wann _____ dein Freund oder deine Freundin 19, 21, 25?

Using the Verbs wissen and kennen

[1]*nobody*

The verbs **wissen** and **kennen** both mean *to know.* **Wissen** means *to know facts,* while **kennen** means *to know or be acquainted/familiar with a person or thing.*

Ich **weiß** deine Telefonnummer nicht.	*I don't know your phone number.*
Ich **kenne** Herrn Meyer nicht persönlich, aber ich **weiß,** wer er ist.	*I don't know Mr. Meyer personally, but I know who he is.*

Note:

- **Wissen** is often used with indirect questions.

Ich **weiß,** wer Goethe ist.	*I know who Goethe is.*
Ich **weiß** nicht, wo das ist.	*I don't know where that is.*

Johann Wolfgang von Goethe, 1749–1832

Übung 14 Die neue Mitbewohnerin

Wendy, an exchange student from San Diego, is new in Göttingen and lives in a dorm. Listen to Wendy's questions and check off the appropriate negative responses.

Don't know. (casual)

	WEISS ICH NICHT.°	KENNE ICH NICHT.°		WEISS ICH NICHT.	KENNE ICH NICHT.
1.	☐	☐	5.	☐	☐
2.	☐	☐	6.	☐	☐
3.	☐	☐	7.	☐	☐
4.	☐	☐	8.	☐	☐

Übung 15 Wissen oder kennen?

Complete the minidialogues with the correct form of **wissen** or **kennen**.

1. A: _____ du Goethe?

   B: Nein, aber ich _____, wer er ist.

   A: _____ du seinen Roman, „Die Leiden (*sufferings*) des jungen Werther"?

   B: Nein, den _____ ich nicht. Aber mein Professor _____ ihn bestimmt.

2. C: _____ du, welcher Film heute im Odeon läuft?

   D: Das _____ ich nicht. Aber Toni, der _____ das bestimmt. Der _____ alles.

3. E: Wo wohnt ihr eigentlich jetzt?

   F: In der Schillerstraße. _____ du die?

   E: Nein. Ich _____ aber, wo die Goethestraße ist.

4. G: _____ ihr schon, wo ihr nächstes Semester studiert?

   H: Nein, wir _____ nur, dass wir nicht hier bleiben.

5. I: Ich _____, wo eine Wohnung frei wird.

   J: Wo denn?

   I: In der Weenderstraße.

   J: Die _____ ich nicht. Wo ist die denn?

6. K: Ihr _____ doch den Peter Sudhoff?

   L: Tut mir leid, den _____ wir nicht.

inquisitive
Übung 16 Ein neugieriger° Mensch

Find out what your partner knows by taking turns asking each other questions.

BEISPIEL: s1: Kennst du den neuen Film von Steven Spielberg?
s2: Nein, den kenne ich nicht. Kennst du den neuen Film von Peter Jackson?
s1: Ja, den kenne ich.

Kennst du …

  das neue Buch von _____?

  den neuen Film von _____?

  die Mutter / den Vater von _____?

  Herrn Professor _____?

  Frau Professor _____?

  die Rockgruppe _____?

  die Stadt _____?

Weißt du …

  die Telefonnummer von _____?

  die Adresse von _____?

  den Vornamen von Herrn / Frau _____?

  wie alt _____ ist?

  wann das nächste Semester beginnt?

Sprache im Kontext

Videoclips

In these videoclips, the people interviewed are talking about their families and various celebrations. As you watch, listen to what they say and think how you would respond to the interviewer's questions.

A. Watch the interviews with Doris and Kurt Borowsky. Mark the following statements **richtig (R)** or **falsch (F)**.

1. Doris

_____ Doris ist verheiratet.

_____ Sie hat zwei Kinder.

_____ Die Kinder heißen Tina und Matthias.

_____ Die Familie feiert Weihnachten, Valentinstag und Ostern.

_____ Das Lieblingsfest von Doris ist Weihnachten.

_____ Doris hat heute Geburtstag.

2. Herr Borowsky

_____ Herr Borowsky wohnt in Berlin.

_____ Er hat eine kleine Familie.

_____ Er hat drei Enkelkinder.

_____ Er hat einen Bruder und zwei Schwestern.

_____ Er ist 67 Jahre alt.

_____ Er hat am 10. Februar Geburtstag.

B. Now listen again to the questions asked by Michael, the interviewer. Write down four questions he asks and use them to interview two other students in the class. Then report your findings about one of the students to the class.

Lesen

Zum Thema

Eine Umfrage (*survey*). Fill out the questionnaire and compare answers in class.

A. Welche Feiertage sind in Ihrer Familie wichtig?

	WICHTIG	UNWICHTIG
1. Geburtstage	☐	☐
2. Hochzeitstage	☐	☐
3. religiöse Feiertage	☐	☐
4. nationale Feiertage	☐	☐
5. Muttertag	☐	☐
6. Vatertag	☐	☐

B. Wie feiern Sie Ihren Geburtstag?

	JA	NEIN
1. Wir haben ein großes Familienfest.	☐	☐
2. Wir gehen ins Restaurant.	☐	☐
3. Familie und Freunde kaufen Geschenke für mich.	☐	☐
4. Ich mache an diesem Tag nichts Besonderes.	☐	☐
5. ??	☐	☐

Auf den ersten Blick

A. Skim over the short texts below. Who are the respondents? What are their ages? What is the general topic?

B. Now scan the texts more closely, looking for words of the following types.

- words relating to family
- words related to places where a celebration is held
- compound nouns: locate five compound nouns in the texts, and determine their components and their English equivalents

C. The two most frequently used words in the texts are the verb **feiern** and the noun **Geburtstag.** How do they relate to the expression **"deinen großen Tag"** in the title? What is implied?

WIE FEIERST DU DEINEN GROSSEN TAG?

Anna, 18: Meine Zwillingsschwester[1] und ich feiern jedes Jahr zusammen[2]. Meistens machen wir eine große Party bei uns zu Hause. Unseren 18. Geburtstag haben wir bei unserer Oma im Partykeller
5 gefeiert. Dort ist mehr Platz.

Stefan, 15: Ich gehe gerne auf Geburtstagspartys, aber ich gebe selber nicht gerne welche[3]. Deswegen feiere ich immer nur mit meinen Eltern und dem Rest der Verwandtschaft.

10 **Patrick, 19:** Seit ich 18 bin, feiere ich meinen Geburtstag nur mit meiner Freundin zusammen. Wir sind jetzt schon seit zweieinhalb Jahren ein Paar.

Lennard, 19: Ich fahre für ein paar Tage nach Paris. Dort feiere ich dann zusammen mit meiner Brieffreundin.

15 **Uta, 42:** Ich habe am 26. März Geburtstag. Zu meinem Geburtstag lade ich meistens abends einige Freunde zu uns nach Hause ein. Ich mache dann ein Buffet. Manche Freunde bringen auch etwas zu essen mit.

Bettina, 40: Ich feiere dieses Jahr einen runden[4] Geburtstag, meinen vierzigsten, und lade natürlich 40 Gäste ein, Freunde und Verwandte. Wir feiern in einem Restaurant in der Innenstadt. Es gibt ein klei-
20 nes Programm mit Gedichten[5] und Musik. Und es gibt auch ein Super-Essen.

Saskia, 30: Der Geburtstag sieht gewöhnlich so bei uns aus: Das Geburtstagskind bekommt den Frühstückstisch schön gedeckt mit Kerzen[6] und Blumen aus dem Garten. Gleich morgens kommen auch die Geschenke von der Familie auf den Tisch. Am Abend kommen immer all unsere Freunde vorbei. Zu essen gibt es ein kleines kaltes Buffet, mit etwas frischem Salat, Brot[7] und Käse. Wir tanzen auch schon
25 mal zu später Stunde.

Teilweise aus: *JUMA* 2/2004, www.juma.de, Umfrage: Kristina Dörnenburg

---

[1]Zwilling- *twin*   [2]*together*   [3]here: *any*   [4]*birthday ending in 0*   [5]*poems*   [6]*candles*   [7]*bread*

Zum Text

A. Now read the statements more closely and answer the following questions about them. As you work through the texts, try to guess meaning from the context as much as possible. Note which additional words you have to look up, if any, to find the information.

1. Wer feiert Geburtstag nur ganz klein und nicht mit Familie?
2. Wer feiert Geburtstag immer zusammen mit einer Schwester?

3. Wer gibt nicht gern Geburtstagspartys, geht aber selbst gerne hin?

4. Wer feiert zu Hause und wer feiert in einem Restaurant?

5. *Ein* Geburtstag ist besonders wichtig (*important*). Welcher Geburtstag ist das? Wie feiert man ihn?

B. What, if anything, did you find surprising about the way these people celebrate their birthdays? What differences, if any, are there between the way people celebrate their birthdays in your area and the way the Germans celebrate theirs?

C. **Wie feiern Sie Ihren Geburtstag?** Now describe briefly how you typically spend your birthday, using the texts you have just read as a model.

Zu guter Letzt

Eine Person vorstellen

Now that you have worked with the topic of family and friends, bring a picture of your family or several friends or a magazine picture depicting your "fictional family" to class.

Schritt 1: Jot down phrases or sentences in German that you might want to use in describing the people in your picture. Make sure that you include names, how the people are related to you if you are describing family members, things they like to do, when they celebrate their birthdays, and so forth.

Schritt 2: Now work in groups of three. Using the items you have jotted down, describe three of the people in the picture. Your description might go something like this:

> Das ist meine Tante. Sie heißt Barbara. Sie hat am 14. April Geburtstag. Sie ist sehr aktiv. Sie kocht gern und läuft gern.

Schritt 3: Each person in the group should ask the other two members two questions about others in the picture you did not describe. Sample questions might be:

> Wer ist das? Wie heißt er/sie? Ist das deine Schwester? dein Bruder?

Schritt 4: Ein Bericht Finally, expand the information about your family or friends in a written report that might include information such as the following:

- wie groß die Familie ist und wo sie wohnt
- wann sie Geburtstag haben
- was Sie und andere Familienmitglieder (*family members*) oder Freunde gern machen (kochen, tanzen, Zeitung lesen, …)
- Lieblings … (-sport, -komponist, -musiker)
- Probleme (kein Geld, zu viel Geld, keine Hobbys, …)

Wortschatz

Der Stammbaum — Family Tree

der **Bruder**, ⸚	brother
die **Eltern** (*pl.*)	parents
der **Enkel**, -	grandson
die **Enkelin**, **-nen**	granddaughter
die **Familie**, **-n**	family
die **Frau**, **-en**	wife
die **Geschwister** (*pl.*)	siblings
die **Großeltern** (*pl.*)	grandparents
die **Großmutter**, ⸚	grandmother
der **Großvater**, ⸚	grandfather
die **Kusine**, **-n**	(female) cousin
der **Mann**, ⸚er	husband
die **Mutter**, ⸚	mother
der **Neffe** (**-n** *masc.*), **-n**	nephew
die **Nichte**, **-n**	niece
die **Oma**, **-s**	grandma
der **Onkel**, -	uncle
der **Opa**, **-s**	grandpa
der **Schwager**, ⸚	brother-in-law
die **Schwägerin**, **-nen**	sister-in-law
die **Schwester**, **-n**	sister
der **Sohn**, ⸚e	son
die **Tante**, **-n**	aunt
die **Tochter**, ⸚	daughter
der **Vater**, ⸚	father
der **Vetter**, **-n**	(male) cousin

Die Wochentage — Days of the Week

der **Montag**	Monday
am Montag	on Monday
der **Dienstag**	Tuesday
der **Mittwoch**	Wednesday
der **Donnerstag**	Thursday
der **Freitag**	Friday
der **Samstag** / der **Sonnabend**	Saturday
der **Sonntag**	Sunday

Die Monate — Months

der **Januar***	January
im Januar	in January
der **Februar**	February
der **März**	March
der **April**	April
der **Mai**	May
der **Juni**	June
der **Juli**	July
der **August**	August
der **September**	September
der **Oktober**	October
der **November**	November
der **Dezember**	December

Feste und Feiertage — Holidays

das **Familienfest**, **-e**	family gathering
(der) **Fasching**	Mardi Gras (*southern Germany, Austria*)
das **Geschenk**, **-e**	gift, present
der **Heilige Abend**	Christmas Eve
die **Hochzeit**, **-en**	wedding
der **Kalender**, -	calendar
(der) **Karneval**	Mardi Gras (*Rhineland*)
der **Muttertag**	Mother's Day
das **Neujahr**	New Year's Day
(das) **Ostern**	Easter
die **Party**, **-s**	party
(das) **Silvester**	New Year's Eve
die **Tradition**, **-en**	tradition
der **Valentinstag**	Valentine's Day
das **Weihnachten**	Christmas
der **Weihnachtsbaum**, ⸚e	Christmas tree

Verben — Verbs

feiern	to celebrate
geben (**gibt**)	to give
gratulieren	to congratulate
heiraten	to marry
kennen	to know (*be acquainted with a person or thing*)
planen	to plan
werden (**wird**)	to become, be
wissen (**weiß**)	to know (*something as a fact*)
wünschen	to wish

Adjektive und Adverbien — Adjectives and Adverbs

leider	unfortunately
morgen	tomorrow
nämlich	namely, that is to say
neu	new
verwandt mit	related to
wichtig	important

***Jänner** is used in Austria.

Ordinalzahlen / Ordinal Numbers

erste	first
der erste Mai	May first
am ersten Mai	on May first
zweite	second
dritte	third
vierte	fourth
fünfte	fifth
sechste	sixth
sieb(en)te	seventh
achte	eighth
neunte	ninth
zehnte	tenth
elfte	eleventh
zwölfte	twelfth
dreizehnte	thirteenth
zwanzigste	twentieth

Possessivartikel / Possessive Adjectives

mein	my
dein	your (*informal sg.*)
sein	his; its
ihr	her; its; their
unser	our
euer	your (*informal pl.*)
Ihr	your (*formal*)

Akkusativpräpositionen / Accusative Prepositions

durch	through
für	for
gegen	against; around (+ *time*)
ohne	without
um	at (+ *time*)
um (... herum)	around (*spatial*)

Akkusativpronomen / Accusative Pronouns

mich	me
dich	you (*informal sg.*)
ihn	him; it
sie	her; it; them
es	it
uns	us
euch	you (*informal pl.*)
Sie	you (*formal*)

Sonstiges / Other

Alles Gute!	All the best!
es gibt	there is, there are
Es tut mir leid.	I'm sorry.
Herzlichen Glückwunsch zum Geburtstag!	Happy birthday!
der Hund, -e	dog
um Mitternacht	at midnight
Wann hast du Geburtstag?	When is your birthday?
Welches Datum ist heute/morgen?	What is today's/ tomorrow's date?

DAS KANN ICH NUN!

1. Wer sind die folgenden Familienmitglieder?

   a. Mein Bruder und meine Schwester sind meine _____. **b.** Meine Mutter und mein Vater sind meine _____. **c.** Familie Renner hat drei _____: einen Sohn und zwei _____.

2. Drei wichtige Feiertage sind: _____, _____, und _____.

3. Zum Geburtstag wünscht man „_____ _____ zum Geburtstag!"

4. Wann haben Sie Geburtstag? Mein Geburtstag ist _____. Dann _____ ich _____ Jahre alt.

5. Wie sagt man das auf Deutsch?

   a. Is that your car, Mrs. Singer? **b.** Do you know our parents? **c.** His brother knows that. **d.** My sister knows him.

6. Welche Präpositionen mit dem Akkusativ fehlen hier?

   a. Ich kaufe ein Geschenk _____ meinen Freund. **b.** Meine Freunde gehen heute _____ mich auf die Party bei Klaus. **c.** Meine Oma geht oft _____ den Park.

7. Nennen Sie die Wochentage mit den Buchstaben D und M am Anfang.

   a. D_____ und D_____
   b. M_____ und M_____

Erstes Zwischenspiel

Persönlichkeiten: Drei Kurzbiographien

Wolfgang Amadeus Mozart (1756–1791)

Geburtsort: Salzburg

Geburtsdatum: 27. Januar 1756

Sternzeichen: Wassermann[1]

Vater: Leopold

Mutter: Maria Anna

Wolfgang Amadeus Mozart, ca. 1783

Leopold Mozart und seine Kinder Wolfgang und „Nannerl", 1763

Geschwister: Marianne, genannt „Nannerl"

Verheiratet[2] mit: Constanze geb. Weber

Kinder: Karl und Wolfgang

Wohnort: Wien

Beruf: Kapellmeister und Komponist

Hauptwerke: Opern (z.B. „Don Giovanni", „Die Zauberflöte"); 41 Symphonien; Kirchenmusik (z.B. „Krönungsmesse"[3], „Requiem"); Konzerte und Kammermusik (z.B. „Eine kleine Nachtmusik")

Hobbys: Musik, Tanzen, Geselligkeit[4], Reisen for example

Lieblingskomponist: Joseph Haydn

[1] *Aquarius* [2] *married* [3] *Coronation Mass* [4] *conviviality*

Paula Modersohn-Becker: Worpsweder Landschaft, um 1900

Paula Modersohn-Becker (1876–1909)

Geburtsort: Dresden

Geburtsdatum: 8. Februar 1876

Sternzeichen: Wassermann

Vater: Woldemar

Mutter: Mathilde

Geschwister: sechs; vier jüngere, zwei ältere

Verheiratet mit: Otto Modersohn

Kinder: Mathilde

Paula Modersohn-Becker, Selbstbildnis

Wohnort: zuletzt in Worpswede[1]

Beruf: Malerin

Hauptwerke: Landschaftsmalerei[2], Porträts, Stilleben

Hobbys: Musik, Tanzen, Kochen, Lesen, Zeichnen

Lieblingsdichter: Rainer Maria Rilke

[1] *Worpswede ist ein Künstlerdorf in der Nähe von Bremen.* [2] *landscape painting*

Albert Einstein (1879–1955)

Geburtsort: Ulm

Geburtsdatum: 14. März 1879

Sternzeichen: Fisch

Vater: Hermann

Mutter: Pauline

Geschwister: Maria („Maja")

Verheiratet mit: zuerst Mileva, dann Elsa

Kinder: Hans und Eduard

Wohnort: zuletzt in Princeton, New Jersey

Beruf: Physiker (Nobelpreis, 1921)

Hauptwerk: Relativitätstheorie

Hobbys: Musik, Geige[1] spielen, Segeln[2]

Lieblingskomponist: Mozart

Lieblingsphilosoph: Immanuel Kant

[1]*violin*   [2]*sailing*

Albert Einstein als Kind, mit seiner Schwester Maja

Albert Einstein beim Segeln

Aktivität 1   Darf ich vorstellen?

Suppose you had to introduce Mozart, Einstein, or Modersohn-Becker to someone at a party. Make three statements about each that characterize who they are.

BEISPIEL: Darf ich vorstellen, das ist Herr/Frau …
Er/Sie ist …
Er/Sie schreibt/malt/wohnt in …

Aktivität 2   Rollenspiel

Imagine that you could interview the people you just read about. With a partner, select one of the three, then create the interview. You could begin as follows:

BEISPIEL: s1: Wo sind Sie geboren, Frau Modersohn-Becker?
s2: In Dresden.
s1: Sind Sie verheiratet? …

Aktivität 3   Ein Steckbrief°

Choose a well-known historical person and gather information to write a **Steckbrief** about her or him. Present the information in class without revealing who the person is. Let the members of the class guess her or his identity.

wanted poster

Mein Tag

Um wie viel Uhr beginnt die Vorlesung hier?

In diesem Kapitel

- **Themen:** Telling time, times of the day, daily plans, movies, music, theater
- **Grammatik:** Separable-prefix verbs; modal verbs; **möchte;** the imperative; **bitte, doch, mal**
- **Kultur:** German theater
- **Lesen:** „Immer das gleiche" (Christine Wuttke)

Alles klar?

A. In diesem ⟨image⟩ (Brief) sehen Sie fünf ⟨image⟩ (Bilder). Die Bilder stehen für fünf Wörter oder Ausdrücke. Die Ausdrücke sind alphabetisch geordnet.

Fahrrad

Haus(e)

Herz

Sonntag

Tasse Kaffee

Lesen Sie den Brief nun mit den Wörtern.

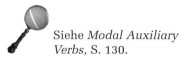

Seid Ihr ☀ -tag zu 🏠 ? Wir kommen per 🚲 vorbei. Auf eine kleine ☕ ♥liche Grüße Susanne ü Peter

B. Sie hören jetzt eine telefonische Einladung. Hören Sie bitte zu und markieren Sie die richtige Information.

1. Die Einladung ist für _____.
   a. Sonntag
   b. Samstag
   c. Freitag

2. Erika und Thomas wollen _____.
   a. Dirk zu Kaffee und Kuchen einladen
   b. mit Dirk auf eine Party gehen
   c. mit Dirk ins Café gehen

3. Dirk soll _____ kommen.
   a. um 3 Uhr
   b. um 5 Uhr
   c. um 4 Uhr

Siehe *Modal Auxiliary Verbs,* S. 130.

Wörter im Kontext

THEMA 1: Die Uhrzeit

Wie spät ist es?
Wie viel Uhr ist es?

Es ist eins.

Es ist **ein Uhr.**
Es ist dreizehn Uhr.

Es ist zehn (Minuten)
nach eins.

Es ist ein Uhr zehn.
Es ist dreizehn Uhr zehn.

Es ist **Viertel nach** eins.

Es ist ein Uhr fünfzehn.
Es ist dreizehn Uhr
fünfzehn.

Es ist **halb** zwei.

Es ist ein Uhr dreißig.
Es ist dreizehn Uhr
dreißig.

Es ist zwanzig (Minuten)
vor zwei.

Es ist ein Uhr vierzig.
Es ist dreizehn Uhr
vierzig.

Es ist **Viertel vor** zwei.

Es ist ein Uhr
fünfundvierzig.
Es ist dreizehn Uhr
fünfundvierzig.

Es ist zehn (Minuten)
vor zwei.

Es ist ein Uhr fünfzig.
Es ist dreizehn Uhr
fünfzig.

Eine **Minute** hat sechzig **Sekunden,** eine **Stunde** sechzig Minuten
und ein Tag vierundzwanzig Stunden.

Time announcements

Aktivität 1 Zeitansagen°

Markieren Sie die Uhrzeiten, die Sie hören.

1. **a.** 7.38 **b.** 17.35 **c.** 17.30
2. **a.** 3.06 **b.** 2.06 **c.** 20.16
3. **a.** 14.00 **b.** 14.15 **c.** 14.05
4. **a.** 12.25 **b.** 10.24 **c.** 11.25
5. **a.** 19.45 **b.** 9.45 **c.** 19.40
6. **a.** 13.00 **b.** 3.40 **c.** 13.40
7. **a.** 0.15 **b.** 0.05 **c.** 0.45
8. **a.** 20.05 **b.** 20.50 **c.** 21.50

114 Kapitel 4 ■ Mein Tag

SPRACHTIPP

In official timetables—for instance, in radio, television, movie, and theater guides—time is expressed according to the twenty-four-hour system.

| 1.00–12.00 Uhr | *1:00 A.M. to 12:00 noon* |
| 13.00–24.00 Uhr | *1:00 P.M. to 12:00 midnight* |

Midnight may also be referred to as **0 (null) Uhr.**

When writing time in numbers, German speakers usually separate hours and minutes with a period, instead of a colon as in English.

ANALYSE

Sehen Sie sich die Zeichnung an und be-antworten Sie die Fragen.

- Wie spät ist es in New York?
- Wie spät ist es in Tokio?
- Wie spät ist es in Bombay?
- Die vierte Uhr zeigt (*shows*) die „gute alte Zeit". Warum hat der Mann wohl (*probably*) diese Uhr gern?

  a. Er hat Kuckucksuhren gern.

  b. Heute ist alles so hektisch.

  c. Die Kuckucksuhr geht langsamer als die anderen Uhren.

  d. ??

Aktivität 2   Wie viel Uhr ist es? Wie spät ist es?

BEISPIEL: Wie viel Uhr ist es? (Wie spät ist es?) →
    Es ist Viertel nach sieben.

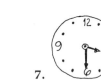

1.

2.

3.

Es ist zwolf uhr zehn
"   "   zehn nach zwolf

4.

5.

6.

7.

Aktivität 3   Was macht Hans-Jürgen am Wochenende?

Sehen Sie sich die Bilder an und ergänzen Sie Hans-Jürgens Pläne für das **Wochenende.**

7.05   **7.20**   **7.45–8.30**

1. Um _____ schläft Hans-Jürgen noch. Dann klingelt der Wecker.
2. Um _____ **steht** er endlich **auf.**
3. Von _____ bis _____ geht er joggen.

9.30

11.20   **12.15**

4. Um _____ **frühstückt** er und liest die Zeitung.
5. Um _____ **ruft** er einen Freund **an.**
6. Um _____ **trifft** er eine Freundin im Café.

Neue Wörter

das Wochenende weekend
steht ... auf (aufstehen)
  gets up
frühstückt (frühstücken)
  eats breakfast
ruft ... an (anrufen) calls
  up
trifft (treffen) meets

13.40

15.00

19.15

WARNER BROS. - presents -

7. Um _____ **geht** er **einkaufen.**

8. Um _____ spielt Hans-Jürgen Fußball auf dem Sportplatz.

9. Um _____ ist er mit Freunden im Kino.

Neue Wörter
geht … einkaufen **(einkaufen gehen)** goes shopping **gewöhnlich** usually **pro Woche** per week

Aktivität 4 Mein Zeitbudget

Wie viel Zeit verbringen (*spend*) Sie **gewöhnlich** mit diesen Dingen?

Schritt 1: Tragen Sie in die Tabelle ein, wie viel Zeit Sie **pro Woche** mit jeder Tätigkeit verbringen.

Tätigkeit	Montag bis Freitag	Wochenende	Insgesamt
Vorlesungen - *lecture* Labor - *lab* Lesen = *reading* Schreiben *writing*			
Nebenarbeit - *side job*			

Essen:
  Frühstück
  Mittagessen
  Abendessen			

Einkaufen Sport Schlafen			

Zeit für mich:
  Fernsehen
  Zeitung/Bücher lesen
  Freunde besuchen *visiting*
  Musik hören			

Schritt 2: Stellen Sie wenigstens 5 Fragen an einen Partner / eine Partnerin. Fragen Sie:

- Wie viel Zeit verbringst du in Vorlesungen? im Labor? mit Lesen? …
- Wie viel Zeit hast du für dich?

Schritt 3: Berichten Sie der Klasse, wie Ihr Partner / Ihre Partnerin seine/ihre Zeit verbringt.

BEISPIEL: Laura verbringt fünfzehn Stunden pro Woche mit Vorlesungen und zehn Stunden pro Woche mit Nebenarbeit. Sie hat nicht viel Zeit für Fernsehen aber hört oft Musik.

THEMA 2: Pläne machen
Hans-Jürgens Wochenplan

Hans-Jürgen **hat** viel **vor** und plant seine Zeit immer sehr genau. Dies ist sein Wochenplan für die nächsten vier Tage.

Neue Wörter

hat ... vor (vorhaben) is planning
einladen invite
der Vortrag lecture
die Vorlesung (university) lecture
abholen pick up
ausgehen go out
aufräumen straighten up
die Bibliothek library
kommt ... vorbei (vorbeikommen) comes by
spazieren gehen go for a walk
fernsehen watch TV

15. DONNERSTAG
08.00 Karin im **Fitnesscenter** treffen
12.00 mit Thomas essen
15.30 Erika auf eine Tasse Kaffee **einladen**
19.30 zum **Vortrag** gehen

16. FREITAG
07.00 schwimmen gehen
10.15 in die Biologie-**Vorlesung** gehen
15.00 Konzerttickets **abholen**
20.00 mit Astrid und Max **ausgehen**

17. SAMSTAG
09.00 Wohnung **aufräumen**
14.00 Kurt in der **Bibliothek** treffen
21.00 Astrid **kommt vorbei**

18. SONNTAG
11.00 spät frühstücken
16.00 mit Astrid **spazieren gehen**
21.45 **fernsehen**: »Sabine Christiansen«[1]

[1] a talk show host dealing mostly with political topics

Tageszeiten

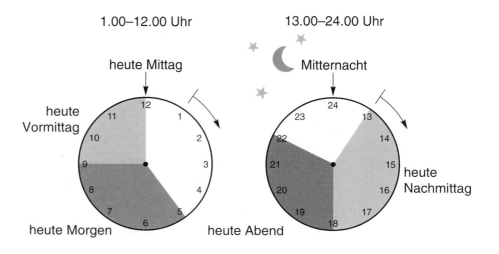

1.00–12.00 Uhr   13.00–24.00 Uhr

heute Mittag   Mitternacht

heute Vormittag   heute Nachmittag

heute Morgen   heute Abend

To say *this morning, this evening,* etc., combine **heute** with a period of the day such as **Morgen: heute Morgen** = *this morning.* Do the same for phrases combined with *tomorrow:* **morgen Nachmittag** = *tomorrow afternoon;* **heute Abend** = *this evening.*

The phrase for *tomorrow morning* is either **morgen früh** or **morgen Vormittag** (to avoid the awkward **morgen Morgen**).

The times of day can also combine with the days of the week: **Samstagabend** = *Saturday evening.* Note that these are written as one word.

A. Was **möchte** Hans-Jürgen machen – und wann? Sehen Sie sich Hans-Jürgens Wochenplan an und organisieren Sie seine Pläne.

am Donnerstag, 15. Oktober

☐ **Heute Morgen** möchte Hans-Jürgen ins Fitnesscenter gehen.
☐ Heute **Mittag** möchte er _____.
☐ Heute **Nachmittag** möchte er _____.
☐ Heute Abend möchte er zu einem _____ gehen.

am Freitag, 16. Oktober

☐ **Morgen früh** möchte Hans-Jürgen schwimmen gehen.
☐ Morgen **Vormittag muss** er _____.
☐ Morgen Nachmittag **soll** er _____.
☐ **Morgen Abend** möchte er _____.

am Samstag, 17. Oktober

☐ Samstagmorgen muss Hans-Jürgen die Wohnung aufräumen.
☐ Samstagnachmittag möchte er _____.
☐ Samstagabend _____ Astrid _____.
☐ Samstags ist er oft bis spät in der **Nacht** bei Freunden.

am Sonntag, 18. Oktober

☐ Sonntagvormittag möchte er _____.
☐ Sonntagnachmittag möchte er _____.
☐ Sonntagabend möchte er _____.

B. Und Sie? Was möchten oder müssen Sie machen – und wann?

Neue Wörter	
möchte	would like to
der Morgen	morning; tomorrow
der Mittag	noon
der Nachmittag	afternoon
früh	early
der Vormittag	morning, before noon
der Abend	evening
muss (müssen)	must
soll (sollen)	is supposed to
die Nacht	night

Siehe *Modal Auxiliary Verbs,* S. 128.

When you do something on a regular basis, use the following adverbs to express the day or the time.

montags	**morgens**
dienstags	**vormittags**
mittwochs	**mittags**
donnerstags	**nachmittags**
freitags	**abends**
samstags/sonnabends	**nachts**
sonntags	

In German, general time precedes specific time.

GENERAL   SPECIFIC
Ich habe donnerstags um 13.00 Uhr Chemie.

Aktivität 5 Hin und her: Zwei Stundenpläne

Schritt 1: Sven und Frank sind 18 Jahre alt und gehen aufs Gymnasium (*secondary school*). Vergleichen Sie ihre Stundenpläne. Welche Kurse haben sie zusammen (*together*)?

BEISPIEL: s1: Welchen Kurs hat Frank montags um acht?
s2: Montags um acht hat Frank Informatik. Welchen Kurs hat Sven montags um acht?
s1: Montags um acht hat Sven Englisch.

Schritt 2: Sven und Frank möchten Tennis spielen. Wann ist die beste Zeit? Wann haben sie beide frei?

Zeit	Montag	Dienstag	Mittwoch	Donnerstag	Freitag	Samstag
8 – 8⁴⁵	Englisch	Informatik	Chemie	Physik	frei	Deutsch
8⁴⁵ – 9³⁰	Englisch	Informatik	Chemie	Physik	Kunst	Deutsch
9³⁵ – 10²⁰	Religion	Deutsch	Erdkunde	Deutsch	Sozialkunde	
10⁴⁰ – 11²⁵	Religion	Mathematik	Mathematik	Mathematik	Deutsch	
11³⁰ – 12¹⁵	Erdkunde	Kunst	Sozialkunde	Geschichte	Geschichte	
12¹⁵ – 13⁰⁰	Mathematik	Physik	Informatik	Englisch	Chemie	
13¹⁵ – 14⁰⁰				Sport		
14⁰⁰ – 14⁴⁵				Sport		

Svens Stundenplan

How does your schedule look?

Aktivität 6 Wie sieht Ihr Stundenplan aus?°

Schritt 1: Schreiben Sie Ihren Stundenplan. Wann sind Ihre Kurse? Wann arbeiten Sie? Dann vergleichen Sie Ihren Stundenplan mit dem von zwei anderen Studenten/Studentinnen in Ihrem Kurs.

BEISPIEL: s1: Was hast du donnerstags um 10?
s2: Donnerstags um 10 habe ich _____. Und du?

Schritt 2: Wer hat Kurse mit Ihnen zusammen? Berichten (*Report*) Sie der Klasse.

Aktivität 7 Bist du heute Abend zu Hause?

Sie wollen einen Freund / eine Freundin besuchen. Sagen Sie, wann Sie vorbeikommen und wie lange Sie bleiben möchten. Benutzen Sie folgendes Sprechschema.

S1	S2
1. Bist du _____ zu Hause?	**2a.** Ja, ich bin zu Hause. **b.** Nein, ich bin leider nicht zu Hause.
3a. Kann ich dann _____ vorbeikommen? **b.** Schade. Wann kann ich denn mal vorbeikommen?	**4a.** Ja, gern. Ich sehe dich also _____. **b.** Kannst du _____ kommen?
5a. Schön. **b.** Ja, gern.	**6.** Wie lange kannst du denn bleiben?
7. _____ Stunde(n).	

THEMA 3: Kino, Musik und Theater

JAN: Ich **gehe** heute Abend **ins Theater.** Willst du mit?

ULLA: Nein, danke. Ich bin kein Theaterfan. Ich **möchte lieber ins Kino.**

JAN: So. Du bist ein Kinofan. Was für (*what kind of*) **Filme** siehst du denn gern?

ULLA: **Am liebsten** Horrorfilme und Psychothriller – die sind so **spannend.**

Was für Filme sehen Sie gern?

☐ Horrorfilme
☐ **Komödien**
☐ Psychothriller
☐ Liebesfilme

☐ **Krimis**
☐ Science-fiction-Filme
☐ Abenteuerfilme
☐ Wildwestfilme

Was sehen Sie gern auf der Bühne (*on stage*)?

☐ **Tragödien**
☐ Lustspiele (*comedies*)
☐ Musicals

☐ **Theaterstücke**
☐ **Opern**
☐ Tanz und **Ballett**

Was für Musik hören Sie gern?

☐ klassische Musik
☐ Heavy Metal
☐ Rockmusik
☐ Techno
☐ alternative Musik

☐ Jazz
☐ Soul
☐ Western-Musik
☐ Rap
☐ Hip-Hop

Neue Wörter

möchte lieber would rather
am liebsten most preferably
spannend suspenseful; exciting
die Komödie (Komödien, *pl.*) comedy
der Krimi (Krimis, *pl.*) detective story
die Tragödie (Tragödien, *pl.*) tragedy
das Theaterstück (Theaterstücke, *pl.*) plays
die Oper (Opern, *pl.*) opera

KULTURTIPP

In Deutschland gibt es in den Groß- und Kleinstädten über 400 öffentliche und private Theater. Der deutsche Staat subventioniert (*subsidizes*) die meisten von ihnen. Deshalb sind die Preise für die Theaterkarten nicht zu teuer. Viele Deutsche haben ein Theaterabonnement (*subscription*). Die deutschen Theater spielen gerne klassische Stücke, die oft modernisiert oder politisiert sind. Das macht sie aktuell und interessant.

Stadttheater Göttingen

Das Thalia in Hamburg

invitations

Aktivität 8 Zwei Einladungen°

Sie hören zwei Dialoge. Wer spricht? Wohin möchten die Sprecher gehen? Warum ist es nicht möglich (*possible*)? Markieren Sie die richtige Information.

<table>
<tr><td>DIALOG 1</td><td>DIALOG 2</td></tr>
<tr><td>

1. Die Sprecher sind …
   a. ein Professor und ein Student.
   b. zwei Studentinnen.
   c. eine Studentin und ein Freund.

2. Der eine Sprecher möchte …
   a. zu Hause arbeiten.
   b. ins Kino.
   c. ins Konzert.

3. Die Sprecherin muss leider …
   a. arbeiten.
   b. in eine Vorlesung.
   c. einen Brief schreiben.

</td><td>

1. Die Sprecher sind …
   a. zwei Studenten.
   b. zwei Professoren.
   c. ein Student und eine Freundin.

2. Die eine Sprecherin möchte …
   a. ins Kino.
   b. in eine Vorlesung.
   c. Karten spielen.

3. Der andere Sprecher …
   a. hat eine Vorlesung.
   b. hat Labor.
   c. muss in die Bibliothek.

</td></tr>
</table>

generally

Aktivität 9 Was machst du so° am Wochenende?

Interviewen Sie Studenten/Studentinnen in der Klasse und finden Sie folgende Personen. Wer „ja" antwortet, muss unterschreiben.

BEISPIEL: s1: Gehst du tanzen, spazieren, laufen oder wandern?
s2: Ja, ich gehe tanzen.
s1: Unterschreib bitte hier.

Siehe *Separable-Prefix Verbs*, S. 124.

AM WOCHENENDE

1. _____ Wer geht tanzen, spazieren, laufen oder wandern?
2. _____ Wer steht früh auf?
3. _____ Wer steht spät auf?
4. _____ Wer räumt das Zimmer, die Wohnung, den Schreibtisch auf?
5. _____ Wer geht ins Kino, ins Theater, in die Oper, ins Konzert, zu einer Technoparty?
6. _____ Wer lädt Freunde ein?
7. _____ Wer sieht fern?
8. _____ Wer surft im Internet?

SPRACHTIPP

To say where you are going, use the following expressions.

Ich gehe
{
ins Kino.
ins Theater.
ins Konzert.
in die Oper.
in die Disko.
}

Aktivität 10 Was hast du vor?

Schauen Sie sich die Programme für Kino, Theater und Musik an. Sagen Sie, wohin Sie gehen wollen.

Vorverkauf Hardenbergstr. 6, Mo.- Fr. von 8 -16.30 Uhr

15. März, 16.00 Uhr und 20.00 Uhr sowie
2. und 3. Mai, jeweils 20.00 Uhr
4. Mai, 18.00 Uhr und 15. Juni, 18.00 Uhr

ICC BERLIN

Das Musical-Ereignis!
Endlich in deutscher Sprache!
PHANTOM DER OPER
Von Arndt Gerber u. Paul Wilhelm
nach dem Roman von G. Leroux
**Internationales Musical-Ensemble
mit Ballett, Chor und Orchester**

Karten: Kasse ICC und alle Vorverkaufsstellen

Theater in Berlin

KOMÖDIE AM KU'DAMM
19.30 Uhr **TAXI, TAXI**
Turbulenter Schwank
THEATER am KU'DAMM
Zusätzlich am Wochenende
Wilhelm heeßt er
Revue-Musical

FAME Das Musical im Schiller Theater
Tickets: 030 · 31 11 31 11

THEATER	Montag, 10. 3.	Dienstag, 11. 3.
Deutsche Oper Berlin 341 02 49	20.00 Kammermusik im Foyer: **Ensemble „das neue Werk" Berlin**	17.00 Foyer: **„Klein-Siegfried"**
Berliner Kammerspiele 391 55 43	**Biedermann und die Brandstifter** von Max Frisch Freitag und Sonnabend 18.00 Uhr	

S1	S2
1. Was hast du am Samstag vor?	2. Ich gehe ins Kino / ins Theater / in die Oper / ? Willst du mit?
3. Was gibt es denn?	4. Einen Film / ein Musical / eine Oper / ? von (+ *name*).
5a. So? Wann fängt er/es/sie denn an? b. Ach, ich bleibe lieber zu Hause.	6a. ____. b. Schade.

Hier klicken!

Weiteres zum Thema Konzert und Theater finden Sie bei **Deutsch: Na klar!** im World-Wide-Web unter www.mhhe.com/dnk5.

Grammatik im Kontext

Verben mit trennbaren Präfixen

Separable-Prefix Verbs°

You are already familiar with sentences such as the following:

Susanne und Peter **kommen** per Fahrrad **vorbei.**	*Susanne and Peter **are coming by** on their bikes.*
Ich gehe heute tanzen. **Kommst** du **mit?**	*I am going dancing today. Will you **come along?***

German, like English, has many two-part verbs that consist of a verb and a short complement that affects the meaning of the main verb. Examples of such two-part verbs in English are *to come by, to come along, to call up, to get up.*

Wüstenrot-Rendite[1]-Programm mit 470 Euro pro anno.

Jede Million fängt klein an.[2]

[1] *yield on investment*
[2] fängt ... an: *begins*
[3] *simple*

Kommen ... vorbei, fängt ... an, rufe ... an, and **kommst ... mit** are examples of such two-part verbs in German. They are also called separable-prefix verbs. In the infinitive, the separable part of these verbs forms the verb's prefix. The prefixes are always stressed.

ánrufen

ánfangen

vor**béi**kommen

mítkommen

In a statement or a question, the prefix is separated from the conjugated verb and placed at the end of the sentence.

—**Kommst** du heute Abend **vorbei?**	*Are you coming by tonight?*
—Ja, aber ich **rufe** vorher **an.**	*Yes, but I'll call first.*

Here are examples of some commonly used separable-prefix verbs.

VERB	BEISPIEL
abholen (holt … ab) to pick up	Ich **hole** dich um 6 Uhr **ab.**
anfangen (fängt … an) to begin	Wann **fängt** die Vorlesung **an**?
anrufen (ruft … an) to call up	Ich **rufe** dich morgen **an.**
aufhören (hört … auf) to end, quit	Der Regen **hört** nicht **auf.**
aufräumen (räumt … auf) to straighten up	Er **räumt** sein Zimmer **auf.**
aufstehen (steht … auf) to got up	Er **steht** um 9 Uhr **auf.**
aufwachen (wacht … auf) to wake up	Wann **wachst** du gewöhnlich **auf**?
einkaufen (kauft … ein) to shop	Herr Lerche **kauft** immer morgens **ein.**
einladen (lädt … ein) to invite	Ich **lade** dich zum Essen **ein.**
einschlafen (schläft … ein) to fall asleep	Ich **schlafe** gewöhnlich nicht vor Mitternacht **ein.**
mitbringen (bringt … mit) to bring along	Ich **bringe** eine Pizza **mit.**
mitkommen (kommt … mit) to come along	**Kommst** du **mit**?
mitnehmen (nimmt … mit) to take along	**Nimmst** du einen Regenschirm **mit**?
vorbeikommen (kommt … vorbei) to come by	Wir **kommen** Sonntag **vorbei.**
vorhaben (hat … vor) to plan to do	Was **hast** du heute **vor**?
zurückkommen (kommt … zurück) to come back	Wann **kommst** du **zurück**?

[1]*ad*
[2]geben … auf *place*

Note:

- A separable-prefix verb shows all the same stem-vowel changes or other irregularities in the present tense as the base verb.

  Hans **schläft** immer lange.   Er **schläft** um 23 Uhr **ein.**
  Er **nimmt** den Schirm.   Er **nimmt** den Schirm **mit.**

- Separable-prefix verbs are listed in the vocabulary of this book as follows:

  auf•hören   ein•schlafen (schläft ein)   vor•haben (hat vor)

The Sentence Bracket°

Die Satzklammer

Separable-prefix verbs show a sentence structure that is characteristic for German: the conjugated verb and its complement form a bracket around the core of the sentence. The conjugated verb is the second element of the sentence, and the separable prefix is the last element.

	SATZKLAMMER		
Ich	**rufe**	dich heute Abend	**an.**
Wann	**kommst**	du heute	**vorbei?**
Peter	**geht**	leider nicht	**mit.**

Another example of the sentence bracket (**Satzklammer**) can be seen in sentences with compound verbs such as **einkaufen gehen** (*to go shopping*), **tanzen gehen** (*to go dancing*), and **spazieren gehen** (*to go for a walk*).

	SATZKLAMMER		
Ich	**gehe**	morgens	**einkaufen.**
Klaus und Erika	**gehen**	Sonntag mit Freunden	**tanzen.**
Daniel	**geht**	mit dem Hund	**spazieren.**

In the sentences above, the verb **gehen** and the infinitives **einkaufen, tanzen,** and **spazieren** form a bracket around the sentence core. You will encounter the concept of the sentence bracket in many other contexts involving verbs.

Übung 1 Daniels Tagesablauf

Daniel ist Künstler (*artist*), aber die Kunst (*art*) allein bringt nicht genug Geld ein. Sie hören jetzt eine Beschreibung von Daniels Tagesablauf. Markieren Sie alle passenden Antworten auf jede Frage.

1. Wann wacht Daniel gewöhnlich auf?
   a. sehr früh
   b. sehr spät
   c. um 5 Uhr

2. Wohnt Daniel allein oder mit jemandem zusammen?
   a. allein
   b. mit seinem Bruder
   c. mit seiner Freundin

3. Was tut Daniel für die Familie Schröder?
   a. Er geht einkaufen.
   b. Er geht mit dem Hund spazieren.
   c. Er macht Reparaturen.

4. Wann fängt Daniels Arbeit im Hotel an?
   a. um 6 Uhr
   b. um 7 Uhr
   c. um 5 Uhr

5. Wann kommt Daniel nach Hause zurück?
   a. um 12 Uhr nachts
   b. um 6 Uhr abends
   c. so gegen 3 Uhr nachmittags

6. Was macht Daniel dann zuerst?
   a. Er geht schlafen.
   b. Er geht einkaufen.
   c. Er räumt das Zimmer auf.

7. Wann fängt Daniels Leben für die Kunst an?
   a. spät nachmittags
   b. am Wochenende
   c. so gegen Mitternacht

8. Wie verbringt Daniel manchmal seinen Abend?
   a. Er sieht fern.
   b. Er lädt Freunde ein.
   c. Er ruft Freunde an.

9. Wann schläft Daniel gewöhnlich ein?
   a. um 12 Uhr nachts
   b. nicht vor 1 Uhr nachts
   c. so gegen halb eins

Übung 2 Was Daniel macht

Erzählen Sie jetzt mit Hilfe der Fragen und Antworten in **Übung 1**, was Daniel jeden Tag macht.

BEISPIEL: Daniel wacht gewöhnlich sehr früh auf.

Übung 3 Eine Verabredung°

A date

Die folgenden Sätze sind eine Konversation zwischen Hans und Petra. Ergänzen Sie zuerst die Verben mit den fehlenden (*missing*) Präfixen. Arrangieren Sie dann die Sätze als Dialog, und üben Sie den Dialog mit einem Partner / einer Partnerin.

_____ Um acht. Ich komme um halb acht _____ und hole dich _____.

_____ Ja, ich gehe ins Kino. Im Olympia läuft ein neuer Film mit Keanu Reeves. Kommst du _____?

_____ Schön. Hinterher lade ich dich zu einem Bier _____.

_____ Gerne. Wann fängt der Film denn _____?

_1_ Hast du für heute Abend schon etwas _____?

Übung 4 Was ich so mache

Was machen Sie **immer, manchmal, selten, nie, oft, gewöhnlich?** Vergleichen Sie sich (*compare yourself*) mit den Personen in den folgenden Sätzen.

BEISPIEL: Daniel steht gewöhnlich früh auf. →
　　　　　Ich stehe nie früh auf.

1. Daniel steht gewöhnlich sehr früh auf.
2. Daniel geht nie am Wochenende einkaufen.
3. Lilo geht oft mit ihrem Hund spazieren.
4. Hans räumt selten sein Zimmer auf.
5. Lilo schläft gewöhnlich beim Fernsehen ein.
6. Daniel lädt manchmal abends Freunde ein.
7. Daniel schläft selten vor 1 Uhr nachts ein.
8. Lilo ruft ihre Eltern oft an.
9. Daniel geht selten mit Freunden aus.

Übung 5 Wie sieht dein Tag aus?

Schritt 1: Arbeiten Sie zu zweit und stellen Sie einander folgende Fragen. Formulieren Sie Ihre Antworten mit Hilfe der Ausdrücke auf der nächsten Seite. Schreiben Sie die Antworten auf.

- Was machst du gewöhnlich jeden Tag?
- Was machst du oft?
- Was machst du manchmal?
- Was machst du nie?

einkaufen gehen   Zimmer aufräumen   arbeiten   spät aufwachen

nach ein Uhr einschlafen   Freunde/Eltern anrufen

mit Freunden ausgehen   vor sechs Uhr aufstehen

Freunde zu einer Party einladen   spazieren gehen

BEISPIEL: Ich stehe gewöhnlich vor sechs Uhr auf. Ich schlafe nie nach ein Uhr ein. …

Schritt 2: Geben Sie jetzt einen kurzen Bericht von etwa vier Sätzen.

BEISPIEL: Keith steht gewöhnlich vor sechs Uhr auf. Er räumt nie sein Zimmer auf. Er geht manchmal einkaufen. Jeden Tag geht er mit Freunden aus.

Modalverben

Modal Auxiliary Verbs°

Modal auxiliary verbs (for example, *must, can, may*) express an attitude toward an action.

Morgen **möchten** wir Tennis **spielen.**	*Tomorrow we **would like to play** tennis.*
Am Wochenende **wollen** wir Freunde **besuchen.**	*On the weekend we **want to visit** friends.*
Ich **kann** morgen **vorbeikommen.**	*I **can come by** tomorrow.*

Note:

- The modal auxiliary verb is the conjugated verb and is in the second position in a statement.
- Its complement—the verb that expresses the action—is in the infinitive form and stands at the end of the sentence.
- In German, sentences with modal auxiliaries and a dependent infinitive demonstrate the pattern of the sentence bracket (**Satzklammer**) that you learned earlier in this chapter.

¹novels

		SATZKLAMMER	
Morgen	**möchten**	wir Tennis	**spielen.**
Peter	**muss**	morgen leider	**arbeiten.**
Ich	**kann**	dich heute	**besuchen.**
Heute Abend	**wollen**	wir ins Kino	**gehen.**

German has the following modal verbs.

dürfen	to be allowed to, may	**Dürfen** wir hier rauchen? *May we smoke here?*
können	to be able to, can	Ich **kann** dich gut verstehen. *I can understand you well.*
mögen	to like, care for	**Mögen** Sie Bücher? *Do you like books?*
müssen	to have to, must	Er **muss** heute arbeiten. *He has to work today.*
sollen	to be supposed to, shall	Wann **sollen** wir vorbeikommen? *When are we supposed to come by?*
wollen	to want to, plan to do	**Willst** du mitgehen? *Do you want to go along?*

The Present Tense of Modals

Modals are irregular verbs. With the exception of **sollen,** they have stem-vowel changes in the singular. Note also that the first- and third-person singular forms are identical and have no personal ending.

	dürfen	können	mögen	müssen	sollen	wollen
ich	**darf**	**kann**	**mag**	**muss**	**soll**	**will**
du	d**a**rfst	k**a**nnst	m**a**gst	musst	sollst	willst
er sie } es	**darf**	**kann**	**mag**	**muss**	**soll**	**will**
wir	dürfen	können	mögen	müssen	sollen	wollen
ihr	dürft	könnt	mögt	müsst	sollt	wollt
sie	dürfen	können	mögen	müssen	sollen	wollen
Sie	dürfen	können	mögen	müssen	sollen	wollen

SIE DÜRFEN HIER NICHT PARKEN

Möchte (*would like to*), one of the most common modal verbs, is the subjunctive of **mögen.** Note that the first- and third-person singular forms are identical.

Wir **möchten** morgen Tennis
spielen.

*We would like to play tennis
tomorrow.*

möchte			
ich	**möchte**	wir	möchten
du	möchtest	ihr	möchtet
er sie es	**möchte**	sie	möchten
Sie möchten			

Note:

- The modal **mögen** is generally used without a dependent infinitive.

  Er **mag** seine Arbeit im Hotel.   *He likes his work in the hotel.*

- The infinitive in a sentence with a modal verb may be omitted when its meaning is understood.

  Ich **muss** jetzt in die Vorlesung
  (**gehen**).

  I have to go to the lecture now.

  Ich **möchte** jetzt nach Hause
  (**gehen**).

  I would like to go home now.

  Er **will** das nicht (**machen**).   *He doesn't want to do that.*

ANALYSE

Scan the headlines and visuals.

- Identify all modal auxiliary verbs in the headlines and visual. Give the English equivalents of the sentences.
- What verbs express the action in those sentences?
- Mark the two parts of each sentence bracket.

Ich möchte mehr Informationen über Greenpeace!

So schön (spannend, aufregend) kann Fernsehen sein

Die Studenten wollen streiken

JEDER KANN AUS-
GLEITEN UND
FALLEN
MAN DARF NUR
NICHT
LIEGENBLEIBEN [1]

AUS INDIEN

[1]Jeder ... *Anyone can slip and fall;
the trick is not to stay down.*

Übung 6 Was kann man da machen?

BEISPIEL: in der Bibliothek →
        s1: Was kann man in der Bibliothek machen?
        s2: Da kann man Bücher lesen!

1. im Restaurant	**a.** Filme sehen
2. im Kino	**b.** einkaufen
3. im Internetcafé	**c.** tanzen
4. in der Disko	**d.** Freunde treffen
5. im Kaufhaus	**e.** Bücher lesen
6. im Park	**f.** etwas essen
7. in der Bibliothek	**g.** spazieren gehen
	h. am Computer arbeiten

SPRACHTIPP

The indefinite pronoun **man** (*one, people, you, they*) is used to talk about a general activity.

   Man darf hier nicht parken.

   You (One) may not park here. (Parking is not allowed here.)

Man is used with the third-person singular verb form.

Übung 7 Was darf man hier machen oder nicht machen?

BEISPIEL: Man darf hier nicht parken.

1.

2.

3.

4.

5.

6.

campen	spielen
schnell fahren	rauchen (*smoke*)
schwimmen	von 8 bis 14 Uhr parken
parken	

Übung 8 Was möchtest du lieber° machen?

would you rather

Fragen Sie einen Partner / eine Partnerin, was er/sie lieber machen möchte.

BEISPIEL: schwimmen gehen oder Tennis spielen? →
        s1: Was möchtest du lieber machen: schwimmen gehen oder
           Tennis spielen?
        s2: Ich möchte lieber Tennis spielen.

1. Zeitung lesen oder im Internet surfen?
2. fernsehen oder einkaufen gehen?
3. ins Café oder ins Kino gehen?
4. deine Familie anrufen oder eine E-Mail schreiben?
5. ein Picknick machen oder spazieren gehen?
6. eine Party zu Hause machen oder ausgehen?

Übung 9 Im Deutschen Haus

Chris und Jeff wohnen im Deutschen Haus an einer amerikanischen Universität. Sie sollen so oft wie möglich deutsch miteinander sprechen. Hören Sie zu, und kreuzen Sie die richtige Information an.

	DAS STIMMT	DAS STIMMT NICHT
1. Chris muss für einen Test arbeiten.	☐	☐
2. Er redet laut (*aloud*) und stört (*disturbs*) seinen Mitbewohner Jeff.	☐	☐
3. Jeff wird jetzt böse (*annoyed*).	☐	☐
4. Chris kann nur laut lernen.	☐	☐
5. Chris geht in die Bibliothek.	☐	☐

Übung 10 Was sind die Tatsachen°?

facts

Was wissen Sie über die beiden Bewohner des Deutschen Hauses? Bilden Sie Sätze.

Chris	soll	ins Badezimmer gehen
Jeff	muss	deutsche Grammatik lernen
	kann	ein A bekommen
	will	nur laut Deutsch lernen
	möchte	Jeff nicht stören
		auch arbeiten
		jetzt auch schlafen
		nicht arbeiten
		lesen

Übung 11 Pläne für eine Party

Brigitte, Lisa und Anja haben endlich ein Dach (*roof*) über dem Kopf: eine Wohnung auf einem alten Bauernhof (*farm*). Jetzt planen sie eine Party. Setzen Sie passende Modalverben in die Lücken ein.

BRIGITTE: Also wen _____¹ (*want to*) wir denn einladen?

LISA: Die Frage ist: Wie viele Leute _____² (*can*) wir denn einladen? Wir haben ja nicht so viel Platz.

ANJA: Im Wohnzimmer _____³ (*can*) bestimmt zwanzig Leute sitzen.

LISA: Und tanzen _____⁴ (*can*) wir im Garten.

ANJA: Und wer _____⁵ (*is supposed to*) für so viele Leute kochen?

LISA: Ich _____⁶ (*want*) lieber nur ein paar Leute einladen.

ANJA: Wir sagen, jeder _____⁷ (*is supposed to*) etwas zum Essen mitbringen.

BRIGITTE: Ich _____⁸ (*would like to*) Kartoffelsalat mit Würstchen machen.

LISA: Gute Idee. Das ist einfach, und das _____⁹ (*like*) alle.

ANJA: Tut mir leid, aber ich _____¹⁰ (*like*) Kartoffelsalat nicht.

BRIGITTE: Ich _____¹¹ (*can*) auch was Italienisches machen, Pizza oder Lasagne.

LISA: Wir _____¹² (*may*) aber nicht nur Bier servieren, wir _____¹³ (*have to*) auch Mineralwasser oder Cola servieren, für die Autofahrer.

Übung 12 Ein Picknick im Grünen

Einige Mitbewohner im internationalen Studentenwohnheim planen ein Picknick. Wer bringt was mit?

BEISPIEL: Andreas will ein Frisbee mitbringen. Er soll auch Mineralwasser mitbringen.

Jürgen aus München	wollen	Brot und Käse (*cheese*)	kaufen
Stephanie aus den USA	müssen	Mineralwasser	mitbringen
Paola und Maria aus Italien	möchte	Bier	machen
Nagako aus Tokio	sollen	ein Radio	
Michel aus Frankreich	können	ein Frisbee	
ich		eine Pizza	
		Kartoffelsalat	
		eine Kamera	
		einen Fußball	

Übung 13 Kommst du mit?

Arbeiten Sie mit einem Partner / einer Partnerin zusammen. Laden Sie ihn/sie ein, etwas mit Ihnen zu unternehmen (*do*). Er/Sie soll die Einladung ablehnen (*decline*) und einen Grund (*reason*) dafür angeben.

BEISPIEL: s1: Ich will heute Tennis spielen. Möchtest du mitkommen?
s2: Nein, leider kann ich nicht. Ich muss nämlich arbeiten.
oder: s2: Ich möchte schon. Leider muss ich …

s1	s2
heute Abend ins Rockkonzert gehen	arbeiten
ins Kino gehen	meine Eltern besuchen
nach (+ *place*) fahren	zu Hause bleiben. (Mein Wagen ist kaputt.)
ins Café gehen	mein Zimmer aufräumen
Tennis spielen	Deutsch lernen
Mini-Golf spielen	eine Arbeit schreiben
zu einer Party gehen	??
tanzen gehen	
??	

The Imperative°

Der Imperativ

The imperative is the verb form used to make requests and recommendations and to give instructions, advice, or commands. You are already familiar with imperative forms used in common classroom requests.

Wiederholen Sie bitte.	*Repeat, please.*
Hören Sie zu!	*Listen!*
Sagen Sie das auf Deutsch.	*Say that in German.*
Nehmen Sie Platz!	*Be seated!*

These are examples of formal imperatives, used for anyone you would address as **Sie.** There are two additional imperative forms, used for informally addressing one or several people whom you would address individually as **du.** Imperatives in written German often end in an exclamation point, especially to emphasize a request or a command.

OVERVIEW OF IMPERATIVE FORMS			
Infinitive	*Formal*	*Informal Singular*	*Informal Plural*
kommen	**Kommen Sie** bald.	**Komm** bald.	**Kommt** bald.
fahren	**Fahren Sie** langsam!	**Fahr** langsam!	**Fahrt** langsam!
anrufen	**Rufen Sie** mich **an.**	**Ruf** mich **an.**	**Ruft** mich **an.**
sprechen	**Sprechen Sie** langsam!	**Sprich** langsam!	**Sprecht** langsam!
arbeiten	**Arbeiten Sie** jetzt!	**Arbeite** jetzt!	**Arbeitet** jetzt!
sein	**Seien Sie** freundlich.	**Sei** freundlich.	**Seid** freundlich.

Formal Imperative

The formal imperative is formed by inverting the subject **(Sie)** and the verb in the present tense.

Note:

- The formal imperative has the same word order as a yes/no question; only punctuation or intonation identifies it as an imperative.
- The imperative of the verb **sein** is irregular.

  Seien Sie bitte freundlich!   *Please be friendly.*

Bitte nehmen Sie Platz

Particles and **bitte** with the Imperative

Requests or commands are often softened by adding the word **bitte** and particles such as **doch** and **mal. Bitte** can stand at the beginning, in the middle, or at the end of the sentence. The particles **doch** and **mal** follow the imperative form. They have no English equivalent.

Hören Sie **bitte** zu!	*Please listen.*
Bitte nehmen Sie Platz.	*Please have a seat.*
Kommen Sie **doch** heute vorbei.	*Why don't you come by today?*
Rufen Sie mich **mal** an.	*Give me a call (some time).* *(Why don't you give me a call some time?)*

office hour   **Übung 14   In der Sprechstunde°**

Mary Lerner geht zum Professor in die Sprechstunde. Kreuzen Sie an, ob es um eine Frage oder eine Aufforderung (*request or command*) geht.

	FRAGE	AUFFORDERUNG		FRAGE	AUFFORDERUNG
1.	☐	☐	8.	☐	☐
2.	☐	☐	9.	☐	☐
3.	☐	☐	10.	☐	☐
4.	☐	☐	11.	☐	☐
5.	☐	☐	12.	☐	☐
6.	☐	☐	13.	☐	☐
7.	☐	☐	14.	☐	☐

Informal Imperative

The singular informal imperative is used for anyone you address with **du**. It is formed for most verbs simply by dropping the **-st** ending from the present tense **du**-form of the verb.

kommen: du **kommst**	→	**Komm!**
anrufen: du **rufst an**	→	**Ruf an!**
arbeiten: du **arbeitest**	→	**Arbeite!**
sprechen: du **sprichst**	→	**Sprich!**
nehmen: du **nimmst**	→	**Nimm!**
But: sein: du **bist**	→	**Sei!**

Verbs that show a vowel change from **a** to **ä** (or **au** to **äu**) in the present tense have no umlaut in the imperative.

du **fährst** → **Fahr!**

du **läufst** → **Lauf!**

Mach Dir ein paar schöne Stunden... geh ins **Kino**

Schreib mal wieder.

Deutsche Post AG

Schau mal hoch.

The plural informal imperative is used to request something from several persons whom you individually address with **du**.

Kommt doch mal zu uns.	*Why don't you come see us. (lit., Come to us.)*
Fahrt jetzt nach Hause.	*Drive home now.*
Gebt mir bitte etwas zu essen.	*Please give me something to eat.*
Seid doch ruhig!	*Be quiet!*

This imperative form is identical to the **ihr**-form of the present tense, but without the pronoun **ihr**.

Übung 15 Macht das, bitte!

Ergänzen Sie die Tabelle.

FORMAL	INFORMAL SING.	INFORMAL PL.
1. Kommen Sie, bitte!	Komm, bitte!	_____, bitte!
2. _____ leise, bitte!	Sprich leise, bitte!	_____ leise, bitte!
3. Laden Sie uns bitte ein.	_____ uns bitte _____.	_____ uns bitte _____.
4. _____ doch ruhig!	Sei doch ruhig!	_____ doch ruhig!
5. Fahren Sie langsam!	_____ langsam!	Fahrt langsam!
6. Rufen Sie mich mal an.	_____ mich mal _____.	Ruft mich mal an.
7. _____ das Buch mit.	_____ das Buch mit.	Nehmt das Buch mit.
8. Machen Sie schnell!	Mach schnell!	_____ schnell!
9. Hören Sie doch auf!	_____ doch _____!	_____ doch _____!

Übung 16 Wir duzen einander unter Studenten.°

We students say du to each other.

Stellen Sie sich vor, Sie sind neu im Studentenwohnheim und reden alle Ihre Mitbewohner zuerst mit **Sie** an. Jetzt müssen Sie **du** benutzen, denn alle Studenten duzen einander. Setzen Sie die Imperativsätze in die **du**-Form.

BEISPIEL: Bitte, kommen Sie herein. → Bitte, komm herein.

1. Bitte, sprechen Sie etwas langsamer.
2. Hören Sie bitte zu.
3. Arbeiten Sie nicht so viel!
4. Fahren Sie doch am Wochenende mit mir nach Heidelberg.
5. Bleiben Sie doch noch ein bisschen.
6. Besuchen Sie mich mal.
7. Rufen Sie mich morgen um 10 Uhr an!
8. Gehen Sie doch ins Kino mit.
9. Kommen Sie doch morgen vorbei.
10. Nehmen Sie die Zeitung mit.
11. Sehen Sie mal, hier ist ein Foto von meiner Familie.
12. Seien Sie bitte ruhig!

Übung 17 Pläne unter Freunden

Sie möchten Ihren Freunden sagen, was sie alles tun sollen. Machen Sie aus den Fragen Imperativsätze. Benutzen Sie dabei auch **doch, mal** oder **bitte.**

BEISPIEL: Kommt ihr heute Abend vorbei? →
          Kommt bitte heute Abend vorbei!

1. Ladet ihr mich ein?
2. Ruft ihr mich morgen an?
3. Holt ihr mich ab?
4. Sprecht ihr immer deutsch?
5. Hört ihr zu?
6. Geht ihr mit?
7. Kommt ihr morgen vorbei?
8. Seid ihr morgen pünktlich?

Übung 18 Situationen im Alltag

Ergänzen Sie die passende Form des Imperativs von **sein.**

1. Ich muss Sie warnen: Autofahren in Deutschland ist ein Abenteuer. _____ bitte vorsichtig!

2. Sie gehen mit zwei Freunden ins Konzert. Diese Freunde sind nie pünktlich und das irritiert Sie. Sie sagen zu ihnen: „_____ aber bitte pünktlich!"

3. Ihr Mitbewohner / Ihre Mitbewohnerin im Studentenwohnheim ist sehr unordentlich. Sie erwarten Ihre Eltern zu Besuch und bitten ihn/sie: „_____ so nett und räum deine Sachen auf!"

4. Drei Mitbewohner im Studentenwohnheim spielen um drei Uhr morgens immer noch laute Musik. Sie klopfen irritiert gegen die Wand und rufen: „Zum Donnerwetter, _____ endlich ruhig!"

5. Frau Kümmel zu Frau Honig: „_____ bitte so nett und kommen Sie morgen vorbei!"

Sprache im Kontext

Videoclips Video

A. Wie sind die Tagesroutinen von Jan und Beatrice? Was machen sie morgens und abends? Schauen Sie sich die Interviews mit Jan und Beatrice an und ergänzen Sie die Tabelle.

	JAN	BEATRICE
MORGENS	*7 Uhr – aufstehen* _____ _____ _____	_____ _____ _____ _____
ABENDS	_____ _____ _____	_____ _____ *0–1 Uhr – ins Bett gehen*

B. Schauen Sie sich das Interview mit Jasmin an und ergänzen Sie die Informationen.

1. Jasmin _____ um 8 Uhr.
2. Um _____ oder _____ Uhr kommt sie von der Arbeit nach Hause.
3. Sie geht ungefähr um 22 Uhr ins _____.
4. Am Wochenende _____ sie lange, macht Sport oder geht _____.
5. Sie geht gern _____ _____.

C. Und Sie? Machen Sie eine Tabelle für Ihre eigene (*own*) Tagesroutine. Erzählen Sie dann einem Partner / einer Partnerin, wie Ihr typischer Tag aussieht.

Lesen

Das folgende Lesestück beschreibt die tägliche Routine und die Freuden (*joys*) des Alltags.

Zum Thema

Immer das Gleiche (*the same thing*)?

A. Ergänzen Sie die Tabelle. Wie sieht Ihr Alltag aus? Und Ihr Wochenende?

MEIN ALLTAG		MEIN WOCHENENDE	
Uhrzeit	*Aktivität*	*Uhrzeit*	*Aktivität*
	aufstehen		
	ins Bett gehen		

B. Machen Sie etwas Besonderes (*something special*) am Wochenende? Berichten Sie mit Hilfe der Tabelle.

BEISPIEL: Gewöhnlich stehe ich um 7 Uhr auf. Aber am Wochenende schlafe ich lange.

Auf den ersten Blick

Überfliegen Sie (*skim*) den Text auf der nächsten Seite, „Immer das gleiche." Suchen Sie Wörter, die in die folgenden Kategorien passen: **Schule, zu Hause** und **unterwegs** (*on the road*).

BEISPIEL: SCHULE: lernen ...
      ZU HAUSE: die kleineren Geschwister ...
      UNTERWEGS: die vielen Menschen ...

IMMER DAS GLEICHE

von Christine Wuttke

Jeden Tag das gleiche.
Ich geh' in die Schule,
lern was – oder auch nicht.
Sehe immer die vielen Menschen,
5 die unterwegs sind,
entweder mit der Straßenbahn[1]
oder zu Fuß
oder auch mit dem Auto.
Und ich fahr lächelnd[2] an den
10 Autoschlangen[3] vorbei.
Auch wenn[4] man als Radfahrer
Mühe[5] hat, vorwartszukommen,
ist man doch oft schneller.
In der Schule sind es dann überall
15 dieselben Erzählungen[6] der Lehrer:
Ihr lernt für euch, nicht für mich.
Und was sonst noch so typisch ist.
In den Arbeiten frage ich mich,
was das Klima[7] ist, was der Transformator ist,
20 oder was ist der Satz aus der Wassermusik.
Und ich kann mal wieder nur abgucken[8].
Endlich wieder zu Hause,
haben die kleineren Geschwister sogar
mal das Fernsehen abgestellt[9] und spielen
25 im Kinderzimmer.
Dann geh' ich zum Klavierunterricht[10],
zu Freunden oder in die Stadt,
und zähle die Werbeplakate[11]
an den Schaufenstern.
30 Abends im Bett denke ich dann,
wie „friedlich"[12] der Tag doch wieder war.
Immer das gleiche.

Oder ist es nicht jeden Tag was Besonderes[13],
was man erlebt[14]?
35 Aber doch das gleiche?
Sehe ich nicht jeden Tag andere Leute
auf den Straßen?
Reden die Lehrer nicht doch immer
was anderes?
40 Schreiben sie nicht jedesmal andere Arbeiten,
in denen[15] man auch mal was weiß?
Aber es ist jeden Tag das gleiche.

Immer das Gleiche? Physik-Vorlesung an der Uni Potsdam

---

[1]*street car* [2]*smiling* [3]*lines of cars* [4]*Auch ... Even if* [5]*difficulty* [6]*stories* [7]*climate*
[8]*to copy from someone/cheat* [9]*haben ... abgestellt turned off* [10]*piano lesson*
[11]*advertising posters* [12]*peaceful* [13]*was ... something special* [14]*experiences*
[15]*which*

As you read a text, you may be tempted to look up most of the words you do not know. Before reaching for the dictionary, however, try to guess the meaning of words from the context. If you find you really must use a dictionary, consider the following:

- Many compound words are not listed in dictionaries. To discover their meaning, look up the components and determine the meaning of the compound from the definitions of its components.

- Some forms found in texts differ from those listed in dictionaries. For example, nouns and pronouns are listed in the nominative singular; verbs are listed under their infinitive forms.

- Some words have multiple meanings. Read through all possible meanings and choose the correct meaning of the word based on its use in the text.

For practice in using a dictionary, do the following exercise:

- Can you figure out what **Autoschlange** means by looking up its components?

- Under which entry would you find **jeden?** And what about the phrase **ich fahr ... vorbei?**

- How many different meanings can you find for the word **Satz?** Which of those meanings most closely fits the context of the word as it is used in the poem **Immer das gleiche?**

- Underline all words in the text that you do not understand. Choose five and look them up. In what form do they appear in the dictionary? How many meanings are given? Which meaning best fits the context?

Zum Text

A. Lesen Sie den Text und beantworten Sie die Fragen.

1. Ist die Autorin Schülerin, Universitätsstudentin oder Lehrerin? Woher wissen Sie das?

2. Wie alt ist sie wohl?

3. Wo lebt die Autorin? In einer Stadt oder auf dem Land? Wie beweist (*shows*) der Text das?

4. Wie groß ist ihre Familie?

B. In most of the text the author uses declarative sentences stating what she does every day. In the last verse she uses words such as **aber** and **oder** and asks herself whether each day really is the same. What does she say about each day that might make it different, even if she still has the same routine?

Zu guter Letzt

Ein Besuch

Your cousin Stacy, who is learning German in high school, wants to come to visit you on campus because she will be applying to colleges next year. She will arrive on Thursday. You want to impress her with your German as well as show her around for a couple of days.

Schritt 1: So that you can get an overview of your time, jot down your usual Thursday-through-Sunday activities in the grid on the next page. Be sure to indicate the exact times at which you have things going on.

Zeit	Donnerstag	Freitag	Samstag	Sonntag
Vormittag				
Nachmittag				
Abend				

Schritt 2: Now write down six activities that you would like to do with your cousin while she is here, and put them into the schedule, too. They might include items such as:

- ins Restaurant gehen
- ins Kino gehen
- die Universität besichtigen (*tour*)
- Stacy in den Deutschkurs mitbringen

Schritt 3: Write your cousin an e-mail to tell her what you are planning for the two of you and when you will be doing those things.

Schritt 4: Working in pairs, describe to your partner what you are planning to do with your cousin. Ask at least three questions about your partner's plans.

Wortschatz

Tage und Tageszeiten — Days and Times of Day

der **Morgen**	morning
der **Vormittag**	morning, before noon
der **Mittag**	noon
der **Nachmittag**	afternoon
der **Abend**	evening
die **Nacht**	night
heute Morgen	this morning
heute Nachmittag	this afternoon
morgen früh	tomorrow morning
morgen Abend	tomorrow evening
morgens	in the morning, mornings
vormittags	before noon
mittags	at noon
nachmittags	in the afternoon, afternoons
abends	in the evening, evenings
nachts	at night, nights
montags	Mondays, on Monday(s)
dienstags	Tuesdays, on Tuesday(s)
mittwochs	Wednesdays, on Wednesday(s)
donnerstags	Thursdays, on Thursday(s)
freitags	Fridays, on Friday(s)
samstags; sonnabends	Saturdays, on Saturday(s)
sonntags	Sundays, on Sunday(s)

Unterhaltung / Entertainment

das **Ballett, -e**	ballet
die **Disko, -s**	disco; dance club
in die Disko gehen	to go clubbing
das **Fernsehen**	watching television
der **Film, -e**	film
das **Kino, -s**	cinema, (movie) theater
ins Kino gehen	to go to the movies
die **Komödie, -n**	comedy
das **Konzert, -e**	concert
ins Konzert gehen	to go to a concert
der **Krimi, -s**	crime, detective, mystery film or book
die **Oper, -n**	opera
in die Oper gehen	to go to the opera
das **Theater, -**	(stage) theater
ins Theater gehen	to go to the theater
das **Theaterstück, -e**	play (stage) drama
die **Tragödie, -n**	tragedy

Verben mit trennbaren Präfixen / Verbs with Separable Prefixes

ab•holen	to pick up (*from a place*)
an•fangen (fängt an)	to begin
an•rufen	to call up
auf•hören (mit)	to stop (*doing something*)
auf•räumen	to clean up, straighten up
auf•stehen	to get up; to stand up
auf•wachen	to wake up
aus•gehen	to go out
ein•kaufen (gehen)	to (go) shop(ping)
ein•laden (lädt ein)	to invite
ein•schlafen (schläft ein)	to fall asleep
fern•sehen (sieht fern)	to watch television
mit•kommen	to come along
mit•nehmen (nimmt mit)	to take along
vorbei•kommen	to come by
vor•haben (hat vor)	to plan (*to do*)
zu•hören	to listen
zurück•kommen	to return, come back

Modalverben / Modal Verbs

dürfen (darf)	to be permitted to; may
können (kann)	to be able to; can
mögen (mag)	to care for; to like
möchte	would like to
müssen (muss)	to have to; must
sollen	to be supposed to; ought, should
wollen (will)	to want to; to plan to

Uhrzeiten / Time

die **Minute, -n**	minute
die **Sekunde, -n**	second
die **Stunde, -n**	hour
Um wie viel Uhr?	At what time?
Wie spät ist es? / Wie viel Uhr ist es?	What time is it?
Es ist eins. / Es ist ein Uhr.	It's one o'clock.
halb: halb zwei	half: half past one, one-thirty
nach: fünf nach zwei	after: five after two
um: um zwei	at: at two
Viertel: Es ist Viertel nach/vor zwei.	quarter: It's a quarter after/to two.
vor: fünf vor zwei	to, of: five to/of two

Sonstiges / Other

frühstücken	to eat breakfast
spazieren gehen	to go for a walk
Ich gehe spazieren.	I'm going for a walk.
treffen (trifft)	to meet
die **Bibliothek, -en**	library
das **Fitnesscenter, -**	gym
der **Plan, ¨e**	plan
die **Tasse, -n**	cup
eine Tasse Kaffee	a cup of coffee
die **Vorlesung, -en**	(university) lecture
der **Vortrag, ¨e**	lecture
die **Woche, -n**	week
pro Woche	per week
das **Wochenende, -n**	weekend
am liebsten: möchte am liebsten	would like to (do) most
doch	(*intensifying particle often used with imperatives*)
früh	early
gemütlich	cozy, cozily
gewöhnlich	usual(ly)
lieber: möchte lieber	would rather
mal	(*softening particle often used with imperatives*)
man	one, people, you, they
Hier darf man nicht parken.	You may not park here.
spannend	suspenseful, exciting
spät	late

1. Wie viel Uhr ist es? Sagen Sie die Zeit auf Deutsch:

   6.00; 9.30; 12.45; 14.07; 17.15.

2. Was machen Sie gewöhnlich zwischen 6 Uhr morgens und 18 Uhr abends? Nennen Sie drei Dinge (*things*).

3. Was möchten Sie am Wochenende machen? Nennen Sie drei Dinge.

4. Bilden Sie Sätze.

   a. ich / morgens / um 7 Uhr / aufstehen
   b. die Vorlesung / um 11 Uhr / aufhören
   c. wir / einladen / 20 Leute / zur Party
   d. was / du / vorhaben / am Wochenende / ?

5. Wie sagt man das auf Deutsch?

   a. Please drop by at 6:00 p.m. (*familiar singular*)
   b. I can't go to the movies. I have to work.
   c. Please call me on Saturday morning. (*formal*)
   d. Would you like to go to the movies tonight? (*familiar plural*)
   e. Parking is not allowed here. (*familiar singular*)

KAPITEL

5

Einkaufen

Was kann man auf dem Markt kaufen?

In diesem Kapitel

- **Themen:** Clothes, colors, types of foods, names of stores and shops
- **Grammatik:** Dative case; verbs that require dative; dative prepositions **wo, wohin,** and **woher**
- **Kultur:** Clothing sizes, shopping, prices, weights and measures
- **Lesen:** „Im Hutladen" (Karl Valentin)

Videoclips
Einkaufen: was und wo?

144

Alles klar?

A. Sie sehen im Bild ein Kaufhaus in Deutschland. Man kann da vieles kaufen. Wo findet man alles?

BEISPIELE: Computer findet man im vierten Stock.
Bücher findet man im Erdgeschoss.

1. Schreibwaren
2. Schuhe
3. Pullover
4. Sportartikel
5. Telefonapparate
6. Teppiche
7. Make-up
8. Brokkoli
9. DVD-Spieler
10. Parfüm
11. Fernseher
12. Kaffeetassen
13. Butter
14. Shampoo

im Erdgeschoss

im vierten Stock

im dritten Stock

im Untergeschoss

im ersten Stock

im zweiten Stock

4	Computer TV/DVD/CD Center Foto/Optik Elektrogeräte Telefon/Handy Shop Kundenrestaurant Toiletten
3	Bettwäsche Gardinen Teppiche Orientteppiche Geschenkartikel Glas/Porzellan Haushaltswaren Reisebüro
2	Jeans-Wear Mode-Boutiquen Kinderkonfektion Babywäsche Schuhe Sport/Fahrräder Camping Friseursalon
1	Damenkonfektion Damenwäsche Herrenkonfektion Herrenartikel Accessoires Handschuhe Bademoden Uhren/Schmuck
E	Lederwaren Lotto/Tabak Zeitschriften Parfümerie Kosmetik/Drogerie Schreibwaren Bücher Süßigkeiten
U	Lebensmittel Toiletten

[1]E = Erdgeschoss (*ground floor*)
[2]U = Untergeschoss (*basement*)

B. Sie hören nun vier Ansagen (*announcements*) im Kaufhaus. Markieren Sie, was die Sprecher beschreiben.

1. Kosmetik   Kameras   Fahrräder
2. Schmuck   Betten   Schuhe
3. Bücher   Kaffeemaschinen   Lederjacken
4. Jeans   Lampen   Fernseher

Wörter im Kontext

Neue Wörter

die Klamotte (Klamotten, *pl.*) duds, rags (*slang for clothing*)
das Hemd shirt
das Kleid dress
das Sakko sport coat
die Badehose swim trunks
der Anzug suit
die Socke (Socken, *pl.*) socks
der Badeanzug (woman's) bathing suit
der Rock skirt
der Rucksack backpack
der Schal scarf
der Hausschuh (Hausschuhe, *pl.*) slippers
der Koffer suitcase
trägt (tragen) is wearing

THEMA 1: Kleidungsstücke

A. Klamotten, Klamotten! Was sehen Sie im Schrank? Kreuzen Sie an!

Ich sehe ...

- ☐ ein **Hemd**
- ☐ ein **Kleid**
- ☐ ein Polohemd
- ☐ ein **Sakko**
- ☐ ein Sweatshirt
- ☐ eine **Badehose**
- ☐ einen **Anzug**
- ☐ **Socken**
- ☐ ein **T-Shirt**
- ☐ einen **Badeanzug**
- ☐ einen Wintermantel
- ☐ einen **Rock**
- ☐ einen **Rucksack**
- ☐ einen **Schal**
- ☐ **Hausschuhe**
- ☐ **Jeans**
- ☐ einen **Koffer**
- ☐ einen **Pullover**

B. Wer trägt was?

BEISPIEL: Die Frau trägt einen Hut, einen Mantel, eine Bluse, ...

C. Was haben Sie alles zu Hause in Ihrem Kleiderschrank?

BEISPIEL: Ich habe ein Sakko, 15 T-Shirts, Hemden, 5 Hosen, Socken, und Schuhe in meinem Kleiderschrank.

Die Koffer-Checkliste notiert Kleidungsstücke für den Urlaub (*vacation*).

- Welche Kleidungsstücke sind für den Winter? Welche sind für den Sommer?
- Welche Sachen auf dieser Liste tragen Sie besonders gern?
- Suchen Sie aus der Liste vier zusammengesetzte Wörter (*compounds*).

Bilden Sie nun Ihre eigenen Wörter.

BEISPIEL: Bade- + Hose = Badehose

$$\left.\begin{array}{l} \text{Bade-} \\ \text{Cord-} \\ \text{Baumwoll-} \\ \text{Trainings-} \\ \text{Leder-} \\ \text{Regen-} \end{array}\right\} + \left\{\begin{array}{l} \text{Anzug} \\ \text{Mantel} \\ \text{Hose} \\ \text{Hemd} \\ \text{Jacke} \\ \text{Schuhe} \end{array}\right.$$

Koffer-Checkliste
Für den Urlaub

☐ T-Shirts	☐ Sweatshirts
☐ Shorts	☐ Baumwollhosen
☐ Cordhosen	☐ Trainings- und Jogginganzüge
☐ Regenmantel	☐ Sportschuhe
☐ Sandalen	☐ Unterwäsche
☐ Badeanzug	☐ Jacke
☐ Badehose	☐ Handschuhe
☐ Blusen	☐ Stiefel
☐ Röcke	☐ Pullover
☐ Kleider	☐ Mütze
☐ Hemden	

Aktivität 1 Eine Reise nach Südspanien

Sie hören ein Gespräch zwischen Bettina und Markus. Sie planen für die Semesterferien eine Reise an die Küste von Südspanien mit einer Gruppe von Freunden. Was nimmt man da mit? Sind die Aussagen richtig oder falsch?

	RICHTIG	FALSCH
1. Bettina und Markus nehmen einen Koffer und einen Rucksack mit.	☐	☐
2. Markus nimmt Shorts, ein paar T-Shirts und Jeans mit.	☐	☐
3. Bettina braucht unbedingt einen neuen Badeanzug.	☐	☐
4. Markus empfiehlt ihr, sie soll einen Bikini in Spanien kaufen.	☐	☐
5. Markus hat einen besonderen Gürtel für sein Geld.	☐	☐
6. Bettina steckt ihr Geld in die Schuhe.	☐	☐

Aktivität 2 Was tragen Sie gewöhnlich?

Sagen Sie, was Sie in den folgenden Situationen tragen.

BEISPIEL: Ich trage gewöhnlich Jeans und ein T-Shirt zur Uni. Zur Arbeit trage ich ein Sporthemd, eine Hose und ein Sakko.

zur Arbeit	einen Anzug
zur Uni	einen Badeanzug
im Winter	ein Kleid
im Urlaub auf Hawaii	ein Abendkleid
zu Hause	einen Wintermantel
auf einer Fete	Jeans
zu einer Hochzeit	ein T-Shirt
??	??

The impersonal expression **es gibt** means *there is* or *there are*. It can also be used to say where you can get something. The object of **es gibt** is always in the accusative case.

Es gibt in dieser Stadt einen Markt.	*There is a market in this town. (It exists.)*
Wo gibt es schicke Blusen?	*Where can you get stylish blouses?*

Use the preposition **bei** and the name of the place to say where you can get something.

Blusen gibt es **bei** Gisie.	*You can get blouses at Gisie's (shop).*

Schicke Blusen Wo? bei Gisie Papendiek 29

clothing ## Aktivität 3 Ich brauche neue Bekleidung°.

Was brauchen Sie, und wo gibt es das? Was kostet das?

BEISPIEL: s1: Ich brauche dringend ein Hemd. Wo gibt es hier Hemden?
s2: Hemden gibt es bei Strauss.
s1: Weißt du, wie viel ein Hemd da kostet?
s2: Es gibt Hemden für 24,90 Euro.

Stiefel	Schuhe
Hose	Gürtel
Bluse	Krawatte

FRÜHLINGS-KRAWATTE **14.⁹⁰** reine Seide

CHINO-HOSE **39.⁹⁰** 100% Baumwolle, Gr. 48–56

auch in navy und weiß mit Atelier-Innenverarbeitung

Dessin-Beispiele

Strauss INNOVATION

STREIFEN-HEMD **24.⁹⁰** 100% Casual Cotton Gr. S–XXL

mit Metall-Schnalle

COTTON-GÜRTEL **14.⁹⁰**

ARIANE* ~~19,90~~ **14,90 €**

Graceland ~~19,90~~ **14,90 €**

THE SHOP

DEICHMANN

Aktivität 4 Koffer packen!°

Let's pack our bags!

Spielen Sie in Gruppen von vier bis fünf Personen. So spielt man es:

BEISPIEL: s1: Ich packe fünf Bikinis in meinen Koffer.
s2: Ich packe fünf Bikinis und Sportschuhe in meinen Koffer.
s3: Ich packe fünf Bikinis, Sportschuhe und Ledersandalen in meinen Koffer.

Wer etwas vergisst (*forgets*) oder falsch sagt, scheidet aus (*drops out*).

THEMA 2: Beim Einkaufen im Kaufhaus

Bernd Thalhofer geht einkaufen, denn er braucht ein paar neue Hemden.

VERKÄUFER:	Bitte schön. Kann ich Ihnen **helfen?**
BERND:	Ich brauche ein paar neue Sporthemden.
VERKÄUFER:	Welche **Größe** brauchen Sie?
BERND:	Größe 42.
VERKÄUFER:	Und welche **Farbe?**
BERND:	Grün oder blau.
VERKÄUFER:	**Wie gefällt Ihnen** dieses **gestreifte** Hemd in Marineblau? Sehr dezent (*tasteful*) und **modisch.**
BERND:	Ich finde, **die Farbe steht mir** nicht. Haben Sie das in Hellblau?
VERKÄUFER:	Ja, hier ist ein Hemd in Hellblau.
BERND:	Ist das aus Baumwolle oder Synthetik?
VERKÄUFER:	Das ist 100 Prozent Baumwolle. Möchten Sie es **anprobieren?**
BERND:	Nein, das ist nicht **nötig.** Größe 42 **passt** mir bestimmt. Wie viel kostet dieses Hemd?
VERKÄUFER:	40 Euro.
BERND:	Gut. Ich nehme drei Hemden.
VERKÄUFER:	**Alle** in Hellblau?
BERND:	Nein, geben Sie mir bitte zwei in Blau und ein Hemd in Weiß.
VERKÄUFER:	**Das macht zusammen** 120 Euro. Bitte **zahlen** Sie vorne an der **Kasse!**
BERND:	Danke schön.
VERKÄUFER:	Bitte sehr.

Neue Wörter

helfen help
die Größe size
die Farbe color
Wie gefällt Ihnen …? How do you like . . . ?
modisch fashionable
Die Farbe steht mir. The color looks good on me.
anprobieren try on
nötig necessary
passt (passen) fits
das macht zusammen all together
zahlen pay
die Kasse cashier, check-out
empfiehlt (empfehlen) recommends
glaubt (glauben) believes
zeigt (zeigen) shows
schenkt (schenken) is giving
dankt (danken) thanks

kariert

gestreift

weiß
rot
orange
gelb
grün
blau
lila
beige
braun
grau
schwarz

■ Was passiert im Kaufhaus? Stimmt das oder stimmt das nicht?

	DAS STIMMT	DAS STIMMT NICHT
1. Bernd braucht ein paar Sporthemden.	☐	☐
2. Er trägt Größe 42.	☐	☐
3. Der Verkäufer **empfiehlt** Bernd ein Hemd in Marineblau.	☐	☐
4. Bernd **glaubt,** Marineblau steht ihm sehr gut.	☐	☐
5. Der Verkäufer **zeigt** Bernd ein Hemd aus Baumwolle.	☐	☐
6. Bernd **schenkt** seinem Onkel die Hemden.	☐	☐
7. Bernd **dankt** dem Verkäufer.	☐	☐

Aktivität 5   Im Kaufhaus

Ergänzen Sie die fehlenden Informationen aus dem Dialog im Thema 2.

1. Der Kunde braucht _____.
2. Der Verkäufer möchte _____ und _____ wissen.
3. Der Kunde braucht _____ 42.
4. Größe 42 _____ ihm.
5. Das Hemd in Marineblau _____ ihm nicht.
6. Das Hemd ist aus _____ _____.
7. Der Kunde _____ 120 Euro für drei Hemden.

Aktivität 6   Gespräche im Geschäft

Was brauchen die Leute? In welcher Größe und in welcher Farbe? Ergänzen Sie die Tabelle.

	WAS?	IN WELCHER GRÖSSE?	IN WELCHER FARBE?
Dialog 1			
Dialog 2			
Dialog 3			
Dialog 4			

Hier klicken!

Weiteres zum Thema Einkaufen finden Sie bei **Deutsch: Na klar!** im World-Wide-Web unter www.mhhe.com/dnk5.

Aktivität 7 Wer trägt was?

Finden Sie folgende Personen und bilden Sie Fragen. Wer **ja** sagt muss rechts unterschreiben (*sign*).

BEISPIEL: Wer trägt gern Rot?
Frage: Trägst du gern Rot?

FRAGE   UNTERSCHRIFT

1. Wessen (*Whose*) Lieblingsfarbe ist Lila? _____
2. Wem steht Blau sehr gut? _____
3. Wem steht Grün nicht gut? _____
4. Wer trägt gern bunte (*colorful*) Sachen? _____
5. Wer trägt gern gestreifte oder karierte Sachen? _____
6. Wer trägt Größe 39 in Hemden oder Größe 10 in Blusen? _____
7. Wer braucht die Schuhgröße 42? _____

Aktivität 8 Wer ist das?

Beschreiben Sie, was und welche Farben jemand in Ihrem Deutschkurs trägt. Sagen Sie den Namen der Person nicht. Die anderen im Kurs müssen erraten (*guess*), wer das ist.

BEISPIEL: Diese Person trägt eine Bluse. Die Bluse ist rotweiß gestreift. Sie trägt auch Jeans; die sind blau. Und ihre Schuhe sind, hm, lila. Wer ist das? —Das ist Winona.

Aktivität 9 Ein Gespräch

Schritt 1: Arbeiten Sie mit einem Partner / einer Partnerin. Benutzen Sie die Wörter und Ausdrücke im Kasten und schreiben Sie zusammen ein Gespräch zwischen einem Verkäufer / einer Verkäuferin und einem Kunden / einer Kundin. Was für Kleidung möchten Sie kaufen? Wie beginnt das Gespräch?

(welche) Farbe   (welche) Größe   Ich möchte gern ____.   Was kostet ____?
____ Euro   preiswert   passt mir (nicht)   ist mir zu groß
Bitte sehr.   ist mir zu klein   ist mir zu teuer   Wie gefällt Ihnen ____?
Ich brauche ____.   steht mir (nicht)   anprobieren
Das macht zusammen ____.   Ich nehme ____.   Danke schön.

Schritt 2: Spielen Sie jetzt das Gespräch mit dem Partner / der Partnerin.

Siehe *Verbs with a Dative Object Only*, S. 162.

THEMA 3: Lebensmittel

A. Geben Sie die englischen Bedeutungen für die folgenden Wörter. Fragen Sie andere Studentinnen / Studenten im Kurs, wenn Sie Wörter nicht kennen.

der Apfel	die Gurke	das Salz
der Aufschnitt	das Hähnchen	der Schinken
die Banane	der Joghurt	das Schnitzel
das Bier	die Karotte	das Schweinefleisch
der Blumenkohl	die Kartoffel	der Tee
der Brokkoli	der Käse	das Toilettenpapier
das Brot	der Keks	die Tomate
das Brötchen	der Kuchen	die Traube
die Butter	die Milch	der Truthahn
das Ei	das Müsli	das Wasser
das Eis	der Pfeffer	die Wurst
die Erdbeere	die Rasiercreme	die Zahnpasta
frisch	das Rindfleisch	zart
gefroren	der Saft	der Zucker

B. Nennen Sie drei **Lebensmittel** oder Produkte für jede Kategorie:

OBST	GEMÜSE	FLEISCH	GETRÄNKE
_____	_____	_____	_____
_____	_____	_____	_____
_____	_____	_____	_____

C. Mini-Umfrage: Interviewen Sie drei Studentinnen/Studenten. Was essen sie **jeden** Tag zum **Frühstück?** Zum **Mittagessen?** Zum **Abendessen?**

KULTURTIPP

Heute kaufen Deutsche oft in großen, modernen **Supermärkten** ein. Es gibt aber immer noch viele Spezialgeschäfte, besonders in kleinen Städten, wie die **Metzgerei**, die **Bäckerei**, die **Konditorei**, den **Getränkeladen** und den **Obst- und Gemüsestand** auf dem Markt. **Medikamente** auf Rezept kann man in Deutschland nicht in einer **Drogerie** kaufen, sondern nur in einer **Apotheke**. Im **Bioladen** gibt es Produkte, die nicht mit chemischen Mitteln behandelt (*treated*) sind.

SPRACHTIPP

The metric system is used in German-speaking countries. The following abbreviations are commonly used:

1 kg = 1 Kilogramm = 1000 Gramm = 2.2 Pfund

500 g = 500 Gramm = 1 Pfund

1000 ml = 1000 Milliliter

0,75 l = 0,75 Liter

1 l = 1 Liter

Kl. I = Klasse I (*top quality*)

Stck. = Stück (*piece*)

Aktivität 10 Kleine Läden

Was kauft man wo? Sagen Sie, wo man diese Dinge kaufen kann.

BEISPIEL: Brötchen kauft man in der Bäckerei.

am Obst- und Gemüsestand	im Bioladen	in der Bäckerei
in der Drogerie	in der Konditorei	in der Metzgerei

1. Brötchen
2. Trauben
3. Rindfleisch
4. Zahnpasta
5. Schinken
6. Blumenkohl
7. Vollkornbrot
8. Bio-Milch
9. Apfelstrudel

die Lebensmittel (*pl.*)
  groceries
das Obst fruit
das Gemüse vegetables
das Fleisch meat
das Getränk (**Getränke**, *pl.*)
  drink
jeden each, every
das Frühstück breakfast
das Mittagessen lunch
das Abendessen dinner
die Metzgerei meat market
die Bäckerei bakery
die Konditorei pastry shop
der Laden store
die Drogerie toiletries and
  sundries store
die Apotheke pharmacy
der Bioladen natural foods
  store

Aktivität 11   Wo? Was? Wie viel?

Sie hören drei Dialoge: in einer Bäckerei, auf dem Markt und in einer Metzgerei. Kreuzen Sie das richtige Geschäft an. Ergänzen Sie die Tabelle.

	MARKT	BÄCKEREI	METZGEREI	WAS?	PREIS?
Dialog 1					
Dialog 2					
Dialog 3					

In der Metzgerei kauft man Fleisch.

SPRACHTIPP

The following words will help you organize your writing and help you put statements in order of occurrence.

> **zuerst**   first
> **deshalb**   therefore
> **dann**   then
> **zuletzt**   finally

Using these connectors will enable you to narrate effectively in German. Remember that if you begin your sentence with one of these connectors, your verb will immediately follow it.

Aktivität 12 Einkaufstag für Jutta

Jutta muss einkaufen. Sie gibt nämlich eine Party. Schreiben Sie einen Text zu jedem Bild. Benutzen Sie Elemente aus beiden Spalten (*columns*) unten.

So beginnt die Geschichte:

Jutta gibt am Wochenende eine Party. Deshalb geht sie heute einkaufen ...

Dort kauft sie ...	Obst und Gemüse – alles ganz frisch.
Zuletzt geht sie ...	Brot, Brötchen und Käsekuchen.
Zuerst geht sie ...	und geht nach Hause.
Da gibt es ...	zur Bäckerei.
Dann geht sie ...	zum Lebensmittelgeschäft.
Jutta braucht auch ...	zur Metzgerei.
Deshalb geht sie auch	Würstchen zum Grillen.
Jetzt hat sie alles ...	Kaffee, Zucker, Milch und Käse.
In der Bäckerei kauft sie ...	auf den Markt.
Auf dem Markt kauft sie ...	Blumenkohl und Kartoffeln.
	Äpfel, Bananen und Trauben – alles ganz frisch.

1.

2.

3.

4.

5.

Aktivität 13 Preiswert einkaufen!

Stellen Sie sich vor, Sie haben nur 10 Euro für Essen und Trinken übrig und müssen damit ein ganzes Wochenende auskommen. Wählen Sie Waren aus den Anzeigen (*ads*) aus. Vergleichen Sie (*compare*) Ihre Listen im Plenum.

BEISPIEL: Wir kaufen ein Kastenweißbrot für €1,59; Schinkenaufschnitt für €1,79; zwei Joghurtbecher für €0,78; zwei Suppen für €0,98; 1 Kilo Tomaten für €1,95; und Eiscreme für €2,69.

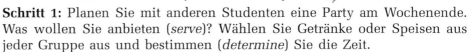

Aktivität 14 Ein Menü für eine Party

Schritt 1: Planen Sie mit anderen Studenten eine Party am Wochenende. Was wollen Sie anbieten (*serve*)? Wählen Sie Getränke oder Speisen aus jeder Gruppe aus und bestimmen (*determine*) Sie die Zeit.

Zeit	heute Abend, am Wochenende, am Samstag, ???
zum Essen	Würstchen, Steaks, Hamburger, Kartoffelsalat, Kartoffelchips, Pommes frites, Salat, Gemüse, ???
zum Nachtisch	Eis, Pudding, frische Erdbeeren, Käsekuchen, ???
zum Trinken	Mineralwasser (Sprudel), Bier, Wein, ???

Schritt 2: Sprechen Sie über Ihre Pläne mit zwei oder drei anderen Studentinnen/Studenten im Kurs. Folgen Sie dem Modell.

S1	S2
1. Wollen wir ____ ____ grillen?	2. Gut. Machen wir ____ mit ____.
3. Und was servieren wir zum Nachtisch?	4. Warum nicht ____ oder ____? Was sollen wir dazu trinken?
5. ____ und ____ natürlich!	6a. Na, gut. b. Also, ____ schmeckt doch nicht dazu. Ich schlage vor (*suggest*), wir trinken ____.

Grammatik im Kontext

The Dative Case°

Der Dativ

As you have learned, the nominative case is the case of the subject; the accusative case is used for direct objects and with a number of prepositions. These cases are signaled by special endings of articles and possessive adjectives, as well as by different forms for personal pronouns.

NOMINATIVE		ACCUSATIVE
Subject		*Direct Object*
Wer	braucht	einen Rucksack?
Uwe	braucht	einen Rucksack.
Subject		*Prepositional Object*
Der Rucksack	ist	für ihn.

Like the nominative and accusative cases, the dative has special forms for pronouns and endings for articles and possessive adjectives. In previous chapters, you learned two common expressions that use dative pronouns.

Lesen macht **mir** Spaß.	*I like to read.* (lit.: *Reading is fun for me.*)
Wie geht es **dir**?	*How are you?* (lit.: *How is it going for you?*)

The dative case serves several distinct functions. It is used primarily:

- for indirect objects (indicating the person to/for whom something is done); it answers the question **wem** (whom? to/for whom?).

Wem zeigt der Verkäufer einen Rucksack?	*To whom is the salesperson showing a backpack?*
Der Verkäufer zeigt **der Studentin** einen Rucksack.	*The salesperson is showing the student a backpack.*

- with certain verbs, such as **gefallen**.

Der Rucksack **gefällt ihm**. *He likes the backpack. (lit.: The backpack pleases him.)*

- with specific prepositions, such as **mit** and **zu**.

Der Kunde geht **mit dem** Rucksack **zur** Kasse. *The customer goes to the cash register with the backpack.*

- in certain expressions, such as **Spaß machen**.

Wandern **macht ihm Spaß**. *He likes to hike. (lit.: Hiking is fun for him.)*

Personal Pronouns in the Dative

The following chart shows the personal pronouns in the dative case.

SINGULAR		PLURAL	
NOMINATIVE	**DATIVE**	**NOMINATIVE**	**DATIVE**
ich	**mir** *to/for me*	wir	**uns** *to/for us*
du	**dir** *to/for you (informal)*	ihr	**euch** *to/for you (informal)*
Sie	**Ihnen** *to/for you (formal)*	Sie	**Ihnen** *to/for you (formal)*
er	**ihm** *to/for him; to/for it*		
sie	**ihr** *to/for her; to/for it*	sie	**ihnen** *to/for them*
es	**ihm** *to/for it*		

ANALYSE

Scan the following ads.

- Find the dative object pronouns. What are the verbs that require the dative to be used?
- What is the nominative form of each of the dative pronouns?

Wir wünschen unseren Gästen ein gesundes Neues Jahr.

Ab Januar möchten wir Ihnen unsere neue Speiseauswahl anbieten.[1]

**Restaurant
Haus Kuckuck**

Horst und Christine Schmidt

Liebe Mutti,
Zum Geburtstag wünschen wir dir alles, alles Gute
Vati und die ganze Bande[2]

**DA SCHAUT JEMAND
AUF IHR GELD!
WOLLEN SIE ES IHM GEBEN?**

Sicher nicht. Schenken Sie dem Mann nicht weiter Ihr Geld.

**Wenn Sie uns
schreiben wollen ...**

[1]möchten ... *we would like to offer you our new menu*

[2]die ... *the whole gang*

Übung 1   Wem macht das Spaß?

Wie sagt man das anders? Setzen Sie Personalpronomen im Dativ in die Lücken.

BEISPIEL: Ich gehe gern einkaufen. Einkaufen gehen macht _mir_ Spaß.

1. Ich fotografiere gern. Fotografieren macht _____ Spaß.
2. Mein Bruder Alex isst gern. Essen macht _____ Spaß.
3. Mein Freund und ich, wir tanzen gern. Tanzen macht _____ Spaß.
4. Die Studenten gehen gern in die Disko. In die Disko gehen macht _____ Spaß.
5. Ich surfe gern im Internet. Im Internet surfen macht _____ Spaß.
6. Meine Schwester telefoniert gern. Telefonieren macht _____ Spaß.
7. Esst ihr gern Apfelstrudel frisch vom Bäcker? Apfelstrudel essen macht _____ bestimmt Spaß.
8. Wir gehen gern einkaufen. Einkaufen gehen macht _____ Spaß.
9. Was machst du gern? Was macht _____ Spaß?

Übung 2   Das macht mir Spaß.

Schritt 1: Was macht dir Spaß? Was macht dir keinen Spaß? Arbeiten Sie mit einer Partnerin / einem Partner.

BEISPIEL: s1: Was macht dir Spaß?
s2: Fotografieren macht mir Spaß.
s1: Und was macht dir keinen Spaß?
s2: Einkaufen gehen macht mir keinen Spaß.

Schritt 2: Berichten Sie nun im Plenum über Ihre Partnerin / Ihren Partner.

BEISPIEL: Fotografieren macht Bob Spaß. Einkaufen gehen macht ihm keinen Spaß.

Übung 3   Hallo, wie geht's?

Ergänzen Sie die fehlenden Personalpronomen im Dativ.

1. A: Hallo, Brigitte, wie geht es _____?
   B: Danke, es geht _____ gut.
   A: Und wie geht's deinem Freund?
   B: Ach, es geht _____ nicht besonders gut. Er hat viel Stress.

2. C: Hallo, Petra und Christoph. Na, wie geht es _____ denn?
   D: Danke, es geht _____ gut.
   C: Und was machen die Kinder?
   D: Ach, es geht _____ immer gut.

3. E: Guten Tag, Herr Professor Distelmeier.
   F: Guten Tag, Herr Liederlich. Wie geht es _____?
   E: Es geht _____ schlecht. Ich habe zu viel Arbeit.

4. G: Tag, Frau Brinkmann. Wie geht es _____?
   H: Danke, es geht _____ gut. Und _____?
   G: Danke, auch gut. Und wie geht es Ihrer Mutter?
   H: Ach, es geht _____ nicht besonders. Sie schläft so schlecht.

Articles and Possessive Adjectives in the Dative

The following chart shows the dative endings for definite and indefinite articles, possessive adjectives, and **der**-words. Note that the masculine and neuter endings are identical.

MASCULINE	NEUTER	FEMININE	PLURAL
dem (k)ein**em** mein**em** } Mann dies**em**	dem (k)ein**em** mein**em** } Kind dies**em**	der (k)ein**er** mein**er** } Frau dies**er**	d**en** kein**en** mein**en** } Männern Frauen Kindern dies**en**
dem Kunden			**den** Kunden

Geben Sie Ihrem Haar einen modischen Kick... HENNA PLUS

Note:

- Nouns in the dative singular do not normally take an ending, except for the special masculine nouns that take an **-n** or **-en** in the accusative as well **(Kapitel 2).**

Nominative	Accusative	Dative
der Kunde	den Kunde**n**	dem Kunde**n**
der Student	den Student**en**	dem Student**en**

- In the dative plural, all nouns add **-n** to the plural ending, unless the plural already ends in **-n.** Exception: Those nouns whose plural ends in **-s** do not add **-n.**

	Plural	Dative Plural
	die Männer	den Männer**n**
	die Frauen	den Frauen
but:	die Autos	den Autos
	die Handys	den Handys

The Dative Case for Indirect Objects

As in English, many German verbs take both a direct object and an indirect object. The direct object, in the accusative, will usually be a thing; the indirect object, in the dative, will normally be a person.

		DATIVE indirect object	ACCUSATIVE direct object
Michael	kauft	**seiner Freundin**	einen Ring.
Der Verkäufer	zeigt	**ihm**	vier Ringe.

Following are some of the verbs that can take two objects in German:

empfehlen (empfiehlt)	to recommend
geben (gibt)	to give
glauben	to believe
leihen	to lend, borrow
schenken	to give as a gift
zeigen	to show

Position of Dative and Accusative Objects

Ich schenke **meinem Bruder ein Handy** zum Geburtstag.	*I'm giving my brother a cell phone for his birthday.*
Ich gebe **es meinem Bruder**.	*I'm giving it (the cell phone) to my brother.*
Wann gibst du **es ihm**?	*When are you giving it to him?*

Note:

- The dative object precedes the accusative object when the accusative object is a noun.
- The dative object follows the accusative object when the direct object (accusative) is a personal pronoun.

Übung 4   Situationen im Alltag

Sie hören fünf Dialoge. Kreuzen Sie für jeden Dialog den Satz an, der zu dem Thema passt.

1. Hans braucht unbedingt etwas Geld.
   - ☐ Sein Freund kann ihm nichts leihen.
   - ☐ Sein Freund gibt ihm einen Scheck.
2. Zwei Studentinnen brauchen Hilfe.
   - ☐ Ein Freund gibt ihnen etwas Geld.
   - ☐ Ein Herr zeigt ihnen den Weg zum Café.
3. Helmut hat Geburtstag.
   - ☐ Marianne schreibt ihm eine Karte.
   - ☐ Marianne schenkt ihm eine CD.
4. Eine Studentin erzählt einem Studenten über ihren Tagesablauf.
   - ☐ Sie empfiehlt ihm Yoga.
   - ☐ Sie hat keine Zeit für Yoga.
5. Achim sagt, er lebt nur von Brot und Wasser.
   - ☐ Er hat kein Geld.
   - ☐ Man kann ihm nicht alles glauben, was er sagt.

Übung 5   Wortsalat!

Bilden Sie Sätze.

BEISPIEL: meinem Freund / macht / keinen Spaß / Telefonieren →
   Telefonieren macht meinem Freund keinen Spaß.

1. einen Wecker / die Mutter / zum Geburtstag / ihrem Sohn / kauft
2. gibt / ihm / sie / wann / ihn / ?
3. den Studenten / zeigt / der Professor / eine Landkarte von Deutschland
4. dem Kunden / die Verkäuferin / einen preiswerten Computer / empfiehlt

5. du / das Handy / zum Geburtstag / gibst / wem / ?

6. kauft / einen Ring / der Kunde / seiner Freundin

7. seiner Freundin / schenkt / zum Valentinstag / er / diesen Ring

Übung 6   So ein Stress!

Horst hat eine große Familie und viele Freunde. Wem schenkt Horst was?

BEISPIEL: Sein Onkel hört gern klassische Musik.
   a. Er schenkt seinem Onkel eine CD.
   b. Er schenkt ihm eine CD.

1. Seine Oma reist oft nach Hawaii.

2. Sein Bruder ist sportlich sehr aktiv.

3. Sein Vetter Klaus findet Fische interessant.

4. Seine Schwester Heike telefoniert pausenlos.

5. Seine Freundin Ute wandert gern.

6. Seine Tante Adelgunde liebt exzentrische Mode.

7. Sein Vater hat schon alles.

8. Seine Mutter trinkt morgens, mittags und abends Kaffee.

9. Seine Eltern planen eine Reise nach Spanien.

 ein Aquarium mit zwei Goldfischen

 das Handy

 die Krawatte

 die Sonnenbrille

 der Kaffeebecher

 der Reiseführer

  die Inline-Skates

   der Rucksack

 der Hut

Verbs with a Dative Object Only

A number of common German verbs always take an object in the dative case. Note that these dative objects usually refer to people.

danken	Ich **danke** dir für die Karte.	*I thank you for the card.*
gefallen	Wie **gefällt** Ihnen dieses Hemd?	*How do you like this shirt?**
gehören	Der Mercedes **gehört** meinem Bruder.	*The Mercedes belongs to my brother.*
helfen	Der Verkäufer **hilft** dem Kunden.	*The salesperson is helping the customer.*

———

*Lit.: *How does this shirt please you?*

passen	Größe 48 **passt** mir bestimmt.	*Size 48 will surely fit me.*
stehen	Das Kleid **steht** dir gut.	*The dress looks good on you.*

A number of frequently used idiomatic expressions also require dative objects.

Wie geht es **dir?**	*How are you?*
Das tut **mir** leid.	*I'm sorry.*
Das ist **mir** egal.	*I don't care.*

Verbs that take only a dative object are indicated in the vocabulary lists of this book as follows: (+ *dat.*)

Übung 7   Ein schwieriger° Kunde

difficult

Ergänzen Sie den Dialog mit passenden Verben und Pronomen im Dativ. Suchen Sie passende Verben aus der folgenden Liste:

danken	**helfen**	**stehen**
empfehlen	**leidtun**	**(zu) teuer sein**
gefallen	**passen**	**zeigen**

VERKÄUFER: Kann ich _____[1] _____[2]? (*help you*)

KUNDE: Ja. Ich brauche ein Geschenk für meine Freundin. Können Sie _____[3] vielleicht etwas _____[4]? (*recommend to me*)

VERKÄUFER: Eine Bluse vielleicht?

KUNDE: _____[5] Sie _____[6] bitte eine Bluse in Größe 50. (*Show me*)

VERKÄUFER: Größe 50? Ist das nicht zu groß?

KUNDE: Ich glaube, Größe 50 _____[7] _____[8] bestimmt. (*fits her*)

VERKÄUFER: Hier habe ich eine elegante Seidenbluse. In Schwarz.

KUNDE: Nein, Schwarz _____[9] _____[10] nicht. (*look good on her*)

VERKÄUFER: Wie _____[11] _____[12] diese Bluse in Lila? (*do you like*)

KUNDE: Schrecklich. Diese Farbe _____[13] _____[14] überhaupt nicht. (*I like*)

VERKÄUFER: Hier habe ich ein Modell aus Paris für 825 Euro. Ich garantiere, diese Bluse _____[15] _____[16] bestimmt. (*she will like*)

KUNDE: Sie machen wohl Spaß. Das _____[17] _____[18] _____[19]. (*is too expensive for me*)

VERKÄUFER: Kann ich _____[20] etwas anderes _____[21]? (*show you*)

KUNDE: Können Sie _____[22] vielleicht ein T-Shirt _____[23]? (*show me*)

VERKÄUFER: Ja, natürlich. Hier habe ich ein ganz …

KUNDE: Oh, je. Es ist schon halb sechs. Es tut _____[24] _____[25]. (*I'm sorry.*) Ich muss sofort gehen. Ich _____[26] _____[27] für Ihre Hilfe. (*thank you*) Auf Wiedersehen.

Übung 8 Sei ehrlich°!

Schritt 1: Wem gehört das?

BEISPIEL: s1: Wem gehört der große Hut?
s2: Der gehört dem Fotomodell Jutta.

> die karierte Hose   der große Hut   das komische Hemd   die langen Stiefel

Jutta	Michael	Mark	Sabine
(das Fotomodell)	(ihr Freund)	(ihr Bruder)	(ihre Schwester)

Schritt 2: Wie gefällt dir das? Führen Sie ein Gespräch.

BEISPIEL: s1: Wie gefällt dir der große Hut?
s2: Der Hut gefällt mir. Er steht ihr gut!

			gut
der große Hut	gefallen/gefällt		nicht gut
das komische Hemd	passen/passt	ihm	zu eng
die karierte Hose	sind/ist	ihr	zu groß
die langen Stiefel	stehen/steht	mir	zu kurz
			zu lang

Prepositions with the Dative Case

Prepositions that require the dative case of nouns and pronouns include:

aus	from, out of	Richard kommt gerade **aus** dem Haus.
		Alexandra kommt **aus** Jena.
	(made) of	Das Hemd ist **aus** Polyester.
bei	near	Die Bäckerei ist **beim** Marktplatz.
	at (the place of)	Schicke Blusen gibt es **bei** Gisie.
	for, at (a company)	Manfred arbeitet **bei** VW.
	with	Sybille wohnt **bei** ihrer Großmutter.
mit	with	Herr Schweiger geht **mit** seiner Frau einkaufen.
		Katja wohnt **mit** ihrer Freundin Beate zusammen.
	by (means of)	Wir fahren **mit** dem Bus.
nach	to	Der Bus fährt **nach** Frankfurt.
		Ich fahre jetzt **nach** Hause.
	after	**Nach** dem Essen gehen wir einkaufen.

seit	since	**Seit** gestern haben wir schönes Wetter.
	for (time)	**Seit** einem Monat kauft sie nur noch Bio-Brot.
von	from	Das Brot ist frisch **vom** Bäcker. Frank kommt gerade **vom** Markt.
	by (origin)	Dieses Buch ist **von** Peter Handke.
zu	to	Wir gehen heute **zum** Supermarkt. Dirk muss schon um fünf Uhr **zur** Arbeit.
	at	Er ist jetzt wieder **zu** Hause.
	for	**Zum** Frühstück gibt es Müsli.

Note:

- **Nach Hause** and **zu Hause** are set expressions. **Nach Hause** is used to say that someone is *going* home, while **zu Hause** means someone is *at* home.

- The following contractions are common:

bei dem → **beim**	Jürgen kauft sein Brot nur **beim** Bäcker.
von dem → **vom**	Er kommt gerade **vom** Markt.
zu dem → **zum**	Er muss jetzt noch **zum** Bäcker.
zu der → **zur**	Dann geht er **zur** Bank.

Übung 9 Ein typischer Tag

Sie hören eine Beschreibung von Maxis Tagesablauf. Was stimmt? Was stimmt nicht? Geben Sie die richtige Information an.

	DAS STIMMT	DAS STIMMT NICHT
1. Maxi wohnt seit einem Monat in Göttingen.	☐	☐
2. Maxi wohnt allein in einer Wohnung.	☐	☐
3. Sie kann zu Fuß zur Universität gehen.	☐	☐
4. Maxi kommt gerade aus der Bibliothek.	☐	☐
5. Dann geht sie in die Mensa.	☐	☐
6. Maxi und Inge gehen zum Supermarkt.	☐	☐
7. Beim Bäcker kaufen sie ein Brot.	☐	☐
8. Maxi muss noch zur Bank.	☐	☐

Mühlenbäckerei
BORGMANN
Mühlenstraße 11 · Kranenburg
Inh. Ralf Borgmann
Telefon 0 28 26 / 2 65

¹*Vom ... From grain to bread*

Übung 10 Auskunft° geben

Information

Ergänzen Sie die fehlenden Präpositionen.

1. Sag mal, wo gibt es hier denn schicke Blusen? —_____ Gisie.

2. Die Bluse steht dir gut. Ist sie _____ Polyester?

3. Ist diese Bluse neu? —Ja, sie ist ein Geschenk _____ meiner Mutter.

4. Das Brot schmeckt ausgezeichnet. Woher hast du es? —Es ist _____ der Bäckerei.

5. Gehst du zu Fuß zum Supermarkt? —Nein, ich fahre _____ dem Wagen.

6. Bitte, komm nach dem Einkaufen sofort _____ Hause.

7. Ich plane schon _____ drei Monaten eine Grillparty.

8. Wollen wir die Party _____ dir oder _____ mir _____ Hause machen?

| aus | bei | mit | nach |
| seit | von | zu | |

Übung 11 Michaels Tag

Setzen Sie die fehlenden Präpositionen, Artikel und Endungen ein.

1. Michael wohnt _____ sein_ Bruder zusammen in einer alten Villa in Berlin.
2. Er geht schon _____ 6 Uhr _____ _____ Haus.
3. Er fährt _____ sein_ Motorrad _____ Arbeit.
4. Er arbeitet _____ Hotel Zentral.
5. Er arbeitet da schon _____ ein_ Jahr. Die Arbeit gefällt ihm sehr.
6. Er arbeitet _____ Leute_ _____ vielen Länder_ zusammen, z. B. _____ Jugoslawien, Spanien, Afghanistan und Amerika.
7. Abends _____ _____ Arbeit trifft er oft ein paar Freunde.
8. Dann geht er _____ sein_ Freunde_ in eine Kneipe.
9. Michael kocht gern. _____ Frühstück gibt es oft so etwas wie Rührei _____ Zwiebeln und Zucchini.
10. Das ist ein Rezept _____ Mexiko.
11. Er hat das Rezept _____ sein_ Freundin Marlene.

Übung 12 Seit wann ist das so?

Arbeiten Sie mit einem Partner / einer Partnerin zusammen. Stellen Sie Fragen.

BEISPIEL: S1: Seit wann wohnst du hier?
S2: Seit drei Semestern.

1. Deutsch lernen
2. Auto fahren können
3. den Professor / die Professorin kennen
4. hier wohnen
5. an dieser Uni studieren
6. ??

Interrogativpronomen

Interrogative Pronouns° *wo, wohin,* and *woher*

The interrogative pronouns **wo** and **wohin** both mean *where.* **Wo** is used to ask where someone or something is located, **wohin** to ask about the direction in which someone or something is moving. **Woher** is used to ask where someone or something comes from.

Wo bist du denn jetzt?	Zu Hause.
Wo wohnst du?	In Berlin.
Wo kauft Maxi ihr Brot?	Beim Bäcker.
Wohin gehst du? (**Wo** gehst du **hin**?)	Zur Bibliothek.
Wohin fährst du? (**Wo** fährst du **hin**?)	Nach Deutschland.
Woher kommen die Orangen? (**Wo** kommen die Orangen **her**?)	Aus Spanien.
Woher hast du die gute Wurst? (**Wo** hast du die gute Wurst **her**?)	Vom Metzger.

Note that the words **wohin** and **woher** are frequently split (**wo ... hin, wo ... her**), especially in conversation.

Übung 13 Wo, wohin, woher?

Bilden Sie die Fragen zu den Antworten.

BEISPIEL: Ich muss heute noch <u>zur Bank</u>. →
        Wohin musst du heute noch? [*oder*]
        Wo musst du heute noch hin?

1. Brötchen gibt es <u>beim Bäcker</u>.
2. Mark muss heute noch <u>zur Metzgerei</u>.
3. Sein Freund kommt gerade <u>vom Bioladen</u>.
4. Wir gehen später <u>zum Supermarkt</u>.
5. Antje ist heute <u>zu Hause</u>.
6. Die Leute kommen gerade <u>aus dem Kino</u>.
7. Sie gehen jetzt alle <u>nach Hause</u>.
8. Die Studentinnen trinken einen Kaffee <u>im Café Kadenz</u>.

Sprache im Kontext

Videoclips

A. Schauen Sie sich das Interview mit Sara an. Lesen Sie die Fragen und streichen (*cross out*) Sie die Antwort durch, die nicht stimmt.

BEISPIEL: Was trägt Sara jetzt? [Jacke, ~~Hut~~, Bluse]

1. Welche Blusengröße hat Sara? [38, 83]
2. Welche Schuhgröße hat sie? [51, 41]
3. Was nimmt Sara mit in Urlaub? [Jeans, Bikini, kurze Hosen]
4. Was trägt sie zu Hause? [Pyjama, Shorts, Kleider]
5. Sara kauft Lebensmittel. Was für Gemüse kauft sie? [Gurke, Karotten, grüne Bohnen]
6. Was für Obst kauft sie? [Äpfel, Erdbeeren, Orangen]
7. Sara muss auch Kosmetik kaufen. Was muss sie kaufen? [Zahnpasta, Shampoo, Toilettenpapier]

B. Schauen Sie sich das Interview mit Harald an und beantworten Sie die Fragen.

1. Was für eine Hemdengröße hat Harald?
2. Was für eine Schuhgröße hat er?
3. Was trägt er im Sommerurlaub?
4. Was trägt er zur Arbeit?
5. Was für Lebensmittel kauft er?

C. Schauen Sie sich das Interview mit Jasmin an. Was für Getränke kauft sie?

D. Jasmin nennt auch ein Rezept für Auberginen. Wie bereitet (*prepare*) sie sie vor?

Lesen

Zum Thema

A. Wo kaufen Sie ein? Kreuzen Sie an, wo Sie oft, manchmal oder nie einkaufen.

	OFT	MANCHMAL	NIE
auf dem Flohmarkt (*flea market*)	☐	☐	☐
auf dem Markt	☐	☐	☐
im Supermarkt	☐	☐	☐
in der Drogerie	☐	☐	☐
in einer Boutique	☐	☐	☐
in einem Einkaufszentrum	☐	☐	☐
aus einem Versandkatalog	☐	☐	☐
im Internet	☐	☐	☐

B. Schauen Sie sich die Liste in **A** an. Sagen Sie, was man dort kaufen kann.

Auf den ersten Blick

Lesen Sie den Titel und überfliegen (*scan*) Sie die ersten paar Zeilen des Textes.

1. Was für ein Text ist dies?

   a. ein Artikel aus einer Zeitung

   b. ein Dialog

   c. eine Werbung für einen Hutladen

2. Suchen Sie im Text zusammengesetzte Wörter mit **Hut** oder **Hüte**. Versuchen Sie zu erraten (*guess*), was diese Wörter bedeuten, z. B. **Filzhüte** = **Filz** + **Hüte**; **Filz** = *felt*; **Hüte** = Plural von **Hut.**

3. Überfliegen Sie die ersten vier Zeilen. Was ist Ihre Meinung zu den Aussagen a–c, unten? Wo sehen Sie einen Beweis (*evidence*) für Ihre Meinung?

   a. Die Verkäuferin und der Kunde führen ein ganz normales Gespräch in einem Hutladen.

   b. Die Verkäuferin stellt ganz normale Fragen.

   c. Der Kunde ist schwierig.

von Karl Valentin

VERKÄUFERIN:	Guten Tag. Sie wünschen?
KARL VALENTIN:	Einen Hut.
VERKÄUFERIN:	Was soll das für ein Hut sein?
K. V.:	Einer zum Aufsetzen°.

5 **VERKÄUFERIN:** Ja, anziehen können Sie niemals einen Hut, den muß man immer aufsetzen.

K. V.: Nein, immer nicht – in der Kirche° zum Beispiel kann ich den Hut nicht aufsetzen.

VERKÄUFERIN: In der Kirche nicht – aber Sie gehen doch nicht immer
10 in die Kirche.

K. V.: Nein, nur da und hie.

VERKÄUFERIN: Sie meinen nur hie und da°!

K. V.: Ja, ich will einen Hut zum Auf- und Absetzen°.

VERKÄUFERIN: Jeden Hut können Sie auf- und absetzen! Wollen Sie
15 einen weichen° oder einen steifen° Hut?

K. V.: Nein – einen grauen.

VERKÄUFERIN: Ich meine, was für eine Fasson°?

K. V.: Eine farblose° Fasson.

VERKÄUFERIN: Sie meinen, eine schicke Fasson – wir haben allerlei
20 schicke Fassonen in allen Farben.

K. V.: In allen Farben? – Dann hellgelb!

VERKÄUFERIN: Aber hellgelbe Hüte gibt es nur im Karneval – einen hellgelben Herrenhut können Sie doch nicht tragen.

K. V.: Ich will ihn ja nicht tragen, sondern aufsetzen.

25 **VERKÄUFERIN:** Mit einem hellgelben Hut werden Sie ja ausgelacht°.

K. V.: Aber Strohhüte sind doch hellgelb.

VERKÄUFERIN: Ach, Sie wollen einen Strohhut?

K. V.: Nein, ein Strohhut ist mir zu feuergefährlich°!

VERKÄUFERIN: Asbesthüte° gibt es leider noch nicht! – Schöne
30 weiche Filzhüte hätten wir.

K. V.: Die weichen Filzhüte haben den Nachteil°, daß man sie nicht hört, wenn sie einem vom Kopf auf den Boden fallen°.

VERKÄUFERIN: Na, dann müssen Sie sich eben einen Stahlhelm
35 kaufen, den hört man fallen.

K. V.: Als Zivilist darf ich keinen Stahlhelm tragen.

VERKÄUFERIN: Nun müssen Sie sich aber bald entschließen°, was Sie für einen Hut wollen.

K. V.: Einen neuen Hut!

40 **VERKÄUFERIN:** Ja, wir haben nur neue.

K. V.: Ich will ja einen neuen.

VERKÄUFERIN: Ja, aber was für einen?

K. V.: Einen Herrenhut!

VERKÄUFERIN: Damenhüte führen wir nicht!

45 **K. V.:** Ich will auch keinen Damenhut!

VERKÄUFERIN: Sie sind sehr schwer zu bedienen°, ich zeige Ihnen einmal mehrere Hüte!

K. V.: Was heißt mehrere, ich will doch nur einen. Ich habe ja auch nur einen Kopf°.

...

Glosses (right margin):
zum ... *for putting on*
church
hie ... *now and then*
to take off (a hat)
soft / firm, stiff
shape
colorless
ridiculed
flammable
asbestos hats
disadvantage
auf ... *fall to the ground*
sich ... *decide*
schwer ... *difficult to serve*
head

der Zylinder

der Strohhut

der Filzhut

der Stahlhelm

der Damenhut

Hier klicken!

Weiteres zum Thema Shopping finden Sie bei **Deutsch: Na klar!** im World-Wide-Web unter www.mhhe.com/dnk5.

Zum Text

Lesen Sie den Dialog mit verteilten Rollen im Kurs vor.

1. Was will der Kunde eigentlich? Wo sagt er genau, was er will?
2. Finden Sie Beispiele im Text, wo und wie der Kunde die Verkäuferin irritiert. Wie reagiert die Verkäuferin?
3. Humor in einer fremden Sprache ist oft schwer zu verstehen. Karl Valentin war ein beliebter Humorist. Finden Sie diesen Dialog komisch oder humorvoll? Wenn ja, was macht ihn komisch?
4. Sie lesen hier nur einen Auszug aus dem Dialog. Glauben Sie, dass der Kunde schließlich einen Hut kauft? Was würden Sie als Verkäufer/ Verkäuferin mit diesem Kunden machen?

Zu guter Letzt

Eine Umfrage in der Klasse

Wie geben Studentinnen und Studenten in Ihrer Klasse ihr Geld aus?

Schritt 1: Füllen Sie zuerst den Fragebogen (*questionnaire*) unten selbst aus.

Schritt 2: Interviewen Sie jetzt drei Studenten/Studentinnen und notieren Sie dabei Namen, Alter und Hauptfach (*major*). Benutzen Sie den Fragebogen (*questionnaire*) und notieren Sie die Antworten.

FRAGEBOGEN

---

1. Gehen Sie gern einkaufen? Warum (nicht)?

2. Wofür geben Sie das meiste Geld aus?

☐ Miete   ☐ Studiengebühren
☐ Auto   ☐ Essen im Restaurant
☐ Kleidung   ☐ Lebensmittel
☐ Unterhaltung   ☐ etwas anderes

3. Was kaufen Sie und wie oft kaufen Sie es?

WAS?		WIE OFT?
☐ Kaffee/Bier	jeden Tag	
☐ Bücher	einmal	in der Woche
☐ Kleidung	zweimal	im Monat
☐ CDs, DVDs	dreimal	im Jahr
☐ Lebensmittel	alle fünf Jahre	
☐ ein Auto	???	
☐ Möbel		

Schritt 3: Für welche anderen Dinge, die nicht auf dieser Liste stehen, geben Studenten/Studentinnen ihr Geld aus? Notieren Sie sie.

Schritt 4: Was haben Sie herausgefunden? Fassen Sie die Informationen über eine Person, die Sie interviewt haben, schriftlich (*in writing*) zusammen und geben Sie der Person dieses Profil.

Wortschatz

Lebensmittel — Groceries, Food

der **Apfel**, ¨	apple
der **Aufschnitt**	cold cuts
die **Banane**, -n	banana
das **Bier**, -e	beer
der **Blumenkohl**	cauliflower
der **Brokkoli**	broccoli
das **Brot**, -e	(loaf of) bread
das **Brötchen**, -	roll
die **Butter**	butter
das **Ei**, -er	egg
das **Eis**	ice cream; ice
die **Erdbeere**, -n	strawberry
das **Fleisch**	meat
das **Gemüse**	vegetables
das **Getränk**, -e	drink
die **Gurke**, -n	cucumber
das **Hähnchen**	chicken
der **Joghurt**	yogurt
die **Karotte**, -n	carrot
die **Kartoffel**, -n	potato
der **Käse**	cheese
der **Keks**, -e	cookie
der **Kuchen**, -	cake
die **Milch**	milk
das **Müsli**, -	granola; cereal
das **Obst**	fruit
der **Pfeffer**	pepper
das **Rindfleisch**	beef
der **Saft**, ¨e	juice
das **Salz**	salt
der **Schinken**, -	ham
das **Schnitzel**, -	cutlet
das **Schweinefleisch**	pork
der **Tee**	tea
die **Tomate**, -n	tomato
die **Traube**, -n	grape
der **Truthahn**, ¨e	turkey
das **Wasser**	water
die **Wurst**, ¨e	sausage
der **Zucker**	sugar

Geschäfte — Stores, Shops

die **Apotheke**, -n	pharmacy
die **Bäckerei**, -en	bakery
die **Drogerie**, -n	toiletries and sundries store
die **Konditorei**, -en	pastry shop

der **Laden**, ¨	store
der **Bioladen**, ¨	natural foods store
der **Getränkeladen**, ¨	beverage store
der **Markt**, ¨e	(open-air) market, marketplace
die **Metzgerei**, -en	butcher shop
der **Obst- und Gemüsestand**, ¨e	fruit and vegetable stand
der **Supermarkt**, ¨e	supermarket

Kleidungsstücke — Articles of Clothing

der **Anzug**, ¨e	suit
der **Badeanzug**, ¨-e	bathing suit
die **Bluse**, -n	blouse
der **Gürtel**, -	belt
das **Hemd**, -en	shirt
die **Hose**, -n	pants, trousers
die **Badehose**, -n	swim trunk
der **Hut**, ¨e	hat
die **Jacke**, -n	jacket
die **Jeans** (*pl.*)	jeans
die **Klamotte**, -n	duds, rags (*slang for clothing*)
das **Kleid**, -er	dress
die **Krawatte**, -n	necktie
der **Mantel**, ¨	coat
die **Mütze**, -n	cap
der **Pullover**, -	pullover sweater
der **Rock**, ¨e	skirt
das **Sakko**, -s	sport coat
der **Schal**, -s	scarf
der **Schlips**, -e	necktie
der **Schuh**, -e	shoe
der **Hausschuh**, -e	slipper
der **Tennisschuh**, -e	tennis shoe
die **Socke**, -n	sock
der **Stiefel**, -	boot
der **Strumpf**, ¨e	stocking; sock
das **T-Shirt**, -s	T-shirt

Sonstige Substantive — Other Nouns

das **Abendessen**	evening meal
die **Brille**, -n	(pair of) eyeglasses
die **Farbe**, -n	color
das **Frühstück**	breakfast

die **Größe, -n**	size
die **Kasse, -n**	cash register; check-out, cashier
der **Koffer, -**	suitcase
das **Medikament, -e**	medicine
das **Mittagessen**	midday meal; lunch
die **Rasiercreme, -s**	shaving cream
der **Rucksack, ¨e**	backpack
die **Tasche, -n**	handbag, purse
das **Toilettenpapier**	toilet paper
die **Zahnpasta**	toothpaste

Farben / Colors

beige	beige
blau	blue
braun	brown
gelb	yellow
grau	gray
grün	green
lila	purple
orange	orange
rot	red
schwarz	black
weiß	white

Verben / Verbs

an•probieren	to try on
danken (+ *dat.*)	to thank
empfehlen (empfiehlt)	to recommend
gefallen (gefällt) (+ *dat.*)	to be pleasing
Wie gefällt Ihnen ...?	How do you like . . . ?
gehören (+ *dat.*)	to belong to (*a person*)
glauben	to believe
helfen (hilft) (+ *dat.*)	to help
leihen	to lend; borrow
passen (+ *dat.*)	to fit
schenken	to give (*as a gift*)
schmecken (+ *dat.*)	to taste (good)
stehen (+ *dat.*)	to look good (*on a person*)
Die Farbe steht mir.	The color looks good on me.
tragen (trägt)	to wear; carry
zahlen	to pay
zeigen	to show

Sonstige Adjektive und Adverbien / Other Adjectives and Adverbs

frisch	fresh(ly)
gefroren	frozen
gestreift	striped
kariert	plaid
modisch	fashionable, fashionably
nötig	necessary
zart	tender

Dativpronomen / Dative Pronouns

mir	(to/for) me
dir	(to/for) you (*informal sg.*)
ihm	(to/for) him/it
ihr	(to/for) her/it
uns	(to/for) us
euch	(to/for) you (*informal pl.*)
ihnen	(to/for) them
Ihnen	(to/for) you (*formal*)

Dativpräpositionen / Dative Prepositions

aus	from; out of, (made) of
bei	at; near; with
mit	with; by means of
nach	after; to
seit	since; for (+ *time*)
von	of; from; by
zu	to; at; for

Sonstiges / Other

alle	all; every
das macht zusammen	all together, that comes to
egal: Das ist mir egal.	I don't care.
jeder	each, every
nach Hause	(to) home
wem?	(to/for) whom?
wohin?	(to) where?
zu Hause	at home

1. Welche Kleidungsstücke tragen Sie jeden Tag?

2. Nennen Sie fünf Farben! Beginnen Sie mit Ihrer Lieblingsfarbe!

3. Sie reisen nach Hawaii. Was nehmen Sie im Koffer mit?

4. Was essen Sie jeden Tag? Was ist Ihr Lieblingsessen? Was trinken Sie jeden Tag?

5. Welche Frage passt?

    a. _____? —Die Jacke gefällt mir gut.

    b. _____? —Ja, bitte, zeigen Sie mir Tennisschuhe, Größe 42.

    c. _____? —Dieser Pullover ist zu klein.

    d. _____? —Ich schenke es (das T-Shirt) meinem Bruder.

6. Wo kauft man das?

    a. ein Sporthemd   b. Obst und Gemüse
    c. Würstchen zum Grillen   d. Brot und Brötchen   e. Kaffee, Milch und Käse

7. Ergänzen Sie: **wo, woher,** oder **wohin!**

    a. _____ fährst du zum Einkaufen?   b. _____ kommen diese Orangen?   c. _____ kauft man frisches Obst und Gemüse am besten?

8. Mit wem machen Sie das gern?

    a. einkaufen gehen   b. auf Partys gehen
    c. essen gehen

Wir gehen aus

Guten Appetit!

In diesem Kapitel

- **Themen:** Places to eat and drink, ordering in a restaurant
- **Grammatik:** Two-way prepositions; describing location; describing placement; expressing time with prepositions; simple past tense of **sein, haben,** and modal verbs
- **Kultur:** Regional food specialties, menus, sharing tables in restaurants, paying the bill
- **Lesen:** „Die Soße" (Ekkehard Müller)

Videoclips
Bedienung, bitte

Alles klar?

Pizzeria AS

Internationale Spezialitäten
Italienisch - Chinesisch - Mexikanisch

Wir liefern Ihre Bestellung frei Haus[1] ab 8,00 Euro

0228
62 42 89
79 80 64

Internationale Spezialitäten
Italienisch - Chinesisch - Mexikanisch

TAGES-ANGEBOTE
unser Angebot außer Feiertag

Montag: Pizzatag
(außer Pizza-Pfannen)

5,00 Euro
(außer Pfannenpizzen und Calzoneria)

Dienstag: Gyrostag

5,00 Euro

Mittwoch: Nudeltag
(außer chin. Nudeln)

5,00 Euro

Donnerstag: Risotto- &
Salattag (außer chinesisch)

5,00 Euro

Geburtstag und Partyservice

Öffnungszeiten:
Mo - Fr von 17.00 - 23.00 Uhr
Sa und Feiertage von 17.00 - 23.00 Uhr
So von 14.00 - 23.00 Uhr

Bei einer Bestellung ab 23,- Euro erhalten Sie
eine Flasche italienischen Wein oder 1 Liter
alkoholfreies Getränk !!

Bestellservice
ab 8,- Euro Mindestbestellung

Von Weichs-Str. 18
53121 Bonn-Endenich

[1]frei ... *free delivery*

A. „Pizzeria AS" ist ein Restaurant in Bonn.

- Schauen Sie sich die Karten in der Werbung für Pizza AS an. Was bedeutet der Name „AS"?
- Pizzeria AS ist nicht nur ein Pizzarestaurant. Was für internationales Essen bekommt man da?
- An welchen Tagen hat das Restaurant Tagesangebote?
- Welches Tagesangebot interessiert Sie besonders?
- Wie viel Geld muss man mindestens ausgeben, wenn man etwas frei Haus bestellt?
- Was bekommt man, wenn man mehr als 23 Euro für Essen ausgibt?

B. Doris hat die Uni gewechselt und studiert jetzt in Berlin. Sie ist beim Info-Büro des Astas an der FU. Hören Sie jetzt ihr Gespräch mit der Asta-Referentin (*adviser*) und ordnen Sie die Charakterisierungen dem richtigen Restaurant zu.

RESTAURANT		CHARAKTERISIERUNG	
1. _____ Brazil	**a.** gemütlich	**e.** österreichische Küche
2. _____ Kartoffelkeller	**b.** in der Oranienburger Straße	**f.** rappelvoll (*coll. crowded*)
3. _____ Kellerrestaurant	**c.** macht viel Spaß	**g.** Rezepte von Helene Weigel
4. _____ Ristorante Italiano	**d.** nicht so teuer	**h.** vegetarisch

Wörter im Kontext

THEMA 1: Lokale

Restaurant „Schublade"

Inhaber	Stefan Höller	Spezialitäten: Frische Salate, Steaks. Auf Vorbestellung: „Heufresser Menue" Brennnesselsuppe – Schweinefilet in Heu gegart mit Bratkartoffeln – Salatteller – Apfelspalten in Karamell mit Vanilleeis + Sahne
	Hauptstraße 17	
	53804 Much, Zentrum	
Telefon	0 22 45 – 44 11	
Öffnungszeiten	Di - So ab 18.00 Uhr	
Ruhetag	Mo	
Plätze unten/oben	100/40	

a.

Neue Wörter

vom Fass   draft
tägl. = täglich   daily
geöffnet   open
die Küche   cuisine; kitchen
geschlossen   closed
zum Mitnehmen   food to go, take-out
der Ruhetag   day that a business is closed

Siehe *Expressing Time with Prepositions,* S. 193.

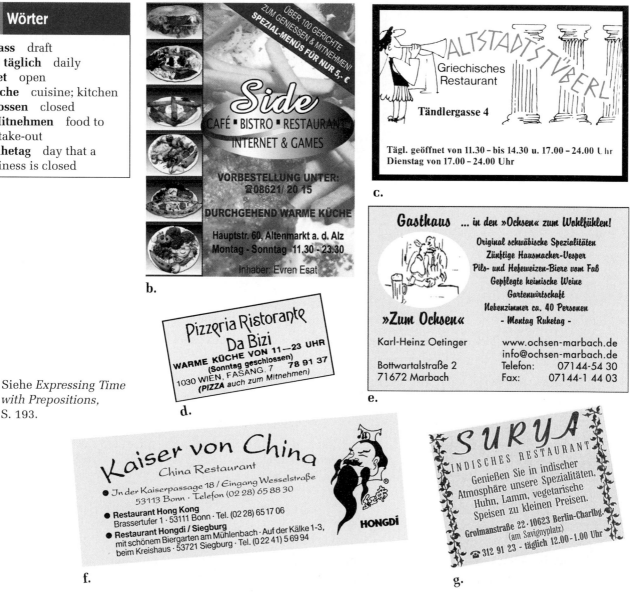

ÜBER 100 GERICHTE
ZUM GENIESSEN & MITNEHMEN!
SPEZIAL-MENÜS FÜR NUR 5,- €

Side
CAFÉ ▪ BISTRO ▪ RESTAURANT
INTERNET & GAMES

VORBESTELLUNG UNTER:
☎08621/ 20 15

DURCHGEHEND WARME KÜCHE

Hauptstr. 60, Altenmarkt a. d. Alz
Montag - Sonntag · 11.30 - 23.30

Inhaber: Evren Esat

b.

ALTSTADTSTÜBERL
Griechisches Restaurant

Tändlergasse 4

Tägl. geöffnet von 11.30 - bis 14.30 u. 17.00 - 24.00 Uhr
Dienstag von 17.00 - 24.00 Uhr

c.

Pizzeria Ristorante Da Bizi
WARME KÜCHE VON 11—23 UHR
(Sonntag geschlossen)
1030 WIEN, FASANG. 7   78 91 37
(PIZZA auch zum Mitnehmen)

d.

Gasthaus ... in den »Ochsen« zum Wohlfühlen!

Original schwäbische Spezialitäten
Zünftige Hausmacher-Vesper
Pils- und Hefeweizen-Biere vom Faß
Gepflegte heimische Weine
Gartenwirtschaft
Nebenzimmer ca. 40 Personen

»Zum Ochsen«   - Montag Ruhetag -

Karl-Heinz Oetinger

Bottwartalstraße 2
71672 Marbach

www.ochsen-marbach.de
info@ochsen-marbach.de
Telefon: 07144-54 30
Fax: 07144-1 44 03

e.

Kaiser von China
China Restaurant
● In der Kaiserpassage 18 / Eingang Wesselstraße
  53113 Bonn · Telefon (02 28) 65 88 30
● **Restaurant Hong Kong**
  Brassertufer 1 · 53111 Bonn · Tel. (02 28) 65 17 06
● **Restaurant Hongdi / Siegburg**
  mit schönem Biergarten am Mühlenbach · Auf der Kälke 1-3,
  beim Kreishaus · 53721 Siegburg · Tel. (0 22 41) 5 69 94

HONGDI

f.

SURYA
INDISCHES RESTAURANT
Genießen Sie in indischer
Atmosphäre unsere Spezialitäten,
Huhn, Lamm, vegetarische
Speisen zu kleinen Preisen.
Grolmanstraße 22 · 10623 Berlin-Charlbg.
(am Savignyplatz)
☎ 312 91 23 - täglich 12.00 - 1.00 Uhr

g.

Wo gibt es das?

Schauen Sie sich die Anzeigen im **Thema 1** an. In welches Lokal können Leute gehen, die

- gern griechisch essen?
- gern im Biergarten sitzen?
- gern Bier vom Fass trinken?
- etwas zum Mitnehmen möchten?

- Vegetarier sind?
- gern schwäbische Spezialitäten essen?
- gern Wein trinken?
- nicht viel Geld haben?

Und Sie? In welches Lokal möchten Sie gehen? Warum?

KULTURTIPP

German has many different words for places where one can eat or drink something.

das **Café**	café serving mainly desserts—**Kaffee und Kuchen**—but also offering a limited menu
der **Gasthof** / das **Gasthaus**	small inn with pub or restaurant
die **Gaststätte**	full-service restaurant
der **Imbiss**	fast-food stand; snack counter
die **Kneipe**	small, simple pub or bar; typical place where students gather (**Studentenkneipe**)
das **Lokal**	general word for an establishment that serves food and drinks
das **Restaurant**	generic word for *restaurant*
das **Wirtshaus**	pub serving mainly alcoholic beverages and some food

Often the word **Stube** or **Stüberl** will appear as a part of the name, as in **Altstadtstüberl** or **Mühlenstube**. **Stube** is an older word for *room* and suggests a cozy atmosphere.

Ein Café in Hamburg

Ein Gasthof in Bad Suderode

Ein Imbiss in Berlin

Eine Kneipe in Berlin

To suggest to a friend that you do something together, you can use the expression **Lass uns (doch) …** :

Lass uns doch ins Restaurant gehen!   *Let's go to a restaurant!*
Lass uns türkisch essen!   *Let's eat Turkish food!*

Aktivität I   Lass uns essen!

Sie haben Hunger. Der Magen knurrt schon. In kleinen Gruppen, besprechen Sie, wie Sie essen möchten. Wozu entscheiden Sie sich?

s1: Lass uns essen. Sag mir, wie?

s2: Lass uns vegetarisch essen.

s3: Nein, lass uns … essen.

Knurr! Knuurr!

Lass uns essen. Sag mir, wie:

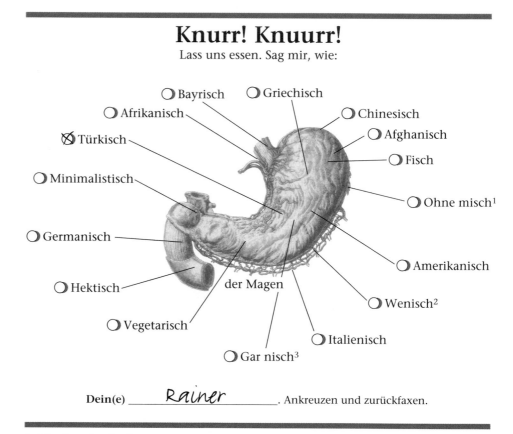

○ Bayrisch
○ Griechisch
○ Afrikanisch
○ Chinesisch
⊗ Türkisch
○ Afghanisch
○ Minimalistisch
○ Fisch
○ Germanisch
○ Ohne misch[1]
○ Hektisch
○ Amerikanisch
der Magen
○ Wenisch[2]
○ Vegetarisch
○ Italienisch
○ Gar nisch[3]

Dein(e) _____ *Rainer* _____ . Ankreuzen und zurückfaxen.

[1]mich [2]wenig [3]nichts

Aktivität 2 Umfrage

Beantworten Sie die Fragen.

1. Gehen Sie oft aus essen? Wie oft? Einmal die Woche, einmal im Monat?
2. Essen Sie gern griechisch, chinesisch, italienisch … ?
3. Wie heißt Ihr Lieblingsrestaurant? Welche Spezialitäten gibt es dort?
4. Wann hat Ihr Lieblingsrestaurant Ruhetag? Oder ist es an allen Tagen der Woche geöffnet?
5. Was trinken Sie normalerweise, wenn Sie ausgehen?
6. Gibt es Cafés in Ihrer Stadt? Was kann man dort essen und trinken?

Aktivität 3 Ich habe Hunger. Ich habe Durst.

Wo gibt es was zu essen und zu trinken in Ihrer Stadt?

VORSCHLÄGE (*RECOMMENDATIONS*) FÜR ESSEN UND TRINKEN:

Pizza, Bier (vom Fass), griechische Küche, indische Spezialitäten (z.B. Lamm), internationale Küche (z.B. chinesische oder italienische Spezialitäten), ein Eis, eine Tasse Kaffee.

S1	S2
1. Ich habe Hunger. Ich habe Durst.	2. Magst du _____? Isst du gern _____? Möchtest du _____?
3. Ja. Wo kann man das bekommen?	4. Im _____.
5. Wann ist es geöffnet? Ist es heute geöffnet?	6a. Ich weiß es nicht genau. b. Täglich von _____ bis _____.

Das Wirtshaus Gatow in Berlin serviert traditionelle deutsche Küche.

Bad Oeynhausen
Herforder Str. 52
Tel. (05731) 3565
Fax (05731) 3536

Minden
Königswall 1-3
Tel. (0571) 21368
Fax (0571) 850581

die Knolle [1] ©
das urige [2] Kartoffelhaus

Kleine Vorspeisen

Frittierte, frische Champignons..................... 3,10
mit Kräuterquark und kleinem Salatbuquette

Kartoffelspieß.. 3,10
Kartoffeln, Speck, Zwiebeln, Paprika
mit Knoblauchcreme und Kräuterquark

Riesen Salatteller

Kleiner gemischter Salat................................. 3,20
Großer gemischter Salatteller.......................... 6,60
mit Schinkenstreifen, Ei und Kräutercroutons

Salat "Korsika"... 7,50
mit Schinken, Ei, Schafskäse, Zwiebeln und Oliven

Hausgemachte Reibekuchen [3]

mit geräuchertem Lachs................................. 8,40
und Senf-Dill-Sauce

mit Apfelmus.. 4,60

Vegetarisches, healthy gesund und lecker...

Gemüse-Pilz-Pfanne.................................... 7,20
mit Schupfnudeln [4] und Kräutern

Gebratene [5] Schupfnudeln............................. 7,30
mit Zwiebeln, Lauch und Kräuterquark

Kartoffel-Käse-Rösti................................... 7,20
mit Tomaten, Basilikum und Mozzarella

Vom Grill und aus der Pfanne

Kartoffelhauspfanne "Die Knolle"................. 13,10
mit 2 Schweinemedaillons, Schweinerückensteak,
Speckbohnen, frischen Champignons,
Sauce Bérnaise und Bratkartoffeln

"Schwaben Pfanne"................................... 13,50
3 Schweinemedaillons mit Champignons à la
Creme, Sauce Hollandaise, Schupfnudeln
und Brokkoli, überbacken mit Käse

hausgemachtes Gulasch............................... 12,40
vom Rind und vom Schwein, frische Paprika,
frische Champignons, Zwiebeln, Apfelrotkohl und
Kartoffelklöße

Grillteller "Die Knolle"............................. 14,60
mit Rinderfilet, Schweinerückensteak,
Putenmedaillon, Grillspeck, Nackensteak, frischen
Champignons und Zwiebeln, dazu Kräuterbutter,
würzige Sauce und Pommes

Geflügel [6]

"Geflügelpfanne" Knolle............................. 13,40
3 Putenmedaillons, frische Champignons, feines
Gemüse mit Sauce Bérnaise und Bratkartoffeln

kleinere Portion...................................... 10,10

Geflügel-Grillteller.................................. 13,60
2 Putenmedaillons, 1 Hähnchenbrustfilet,
Pfeffersauce, Bratkartoffeln und gemischter Salat

kleinere Portion...................................... 10,20

Lieblingsgerichte vom "Alten Fritz" überbacken mit Käse

"Schöne Gärtnerin"................................... 8,70
Kartoffelauflauf mit Brokkoli, Blumenkohl,
Schinken und Käsesauce

Kartoffelauflauf "Hühnerdieb"...................... 9,40
mit Hähnchenfleisch, Champignons, Brokkoli,
Mais und Käsesauce

Kartoffelauflauf "Indisch".......................... 9,40
mit Geflügelstreifen, Currysauce, Mais, Tomaten,
und Porree

Kartoffel-Beziehungskisten
frische Bratkartoffeln aus der Pfanne mit ...

drei gebratenen Landeiern........................... 5,10
und Gewürzgurke

Nürnberger Pfanne.................................... 7,50
6 Nürnberger, Sauerkraut und Bratkartoffeln

Matjesfilet mit Hausfrauensauce..................... 9,70

Seemannspfännchen.................................. 7,50
Champignons, Shrimps, Schnittlauch und
Spiegelei

Nachtisch

Sylter Rote Grütze.................................... 2,40
mit Vanillesauce

Warmer Apfelstrudel................................. 2,90
auf Vanillesauce

Schokoeisbecher..................................... 2,90
mit Eierlikör und Schlagcreme

Getränke

Pilsener............................ 0,21 1,90
Apfelsaft, Orangensaft........... 0,21 1,90
Sprudel, Cola, Fanta.............. 0,21 2,20

Nach dem Original bearbeitet © 2006 by www.pagewerbung.de, Bad Oeynhausen, Germany

[1] *spud*   [2] *cozy*   [3] *potato pancakes*   [4] *small potato dumplings*   [5] *fried*   [6] *fowl*

A. Suchen Sie die Wörter unten auf der Speisekarte im **Thema 2.** Können Sie vom Kontext erraten (*guess*), wie die Wörter auf Englisch heißen?

1. _M_ das **Apfelmus**
2. _e_ die **Bohne**
3. _____ das **Gericht**
4. _____ der **Grill**
5. _____ der **Mais**
6. _____ die **Olive**
7. _l_ die **Paprika**
8. _____ die **Pfanne**
9. _____ die **Pommes (frites)** (*pl.*)
10. _o_ der **Salat**
11. _d_ das **Sauerkraut**
12. _f_ der **Speck**
13. _c_ das **Spiegelei**
14. _____ der **Teller**
15. _____ die **Zwiebel**

a. pan
b. French fries
c. fried egg
d. sauerkraut
e. bean
f. bacon
g. onion
h. olive
i. corn
j. plate
k. grill, barbecue
l. bell pepper
m. applesauce
n. dish (*a prepared item of food*)
o. salad

B. Eine Mahlzeit (*meal*) besteht oft aus mehreren Gängen (*courses*): **Vorspeise, Hauptgericht, Beilage** und **Nachspeise (Nachtisch).** Dazu gibt es Getränke. Welche Speise gehört nicht in die Kategorie? Streichen Sie aus, was nicht dazu gehört.

1. Vorspeise: **Suppe, Schweinebraten**
2. Hauptgericht: **Auflauf, Leberkäs, Senf, Weißwurst**
3. Beilage: **Nudeln, Bratkartoffeln, Schnitzel, Reis**
4. Nachtisch: **Apfelstrudel, Brezeln, Eisbecher**
5. Getränke: **Sprudel, Wein, Sahne, Pilsener**

ANALYSE

Spaß mit der Speisekarte. Schauen Sie sich die Speisekarte auf der vorigen Seite noch mal an und beantworten Sie die folgenden Fragen.

- Das Restaurant „Knolle" ist ein Kartoffelrestaurant. Was kann man bestellen, wenn man Kartoffeln *nicht* mag?
- Finden Sie **Kartoffelauflauf „Indisch"** auf der Speisekarte. Was ist an (*about*) diesem Auflauf indisch?
- Bei welchen anderen Speisen finden Sie geographische Namen?

Neue Wörter

die Vorspeise appetizer
das Hauptgericht main dish
die Beilage side dish
die Nachspeise dessert
der Nachtisch dessert
die Suppe soup
der Schweinebraten pork roast
der Auflauf casserole
der Leberkäs Bavarian style meatloaf
der Senf mustard
die Weißwurst white sausage
die Bratkartoffeln (*pl.*) fried potatoes
die Brezel pretzel
der Eisbecher dish of ice cream
der Sprudel carbonated mineral water
die Sahne cream
das Pilsener Pilsner beer

Every area has its own regional specialties, while some dishes are available almost anywhere. Bavarian favorites include **Schweinshaxen** (pig's feet), **Spanferkel** (suckling pig), **Leberkäs** (a type of meatloaf), and **Weißwurst** (a type of veal sausage).

North German dishes include **Matjeshering** (salted young herring) and **Hamburger Labskaus,** a sailor's casserole made of cured meat, pickled herring, and various other ingredients topped with a fried egg. In the Southwest and parts of Switzerland one commonly finds **Spätzle** or **Spätzli,** egg noodles generally served with butter and cheese. The Westphalians are known for their **Pumpernickel** bread, the Thuringians for their **Thüringer Bratwurst,** and the Viennese for the **Wiener Schnitzel,** a breaded, pan-fried veal cutlet. Meat is frequently pork (**Schweinefleisch**). Beef (**Rindfleisch**) is also found on menus but is generally more expensive. Many restaurants have lighter fare such as chicken breast (**Hähnchen**) and turkey (**Truthahn** or **Pute**). Favorite dessert items include **Rote Grütze,** a compote made from crushed strawberries, currants, and cherries, and—in Bavaria—**Kaiserschmarren,** a sweet crepelike omelet.

Be prepared to get a bottle of **Sprudel** (*mineral water*) if you request water in a restaurant, and don't expect to get a lot of ice with it. It is not customary to serve a guest tap water, whether in a restaurant or a private home.

Weißwurst mit Sauerkraut

Matjeshering auf Gemüse

Rote Grütze

Aktivität 4 So viele Speisen!

Welche Speise oder welches Wort ist das?

1. B e l a t f r a n k f o r t   _____
2. S t a l a   _____
3. S c k e p   _____
4. S t u r e u k a r a   _____
5. N e l d u   _____
6. V e p r e s o s i   _____
7. Z e b w e i l   _____
8. H h h e n ä c n   _____
9. P e n a n f   _____
10. H i g e t u t p a c h r   _____
11. A l u f u f a   _____

Aktivität 5 Was bestellen° Norbert und Dagmar?   *are ordering*

Hören Sie zu und ergänzen Sie die Tabelle.

	NORBERT	DAGMAR
Vorspeise		*Champignons*
Hauptgericht		
Beilage	*Reis*	
Getränk		

Hier klicken!

Weiteres zum Thema Restaurant und Gerichte finden Sie bei **Deutsch: Na klar!** im World-Wide-Web unter www.mhhe.com/dnk5.

Aktivität 6 Was sollen wir bestellen?

Schauen Sie sich die Speisekarte auf Seite 180 an und besprechen Sie zu zweit oder zu dritt, was Sie bestellen möchten. Pro Person können Sie nur 20 Euro ausgeben.

BEISPIEL: Ich nehme Kartoffelspieß als Vorspeise. Als Hauptgericht nehme ich Matjesfilet mit Hausfrauensauce. Und als Nachspeise nehme ich rote Grütze.

Notieren Sie Ihre Bestellung:

Vorspeise:	€ 3,10	Vorspeise:
Hauptgericht:	€ 9,70	Hauptgericht:
Nachspeise:	€ 2,40	Nachspeise:
Summe:	€ 15,20	Summe:

Aktivität 7 Im Restaurant

Bilden Sie kleine Gruppen. Eine Person spielt den Ober oder die Kellnerin und nimmt die Bestellungen der Gäste an.

S1	S2
OBER/KELLNERIN	GAST
1. Bitte schön. Was darf's sein?	**2.** Ich möchte gern _____.
3. Und zu trinken?	**4.** Bringen Sie mir bitte _____.
5. Sonst noch was? (*Anything else?*)	**6a.** Ja, _____. **b.** Nein, das ist alles.

KULTURTIPP

When you are in a restaurant and want to get the server's attention, it is polite to say **bitte schön.** Young people often call out **hallo,** but this is very informal. In more formal restaurants, you may hear people call **Herr Ober** if the server is male. Use the generic term **Bedienung (bitte)** to call for a server.

In all but the most exclusive restaurants in German-speaking countries, it is acceptable for people to ask to share a table if it is very crowded. Simply ask: **Ist hier noch frei?** The answer might be: **Ja, hier ist noch frei.** Or: **Nein, hier ist besetzt.**

THEMA 3: Im Restaurant

Welches Bild passt zu welchem Mini-Dialog?

a.

b.

c.

d.

e.

f.

Neue Wörter

der Ober waiter
die Speisekarte menu
bestellen order
Was bekommen Sie? What will you have?
war (sein) was
hatte (haben) had
vielen Dank many thanks
Entschuldigen Sie. Excuse me.
Ist hier noch frei? Is this seat available?
Hier ist besetzt. This seat is taken.
da drüben over there
der Platz room, space
das Messer knife
der Löffel spoon
die Serviette napkin
die Gabel fork
ziemlich rather
voll full
hoffentlich I/we/let's hope
warten wait
mussten (müssen) had to

1. _____ — Herr **Ober,** die **Speisekarte,** bitte!

2. _____ — Wir möchten **bestellen.**
   — Ja, bitte, **was bekommen Sie?**
   — Ich nehme das Hähnchen.

3. _____ — Also, das **war** viermal Schnitzel und viermal Rotwein …
   — Nein, ich **hatte** den Grillteller.
   — Ach, ja. Das macht zusammen 68,40 Euro.
   — 70,– Euro.
   — **Vielen Dank.**

4. _____ — **Entschuldigen Sie,** bitte! **Ist hier noch frei?**
   — Nein, **hier ist besetzt,** aber **da drüben** ist **Platz.**

5. _____ — Herr Ober, ich habe **Messer, Löffel** und **Serviette,** aber keine **Gabel.**
   — Und ich habe keine Serviette.

6. _____ — Hier ist es aber **ziemlich voll. Hoffentlich** müssen wir nicht lange auf einen Platz **warten.**
   — Ja, wir **mussten** lange nach einem Parkplatz suchen.

Aktivität 8   Im Brauhaus Matz

Zwei Freunde, Jens und Stefanie, sind im Brauhaus Matz. Hören Sie zu, und ergänzen Sie den Text mit Informationen aus dem Dialog.

Stefanie und Jens suchen _____ _____[1] in einem Restaurant. Es ist ziemlich _____.[2] Jens sieht zwei Leute an einem _____.[3] Da ist noch _____[4] für zwei Leute. Er geht an den Tisch und fragt: „Ist _____ _____ _____[5]?" Die Antwort am ersten Tisch ist: „_____.[6]" Die Antwort am zweiten Tisch ist: „_____.[7]"

Aktivität 9 Ist hier noch frei?

Bilden Sie mehrere Gruppen. Einige Personen suchen Platz.

S1	S2
1. Entschuldigen Sie. Ist hier noch frei?	**2a.** Ja, hier ist noch _____. **b.** Nein, hier ist leider _____. Aber da drüben ist noch _____.
3a. Danke schön. **b.** (*geht zu einem anderen Tisch*)	

Aktivität 10 Wir möchten zahlen, bitte.

Was haben diese Leute bestellt? Wie viel kostet es? Kreuzen Sie an, was Sie hören.

		GETRÄNKE		ESSEN		BETRAG
Dialog 1		2 Bier		Knackwürste*		€10,00
		3 Cola		Weißwürste		€15,00
	X	3 Bier		Bockwürste†		€18,50
				Sauerkraut		
				Brot		

---

*a type of German frankfurter
†a type of German sausage similar to a hot dog in flavor and consistency

	GETRÄNKE	ESSEN	BETRAG
Dialog 2	2 Tassen Tee	2 Stück Käsekuchen	€6,25
	2 Tassen Kaffee	1 Stück Käsekuchen	€4,25
	1 Tasse Kaffee	1 Stück Obsttorte	€9,55
Dialog 3	2 Bier	Leberknödelsuppe*	€35,40
	5 Bier	Schweinskotelett	€39,40
	3 Bier	Brezeln	€43,40
		Weißwürste	
		Sauerkraut	

*liver dumpling soup

Grammatik im Kontext

Wechselpräpositionen

Two-Way Prepositions°

So far you have learned two kinds of prepositions: prepositions that are always used with the accusative case and others that are always used with the dative case.

In addition, a number of prepositions take either the dative or the accusative, depending on whether they describe a location or a direction. The most common two-way prepositions are these:

an	at, near, on
auf	on, on top of, at
hinter	behind, in back of
in	in
neben	next to
über	above, over
unter	under, beneath, below; among
vor	in front of; before
zwischen	between

Auf dem Bauernhof kann man gut frisches Obst und Gemüse kaufen.

Note:

- When answering the question **wo,** these prepositions take the dative case.

WO?	STATIONARY LOCATION (DATIVE)
Wo kauft man Brot?	In **der** Bäckerei.
Wo zahlt der Kunde?	An **der** Kasse.
Wo kauft man frisches Gemüse?	Auf **dem** Bauernhof.
Wo soll ich warten?	Vor **dem** Geschäft.

- When answering the question **wohin,** they take the accusative case.

WOHIN?	DIRECTION (ACCUSATIVE)
Wohin geht Frau Glättli?	In **die** Bäckerei.
Wohin geht der Kunde?	An **die** Kasse.
Wo gehst du hin?	Auf **den** Markt.
Wo geht Herr Sauer hin?	In **das** Geschäft.

- The following contractions are common.

an dem → **am**	Das Kaufhaus steht **am** Markt.
an das → **ans**	Geh doch **ans** Fenster!
in dem → **im**	Frau Kraus isst **im** Restaurant.
in das → **ins**	Nikola geht gleich **ins** Geschäft.

CAFE DERKS
BÄCKEREI KONDITOREI

Ihr Fachgeschäft[1]
für Brot und feinste Backwaren

Derks, am Markt
Derks, am Rathaus

[1]specialty store

ANALYSE

Suchen Sie in den folgenden Anzeigen alle Präpositionen mit Dativ- oder Akkusativobjekten. Ordnen Sie sie ein.

WO? (DATIV)	**WOHIN?** (AKKUSATIV)
BEISPIEL: im alten Forsthaus	_____

Restaurant
Schubert-Stüberln

Küchenchef
Franz Zimmer

hinter dem Burgtheater, vis-à-vis der Universität,
beim Dreimäderlhaus

Schreyvogelgasse 4, 1010 Wien
Telefon für Tischreservierung 63 71 87

Mach' Dir ein paar schöne Stunden... geh' ins Kino

Kulinarische Notizen
Ein Brevier für Genießer.
Biergartenromantik im alten Forsthaus

Parken! Problemlos!
3.000 kostenlose Parkplätze direkt vor der Tür.

Fahren Sie in unser großes Parkhaus an der Pelkovenstraße.

PP

OLYMPIA Einkaufszentrum
Hanauer Straße · Telefon 1 41 60 02

After work

Übung 1   Am Feierabend°

Was machst du gern/oft/manchmal/nie am Feierabend?

BEISPIEL: s1: Gehst du gern ins Café?
s2: Ja, ich gehe gern ins Café. [*oder*] Nein, ich gehe nicht gern ins Café.

der Biergarten	das Kino	der Sportclub
das Café	die Kneipe	die Stadt
die Disko	das Lokal	der Supermarkt
das Fitnesszentrum	das Restaurant	das Theater

Übung 2   Wo kauft Mark ein?

Mark muss heute einkaufen. Hier ist sein Einkaufszettel. Wo gibt es das?

BEISPIEL: Käsekuchen →
Käsekuchen gibt es in der Konditorei.

die Bäckerei

die Buchhandlung

die Konditorei

der Markt

die Metzgerei

das Schuhgeschäft

der Supermarkt

Einkaufszettel

250 g Aufschnitt
Käsekuchen
150 g Emmentaler Käse
6 Brötchen
12 Würstchen zum Grillen
1 Pfund Kaffee
Schwarzbrot
2 Flaschen Sprudel
4 Tomaten
nicht vergessen:
Wörterbuch
Tennisschuhe

Übung 3   Ein Einkaufszentrum

Wie kommt man dahin und was kann man dort machen? Schauen Sie sich die Werbung (unten) an und beantworten Sie die Fragen.

BEISPIEL: Wie kommt man zum Einkaufszentrum Spahn? →
Man kommt mit dem Bus dahin.

NÜTZLICHE WÖRTER

die Boutique

der Bus

die Buslinie

die Cafeteria

der Parkplatz

die Spielecke

das Studio

¹*children's play corner*

1. Mit welcher Buslinie kann man dahin fahren?
2. Wo gibt es etwas zu essen?
3. Wo kann man Lampen kaufen?
4. Wo kann man parken?
5. Wo gibt es Geschenke zu kaufen?
6. Wohin kann man seine Kinder bringen?

Übung 4 Wo sollen wir nur parken?

Sie und ein Freund / eine Freundin haben heute viel vor. Sie wollen mit dem Auto in die Stadt. Wo können Sie parken?

BEISPIEL: Sie möchten ins Kino. →
Lass uns hinter dem Kino parken.

1. Sie gehen ins Theater.
2. Sie brauchen eine Winterjacke. Sie müssen ins Kaufhaus.
3. Sie brauchen Obst und Gemüse und wollen auf den Markt.
4. Sie müssen in die Universität.
5. Sie müssen in die Apotheke.
6. Sie brauchen Würstchen zum Grillen. Sie müssen in die Metzgerei.
7. Sie möchten im Café eine Tasse Kaffee trinken.

Describing Location

The verbs **hängen, liegen, sitzen, stecken,** and **stehen** indicate where someone or something is located.

hängen	to be (hanging)
liegen	to be (lying)
sitzen	to be (sitting)
stecken	to be (placed)
stehen	to be (standing)

When a two-way preposition is used with one of these verbs indicating location, the object of the preposition is in the dative case. Remember, the interrogative pronoun **wo** asks where someone or something is located.

Wo hängt das Bild?	*Where is the picture hanging?*
Es hängt **im** Wohnzimmer.	*It's hanging in the living room.*
Wo liegt die Rechnung?	*Where is the bill?*
Sie liegt **neben der** Serviette.	*It's next to the napkin.*
Wo sitzen die Studenten?	*Where are the students sitting?*
Sie sitzen **auf einer** Bank **im** Park.	*They're sitting on a bench in the park.*
Wo steckt der Schlüssel?	*Where is the key?*
Er steckt **in der** Tür.	*It's in the door.*
Wo steht das Motorrad?	*Where is the motorcycle?*
Es steht **auf dem** Parkplatz **beim** Markt.	*It's in the parking lot by the market.*

Übung 5 Idylle im Grünen

Claudia und Jürgen verbringen (*are spending*) einen Samstagnachmittag im Grünen. Beantworten Sie die Fragen zum Bild.

1. Wo liegt Jürgen?
2. Wo sitzt Claudia?
3. Wo hängt eine Spinne?
4. Wo sitzt der Hund?
5. Wo sitzt der Vogel?
6. Wo steht der Picknickkorb?
7. Wo steckt die Weinflasche?
8. Wo liegt das Buch?

der Vogel

der Baum

die Spinne

der Hund

die Wiese

der Picknickkorb

die Flasche

pub with a beer garden

Übung 6 In einem Gartenlokal°

Ergänzen Sie das passende Verb: **hängen, liegen, sitzen, stecken** oder **stehen**.

Andreas und Thomas ____[1] in einem Gartenlokal. Das Lokal heißt „Im Forsthaus". Es ____[2] sehr schön im Grünen nicht weit von Bonn. Vor dem Lokal ____[3] viele Autos. Im Biergarten ____[4] Papierlaternen. Auf dem Tisch vor Andreas und Thomas ____[5] zwei Gläser Bier. Unter dem Tisch direkt neben ihnen ____[6] ein Hund. Er gehört zu den Gästen am Nebentisch. Um den Tisch ____[7] vier Leute. Der Ober ____[8] jetzt neben Andreas. Ein Bleistift (*pencil*) ____[9] in seiner Tasche. Die Rechnung ____[10] schon auf dem Tisch.

Describing Placement

The verbs **legen, setzen,** and **stellen,** as well as **hängen** and **stecken,** can indicate where someone or something is being put or placed.

hängen	to hang, to put/place
legen	to lay, to put/place
setzen	to set, to put/place
stecken	to put/place
stellen	to stand, to put/place

When a two-way preposition is used with one of these verbs indicating placement, the object of the preposition is in the accusative case. Remember, the interrogative pronoun **wohin** asks where someone or something is being put or placed.

Wohin hängt der Mann den Mantel?	*Where is the man hanging the coat?*
Er hängt ihn **an den** Haken.	*He's hanging it on the hook.*
Wo legt der Kellner die Rechnung **hin?**	*Where is the waiter putting the bill?*
Er legt sie **auf den** Tisch.	*He's laying it on the table.*
Wohin setzt die Frau das Kind?	*Where is the woman putting the child?*
Sie setzt es **auf den** Stuhl.	*She's putting him/her on the chair.*
Wo steckt die Kellnerin das Geld **hin**?	*Where is the waitress putting the money?*
Sie steckt es **in die** Tasche.	*She's putting it in the purse.*
Wohin stellt die Kellnerin den Teller?	*Where is the waitress putting the plate?*
Sie stellt ihn **auf den** Tisch.	*She's placing it on the table.*

Die Kellnerin stellt den Teller auf den Tisch.

SPRACHTIPP

The verb **setzen** is frequently used with a personal pronoun that reflects the subject of the sentence. Used in this reflexive way, the verb means *to sit down.*

Ich setze **mich** an den Tisch.	*I sit down at the table.*
Wir setzen **uns.**	*We sit down.*

In the third-person singular and plural this reflexive pronoun is always **sich.**

Die Studenten setzen **sich** auf die Bank.	*The students sit down on the bench.*

Übung 7 Im Lokal

Andreas trifft ein paar Freunde im „Nudelhaus". Ergänzen Sie die Sätze mit **hängen, legen, setzen, stecken** oder **stellen.**

1. Andreas und drei Studienfreunde ＿＿ sich an einen Tisch beim Fenster.
2. Andreas ＿＿ seinen Rucksack unter den Stuhl.
3. Michael ＿＿ seinen Rucksack an seinen Stuhl.
4. Endlich kommt der Kellner und ＿＿ die Speisekarte auf den Tisch.
5. Die vier bestellen zuerst etwas zu trinken. Der Kellner ＿＿ vier Colas auf den Tisch.
6. Da kommt noch ein Freund, Phillip, an den Tisch zu ihnen. Andreas ＿＿ noch einen Stuhl an den Tisch.
7. Phillip ＿＿ sich neben Andreas.
8. Er ＿＿ seine Bücher auf den Tisch.
9. Sein Handy ＿＿ er in seinen Rucksack.

SPRACHTIPP

The verb **stehen** is used idiomatically to say that something has been stated (in print).

—Hier gibt es auch vegetarische Kost.

They have vegetarian food here.

—Wo **steht** das?

Where does it say that?

Übung 8 Ein Abend im Kartoffelkeller!

Ergänzen Sie die Sätze mit einem passenden Verb: **liegen, sitzen, stehen, legen, setzen** oder **stellen.**

1. Im Zentrum von Berlin ＿＿ das Restaurant „Kartoffelkeller".
2. Im Restaurant ist es heute sehr voll. An allen Tischen ＿＿ schon Leute und einige suchen noch Platz.
3. Ein paar Leute ＿＿ draußen vor dem Lokal und warten, dass jemand geht.
4. Man ＿＿ hier auch sehr gemütlich. Und die Preise sind nicht so hoch. Deshalb ist es unter Studenten populär.
5. Endlich kommt eine Kellnerin und ＿＿ die Speisekarte auf den Tisch.
6. Auf der Speisekarte ＿＿: „Spezialität unseres Hauses ist Kartoffelsuppe mit Brot."
7. Die Kellnerin ＿＿ neben dem Tisch und wartet auf die Bestellung.
8. Am Nebentisch ＿＿ einige Studenten und diskutieren laut.
9. Ein Student ＿＿ sich an die Theke (*counter*) und bestellt ein Bier.
10. Der Kellner ＿＿ das Bier vor ihn auf die Theke.

Übung 9 Die verlorene Theaterkarte

Michael kann seine Theaterkarte nicht finden. Wo steckt sie wohl? Eine Person denkt sich aus, wo die Karte ist. Die anderen müssen raten (*guess*), wo die Karte ist.

BEISPIEL: s1: Steckt die Theaterkarte in seiner Hosentasche?
s2: Nein.
s1: Liegt die Theaterkarte auf dem Schreibtisch?
s2: Nein. (usw.)

das Weinglas
die Papiere (pl.)
die Büchertasche
die Sporttasche

Expressing Time with Prepositions

The following two-way prepositions always take the dative case when expressing time:

vor drei Tagen	*three days ago*
vor dem Theater	*before the play*
in einer Stunde	*in one hour*
zwischen 5 und 7 Uhr	*between 5 and 7 o'clock*

You have learned several other prepositions expressing time—not two-way prepositions—that also take the dative case.

nach dem Theater	*after the play*
seit einem Jahr	*for a year*
von 5 bis 7 Uhr	*from 5 to 7 o'clock*

The prepositions **um** and **gegen** always take the accusative case.

bis (um) 5 Uhr	*until 5 o'clock*
(so) gegen 7 Uhr	*around 7 o'clock*

Note: In German, expressions of time always precede expressions of place.

	TIME	PLACE
Wir kommen	**so gegen zehn Uhr**	nach Hause.
Ich gehe	**heute**	ins Kino.

Vor und nach dem Theater an die schönste Bar in der Stadt

Paletti

direkt im Stadtkino

Übung 10   Was machst du gewöhnlich um diese Zeit?

Arbeiten Sie mit einem Partner / einer Partnerin zusammen.

BEISPIEL: s1: Was machst du nach dem Deutschkurs?
s2: Da gehe ich in die Bibliothek.

von _____ bis _____	arbeiten
zwischen _____ und _____	schlafen
so gegen _____	essen
um _____	ausgehen
vor _____	einkaufen gehen
nach _____	fernsehen
??	??

Expressing Events in the Past

Like English, German has several tenses to express events in the past. The most common are the simple past tense (**das Imperfekt**) and the present perfect tense (**das Perfekt**).

- The present perfect tense (introduced in **Kapitel 7**) is preferred in conversation.
- The simple past tense is used primarily in writing. However, in the case of **haben, sein,** and the modals, the simple past is more common in conversation. In this chapter you will learn the simple past tense of these verbs; the simple past tense of all other verbs will be introduced in **Kapitel 10**.

The Simple Past Tense of **sein** and **haben**

	sein	**haben**
ich	war	hatte
du	warst	hattest
er, sie, es	war	hatte
wir	waren	hatten
ihr	wart	hattet
sie	waren	hatten
Sie	waren	hatten

Read the cartoon.

- What forms of the verbs **haben** and **sein** are used?
- The answer to the friend's question contains no verb or object because they are understood. What would the complete sentence be?
- How would the friend pose her questions if the speakers were adults addressing each other formally?

Du warst in Paris? Hattest du denn keine Schwierigkeiten¹ mit deinem Französisch?

Ich nicht, aber die Franzosen!

¹difficulties

Übung 11 Ausreden und Erklärungen°

Excuses and explanations

Ergänzen Sie **haben** oder **sein** im Imperfekt.

1. A: Warum _____ Sie gestern und vorgestern nicht im Deutschkurs, Herr Miller?

   B: Es tut mir leid, Herr Professor, aber meine Großmutter _____ krank (*sick*).

2. C: Rolf, _____ du gestern Abend noch in der Bibliothek?

   D: Nein, die _____ geschlossen. Außerdem _____ ich keine Lust zu arbeiten. Ich _____ aber im Kino!

3. E: Warum _____ Michael und Peter nicht auf der Party bei Ulla?

   F: Sie _____ keine Zeit.

4. G: Ihr _____ doch gestern im Café Käuzchen, nicht?

   H: Nein, wir _____ im Café Kadenz. Im Käuzchen _____ es zu voll.

   G: Wie _____ es denn?

   H: Die Musik _____ gut, aber der Kaffee _____ schlecht.

Übung 12 Wo warst du denn?

Fragen Sie Ihren Partner / Ihre Partnerin!

BEISPIEL: S1: Wo warst du denn Freitagabend?
   S2: Da war ich im Theater.
   S1: Wie war's denn?
   S2: Sehr langweilig.

WO	WIE
auf dem Sportplatz	interessant
auf einer Party	langweilig
bei Freunden	nicht besonders gut
im Kino	schön
im Restaurant	??
im Theater	
zu Hause	
??	

The Simple Past Tense of Modals

	dürfen	können	mögen	müssen	sollen	wollen
ich	durfte	konnte	mochte	musste	sollte	wollte
du	durftest	konntest	mochtest	musstest	solltest	wolltest
er, sie, es	durfte	konnte	mochte	musste	sollte	wollte
wir	durften	konnten	mochten	mussten	sollten	wollten
ihr	durftet	konntet	mochtet	musstet	solltet	wolltet
sie	durften	konnten	mochten	mussten	sollten	wollten
Sie	durften	konnten	mochten	mussten	sollten	wollten

Note:

- As with **haben** and **sein,** the first- and third-person singular forms and first- and third-person plural forms of the simple past tense of modals are identical.
- Modals have no umlaut in the simple past tense.

Peter **wollte** gestern in die Disko. Ich **musste** aber zu Hause bleiben.	*Peter wanted to go clubbing yesterday. But I had to stay home.*
Wir **konnten** keinen Parkplatz finden.	*We couldn't find a parking space.*

[1]*In case*

Übung 13   Ich wollte ... aber ich musste ...

Was wolltest du am Wochenende machen? Was musstest du machen?

A. Ergänzen Sie **wollen** im Imperfekt.

1. Ich _____ zuerst mal lange schlafen.
2. Mein Freund _____ mit mir ausgehen.
3. Bei gutem Wetter _____ wir Freunde im Park treffen.
4. Unsere Freunde _____ uns abholen.
5. _____ du am Wochenende nicht lange schlafen und dann ausgehen?

B. Ergänzen Sie **müssen** im Imperfekt.

1. Ja, aber ich _____ früh aufstehen; ich _____ nämlich arbeiten.
2. Meine Freundin _____ auch arbeiten.
3. Am Nachmittag _____ wir einkaufen gehen.
4. Meine Freunde _____ ohne mich ausgehen.

Übung 14 Kleine Probleme

Ergänzen Sie die fehlenden Modalverben im Imperfekt.

Gestern Abend waren wir im Theater. Wir ____[1] (wollen) in der Nähe vom Theater parken. Da ____[2] (dürfen) man aber nicht parken. Wir ____[3] (können) keinen Parkplatz auf der Straße finden. Deshalb ____[4] (müssen) wir ins Parkhaus fahren. Katrin ____[5] (sollen) vor dem Theater auf uns warten. Sie ____[6] (müssen) lange warten. Nach dem Theater ____[7] (wollen) wir noch ins Café Kadenz. Da ____[8] (können) wir keinen Platz bekommen. Wir ____[9] (müssen) also nach Hause fahren.

Übung 15 Bei mir zu Hause

Wie war das bei Ihnen zu Hause?

BEISPIEL: Als (As a) Kind mochte ich keinen Fisch essen.
Mein Vater wollte abends in Ruhe die Zeitung lesen.

ich	dürfen	Fisch/Brokkoli/Salat essen
wir Kinder	können	Gemüse essen
mein Vater	mögen	am Wochenende das Auto waschen
??	müssen	jeden Tag Hausaufgaben machen
	sollen	abends in Ruhe die Zeitung lesen
	wollen	abends nicht fernsehen
		nur am Wochenende ins Kino gehen
		um zehn im Bett sein
		??

Übung 16 Hin und her: Warum nicht?

Fragen Sie Ihren Partner / Ihre Partnerin, warum die folgenden Leute nicht da waren.

BEISPIEL: s1: Warum war Andreas gestern Vormittag nicht in der Vorlesung?
s2: Er hatte keine Lust.

PERSON	WANN	WO	WARUM
Andreas	gestern Vormittag	in der Vorlesung	keine Lust haben
Anke	Montag	zu Hause	
Frank			keine Zeit haben
Yeliz	heute Morgen	in der Vorlesung	
Mario			kein Geld haben
Ihr Partner / Ihre Partnerin			

Sprache im Kontext

Videoclips

A. Schauen Sie sich das Interview mit dem Besitzer des Restaurants an und ergänzen Sie die Sätze.

1. Das Restaurant heißt ___.
   a. Geigenhafen
   b. Gugelhof
   c. Gartenlaube

2. Es gibt Spezialitäten vom ___, von Baden und von der Schweiz.
   a. Elsass
   b. Rheinland
   c. Mittelmeer

3. Eine Spezialität des Restaurants ist ___.
   a. Lamm provenzal
   b. Tarte flambée
   c. Steak tartare

B. Schauen Sie sich die Szene im Restaurant an, wo die Gäste Essen bestellen. Wer bestellt was?

1. ___ Michael	**a.** Putenspieß	
2. ___ Claudia	**b.** Kartoffelauflauf	
3. ___ Ali	**c.** Schweineschnitzel	
4. ___ Sara	**d.** Tomatensuppe	

C. Die Gäste sprechen über ihre Essgewohnheiten. Hören Sie zu und beantworten Sie folgende Fragen.

1. Wo isst Ali gern?
2. Was isst Claudia gern?
3. Was ist Saras Lieblingsessen?
4. Wer isst gern Falafel?
5. Was für Fastfood isst Claudia gern?

D. Und Sie? Was essen und trinken Sie gern, wenn Sie ins Restaurant gehen?

Lesen

Zum Thema

A. Beantworten Sie die folgenden Fragen, bevor Sie den Text lesen.

1. Kochen Sie gern?
2. Sind Sie ein guter Koch / eine gute Köchin?
3. Wie oft kochen Sie pro Woche?
4. Was kochen Sie am liebsten?

5. Was kochen Sie oft, wenn Sie Freunde einladen?

6. Kochen Sie lieber allein oder mit jemandem zusammen?

B. Interviewen Sie einen Studenten / eine Studentin in der Klasse und stellen Sie ihm/ihr die Fragen in **A.**

Auf den ersten Blick

A. Lesen Sie den Titel und die erste Zeile im Text und beantworten Sie die folgenden Fragen.

1. Was ist das Thema?

2. Was macht der Mann?
   a. Er isst.
   b. Er kocht.
   c. Er singt.

3. Mit wem spricht der Mann?
   a. mit seiner Frau
   b. mit sich selbst
   c. mit jemandem am Telefon

B. Verbinden Sie das deutsche Wort mit der englischen Bedeutung.

1. angebrannt	*monologue, soliloquy*
2. brennen	*splendid*
3. das Selbstgespräch	*burnt*
4. der Essig	*salty*
5. herrlich	*to burn*
6. verkochen	*sharp, spicy*
7. scharf	*to cook down*
8. sauer	*sauce*
9. salzig	*vinegar*
10. die Soße	*sour*

C. Überfliegen Sie (*scan*) jetzt den Text. Welche Lebensmittel kommen im Text *nicht* vor? Kreuzen Sie an!

☐ Salz   ☐ Essig   ☐ Paprika
☐ Zwiebeln   ☐ Tomaten   ☐ Knoblauch
☐ Wurst   ☐ Pfeffer   ☐ Karotten
☐ Wein   ☐ Kartoffeln ☐ Oliven

D. Was für eine (*what kind of*) Soße kocht der Mann? Eine Soße für einen Schweinebraten? für ein Schnitzel vielleicht? Was meinen Sie? Begründen Sie Ihre Antwort.

DIE SOSSE

von Ekkehard Müller

Selbstgespräch eines Mannes beim Kochen:

Hoffentlich ist die Soße richtig. Hoffentlich schmeckt sie gut.
Nein. Da fehlt° noch etwas.   *is missing*
Ich muss sie noch mehr salzen.
5 Oh weh! Das war zu viel.
Was mache ich jetzt?
Ich muss sie mit Wasser verdünnen°. Oh weh. Das war auch zu viel.   *dilute*
Jetzt schmeckt sie nach gar nichts.
Macht nichts. Das Wasser wird wieder verkochen.
10 Und das Salz???

Jetzt muss ich noch Zwiebeln schneiden.
Ich hätte° sie schon vorher …   *should have*
Au, das brennt in den Augen.
So. Die Zwiebeln sind auch schon drin. Wie schmeckt sie jetzt?
15 Besser. Viel besser.
Aber es fehlt noch etwas.

Ich muss noch Wein dazugeben.
Hm. Der schmeckt aber gut.
Und noch ein Glas.
20 Ausgezeichnet!
Oh weh! Jetzt habe ich keinen Wein mehr für die Soße.
Was mache ich?
Ich nehme Essig.

Brrrrrrrrr, zu sauer!
25 Wie rette° ich die Soße?   *save*
Ich weiß es. Mit Tomatenketchup. Das schadet nie°.   schadet … *never hurts*
Hier schon.
Jetzt muss noch Pfeffer rein. Endlich scharf!
Und Paprika. Und Knoblauch°.   *garlic*
30 Schade, dass Knoblauch wie der Teufel stinkt.
Und jetzt, jetzt kommen noch Oliven in die Soße.
Ich mag Oliven.
Oliven erinnern° mich an Italien.   *remind*
Und Italien erinnert mich an Sonne.
35 Und an das Meer.
Und an Fischer.
Ah, die Sonne!
Ah, das Meer!
Ah, die Fischer!
40 Und der Duft° der Bäume im Frühling!   *fragrance*
Herrlich!
Was raucht denn hier?
Ich gehe ins Gasthaus. Die Soße ist angebrannt.

Zum Text

A. Lesen Sie den ganzen Text einmal durch und beantworten Sie dann die folgenden Fragen.

1. Mit der Soße gibt es immer wieder ein neues Problem, aber der Mann weiß immer wieder eine Lösung (*solution*). Wie löst er die folgenden Probleme?

BEISPIEL: Die Soße hat zu viel Salz. → Er verdünnt die Soße mit Wasser.

    a. Er hat keinen Wein mehr für die Soße.
    b. Die Soße ist zu sauer.
    c. Die Soße ist nicht scharf genug (*enough*).

2. Warum hat der Mann keinen Wein mehr für die Soße?

3. Warum nimmt der Mann Olivon für die Soße?

4. Immer wieder macht der Mann Kommentar wie „Oh weh!", wenn er neue Zutaten (*ingredients*) in die Soße mischt. Suchen Sie andere Kommentare im Text.

5. Was passiert mit der Soße am Ende? Warum? Wohin geht der Mann dann?

B. Ist Ihnen schon mal etwas Ähnliches (*something similar*) passiert? Was haben Sie gekocht? Erzählen Sie. Schreiben Sie einen kurzen Bericht (*report*).

Zu guter Letzt

Ihr Lieblingsrestaurant bewerten

Haben Sie ein Lieblingsrestaurant? Gemeinsam mit anderen Studenten/ Studentinnen werden Sie jetzt ein Bewertungsformular (*evaluation form*) für ein Restaurant entwickeln (*develop*), ausfüllen und darüber berichten.

Schritt 1: Machen Sie eine Liste mit Fragen über Ihr Lieblingsrestaurant, zum Beispiel: Warum essen Sie dort? Wie ist die Atmosphäre? Essen Sie oft dort? Wie oft? Mit wem? Was? Wie ist die Bedienung? Wie sind die Preise? Weitere Fragen?

Schritt 2: Arbeiten Sie in Gruppen zu dritt. Stellen Sie das Bewertungsformular zusammen. Benutzen Sie Fragen aus **Schritt 1**. Erstellen Sie mindestens 10 Fragen für Ihr Formular. Geben Sie dazu auch mögliche Antworten an, z.B.

1. Wie oft essen Sie da?
    ___-mal pro Woche
    ___-mal pro Monat
    ___-mal im Jahr
2. Wie ist die Atmosphäre?
    ☐ ruhig
    ☐ laut und lustig
    ☐ angenehm
3. …

Beantworten Sie die Fragen noch nicht!

Schritt 3: Machen Sie Fotokopien des Formulars und tauschen Sie es mit einer anderen Gruppe aus. Jede/r bekommt also ein Formular zum Ausfüllen. Füllen Sie das Formular mit Bezug auf (*with reference to*) Ihr eigenes Lieblingsrestaurant aus.

Schritt 4: Berichten Sie der Klasse über Ihr Lieblingsrestaurant. Beschreiben Sie verschiedene Aspekte des Restaurants. Die Klasse entscheidet (*decides*) Folgendes: Ist das Restaurant: 1. exzellent, 2. sehr gut, 3. gut, 4. mittelmäßig oder 5. unterdurchschnittlich?

Wortschatz

Lokale — Eating and Drinking Establishments

der **Biergarten**, ⸚	beer garden
das **Café**, -s	café
die **Gaststätte**, -n	full-service restaurant
der **Imbiss**, -e	fast-food stand
die **Kneipe**, -n	pub, bar
das **Lokal**, -e	restaurant, pub, bar
das **Restaurant**, -s	restaurant
das **Wirtshaus**, ⸚er	pub

Im Restaurant — In the Restaurant

das **Apfelmus**	applesauce
der **Apfelstrudel**	apple strudel
der **Auflauf**	casserole
die **Bedienung**	service
die **Beilage**, -n	side dish
die **Bohne**, -n	bean
die **Bratkartoffeln** (*pl.*)	fried potatoes
die **Brezel**, -n	pretzel
der **Eisbecher**, -	dish of ice cream
die **Gabel**, -n	fork
das **Gericht**, -e	dish (*of prepared food*)
der **Grill**	grill, barbeque
das **Hauptgericht**, -e	main dish
der **Kellner**, - / die **Kellnerin**, -nen	waiter / waitress, server
die **Küche**	food, cuisine; kitchen
der **Leberkäs**	Bavarian style meatloaf
der **Löffel**, -	spoon
der **Mais**	corn
das **Messer**, -	knife
die **Nachspeise**, -n	dessert
der **Nachtisch**, -e	dessert
die **Nudel**, -n	noodle
der **Ober**, -	waiter
die **Olive**, -n	olive
die **Paprika**	bell pepper
die **Pfanne**, -n	pan

das **Pilsener**, -	Pilsner beer
der **Platz**, ⸚e	place, seat
die **Pommes frites** (*pl.*)	french fries
die **Rechnung**, -en	bill
der **Reis**	rice
der **Ruhetag**, -e	*day that a business is closed*
die **Sahne**	cream; whipped cream
der **Salat**, -e	salad; lettuce
das **Sauerkraut**	sauerkraut
der **Schweinebraten**, -	pork roast
der **Senf**	mustard
die **Serviette**, -n	napkin
der **Speck**	bacon
die **Speise**, -n	dish (of prepared food)
die **Speisekarte**, -n	menu
das **Spiegelei**, -er	fried egg (sunny-side up)
der **Sprudel**	mineral water
die **Suppe**, -n	soup
der **Teller**, -	plate
die **Vorspeise**, -n	appetizer
der **Wein**, -e	wine
die **Weißwurst**, ⸚e	white sausage
die **Zwiebel**, -n	onion

Verben — Verbs

bekommen	to get
Was bekommen Sie?	What will you have?
bestellen	to order
entschuldigen	to excuse
Entschuldigen Sie!	Excuse me!
hängen	to hang; to be hanging
lassen	to let
Lass uns (doch) …	Let's . . .
legen	to lay, put (*in a lying position*)
liegen	to lie; to be located
setzen	to set; to put (*in a sitting position*)
sitzen	to sit

stecken	to place, put (*inside*); to be (*inside*)
stehen	to stand; to be located
stellen	to stand up; place, put (*in an upright position*)
warten	to wait

Adjektive und Adverbien
Adjectives and Adverbs

alkoholfrei	nonalcoholic
besetzt	occupied, taken
Hier ist besetzt.	This place is taken.
da drüben	over there
geöffnet	open
geschlossen	closed
getrennt	separate(ly)
hoffentlich	I hope
täglich	daily
vegetarisch	vegetarian
voll	full; crowded
ziemlich	somewhat, rather

Wechsel-präpositionen
Dative/Accusative Prepositions

an	at, on, to, near
auf	on, on top of, at
hinter	behind, in back of
in	in; to (*a place*)

neben	next to, beside
über	over, above
unter	under, below, beneath; among
vor	before, in front of
zwischen	between

Präpositionen (Temporal)
Prepositions (Temporal)

bis (um): bis (um) fünf Uhr	until: until five o'clock
(so) gegen: (so) gegen fünf Uhr	around/about: around five o'clock
in (+ *dat.*): in zwei Tagen	in: in two days
nach: nach Dienstag	after: after Tuesday
seit: seit zwei Jahren	since, for: for two years
von: von zwei bis drei Uhr	from: from two to three o'clock
vor (+ *dat.*): vor zwei Tagen	ago: two days ago
zwischen: zwischen zwei und drei Uhr	between: between two and three o'clock

Sonstiges
Other

Ist hier noch frei?	Is this seat available?
Vielen Dank!	Many thanks!
vom Fass	on top; draft
zum Mitnehmen	(food) to go; take-out

▼ DAS KANN ICH NUN!

1. Nennen Sie drei andere Lokalitäten, wo man essen und trinken kann.

   a. das Restaurant **b.** _____ **c.** _____
   d. _____

2. Was ist Ihr Lieblingsessen? Ihr Lieblingsgetränk? Ihre Lieblingsnachspeise?

3. „Wo" oder „wohin"?

   a. _____ wollen wir gehen? **b.** _____ ist noch ein Platz frei?

4. Setzen Sie passende Präpositionen und Artikel ein.

   a. _____ _____ Konzert gehen Uwe und Ute _____ _____ Kneipe. **b.** Ihr Auto steht _____ _____ Restaurant. **c.** Uwe setzt sich _____ _____ Tisch. **d.** Sein Hund liegt _____ _____ Tisch.

5. Wie sagen Sie das?

   a. Ask if this seat is taken. **b.** Ask a server to bring you the menu. **c.** Order some mineral water and a dish of ice cream.
   d. Let the server know that you would like to pay.

6. Ergänzen Sie **sein** oder **haben** im Imperfekt. Wo _____ du gestern? —Ich _____ in der Uni. Wir _____ eine Gastvorlesung von einem Professor aus USA.

7. Setzen Sie ein passendes Modalverb im Imperfekt ein.

   a. Ich _____ nach der Vorlesung sofort in die Mensa. **b.** Wir _____ leider nicht mitkommen. **c.** Wir _____ nämlich zwei Stunden in der Vorlesung bleiben.

Zweites Zwischenspiel

Begegnung mit der Kunst der Gegenwart

Was ist Kunst? Das Wort „Kunst" kommt von „können". Ein Künstler oder eine Künstlerin ist ein „Könner"; jemand, der etwas „kann", z.B. malen, zeichnen, formen, komponieren, schreiben. Was erwarten Sie als Kunstbetrachter[1] von einem Kunstwerk? Soll es z.B. „schön" sein, provozieren, zum Nachdenken anregen[2] oder die Realität darstellen[3]?

Die Beispiele moderner und zeitgenössischer[4] deutscher Kunst auf diesen Seiten zeigen Kunst im Kontext von alltäglichen Dingen und ungewöhnlichen Medien. Viele Leute bewundern[5] diese Werke, andere nennen sie Werke von „Dilettanten und hochgemuten[6] Nichtskönnern". Was meinen Sie? (Zitat: aus S. 7, Faust / de Vries. „Hunger nach Bildern")

*Tisch mit Aggregat,
1958/87. Joseph Beuys*

*„Flaschenpost", 1990.
Rolf Glasmeier*

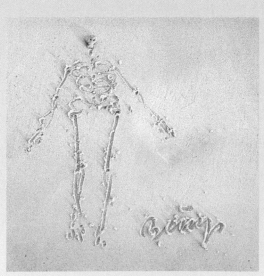

Sandzeichnung. 1975, Joseph Beuys

Aktivität 1   Kunstbewertung

A. Was halten Sie von diesen Kunstgebilden? Wie würden Sie sie charakterisieren?

BEISPIEL: Ich finde die „Flaschenpost" sehr witzig.

- ☐ aggressiv
- ☐ hässlich
- ☐ humorvoll
- ☐ komplex
- ☐ radikal
- ☐ schön
- ☐ verrückt
- ☐ kitschig
- ☐ witzig
- ☐ provozierend
- ☐ dilettantisch
- ☐ komisch
- ☐ originell
- ☐ faszinierend
- ☐ spektakulär
- ☐ kindisch
- ☐ phantasievoll
- ☐ kreativ
- ☐ tief[7]
- ☐ ??

[1]*viewer of art*   [2]*incite*   [3]*represent*   [4]*contemporary*
[5]*admire*   [6]*arrogant*   [7]*profound*

B. Besprechen Sie die folgender Fragen im Plenum.

1. Welches dieser Kunstwerke gefällt Ihnen besonders gut? Wenn Ihnen keins davon gefällt, warum nicht?

2. Erinnert Sie das eine oder andere dieser Kunstwerke an etwas, was Sie schon einmal, vielleicht in einem Museum, gesehen haben? Sind Ihnen die Namen der Künstler bekannt? Wenn ja, welche Namen?

3. Wer ist Ihr Lieblingskünstler / Ihre Lieblingskünstlerin?

4. Was für Kunstwerke oder Reproduktionen von Kunstwerken haben Sie in Ihrem Zimmer oder in Ihrer Wohnung?

5. Wenn Sie eins dieser Kunstwerke erwerben[1] könnten, welches würden Sie wählen, und warum?

```
                              i
                            in
                          inf
                        info
                      infor
                    inform
                  informi
                informie
              informier
            informieren        claus bremer

haltungen     nur nur nur nur nur nur nur nur nur nur nur nu n
altungen      nicht nicht nicht nicht nicht nicht nicht nicht nicht nicht
ltungen       nicht nicht nicht nicht nicht nicht nicht nicht nich
tungen        nicht nicht nic
ungen                      n
ngen
gen
en
n
```

```
provozieren
provozieren
provozieren
provozieren
provozieren
provozieren
provozieren
provozieren
provozieren
rovozieren
ovozieren
vozieren
ozieren
zieren
ieren
eren
ren
en
n
```

Konkrete Poesie

Hier sind zwei Beispiele konkreter Poesie. Charakteristisch für sie ist der visuelle Aspekt. Das Visuelle kann z.B. ein Piktogramm sein oder eine Figur, die mit Buchstaben und Wörtern gefüllt ist. Was halten Sie von Claus Bremers und Reinhard Döhls konkreter Poesie?

```
    pfelApfelApfelAp
  pfelApfelApfelApfelApfe
 pfelApfelApfelApfelApfelAp
 ApfelApfelApfelApfelApfelA
 pfelApfelApfelApfelApfelApfe
 ApfelApfelApfelApfelApfelAp
 pfelApfelApfelApfelApfelApfe
 ApfelApfelApfelWurmApfelA
  elApfelApfelApfelApfelApfe
   elApfelApfelApfelApfelAr
    ApfelApfelApfelApfel
     ApfelApfelApfelA
      ApfelApfelA
```

reinhard döhl

„Der Leser". 1981, Georg Jiri Dokoupil

Aktivität 2   Sie sind dran[2].

A. Schreiben Sie jetzt Ihr eigenes konkretes Gedicht.

B. Schreiben Sie ein Gedicht im Fünfzeilenformat:

Erste Zeile:	ein Substantiv
Zweite Zeile:	zwei Adjektive
Dritte Zeile:	drei Verben im Infinitiv
Vierte Zeile:	ein Satz, eine Frage oder ein Ausdruck
Fünfte Zeile:	Wiederholung der ersten Zeile, oder ein anderes Substantiv

[1]acquire   [2]Sie ... It's your turn.

Freizeit und Sport

Zwei junge Leute auf einer
Wanderung in der Schweiz

In diesem Kapitel

- **Themen:** Sports and leisure pastimes, locations, seasons, weather expressions
- **Grammatik:** Coordinating conjunctions, present perfect tense, comparative
- **Kultur:** Sports, hobbies, clubs, temperature conversion
- **Lesen:** „Vergnügungen" (Bertolt Brecht)

Videoclips
Pläne für die Freizeit

Alles klar?

A. Schauen Sie sich die Grafik an und beantworten Sie die Fragen.

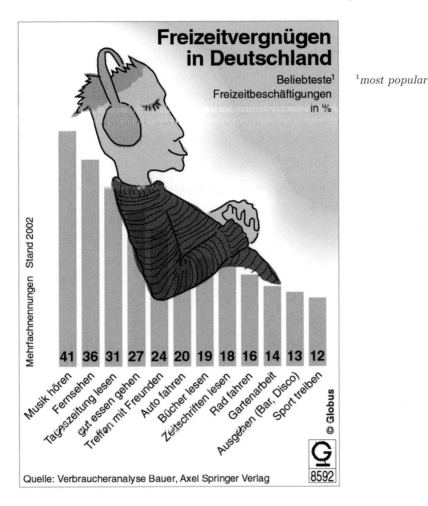

Freizeitvergnügen in Deutschland — Beliebteste[1] Freizeitbeschäftigungen in %

[1]*most popular*

Mehrfachnennungen Stand 2002

Musik hören	Fernsehen	Tageszeitung lesen	gut essen gehen	Treffen mit Freunden	Auto fahren	Bücher lesen	Zeitschriften lesen	Rad fahren	Gartenarbeit	Ausgehen (Bar, Disco)	Sport treiben
41	36	31	27	24	20	19	18	16	14	13	12

© Globus

Quelle: Verbraucheranalyse Bauer, Axel Springer Verlag

8592

- Was ist die beliebteste Freizeitbeschäftigung der Deutschen?
- Welche Freizeitbeschäftigung haben nur 12% der Deutschen gern?
- Was ist die beliebteste Freizeitbeschäftigung in Ihrem Land?
- Welche Freizeitbeschäftigung ist in Ihrem Land nicht so beliebt?

B. Sie hören nun drei kurze Dialoge. Wie verbringen Ulrike, Wolfgang und Antje ihre Freizeit?

1. Ulrike
    a. Tanzen   **b.** sich mit Freunden treffen   **c.** Kochen   **d.** Lesen

2. Wolfgang
    a. Fußball spielen   **b.** Fernsehen   **c.** Musik hören   **d.** Rad fahren

3. Antje
    a. ins Kino gehen   **b.** Sport treiben   **c.** Musik spielen   **d.** im Internet surfen

Wörter im Kontext

Types of sports

THEMA 1: Sportarten°

Wo macht man das? Kombinieren Sie!

BEISPIEL: Man wandert im Wald oder am Fluss.

wandern	auf dem **Tennisplatz**
Rad fahren	im Fitnesscenter
angeln	auf dem **See**
tauchen	auf der Straße
reiten	im **Wald**
segeln	am **Fluss**
Bodybuilding machen	im **Meer**
turnen	in der **Turnhalle**
schwimmen	im **Schwimmbad**
Tennis spielen	auf der **Wiese**
	in den **Bergen**

Neue Wörter

der See   lake
der Wald   forest
der Fluss   river
das Meer   sea, ocean
die Turnhalle   gymnasium
die Wiese   meadow
turnen   do gymnastics
der Berg (Berge, *pl.***)**
   mountain

1. Lisa turnt jeden zweiten Tag.

2. Uwe und Erich machen dreimal die Woche Bodybuilding.

3. Kerstin fährt Rad.

4. Heinz angelt oft im Sommer.

5. Manfred segelt gern.

6. Renate taucht gern.

7. Eva reitet jeden Tag.

Die Karte „Naherholung" zeigt, welche Sportmöglichkeiten es in und um Göttingen gibt. Schauen Sie sich die Bildsymbole auf der Karte an. Welche Sportarten kann man hier treiben? Wo kann man das machen?

BEISPIELE: Man kann auf dem Kiessee segeln.
　　　　　Man kann im Jahnstadion Fußball spielen.

 im **Verein** kegeln　　　wandern　　　Golf spielen

Fußball spielen　　　angeln　　　reiten

tauchen, schwimmen　　segeln　　　**joggen**

Tennis spielen　　　**Schlittschuh laufen**

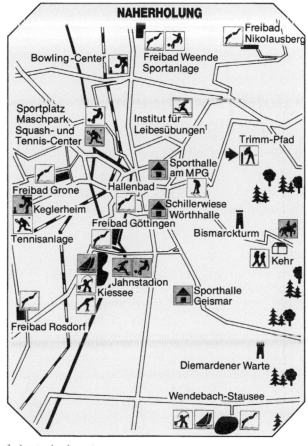

¹physical education

Neue Wörter

der Verein　club
das Freibad　outdoor swimming pool
der Sportplatz　athletic field
die Sporthalle　sports arena
das Hallenbad　indoor swimming pool
das Stadion　stadium
das Eisstadion　ice-skating rink

Aktivität 1　Was braucht man für diese Sportarten?

Bilden Sie Sätze mit Elementen aus beiden Spalten (columns).

BEISPIEL: Zum Wandern braucht man Wanderschuhe.

zum Angeln　　　　　　　ein Fahrrad
zum Reiten　　　　　　　ein Segelboot
zum Wandern　　　　　　einen Ball
zum Tauchen　　　　　　eine Angelrute (fishing pole)
zum Fußball spielen　　　ein Pferd (horse)
zum Rad fahren　　　　　Wanderschuhe
zum Segeln　　　　　　　Schwimmflossen (fins)

SPRACHTIPP

To say how often you do something, use the following expressions:

jeden Tag	every day
einmal/zweimal die Woche	once/twice a week
dreimal im Monat	three times a month
einmal im Jahr	once a year

Aktivität 2   Ein Gespräch über Sport

Bilden Sie kleine Gruppen und diskutieren Sie. Welche Sportarten treiben Sie gern? Wie oft?

BEISPIEL: s1: Ich jogge gern, und ich wandere auch gern.
s2: Wie oft machst du das?
s1: Ich gehe einmal im Monat wandern, aber ich jogge jeden Tag.

THEMA 2: Hobbys und andere Vergnügungen°

pleasures

Wie **verbringen** Sie Ihre **Freizeit**? Kreuzen Sie an!

☐ **Sport treiben**	☐ spazieren gehen
☐ Musik hören	☐ **Briefmarken sammeln**
☐ mit Freunden ausgehen	☐ **Spielkarten** sammeln
☐ Motorrad fahren	☐ **bloggen**
☐ ins Museum gehen	☐ **zeichnen**
☐ **Karten** spielen	☐ fotografieren
☐ Ski fahren	☐ Klavier spielen
☐ Computerspiele spielen	☐ **malen**
☐ **Schach spielen**	☐ am **Wagen** arbeiten
☐ fernsehen	☐ im Garten arbeiten
☐ **faulenzen**	☐ **Briefe** schreiben
☐ Windsurfing gehen	☐ ??

Neue Wörter

Freizeit verbringen spend free time
Sport treiben play sports
die Briefmarke (Briefmarken, *pl.***)** postage stamp
sammeln collect
die Spielkarte (Spielkarten, *pl.***)** playing card
zeichnen draw
malen paint (pictures)
Schach spielen play chess
faulenzen do nothing, be lazy
der Brief (Briefe, *pl.***)** letter
beliebt popular

Sie gehen oft ins Museum.

Sie bloggt.

Sie malt.

Er arbeitet am Wagen.

Sie spielen Schach.

Er faulenzt.

Vergleichen Sie Ihre Liste mit der Liste von anderen Personen im Kurs. Können Sie drei gemeinsame Dinge finden? Was ist besonders **beliebt?**

Aktivität 3 In der Freizeit

Sie hören drei junge Leute über ihre Freizeit sprechen. Kreuzen Sie an, was sie machen.

1. Nina …
   a. hört Musik. □
   b. geht mit Freunden aus. □
   c. spielt Computerspiele. □
   d. fotografiert. □
   e. zeichnet. □
   f. malt. □

2. Thomas …
   a. hat keine Freizeit. □
   b. träumt (*dreams*) vom Motorrad fahren. □
   c. fährt Ski im Traum. □
   d. arbeitet am Wagen. □
   e. bloggt. □

3. Annette …
   a. geht Windsurfen. □
   b. geht zum Flohmarkt. □
   c. spielt Karten. □
   d. sammelt Spielkarten. □
   e. sammelt Briefmarken. □
   f. surft im Internet. □

Aktivität 4 Wie hast du deine Freizeit verbracht?°

How did you spend your free time?

Fragen Sie einen Partner / eine Partnerin: Wie hast du in den letzten acht Tagen deine Freizeit verbracht?

BEISPIEL: Ich habe Musik gehört. Ich bin mit Freunden ausgegangen. Ich habe jeden Tag ferngesehen.

 Siehe *Expressing Events in the Past*, S. 217.

mit Freunden	bin … ausgegangen
mit einem Freund	bin … in die Disko / ins Kino gegangen
mit einer Freundin	habe … Musik gehört/gespielt
allein	habe … ferngesehen/gebloggt

Aktivität 5 Möchtest du mitkommen?

Machen Sie eine Verabredung (*date*).

S1	S2
1. Ich gehe heute Bowling. Möchtest du mitkommen? ins Kino/Theater/Stadtbad/… in ein Rockkonzert / …	**2a.** Ja, gern, um wie viel Uhr denn? **b.** Ich kann nicht.
3a. Um _____ Uhr. Nach dem Abendessen um _____. Nach der Vorlesung um _____. **b.** Warum denn nicht?	**4a.** Wo wollen wir uns treffen (*meet*)? **b.** Ich muss arbeiten. Ich habe kein Geld / keine Zeit / …
5a. Vor dem Kino. / Vor der Bibliothek. / Im Studentenheim. / Bei mir zu Hause. / … **b.** Schade.	**6.** Gut. Ich treffe dich dann um _____.

Aktivität 6 Pläne für einen Ausflug°

excursion

Verena und Antje machen Pläne fürs Wochenende. Sie wohnen beide in Düsseldorf. Hören Sie sich den Dialog an, und markieren Sie dann die richtigen Antworten.

	DAS STIMMT	DAS STIMMT NICHT	KEINE INFORMATION
1. Verena und Antje planen einen Ausflug.	□	□	□
2. Sie wollen im Neandertal wandern.	□	□	□
3. Es dauert nur eine Stunde bis zum Neandertal.	□	□	□
4. Der Weg führt durch den Wald.	□	□	□
5. Auf dem Wege dahin wollen sie ein Picknick machen.	□	□	□
6. Antje will ihren Freund Stefan einladen.	□	□	□

THEMA 3: Jahreszeiten und Wetter

Die Jahreszeiten

Die **Jahreszeiten**: der **Frühling**, der **Sommer**, der **Herbst**, der **Winter**.
Welches Bild passt zu welcher Jahreszeit?

1. Der Berliner Wannsee im ———.

2. Am Kornmarkt in Heidelberg im ———.

3. Der Grundlsee in Österreich im ———.

4. Das Städtchen Creuzburg im ———.

Das Wetter

DIE SONNE	DIE WOLKEN	DER REGEN	DAS GEWITTER	DER SCHNEE
Die Sonne scheint.	**Es ist bewölkt.**	**Es regnet.**	**Es gibt ein Gewitter.**	**Es gibt Schnee.**
Es ist sonnig.	**Es ist kühl.**	**Es ist regnerisch.**	**Es blitzt und donnert.**	**Es schneit.**
Es ist angenehm/ heiter/warm/heiß.		**Es gibt einen Schauer.**	**Es ist schwül.**	**Es ist kalt.**

A. Welche Jahreszeit ist das: Winter, Sommer, Frühling oder Herbst?

BEISPIEL: Die Blätter fallen von den Bäumen. →
Das ist Herbst.

1. Die Blätter (*leaves*) sind nicht mehr **so** grün **wie** im Sommer und **fallen** von den Bäumen. Es kann auch regnerisch werden.
2. Leute schwimmen im Freibad. An manchen Tagen ist der **Himmel wolkenlos.**
3. Es regnet viel und die Blumen blühen. Man braucht oft einen **Regenschirm.** Die Tage werden **länger als** im Winter.
4. Die Tage sind kurz. Für viele Menschen **dauert** diese Jahreszeit zu lang.
5. Es wird **kühler** als im Sommer und die Tage werden etwas **kürzer.**
6. Es ist sehr heiß und manchmal sogar schwül und unangenehm.
7. **Drinnen** ist es schön warm, **draußen** aber wirklich **kalt. Die Sonne scheint** selten. Ein starker **Wind** bläst und der Himmel ist oft **bewölkt.**

B. Welcher **Wetterbericht** passt zu welchem Bild?

1. _____ Im Norden beginnt es zu regnen, und morgen regnet es den ganzen Tag. Am Abend: **Regen,** eventuell auch **Hagel.**
2. _____ Im Moment ist es **bewölkt.** Die **Temperatur** heute Nachmittag ist nur 7 **Grad,** aber heute Abend wird es **kalt** und **windig.**
3. _____ In der Karibik ist es sonnig, heiter und warm. Wir haben den ganzen Tag **angenehme** Temperaturen. Morgen wird es wieder heiß.
4. _____ Im Süden gibt es **starke Gewitter.** Was **passiert? Es blitzt und donnert.**
5. _____ In den Bergen schneit es im Moment. Die Skifahrer sind begeistert über den Schnee.
6. _____ Im Rheinland gibt es heute Morgen **Nebel,** nachher einzelne **Wolken.** Auch morgen neblig und kühl.

Siehe *Expressing Comparisons: The Comparative,* S. 225.

Neue Wörter

angenehm pleasant
heiter bright
heiß hot
schwül humid
so ... wie as . . . as
der Himmel sky
wolkenlos cloudless
der Regenschirm umbrella
länger (lang) longer
als than
dauert (deuern) lasts
kühler (kühl) cooler
kürzer (kurz) shorter
drinnen inside
draußen outside
der Wetterbericht weather report
der Hagel hail
der Grad (Grad, *pl.*) degree
windig windy
starke (stark) strong
das Gewitter (Gewitter, *pl.*) thunderstorm
passiert (passieren) happens
es blitzt there's lightning
es donnert it's thundering
es schneit it's snowing
der Nebel fog

a.

b.

c.

d.

e.

f.

Aktivität 7 Das Wetter in Deutschland

Schritt 1: Lesen Sie den Text zum Wetterbericht und beantworten Sie die Fragen.

[1]largely [2]early [3]lockert sich auf *breaks up* [4]*sight* [5]*gusty*

1. Dieser Wetterbericht ist wahrscheinlich für einen Tag im _____.

    a. August
    b. Sommer
    c. Februar
    d. Mai

2. Wo gibt es heute Schnee?

    a. an den Küsten
    b. im Westen
    c. im Norden und im Osten
    d. an den Küsten und im Westen

3. An den Küsten soll es am Nachmittag _____ geben.

    a. Sonnenschein
    b. Nebel
    c. starke Gewitter
    d. Hagel

4. An der Nordküste ist die Tagestemperatur _____.

    a. 4 Grad Celsius
    b. 5 Grad Celsius
    c. 3 Grad Celsius
    d. 0 Grad Celsius

5. Der Wind weht schwach bis mäßig aus _____.

    a. Nordwest
    b. Nordost
    c. Südwest
    d. den Bergen

Schritt 2: Schauen Sie sich jetzt die Wetterkarte noch mal an, und vergleichen (*compare*) Sie das Wetter in einer Stadt mit dem Wetter in einer anderen Stadt.

BEISPIELE: In Kiel ist es sonniger als in Frankfurt.
In Nürnberg ist es genau so kalt wie in München.

Aktivität 8 Wetterberichte im Radio

Sie hören fünf kurze Wetterberichte für fünf Städte in Europa. Kreuzen Sie die richtigen Informationen an und notieren Sie die Temperaturen in Grad Celsius.

	ZÜRICH	WIEN	BERLIN	PARIS	LONDON
sonnig	☐	☐	☐	☐	☐
warm	☐	☐	☐	☐	☐
bewölkt bis heiter	☐	☐	☐	☐	☐
(stark) bewölkt	☐	☐	☐	☐	☐
Nebel	☐	☐	☐	☐	☐
Schauer	☐	☐	☐	☐	☐
Regen	☐	☐	☐	☐	☐
Wind	☐	☐	☐	☐	☐
Gewitter	☐	☐	☐	☐	☐
Grad Celsius	_____	_____	_____	_____	_____

KULTURTIPP

The Fahrenheit temperature scale is used in the United States, but the Celsius scale is used elsewhere. Swedish astronomer Anders Celsius (1701–1744) first used a scale similar to the present day Celsius scale. The German physicist Daniel Fahrenheit (1686–1736) defined the Fahrenheit unit and also invented the mercury thermometer.

   To convert Celsius to Fahrenheit: divide by 5, multiply by 9, and add 32. To convert Fahrenheit into Celsius: Subtract 32, divide by 9, and multiply by 5.

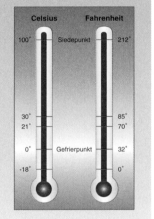

Aktivität 9 So ist das Wetter in …

Woher kommen Sie? Wie ist das Wetter dort?

BEISPIEL: Ich komme aus San Franzisko. Dort ist das Wetter im Sommer oft kühl und neblig. Im Frühling ist es meistens sonnig. Und im Winter regnet es.

Aktivität 10 Ihr Wetterbericht

Schreiben Sie einen Wetterbericht für Ihr Gebiet (*area*).

BEISPIEL: Das Wetter für Donnerstag: schwül und heiß. Temperaturen: 30–35 Grad Celsius. Das Wetter für morgen: morgens Nebel, dann sonnig, 30 Grad.

Grammatik im Kontext

koordinierende Konjunktionen

Connecting Ideas: Coordinating Conjunctions°

Coordinating conjunctions connect words, phrases, or sentences. You already know **und** and **oder.**

> Herr **und** Frau Baumann sitzen vor dem Fernseher.
>
> War der Film langweilig **oder** amüsant?

Other coordinating conjunctions are the following:

> **aber** but, however   **sondern** but, rather   **denn** because, for

> Erst muss ich heute arbeiten, **und** dann gehe ich Tennis spielen.
>
> Ich spiele gern Tennis, **aber** mein Freund spielt lieber Karten.
>
> Willst du mit zum Sportplatz, **oder** willst du zu Hause bleiben?
>
> Ich möchte zum Sportplatz, **denn** da gibt es ein Fußballspiel.
>
> Ich bleibe nicht zu Hause, **sondern** ich gehe zum Sportplatz.

Note:

- When used to connect sentences, coordinating conjunctions do not affect word order. Each sentence can be stated independently of the other.

Expressing a Contrast: **aber** vs. **sondern**

The conjunction **aber** is normally used for English *but* to express the juxtaposition of ideas. The adverb **zwar** is often added to the first contrasted element to accentuate the juxtaposition.

Das Spiel war kurz, **aber** spannend.	*The game was short but exciting.*
Ich spiele **zwar** gern Tennis, **aber** nicht bei dem Wetter.	*I do like playing tennis, but not in this weather.*
Der Film hat **zwar** nicht lange gedauert, **aber** er war sehr interessant.	*Admittedly the movie didn't last very long, but it was very interesting.*

If however, a negative such as **nicht** or **kein** is part of the first contrasted element *and* two mutually exclusive ideas are juxtaposed, **sondern** must be used.

Es ist **nicht** warm, **sondern** kalt draußen.	*It isn't warm but rather cold outside.*

The weather outside isn't warm and cold at the same time; therefore **warm** and **kalt** are mutually exclusive and **sondern** must be used.

Das ist **kein** Regen, **sondern** Hagel!	*That's not rain but hail!*

The precipitation in question is either rain or hail but not both; therefore **Regen** and **Hagel** are mutually exclusive and **sondern** must be used.

Übung 1 Wie ist das Wetter?

Gebraucht man hier **aber** oder **sondern?** Ergänzen Sie die Sätze.

1. Gestern war es zwar kalt, _____ sonnig.
2. Bei uns gibt es im Winter keinen Schnee, _____ nur viel Regen.
3. Im Frühling wird es hier nie heiß, _____ im Sommer wird es manchmal sehr heiß.
4. Die Sonne scheint zwar, _____ ich glaube, es gibt heute ein Gewitter.
5. Es gibt heute keinen Regen, _____ Schnee.
6. Heute ist das Wetter angenehm, _____ morgen wird es heiß.
7. Es regnet zwar nicht, _____ ich nehme doch lieber einen Regenschirm mit.

Übung 2 Freizeitpläne

Ergänzen Sie: **und, aber, oder, denn, sondern.**

Jörg _____[1] seine Freundin Karin planen einen Ausflug _____[2] ein Picknick. Die Frage ist: wohin _____[3] wann? Heute geht es leider nicht, _____[4] es regnet, _____[5] morgen haben beide keine Zeit. Also müssen sie bis zum Wochenende warten. Sie wollen diesmal nicht mit dem Auto ins Grüne fahren, _____[6] mit ihren Fahrrädern. Das dauert zwar länger, _____[7] es macht bestimmt mehr Spaß. Sie wollen an einen See, _____[8] da können sie schwimmen gehen. Danach wollen sie ein Picknick im Wald _____[9] am See machen. Karin ist nicht für die öffentlichen (*public*) Picknickplätze, _____[10] da sind meistens zu viele Leute, Kinder _____[11] Hunde, Onkel _____[12] Tanten. Jörg lädt seinen Freund Andreas ein, _____[13] der kann leider nicht mit. Es tut ihm leid, _____[14] er muss arbeiten.

Expressing Events in the Past: The Present Perfect Tense°

das Perfekt

In German, the present perfect tense is generally used to talk about past events, although a number of common verbs (**sein, haben,** and the modals) typically use the simple past tense (**Imperfekt**) in conversation. There is essentially no difference in meaning between the two tenses.

Gestern **habe** ich Fußball **gespielt.**	*I played soccer yesterday.*
Wer **hat** denn **gewonnen?**	*Who won?*
Wir **haben** fünf zu null **verloren.**	*We lost five to zero. Then*
Dann **sind** wir in die Kneipe **gegangen.**	*we went to the pub.*

Note:

- The present perfect tense in German, as well as English, is a compound tense. It consists of two parts: the present tense of the auxiliary verb **haben** or **sein** and a past participle (**Partizip Perfekt**). (You will learn about the auxiliaries on page 221.)
- The auxiliary verb (**haben** or **sein**) and the past participle form a sentence bracket (**Satzklammer**).

		┌─── SATZKLAMMER ───┐	
Unsere Mannschaft	**hat**	fünf zu null	**verloren.**
Dann	**sind**	wir in die Kneipe	**gegangen.**

Uwe und Klaus reden über ihr Lieblingsthema: Fußball.

UWE: Hast du schon gehört? Bayern München hat gestern gegen Dynamo Dresden verloren. Null zu zwei!

KLAUS: Unglaublich! Hast du das in der Zeitung gelesen?

UWE: Ich habe es im Fernsehen gesehen.

KLAUS: Wie lange hat das Spiel gedauert?

UWE: Etwas über zwei Stunden. Dynamo Dresden hat sehr gut gespielt. Letzte Woche haben sie auch gegen Bremen gewonnen; eins zu null.

KLAUS: Ja, aber gegen den FC [Fußballclub] Nürnberg haben sie drei zu null verloren.

- Identify the past participles in the dialogue.
- What endings do these participles have?
- With what syllable do nearly all of the participles begin?
- What are the infinitives of these verbs?

German, like English, distinguishes between two types of verbs: so-called weak verbs (**schwache Verben**) and strong verbs (**starke Verben**). They form their past participles differently.

Weak Verbs

Ich habe **gehört**, Dynamo Dresden hat sehr gut **gespielt**.	*I heard that Dynamo Dresden played very well.*
Wir haben lange **gewartet**.	*We waited for a long time.*

Note:

- Weak verbs form the past participle by combining the verb stem with the prefix **ge-** and the ending **-(e)t**.
- The ending **-et** is used when the verb stem ends in **-t, -d,** or a consonant cluster such as **-gn-** or **-fn-**.

INFINITIVE	PREFIX	STEM	ENDING	PAST PARTICIPLE
hören	**ge-**	hör	**-t**	gehört
wandern	**ge-**	wander	**-t**	gewandert
warten	**ge-**	wart	**-et**	gewartet
regnen	**ge-**	regn	**-et**	geregnet

Weak verbs ending in **-ieren** form the past participle without adding a prefix, but they do add a final **-t.**

INFINITIVE	PAST PARTICIPLE
diskutieren	diskutiert
fotografieren	fotografiert

Nürnberger Bratwurstglöckl! am Dom

Reserviert

für 5 Personen

Ab[1] 20.00 Uhr

[1]starting at

Übung 3 In meiner Kindheit

Drei Leute erzählen über ihre Hobbys als Kinder. Was hat ihnen Spaß gemacht? Was stimmt, und was wissen wir nicht?

	DAS STIMMT	KEINE INFORMATION
1. Herr Harter hat gern …		
Trompete gespielt.	☐	☐
Briefmarken gesammelt.	☐	☐
viel Fernsehen geschaut.	☐	☐
2. Frau Beitz hat gern …		
mit ihrem Hund gespielt.	☐	☐
gemalt.	☐	☐
Comic-Hefte gesammelt.	☐	☐
3. Herr Huppert hat gern		
Bücher von Karl May gesammelt.	☐	☐
Cowboy gespielt.	☐	☐
im Schulorchester gespielt.	☐	☐
Fußball gespielt.	☐	☐

Übung 4 Haben Sie das als Kind gemacht?

Kreuzen Sie an, was Sie als Kind gern gemacht haben. Bilden Sie dann Sätze nach dem Muster.

BEISPIEL: Ich habe gern gemalt, aber ich habe nic mit Puppen gespielt.

Briefmarken sammeln	☐
Insekten sammeln	☐
Comic-Hefte sammeln	☐
_??_ sammeln	☐
mit Puppen (*dolls*) spielen	☐
ein Instrument spielen, z.B. Klavier oder Gitarre	☐
Fußball oder Baseball spielen	☐
Computerspiele spielen	☐
fernsehen	☐
malen	☐
Pop-Musik hören	☐
Hausarbeiten machen	☐
angeln	☐
im Internet surfen	☐

Übung 5 Im Nudelhaus

Wie haben Inge und Claudia den Abend verbracht? Setzen Sie das Partizip Perfekt ein.

Inge und Claudia haben ein gemütliches Restaurant in der Stadt _____¹ (suchen). Draußen hat es _____² (blitzen) und _____³ (donnern), ein Gewitter! Im Nudelhaus war es sehr voll. Der Kellner hat sie _____⁴ (fragen): Haben Sie einen Tisch _____⁵ (reservieren)? Sie haben ziemlich lange auf einen Platz _____⁶ (warten). Der Kellner hat die Speisekarte auf den Tisch _____⁷ (legen). Am Nebentisch haben einige Leute Karten _____⁸ (spielen). Sie haben laut _____⁹ (lachen [*to laugh*]). Das Essen hat sehr gut _____¹⁰ (schmecken). Es hat nur 15 Euro _____¹¹ (kosten). Auf dem Weg nach Hause hat es immer noch _____¹² (regnen).

Strong Verbs

| Heute Morgen **habe** ich Zeitung **gelesen.** | *This morning I read the newspaper.* |
| Dann **habe** ich einen Kaffee **getrunken.** | *Then I drank a cup of coffee.* |

Note:

- Strong verbs form the past participle by placing the prefix **ge-** before the stem of the verb and adding the ending **-en.**
- Many strong verbs show vowel and consonant changes in the past participle.

INFINITIVE	PREFIX	STEM	ENDING	PAST PARTICIPLE
lesen	**ge-**	les	**-en**	gelesen
nehmen	**ge-**	nomm	**-en**	genommen
sitzen	**ge-**	sess	**-en**	gesessen
trinken	**ge-**	trunk	**-en**	getrunken

Following are several other familiar strong verbs and their past participles. A complete list of strong and irregular verbs is in Appendix C.

INFINITIVE	PAST PARTICIPLE	INFINITIVE	PAST PARTICIPLE
essen	gegessen	schreiben	geschrieben
finden	gefunden	sehen	gesehen
geben	gegeben	sprechen	gesprochen
helfen	geholfen	stehen	gestanden
schlafen	geschlafen	tragen	getragen

Übung 6 Infinitiv und Partizip

Vervollständigen Sie die Tabelle.

	INFINITIV	PARTIZIP PERFEKT
1.	trinken	_____
2.	_____	gegessen
3.	_____	gestanden
4.	finden	_____
5.	helfen	_____
6.	_____	gesehen
7.	sprechen	_____
8.	_____	gegeben
9.	sitzen	_____

Übung 7 Wie war's im Restaurant Nudelhaus?

Setzen Sie passende Partizipien aus der Liste in **Übung 6** ein.

1. Viele Leute haben vor dem Restaurant _____ und auf einen Platz gewartet.

2. Wir konnten zuerst keinen Platz finden. Dann haben wir endlich einen Platz _____.

3. Ich habe grüne Schinkennudeln _____, und wir haben Pilsener _____.

4. Am Tisch neben uns haben Touristen aus Brasilien _____.

5. Sie haben Portugiesisch _____.

6. Sie konnten nur wenig Deutsch. Wir haben ihnen mit der Speisekarte _____.

7. Sie haben mir ihre Visitenkarte (*business card*) mit E-Mail-Adresse _____. Ich soll sie in Brasilien besuchen!

```
        NUDELHAUS
       ROTE STR. 13
      37073 GÖTTINGEN
      TEL: 0551/42263

   #0001        06-01-06
   RECHNUNG-#        35
   GAST/TISCH#     3

  2 HEFEWEIZEN      €4,00
  1 GRUENE SCHINKEN €5,50
  1 VOLLKORNNUDELN  €5,25

  BAR-TL     €14,75

  F: UEDIENIE SIE
          KELLNER 1
```

The Use of **haben** or **sein** as Auxiliary

Most verbs use **haben** as the auxiliary verb in the present perfect tense.

Unsere Mannschaft **hat** das Fußballspiel **gewonnen**.	*Our team won the soccer game.*
Die Fans **haben** auf den Straßen **getanzt**.	*The fans danced in the streets.*

Sein is used with verbs that indicate movement from one place to another (e.g., **gehen** and **fahren**).

Rudi **ist** zum Fußballplatz **gegangen**.	*Rudi went to the soccer field.*
Nach dem Spiel **ist** er nach Hause **gefahren**.	*After the game he went home.*

Other verbs that show motion from one place to another are **kommen (ist gekommen)**, **laufen (ist gelaufen)**, **fliegen (ist geflogen)** and **reiten (ist geritten)**.

Sein is also used with verbs that indicate a change of condition (e.g., **werden**).

Gestern **ist** Peter 21 **geworden**.	*Yesterday Peter turned 21.*

In the previous example, the verb **werden** expresses a change in age (**ist 21 geworden**).

Other important verbs using **sein** in the present perfect tense are **sein, bleiben**, and **passieren**.

Wo **ist** Rudi gestern **gewesen**?	*Where was Rudi yesterday?*
Wir **sind** zu Hause **geblieben**.	*We stayed home.*
Unsere Mannschaft hat verloren? Wie **ist** das **passiert**?	*Our team lost? How did that happen?*

Note:

- Verbs conjugated with **sein** in the present perfect tense will be listed in the vocabulary sections as follows: **kommen, ist gekommen**.

Übung 8 Was hast du in deiner Freizeit gemacht?

Ergänzen Sie die Sätze mit der passenden Form von **sein** oder **haben**.

1. Ich _____ nichts gemacht. Es _____ die ganze Woche geregnet.
2. Ich _____ mit Freunden ins Kino gegangen.
3. Wir _____ einen alten Film mit Charlie Chaplin im Rialto gesehen.
4. Wir _____ zu Hause geblieben und _____ Karten gespielt.
5. Meine Eltern _____ zu Besuch gekommen. Ich hatte nämlich Geburtstag.
6. Ich _____ 21 geworden. Meine Freunde _____ mir eine große Party gemacht.
7. Mein Freund und ich _____ zum Wochenende nach London geflogen.
8. Wir _____ in die Berge gefahren und _____ an einem Fluss geangelt.

Übung 9 Hin und her: Wochenende und Freizeit

Wer hat was gemacht? Arbeiten Sie zu zweit.

BEISPIEL: s1: Was hat Dagmar gemacht?
　　　　　　 s2: Sie ist ins Alte Land gefahren.

**Fremdenverkehrsverein[1]
Altes Land e. V.[2]**

[1]*Tourism Office*
[2](= eingetragener Verein) *registered association*

WER	WAS
Dagmar	
Thomas	zum Sportplatz gehen
Jürgen	
Stefanie	einen Detektivroman lesen
Susanne	
Felix und Sabine	eine Radtour machen
die Kinder	

KULTURTIPP

In ihrer Freizeit treiben viele Deutsche gern Sport; besonders beliebt sind Fußball, Rad fahren, Schwimmen und Tennis. Andere bleiben lieber zu Hause und machen Gartenarbeit, pflegen (*take care of*) ihren Wagen, spielen mit ihren Haustieren, sammeln Briefmarken, lesen oder sehen fern. Viele Deutsche haben ein Hobby, das sie in einem Verein ausüben. In vielen Städten gibt es Gesangs- und Heimatvereine sowie (*as well as*) Vereine für Schützen (*marksmen*), Amateurfunker (*ham radio operators*) und Kegler.

Radfahrer auf der Landstraße

Mixed Verbs

On pages 218 through 220 you learned about past participle formation for weak and strong verbs. A few verbs include features of both weak and strong verbs in the past participle. They are called mixed verbs. Like weak verbs, the participles of mixed verbs end in **-t**; like most strong verbs, their verb stem undergoes a change.

INFINITIVE	PAST PARTICIPLE
bringen	gebracht
kennen	gekannt
wissen	gewusst

Past Participles of Verbs with Prefixes

Many German verbs consist of a base verb, such as **rufen** or **stellen**, and a prefix, such as **an-** or **be-**, to form verbs such as **anrufen** (*to call*) and **bestellen** (*to order*). The verb **anrufen**, as you learned in **Kapitel 4**, belongs to the group of verbs that have separable prefixes.

Ich **rufe** meinen Bruder **an.**	*I am calling my brother.*

When used in the present perfect tense, separable-prefix verbs form the past participle by inserting the **ge-** prefix between the separable prefix and the verb base. These verbs may be strong, weak, or mixed.

Ich habe meinen Bruder **angerufen.**	*I called my brother.*
Ich bin heute Morgen spät **aufgewacht.**	*I got up late this morning.*

Other examples of separable-prefix verbs and their past participles include:

INFINITIVE	PAST PARTICIPLE
aufstehen	(ist) aufgestanden
ausgeben	ausgegeben
ausgehen	(ist) ausgegangen
einkaufen	eingekauft
einladen	eingeladen
zurückkommen	(ist) zurückgekommen

Other prefixed verbs, such as **bestellen** and **verbringen,** begin with prefixes that are not separable from the base, such as **be-, emp-, ent-, er-, ge-,** and **ver-.**

Hoffentlich **gewinnen** wir das Spiel.	*I hope we win the game.*
Der Gast **bestellt** eine Pizza.	*The guest orders a pizza.*
Er **verbringt** den ganzen Abend auf dem Fußballplatz.	*He spends the entire evening at the soccer field.*

A verb with an inseparable prefix forms the past participle without an additional **ge-** prefix. These verbs may be either strong, weak, or mixed.

Wir haben das Spiel **gewonnen**.	*We won the game.*
Der Gast hat eine Pizza **bestellt**.	*The guest ordered a pizza.*
Er hat den ganzen Abend auf dem Fußballplatz **verbracht**.	*He spent the entire evening at the soccer field.*

Other examples of inseparable-prefix verbs and their past participles include:

INFINITIVE	PAST PARTICIPLE
bezahlen	bezahlt
erzählen	erzählt
gefallen	gefallen
gewinnen	gewonnen
verbringen	verbracht
verlieren	verloren

Übung 10   Verbformen

Ergänzen Sie die fehlenden Verbformen.

	INFINITIV	HILFSVERB	PARTIZIP PERFEKT
1.	aufstehen	_____	aufgestanden
2.	bestellen	_____	_____
3.	einladen	hat	_____
4.	_____	ist	eingeschlafen
5.	_____	_____	gefallen
6.	_____	_____	mitgekommen
7.	_____	hat	verloren

Übung 11   Kleine Situationen

Ergänzen Sie das Partizip Perfekt.

Verloren/Gefunden

Großer, graugetigerter Kater, rotes Halsband mit Glöckchen. Wer hat ihn gesehen oder gefunden? Hört auf den Namen Charly. Finderlohn.

1. Aus der Zeitung: Großer, graugetigerter Kater, rotes Halsband mit Glöckchen ____ (verlieren). Wer hat ihn ____ oder ____ (sehen, finden)? Er hört auf den Namen Charly.

2. In den letzten Tagen ist es recht kalt ____ (werden).

3. Wir haben gestern Abend noch lange über die Probleme mit dem Studium ____ (diskutieren). Ich bin erst um drei Uhr nachts ____ (einschlafen). Und dann bin ich um sechs Uhr ____ (aufstehen).

4. Wir haben für acht Uhr einen Tisch im Nudelhaus ____ (reservieren). Wir haben alle eine Pizza ____ (bestellen).

5. A: Wo hast du deinen Freund kennen ____ (lernen)?
   B: Jemand hat ihn zu einer Party ____ (einladen). Gleich am nächsten Tag hat er mich ____ (anrufen).

6. C: Wie hat es euch im Nudelhaus ____ (gefallen)?
   D: Sehr gut. Warum bist du nicht ____ (mitkommen)?
   C: Ich habe nicht ____ (wissen), wo ihr wart.

Übung 12 Mein Wochenende

Schritt 1: Sprechen Sie mit jemand (*someone*) über Ihr Wochenende. Nennen Sie drei Aktivitäten. Folgen Sie dem Beispiel.

BEISPIEL: s1: Was hast du letztes Wochenende gemacht?
        s2: Zuerst habe ich meine Freundin angerufen.
        s1: Und dann?

Hier sind einige mögliche Aktivitäten:

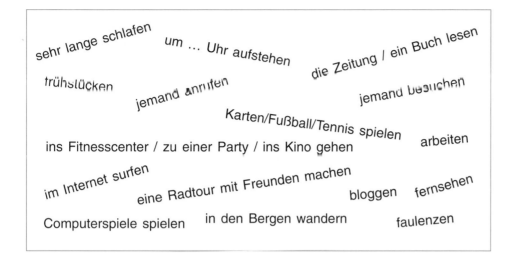

sehr lange schlafen • um … Uhr aufstehen • die Zeitung / ein Buch lesen • frühstücken • jemand anrufen • jemand besuchen • Karten/Fußball/Tennis spielen • ins Fitnesscenter / zu einer Party / ins Kino gehen • arbeiten • im Internet surfen • eine Radtour mit Freunden machen • bloggen • fernsehen • Computerspiele spielen • in den Bergen wandern • faulenzen

Schritt 2: Berichten Sie dann im Plenum.

Expressing Comparisons: The Comparative°

der Komparativ

Adjectives and adverbs have three forms: the basic form **(die Grundform)**, the comparative **(der Komparativ)**, and the superlative **(der Superlativ)**. In this chapter you will learn about the comparative.

Es wird **kühler.**	*It is getting cooler.*
Es regnet **öfter.**	*It rains more often.*
Die Tage werden **kürzer.**	*The days are getting shorter.*

In German, the comparative is formed by adding **-er** to the basic form of the adjective or adverb. (Remember that in German, adverbs are identical to adjectives.) Unlike English, German has only one way to form the comparative, whereas English has two:

cool → cool**er**

often → **more** often

Note:

- Most adjectives of one syllable with the vowel **a, o,** or **u** have an umlaut in the comparative.

groß → gr**ö**ßer

kurz → k**ü**rzer

oft → **ö**fter

warm → w**ä**rmer

- Some adjectives that end in **-er** or **-el** drop an **e** when adding the **-er**.

  teue**r** → teurer   dunke**l** → dunkler

A small number of adjectives and adverbs have irregular forms in the comparative. Here are some common ones.

gern	→ lieber	hoch	→ höher
gut	→ besser	viel	→ mehr

Ich reite **gern,** aber ich wandere **lieber.**	*I like to ride, but I prefer hiking.*
Gestern war das Wetter **gut**, aber heute ist es noch **besser.**	*Yesterday the weather was good, but today it is even better.*
Im Sommer regnet es hier nicht **viel**, aber im Winter regnet es **mehr.**	*It doesn't rain much here in the summer, but in winter it rains more.*

The adverb **immer** is used with a comparative form to express the notion of "more and more."

Das Wetter wird **immer besser.**	*The weather is getting better and better.*
Die Tage werden **immer länger.**	*The days are getting longer and longer.*
Die Sommerabende werden **immer angenehmer.**	*The summer evenings are getting more and more pleasant.*

The conjunction **als** (*than*) can link the two parts of a comparison.

Das Wetter ist besser im Süden **als** im Norden.	*The weather is better in the South than in the North.*

The particle **noch** (*even*) intensifies a comparative.

Wandern macht mir **noch** mehr Spaß als Schwimmen.	*Hiking is even more fun than swimming.*

ANALYSE

Freundlicher, bis 23 Grad

Es wird wieder sommerlicher. Der Himmel ist wechselnd bewölkt mit sonnigen Abschnitten. Die Temperatur steigt auf 23 Grad.

WETTER
Der Himmel ist heute meist nur leicht bewölkt, und nach 23/10 Angaben der Meteorologen soll es auch trocken bleiben. Mittwoch und Donnerstag wird es noch wärmer.

- Scan the excerpts from German weather reports and identify adjectives and adverbs in the comparative. What are the basic forms of those adjectives and adverbs?

- The adjectives in the comparative imply a contrast to the weather elsewhere or at some other time. State this contrast by forming phrases using **als**.

Kiel 20/10
Rostock 20/12
Hamburg 21/11
Bremen 21/11
Hannover 22/11
Berlin 23/13
Magdeburg 23/12

Heute in Norddeutschland
Im Norden Deutschlands gibt es heute einen Mix aus Sonne und Wolken. An der Nordsee ist der Himmel wolkiger.

Übung 13　Wie war das Wetter?

Ergänzen Sie die Sätze mit dem Adjektiv im Komparativ.

BEISPIEL: In Berlin war es warm, aber in Hamburg war es noch ___*wärmer*___.

1. Im Westen war es bewölkt, aber im Norden war es noch _____.
2. Heute ist es kalt und windig, aber gestern war es noch _____ und _____.
3. Am Meer war es sonnig, aber in den Bergen war es noch _____.
4. Am Nachmittag war es angenehm, aber am Abend war es noch _____.
5. Zu Weihnachten hat es viel geschneit, aber an Neujahr hat es noch _____ geschneit.
6. Das Wetter in Österreich hat mir mir gut gefallen, aber in Italien hat mir das Wetter noch _____ gefallen.
7. Auf dem Land gibt es oft Gewitter im Sommer, aber in den Bergen gibt es noch _____ Gewitter.

Übung 14　Vergleiche

Bilden Sie Sätze nach dem Muster.

BEISPIEL: in Berlin = 35 Grad Celsius / in Frankfurt = 25 Grad C (heiß) →
　　　　　In Berlin ist es heißer als in Frankfurt.

1. in Österreich = 20 Grad C / in der Schweiz = 25 Grad C (warm)
2. in den Bergen = −2 Grad C / in der Stadt = 10 Grad C (kalt)
3. die Tage im Winter / die Tage im Sommer (kurz)
4. die Tage im Sommer / die Tage im Winter (lang)
5. das Wetter im Frühling / das Wetter im Herbst (angenehm)
6. segeln / angeln (interessant)
7. das Wetter heute / das Wetter gestern (gut)
8. die Temperatur gestern / die Temperatur heute (hoch)
9. in London / in Kairo (es regnet viel)

Expressing Equality

An adjective or adverb combined with **so ... wie** (*as . . . as*) expresses equality. The phrase **nicht so ... wie** expresses inequality.

Das Wetter im Norden ist **so** schlecht **wie** im Süden.	*The weather in the North is as bad as in the South.*
Im Süden regnet es **nicht so** viel **wie** im Norden.	*It doesn't rain as much in the South as in the North.*

The adverb **genauso** (*just/exactly as*) can replace **so** to emphasize the point being made.

Österreich ist **genauso** schön **wie** die Schweiz.	*Austria is just as beautiful as Switzerland.*

Übung 15   So ist das!

Ergänzen Sie die folgenden Sätze mit **so ... wie** oder **nicht so ... wie** und einem Adjektiv aus der folgenden Liste.

> bequem, gern, groß, gut, intelligent, interessant, klein, lang, schnell, schön, teuer, viel

BEISPIEL: Wandern gefällt mir _____ Reiten. →
Wandern gefällt mir ___*so gut wie*___ Reiten.
oder Wandern gefällt mir ___*nicht so gut wie*___ Reiten.

1. Schwimmen gefällt mir _____ Rad fahren.
2. Ein Volkswagen ist _____ ein Mercedes.
3. Ich glaube, ein BMW kann _____ ein Mercedes fahren.
4. Ich bin _____ mein Freund / meine Freundin.
5. Ich finde den Ozean _____ die Berge.
6. Während der Woche schlafe ich morgens _____ am Wochenende.
7. Ich finde Politik _____ Sport.
8. Ich esse Tofu _____ Hamburger.
9. Ich höre klassische Musik _____ Popmusik.
10. Ich finde Turnschuhe _____ Wanderschuhe.

Übung 16   Was meinst du?

Arbeiten Sie zu zweit und wechseln Sie einander ab (*take turns*). Folgen Sie dem Beispiel.

BEISPIEL: Ich gehe lieber _____ als _____. (ins Kino, in die Disko, ins Theater, ...)
  s1: Ich gehe lieber ins Kino als ins Theater. Und du?
  s2: Ich gehe genauso gern ins Theater wie ins Kino.
oder Ich gehe nicht so gern ins Kino wie ins Theater.
oder Ich gehe auch lieber ins Kino als ins Theater.

1. Ich mag _____ lieber als _____. (Fotografieren, Malen, Zeichnen, ...)
2. Ich mag _____ lieber als _____. (Musik hören, Bloggen, Fernsehen, ...)
3. Ich finde _____ schöner als _____. (klassische Musik, Rapmusik, Heavymetal, ...)
4. Ich trage _____ lieber als _____. (Sandalen, Stiefel, Turnschuhe, ...)
5. _____ gefällt mir besser als _____. (Rad fahren, Schlittschuh laufen, Inlineskaten, ...)
6. Ich finde _____ interessanter als _____. (Wien, Berlin, Zürich, ...)
7. _____ gefällt mir besser als _____. (Camping, Wandern, Segeln, ...)
8. _____ schlafe ich länger als _____. (an Wochentagen, am Wochenende, montags, ...)

Sprache im Kontext

Videoclips

A. Jan, Dennis und Beatrice sprechen über ihre Freizeit. Was machen sie nicht in der Freizeit? Streichen Sie die Aktivitäten durch, die sie *nicht* machen.

1. Jan …
verbringt seine Freizeit
  im Freien
geht ins Kino
trifft Freunde
sieht fern
macht Sport

2. Dennis …
geht ins Kino
geht ins Museum
treibt Sport
trifft Freunde

3. Beatrice …
geht ins Kino
trifft gern Freunde
macht Sport
hört Musik

B. Herr Borowsky verbringt seine Freizeit ein bisschen anders. Wie verbringt er seine Freizeit?

C. Welche Sportarten treiben Jan und Dennis?

D. Wo haben diese Leute den Urlaub verbracht? Kombinieren Sie.

1. _____ Jan   **a.** in Ägypten

2. _____ Beatrice   **b.** in Wien

3. _____ Herr Borowsky   **c.** in Guatemala

4. _____ Dennis   **d.** auf den Kanarischen Inseln und in Bayern

E. Und Sie? Was machen Sie in der Freizeit? Wo haben Sie letztes Jahr Ihren Urlaub verbracht?

Lesen

Zum Thema

A. Wie viel Freizeit hat man in verschiedenen Ländern? Schauen Sie sich die Tabelle „Arbeitsfrei" an. Beantworten Sie die folgenden Fragen mit Hilfe der Tabelle.

1. Wie viele Urlaubstage haben die Deutschen im Jahr?

2. Welches Land hat mehr Urlaubstage – die Schweiz oder Österreich?

3. Wer hat mehr Freizeit – die Belgier oder die Niederländer?

4. Wie viele Urlaubstage haben die US-Amerikaner?

B. Was machen die Deutschen in ihrer Freizeit? Schauen Sie sich die Grafik auf Seite 211 an. Vergleichen Sie Ihre Freizeitbeschäftigungen mit denen der Deutschen.

- Was machen Sie gern in Ihrer Freizeit?
- Stehen Ihre Freizeitaktivitäten auf der Liste?

[1]Durchschnittlicher ... *average annual vacation*

Arbeitsfrei
Durchschnittlicher Jahresurlaub[1] für Arbeitnehmer in der Industrie

Land	Tage
Deutschland	30 Tage
Luxemburg	28
Österreich	26,5
Ungarn	26
Niederlande	25,3
Dänemark	25
Frankreich	25
Norwegen	25
Schweden	25
Tschechien	25
Großbritannien	24,4
Schweiz	24,4
Spanien	23
Griechenland	22
Portugal	22
Belgien	20
Finnland	20
Irland	20
Italien	20
Polen	20
Japan	18
USA	12

Stand 2004

Quelle: iw, BDA   © Globus   9869

C. Machen Sie eine Liste der sechs beliebtesten Freizeitaktivitäten in Ihrer Klasse. Vergleichen Sie Ihre Klasse mit den Deutschen.

1. Was ist die beliebteste Freizeitbeschäftigung in Ihrer Klasse?

2. Was steht an zweiter Stelle (*place*) für die Klasse?

3. Steht diese Aktivität auf der Liste der Deutschen?

4. Welche Unterschiede (*differences*) und Ähnlichkeiten (*similarities*) gibt es?

Auf den ersten Blick

A. Assoziationen: Woran denken Sie, wenn Sie _____ hören?

BEISPIEL: Schnee →

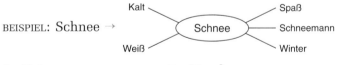

1. Reisen   **5.** Hund

2. Schwimmen   **6.** Buch

3. freundlich sein   **7.** neue Musik

4. bequeme Schuhe   **8.** Singen

B. Lesen Sie den Titel und überfliegen (*scan*) Sie den Text.

1. Was für ein Text ist das?
 a. ein Artikel aus einer Zeitung
 b. ein Gedicht (*poem*)
 c. ein Brief

2. Wie heißt der Autor? Was wissen Sie über ihn?

3. Kennen Sie andere Werke (*works*) von ihm? Wenn ja, welche?

VERGNÜGUNGEN

von Bertolt Brecht

Der erste Blick[1] aus dem Fenster am Morgen
Das wiedergefundene alte Buch
Begeisterte Gesichter[2]
Schnee, der Wechsel der Jahreszeiten
5 Die Zeitung
Der Hund
Die Dialektik
Duschen, Schwimmen
Alte Musik
10 Bequeme Schuhe
Begreifen[3]
Neue Musik
Schreiben, Pflanzen
Reisen
15 Singen
Freundlich sein.

Bertolt Brecht 1898–1956

---

[1]*glance* [2]*Begeisterte … enthusiastic faces* [3]*understanding*

Zum Text

A. Die Wörter **Duschen, Pflanzen, Reisen** können die Pluralformen sein von: **Dusche** (*shower*), **Pflanze** (*plant*), **Reise** (*trip*); oder sie können auch Verbalformen sein: **Duschen** = *taking a shower;* **Pflanzen** = *planting;* **Reisen** = *traveling.* Wie versteht Brecht diese Wörter wahrscheinlich? Als Dinge (Objekte) oder als Aktivitäten? Warum ist das wichtig?

B. Sind Brechts Vergnügungen ungewöhnlich oder ganz normal? Welche finden Sie ungewöhnlich? Warum?

C. Schreiben Sie ein Gedicht mit dem Titel „Vergnügungen". Tauschen Sie Ihr Gedicht mit dem von einem Partner / einer Partnerin aus. Lesen Sie das Gedicht Ihres Partners / Ihrer Partnerin vor.

Zu guter Letzt

Freizeitvergnügungen in der Stadt

Schreiben Sie einen Prospekt über Ihre Universitätsstadt für deutsche Touristen. Was gibt es dort alles zu unternehmen?

Schritt 1: In Gruppen zu viert schauen Sie sich **Thema 1** und **2** an und notieren Sie mindestens 10 Freizeitaktivitäten, die man in Ihrer Stadt machen kann.

BEISPIEL: wandern, segeln, …

Schritt 2: Suchen Sie Fotos aus Zeitschriften, Werbungen oder dem Internet über diese Freizeitaktivitäten und wo man diese Aktivitäten macht. Verwenden Sie sie im Prospekt. Beschreiben Sie zuerst die Plätze in je zwei bis drei Sätzen und sagen Sie, was man dort machen kann.

BEISPIEL: Nicht weit von der Uni gibt es einen Wald mit einem See. Dort kann man wandern und segeln.

Sprache im Kontext **231**

Schritt 3: Tauschen Sie Ihren Prospekt mit dem von einer anderen Gruppe aus. Die andere Gruppe soll die Orte noch weiter beschreiben und auch sagen, was man dort noch machen kann.

BEISPIEL: Der Wald heißt Huesten Woods. Viele Studenten fahren dort auch Rad.

Schritt 4: Inkorporieren Sie die Ideen der anderen Gruppe und schreiben Sie den Prospekt zu Ende.

BEISPIEL: Nicht weit von der Uni gibt es einen Wald. Er heißt Huesten Woods. Dort kann man wandern und segeln. Viele Studenten fahren dort auch Rad.

Wortschatz

Sport und Vergnügen / Sports and Leisure

angeln	to fish
bloggen	to blog
Bodybuilding machen	to do bodybuilding, weight training
der **Brief**, -e	letter
die **Briefmarke**, -n	postage stamp
faulenzen	to be lazy, lie around
die **Freizeit**	free time
der **Fußball**, ⸚e	soccer; soccer ball
Fußball spielen	to play soccer
joggen	to jog
die **Karte**, -n	card
malen	to paint
Rad fahren (fährt Rad), ist Rad gefahren	to bicycle, ride a bike
reiten, ist geritten	to ride (horseback)
sammeln	to collect
Schach spielen	to play chess
Schlittschuh laufen (läuft), ist gelaufen	to ice-skate
segeln	to sail
die **Spielkarte**, -n	playing card
der **Sport**, *pl.* **Sportarten**	sports, sport
Sport treiben, getrieben	to play sports
tauchen	to dive
Tennis spielen	to play tennis
turnen	to do gymnastics
(Zeit) verbringen, verbracht	to spend (time)
der **Verein**, -e	club, association
der **Wagen**, -	car
zeichnen	to draw

Orte / Locations

der **Berg**, -e	mountain
das **Eisstadion**, *pl.* **Eisstadien**	ice-skating rink
der **Fluss**, ⸚e	river
das **Freibad**, ⸚er	outdoor swimming pool
das **Hallenbad**, ⸚er	indoor swimming pool
das **Meer**, -e	sea, ocean
das **Schwimmbad**, ⸚er	swimming pool
der **See**, -n	lake
die **Sporthalle**, -n	sports arena
der **Sportplatz**, ⸚e	athletic field
das **Stadion**, *pl.* **Stadien**	stadium
der **Tennisplatz**, ⸚e	tennis court
die **Turnhalle**, -n	gymnasium
der **Wald**, ⸚er	forest
die **Wiese**, -n	meadow

Die Jahreszeiten / Seasons

das **Frühjahr**	spring
der **Frühling**	spring
der **Herbst**	autumn, fall
der **Sommer**	summer
der **Winter**	winter

Das Wetter / Weather

das **Gewitter**, -	thunderstorm
der **Grad**	degree(s)
35 Grad	35 degrees
der **Hagel**	hail
der **Himmel**	sky
der **Nebel**	fog
der **Regen**	rain
der **Regenschauer**, -	rain shower

der **Regenschirm**, -e	umbrella	**windig**	windy
der **Schnee**	snow	**wolkenlos**	cloudless
die **Sonne**	sun		
Die Sonne scheint.	The sun is shining.		

der Sonnenschein — sunshine
die Temperatur, -en — temperature
der Wetterbericht, -e — weather report
der Wind, -e — wind
die Wolke, -n — cloud

blitzen — to flash
Es blitzt. — There's lightning.
donnern — to thunder
Es donnert. — It's thundering.
regnen — to rain
Es regnet. — It's raining.
schneien — to snow
Es schneit. — It's snowing.

angenehm — pleasant
bewölkt — overcast, cloudy
heiß — hot
heiter — fair, bright
kalt; kälter — cold; colder
kühl — cool
kurz; kürzer — short; shorter
lang; länger — long; longer
neblig — foggy
regnerisch — rainy
schwül — muggy, humid
sonnig — sunny
stark; stärker — strong; stronger
warm; wärmer — warm; warmer

Verben / Verbs

bringen, gebracht — to bring
dauern — to last; to take
fallen (fällt), ist gefallen — to fall
fliegen, ist geflogen — to fly
passieren, ist passiert — to happen
reservieren — to reserve
verlieren, verloren — to lose

Sonstiges / Other

als — than
beliebt — popular
denn — because, for
draußen — outside
dreimal — three times
drinnen — inside
einmal — once
einmal die Woche — once a week
einmal im Monat — once a month
einmal im Jahr — once a year
früher — earlier, once, used to (*do, be, etc.*)
genauso — just/exactly as
gestern — yesterday
jeden Tag — every day
oder — or
so … wie — as . . . as
sondern — but, rather
zweimal — twice

▼ DAS KANN ICH NUN!

1. Nennen Sie drei Sportarten. Wie oft treiben Sie Sport?

2. Setzen Sie passende Wörter ein.

 a. Zum _____ braucht man ein Segelboot.
 b. Zum Reiten braucht man ein _____.
 c. Man _____ an einem Fluss oder an einem See.

3. Nennen Sie drei Freizeitaktivitäten. Was machen Sie gern in Ihrer Freizeit?

4. Wie gut können Sie das? Verwenden Sie **besser als** oder **(nicht) so gut wie** in Ihren Antworten.

 a. Schach spielen vs. Karten spielen
 b. Fahrrad fahren vs. Schlittschuh laufen
 c. singen vs. tanzen

5. Wie heißen die vier Jahreszeiten? Beschreiben Sie sie.

6. Setzen Sie eine passende Konjunktion ein.

 a. Ist es kalt _____ warm draußen? **b.** Ich bin nicht zum Sportplatz gegangen, _____ ich bin zu Hause geblieben. **c.** Mein Freund segelt gern, _____ ich reite lieber.

7. Setzen Sie die richtige Form von **haben** oder **sein** ein.

 a. Wann _____ das passiert? **b.** Wo _____ der Mann gestanden? **c.** Wann _____ seine Frau gekommen? **d.** Wann _____ sie ihn nach Hause gebracht? **e.** Wir _____ die ganze Zeit bei ihm geblieben.

8. Wie sagt man das im Perfekt?

 a. Wir gehen aus. **b.** Er spielt Fußball. **c.** Ich weiß das leider nicht. **d.** Er bestellt eine Pizza im Restaurant. **e.** Das Wetter wird besser.

Wie man fit und gesund bleibt

Rückenstraße

Muskeltraining im
Fitness-Studio

Videoclips
Gesund leben

In diesem Kapitel

- **Themen:** Health and fitness, the human body, common illnesses and health complaints, morning activities
- **Grammatik:** Subordinating conjunctions, reflexive pronouns and verbs
- **Kultur:** Health spas in Germany, doctor visits, **Apotheken** and **Drogerien,** German breakfast
- **Lesen:** „Sage mir, was du isst …" (Monika Hillemacher)

Alles klar?

A. Schauen Sie sich die Anzeige für Baden-Baden an, einen Kurort (*spa*) in Deutschland. Was kann man in Baden-Baden unternehmen (*do*)? Machen Sie eine Liste.

Hier klicken!

Weiteres zum Thema Kurorte finden Sie bei **Deutsch: Na klar!** im World-Wide-Web unter www.mhhe.com/dnk5

BEISPIEL:

SPORT	UNTERHALTUNG	GESUNDHEIT
schwimmen	ins Theater gehen	in die Sauna gehen

B. Was machen diese Leute in Baden-Baden? Kreuzen Sie an.

	HERR/FRAU LOHMANN	HERR KRANZLER	FRAU DIETMOLD
Golf	☐	☐	☐
Karten spielen	☐	☐	☐
Massage	☐	☐	☐
Mini-Golf	☐	☐	☐
Sauna	☐	☐	☐
Schwimmen	☐	☐	☐
Spazierengehen	☐	☐	☐
Tanzen	☐	☐	☐
Theater	☐	☐	☐
Thermalbad	☐	☐	☐
Tischtennis	☐	☐	☐
Trinkkur	☐	☐	☐
Wandern	☐	☐	☐

There are many health spas **(Heilbäder und Kurorte)** throughout Germany, and Germans can choose to spend several weeks at a spa after an illness or when they feel stressed from their jobs. The national health-care system **(Krankenkasse)** subsidizes such a stay to a degree if rest and recuperation **(Kur und Erholung)** are prescribed by a physician. The necessity of such treatment is evaluated on a case-by-case basis. Faced with increasing health-care costs, fewer demands for **Kur und Erholung** at health spas, and the recent trends toward **Wellness**, these resorts are having to reinvent themselves. To be sure, the traditional **Kur** is still available, but at more cost to the patient. These **Kurorte** now offer additional activities such as exercise and **Wellness** programs, family excursions, and, at some, even gambling. Some resorts now offer conference facilities so that participants can combine meetings with some type of recreation. At some health spas people go on a **Trinkkur:** at prescribed intervals they drink a glass of the healthful mineral waters for which some spas are famous.

Wörter im Kontext

Neue Wörter

die Gesundheit health
tue (tun) do
versuche (versuchen) try
die Arbeit work
meistens mostly
zu Fuß on foot
der Kräutertee herbal tea
ab und zu now and then
deshalb for that reason
rauche (rauchen) smoke
d.h. = das heißt that is
wenig little
regelmäßig regularly
besonders especially
die Luft air
mich fit halten (sich fit halten) keep fit
mich beeilen (sich beeilen) hurry up
mindestens at least
mache Urlaub (Urlaub machen) go on vacation
anstrengend strenuous
die Krankenschwester nurse
achte auf (achten auf) pay attention to
die Biolebensmittel (*pl.*) organic foods
entweder ... oder either . . . or
mich entspannen (sich entspannen) relax

THEMA 1: Fit und gesund

Was machen diese Leute, um **fit** zu bleiben?

TINA: Für meine **Gesundheit tue** ich viel. Ich esse vegetarisch, **versuche** so gut es geht, den **Stress** in meinem Leben zu reduzieren. Zur **Arbeit** gehe ich **meistens zu Fuß.** Ich trinke viel **Kräutertee** und nur selten **Alkohol,** und **ab und zu** ein Glas Wein zum Essen.

WALTER: **Fitness** ist mir sehr wichtig. **Deshalb rauche** ich nie und esse gesund, **d.h. (das heißt) wenig** Fleisch und viel Gemüse. Ich treibe **regelmäßig** Sport, **besonders** an der frischen **Luft.** Ich möchte **mich fit halten.** So, und jetzt muss ich **mich beeilen.** Ich muss ins Fitnesscenter.

ANITA: **Mindestens** zweimal im Jahr **mache** ich **Urlaub,** denn meine Arbeit ist sehr **anstrengend.** Ich bin nämlich **Krankenschwester.** Ich **achte auf** meine Gesundheit und esse nur **Biolebensmittel, entweder** direkt vom Bauernhof **oder** vom Bioladen. Ich mache jede Woche Yoga. Da kann ich **mich** richtig **entspannen.**

A. Was machen Tina, Walter und Anita für ihre Gesundheit? Kombinieren Sie!

1. Stress _____
2. regelmäßig _____
3. mit Yoga _____
4. Kräutertee _____
5. gesund _____
6. auf die Gesundheit _____
7. ab und zu _____
8. oft Urlaub _____
9. nie _____
10. Biolebensmittel _____

a. trinken
b. machen
c. Alkohol trinken
d. achten
e. rauchen
f. sich entspannen
g. reduzieren
h. essen
i. Sport treiben
j. essen

B. Tina, Walter und Anita leben gesund. Wählen Sie die richtige Antwort.

1. Wie kommt Tina zur Arbeit?
   a. zu Fuß **b.** mit dem Rad **c.** mit dem Auto
2. Wie oft trinkt Tina ein Glas Wein?
   a. nie **b.** ab und zu **c.** einmal in der Woche
3. Wie viel Fleisch isst Walter?
   a. viel **b.** wenig **c.** keins
4. Wie oft treibt Walter Sport?
   a. einmal im Monat **b.** regelmäßig **c.** nie
5. Was für Lebensmittel isst Anita?
   a. Biolebensmittel **b.** Lebensmittel vom Supermarkt
6. Wie oft macht Anita Urlaub?
   a. mindestens zweimal im Jahr **b.** einmal im Jahr **c.** nicht mehr als alle zwei Jahre
7. Wie entspannt sich Anita?
   a. Sie joggt. **b.** Sie läuft Schlittschuh. **c.** Sie macht Yoga.

Aktivität 1 Meine Fitnessroutine

Schritt 1: Was machen Sie, um fit und gesund zu bleiben? Kreuzen Sie an!

1. ☐ joggen
2. ☐ ins Fitnesscenter gehen
3. ☐ vegetarisch essen
4. ☐ meditieren
5. ☐ Urlaub machen
6. ☐ wenig Alkohol trinken
7. ☐ Stress reduzieren
8. ☐ nicht rauchen
9. ☐ mich entspannen
10. ☐ viel an die frische Luft gehen
11. ☐ viel zu Fuß gehen
12. ☐ Yoga machen
13. ☐ viel Wasser trinken
14. ☐ ??

Schritt 2: Sagen Sie nun, wie oft Sie das tun.

BEISPIEL: Ich trinke jeden Tag viel Wasser.

nie	jeden Tag
selten	mindestens/meistens einmal/zweimal die Woche
ab und zu	einmal/zweimal/dreimal im Jahr
manchmal	??
regelmäßig	

Siehe *Reflexive Pronouns and Verbs,* S. 248.

Schritt 3: Sagen Sie nun, warum Sie das tun oder nicht tun.

BEISPIELE: Ich jogge nicht. Das ist mir zu langweilig.
 Ich esse vegetarisch. Das ist gut für die Gesundheit.

macht mir (keinen) Spaß	ist zu anstrengend
ist gut/schlecht für die Gesundheit	ist (un)gesund
macht krank	reduziert Stress
kostet zu viel Geld	ist mir zu langweilig
habe keine Zeit/Lust dazu (*for that*)	??

fitness adviser ### Aktivität 2 Beim Fitnessberater°

Spielen Sie ein Gespräch zwischen einem Fitnessberater und einer Klientin. Was darf man tun? Was soll man nicht tun?

BEISPIEL: s1: Darf ich Wein trinken?
 s2: Ja, aber nicht zu viel. Trinken Sie lieber viel Wasser.
 s1: Und wie viele Stunden soll ich pro Nacht schlafen?
 s2: Mindestens sieben Stunden.

Fleisch essen	Kräutertee trinken
Vitamintabletten einnehmen	Kaffee trinken
Urlaub machen	??
Sport treiben	

body # THEMA 2: Der menschliche Körper°

Ein Telefongespräch

CHRISTOPH: Schmidt.

UTA: Hallo, Christoph? Hier ist Uta.

CHRISTOPH: Ja, grüß dich, Uta.

UTA: Nanu! Was ist denn los? Du **klingst** ja so **deprimiert**.

CHRISTOPH: Ich liege im Bett. Ich **fühle mich hundsmiserabel**.

UTA: **Was fehlt dir** denn?

CHRISTOPH: Ich habe eine **Erkältung**, vielleicht **sogar** die **Grippe**. Der Hals **tut** mir **weh**, ich kann **kaum schlucken, mir ist schlecht**. Ich habe **Fieber, Halsschmerzen, Husten** und **Schnupfen.** Ich habe auch **Kopfschmerzen** und bin so **müde** und **schlapp**. Und morgen muss ich eine Arbeit bei Professor Höhn **abgeben**.

UTA: **So ein Pech**. Warst du schon beim **Arzt?**

CHRISTOPH: Nein.

UTA: Wie lange bist du denn schon **krank?**

CHRISTOPH: Seit **fast** zwei Wochen schon.

UTA: Du bist **verrückt**! Geh doch **gleich** zum Arzt. Er kann dir sicher was* **verschreiben**.

CHRISTOPH: Aber ich kriege (*get*) wohl keinen **Termin**.

UTA: **Das macht nichts**. Geh einfach in die **Sprechstunde**.

CHRISTOPH: Na gut. Ich danke dir für den **Rat**.

UTA: **Nichts zu danken** … Ich wünsche dir **gute Besserung**!

> Ich fühle mich hundsmiserabel.

Neue Wörter

klingst (klingen) sound
deprimiert depressed
fühle mich (sich fühlen) feel
hundsmiserabel really lousy
Was fehlt dir? What's wrong with you?
die Erkältung cold
sogar even
die Grippe flu
tut weh (wehtun) hurts
kaum scarcely
schlucken swallow
mir ist schlecht I feel bad, I feel sick to my stomach
das Fieber fever
die Halsschmerzen (*pl.*) sore throat
der Husten cough
der Schnupfen runny nose, sniffles
die Kopfschmerzen (*pl.*) headache
müde tired
schlapp worn-out
abgeben drop off, give to
so ein Pech what bad luck
der Arzt doctor
krank sick
fast almost
verrückt crazy
gleich right away
verschreiben prescribe
der Termin appointment
Das macht nichts. That doesn't matter.
die Sprechstunde office hours
der Rat advice
nichts zu danken don't mention it
gute Besserung get well soon

A. Stimmt das oder stimmt das nicht?

	DAS STIMMT	DAS STIMMT NICHT
1. Uta spricht mit Christoph am Telefon.	☐	☐
2. Christoph fühlt sich heute viel besser.	☐	☐
3. Er war gestern beim Arzt.	☐	☐
4. Uta ist deprimiert.	☐	☐
5. Uta gibt Christoph Rat.	☐	☐
6. Sie bringt Christoph zum Arzt.	☐	☐

B. Was ist los mit Christoph? Ergänzen Sie!

1. Christoph klingt _____.
2. Er fühlt sich _____.
3. Er hat eine _____.
4. Der Hals _____ ihm _____.
5. Er hat auch _____, _____, _____ und _____.
6. Christoph ist seit zwei Wochen _____.

***Was,** as used here, is a shortened form of **etwas**. It occurs often in colloquial German.

Aktivität 3 Christophs Geschichte

Erzählen Sie Christophs Geschichte. Benutzen Sie die Bilder.

Aktivität 4 Im Aerobic-Kurs

Sie hören eine Aerobic-Lehrerin beim Training im Aerobic-Kurs. Nummerieren Sie alle Körperteile in der Reihenfolge von 1–10, so wie Sie sie hören. Einige Wörter auf der Liste kommen nicht im Hörtext vor.

_____ Arme	_____ Füße	_____ Knie	_____ Muskeln
_____ Bauch	_____ Hals	_____ Kopf	_____ Rücken
_____ Beine	_____ Hände	_____ Ohren	_____ Schultern
_____ Finger			

KULTURTIPP

Die Deutschen, so heißt es, sind die Arztbesuchseuropameister[1]. Niemand in Europa geht so oft und so gern zum Arzt wie die Deutschen. Elfmal pro Jahr gehen sie zum Arzt. Sechsmal tun es die Franzosen, dreimal die Schweden. 90 Prozent der Deutschen suchen mindestens einmal im Jahr einen Arzt auf. Verglichen mit den Schweizern (69 Prozent) und den Italienern (48 Prozent), steht den Deutschen die Goldmedaille zu. (Aus: *Die Zeit*)

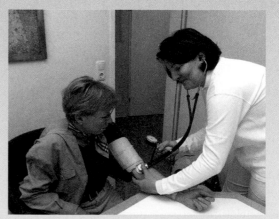

Was fehlt Ihnen?

[1]**Meister** = *champions*

Aktivität 5 Beschwerden°

Complaints

Was fehlt diesen Leuten? Was sollten sie dagegen tun? Markieren Sie Ihre
Antworten.

DIALOG 1

Leni hat:	Rückenschmerzen.	eine Erkältung	Kopfschmerzen
Doris empfiehlt:	Geh zum Arzt.	Leg dich ins Bett.	Nimm Aspirin.

DIALOG 2

Doris hat:	Kopfschmerzen	Bauchschmerzen	Fieber
Leni empfiehlt:	Geh zum Arzt.	Trink Kamillentee.	Leg dich ins Bett.

DIALOG 3

Patient hat:	keine Energie	Halsschmerzen	kann nicht schlafen
Arzt empfiehlt:	mehr Schlaf	Kur im Schwarzwald	Tabletten gegen Stress

---

SPRACHTIPP

Use the following phrase to talk about how you feel:

Ich **fühle mich** nicht wohl.	*I don't feel well.*

The person with the symptoms refers to himself or herself with a pronoun in the dative case.

Mir ist schlecht.	*I feel sick to my stomach.*
Mir ist warm/kalt.	*I feel warm/cold.*

The verb **fehlen** with the dative case is frequently used to ask "What is the matter?"

Was fehlt dir/ihm denn?	*What's the matter with you/him?*

Use the verb **wehtun** with the dative case to say that something hurts.

Die Füße **tun mir/ihm/ihr weh.**	*My/His/Her feet hurt.*

Aktivität 6 Was fehlt dir denn?

Fragen Sie Ihren Partner / Ihre Partnerin: „Was fehlt dir denn?" Antworten
Sie auf seine/ihre Beschwerden mit einem guten Rat.

BEISPIEL: s1: Ich fühle mich so schlapp.
           s2: Geh nach Hause und leg dich ins Bett.

BESCHWERDEN	RATSCHLÄGE
Ich fühle mich so schlapp.	Nimm ein paar Aspirin.
Der Hals tut mir weh.	Geh ...
Ich habe ...	in die Sauna.
Kopfschmerzen.	nach Hause.
Rückenschmerzen.	zum Arzt.
Husten.	Leg dich ins Bett.
Schnupfen.	Nimm mal Vitamin C.
eine Erkältung.	Trink heißen Tee mit Rum.
Fieber.	??
Ich kann nicht schlafen.	
Mir ist schlecht.	

EMS

EMSER
PASTILLEN[1]
Naturkraft
gegen
Erkältung

Für den Hals · jederzeit: EMSER PASTILLEN

[1]*lozenges*

Wörter im Kontext   **241**

THEMA 3: Morgenroutine

a.

b.

c.

d.

e.

f.

g.

h.

A. Was bedeuten die Wörter und Ausdrücke? Kombinieren Sie!

1. _____ sich duschen   **a.** *to shave*
2. _____ sich setzen   **b.** *to stretch*
3. _____ sich kämmen   **c.** *to brush one's teeth*
4. _____ sich strecken   **d.** *to shower*
5. _____ sich das Gesicht waschen   **e.** *to sit down*
6. _____ sich rasieren   **f.** *to comb one's hair*
7. _____ sich anziehen   **g.** *to wash one's face*
8. _____ sich die Zähne putzen   **h.** *to get dressed*

B. Was machen Herr und Frau Lustig morgens? Was passt zu welchem Bild?

1. _____ Er **rasiert sich.**
2. _____ Sie **streckt sich.**
3. _____ Sie **kämmt sich.**
4. _____ Sie **putzt sich die Zähne.**
5. _____ Er **duscht sich.**
6. _____ Er **setzt sich** an den Tisch.
7. _____ Sie **wäscht sich** das **Gesicht.**
8. _____ Er **zieht sich an.**

Aktivität 7 Meine Routine am Morgen

Was machen Sie jeden Morgen? Hier sind einige Dinge, die man morgens oft macht. In welcher Reihenfolge machen Sie alles jeden Morgen? Nummerieren Sie die Aktivitäten von 1 bis 8.

_____ Ich ziehe mich an.

_____ Ich dusche mich.

_____ Ich wasche mir das Gesicht.

_____ Ich kämme mich.

_____ Ich strecke mich.

_____ Ich rasiere mich.

_____ Ich setze mich an den Frühstückstisch.

_____ Ich putze mir die Zähne.

Aktivität 8 Hin und her: Meine Routine — deine Routine

Jeder hat eine andere Routine. Was machen diese Leute und in welcher Reihenfolge? Machen Sie es auch so?

BEISPIEL: s1: Was macht Alexander morgens?
s2: Zuerst rasiert er sich und putzt sich die Zähne. Dann kämmt er sich. Danach setzt er sich an den Tisch und frühstückt.

WER	WAS ER/SIE MORGENS MACHT
Alexander	zuerst / sich rasieren / sich die Zähne putzen dann / sich kämmen danach / sich an den Tisch setzen / frühstücken
Elke	
Tilo	zuerst / sich duschen / sich rasieren dann / sich an den Tisch setzen / frühstücken danach / sich die Zähne putzen
Kamal	
Sie	zuerst / ?? dann / ?? danach / ??
Ihr Partner / Ihre Partnerin	zuerst / ?? dann / ?? danach / ??

Grammatik im Kontext

Connecting Sentences: Subordinating Conjunctions°

Subordinating conjunctions are used to connect a main clause and a dependent clause. Four frequently used subordinating conjunctions are **dass** (*that*), **ob** (*whether, if*), **weil** (*because*), and **wenn** (*whenever, if*).

Ich hoffe, **dass** du bald gesund wirst.	*I hope that you'll get well soon.*
Weißt du, **ob** Mark krank ist?	*Do you know whether Mark is ill?*
Mark bleibt zu Hause, **weil** er eine Erkältung hat.	*Mark is staying at home because he has a cold.*
Ich gehe ins Fitnesscenter, **wenn** ich Zeit habe.	*I go to the fitness center whenever I have time.*

Note:

- In dependent clauses the conjugated verb is placed at the end.
- In the case of a separable-prefix verb, the prefix is joined with the rest of the verb.
- A comma always separates the main clause from the dependent clause.

MAIN CLAUSE	DEPENDENT CLAUSE
Er bleibt zu Hause,	weil er eine Erkältung **hat.**
Ich weiß nicht,	ob er schon zum Arzt gegangen **ist.**
Er hat gesagt,	dass er zu Hause bleiben **muss.**
Ich bin sicher,	dass er **mitkommt.**

If the dependent clause precedes the main clause, the main clause begins with the conjugated verb, followed by the subject.

DEPENDENT CLAUSE	MAIN CLAUSE
Weil Mark krank war,	**musste** er zu Hause bleiben.
Wenn wir Zeit haben,	**gehen** wir am Wochenende ins Fitnesscenter.
Ob Hans Zeit hat,	**weiß** ich nicht.

Indirect Questions

An indirect question is made up of an introductory clause and a question. Interrogative pronouns function like subordinating conjunctions in indirect questions. The conjugated verb is placed at the end.

DIRECT QUESTION	INDIRECT QUESTION
Warum kauft Herr Stierli so viel Vitamin B?	Ich weiß nicht, **warum** Herr Stierli so viel Vitamin B **kauft.**
Was hat er vor?	Ich möchte wissen, **was** er **vorhat.**

A yes/no question is introduced by the conjunction **ob** in the indirect question.

Geht er zu einer Party?	Ich möchte wissen, **ob** er zu einer Party **geht.**

Übung 1   Es geht ihm hundsmiserabel.

Suchen Sie in Spalte B passende Nebensätze für die Sätze in Spalte A. Bei manchen Sätzen gibt es mehrere richtige Antworten.

A	B
1. Tobias liegt im Bett, _____	**a.** dass er schon seit vier Tagen krank ist.
2. Inge möchte wissen, _____	**b.** wie es ihm geht.
3. Inge hofft (*hopes*), _____	**c.** weil er die Grippe hat.
4. Er sagt ihr, _____	**d.** wenn er wieder gesund ist.
5. Sie fragt ihn, _____	**e.** dass er endlich zum Arzt geht.
6. Sie besucht ihn, _____	**f.** ob er schon beim Arzt war.

Übung 2   Ein großer Erfolg°   *success*

Schauen Sie sich den Cartoon „Herr Stierli" an. Beantworten Sie die Fragen, indem Sie die Konjunktion **weil** benutzen (*use*).

1. Warum ist Herr Stierli zur Apotheke gegangen? (Er wollte Vitamin B kaufen.)
2. Warum hat er fünf Packungen Vitamin B gekauft? (Er hat mehr Energie gebraucht.)
3. Warum war Herr Stierli sehr stolz (*proud*)? (Er war sehr populär bei den Gästen auf der Party.)
4. Warum hat er so großen Erfolg? (Er hat so viel Vitamin B eingenommen.)

Übung 3 Was meinen Sie?°

BEISPIEL: s1: Obst ist die beste Nahrung (*food*).
s2: Ich bezweifle, dass Obst die beste Nahrung ist.

REDEMITTEL

Ich bezweifle, dass …

Ich glaube auch, dass …

Ich bin sicher, dass …

Essen macht Spaß *Jeder Deutsche trinkt im Leben 3060 Liter Bier*

MOZART GEGEN STRESS

1. Vitamin C ist gut gegen Erkältungen.
2. Klassische Musik ist gut gegen Stress.
3. Rauchen gefährdet (*endangers*) die Gesundheit.
4. Yoga reduziert Stress.
5. Gesund ist, was gut schmeckt.
6. Hühnersuppe ist gut gegen Erkältungen.
7. Bier macht dick.
8. Vegetarisches Essen ist ideal.
9. Zu viel Zucker macht aggressiv.
10. Knoblauch (*garlic*) hilft gegen Vampire.

Übung 4 Wie gesundheitsbewusst° sind Sie?

Fragen Sie einen Partner / eine Partnerin, was er/sie für Fitness und die Gesundheit tut, und warum.

BEISPIEL: s1: Gehst du regelmäßig ins Fitnesscenter?
s2: Nein.
s1: Warum nicht?
s2: Weil ich das langweilig finde.

S1: FRAGEN	S2: ANTWORTEN
vegetarisch essen	finde das langweilig
Vitamintabletten einnehmen	kostet zu viel
zu Fuß zur Arbeit / zur Uni gehen	mag ich (nicht)
Kräutertee / Kaffee / viel Wasser trinken	reduziert Stress
	macht mir (viel/keinen) Spaß
rauchen	habe keine Zeit dazu
Yoga machen	ist sehr gesund/ungesund
regelmäßig ins Fitnesscenter gehen	
Biolebensmittel kaufen	
auf Kalorien achten	

KULTURTIPP

In deutschsprachigen Ländern kauft man Medikamente, sogar Aspirin, in der **Apotheke**. Vitamine, pflanzliche Heilmittel (z.B. Baldrian), Zahnpasta, Seife und Kosmetikartikel kauft man in der **Drogerie** oder auch im Supermarkt.

Medikamente gibt es in der Apotheke.

Übung 5 Das mache ich, wenn …

Sagen Sie, wann Sie das machen.

BEISPIEL: Ich gehe zum Arzt, wenn ich krank bin.

Ich gehe zum Arzt, …	Ich brauche Zahnpasta.
zum Zahnarzt, …	Ich habe zu viel gegessen.
in die Sauna, …	Ich brauche Aspirin.
in die Drogerie, …	Ich fühle mich hundsmiserabel.
in die Apotheke, …	Ich habe die Grippe.
Ich bleibe im Bett, …	Ich fühle mich schlapp.
Ich nehme viel Vitamin C ein, …	Ich habe eine Erkältung.
Ich esse Hühnersuppe, …	Ich bin krank.
Ich trinke Kräutertee, …	Ich habe Zahnschmerzen.
	??

Übung 6 Was tun Sie gewöhnlich?

Sagen Sie, was Sie in diesen Situationen machen.

BEISPIEL: Wenn ich eine Erkältung habe, trinke ich viel Kräutertee.

Wenn ich eine Erkältung habe,	im Bett bleiben
Wenn ich nicht einschlafen kann,	Kräutertee trinken
Wenn ich gestresst bin,	heiße Milch trinken
Wenn ich mich schlapp fühle,	Rotwein mit Rum trinken
Wenn ich mich hundsmiserabel fühle,	in die Sauna gehen
	viel Vitamin C einnehmen
	Hühnersuppe essen
	ein Buch lesen
	meditieren
	Musik hören
	??

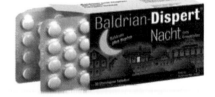

Übung 7 Ich muss es mir überlegen°.

think it over

Stefans Freunde wollen mit ihm Bungeejumping gehen. Stefan ist aber sehr skeptisch, weil er das noch nie gemacht hat. Was will er genau wissen?

BEISPIEL: Wo kann man das lernen? →
Er will wissen, wo man das lernen kann.

Er will wissen, …

1. Wo kann man das denn tun?
2. Wie gefährlich (*dangerous*) ist das eigentlich?
3. Warum muss es ausgerechnet Bungeejumping sein?
4. Was für Kleidung muss man dabei tragen?
5. Muss man nicht zuerst ein Training machen?
6. Wer geht sonst noch mit?
7. Wer hat diese verrückte Idee gehabt?

Reflexive Pronouns and Verbs°

Wander-Vögel

informieren sich
jeden Samstag im
REISE-JOURNAL
der Rheinischen Post

When the subject and pronoun object of a sentence refer to the same person, the object is called a reflexive pronoun.

Wir informieren **uns** über Fitnesscenter.	*We're gathering information about fitness centers.*
Die Studenten informieren **sich** über die Kosten.	*The students are informing themselves about the costs.*
Informieren **Sie sich** bitte zuerst über die Kosten.	*Please get informed first about the costs.*

Note:

- The reflexive pronoun comes after the conjugated verb.

  Christoph fühlt **sich** nicht wohl.

- It follows pronoun subjects in questions and the formal imperative.

  Fühlst du **dich** nicht wohl?
  Informieren Sie **sich** zuerst!

- Reflexive pronouns are identical to personal pronouns except for the third-person forms and the formal **Sie**-forms, all of which are **sich.**

REFLEXIVE PRONOUNS					
ACCUSATIVE	DATIVE		ACCUSATIVE	DATIVE	
mich	mir	*myself*	uns	uns	*ourselves*
dich	dir	*yourself*	euch	euch	*yourselves*
sich	sich	*yourself (formal)*	sich	sich	*yourselves (formal)*
sich	sich	*himself/herself*	sich	sich	*themselves*

Verbs with Accusative Reflexive Pronouns

German uses reflexive pronouns much more extensively than English. Some verbs are always used with an accusative reflexive pronoun, for example, **sich erkälten** (*to catch cold*). The English equivalent of many such verbs has no reflexive pronoun at all.

Er hat **sich erkältet.**	*He caught a cold.*
Wir müssen **uns beeilen.**	*We have to hurry.*

Other German verbs can be used with or without a reflexive pronoun, depending on the desired meaning. The reflexive use of such verbs is often expressed in English with a different verb altogether.

Sie **setzt** das Kind auf das Sofa.	Sie **setzt sich** auf das Sofa.
*She **puts** the child on the sofa.*	*She **sits** down on the sofa.*
Ich **lege** das Buch auf den Tisch	Ich **lege mich** ins Bett.
*I **lay** the book on the table.*	*I **lie** down on the bed.*

Infinitive: **sich setzen** (*to sit down*)	
ich setze **mich**	wir setzen **uns**
du setzt **dich**	ihr setzt **euch**
er sie } setzt **sich** es	sie setzen **sich**
Sie setzen **sich**	

Verbs that are *always* used with an accusative reflexive pronoun include the following:

sich ausruhen	to rest
sich beeilen	to hurry
sich entspannen	to relax
sich erholen	to recuperate
sich erkälten	to catch cold

Verbs that are *typically* used with an accusative reflexive pronoun include the following:

sich (hin)legen	to lie down
sich (hin)setzen	to sit down
sich informieren (über)	to inform oneself (about)
sich (wohl) fühlen	to feel (well)

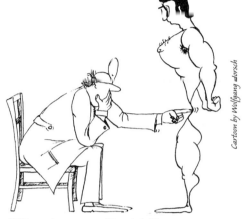

Cartoon by Wolfgang Horsch

„Bitte entspannen Sie sich!"

ANALYSE

Schauen Sie sich den Cartoon an.

- Lesen Sie, was Wurzel denkt, und identifizieren Sie die Sätze mit reflexiven Verben.
- Wie fühlt sich Wurzel heute?
- Fühlt er sich gewöhnlich so gut? Wie oft hat er sich schon so gefühlt?
- Warum fühlt er sich am Ende ganz deprimiert?

[1]unusual
[2]sign

Übung 8 Beim Arzt

Sie hören eine Besprechung zwischen Herrn Schneider und seinem Arzt. Markieren Sie die richtigen Antworten auf die Fragen.

1. Warum hat Herr Schneider einen Termin beim Arzt?
   a. Er hat einen chronischen Schluckauf (*hiccups*).
   b. Er hat sich beim Fitnesstraining verletzt.
   c. Er fühlt sich so schlapp.

2. Was ist die Ursache (*cause*) seines Problems?
   a. Seine Arbeit bringt viel Stress mit sich.
   b. Er sitzt den ganzen Tag am Schreibtisch.
   c. Seine Arbeit ist so langweilig.

¹*each time*

3. Was empfiehlt ihm der Arzt?
   a. Er soll sich eine andere Arbeit suchen.
   b. Er soll sich im Schwarzwald vom Stress erholen.
   c. Er soll Sport treiben.

4. Wie reagiert Herr Schneider auf diese Vorschläge?
   a. Er ist sehr enthusiastisch.
   b. Er hat keine Zeit für eine Kur im Schwarzwald.
   c. Er interessiert sich nicht für Sport.

5. Was verschreibt ihm der Arzt?
   a. einen täglichen Spaziergang
   b. regelmäßig meditieren
   c. Vitamintabletten

6. Warum meint der Arzt, dass Herr Schneider mit seinen Nerven am Ende ist?
   a. Er hat einen Schluckauf und weiß es nicht.
   b. Er entspannt sich oft.
   c. Er redet zu viel und zu schnell.

Verbs with Reflexive Pronouns in the Accusative or Dative

A number of German verbs may be used with a reflexive pronoun in either the accusative or the dative case. They include:

sich anziehen	*to get dressed*
sich kämmen	*to comb one's hair*
sich verletzen	*to injure oneself*
sich waschen	*to wash oneself*

REFLEXIVE PRONOUN IN ACCUSATIVE	REFLEXIVE PRONOUN IN DATIVE
Ich ziehe **mich** an.	Ich ziehe **mir** die Jacke an.
I get dressed.	*I put my jacket on.*
Ich wasche **mich**.	Ich wasche **mir** die Hände.
I wash myself.	*I wash my hands.*
Du hast **dich** verletzt.	Du hast **dir** den Fuß verletzt.
You've injured yourself.	*You've injured your foot.*
Ich kämme **mich**.	Ich kämme **mir** die Haare.
I'm combing my hair.	*I'm combing my hair.*

Note:

- The reflexive pronoun functions as the indirect object in the dative case if the sentence also has a direct object in the accusative—**die Jacke, die Hände, den Fuß,** and **die Haare** in the examples above.

- For the verb **sich kämmen** the meaning is the same whether an accusative reflexive is used or a dative reflexive with the direct object **die Haare.**

- The expression **sich die Zähne putzen** is used only with the dative reflexive pronoun, to mean *to brush one's teeth.*

  Ich putze **mir** die Zähne.   *I'm brushing my teeth.*

Übung 9   Morgenroutine

Morgens geht es bei der Familie Kunze immer recht hektisch zu. Ergänzen Sie die fehlenden Reflexivpronomen.

Herr Kunze duscht _____[1] zuerst. Dann rasiert er _____.[2] Seine Frau ruft: „Bitte, beeil _____,[3] ich muss _____[4] auch noch duschen."
   Cornelia, die siebzehnjährige Tochter, erklärt: „Ich glaube, ich habe _____[5] erkältet. Ich fühle _____[6] so schlapp. Ich lege _____[7] wieder hin." Frau Kunze zu Cornelia: „Zieh _____[8] bitte sofort an! Du fühlst _____[9] so schlapp, weil du so spät ins Bett gegangen bist." Cornelia: „Ich ziehe _____[10] ja schon an."
   Frau Kunze zu Thomas, dem siebenjährigen Sohn: „Es ist schon halb acht, und du musst _____[11] noch kämmen. Hast du _____[12] überhaupt schon gewaschen? Und hast du _____[13] auch die Zähne geputzt?"
   Sabine, die zwölfjährige Tochter, duscht _____[14] schon seit fünfzehn Minuten.
   Herr und Frau Kunze setzen _____[15] endlich an den Frühstückstisch. Herr Kunze zu seiner Frau: „Wir müssen _____[16] beeilen. Wo sind die Kinder?" Er ruft ungeduldig: „Könnt ihr _____[17] nicht ein bisschen beeilen? Es ist schon acht Uhr."
   So ist es jeden Morgen: Alle müssen _____[18] beeilen.

Übung 10   Ratschläge°   *Advice*

Was kann man Ihnen in diesen Situationen raten?

BEISPIEL: s1: Ich habe die Grippe.
          s2: Leg dich ins Bett.
          oder Du musst dich ins Bett legen.

1. Sie haben die Grippe.
2. Sie haben sich erkältet.
3. Sie fühlen sich hundsmiserabel.
4. Sie haben den ganzen Tag in der Bibliothek verbracht.
5. Sie müssen in einer Minute an der Bushaltestelle sein.
6. Sie haben sich die große Zehe verletzt.

sich beeilen
sich gut erholen
sich ins Bett legen
sich entspannen
sich (ins Café) setzen
sich wärmer anziehen
sich ausruhen
??

Trimm Dich am Feierabend

Übung 11 Wie oft machen Sie das?

Fragen Sie jemand, wie oft er/sie die folgenden Dinge macht.

BEISPIEL: sich die Zähne putzen →
  s1: Putzt du dir jeden Tag die Zähne?
  s2: Natürlich putze ich mir jeden Tag die Zähne.

sich die Zähne putzen	nie
sich die Haare kämmen	ab und zu
sich rasieren	oft
sich die Haare waschen	jeden Tag/Morgen/Abend
sich duschen	einmal/zweimal die Woche

Expressing Reciprocity

A reflexive pronoun is used to express reciprocity.

Martina und Jörg **lieben sich.**	*Martina and Jörg love each other.*
Sie **treffen sich** im Park.	*They meet (each other) in the park.*
Sie **kennen sich** seit zwei Wochen.	*They have known each other for two weeks.*
Sie **rufen sich** oft an.	*They call each other frequently.*

Übung 12 Der neue Freund

Martina erzählt ihrer Freundin Katrin über ihren neuen Freund Jörg. Benutzen Sie die Verben unten in einem kleinen Bericht.

Hier ist der Anfang:
Wir haben uns vor zwei Wochen kennen gelernt.

1. sich kennen lernen (wo)
2. sich anrufen (wie oft)
3. sich treffen (wo, wie oft)
4. sich sehr gut verstehen
5. sich lieben

Sprache im Kontext

Videoclips

A. Im Interview erklären diese Leute, warum sie ihre Lebensmittel im Bioladen kaufen. Verbinden (*Connect*) Sie die Person mit dem Grund (*reason*).

1. Frau Simon
2. Maria
3. Peter

Der Käse aus dem Bioladen schmeckt besser als Käse aus einem Supermarkt.

Bauern gebrauchen keine Chemikalien für die Bioprodukte.

Biosäfte sind gesünder als die herkömmlichen Säfte.

B. Und Sie? Kaufen Sie auch im Bioladen ein? Warum? (Warum nicht?)

C. Welche Symptome haben diese Leute, wenn sie krank sind? Markieren Sie Oliver und/oder Maria.

OLIVER   MARIA

☐   ☐   hat oft eine Erkältung
☐   ☐   hat Halsschmerzen
☐   ☐   hat Fieber und Husten
☐   ☐   hat Schnupfen
☐   ☐   hat manchmal die Grippe

D. Welche Symptome haben Sie, wenn Sie krank sind?

E. Und was machen diese Leute, wenn sie krank sind?

1. Oliver badet heiß, schwitzt (*sweats*), _____ sich ins Bett, _____ viel und trinkt _____.

2. Maria legt sich auf die _____, trinkt Tee mit Honig und versucht, abzuschalten (*switch off*).

F. Was machen Sie, wenn Sie krank sind?

Lesen

Zum Thema

A. Wie gesund essen Sie? Was betrifft Sie? Kreuzen Sie an.

1. Gesund essen ist mir wichtig. ☐
2. Ich esse regelmäßig drei Mahlzeiten am Tag. ☐
3. Ich habe nie Zeit zum Frühstücken. ☐
4. Ich habe oft keine Zeit zum Essen oder esse sehr schnell. ☐
5. Ich esse oft vor dem Fernseher. ☐
6. Ich esse gern und oft Fastfood. ☐
7. Ich esse möglichst viele Bioprodukte. ☐
8. Ich bin Vegetarier/Vegetarierin. ☐
9. Ich möchte abnehmen (*lose weight*). ☐
10. Ich möchte zunehmen (*gain weight*). ☐
11. Ich esse sehr gesund. ☐

B. Was sind Ihre Essgewohnheiten (*eating habits*)? Füllen Sie den Fragebogen aus.

Essen Sie gesund?

Wie oft essen bzw. trinken Sie …	täglich	mehrmals pro Woche	selten	nie
Getreideprodukte (Vollkornbrot, Weißbrot, Cerealien, Reis, Pasta usw.)	☐	☐	☐	☐
frisches Obst und Gemüse, Fruchtsaft ohne Zucker	☐	☐	☐	☐
Milchprodukte (Vollmilch, Magermilch, Quark, Joghurt, Käse usw.)	☐	☐	☐	☐
Wurst, Schinken, Speck, Aufschnitt	☐	☐	☐	☐
Fleisch (Rindfleisch, Schweinefleisch usw.)	☐	☐	☐	☐
Geflügel	☐	☐	☐	☐
Fisch, Meeresfrüchte	☐	☐	☐	☐
Butter	☐	☐	☐	☐
Süßigkeiten	☐	☐	☐	☐
Cola, Limonade	☐	☐	☐	☐
Bier, Wein, Alkohol	☐	☐	☐	☐
Kaffee, Tee	☐	☐	☐	☐

C. Formulieren Sie nun mit Hilfe der Aussagen in **A** und dem Fragebogen etwas über Ihre Essgewohnheiten.

BEISPIEL: Gesund essen ist mir wichtig. Ich esse nicht sehr oft Fastfood. Fleisch esse ich selten, aber ich esse täglich viel Gemüse und frisches Obst.

D. Vergleichen Sie Ihre Essgewohnheiten untereinander in kleinen Gruppen. Was haben Sie erfahren? Berichten Sie dann im Plenum darüber.

BEISPIEL: Stephanie isst viel Obst und Gemüse, aber Robert isst gesünder als sie. Er isst nie Fastfood und wenig Fleisch.

> ## KULTURTIPP
>
> Auf dem deutschen Frühstückstisch findet man traditionell Brot und Brötchen mit Butter, Marmelade, Honig und Käse, eventuell auch Aufschnitt und ein gekochtes Ei. Cerealien wie Müsli gehören auch zum Frühstück. Zum Trinken gibt es Kaffee oder Tee und Fruchtsaft.

E. Was essen und trinken Sie gewöhnlich zum Frühstück? Kreuzen Sie an.

TRINKEN		ESSEN	
Kaffee	☐	Müsli	☐
Tee	☐	Cornflakes, Cerealien	☐
Milch	☐	Brot, Brötchen oder Toast	☐
Saft	☐	Pfannkuchen	☐
Wasser	☐	Eier	☐
Cola	☐	Speck, Schinken	☐
_____	☐	Obst	☐
		_____	☐

Auf den ersten Blick

A. Schauen Sie sich den Titel, die Untertitel und die Bilder im Text **Sage mir, was du isst …** an. Was ist das Thema?

B. Schauen Sie sich die Bilder der Frühstückstypen und die Untertitel jetzt etwas genauer an. Können Sie sich mit einem dieser Typen identifizieren? Finden Sie einen besonders sympathisch?

C. Was bedeuten die fettgedruckten (*boldfaced*) Ausdrücke?

1. „Sage mir, was du frühstückst und ich sage dir, wer du bist", **behauptet** Professor Gebert.
   a. sagt
   b. fragt
   c. wiederholt

2. Am Wochenende **lassen** Studenten **das Frühstück** besonders gerne **unter den Tisch fallen.**
   a. (Die Studenten) fallen unter den Tisch.
   b. (Die Studenten) essen kein Frühstück.
   c. Das Frühstück fällt unter den Tisch.

3. Der Müsli-Raspler **macht sich viele Gedanken über das Essen.**
   a. denkt viel über das Essen nach
   b. hat kein Interesse am Essen
   c. arbeitet beim Essen

4. Für den Müsli-Raspler sind Studium und Job eher **Nebensache.**
   a. sehr wichtig   **b.** gleich wichtig   **c.** nicht sehr wichtig

5. Der Guck-zurück-Typ **verschlingt wahllos alles,** was er im Kühlschrank findet.
   a. kontrolliert alles   **b.** isst nicht alles   **c.** isst alles

6. Der Beifahrersitz-Frühstücker **kann sich** bei der Diplomarbeit (*thesis*) **nicht festlegen.**
   a. kann (die Diplomarbeit) nicht verstehen
   b. kann sich nicht engagieren
   c. interessiert sich nicht dafür

7. Der Espresso-Mann **stürzt** seinen morgendlichen **Kaffee hinunter.**
   a. lässt den Kaffee fallen
   b. kocht den Kaffee
   c. trinkt den Kaffee sehr schnell

SAGE MIR, WAS DU ISST ...
Was Das Frühstück Über Den Charakter Verrät

von Monika Hillemacher

Haben Sie schon wieder mal keine Zeit gehabt? Typisch! Nur etwa 60 Prozent der Studenten essen morgens Frühstück. Dabei kann man Uni-Stress viel besser mit einem Frühstück im Bauch verkraften°.   *cope with*

Essen und trinken am Morgen kann jeder. Ernährungsexperte
5 Gerhard Jahreis: „Jeder Mensch hat seinen ganz individuellen Rhythmus. Wichtig ist nicht, wann jemand frühstückt, sondern nur, dass und was er frühstückt."

Auf den Fitness-Speiseplan gehören Milch und Milchprodukte wie Trinkmilch, Joghurt und Käse, Müsli, frisches Obst, Vollkornbrot oder
10 -brötchen und ausreichend Getränke wie Kaffee, Tee, Saft oder Wasser. Käse, Quark° und Joghurt sind wahre Kraftpakete°. Und wer oft   *fresh yogurt cheese / power packs*
Vollmilch, Cerealien mit Milch oder Joghurtvarianten auf dem Tisch hat, bleibt schlanker. Frische Produkte sind besser als Multivitaminsaft oder Mineralstofftabletten.
15 Am Wochenende lassen Studenten das Frühstück besonders gerne unter den Tisch fallen. Es gibt dann manchmal einen Brunch mit Freunden und Familie.

„Sage mir, was du frühstückst und ich sage dir,
wer du bist", behauptet Professor Gebert von der
20 Universität Münster: „Der Charakter bestimmt
das Frühstück mit." Der Psychologe und
Soziologe fragt Studenten regelmäßig nach ihren
Frühstücksgewohnheiten. Allerdings schaut er in
erster Linie Männern auf den Teller, weil sie –
anders als ihre Kommilitoninnen° – „Gewohn-   *fellow (female) students*
heitsmenschen° und somit berechenbarer° sind."   *creatures of habit / more predictable*
Das Resultat sind Professor Geberts (nicht ganz
ernst gemeinte) Frühstückstypenklassen.

Der **Marmeladen-Mann** ist der Schwarm°   *heartthrob*
30 aller Kommilitoninnen: Seine Vorliebe für
Erdbeermarmelade lässt ihn auf den ersten

Der Marmeladen-Mann

Blick etwas langweilig erscheinen. Einmal erobert°, bleibt er seiner Herzensdame jedoch genau so treu wie seiner Lieblingsmarmelade.

35   Der **Müsli-Raspler**° startet mit frisch gepresstem O-Saft, biologisch – logisch. Macht sich viele Gedanken über das Essen, die Umwelt°, das Leben im Allgemeinen, grübelt° viel über dies und das. Studium und Job eher Nebensache. Er verliert sich
40 oft in Luftschlössern°.

Der Müsli-Raspler

Der **Beifahrersitz-Frühstücker**° isst und trinkt im Auto, in der Bahn, im Bus, auf dem
45 Rad, im Laufschritt. Diese Spezies macht vieles schnell nebeneinander°, fühlt sich spontan. Spätestens im Examen drohen dann Probleme. Dieser Typ kann sich bei der Diplomarbeit nicht festlegen. Oft schiebt
50 er die Prüfung hinaus°.

Der Beifahrersitz-Frühstücker

Der **Guck-zurück-Typ**° verschlingt wahllos alles, was er im Kühlschrank findet. Professor Gebert nennt ihn ein Spiegelbild° der
55 modernen „Spontan- und Spaß-Gesellschaft°." Nicht einmal für den Kauf von Brot und Butter haben „solche Chaoten° einen
60 Plan." Geschweige denn° für ihr restliches Leben.
    Der **Espresso-Mann** stürzt seinen morgendlichen Kaffee hinunter. Symbol für ein
65 „Leben auf der Überholspur°. Er will alles erleben°. Schnell. Sofort. Langweilig ist es nie, dazu ist sein Leben viel zu kurz."

Der Espresso-Mann

Der Guck-zurück-Typ

Quelle: Monika Hillemacher; adaptiert aus: „Sage mir, was du isst …", UNICUM, April 2005. Illustrationen: © Sabine Kühn, www.sabinekuehn.de.

Margin glossary:
- conquered
- cruncher
- environment
- ponders
- castles in the sky
- multitasking breakfaster
- at the same time
- schiebt … hinaus *postpones*
- take-my-chances type
- reflection
- society
- scatterbrains
- Geschweige … *let alone*
- fast lane / experience

Zum Text

A. Überfliegen Sie den Text bis Zeile 28 und unterstreichen Sie Schlüsselworte (*key words*) in jedem Absatz (*paragraph*), ohne Hilfe eines Wörterbuches. Listen Sie dann mit Hilfe der Schlüsselworte die wichtigen Informationen in jedem Absatz auf und formulieren Sie für jeden Absatz einen Satz, der diese Informationen zusammenfasst (*summarizes*).

B. Lesen Sie nun die humorvollen, „nicht ganz ernst gemeinten" (*not entirely serious*) Beschreibungen der Frühstückstypen etwas genauer. Welche Qualitäten sehen Sie als positiv, welche als negativ?

	POSITIV	NEGATIV
Marmeladen-Mann	_____	_____
Müsli-Raspler	_____	_____
Beifahrersitz-Frühstücker	_____	_____
Guck-zurück-Typ	_____	_____
Espresso-Mann	_____	_____

C. Warum hat Professor Gebert von der Uni in Münster in erster Linie nur Männer nach ihren Frühstücksgewohnheiten befragt?

D. Frühstückstypen in der Klasse

1. Welcher Frühstückstyp sind Sie? Schreiben Sie zwei oder drei Sätze über Ihre Frühstücksgewohnheiten und berichten Sie im Plenum.

BEISPIEL: s1: Ich bin eine Marmeladen-Frau! Ich esse jeden Tag Frühstück! Ich esse aber nur Orangenmarmelade.

s2: Freitags bin ich ein Espresso-Mann und Montags ein Beifahrersitz-Frühstücker. Dienstags, mittwochs und donnerstags schlafe ich lange und esse kein Frühstück.

2. Machen Sie nun eine Liste aller Frühstückstypen in Ihrer Klasse. Welcher Typ ist besonders populär? Haben Sie noch andere Typen in der Klasse, die im Text nicht vorgekommen (*appeared*) sind?

E. Ihre Meinung Professor Gebert behauptet: „Sage mir, was du frühstückst und ich sage dir, wer du bist. Der Charakter bestimmt das Frühstück mit." Stimmt das? Arbeiten Sie zu zweit. Suchen Sie ein oder zwei Argumente für oder gegen diese Behauptung. Was spricht für diese Kategorien? Was spricht gegen diese Kategorien? (Das muss auch nicht ganz ernst gemeint sein!)

BEISPIEL: Ich bin meistens eine Marmeladen-Frau (Orangenmarmelade, bitte!), aber manchmal esse ich, was der Müsli-Raspler isst. Ich bin aber wirklich keine Chaotin! Nicht alles stimmt für alle Leute.

Zu guter Letzt

Ein idealer Fitnessplan

Machen Sie einen idealen Fitnessplan für sich.

Schritt 1: Schreiben Sie eine Liste mit Fitnessaktivitäten, die Sie während der letzten Woche gemacht haben. Analysieren Sie die Liste:

- Sind Sie viel zu Fuß gegangen?
- Haben Sie Sport getrieben?
- Haben Sie sich zu wenig entspannt?
- Was sehen Sie als positiv, was als negativ?

Schreiben Sie nun eine Liste mit allem, was Sie während der letzten Woche gegessen haben. Analysieren Sie die Liste:

- Haben Sie gesund gegessen?
- Haben Sie zu viel Fastfood gegessen?

Schritt 2: Möchten Sie mehr für Ihre Gesundheit tun? Was ist der ideale Fitnessplan für Sie? Machen Sie nun mit Hilfe der Informationen, die Sie in **Schritt 1** gesammelt haben, einen idealen Fitnessplan für sich.

BEISPIEL: MEIN IDEALER FITNESSPLAN

SPORT TREIBEN	ESSEN UND TRINKEN	SONSTIGES
dreimal die Woche joggen	mehr Gemüse essen	weniger Fernsehen
_____	_____	_____
_____	_____	_____
_____	_____	_____

Hier klicken!

Weiteres zum Thema Gesundheit finden Sie bei **Deutsch: Na klar!** im World-Wide-Web unter www.mhhe.com/dnk5.

Schritt 3: Tauschen Sie Ihre Listen und Fitnessplan mit einem Partner / einer Partnerin aus. Lesen Sie die Fitnesspläne und machen Sie dann einander einige Vorschläge (*suggestions*). Sie können sie entweder annehmen (*accept*) oder ablehnen (*reject*).

BEISPIEL: Enstpanne dich öfter und geh zu Fuß zur Uni.

Schritt 4: Revidieren (*revise*) Sie nun Ihren Fitnessplan und machen Sie eventuell Korrekturen oder Änderungen (*changes*).

Wortschatz

Körperteile — Parts of the Body

der **Arm,** -e	arm
das **Auge,** -n	eye
der **Bauch,** ¨e	stomach, belly
das **Bein,** -e	leg
die **Brust,** ¨e	chest; breast
der **Ell(en)bogen,** -	elbow
der **Finger,** -	finger
der **Fuß,** ¨e	foot
das **Gesicht,** -er	face
das **Haar,** -e	hair
der **Hals,** ¨e	throat, neck
die **Hand,** ¨e	hand
das **Kinn,** -e	chin
das **Knie,** -	knee
der **Kopf,** ¨e	head
der **Mund,** ¨er	mouth
der **Muskel,** -n	muscle
die **Nase,** -n	nose
das **Ohr,** -en	ear
der **Rücken,** -	back
die **Schulter,** -n	shoulder
die **Zehe,** -n	toe

Gesundheit und Fitness — Health and Fitness

der **Alkohol**	alcohol
die **Arbeit,** -en	work; assignment; paper
der **Arzt,** ¨e / die **Ärztin,** -nen	physician, doctor
die **Biolebensmittel** (*pl.*)	organic foods
die **Erkältung,** -en	cold
das **Fieber**	fever
die **Fitness**	fitness
die **Gesundheit**	health
die **Grippe**	flu
der **Husten**	coughing, cough
der **Krankenpfleger,** / die **Krankenschwester,** -n	nurse
der **Kräutertee**	herbal tea
die **Luft,** ¨e	air
der **Rat**	advice
die **Schmerzen** (*pl.*)	pains
die **Halsschmerzen**	sore throat
die **Kopfschmerzen**	headache
der **Schnupfen**	nasal congestion; head cold
die **Sprechstunde,** -n	office hours
der **Stress**	stress
der **Termin,** -e	appointment

Verben — Verbs

ab•geben (gibt ab), abgegeben	to drop off, give to
achten auf (+ *acc.*)	to pay attention to
sich an•ziehen, angezogen	to get dressed
sich aus•ziehen, ausgezogen	to get undressed
sich beeilen	to hurry up
sich duschen	to shower
sich entspannen	to relax
sich erholen	to get well, recover

sich erkälten	to catch a cold
sich fit halten (hält), gehalten	to keep fit, in shape
sich (hin•)legen	to lie down
sich (hin•)setzen	to sit down
sich informieren (über)	to inform oneself (about)
sich kämmen	to comb (one's hair)
sich rasieren	to shave
rauchen	to smoke
schlucken	to swallow
sich strecken	to stretch
tun, getan	to do
sich verletzen	to injure oneself
verschreiben, verschrieben	to prescribe
versuchen	to try, attempt
sich waschen (wäscht), gewaschen	to wash oneself
weh•tun, wehgetan (+ dat.)	to hurt
Das tut mir weh.	That hurts.
sich (wohl) fühlen	to feel (well)
sich die Zähne putzen	to brush one's teeth

Adjektive und Adverbien / Adjectives and Adverbs

ab und zu	now and then, occasionally
anstrengend	tiring, strenuous
besonders	especially
deprimiert	depressed
deshalb	therefore
entweder … oder	either … or
fast	almost
fit	fit, in shape
gesund	healthy, healthful, well

gleich	immediately
hundsmiserabel (coll.)	sick as a dog
kaum	hardly, scarcely
krank	sick, ill
manchmal	sometimes
meistens	mostly
mindestens	at least
müde	tired
regelmäßig	regular(ly)
schlapp	weak, worn out
sogar	even
verrückt	crazy
wenig	little, few

Unterordnende Konjunktionen / Subordinating Conjunctions

dass	that
ob	whether
weil	because
wenn	if, when

Sonstiges / Other

d.h. (= das heißt)	that is, i.e.
Das macht nichts.	That doesn't matter.
Gute Besserung!	Get well soon!
klingen	to sound
Du klingst so deprimiert.	You sound so depressed.
Mir ist schlecht.	I'm sick to my stomach.
Nichts zu danken.	No thanks necessary; Don't mention it.
So ein Pech!	What a shame! (What bad luck!)
Urlaub machen	to go on vacation
Was fehlt Ihnen/dir?	What's the matter?
zu Fuß gehen	to go on foot, to walk

▼ DAS KANN ICH NUN!

1. Nennen Sie sechs Körperteile mit Artikel und Plural.

2. Beschreiben Sie Ihre Morgenroutine. Bilden Sie mindestens drei Sätze mit reflexiven Verben.

3. Sie telefonieren mit einem Freund. Er klingt krank, kann kaum sprechen und hustet. Was fragen Sie ihn? Was empfehlen Sie ihm? Was wünschen Sie ihm?

4. Was machen Sie, wenn Sie eine Erkältung haben?

   Wenn ich eine Erkältung habe, …

5. Sie gehen zum Arzt, weil Sie sich hundsmiserabel fühlen. Der Arzt fragt: „Was fehlt Ihnen denn?" Was sagen Sie?

6. Was tun Sie für Fitness und Gesundheit? (Nennen Sie drei Dinge.) Wenn Sie nichts tun, sagen Sie bitte, warum Sie nichts tun.

7. Sie haben sich erkältet, aber Sie müssen unbedingt zur Arbeit. Sie reden mit einem Freund / einer Freundin über diese Situation. Was sagen Sie zu ihm/ihr?

   a. Ich weiß nicht, ob … **b.** Ich kann heute nicht zu Hause bleiben, weil … **c.** Ich glaube nicht, dass …

In der Stadt

Weihnachtslichter am
Kohlmarkt in Wien

In diesem Kapitel

- **Themen:** Hotel and lodging, places in the city, asking for and giving directions
- **Grammatik:** Genitive case, attributive adjectives
- **Kultur:** Services of tourist information offices, Wittenberg history
- **Lesen:** „Die Gitarre des Herrn Hatunoglu" (Heinrich Hannover)

Videoclips
Hier gefällt es mir!

Alles klar?

A. Dresden liegt im Bundesland Sachsen südlich von Berlin an der Elbe. Die Residenzstadt feierte 2006 ihr 800-jähriges Jubiläum. Es gibt viele Sehenswürdigkeiten (*tourist attractions*) in und um die Stadt. Für Jugendliche gibt es in Dresden besonders viel zu erleben.

**Junges Dresden:
Freizeit, Unterhaltung, Szene**

Dresden hat viele Facetten[1]: weltberühmte Museen und Sehenswürdigkeiten, eine romantische Elblandschaft[2], sächsische Gemütlichkeit und eine bunte Szenekultur. Ein Abend in Dresden muss nicht immer Oper, Konzert oder Theater bedeuten. Wer außerdem Lust auf einen Kneipenbummel[3] hat, kommt in der Dresdner Neustadt voll auf seine Kosten[4]. In der Hauptstraße, der Rähnitzgasse und der Königstraße gibt es Restaurants unterschiedlichster Couleur. Internationale und sächsische[5] Küche findet man auch rings um den Albertplatz. Von hier aus geht's die Alaunstraße entlang, wo sich urige[6] Szenekneipen und internationale Spezialitätenrestaurants abwechseln. Neben den individuellen Möglichkeiten der aktiven Erholung im Grünen an Dresdens Elbufern oder im Großen Garten finden Sie vielfältige[7] Angebote in den Erlebnisbädern oder den Sport- und Mehrzweckhallen. Für Skater empfiehlt sich in Dresden das Nachtskaten (von April bis Oktober): Jeden Freitag um 21 Uhr starten ca. 3000 Fans des Sports zu einer nächtlichen, 20 Kilometer langen Tour durch Dresden. Günstige Übernachtungsmöglichkeiten finden Sie in Dresdens Jugendherbergen[8] und Hostels.

[1]*dimensions*   [2]*Elbe river landscape*   [3]*pub crawl*   [4]kommt voll auf seine Kosten *finds everything he/she needs*   [5]*Saxon*   [6]*ancient*
[7]*multifaceted*   [8]*youth hostels*

Suchen Sie die fehlenden Informationen im Text oben.

1. Die _____ in Dresden sind weltberühmt.
2. Wenn man Kultur erleben möchte, kann man abends in die _____, ins _____ oder ins _____ gehen. Wenn man das nicht will, kann man auch in der Dresdner Neustadt einen _____ machen.
3. Wenn man essen will, findet man _____ und _____ Küche rings um den Albertplatz in Dresden.
4. Im Grünen kann man sich an Dresdens _____ oder im _____ _____ erholen.
5. Für Skatingfans gibt es vom April bis Oktober das _____.
6. In Dresden kann man in _____ und in _____ übernachten.

Suchen Sie mehr Informationen über Dresden. Was würden Sie gern dort machen?

B. Sie machen eine Stadtführung (*guided tour*) durch Dresden. Der Fremdenführer (*tour guide*) erzählt einige Tatsachen über die Stadt. Hören Sie zu und kreuzen Sie an, was stimmt und was nicht stimmt.

	DAS STIMMT	DAS STIMMT NICHT
1. Heute leben etwa 500 000 Einwohner in Dresden.	☐	☐
2. Die erste deutsche Lokomotive kommt aus Dresden.	☐	☐
3. Bierdeckel, Kaffeefilter und Shampoo hat man in Dresden erfunden.	☐	☐
4. In Dresden hat Richard Wagner die erste deutsche Oper geschrieben.	☐	☐
5. Die Stadt bietet viel Kultur an: Musik, Museen und Theater.	☐	☐
6. Dresden ist die europäische Hauptstadt des Films.	☐	☐

accommodations

THEMA 1: Unterkunft° online buchen

A&O HOSTEL BERLIN Fhain — Bei uns schlafen Sie zum Frühstückspreis!

HOSTEL
SPECIALS
SERVICE
TICKETS
PARTIES
BILDER
PREISE
GRUPPEN
BERLIN
PARTNER
KONTAKT
DOWNLOADS
SITEMAP
BUCHEN
EMPFEHLEN
PRESSE
JOBS
FAQ

Preisliste

Alle Preise pro Person und Nacht inkl. MwSt.

Alle Preise gelten pro Person und Nacht, inklusive Mehrwertsteuer.[1] Die angegebenen Preise können je nach Verfügbarkeit[2] variieren. Es gelten die bei Buchung genannten Preise als vereinbart.

Möchten Sie die aktuellen Preise für ein bestimmtes Datum wissen? Sehen Sie im Bereich BUCHEN nach.

Einzelzimmer*	ab	30.00 €
Zweibettzimmer*	ab	17.00 €
Kleines Mehrbettzimmer (4-6 Betten) mit Dusche und WC	ab	13.00 €
Kleines Mehrbettzimmer (4-6 Betten)	ab	10,50 €
Großes Mehrbettzimmer (8-10 Betten) mit Dusche und WC	ab	10,50 €
Großes Mehrbettzimmer (8-10 Betten)	ab	10.00 €

* inklusive Frühstück und Bettwäsche

Ergänzungen

Bettwäsche	3,00 € / einmalig
Handtuch	1,00 € / einmalig
Frühstücksbuffet	5,00 € / Tag
Fahrradverleih[3]	10,00 € / Tag
Parkplatz	3,00 € / Tag (max. 6,00 €)
Internetzugang	1,00 € / 20 Minuten

Für Gruppen bietet das A&O HOSTEL Friedrichshain/Kreuzberg besondere Preise und Angebote. (mehr...)

[1]*value-added tax* [2]*availability*
[3]*bicycle rental*

Bad ramsach — oase der erholung und entspannung

home ¦ contact ¦ impressum & links

Hotel & Preise
Aktuelle[1] Angebote
Restaurant
Wohlbefinden
Kuren im Ferienstil
Seminar-Oase
"Top of Ramsach" live
Stellenangebote
Aktuell
Gästebuch

Preise & Gesamt-Angebot (PDF)

Hotel & Preise

Preise 2006

Alle Zimmer ausgestattet[2] mit: Dusche/WC, Balkon, Föhn, Radio, Satelliten-TV, Direktwahltelefon, Internetanschluss (analog), Kühlschrank und Bademantel.
Lassen Sie sich verwöhnen!

Preise pro Zimmer ab 3 Nächten in CHF[3] inkl. Mehrwertsteuer:

Bergseite (Sonnseite)	1. Stock (EZ / DZ)	2. Stock (EZ / DZ)	3/4 Stock (EZ /DZ)
Vollpension	163.00 / 260.00	173.00 / 280.00	183.00 / 300.00
Halbpension	143.00 / 220.00	153.00 / 240.00	163.00 / 260.00
Zi. + Frühstück	108.00 / 150.00	118.00 / 170.00	128.00 / 190.00
Talseite[4] (Aussichtsseite)[5]	**1. Stock (EZ / DZ)**	**2. Stock (EZ / DZ)**	**3/4 Stock (EZ /DZ)**
Vollpension	168.00 / 270.00	178.00 / 290.00	188.00 / 310.00
Halbpension	148.00 / 230.00	158.00 / 250.00	168.00 / 270.00
Zi. + Frühstück	113.00 / 160.00	123.00 / 180.00	133.00 / 200.00

Preise pro Zimmer 1 und 2 Nächte in CHF inkl. Mehrwertsteuer:

1 und 2 Nächte	1. Stock (EZ / DZ)	2. Stock (EZ / DZ)	3/4 Stock (EZ /DZ)
Zi. + Frühstück Hotel	115.00 / 170.00	135.00 / 200.00	135.00 / 200.00

Zimmerservice: 5.00 pro Person und Mahlzeit (ausser Frühstück)

[1]*current* [2]*furnished*
[3]*(abbreviation for Swiss francs)* [4]*valley side* [5]*view side*

Bei Hotelwerbungen findet man oft folgende Bezeichnungen:

Vollpension	*all meals included*
Halbpension	*one meal besides breakfast included*
Pauschalangebot	*package offer*

Die folgenden Abkürzungen sind auch typisch:

EZ	= **das Einzelzimmer**	*single room*
DZ	= **das Doppelzimmer**	*double room*
DU	= **die Dusche**	*shower*
WC	= **die Toilette** (Engl. *water closet*)	*toilet*
inkl.	= **inklusive**	*included, including*

A. Was ist Ihnen wichtig, wenn Sie in einem **Hotel,** einer **Pension** oder einer **Jugendherberge übernachten** wollen? Die **Unterkunft** sollte …

☐ **in der Nähe** des **Bahnhofs** liegen.
☐ in der **Innenstadt** (im **Zentrum**) liegen.
☐ ein Restaurant im Haus haben.
☐ Kabelfernsehen oder Radio haben.
☐ in ruhiger **Lage** sein.
☐ Bad/Dusche/WC im Zimmer haben.
☐ Frühstück **im Preis enthalten.**
☐ einen **Parkplatz** in der Nähe haben.

☐ Hunde **erlauben.**
☐ Telefon im Zimmer haben.
☐ im Bad einen **Föhn** haben.
☐ preiswert sein.
☐ **günstig liegen** (z.B. im Zentrum).
☐ einen **Kühlschrank** im Zimmer haben.
☐ **Internetzugang** haben.
☐ in einer **Fußgängerzone** liegen.
☐ **Bettwäsche** haben.

B. Daniel in Berlin. Daniel war drei Tage in Berlin. Er wollte nicht viel Geld für _____[1] (*lodging*) ausgeben, aber sie sollte _____ _____[2] (*be conveniently located*), am besten in der _____[3] (*inner city*). Er hat dort auch eine preiswerte Unterkunft in einer _____[4] (*youth hostel*) gefunden: ein _____[5] (*single room*) mit WC und _____[6] (*shower*). _____[7] (*breakfast*) und _____[8] (*linens*) waren im Preis enthalten. Das Zimmer hatte kein Telefon und auch keinen _____[9] (*Internet access*). Dafür musste man extra bezahlen.

C. Frau Heilmann macht Kurzurlaub. Frau Heilmann wollte sich ein paar Tage entspannen und hat in Bad Ramsach in der Schweiz Kurzurlaub gemacht. Das Hotel war in ruhiger _____[10] (*location*). Sie hatte ein _____[11] (*single room*) mit Vollpension auf der Talseite des Hotels im zweiten _____[12] (*floor*). Das Zimmer war etwas teuer — es hat 178 CHF pro Nacht gekostet, aber es war sehr schön ausgestattet mit Telefon, WC, _____[13] (*shower*) und einem _____[14] (*refrigerator*) und es hatte auch einen Balkon mit Blick auf das schöne Tal.

Neue Wörter

die Pension bed and breakfast
die Jugendherberge youth hostel
übernachten to stay overnight
die Unterkunft lodging
in der Nähe near
der Bahnhof train station
das Zentrum town center
die Lage location
im Preis enthalten include in the price
erlauben allow
der Föhn hair dryer
günstig liegen be conveniently located
der Kühlschrank refrigerator
der Internetzugang Internet access
die Fußgängerzone pedestrian zone
die Bettwäsche linens

Aktivität 1 Zwei telefonische Zimmerbestellungen

Was stimmt? Markieren Sie die richtigen Antworten.

<table>
<tr><td align="center">ERSTES TELEFONGESPRÄCH</td><td align="center">ZWEITES TELEFONGESPRÄCH</td></tr>
<tr><td>

1. Der Gast braucht ein ...
   a. Einzelzimmer.
   b. Doppelzimmer.
2. Er braucht das Zimmer für ...
   a. eine Nacht.
   b. mehrere (*several*) Nächte.
3. Das Hotel hat ein Zimmer frei ...
   a. ohne Bad.
   b. mit Bad.
4. Frühstück ist im Preis ...
   a. nicht enthalten.
   b. enthalten.
5. Der Gast ...
   a. muss ein anderes Hotel finden.
   b. nimmt das Zimmer.

</td><td>

1. Das Jugendgästehaus hat ...
   a. nur Doppelzimmer.
   b. nur Mehrbettzimmer.
2. Das Haus ist ...
   a. ganz neu.
   b. sehr alt.
3. Die Übernachtung kostet ...
   a. mehr als 20 Euro.
   b. weniger als 20 Euro.
4. Jedes Zimmer hat ...
   a. WC and Dusche.
   b. fünf Betten.
5. Das Gästehaus liegt ...
   a. auf dem Lande.
   b. in der Nähe der Innenstadt.

</td></tr>
</table>

KULTURTIPP

„Tourist i" (*for information*) ist für viele Besucher in deutschen Städten der erste Stopp. Meist liegt er am Hauptbahnhof oder an einem anderen zentralen Ort. Hier können Touristen viel Wissenswertes über die neue Stadt erfahren. Sie können zum Beispiel Empfehlungen für Restaurants bekommen, eine Stadtrundfahrt buchen und Prospekte (*brochures*) von der Stadt erhalten. Hier gibt es auch eine Zimmervermittlung. Da kann der Besucher ein Zimmer in einem Hotel oder einer Pension finden.

Aktivität 2 Unterkunft in Berlin

Sie reisen mit Freunden und suchen eine Unterkunft in Berlin. Schauen Sie sich die Webseite „AO Hostel" im **Thema 1** genau an und überlegen Sie sich, in was für einem Zimmer Sie übernachten wollen. Gebrauchen Sie die folgenden Ausdrücke.

BEISPIEL: Ich schlage vor, wir übernachten in einem Mehrbettzimmer. Das ist nicht so teuer.

Ich schlage vor, ...

Mir gefällt ... besser.

Ich brauche ... im Zimmer.

... ist mir zu teuer.

THEMA 2: Im Hotel 🎧

Teil A: *Herr Thompson* **kommt** *im Hotel „Mecklenheide"* **an.** **Zuerst** *muss er* **sich anmelden.**

REZEPTION: Guten Abend.

GAST: Guten Abend. Ich habe ein Zimmer für zwei Nächte bestellt.

REZEPTION: **Auf welchen Namen,** bitte?

GAST: Thompson.

REZEPTION: Ah, ja. Herr Thompson. Ein Einzelzimmer mit Bad. **Würden Sie** bitte das **Anmeldeformular ausfüllen?**

GAST: Möchten Sie auch meinen **Reisepass** sehen?

REZEPTION: Nein, das ist nicht nötig. Ihr Zimmer liegt im ersten **Stock,** Zimmer 21. Hier ist **der Schlüssel. Der Aufzug** ist hier **rechts.**

GAST: Danke.

REZEPTION: Wir bringen Ihr **Gepäck** aufs Zimmer. Haben Sie nur den einen Koffer?

GAST: Ja … **Übrigens,** wann gibt es morgens Frühstück?

REZEPTION: Zwischen 7 und 10 Uhr im **Frühstücksraum** hier gleich **links** im **Erdgeschoss.**

GAST: Danke sehr.

REZEPTION: Bitte sehr. Ich wünsche Ihnen einen **angenehmen Aufenthalt.**

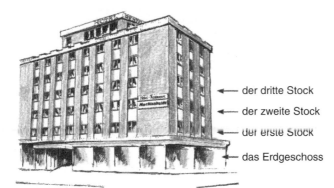

← der dritte Stock
← der zweite Stock
← der erste Stock
← das Erdgeschoss

Teil B: *Herr Thompson ruft die* **Rezeption** *an und* **beschwert sich,** *weil der Fernseher nicht* **funktioniert.**

REZEPTION: Rezeption.

THOMPSON: Guten Abend. Der Fernseher in meinem Zimmer ist **kaputt.** Es gibt kein Bild, keinen Ton, nichts.

REZEPTION: **Das tut mir leid,** Herr Thompson. Ich schicke **sofort** jemand auf Ihr Zimmer. Wenn er den **Apparat** nicht gleich **reparieren** kann, bringen wir Ihnen einen anderen.

THOMPSON: Vielen Dank. **Auf Wiederhören.**

REZEPTION: Auf Wiederhören.

Teil A

kommt … an (ankommen) arrives
zuerst first
sich anmelden register, check in
würden Sie … ausfüllen would you fill out …
das Anmeldeformular registration form
der Reisepass passport
der Schlüssel key
der Aufzug elevator
rechts to the right
das Gepäck luggage
übrigens by the way
links to the left
angenehm pleasant
der Aufenthalt stay

Teil B

die Rezeption reception desk
beschwert sich (sich beschweren) complains
kaputt broken
Das tut mir leid. I'm sorry.
sofort immediately
der Apparat TV set
reparieren repair
auf Wiederhören good-bye (*on the phone*)

Bilden Sie Sätze!

1. _c_ Ich habe ein Einzelzimmer …
2. ___ Würden Sie bitte das Anmeldeformular …
3. ___ Ihr Zimmer liegt …
4. ___ Wir bringen Ihr Gepäck …
5. ___ Ich wünsche Ihnen …
6. ___ Der Fernseher in meinem Zimmer …

a. ist kaputt.
b. bezahlen?
c. bestellt.
d. einen angenehmen Aufenthalt.
e. ausfüllen?
f. aufs Zimmer.
g. im ersten Stock.

Aktivität 3 Im Hotel Mecklenheide

Was passiert? Ergänzen Sie!

1. Herr Thompson bekommt ein _____ mit Bad im ersten _____.
2. Er muss das Anmeldeformular _____.
3. Seinen _____ muss er aber nicht vorzeigen.
4. Er bekommt den _____ zum Zimmer und nimmt den _____ in den ersten Stock.
5. Jemand vom Hotelpersonal bringt sein _____ aufs Zimmer.
6. Er kann zwischen 7 und 10 Uhr im Frühstücksraum im _____ frühstücken.
7. Herr Thompson _____ sich, weil der Fernseher in seinem Zimmer _____ ist.
8. Jemand vom Hotelpersonal soll den Fernseher _____.

Aktivität 4 Die Geschichte von Herrn Thompson

Sehen Sie sich die Bilder von Herrn Thompson im Hotel an. Schreiben Sie für jedes Bild einen Satz und erzählen Sie die Geschichte von Herrn Thompson.

Hier klicken!

Weiteres zum Thema Hotel und Unterkunft finden Sie bei **Deutsch: Na klar!** im World-Wide-Web unter www.mhhe.com/dnk5.

1.

2.

3.

4.

5.

6.

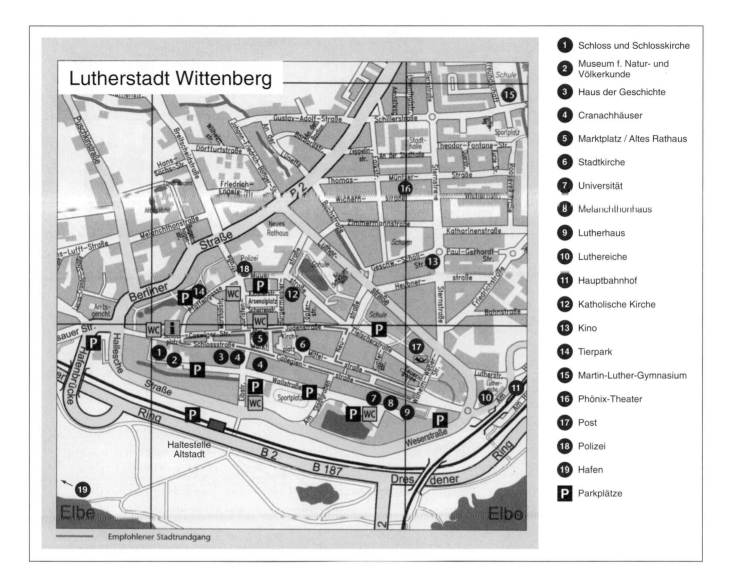

Map legend:
1. Schloss und Schlosskirche
2. Museum f. Natur- und Völkerkunde
3. Haus der Geschichte
4. Cranachhäuser
5. Marktplatz / Altes Rathaus
6. Stadtkirche
7. Universität
8. Melanchthonhaus
9. Lutherhaus
10. Lithereiche
11. Hauptbahnhof
12. Katholische Kirche
13. Kino
14. Tierpark
15. Martin-Luther-Gymnasium
16. Phönix-Theater
17. Post
18. Polizei
19. Hafen
P. Parkplätze

A. Verbinden Sie das deutsche Wort mit dem Englischen.

1. ___ die **Kirche**
2. ___ das **Museum**
3. ___ die **Post**
4. ___ die **Bank**
5. ___ die **Polizei**
6. ___ der **Hafen**
7. ___ das **Schloss**
8. ___ die **Haltestelle**
9. ___ der **Tierpark**
10. ___ das **Rathaus**

a. bank
b. city hall
c. museum
d. castle
e. police
f. post office
g. stop/station (*bus, train, etc.*)
h. harbor
i. zoo
j. church

Nach dem Weg fragen

Neue Wörter

nach dem Weg fragen to ask for directions
Entschuldigung excuse me
gehen Sie ... entlang (entlanggehen) go along
biegen Sie ... ein (einbiegen) turn
immer geradeaus straight ahead
bis zur as far as, up to
gegenüber vom across from the
weit far
ungefähr about, approximately

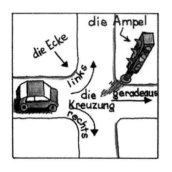

*Ein **Tourist** steht in Wittenberg vor der Stadtkirche und fragt nach dem Weg.*

TOURIST: **Entschuldigung,** wie komme ich am besten zum Lutherhaus?

PASSANT: **Gehen Sie** hier die Mittelstraße **entlang.** Dann **biegen Sie** rechts in die Wilhelm-Weber Straße **ein.** Gehen Sie **immer geradeaus bis zur** Collegienstraße. Da finden Sie das Lutherhaus. Es liegt **gegenüber vom** Restaurant „Am Lutherhaus".

TOURIST: Ist es **weit** von hier?

PASSANT: Nein. **Ungefähr** 15 Minuten zu Fuß.

B. Sie stehen am alten Markt am Rathaus und kennen Wittenberg jetzt sehr gut. Einige Touristen fragen Sie nach dem Weg.

TOURIST 1: Wie komme ich am besten zum Haus der Geschichte?

SIE: _____ _____ (go along) die Elbstraße _____. Dann _____ _____ (turn) rechts _____. Das Haus der Geschichte ist auf der linken Seite.

TOURIST 2: Sind das Schloss und die Schlosskirche _____ (far) von hier?

SIE: Nein, _____ (about) zehn Minuten zu Fuß. Gehen Sie die Schlossstraße _____ _____ (straight ahead). Dann sehen Sie das Schloss und die Schlosskirche.

Aktivität 5   Drei Touristen

Drei Leute fragen nach dem Weg. Wohin wollen sie? Wie kommen sie dahin?

	DIALOG 1	DIALOG 2	DIALOG 3
Wohin man gehen will			
Wie man dahin kommt			

Aktivität 6 Hin und her: In einer fremden° Stadt

unfamiliar

Sie sind in einer fremden Stadt. Fragen Sie nach dem Weg. Benutzen Sie
die Tabelle.

BEISPIEL: s1: Ist das Landesmuseum weit von hier?
s2: Es ist sechs Kilometer von hier, bei der Universität.
s1: Wie komme ich am besten dahin?
s2: Nehmen Sie die Buslinie 7, am Rathaus.

WOHIN?	WIE WEIT?	WO?	WIE?
Landesmuseum	6 km	bei der Universität	Buslinie 7, am Rathaus
Bahnhof	15 Minuten	im Zentrum	mit dem Taxi
Post			
Schloss	15 km	außerhalb der Stadt	mit dem Auto
Opernhaus			

Aktivität 7 In Wittenberg

Schauen Sie sich den Stadtplan von Wittenberg im **Thema 3** an und fragen
Sie jemand im Kurs, wie Sie am besten an einen bestimmten Ort kommen.

BEISPIEL: Sie stehen am Haus der Geschichte (Nummer 3 im Stadtplan). →
s1: Entschuldigung, wie komme ich am besten zum Markt?
s2: Geh geradeaus bis zur Elbstraße. Bieg dann links ein. Der
Markt ist auf der rechten Seite gleich an der Ecke.

SIE STEHEN …

am Haus der Geschichte
vor der katholischen Kirche
am Schloss
am Tierpark
vor der Stadtkirche
vor dem Kino
am Hauptbahnhof
vor dem alten Rathaus
am Markt

SIE WOLLEN …

ins Kino
zum Schloss
zum alten Rathaus
zum Markt
zur Stadtkirche
zum Hauptbahnhof
in den Tierpark

REDEMITTEL

Entschuldigung, wie komme ich am
besten zum/zur _____?
Wie weit ist es bis zum/zur _____?
immer geradeaus
bis zur Kreuzung/Ampel
Geh die _____-straße entlang.
Bieg links/rechts in die _____
-straße ein.
gleich an der Ecke / um die Ecke
auf der rechten/linken Seite
Es ist zehn Minuten zu Fuß.

Siehe *Attributive
Adjectives*, S. 274.

KULTURTIPP

Wittenberg: Ein Blick in die Geschichte

1180   erste urkundliche Erwähnung (*mention*) von Wittenberg

1502   Gründung der Wittenberger Universität

1508   Martin Luther kommt nach Wittenberg. Er wird Theologieprofessor.

1517   Luther veröffentlicht (*publishes*) seine 95 Thesen an der Tür der Schlosskirche. Die Reformation beginnt.

1537   Lucas Cranach, ein berühmter Maler der Reformation, wird Bürgermeister der Stadt.

1618–1648   der dreißigjährige Krieg: Wittenberg erleidet (*suffers*) Schäden.

Martin-Luther-Denkmal am Markt

1817   Schließung der Wittenberger Universität

1883   Eröffnung des Reformationsmuseums „Lutherhaus"

1994   Die Universität wird wieder belebt (*revived*).

Das Lutherhaus in der Collegienstraße

1996   Das Lutherhaus, das Melanchthonhaus und die Stadt- und Schlosskirche werden Teil des Weltkulturerbes (*world cultural heritage*) der UNESCO.

Quelle: www.wittenberg.de (adaptiert)

Aktivität 8   Wie kommt man dahin?

Fragen Sie nach dem Weg in Ihrer Stadt oder auf Ihrem Campus. Wählen Sie passende Fragen und Antworten aus jeder Spalte (*column*).

BEISPIEL: s1: Entschuldigung, wo ist hier die Post?
           s2: Da nehmen Sie am besten den Bus.
           s1: Wo ist die Haltestelle?
           s2: Gleich da drüben an der Kreuzung.

FRAGEN	ANTWORTEN
Wie kommt man hier zum Supermarkt / zur Bibliothek / zur Sporthalle?	immer geradeaus
	bis zur Ampel
	nächste Kreuzung rechts/links
Wie weit ist es bis ins Zentrum?	Da nehmen Sie am besten ＿＿＿ (den Bus, z.B. Linie 8).
Entschuldigung, wo ist hier die Post (Bank, Mensa)?	gleich da drüben / gleich an der Ecke
Wo ist die Haltestelle? ??	fünf Minuten zu Fuß ??

Wie kommt man hier zum Schloss?

Das können Sie selbst googeln

Grammatik im Kontext

The Genitive Case°

Der Genitiv

The genitive case typically indicates ownership, a relationship, or the characteristics of another noun.

Der Wagen **meines Vaters** steht auf dem Parkplatz.	*My father's car is in the parking lot.*
Die Lage **des Hotels** ist günstig.	*The location of the hotel is convenient.*
Das Hotel liegt im Zentrum **der Stadt.**	*The hotel is located in the center of town.*

SINGULAR			PLURAL
Masculine	*Neuter*	*Feminine*	*All Genders*
des / eines / unseres / dieses — Vaters / Gastes *but:* Studenten	des / eines / unseres / dieses — Hotels	der / einer / unserer / dieser — Stadt	der / unserer / dieser — Gäste

Note:

- Most masculine and neuter nouns add **-s** in the singular genitive case.

  die Lage dieses Hotel**s**   *the location of this hotel*

- Masculine and neuter nouns of one syllable often add **-es.**

  die Unterschrift des Gast**es**   *the guest's signature*

- Masculine nouns that add **-n** or **-en** in the dative and the accusative also add **-n** or **-en** in the genitive case.

  das Gepäck des Student**en**   *the student's luggage*

- A noun in the genitive always follows the noun it modifies.

In spoken German, the genitive case is often replaced by the preposition **von** and the dative case.

in der Nähe **vom Bahnhof**   *in the vicinity of the railroad station*

To ask for the owner of something, use the interrogative pronoun **wessen** (*whose*).

Wessen Koffer ist das?	*Whose suitcase is that?*
Wessen Unterschrift ist das?	*Whose signature is that?*

Proper Names in the Genitive

Martinas Koffer	*Martina's suitcase*
Herrn Kramers Reisepass	*Mr. Kramer's passport*
Hessen: das Herz **Deutschlands**	*Hesse: the heart of Germany*

Note:

- A proper name in the genitive normally precedes the noun it modifies.
- Proper names in the genitive add **-s** without an apostrophe, in contrast to English.
- The name of a country or a region in the genitive case may precede or follow the noun it modifies.

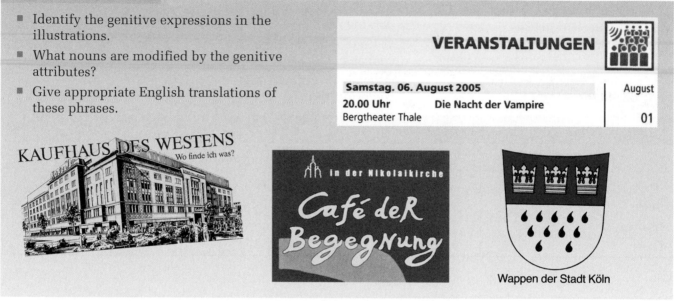

ANALYSE

- Identify the genitive expressions in the illustrations.
- What nouns are modified by the genitive attributes?
- Give appropriate English translations of these phrases.

KAUFHAUS DES WESTENS
Wo finde ich was?

VERANSTALTUNGEN

Samstag. 06. August 2005	August
20.00 Uhr Die Nacht der Vampire	
Bergtheater Thale	01

In der Nikolaikirche
Café deR Begegnung

Wappen der Stadt Köln

Vienna ## Übung 1   Was für eine Stadt ist Wien°?

Sie sind gerade in Wien. Beschreiben Sie die Stadt.

BEISPIEL: Wien ist eine Stadt der Tradition.

Wien ist eine Stadt …

die Kaffeehäuser	die Schlösser
das Theater	die Architektur
die Musik	die Kirchen
die Museen	der Walzer (*waltz*)

Übung 2   Wo ist Ihr Hotel?

Beschreiben Sie die Lage Ihres Hotels in Wien.

BEISPIEL: Unser Hotel liegt in der Nähe eines Cafés.

Unser Hotel liegt in der Nähe …

ein Park	die Ringstraße
ein Schloss	die Post
eine Bank	der Stephansdom (*St. Stephen's Cathedral*)
die Donau (*Danube*)	das Rathaus
die Universität	die U-Bahn
der Bahnhof	das Zentrum

Übung 3 Spiel mit Wörtern

In der deutschen Sprache gibt es viele zusammengesetzte (*compound*) Wörter. Oft kann man sie auseinander (*apart*) nehmen und mit Hilfe eines Genitivobjekts anders ausdrücken.

Schritt 1: Nehmen Sie zuerst die zusammengesetzten Wörter in Spalte A auseinander.

BEISPIEL: die Hotellage → die Lage des Hotels

Schritt 2: Bilden Sie dann Sätze mit Hilfe von Spalte B.

BEISPIEL: Die Lage des Hotels ist sehr günstig in der Nähe des Zentrums.

A	B
1. die Hotellage	a. ist nicht weit von hier entfernt.
2. der Übernachtungspreis	b. liegt auf dem Tisch im Hotelzimmer.
3. der Hotelmanager	c. ist am Wochenende geschlossen.
4. der Autoschlüssel	d. ist in der Tiefgarage im Hotel.
5. das Stadtzentrum	e. beträgt 130 Euro pro Person.
6. die Universitätsbibliothek	f. heißt Johannes Tiefenbach.
7. der Hotelparkplatz	g. ist sehr günstig in der Nähe des Zentrums.

Übung 4 Wem gehört das?

Wessen Sachen sind das? Arbeiten Sie zu zweit.

BEISPIEL: s1: Wessen Gepäck ist das?
          s2: Das ist das Gepäck des Gastes.

1. das Gepäck	meine Schwester
2. der Rucksack	der Student
3. der Reisepass	der Herr auf Zimmer 33
4. die Unterschrift (*signature*)	der Gast
5. die Koffer	die Touristen
6. der Schlüssel	unsere Freunde

Prepositions with the Genitive

A number of prepositions are used with the genitive case. Here are several common ones:

außerhalb	*outside of*	außerhalb der Stadt
innerhalb	*inside of, within*	innerhalb einer Stunde
trotz	*in spite of*	trotz des Regens
während	*during*	während des Sommers
wegen	*because of*	wegen der hohen Kosten

In colloquial German, **trotz, während,** and **wegen** may also be used with the dative case.

Übung 5   Notizen von einer Reise nach Wien

Setzen Sie passende Präpositionen mit dem Genitiv ein.

1. _____ unserer Reise nach Wien haben wir viel gesehen.
2. _____ der höheren Hotelpreise haben wir in einer kleinen Pension übernachtet.
3. Die Pension hat _____ der Stadt gelegen.
4. _____ der vielen Touristen war es in Wien schön.
5. _____ der vielen Besucher mussten wir lange vor der Spanischen Reitschule warten.

inquiries

Übung 6   Erkundigungen°

Sie sind bei der Information und fragen nach dem Weg. Arbeiten Sie zu zweit.

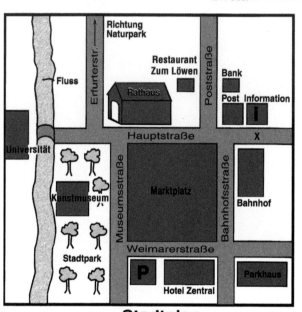

Stadtplan

FÜR DIE FRAGEN

Bitte schön, wo ist …

Entschuldigung, wie komme ich zum/zur …

Bitte, können Sie mir sagen, …

FÜR DIE ANTWORTEN

in der Nähe

in der Mitte

auf der anderen Seite

innerhalb/außerhalb

(direkt) gegenüber (von)

neben

die _____-straße entlanggehen

BEISPIEL: s1: Bitte schön, wo liegt das Rathaus?
 s2: Es liegt direkt gegenüber vom Marktplatz. Gehen Sie rechts die Hauptstraße entlang.

1. das Rathaus
2. das Hotel Zentral
3. ein Parkplatz
4. der Naturpark
5. das Kunstmuseum
6. die Post
7. die Universität
8. eine Bank

Attributive Adjektive

Attributive Adjectives°

You are already familiar with predicate adjectives. Predicate adjectives do not take endings.

Der Bahnhof ist **alt.**

Das Hotel ist **preiswert.**

Die Bedienung ist **freundlich.**

When adjectives precede the nouns they modify, they are called attributive. Attributive adjectives do take endings.

Der **alte** Bahnhof liegt in der Nähe des Hotels.

Das **preiswerte** Hotel liegt außerhalb der Stadt.

Die **freundliche** Bedienung hat mir gefallen.

Adjectives after a Definite Article

Whenever an adjective follows a definite article or other **der**-word, such as **dieser** or **jeder**, it takes the ending **-e** or **-en** (depending on the case and gender).*

	SINGULAR			PLURAL
	Masculine	*Neuter*	*Feminine*	*All Genders*
Nom.	der groß**e** Park	das schön**e** Wetter	die lang**e** Straße	die alt**en** Häuser
Acc.	den groß**en** Park	das schön**e** Wetter	die lang**e** Straße	die alt**en** Häuser
Dat.	dem groß**en** Park	dem schön**en** Wetter	der lang**en** Straße	den alt**en** Häusern
Gen.	des groß**en** Parks	des schön**en** Wetters	der lang**en** Straße	der alt**en** Häuser

SUMMARY OF ENDINGS

	SINGULAR			PLURAL
	Masculine	*Neuter*	*Feminine*	*All Genders*
Nom.	-e	-e	-e	-en
Acc.	-en	-e	-e	-en
Dat.	-en	-en	-en	-en
Gen.	-en	-en	-en	-en

SPRACHTIPP

When two or more attributive adjectives modify a noun, they have the same ending.

Das **kleine historische** Hotel liegt in der Altstadt.

Die **vielen alten** Häuser haben mir gefallen.

Übung 7 Was hat Ihnen in der Stadt gefallen oder nicht gefallen?

Bilden Sie Sätze mit Adjektiven. Folgen Sie dem Beispiel.

BEISPIEL: Die Menschen waren alle sehr freundlich. →
Die freundlichen Menschen haben mir gefallen.

1. Die Häuser waren sehr alt.
2. Das Hotel war klein und gemütlich.
3. Das Frühstück im Hotel war ausgezeichnet.
4. Die Straßen waren sauber.
5. Das Bier war ausgezeichnet.
6. Der Marktplatz war klein.
7. Die Bedienung im Restaurant war leider unfreundlich.
8. Aber der Bürgermeister war sehr freundlich.

Obst aus dem Alten Land

STIFTUNG Kunststätte JOHANN und JUTTA BOSSARD

Das familienfreundliche Museum. Eintritt frei für Kinder bis 16 Jahre.

---

*This type of adjective ending is traditionally referred to as a *weak* adjective ending.

Bei einem Volksfest in Straubing: Die vielen netten Leute haben mir gefallen.

Übung 8 In der Stadt

Setzen Sie passende Adjektive aus der Liste in die Lücken.

klein	alt	modern
groß	neu	(un)bequem

1. Das Rathaus liegt neben der _____ Post.
2. Neben dem _____ Rathaus ist ein Park.
3. In dem _____ Park gibt es einen kleinen See.
4. Vor der _____ Kirche steht eine Statue.
5. In den _____ Hotels übernachten viele Touristen.
6. Auf dem _____ Marktplatz kann man täglich Obst und Gemüse kaufen.
7. In dieser _____ Stadt kann man gut leben.

Übung 9 Was hat Bob mitgebracht?

Bob ist gerade von einer Reise nach Deutschland und Österreich zurückgekommen. Er hat allen etwas mitgebracht. Führen Sie kurze Gespräche mit einem Partner / einer Partnerin. Folgen Sie dem Beispiel.

BEISPIEL: seine Schwester →
    s1: Was hat Bob seiner Schwester mitgebracht?
    s2: Er hat ihr diesen schönen Kalender mitgebracht.

der Kalender

seine Schwester

Hier sind einige Adjektive für Ihre Antworten:

schön	komisch
originell	exzentrisch
interessant	langweilig
fantastisch	nett
praktisch	billig
cool	hässlich

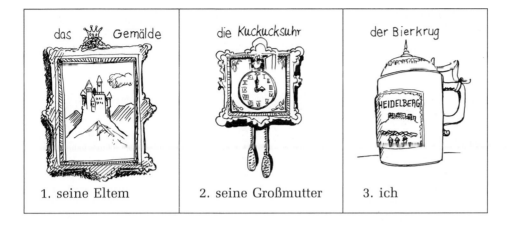

das Gemälde

1. seine Eltem

die Kuckucksuhr

2. seine Großmutter

der Bierkrug

3. ich

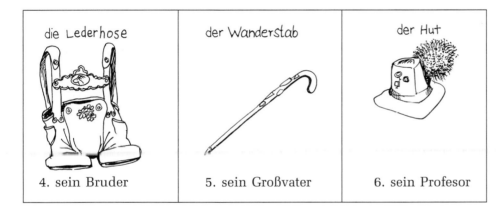

die Lederhose

4. sein Bruder

der Wanderstab

5. sein Großvater

der Hut

6. sein Profesor

Übung 10 Notizen von einem Besuch

Ergänzen Sie die Endungen.

1. Die historisch_____ Stadt hat viele Sehenswürdigkeiten.
2. Das alt_____ Rathaus liegt direkt am Marktplatz.
3. Neben dem alt_____ Rathaus steht das neu_____ Opernhaus.
4. In der Nähe des alt_____ Rathauses liegt auch der Marktplatz.
5. Morgen besuchen wir das alt_____ Rathaus.
6. Trotz des kalt_____ Wetters haben wir einen Spaziergang gemacht.
7. Der Groß_____ Garten ist der Name eines Parks in Dresden.
8. Heute besuchen wir den Groß_____ Garten.
9. Unser Hotel liegt am Groß_____ Garten.
10. Die viel_____ Touristen in Dresden kommen aus der ganzen Welt.

Adjectives after an Indefinite Article

Adjectives preceded by indefinite articles, possessives, or other **ein**-words follow the same pattern as adjectives preceded by **der**-words, except in three instances: the masculine nominative and the neuter nominative and accusative.

Heute war **ein** schön**er** Tag.	*Today was a nice day.*
Das ist **mein** neu**es** Haus.	*This is my new house.*
Ich suche **ein** preiswert**es** Hotel.	*I am looking for a reasonably priced hotel.*
Wo ist **Ihr** neu**er** Wagen?	*Where is your new car?*

	SINGULAR			PLURAL
	Masculine	*Neuter*	*Feminine*	*All Genders*
Nom.	ein groß**er** Park	ein schön**es** Haus	eine lang**e** Straße	keine neu**en** Geschäfte
Acc.	einen groß**en** Park	ein schön**es** Haus	eine lang**e** Straße	keine neu**en** Geschäfte
Dat.	einem groß**en** Park	einem schön**en** Haus	einer lang**en** Straße	keinen neu**en** Geschäften
Gen.	eines groß**en** Parks	eines schön**en** Hauses	einer lang**en** Straße	keiner neu**en** Geschäfte

SUMMARY OF ENDINGS

	SINGULAR			PLURAL
	Masculine	*Neuter*	*Feminine*	*All Genders*
Nom.	-er	-es	-e	-en
Acc.	-en	-es	-e	-en
Dat.	-en	-en	-en	-en
Gen.	-en	-en	-en	-en

Übung 11 Sehenswürdigkeiten in einer Stadt

Ergänzen Sie die Adjektive.

Hier ist …

1. ein deutsch_____ Restaurant.
2. eine bekannt_____ Universität.
3. ein alt_____ Rathaus.
4. eine modern_____ Fußgängerzone.
5. eine historisch_____ Altstadt.
6. ein groß_____ Flughafen.
7. ein berühmt_____ Kunstmuseum.
8. ein gemütlich_____ Biergarten.
9. ein historisch_____ Hotel.
10. ein groß_____, modern_____ Bahnhof.

Übung 12 Was gibt es in Ihrem Heimatort°?

hometown

Stellen Sie Fragen über den Heimatort eines Partners / einer Partnerin in Ihrer Klasse. Benutzen Sie die „Sehenswürdigkeiten" in **Übung 11** für Ihre Fragen. Berichten Sie dann im Plenum.

BEISPIEL: S1: Gibt es in deinem Heimatort ein deutsches Restaurant?
         S2: Nein, es gibt kein deutsches Restaurant da.
    oder Ja, es gibt ein deutsches Restaurant. Es heißt Suppenküche.

Adjectives without a Preceding Article

An attributive adjective that is not preceded by a **der-** or an **ein-**word takes an ending that signals the case, gender, and number of the noun that follows. With the exception of the genitive singular masculine and neuter, those endings are identical to those of the **der-**words.

da**s** Obst → Wo bekommt man hier frisch**es** Obst?	*Where can you get fresh fruit?*
di**e** Brötchen → Hier gibt es jeden Tag frisch**e** Brötchen.	*You can get fresh rolls here every day.*
bei de**m** Wetter → Bei schlecht**em** Wetter bleibe ich zu Hause.	*In bad weather I stay home.*

	SINGULAR			PLURAL
	Masculine	*Neuter*	*Feminine*	*All Genders*
Nom.	schön**er** Park	gut**es** Wetter	zentral**e** Lage	alt**e** Häuser
Acc.	schön**en** Park	gut**es** Wetter	zentral**e** Lage	alt**e** Häuser
Dat.	schön**em** Park	gut**em** Wetter	zentral**er** Lage	alt**en** Häusern
Gen.	schön**en** Parks	gut**en** Wetters	zentral**er** Lage	alt**er** Häuser

SUMMARY OF ENDINGS

	SINGULAR			PLURAL
	Masculine	*Neuter*	*Feminine*	*All Genders*
Nom.	-er	-es	-e	-e
Acc.	-en	-es	-e	-e
Dat.	-em	-em	-er	-en
Gen.	-en	-en	-er	-er

Note:

- An adjective in the genitive singular masculine or neuter always takes the **-en** ending.

Circle all attributive adjectives in the illustrations.
Then determine:

- the gender, case, and number of the noun.
- why a particular adjective ending is used.

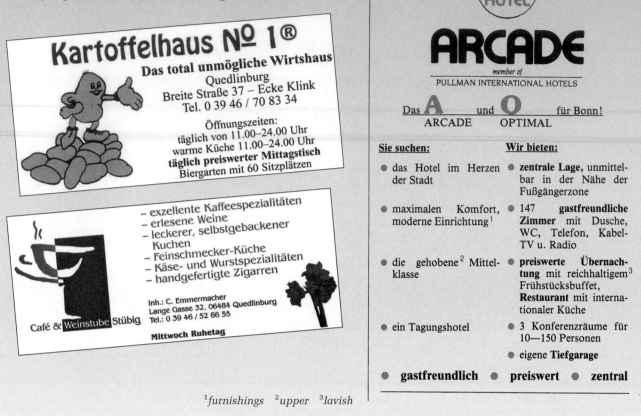

Kartoffelhaus № 1®

Das total unmögliche Wirtshaus

Quedlinburg
Breite Straße 37 – Ecke Klink
Tel. 0 39 46 / 70 83 34

Öffnungszeiten:
täglich von 11.00–24.00 Uhr
warme Küche 11.00–24.00 Uhr
täglich preiswerter Mittagstisch
Biergarten mit 60 Sitzplätzen

– exzellente Kaffeespezialitäten
– erlesene Weine
– leckerer, selbstgebackener Kuchen
– Feinschmecker-Küche
– Käse- und Wurstspezialitäten
– handgefertigte Zigarren

Inh.: C. Emmermacher
Lange Gasse 32, 06484 Quedlinburg
Tel.: 0 39 46 / 52 66 55

Café & Weinstube Stübig

Mittwoch Ruhetag

¹*furnishings*   ²*upper*   ³*lavish*

ARCADE
HOTEL

member of
PULLMAN INTERNATIONAL HOTELS

Das **A** und **O** für Bonn!
ARCADE   OPTIMAL

Sie suchen:

- das Hotel im Herzen der Stadt
- maximalen Komfort, moderne Einrichtung¹
- die gehobene² Mittelklasse
- ein Tagungshotel

Wir bieten:

- **zentrale Lage,** unmittelbar in der Nähe der Fußgängerzone
- 147 **gastfreundliche Zimmer** mit Dusche, WC, Telefon, Kabel-TV u. Radio
- **preiswerte Übernachtung** mit reichhaltigem³ Frühstücksbuffet, **Restaurant** mit internationaler Küche
- 3 Konferenzräume für 10—150 Personen
- eigene **Tiefgarage**

● **gastfreundlich** ● **preiswert** ● **zentral**

Adjectives that end in the vowel **-a** (**lila, rosa**) do not add adjective endings. They remain unchanged.

Meine Oma hat **lila** Haare.   *My grandma has purple hair.*

Übung 13   Kurze Gespräche

Sie hören zwei kurze Gespräche. Ergänzen Sie die Adjektivendungen, so wie Sie sie hören.

DIALOG 1

GERD: Sag mal, seit wann hast du denn blau_____¹ Haare?

GABI: Seit letzt_____² Woche. Gefallen sie dir?

GERD: Na ja, ich war an deine braun_____³ Haare gewöhnt.

GABI: Ich habe ja auch blau_____⁴ Augen. Die blau_____⁵ Haare passen gut zu meinen blau_____⁶ Augen.

GERD: Ein merkwürdig_____⁷ Grund (*masc.*). Na ja, meine Oma hat lila Haare.

DIALOG 2

PASSANT: Entschuldigung, wo ist das Rathaus?

PASSANTIN: Meinen Sie das alt____⁸ oder das neu____⁹?

PASSANT: Oh, es gibt zwei? Ein alt____¹⁰ und ein neu____¹¹? Ich suche das Rathaus mit dem berühmt____¹² Glockenspiel.

PASSANTIN: Also, das ist das alt____¹³ Rathaus. Gehen Sie geradeaus, dann die zweit____¹⁴ Straße links. Das Rathaus liegt auf der recht____¹⁵ Seite.

Das Rathaus in München am Marienplatz

Übung 14 Kleinanzeigen°: Gesucht/Gefunden

Classified ads

Ergänzen Sie die Lücken mit den passenden Adjektivendungen.

1. Studentin sucht schön____ Zimmer in nett____ Wohngemeinschaft.

2. Freundlich____ Englisch-lehrer sucht klein____ Wohnung in zentral____ Lage.

3. Italienisch____ Studentin sucht nett____ Zimmer im Norden der Stadt.

4. **Gesucht.** Klein____, schwarz____ Pudel entlaufen, Nähe Stadtpark. Hört auf den Namen Papageno. Belohnung.

5. **Gefunden.** Groß____, graugetigert____ Kater, Nähe Rosenbachstraße und Meisenweg.

6. **Gefunden.** Freundlich____, klein____ Katze, schwarz mit weiß____ Nase, Landeshauptstraße, Ecke Stadtpark.

Übung 15 Hin und her: Was gibt es hier?

Fragen Sie einen Partner / eine Partnerin nach den fehlenden Informationen.

BEISPIEL: s1: Was gibt es beim Gasthof zum Bären?
s2: Warme Küche.
s1: Was gibt es sonst noch?
s2: Bayerische Spezialitäten.

WO?	WAS?	WAS SONST NOCH?
Gasthof zum Bären		
Gasthof Adlersberg	ein Biergarten / gemütlich	liegt in Lage / idyllisch
Gasthaus Schneiderwirt		
Hotel Luitpold	liegt in Lage / idyllisch	Zimmer / rustikal
Restaurant Ökogarten	Gerichte / vegetarisch	

Adjectives Referring to Cities and Regions

Das Hotel liegt in der **Frankfurter** Innenstadt.

Wo trägt man **Tiroler** Hüte?

Wo isst man **Wiener** Schnitzel?

A city or regional name can be used attributively by adding **-er** to the name of the city or region. This is one of the rare instances where an adjective is capitalized in German. No further changes are made. One country name can also be used in this way: **die Schweiz.**

Essen Sie gern **Schweizer** Käse?

Jenaer Bücherstube

KABARETT
Leipziger Pfeffermühle

Für Ausflugsfahrten brauchen Sie einen echten Hamelner Bus:

RATTENFÄNGER-REISEN HAMELN

RATTENFÄNGER-REISEN HAMELN
Bahnhofstraße 18/20
☎ (0 51 51) 10 84 92 · Fax 10 84 93

Die Bremer Stadtmusikanten

Übung 16   Berichte

Sie sind gerade von einer Reise nach Hause gekommen. Nun müssen Sie berichten.

Was hast du da gesehen oder gemacht?

BEISPIEL: s1: Was hast du in Köln gemacht?
　　　　　 s2: Da habe ich den Kölner Dom besichtigt.

1. in Hamburg / den Hafen besichtigt
2. in Bremen / die Stadtmusikanten gesehen
3. in Düsseldorf / die berühmte Altstadt besucht
4. in Dortmund / Bier getrunken
5. in Berlin / eine Weiße mit Schuss getrunken
   [ein Spezialgetränk aus Bier und Saft]
6. in München / Weißwurst gegessen
7. in der Schweiz / Käse gekauft
8. in Wien / Walzer getanzt

Sprache im Kontext

Videoclips

A. Hotel Jurine: Interview mit Nadine Schulz. Nadine Schulz arbeitet im Hotel. Sie gibt viele Informationen über das Hotel. Was sagt sie?

1. Der Name des Hotels ist ____ ____ des Inhabers.
2. Das Hotel hat 53 ____.
3. Ein Einzelzimmer kostet zwischen ____ und ____ Euro.
4. Ein ____ kostet zwischen 80 und 140 Euro.
5. Die Zimmer haben ____, WC, ____, Telefon, ISDN-Anschluss und Modem für Computer.

B. Wie gefällt Doris und Beatrice das Hotel? Was sagen sie?

Das Hotel ist ...

C. Michael fragt Dennis nach dem Weg zum Alexanderplatz. Was sagt Dennis? Nummerieren Sie die Sätze in der richtigen Reihenfolge.

____ und dann kannst du es nicht verfehlen

____ du gehst am besten immer geradeaus

____ und dann gehst du immer geradeaus circa fünf Minuten

____ vorne an der Ampel gehst du nach links

____ Nächste gleich wieder rechts

Lesen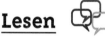

Zum Thema

A. Vorteile (*Advantages*) **und Nachteile** (*disadvantages*) **des Stadtlebens.** Arbeiten Sie zu zweit. Machen Sie eine Liste von den Vorteilen und Nachteilen des Stadtlebens.

B. Zusammenwohnen. Interviewen Sie zwei Leute im Deutschkurs und berichten Sie danach im Plenum.

1. Was ärgert dich (*annoys you*), wenn du zu Hause bist?
2. Was machst du, wenn deine Nachbarn/Nachbarinnen zu laut sind?
   a. Ich beschwere mich persönlich.
   b. Ich beschwere mich beim Hausmanager.
   c. Ich bin dann noch lauter als sie.

C. Was würden Sie machen?

1. Sie müssen für eine Prüfung lernen, und Ihr Mitbewohner / Ihre Mitbewohnerin spielt sehr laute Musik.
2. Sie studieren Musik (Trompete) und müssen jeden Tag üben. Ihre Nachbarn im Haus beschweren sich immer, wenn Sie spielen.

A. In dem folgenden Text stehen die Verben im Imperfekt (*simple past*). Suchen Sie den Infinitiv in der zweiten Spalte.

1. _____ spielte		**a.** schlagen (*to hit*)
2. _____ gab		**b.** sprechen
3. _____ stieß		**c.** grüßen
4. _____ losging		**d.** ausziehen (*to move out*)
5. _____ blies		**e.** einziehen (*to move in*)
6. _____ schlug		**f.** losgehen (*to start, begin*)
7. _____ traf		**g.** anfangen
8. _____ grüßte		**h.** stören (*to disturb*)
9. _____ einzog		**i.** stoßen (*to pound*)
10. _____ auszog		**j.** spielen
11. _____ sprach		**k.** blasen (*to blow*)
12. _____ anfing		**l.** treffen
13. _____ störte		**m.** geben

B. Lesen Sie die ersten zwei Absätze (*paragraphs*). Wo findet die Geschichte statt (*takes place*)? Wie könnte die Geschichte weitergehen?

DIE GITARRE DES HERRN HATUNOGLU

von Heinrich Hannover

Frau Amanda Klimpermunter spielte oft und gern Klavier. Aber sie wohnte in einem großen Mietshaus. Und da gab es manchmal Ärger° mit den Mietern der Nachbarwohnungen. Denn die Wände und Decken des Hauses waren dünn°.

5   In der Wohnung unter Frau Klimpermunter wohnte Herr Maibaum. Wenn oben Klavier gespielt wurde, fühlte sich Herr Maibaum in seiner Ruhe gestört° und schimpfte°. Dann stieß er ein paarmal mit einem Besenstiel an die Decke. Aber Frau Klimpermunter spielte weiter. Und so schaffte sich Herr Maibaum eines Tages eine Trompete an. Und 10 immer, wenn Frau Klimpermunters Klaviermusik losging, trompetete er kräftig° dagegen.

    Das störte nun den Nachbarn des Herrn Maibaum, der sich schon über das Klavier genug geärgert hatte. Und jetzt auch noch die Trompete, das war zuviel. Ein paarmal klopfte° er mit einem Holzpantoffel gegen die 15 Wand. Aber Herr Maibaum trompetete weiter. Und so schaffte sich der Nachbar, er hieß Fromme-Weise, eine Posaune an. Und immer, wenn das Klavier und die Trompete im Haus ertönten, blies er laut wie ein Elefant auf der Posaune.

    Aber das störte nun Frau Morgenschön, die Wand an Wand mit 20 Herrn Fromme-Weise wohnte. Ein paarmal schlug sie mit dem Kochlöffel gegen die Wand, aber das kümmerte ihren Nachbarn nicht. Und so kaufte sie sich eine Flöte und düdelte° dazwischen, wenn die anderen Musikanten im Haus loslegten.

    Das störte Herrn Bollermann, der unter Frau Morgenschön wohnte. 25 Er kaufte sich ein Schlagzeug und haute, wenn die anderen herumtönten, kräftig auf die Pauke. Das gab nun alle Tage einen Höllenlärm im Haus, ein fürchterliches Durcheinander – tüdelüdelüt-bumsbums-trärä-trarabumspeng ... Wenn man sich auf der Treppe traf, grüßte keiner den

trouble

thin

disturbed / yelled, swore

powerfully, vigorously

knocked

noodled

anderen, man knallte° mit den Türen, es gab immer Krach° im Haus, *slammed / noise*
30 auch wenn keiner Musik machte.

Aber dann zog Herr Hatunoglu ins Haus ein, ein Ausländer, wie man
schon am Namen merkt. Er brachte eine Gitarre mit und freute sich,
daß im Haus musiziert wurde. „Da kann ich ja auch ein bißchen Gitarre
spielen", sagte er. Aber obwohl man die Gitarre bei dem Lärm, den die
35 anderen Hausbewohner mit ihren Instrumenten machten, gar nicht
hören konnte, waren sich plötzlich alle einig: „Die Gitarre ist zu laut."
Plötzlich sprachen sie wieder miteinander.

„Finden Sie nicht auch, daß der Herr Hatunoglu mit seiner Gitarre
einen unerträglichen Lärm macht?"
40 „Ja, Sie haben recht, der Mann muß raus."

Sie grüßten sich wieder auf der Treppe und hörten auf, sich gegenseitig
zu nerven. Dem Herrn Hatunoglu aber machten sie das Leben schwer°. *difficult*
Wenn er anfing, auf der Gitarre zu spielen, klopften sie von oben und
von unten und von allen Seiten mit Besenstielen, Kochlöffeln und
45 Holzpantoffeln an Wände und Decken und riefen: „Aufhören! Ruhe im
Haus!"

„Was haben die Leute bloß gegen meine Gitarre?" fragte Herr
Hatunoglu. Und eines Tages zog er aus.

Kaum war Herr Hatunoglu ausgezogen, ging der Krach im Haus
50 wieder los. Sobald Frau Klimpermunter den ersten Ton auf dem Klavier
gespielt hat, packen die anderen Hausbewohner ihre Instrumente aus
und legen los: Tüdelüdelüt-bumsbums-trärä-trara-bumspeng ... Sie
sprechen auch nicht mehr miteinander und grüßen sich nicht mehr auf
der Treppe. Und sie knallen wieder mit den Türen. Aber abends, wenn
55 sie völlig entnervt ins Bett gehen, flüstern sie vor sich hin: „Was war
das doch für eine schöne, ruhige Zeit, als noch der Herr Hatunoglu mit
seiner Gitarre im Haus wohnte."

Zum Text

A. Wer wohnt wo? Setzen Sie die Namen der Bewohner in das Bild ein.
Sehen Sie sich nun auch die Bilder auf Seite 286 an. Welches
Instrument gehört zu welcher Person? Welches „Schlagzeug" gehört
zu welcher Person?

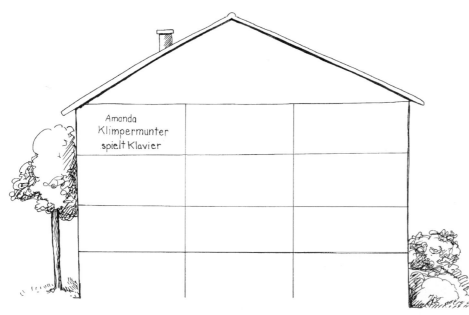

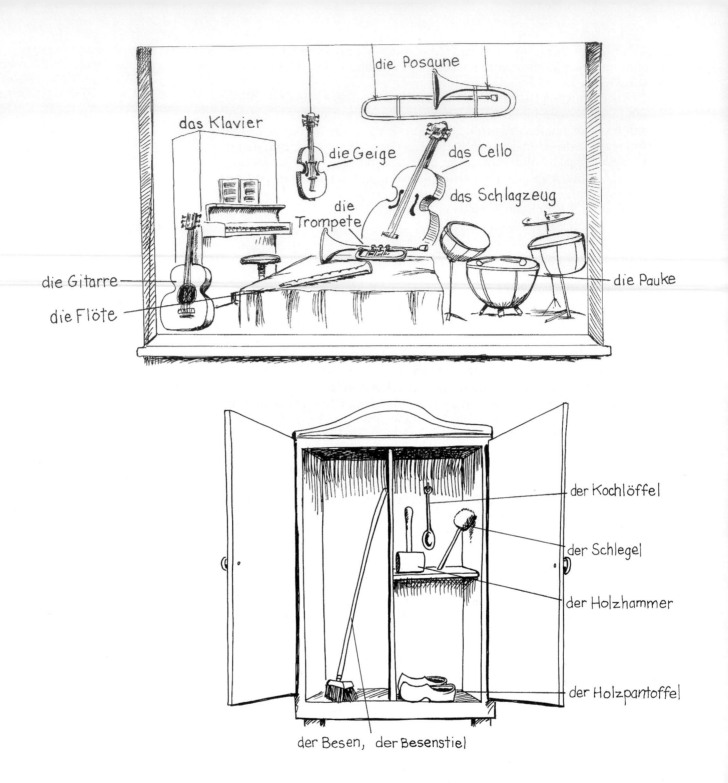

die Posaune

das Klavier

die Geige

das Cello

die Trompete

das Schlagzeug

die Gitarre

die Flöte

die Pauke

der Kochlöffel

der Schlegel

der Holzhammer

der Holzpantoffel

der Besen, der Besenstiel

B. Stimmt das? Stimmt das nicht? Oder steht das nicht im Text?

	DAS STIMMT	DAS STIMMT NICHT	DAS STEHT NICHT IM TEXT
1. Herr Hatunoglu ist unfreundlich.	☐	☐	☐
2. Nachdem Herr Hatunoglu einzieht, sprechen die Nachbarn wieder miteinander.	☐	☐	☐
3. Herr Hatunoglu spielt Gitarre und ist sehr froh, dass die anderen Bewohner so viel Musik machen.	☐	☐	☐
4. Die anderen Bewohner sagen, sie mögen Herrn Hatunoglu nicht, weil er so laut ist.	☐	☐	☐
5. Herr Hatunoglu lädt oft Freunde ein, und sie sind sehr laut.	☐	☐	☐
6. Sobald Herr Hatunoglu auszieht, werden die anderen Bewohner miteinander viel freundlicher.	☐	☐	☐

C. Die folgenden Wörter stehen im Text. Welches Wort gehört nicht in die Gruppe? Sagen Sie warum.

BEISPIEL: Holzpantoffel   Klavier   Besen →
Klavier gehört nicht dazu. Frau Klimpermunter spielt Klavier. Die Nachbarn schlagen mit dem Holzpantoffel und Besen gegen die Wand, wenn sie Musik hören.

1. sich etwas anschaffen   düdeln   trompeten
2. Nachbarn kümmern   die Tür knallen Krach machen
3. klopfen   schlagen   flüstern
4. anschaffen   aufhören   kaufen

D. Wählen Sie eine Person aus der Geschichte „Die Gitarre des Herrn Hatunoglu". Beschweren Sie sich über die Situation im Haus aus der Perspektive dieser Person. Schreiben Sie Ihre Beschwerde (*complaint*) auf, und lesen Sie sie der Klasse vor. Die anderen müssen raten, wer Sie sind.

E. Interviewen Sie Herrn Hatunoglu und eine weitere Person im Haus. Schreiben Sie mindestens drei Fragen für jede Person auf. Arbeiten Sie in Gruppen zu viert. Zwei Studenten / Studentinnen übernehmen die Rollen. Die anderen interviewen die beiden.

Zu guter Letzt

Eine Webseite für Touristen

Entwerfen Sie eine Webseite über Ihre Heimatstadt für Touristen.

Schritt 1: Suchen Sie im Internet einen Stadtplan von Ihrer Heimatstadt oder Ihrer Universitätsstadt. Identifizieren Sie die wichtigsten Sehenswürdigkeiten, z.B. Denkmäler (*monuments*), Gebäude (*buildings*), Plätze und Parks.

Schritt 2: Schreiben Sie einen kurzen Text über fünf bis sieben der wichtigsten Sehenswürdigkeiten in der Stadt. Suchen Sie auch passende Fotos dazu.

Schritt 3: Stellen Sie nun alles zusammen und machen Sie die Webseite. Benutzen Sie die Stadt Wittenberg als Modell (www.wittenberg.de). Vergessen Sie nicht, einen kurzen historischen Überblick zu geben.

Schritt 4: Tauschen Sie Ihre Webseite mit einem Partner / einer Partnerin aus. Jeder muss dann drei Fragen über die Webseite vorbereiten.

Schritt 5: Stellen Sie Ihrem Partner / Ihrer Partnerin die Fragen und notieren Sie die Antworten. Berichten Sie dann der Klasse, was Sie über die Stadt gelernt haben.

Wortschatz

In der Stadt — In the City

die **Ampel, -n**	traffic light
der **Bahnhof, ⸚e**	train station
die **Bank, -en**	bank
die **Fußgängerzone, -n**	pedestrian zone
der **Hafen, ⸚**	harbor, port
das **Hotel, -s**	hotel
die **Innenstadt, ⸚e**	downtown
die **Jugendherberge, -n**	youth hostel
die **Kirche, -n**	church
die **Kreuzung, -en**	intersection
die **Lage, -n**	location
das **Museum,** *pl.* **Museen**	museum
der **Passant (-en** *masc.***), -en /** die **Passantin, -nen**	passer-by
die **Pension, -en**	bed and breakfast, small family-run hotel
die **Polizei**	police, police station
die **Post,** *pl.* **Postämter**	post office
das **Rathaus, ⸚er**	city hall
das **Schloss, ⸚er**	castle, palace
der **Tierpark, -s**	zoo
der **Tourist (-en** *masc.***), -en /** die **Touristin, -nen**	tourist
der **Weg, -e**	way, path; road
das **Zentrum,** *pl.* **Zentren**	center (of town)

Im Hotel — At the Hotel

das **Anmeldeformular, -e**	registration form
der **Apparat, -e**	set, appliance (*such as TV, telephone, camera*)
der **Aufenthalt, -e**	stay; layover
der **Aufzug, ⸚e**	elevator
die **Bettwäsche**	linens
das **Doppelzimmer, -**	room with two beds, double room
die **Dusche, -n**	shower
das **Einzelzimmer, -**	room with one bed, single room
das **Erdgeschoss, -e**	ground floor
der **Föhn, -e**	hair dryer
der **Frühstücksraum, ⸚e**	breakfast room
das **Gepäck**	luggage
der **Internetzugang**	Internet access
die **Kreditkarte, -n**	credit card
der **Kühlschrank, ⸚e**	refrigerator
der **Parkplatz, ⸚e**	parking space; parking lot
der **Preis, -e** im Preis enthalten	price; cost included in the price
der **Reisepass, ⸚e**	passport
die **Rezeption**	reception desk
der **Schlüssel, -**	key
der **Stock,** *pl.* **Stockwerke**	floor, story
die **Übernachtung, -en**	overnight stay
die **Unterkunft, ⸚e**	accommodation
das **WC, -s**	bathroom, toilet

Nach dem Weg fragen — Asking Directions

bis: bis zum/zur	to, as far as
gegenüber von (+ *dative*)	across from
geradeaus immer geradeaus	straight ahead (keep on going) straight ahead
links nach links	left to the left
rechts nach rechts	right to the right
weit	far
die **Ecke, -n** an der Ecke	corner at the corner
die **Haltestelle, -n**	bus stop

die **Mitte**	middle, center
in der Mitte (der Stadt)	in the center (of the city)
die **Nähe**	vicinity
in der Nähe (des Bahnhofs)	near (the train station)

Verben / Verbs

ab•reisen, ist abgereist	to depart
an•kommen, ist angekommen	to arrive
sich an•melden	to check in, register
aus•füllen	to fill out
sich beschweren über (+ acc.)	to complain about
ein•biegen	to turn, to make a turn
entlang•gehen, ist entlanggegangen	to walk along
erlauben	to allow, permit
funktionieren	to work, function
reparieren	to repair
übernachten	to stay overnight

Adjektive und Adverbien / Adjectives and Adverbs

günstig	favorable, convenient(ly)
günstig liegen	to be conveniently located

kaputt	broken
sofort	immediately
übrigens	by the way
ungefähr	about, approximately
zuerst	first, at first

Genitivpräpositionen / Genitive Prepositions

außerhalb	outside of
innerhalb	inside of, within
trotz	in spite of
während	during, while
wegen	because of, on account of

Sonstige Ausdrücke / Other Expressions

Auf welchen Namen?	Under what name?
Auf Wiederhören!	Good-bye! (*on telephone*)
Das tut mir leid.	I'm sorry.
Entschuldigung	excuse me
jemand nach dem Weg fragen	to ask someone for directions
Wie komme ich am besten dahin?	What's the best way to get there?
Würden Sie (bitte) ... ?	Would you (please) . . . ?

DAS KANN ICH NUN!

1. Sie sind beim Informationszentrum einer deutschen Stadt und suchen ein Zimmer. Nennen Sie 3–4 Dinge, die Ihnen wichtig sind.
2. Sie sind an der Rezeption eines Schweizer Hotels. Sie haben eine Reservierung. Was sagen Sie?
3. Sie sind in einer fremden Stadt und suchen das Rathaus. Fragen Sie jemand auf der Straße nach dem Weg.
4. Wie heißen diese Wörter auf Deutsch?
   a. *street crossing* b. *traffic light*
   c. *straight ahead*
5. Sie sind in einem Hotel in einer deutschen Stadt und erzählen einem Freund/einer Freundin etwas über das Hotel. Wie sagen Sie dies auf Deutsch?

   a. *My room is on the first floor.* d. *The hotel is located in the center of town near the railroad station.* c. *Behind the hotel is a big, beautiful park.* d. *In the park there is a small lake.*
6. Sie schreiben eine Postkarte aus Wien. Ergänzen Sie die Adjektivendungen.

   Wien ist eine sehr schön___ Stadt mit viel___ interessanten Museen und historisch___ Kirchen. Neben meinem Hotel liegt ein alt___ Schloss. Hinter dem alt___ Schloss liegt ein wunderschön___ Park. Gestern habe ich im Restaurant ein Wien___ Schnitzel gegessen. Zum Glück haben wir gut___ Wetter.

Das kann ich nun!   **289**

Drittes Zwischenspiel

Die Entwicklung der Stadt

Im Laufe der Zeit hat sich das Bild der Stadt sehr verändert[1]. Viele Städte in Deutschland, wie auch anderswo in Europa, haben aber zum Teil ihren ursprünglichen[2] Charakter aus der mittelalterlichen Zeit erhalten[3]. Sie sind stolz auf ihre Vergangenheit, die oft bis ins Mittelalter und manchmal bis in die Römerzeit zurückreicht. Köln wurde zum Beispiel im Jahre 50 gegründet, Erfurt im 9. Jahrhundert. Die Geschichte Goslars reicht in das 10. Jahrhundert zurück. Gelegentlich sind sogar noch Überreste alter Bauten und Denkmäler[4] aus frühen Zeiten zu sehen.

Aktivität 1   Mittelalterliche Städte

Wie sahen Städte im Mittelalter aus? Was gehörte zum typischen Stadtbild? Kreuzen Sie an.

- ☐ Restaurants
- ☐ Gefängnis[5]
- ☐ Burg/Schloss
- ☐ Universität
- ☐ Kirche/Dom
- ☐ Bürgerhäuser[6]
- ☐ Wachttürme[7]
- ☐ Krankenhaus
- ☐ Markt
- ☐ Geschäfte
- ☐ Parks
- ☐ Bibliothek
- ☐ Schule
- ☐ Fabrik
- ☐ Stadtmauer[8]
- ☐ Rathaus
- ☐ Museum
- ☐ Stadttor[9]

[1]changed [2]original [3]preserved [4]Bauten ... buildings and monuments [5]prison [6]patrician houses [7]watchtowers [8]city wall [9]city gate

Aktivität 2   Nürnberg damals

Schauen Sie sich jetzt die Stadtansicht von Nürnberg aus dem Jahr 1533 an. Identifizieren Sie die Hauptmerkmale der Stadt.

1. _____ Burg
2. _____ Kirche
3. _____ Brücke
4. _____ Bürgerhäuser
5. _____ Stadtmauer
6. _____ Wachtturm

- ■ Welche(s) Gebäude[10] bildete(n) den Kern[11] einer mittelalterlichen Stadt? Warum?
- ■ Wer wohnte in der Stadt? Wer wohnte außerhalb der Stadt?

[10]building(s)   [11]center

Erfurt

Köln

Nürnberg heute

Nürnberg im Jahr 1533

Aktivität 3 Nürnberg heute

Vergleichen Sie die zwei Ansichten von Nürnberg. Obwohl Nürnberg während des Zweiten Weltkriegs fast völlig zerstört[1] wurde, sind noch einige Bauten und Denkmäler aus dem Mittelalter und der Renaissance erhalten. Wie viele der folgenden Bauten und Denkmäler können Sie auf dem Stadtplan finden?

1. St. Sebaldus Kirche (14. Jahrhundert)
2. St. Lorenz Kirche (13.–14. Jahrhundert)
3. das Rathaus (14. Jahrhundert)
4. die Stadtmauer (14.–15. Jahrhundert)
5. der Schöne Brunnen (1389–1396)
6. die Burg (11.–12. Jahrhundert)

Aktivität 4 Auf den Spuren[2] der Stadtentwicklung

Wählen Sie eine Stadt in Ihrem Land aus. Es kann auch Ihre Heimatstadt sein. Beschreiben Sie folgendes:

- Wie sah die Stadt vor 100 Jahren aus?
- Was gehörte damals zum Stadtbild?

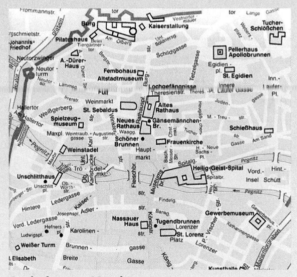

Stadtplan von Nürnberg

- Gab es einen Mittelpunkt der Stadt? Wenn ja, was gehörte dazu? Ein Markt, eine Kirche oder ein anderes Gebäude?
- Welche alten Bauten und Denkmäler sind noch in dieser Stadt erhalten? Welche sind verschwunden[3]? Warum?

[1]*destroyed*   [2]*Auf … On the trail*   [3]*disappeared*

Auf Reisen

Alles einsteigen!

In diesem Kapitel

- **Themen:** Travel, vacations, modes of transportation, items to take on vacation
- **Grammatik:** Superlative, adjectival nouns, simple past tense, conjunction **als,** past perfect tense
- **Kultur:** German vacations, German geography, dealing with a travel agency, buying a train ticket
- **Lesen:** „The American Dream" (Bernd Maresch)

Videoclips
Wohin im Urlaub?

Alles klar?

A. Was planen Sie für Ihren nächsten Urlaub? Was interessiert Sie? Lesen Sie die folgenden Anzeigen.

- Auf welcher Reise kann man eine Fremdsprache lernen?
- Welche Reisen sind für sportliche Leute am geeignetsten (*most suited*)? Welche Sportarten kann man auf diesen Reisen machen?
- Welche Reise verbindet (*connects*) Sport und Kultur? Welche verbindet Action mit Erholung in der Natur?
- Was macht Ihnen persönlich in den Ferien Spaß: eine Fremdsprache lernen? Tennisspielen lernen? eine Kanutour machen? Mountainbiking?

Tennis, Biken, Wassersport, Marathon und vieles mehr
AKTIV URLAUB

SportScheck Reisen

Sun and Fun Sportreisen GmbH
Franz-Joseph-Str 43
D-80801 Munchen

Hammer Str. 418
48153 Münster
Telefon 0251/87188-0

RUCKSACK REISEN
Aktivurlaub, Gruppenreisen und Kanutouren

Wildwasser-Kajak

Eine faszinierende Sportart, die Action und Adrenalin mit intensiver Erholung in unverbrauchter[1] Natur verbindet. Erlernbar für jeden, der bereit ist, im Team zu agieren und Spaß zu haben. Die Reviere[2] in Frankreich, Slowenien und Österreich zählen zu den Klassikern des Wildwassersports.

[1] unspoiled   [2] preserves

SPANISCH in LATEINAMERIKA

z.B. Bolivien
2 Wo Einzelunterricht[3] 25 Std/Wo
Wochenend-Tourenprogramm
Unterkunft m. VP bei Gastfamilie
Kleinkinderbetreuung[4]

schon ab € 700,–

ALR Wolfgang Retz Postfach 380 153/D
Conradstr. 16/4 Berlin 13509
Tel: (030) 805 49 30. Fax: (030) 805 15 52

[3] one-on-one instruction
[4] child care

TENNIS & KULTUR IN PRAG

€ 200,–

1 Wo inkl.: 5x2(4) Std. **Tennistraining**
+ HP + Kulturprogramm · Info + Buchung:
Tel. (089) 53 94 34 od. 53 64 35 · Fax 532 84 70
Tamar-Reisen·Häberlstraße 13·München 80337

B. Sie hören drei Gespräche über den Urlaub. Wo haben die Urlauber ihre Ferien verbracht? Was haben sie unternommen?

WO	WAS
1. **a.** an der Nordsee	**a.** segeln
b. an der Ostsee	**b.** Camping
2. **a.** Mexiko	**a.** Spanisch lernen
b. Bolivien	**b.** tauchen
3. **a.** in den Dolomiten	**a.** Bergsteigen
b. im Schwarzwald	**b.** wandern

Wörter im Kontext

THEMA 1: Ich möchte verreisen

Wie reisen Sie am liebsten?

□ mit dem Wagen

□ mit dem **Flugzeug**

□ mit dem Fahrrad

□ mit dem **Zug** / mit der **Bahn**

□ mit dem **Taxi**

□ mit dem Motorrad

□ mit dem **Schiff**

□ **per Autostop**

□ mit dem **Bus**

BEISPIEL: Ich reise am liebsten mit dem Bus.

A. Und warum? Was finden Sie …

am interessantesten?	am langweiligsten?	am praktischsten?
am **sicher**sten?	am **gefährlich**sten?	am **laut**esten?
am **schnell**sten?	am **langsam**sten?	am bequemsten?

B. Fragen Sie jemand, wie er oder sie **verreisen** möchte.

BEISPIEL: s1: Also Sven, du möchtest verreisen? Wohin?
s2: Nach Marokko.
s1: Wie kommst du dahin?
s2: Mit dem Schiff.
s1: Und warum?
s2: Das ist am interessantesten.

Siehe *Expressing Comparisons: The Superlative,* S. 301.

Neue Wörter

sicher safe
schnell fast
laut loud
gefährlich dangerous
langsam slow
verreisen go on a trip
die Reise trip
vergessen forgotten
der Handschuh (Handschuhe, *pl.*) glove
der Reiseführer travel guide
der Strand beach
das Sonnenschutzmittel suntan lotion, sunscreen
das Handgepäck carry-on luggage
das Bargeld cash
der Reisescheck (Reiseschecks, *pl.*) travelers' check
der Personalausweis ID card
die Fahrkarte (Fahrkarten, *pl.*) ticket
die Platzkarte (Platzkarten, *pl.*) seat-reservation cards
der Fahrplan schedule

Ihre Checkliste vor der Reise – haben Sie nichts vergessen?

In den Koffer packen …

Bekleidung
☐ Unterwäsche
☐ Regenmantel
☐ **Handschuhe**
☐ Jogginganzug
☐ Schlafanzug
☐ Schal
☐ Sportbekleidung

Schuhwerk
☐ Hausschuhe
☐ Turnschuhe

Toilettensachen
☐ Hautcreme
☐ Zahnpasta
☐ Haarshampoo
☐ Zahnbürste

Für Ihre Aktivitäten im Urlaub
☐ Kamera, Filme
☐ **Reiseführer**
☐ Stadtpläne
☐ Landkarten

Für den Strand
☐ **Sonnenschutzmittel**
☐ Sonnenbrille
☐ Badehose/Badeanzug

Für die Berge
☐ Wanderstock
☐ Wanderschuhe
☐ Rucksack

Das sollte im Handgepäck nicht fehlen …
☐ Reiseapotheke
☐ Reiselektüre

Auch das muss mit - aber nicht im Koffer!
☐ **Bargeld**
☐ **Reiseschecks,** Euroschecks
  Achtung! Scheckkarte!
☐ Reisepass, **Personalausweis**
☐ **Fahrkarten**
☐ **Platzkarten**
☐ **Fahrplan**
☐ Kofferschlüssel
☐ Wohnungsschlüssel

Aktivität 1   Alles für die Reise

Diese Wörter haben alle mit Reisen zu tun. Welches Wort in jeder Gruppe passt nicht?

1. Stadtplan, Landkarte, Reiseführer, Zahnbürste
2. Badeanzug, Sportbekleidung, Stadtplan, Regenmantel
3. Bargeld, Turnschuhe, Reiseschecks, Reisepass
4. Wanderschuhe, Wanderstock, Kofferschlüssel, Rucksack

Aktivität 2   Haben Sie etwas vergessen?

Schauen Sie sich die Reise-Checkliste aus **Thema 1** an und nennen Sie zwei Dinge aus der Liste, die Sie unbedingt (*absolutely*) mitnehmen würden.

BEISPIEL: Ich möchte eine Mountainbike-Tour machen. Ich nehme Sonnenschutzmittel und eine Kamera mit.

eine Wanderreise durch Europa

eine Reise nach Hawaii

eine Safari nach Afrika

eine Reise nach _____

Deutsche Arbeitnehmer bekommen im Jahr durchschnittlich (*on average*) sechs Wochen bezahlten Urlaub. Das erklärt, warum der Urlaub ein so wichtiges Thema ist. Wie kann man sechs Wochen freie Zeit sinnvoll planen? Die meisten, vor allem Familien, nehmen den größten Teil des Urlaubs im Sommer, wenn die Kinder Ferien (*school holidays*) haben. Viele Deutsche machen auch im Winter Urlaub: Sie fahren in den Bergen Ski oder suchen ein wärmeres Klima im Süden.

Aktivität 3 Hin und her: Was nehmen sie mit?

Wohin fahren diese Leute im Urlaub? Was nehmen sie mit? Und warum? Ergänzen Sie die Informationen.

BEISPIEL: s1: Wohin fährt Angelika Meier in Urlaub?
s2: Sie fährt in die Türkei.
s1: Warum fährt sie in die Türkei?
s2: Weil …
s1: Was nimmt sie mit?
s2: Sie nimmt …

PERSONEN	WOHIN?	WARUM?	WAS NIMMT ER/SIE MIT?
Angelika Meier	in die Türkei	sich am Strand erholen	Buch, Sonnenbrille, Badesachen
Peter Bayer			
Roland Metz	nach Thüringen	wandern, Weimar besichtigen	Stadtpläne, Reiseführer, Wanderschuhe
Sabine Graf			

Advantages and disadvantages

Aktivität 4 Vorteile und Nachteile°

Alles hat seine Vorteile und Nachteile. Was meinen Sie?

BEISPIELE: Mit dem Fahrrad sieht man viel, aber es ist anstrengend.
Mit dem Auto geht es schneller, aber es ist _____.

mit dem/der _____	geht es	nicht	bequem / anstrengend
Bahn (Zug)	ist es	sehr	billig / teuer
Bus	kostet es	zu	praktisch / unpraktisch
Fahrrad	sieht man		romantisch / langweilig
Flugzeug			schnell / langsam
Wagen (Auto)			sicher / gefährlich
per Autostop			viel / wenig
zu Fuß			
??			

THEMA 2: Eine Wandertour

Teil A: *Ein Gespräch im **Reisebüro** zwischen Claudia Siemens und Herrn Bittner, einem Angestellten im Reisebüro.*

FRAU SIEMENS: Mein Freund und ich möchten dieses Jahr mal einen Aktivurlaub machen. Wir wollen mal was anderes **erleben.** Können Sie etwas **vorschlagen?**

HERR BITTNER: Ja, gern. Wofür interessieren Sie sich denn? Es gibt so viele **Möglichkeiten.** Sind Sie sportlich **aktiv?**

FRAU SIEMENS: Nicht besonders. Manchmal spielen wir Tennis und fahren auch schon mal Rad.

HERR BITTNER: Wie wäre es mit einer Radreise durchs Elsass – oder mit einem Segelkurs an der Ostsee?

FRAU SIEMENS: Ach, ein Segelkurs ist mir zu anstrengend. Ich kann auch nicht gut schwimmen. Und eine Radreise … ich weiß nicht. Was können wir **sonst noch unternehmen?**

HERR BITTNER: Wir haben hier ein **Angebot** für eine viertägige Wandertour im Naturpark Solling-Vogler in der Nähe von Göttingen. Hier ist ein **Reiseprospekt.** Das kann ich sofort für Sie **buchen.**

FRAU SIEMENS: Hmm, klingt gut. Wo übernachtet man denn?

HERR BITTNER: Im **Zelt** natürlich.

FRAU SIEMENS: Ach, ich weiß nicht, ob mein Freund **damit einverstanden ist.** Er liebt die **Natur** zwar, aber in der Natur übernachten? Wir werden es **uns überlegen.**

Teil B: *Ein Gespräch zu Hause zwischen Claudia und ihrem Freund Manfred. Sie zeigt ihm den Reiseprospekt vom Reisebüro.*

CLAUDIA: Also, wie findest du diese Wandertour im Naturpark?

MANFRED: Hmm. Mit einer Wandertour bin ich einverstanden aber in der Natur übernachten? Das ist nicht mein **Ding.** Schauen wir mal im Internet nach. Vielleicht finden wir dort noch andere Möglichkeiten.

CLAUDIA: Ja, schau mal, hier ist etwas. Auch eine Wandertour – eine dreitägige – im Thüringer Wald.

MANFRED: Und wo **beginnt** die Tour?

CLAUDIA: Die Teilnehmer treffen sich mit einem Reiseleiter in Großbreitenbach nicht weit von Ilmenau. Von da aus fährt die Gruppe mit einem Bus zum Park. Die **Fahrt** dauert nicht lange und unterwegs sieht man viel Grünes.

MANFRED: Und wo schläft man unterwegs? Ich **hoffe** nicht im Zelt.

CLAUDIA: Nein, nicht im Zelt. In kleinen **Hütten.**

MANFRED: Hm, klingt gut. Was soll die Reise **insgesamt** kosten?

CLAUDIA: 300 Euro **pro Person.** Sollen wir das sofort buchen?

MANFRED: Mir ist es recht. Das ist günstig.

CLAUDIA: Ich werde Georg und Monika anrufen. Vielleicht wollen die beiden mitkommen. Wir machen das **zu viert.**

Neue Wörter

das Reisebüro travel agency
erleben experience
vorschlagen suggest
die Möglichkeit (Möglichkeiten, *pl.***)** possibility
sonst noch otherwise
unternehmen undertake, do
das Angebot offer
der Reiseprospekt travel brochure
buchen book
das Zelt tent
damit einverstanden ist (sein) will agree to that
uns überlegen (sich überlegen) think over
das Ding thing
die Fahrt trip
hoffe (hoffen) hope
die Hütte (Hütten, *pl.***)** cabin
insgesamt altogether
zu viert as a foursome

SPRACHTIPP

Eine Wandertour von vier Tagen ist eine **viertägige** Wandertour. Eine Fahrt von einer Woche ist eine **einwöchige** Fahrt. Ein Aufenthalt von fünf Monaten ist ein **fünfmonatiger** Aufenthalt. So macht man es:

ein-	-stündig
zwei- +	-tägig
drei-	-wöchig } + Adjektivendung
…	-monatig

In einem Reisebüro

Ergänzen Sie:

1. Im Reisebüro kann man eine Reise

_____.

2. Das Reisebüro hat ein _____ für eine Wandertour.

3. Über die Reise kann man im _____ lesen.

4. Die Tour im Naturpark Solling-Vogler dauert

_____.

5. Manfred ist mit der Wandertour im Thüringer Wald _____.

6. Der Preis für die Wandertour ist _____.

7. Claudia will Georg und Monika einladen und die Reise _____ machen.

Aktivität 5   Eine Wandertour — tolle Idee!

Claudia Siemens trifft sich mit ihren Freunden Georg und Monika im Café und berichtet über die Internetsuche. Ergänzen Sie die Sätze mit Informationen aus dem Gespräch im **Thema 2.**

CLAUDIA: Manfred und ich wollen eine _____¹ machen. Im Internet haben wir etwas Interessantes gefunden – im Thüringer Wald. Habt ihr Lust?

MONIKA: Wie lange dauert denn so eine Tour?

CLAUDIA: _____.²

MONIKA: Und wo übernachtet man?

CLAUDIA: _____.³

GEORG: Was soll das denn kosten?

CLAUDIA: _____.⁴

GEORG: Ist das nicht ein bisschen teuer?

CLAUDIA: _____.⁵

MONIKA: Du, Georg, was meinst du? Sollen wir das machen?

GEORG: Also, ich finde das ist mal was anderes.

MONIKA: Gut, dann sind wir damit _____.⁶ Wir kommen mit!

Aktivität 6   Pläne für einen interessanten Urlaub

Sie hören vier Gespräche im Reisebüro. Wie, wohin und warum wollen die Leute in Urlaub fahren? Wie lange wollen sie dort bleiben?

Hier klicken!

Weiteres zum Thema Reisen finden Sie bei **Deutsch: Na klar!** im World-Wide-Web unter www.mhhe.com/dnk5.

PERSONEN	WIE?	WOHIN?	WARUM?	WIE LANGE?
1. Nicola Dinsing				
2. Marianne Koch und Astrid Preuß				
3. Herbert und Sabine Lucht				
4. Sebastian Thiel				

Aktivität 7 Überredungskünste°

Versuchen Sie, einen Partner / eine Partnerin zu einem Plan für einen gemeinsamen Urlaub zu überreden (*persuade*). Die Anzeigen (*ads*) in **Alles klar?** bieten mögliche Reisen.

s1	s2
1. Ich möchte dieses Jahr nach/in ——. Willst du mit?	2. Was kann man denn da unternehmen?
3. Man kann da zum Beispiel ——.	4. Ist das alles? Was sonst noch?
5. Nein, man kann auch ——.	6. Wo übernachtet man denn?
7. ——.	8. Wie viel soll das kosten?
9. ——.	10. Wie kommt man dahin?
11. ——.	12a. Ich will es mir überlegen. b. Ich weiß nicht, das ist mir zu —— (teuer, langweilig usw.). c. Klingt gut. Ich komme mit.

THEMA 3: Eine Fahrkarte, bitte!

Wo ist das?

1. Am —— kauft man Fahrkarten für den Zug.
2. Der Zug fährt von —— 2 ab.
3. Man bekommt Informationen über Züge bei der ——.
4. Auf dem —— kann man lesen, wann ein Zug ankommt oder abfährt.
5. Die Leute stehen auf dem —— und warten auf den Zug.

Reiseverbindungen

Deutsche Bahn **DB**

BAHNHOF	UHR	ZUG	BEMERKUNGEN[2]

VON   *Bad Harzburg*   *Gültig[1] am Montag, dem 09.08.*
NACH   *Hamburg Hbf*
ÜBER

BAHNHOF   UHR   ZUG   BEMERKUNGEN[2]

Bad Harzburg   ab 10:46 E   3622
  Hannover Hbf   an 12:25
                 ab 12:43 ICE   794   Zugrestaurant
Hamburg Hbf   an 13:56

[1]*valid* [2]*notes*

Am Fahrkartenschalter im Bahnhof

Hier klicken!

Weiteres zum Thema Bahnfahren finden Sie bei **Deutsch: Na klar!** im World-Wide-Web unter www.mhhe.com/dnk5.

MICHAEL: Eine Fahrkarte nach Hamburg, bitte.

ANGESTELLTER: **Hin und zurück?**

MICHAEL: Nein, **einfach, zweiter Klasse,** bitte.

ANGESTELLTER: Das macht €42. Das ist übrigens der Sparpreis für Jugendliche. Haben Sie Ihren Ausweis dabei?

MICHAEL: Ja, natürlich. Wann fährt denn der nächste Zug?

ANGESTELLTER: In dreißig Minuten. In Hannover müssen Sie dann **umsteigen.**

MICHAEL: Habe ich da gleich **Anschluss?**

ANGESTELLTER: Sie haben achtzehn Minuten Aufenthalt. Dann können Sie mit dem ICE weiter nach Hamburg fahren. Für den ICE müssen Sie allerdings noch einen Platz reservieren. Möchten Sie im Großraumwagen sitzen, oder lieber in einem Abteil?

MICHAEL: Lieber in einem Abteil. Nichtraucher, bitte. Wann komme ich in Hamburg an?

ANGESTELLTER: Um 13.56 Uhr.

MICHAEL: Danke schön.

ANGESTELLTER: Bitte sehr.

Aktivität 8 Michaels Pläne

Ergänzen Sie den Text mit Informationen aus dem Dialog.

Michael fährt mit dem _____[1] nach Hamburg. Er kauft seine Fahrkarte am Schalter im _____.[2] Er fährt zweiter _____.[3] Der nächste Zug nach Hannover fährt in _____[4] ab. Michael muss in Hannover _____.[5] Dort hat er gleich _____[6] an den ICE nach Hamburg. Für den ICE muss er einen _____[7] reservieren.

Sie hören drei kurze Dialoge am Fahrkartenschalter. Setzen Sie die richtigen Informationen in die Tabelle ein.

INFORMATION	DIALOG 1	DIALOG 2	DIALOG 3
Fahrkarte nach			
1. oder 2. Klasse			
einfach oder hin und zurück			
für wie viele Personen			
Platzkarten?			

Grammatik im Kontext

Expressing Comparisons: The Superlative°

Der Superlativ

In **Kapitel 7** you learned how to express comparisons using the comparative. In this chapter you will learn about the superlative form of adjectives and adverbs. The superlative indicates the highest degree of a quality or quantity.

Mit dem Zug fährt man **am bequemsten.**	*Traveling by train is the most comfortable.*
Zu Fuß ist es **am schönsten.**	*Walking is the nicest.*
Mit dem Heißluftballon sieht man **am meisten.**	*By hot air balloon you see the most.*

Zu Fuß ist es am schönsten.

Mit dem Heißluftballon sieht man am meisten.

Note:

- The superlative form of adverbs and predicate adjectives is **am ____-sten.**

- German has only one form of the superlative, in contrast to English (*most* and *-(e)st*).

bequem	**am bequemsten**	*the most comfortable*
freundlich	**am freundlichsten**	*the most friendly/the friendliest*
schnell	**am schnellsten**	*the fastest*

Was machen Berliner am liebsten?

Urlaub.

Beratung[1] und Buchung bei uns im TUI Reisebüro.

Sie haben es sich verdient.[2] *Urlaub mit der TUI.*

TUI

[1] *advice* [2] *sich ... earned*

- Most adjectives of one syllable with the vowel **a, o,** or **u** in the stem add an umlaut in the superlative.

hoch	**am höchsten**	*highest*
lang	**am längsten**	*longest*

- Adjectives ending in **-s, -ß, -z,** or **-t** add **-esten** to the basic form.

heiß	**am heißesten**	*hottest*
kurz	**am kürzesten**	*shortest*
laut	**am lautesten**	*loudest*

- Some common irregular forms are these:

gern	**am liebsten**	*most preferred*
groß	**am größten**	*biggest, largest*
gut	**am besten**	*best*
viel	**am meisten**	*most*

Übung 1 Zur Wiederholung: kurz und bündig

Ergänzen Sie die Tabelle mit den fehlenden Formen.

	GRUNDFORM	KOMPARATIV	SUPERLATIV
1.	bequem	bequemer	am bequemsten
2.	_____	jünger	_____
3.	hoch	_____	_____
4.	_____	mehr	_____
5.	_____	lieber	_____
6.	_____	besser	_____
7.	laut	_____	_____
8.	_____	_____	am kürzesten

Übung 2 Wo mag das sein?

Schritt 1: Ergänzen Sie zuerst die Fragen mit dem Superlativ des Adjektivs oder Adverbs in Klammern.

BEISPIEL: Wo regnet es __*am meisten*__ ? (viel)

1. Wo sind die Berge _____? (hoch)
2. Wo schmeckt das Bier _____? (gut)
3. Wo sind die Bierkrüge (*beer mugs*) _____? (groß)
4. Wo verbringen die Deutschen einen warmen Sommerabend _____? (gern)
5. Wo feiert man _____? (viel)
6. Wo singen die Deutschen _____? (laut)
7. Wo fahren die Autos _____? (schnell)
8. Wo übernachtet man _____? (günstig)

Schritt 2: Arbeiten Sie nun zu zweit und beantworten Sie abwechselnd (*taking turns*) die Fragen in **Schritt 1.** Im Kasten sind mögliche Antworten.

BEISPIEL: s1: Wo regnet es am meisten?
  s2: Ich glaube, am meisten regnet es in Norddeutschland.

in Österreich   in einem Biergarten   auf der Autobahn   zu Hause

in einer Jugendherberge   in der Schweiz

beim Karneval in Köln   in Bayern

im Hofbräuhaus in München   in Norddeutschland

Übung 3 Hin und her: Wie war der Urlaub?

Herr Ignaz Huber aus München war drei Wochen im Urlaub in Norddeutschland. Er war zwei Tage in Hamburg, eine Woche in Cuxhaven und nicht ganz zwei Wochen auf der Insel Sylt. Stellen Sie Ihrem Partner / Ihrer Partnerin Fragen über seinen Urlaub. Benutzen Sie den Superlativ.

BEISPIEL: s1: Wo war es am wärmsten?
  s2: Am wärmsten war es in Cuxhaven.

	IN HAMBURG	IN CUXHAVEN	AUF DER INSEL SYLT
1. *Wo war es (kalt/warm)?*			
2. *Wo waren die Hotels (günstig/teuer)?*	150 Euro	90 Euro mit Halbpension	200 Euro
3. *Wo hat es (viel) geregnet?*			
4. *Wo war das Hotelpersonal (freundlich)?*	freundlich	sehr freundlich	unfreundlich
5. *Wo war der Strand (schön)?*			
6. *Wo hat das Essen (gut) geschmeckt?*	ziemlich gut	nicht besonders	ausgezeichnet

Attributive Adjectives in the Comparative

When adjectives in the comparative are used attributively, i.e. before a noun, they take adjective endings.

Ich brauche einen größer**en** Koffer.	*I need a larger suitcase.*
Sie suchen ein günstiger**es** Hotel?	*You're looking for a more reasonably priced hotel?*
Günstiger**e** Hotels findet man in kleiner**en** Städten.	*You'll find more reasonably priced hotels in smaller towns.*
Wo finde ich ein besser**es** Restaurant?	*Where do I find a better restaurant?*

Note:

- Attributive adjectives in the comparative add appropriate adjective endings to the comparative forms:

größer	Hier ist ein größer<u>er</u> Koffer.
besser	Wo gibt es ein besser<u>es</u> Restaurant?
kleiner	Das kleiner<u>e</u> Hotel war günstiger.

- When used attributively, **mehr** and **weniger** (the comparatives of **viel** and **wenig**) do not take adjective endings.

Ich brauche **mehr** Geld für die Reise.	*I need more money for the trip.*
Ich habe jetzt **weniger** Zeit zum Reisen.	*I now have less time for traveling.*

Übung 4 Werners Reisevorbereitungen

Werner erzählt von seinen Reisevorbereitungen. Hören Sie zu und markieren Sie die beste Ergänzung zu jedem Satz.

1. Werner braucht …
   a. mehr Geld. **b.** mehr Zeit. **c.** mehr Arbeit.
2. Er braucht auch …
   a. einen kleineren Koffer. **b.** einen größeren Koffer.
   c. zwei kleinere Koffer.
3. Er nimmt ____ mit.
   a. die kleinere Kamera **b.** die neuere Kamera
   c. die größere Kamera
4. Dies ist Werners …
   a. längster Urlaub. **b.** teuerster Urlaub. **c.** kürzester Urlaub.

Übung 5 Probleme im Urlaub

Herr Ignaz Huber aus München fährt in Urlaub. Aber überall gibt es Probleme.

BEISPIEL: Sein Mietwagen ist zu klein. →
         Er wünscht sich einen größeren Wagen.

1. Das Hotel ist zu teuer.
2. Das Hotelzimmer ist ungemütlich.
3. Das Bett ist zu kurz.
4. Das Bad ist zu klein.
5. Die Bedienung ist unhöflich.
6. Das Essen ist schlecht.
7. Seine Wanderschuhe sind unbequem.
8. Das Wetter ist zu heiß.
9. Der Urlaub ist zu kurz.

Attributive Adjectives in the Superlative

Arnstadt ist die **älteste** Stadt Thüringens.

Arnstadt is the oldest city in Thuringia.

In Thüringen gibt es die **schönsten** Rathäuser.

The most beautiful city halls are in Thuringia.

Das **beste** Bier gibt es in München.

You'll find the best beer in Munich.

Note:

- Attributive adjectives in the superlative add **-(e)st** plus an appropriate adjective ending to the adjective.
- A definite article usually precedes the adjective in the superlative.

Übung 6 Tatsachen° über Deutschland

Facts

Die meisten Antworten finden Sie im **Kulturtipp**.

BEISPIEL: Berlin ist die größte Stadt Deutschlands.

Bayern	ist	das nördlichste Bundesland
Bremen	hat	die meiste Industrie
Frankfurt	produziert	die höchsten Berge
Berlin		die älteste Universität
Heidelberg		das berühmteste Porzellan
Nordrhein-Westfalen		das kleinste Bundesland
Meißen		den größten Flughafen
Rheinland-Pfalz		die größte Stadt
Mecklenburg-Vorpommern		den meisten Wein
Schleswig-Holstein		die meisten Seen
??		??

Die schönsten Rathäuser in Thüringen

Hessen-Thüringen

ADAC Freizeitservice

Wissenswertes über Deutschland

- Zwei Drittel allen Weins kommt aus Rheinland-Pfalz.
- Mecklenburg-Vorpommern hat 600 Seen.
- Nordrhein-Westfalen hat mehr Industrie als die anderen Bundesländer.
- Die meisten Touristen und Besucher landen auf dem Frankfurter Flughafen.
- Berlin hat über drei Millionen Einwohner.
- Meißen produziert das berühmteste Porzellan.
- Die größte Insel ist Rügen (926 km^2).
- Der längste Fluss ist der Rhein (865 km), der zweitlängste ist die Elbe (700 km).
- Der höchste Berg ist die Zugspitze (2962 m), der zweithöchste ist der Watzmann (2713 m).
- Die Universität Heidelberg existiert seit 1386.

Burg Katz am Rhein

Übung 7 Eine Reise nach Österreich

Sie planen eine Reise nach Österreich und brauchen Information. Was möchten Sie wissen?

1. Wie heißt die _____ (schön) Stadt Österreichs?
2. Wie heißt das _____ (preiswert) Hotel in Wien?
3. Wo liegen die _____ (interessant) Sehenswürdigkeiten?
4. Welches ist das _____ (alt) Schloss?
5. In welchem Café gibt es den _____ (gut) Kaffee?
6. Wo gibt es die _____ (freundlich) Leute?
7. Wie heißt der _____ (groß) Vergnügungspark in Österreich?

Substantivierte Adjektive

Adjectival Nouns°

Adjectives can be used as nouns. As nouns, they are capitalized.

Deutsche und Amerikaner bezahlen Rechnungen oft mit Plastik.	*Germans and Americans frequently pay their bills with credit cards.*
Die meisten **Deutschen** zahlen mit Scheckkarte oder in bar.	*Most Germans pay with a debit card or cash.*
Auch die Kreditkarte ist **nichts Ungewöhnliches.**	*Even the credit card is nothing unusual.*

Note:

- An adjectival noun takes the same endings as an attributive adjective.

Ein **deutscher** Tourist hat mich nach dem Weg gefragt.	*A German tourist asked me for directions.*
Ein **Deutscher** hat mich nach dem Weg gefragt.	*A German asked me for directions.*

- The gender and number of an adjectival noun are determined by what it designates: people are masculine or feminine.

ein Deutsch**er** = a German (*man*)	**der** Deutsch**e** = the German (*man*)
eine Deutsch**e** = a German (*woman*)	**die** Deutsch**e** = the German (*woman*)
[zwei] Deutsch**e** = [two] Germans	**die** Deutsch**en** = the Germans

- The case of the adjectival noun depends on its function within the sentence.

Eine Deutsche hat den Zoo gesucht.	*A German (woman) was looking for the zoo.*
Ich habe **der Deutschen** den Weg gezeigt.	*I showed the German (woman) the way.*

- Abstract concepts are neuter. They are frequently preceded by words such as **etwas, nichts,** or **viel.**

Steht in der Zeitung **etwas Neues?**	*Is there anything new in the paper?*
Es gibt **nichts Neues.**	*There is nothing new.*
Er hat **viel Interessantes** von seiner Reise erzählt.	*He told a lot of interesting things about his trip.*

Übung 8   Die Urlauber sind alle aus Deutschland.

Ergänzen Sie die Sätze mit dem Wort **deutsch** als Nomen.

BEISPIEL: Die ___Deutschen___ reisen gern.

1. Das Traumziel (*dream destination*) der _____ ist Spanien.
2. Im Hotel auf Mallorca findet man nur _____.
3. Herr Keller ist aus Deutschland. Er ist _____.
4. Frau Keller ist auch _____.
5. Für die _____ sind Sonne und Meer sehr wichtig.
6. Die _____ liegen den ganzen Tag am Strand in der Sonne.
7. Abends gehen sie mit anderen _____ in die Diskos.
8. Am Ende des Urlaubs fliegen die _____ von der Sonne gebräunt nach Deutschland zurück. Die Bekannten zu Hause sind alle neidisch.

[1]*jealous*

Übung 9   Was erwarten diese Leute vom Urlaub?

BEISPIEL: Ich möchte im Urlaub etwas ___Schönes___ (schön) erleben.

1. Herr Lüders aus Berlin will nichts _____ (anstrengend). Er braucht nur gutes Wetter, Sonne und Meer.
2. Das Reisebüro Fröhlich bietet eine Reise zum Mars zum Sparpreis von nur 5 000 Euro. Das ist wirklich etwas _____ (toll)! Ich buche das sofort.
3. Ingrid und ihr Freund Horst möchten mit dem Rad durch Portugal fahren. Da sieht man viel _____ (interessant).
4. Herr und Frau Lindemann wollen nichts _____ (neu) sehen. Wie jedes Jahr fahren sie in die Alpen.
5. Marion sucht etwas _____ (ungewöhnlich). Sie bucht einen Kochkurs in der Toskana.

Narrating Events in the Past:
The Simple Past Tense°

You recall that in conversation about events in the past, the present perfect tense is preferred except for the verbs **haben, sein,** and modal verbs. These verbs are commonly used in the simple past tense in conversation as well as in written or formal language.

The simple past tense of other verbs is generally used in German to narrate past events in writing or in formal speech. By choosing this tense, the narrator or writer generally establishes a distance from the events.

Weak Verbs°

Weak verbs form the simple past tense by adding the marker **-(e)te** to the stem.

Wir **packten** unsere Sachen in einen Rucksack.	We packed our things in a backpack.
Wir **warteten** auf den Bus.	We waited for the bus.
Die Fahrt **dauerte** drei Stunden.	The trip took three hours.
Wir **übernachteten** in einer Jugendherberge.	We stayed at a youth hostel.

reisen			
ich	reis**te**	wir	reis**ten**
du	reis**test**	ihr	reis**tet**
er sie es	reis**te**	sie	reis**ten**
Sie reis**ten**			

warten			
ich	wart**ete**	wir	wart**eten**
du	wart**etest**	ihr	wart**etet**
er sie es	wart**ete**	sie	wart**eten**
Sie wart**eten**			

Note:

- The first- and third-person singular are identical, as are the first- and third-person plural.
- Verbs with stems ending in **-t** or **-d,** as well as some verbs with a consonant + **-n** in the stem (e.g., **regnen, öffnen**), add **-ete** to the stem.
- Weak verbs with separable and inseparable prefixes have the same past tense stem as the base verb.

In Wien **besuchten** sie die Spanische Reitschule.	In Vienna they visited the Spanish Riding School.
Die Familie **reiste** letzten Donnerstag **ab.**	The family departed last Thursday.

Übung 10 Kleine Erlebnisse° im Urlaub

experiences

Ergänzen Sie die Sätze mit passenden Modalverben im Imperfekt: **dürfen, können, müssen, wollen.**

BEISPIEL: Wir __*wollten*__ per Autostop nach Spanien fahren.

1. Niemand _____ uns mitnehmen.
2. Wir _____ zwei Stunden an der Autobahn warten.
3. Ein Fahrer _____ uns bis nach Freiburg mitnehmen.
4. Wir _____ in der Jugendherberge übernachten, aber dort war kein Platz mehr.
5. Deshalb _____ wir im Park übernachten.
6. Im Park _____ man aber nicht übernachten. Es war verboten.
7. Wir _____ aber noch eine Übernachtung auf einem Bauernhof bekommen.

Eine kleine Pause auf Reisen

Übung 11 Eine Reise nach Spanien

Rainer hat in der Schule über seine Sommerferien geschrieben. Setzen Sie Rainers Sätze ins Imperfekt.

BEISPIEL: Wir haben eine Reise nach Spanien gemacht. →
　　　　　 Wir machten eine Reise nach Spanien.

1. Schon drei Wochen vor der Reise habe ich meinen Koffer gepackt.
2. Bei unserer Abfahrt in Deutschland hat es geregnet.
3. Wir haben auf einem Campingplatz übernachtet.
4. Am Urlaubsort ist es jeden Tag regnerisch gewesen. So ein Pech!
5. Wir haben in einer kleinen Stadt gewohnt.
6. Wir haben alle Museen da besucht.
7. Die Reise hat nicht viel Spaß gemacht.
8. Das Schlimmste (*worst*): In Deutschland ist ein Traumsommer gewesen. Schade. Ohne mich.

Im Stau auf der Autobahn

Strong Verbs°

Strong verbs change their stem vowel in the simple past tense. Many verbs that are strong in English are also strong in German. You will find a comprehensive list of strong verbs in the Appendix.

Familie Stieber **fuhr** im Urlaub nach Spanien.	*The Stieber family drove to Spain on their vacation.*
Sie **standen** lange im Stau auf der Autobahn.	*They were in a traffic jam on the Autobahn for a long time.*
Der Urlaub **fing** nicht gut **an**.	*The vacation did not start out well.*

	fahren	**stehen**	**anfangen**	**verlieren**
ich	fuhr	stand	fing an	verlor
du	fuhr**st**	stand**est**	fing**st** an	verlor**st**
er sie } es	fuhr	stand	fing an	verlor
wir	fuhr**en**	stand**en**	fing**en** an	verlor**en**
ihr	fuhr**t**	stand**et**	fing**t** an	verlor**t**
sie/Sie	fuhr**en**	stand**en**	fing**en** an	verlor**en**

Note:

- The first- and third-person singular are identical; they have no personal endings.
- A past tense stem ending in a **-d, -t,** -or **-s** adds **-est** to the **du**-form and **-et** to the **ihr**-form.
- Like weak verbs, strong verbs with separable and inseparable prefixes have the same past tense stem as the base verb.

Mixed Verbs°

Mischverben

Several verbs change their stem vowel *and* add **-te** to the changed stem in the simple past, combining aspects of both strong and weak verbs. These verbs include:

bringen → brachte	verbringen → verbrachte	
denken → dachte	wissen → wusste	
kennen → kannte		

The simple past tense of **werden** (*to become*) is **wurde.**

The Conjunction als

The conjunction **als** has several important functions in German. You have learned to use it in the comparison of adjectives.

Mit dem Zug fährt man bequemer **als** mit dem Bus.

Additionally, **als** can be used as a subordinating conjunction meaning *when,* referring to a one-time event in the past. Sentences with the conjunction **als** are often in the simple past tense, even in conversation.

Als meine Reise nach Russland begann, war es schon Winter.	*When my trip to Russia began, it was already winter.*
Als ich am Morgen aufwachte, fand ich mich mitten im Dorf.	*When I woke up in the morning, I found myself in the middle of the village.*

ANALYSE

Sonderbares° Erlebnis einer Reise

Bizarre

Der Baron von Münchhausen lebte im 18. Jahrhundert und hatte einige merkwürdige Abenteuer. Man nannte ihn auch den „Lügenbaron" (*"lying baron"*), weil man ihm seine Geschichten nicht glaubte. Lesen Sie die folgende Geschichte und identifizieren Sie alle Verben im Imperfekt. Machen Sie eine Liste mit den Verben und geben Sie den Infinitiv an. Welche Verben sind stark? Welche sind schwach? Sie finden die Liste mit starken Verben im Anhang (*appendix*).

Münchhausens Reise nach Russland

Meine Reise nach Russland begann im Winter. Ich reiste zu Pferde°, weil das am bequemsten war. Leider trug ich nur leichte Kleidung, und ich fror° sehr. Da sah ich einen alten Mann im Schnee. Ich gab ihm meinen Reisemantel und ritt weiter. Ich konnte leider kein Dorf° finden. Ich war müde und stieg vom Pferd ab°. Dann band° ich das Pferd an einen Baumast° im Schnee und legte mich hin. Ich schlief tief und lange. Als ich am anderen Morgen aufwachte, fand ich mich mitten in einem Dorf auf dem Kirchhof°. Mein Pferd war nicht da, aber ich konnte es über mir hören. Ich schaute in die Höhe° und sah mein Pferd am Wetterhahn des Kirchturms° hängen. Ich verstand sofort, was passiert war. Das Dorf war in der Nacht zugeschneit° gewesen. In der Sonne war der Schnee geschmolzen°. Der Baumast, an den ich mein Pferd gebunden hatte°, war in Wirklichkeit die Spitze des Kirchturms gewesen. Nun nahm ich meine Pistole und schoss° nach dem Halfter°. Mein Pferd landete ohne Schaden° neben mir. Dann reiste ich weiter.

zu … on horseback

froze
village
stieg … got off the horse / tied
branch of a tree

churchyard (cemetery)
in … up
am … on the weather vane on top of the church tower / snowed under
melted
gebunden … had tied

shot / halter / damage

diary **Übung 12   Aus Münchhausens Tagebuch°**

Ergänzen Sie die Verben im Imperfekt.

Ich _____¹ (beginnen) meine Reise nach Russland im Winter. Ich
_____² (reisen) zu Pferde, weil das am bequemsten _____.³ (sein)
Leider _____⁴ (frieren) ich sehr, weil ich nur leichte Kleidung
_____.⁵ (tragen) Plötzlich _____⁶ (sehen) ich einen alten Mann im
Schnee. Ich _____⁷ (geben) ihm meinen Mantel und _____⁸
(reiten) weiter. Bald _____⁹ (sein) ich müde und _____¹⁰ vom
Pferd _____.¹¹ (ab•steigen) Ich _____¹² (binden) das Pferd an
einen Baumast im Schnee. Dann _____¹³ ich mich _____¹⁴
(hin•legen) und _____ _____.¹⁵ (ein•schlafen) Als ich am
anderen Morgen _____¹⁶ (auf•wachen), _____¹⁷ (finden) ich mich
mitten in einem Dorf. Ich _____¹⁸ (wissen) zuerst nicht, wo mein
Pferd war. Ich _____¹⁹ (kennen) keinen Menschen in diesem Dorf.

Übung 13   Münchhausens Reise

Sie hören die Geschichte von Münchhausens Reise nach Russland mit
sechs Veränderungen (*changes*). Können Sie sie identifizieren?

Übung 14   Wann war das?

Sagen Sie, wie alt Sie damals waren.

BEISPIEL: den Führerschein machen →
       Ich war 17 Jahre alt, als ich den Führerschein machte.

1. in den Kindergarten kommen
2. das erste Geld verdienen (*to earn*)
3. sich zum ersten Mal verlieben (*to fall in love*)
4. den Führerschein machen
5. meine Familie nach _____ umziehen (*to move*)
6. _____ (besten Freund oder beste Freundin) kennen lernen
7. meine erste Reise ins Ausland machen
8. zum ersten Mal tanzen gehen

The Past Perfect Tense°

The past perfect tense describes an event that precedes another event in the past.

Bevor wir in Urlaub fuhren, **hatten** wir alle Rechnungen **bezahlt.**	*Before we went on vacation we **had paid** all the bills.*
Nachdem wir auf Mallorca **angekommen waren,** gingen wir sofort an den Strand.	*After we **had arrived** in Mallorca, we immediately went to the beach.*

The conjunctions **bevor** and **nachdem** are commonly used to connect sentences with the simple past and past perfect tenses.

To form the past perfect, combine the simple past of **haben** (*hatte*) or **sein** (*war*) and the past participle of the main verb. Verbs using **sein** in the present perfect tense also use **sein** in the past perfect.

PRESENT PERFECT	PAST PERFECT
Ich **bin** gegangen.	Ich **war** gegangen. (*I had gone.*)
Wir **haben** bezahlt.	Wir **hatten** bezahlt. (*We had paid.*)

Übung 15   Die Fahrt hatte kaum begonnen

Ergänzen Sie die Sätze durch Verben im Plusquamperfekt.

1. Ich _____ schon früh aus dem Haus _____ (gehen), denn mein Flugzeug nach Frankfurt flog um 8 Uhr ab.
2. Ich _____ am Tag zuvor ein Taxi _____ (bestellen).
3. Am Flughafen fiel mir ein (*I remembered*), dass ich die Schlüssel in der Haustür _____ _____ (vergessen).
4. Kein Wunder, denn letzte Nacht _____ ich kaum _____ (schlafen).
5. Sobald ich am Flughafen _____ _____ (ankommen), rief ich eine Nachbarin (*neighbor*) an.
6. Der Flug nach Frankfurt war verspätet (*late*). Nachdem wir drei Stunden _____ _____ (warten), konnten wir endlich abfliegen.

Sprache im Kontext

Videoclips

A. Thomas Möllmann arbeitet im Reisebüro. Schauen Sie sich das Interview mit ihm an und ergänzen Sie die folgenden Informationen.

1. Ein Reiseziel, das im Moment „in" ist, ist _____.
2. Andere beliebte Reiseziele der Kunden sind _____ und die _____ _____.
3. Wie kommen die Kunden an den Urlaubsort? Die meisten Kunden _____.

4. Herr Möllmann hat dieses Jahr eine _____ an die _____ gemacht. Er ist mit der _____ gefahren.

5. Herr Möllmann hat vor, in ungefähr sechs Wochen nach _____ zu reisen.

6. Herr Möllmann arbeitet seit ungefähr _____ Jahren im Reisebüro.

B. Was sind beliebte Reiseziele in Ihrem Land?

C. Alex spricht über seine Urlaubspläne und über seinen Urlaub letztes Jahr. Schauen Sie sich das Interview an und machen Sie sich Notizen in der Tabelle. Benutzen Sie dann Ihre Notizen, um wenigstens 3–4 Sätze über den Urlaub von Alex zu schreiben.

Am schönsten ist's im eigenen Land

Wo die Deutschen 2005 ihren Urlaub verbrachten

Deutschland	32,0 %
Spanien	10,6
Italien	7,7
Österreich	6,1
Türkei	5,1
Osteuropa	5,0
Frankreich, Monaco	4,7
Griechenland	3,6
Kroatien, Slowenien	3,4
Skandinavien	3,4
Tunesien, Marokko, Ägypten	2,7
USA, Kanada	2,3
Asien	2,1
Karibik	1,5

Datenbasis: 4000 befragte Personen ab 14 Jahren im Januar 2006.
Quelle: BAT Freizeit-Forschungsinstitut

Urlaub dieses Jahr:	
Wohin? Wie lange?	
Wie kommt er dahin?	
Wo hat er gebucht?	
Urlaub letztes Jahr:	
Wo? Wie lange? Mit wem?	
Was hat er mitgenommen?	
Was hat er erlebt?	

D. Fragen Sie drei Personen in der Klasse, wohin sie dieses Jahr in Urlaub fahren und wo sie letztes Jahr waren. Berichten Sie der Klasse darüber.

Lesen

Zum Thema

A. Ihr letzter Urlaub. Beantworten Sie die folgenden Fragen und vergleichen Sie Ihre Antworten untereinander.

1. Wann haben Sie zum letzten Mal Urlaub gemacht?

2. Wohin sind Sie gefahren?

3. Sind Sie allein oder mit Freunden gefahren?

4. Was haben Sie dort gemacht?

5. Wie war das Wetter dort?

6. Wie lange waren Sie dort?

7. Was hat Ihnen dort (nicht) gefallen?

B. Ein Aktivurlaub. Die Werbung „Sportreisen" auf der nächsten Seite zeigt viele Möglichkeiten für einen Aktivurlaub. Schauen Sie sich die Tabelle mit einem Partner / einer Partnerin an.

- Welche Sportarten gibt es?
- Wo finden diese Aktivitäten statt *(take place)*?
- Was macht man alles da?
- Für welche Sportart muss man am fittesten sein?
- Welche Reise möchten Sie machen? Warum?

SPORTREISEN ...

Sportart	Ort	Leistungen	Reisetermin	Preis	Grad*
Rafting	Colorado/USA	zwei Übernachtungen im Hotel, Transfer, Raftingtour, Bootsführer, alle Mahlzeiten während der Tour, Campingausrüstung, Anreise in Eigenregie[1]	1., 8., 15. und 22.9.	ab 800 € für 7 Tage	••
Katamaransegeln	Levkada/Griechenland	Flug, Übernachtungen im Appartement, kostenlose Benutzung der Katamarane und Segelflotte,[2] Teilnahme am Unterricht[3]	1., 8., 15., 22. und 29.9.	ab 715 € pro Woche	•••
Tauchen	Villi Varu/Malediven	Flug ab Düsseldorf, sechs Übernachtungen mit Vollpension, Sechs-Tage-Tauchpaket à 1 Tauchgang[4] täglich und 2 Hausriff-Tauchgänge (inkl. Boot, Flasche, Blei und Bleigurt)[5]	3., 10., 17. und 24.9.	115 € pro Woche	•
Aktiv-Camp	Berchtesgaden/Deutschland	Schnupperkurs[6] im Klettergarten,[7] River-Rafting auf der Saalach, Mountainbike-Tour, Bergwanderung, Paragliding-Schnupperkurs, sechs Übernachtungen mit Frühstück, Ausrüstung,[8] Führung[9]	6.–12.9.	300 €	•
Surfen	Bonaire/Karibik	Flug ab Amsterdam, Übernachtung im Appartement mit Selbstversorgung[10] oder im Hotel mit Frühstück, Surfboard-Miete 115 Euro pro Woche	6., 13., 20. und 27.9.	ab 1100 € pro Woche	••
Reiten	Costa Blanca/Spanien	Flug, acht Tage mit sieben Übernachtungen im Appartement mit Selbstversorgung, Reitprogramm, Reitführung, Unterlagen, Qualifikation: sicher in den Grundgangarten,[11] gute Kondition	9.–16.9.	ab 1050 €	••

* Zeigt den Grad der körperlichen[12] Fitneß, die der Teilnehmer[13] mitbringen muß: ••• = sehr gut trainiert, •• = körperlich fit, • = auch für Anfänger[14]

[1]Anreise ... *passage excluded* [2]*sailing fleet* [3]Teilnahme ... *participation in instruction* [4]*dive* [5]Blei ... *weight and weight belt* [6]*sampler class* [7]*climbing garden* [8]*equipment* [9]*guide* [10]*no meals provided* [11]sicher ... *secure in all the basic paces* [12]*physical* [13]*participant* [14]*beginners*

Auf den ersten Blick

A. Schauen Sie sich den Text „The American Dream" an. Was für ein Text ist das?
   1. ein Interview   **2.** ein Gedicht   **3.** ein Reisebericht

B. Überfliegen Sie das Lesestück. Der Text berichtet über:
   1. die Arbeitserfahrung eines deutschen Studenten in den USA
   2. eine Reise für Studenten in die USA
   3. eine Beschreibung von Städten und Regionen in den USA

C. Präziser bitte! Suchen Sie diese Informationen im Text!
   1. Wie lange war Bernd insgesamt in den USA?
   2. Was hat er in den USA gemacht?
   3. In welchen Bundesstaaten hat er gearbeitet?

von Bernd Maresch

Jobben in den USA

Just another summer of my life?! „ … aber es wird noch ein bisschen
dauern, es ist gerade rush-hour in New York City", säuselt° mir die   *murmurs*
freundliche amerikanische Stimme ins Ohr. Vor ein paar Minuten sind
wir im JFK-Airport gelandet. Nun bin ich im Land der unbegrenzten
5 Möglichkeiten, die Vordiplomprüfungen sind vorbei, die
Semesterferien liegen vor mir, und warum sollte ich diese nicht
jobbenderweise° in den USA verbringen, um die Mythen dieses Landes   *while working*
kennen zu lernen?

New York Times Square: Im Land der unbegrenzten Möglichkeiten

Was folgte, waren drei aufregende Monate, die ich als „American
10 Dream" bezeichne: In Manhattan arbeitete ich zusammen mit 20 jungen
Leuten aus zwölf Nationen im „New York Student Center". Mit einem
Drücken° im Magen starte ich zu meinem ersten Auftrag: Ich sollte eine   *sinking feeling*
Gruppe von 35 Briten am JFK in Empfang nehmen° und sie über   *in … to receive*
die „dos & don'ts" dieser Stadt aufklären. Es war ein seltsames Gefühl,
15 allein in einer fremden Stadt vor einer Gruppe englischsprechender
Menschen zu stehen und ihnen in ihrer Muttersprache mit meinem
deutsch-akzentuiertem Englisch das Programm zu erklären.

Dennis Hopper in Manhatten und Bruce Willis im Central Park

New York zeigte sich von seiner weltstädtischen° Seite. Zu acht   *cosmopolitan*
20 wohnten wir in einem großzügigen° Appartement, das wir in der Nähe   *spacious*
von SoHo anmieteten. Die Seiten meines Tagebuchs der folgenden
Wochen lesen sich wie ein Star-Report aus der Yellow-Press: Wir trafen
Dennis Hopper bei Dreharbeiten° mitten auf den Straßen von   *filming*
Manhattan und Bruce Willis beim Rollerbladen im Central Park. Bon
25 Jovi gab ein Spontan-Konzert am Times Square vor dem Auftritt bei
David Letterman.
    Nach sechs Wochen wechselte ich den Schauplatz. Arbeiten mit
Rangern in einem von Utahs Nationalparks. Die pralle° Natur stand   *intense*
freilich im krassen° Gegensatz zum New Yorker Großstadtleben. Unsere   *stark*
30 Crew lebte selbstversorgend in „bunk houses" inmitten des Uinta
National Forest. Arbeitslohn erhielten wir in Form von Unterkunft
und Verpflegung°.   Unterkunft … *room and board*

Jeep, Motorboot und Pferde

Wir mussten hart zupacken°: Holzzäune errichten°, Pipelines für
35 Tränken° der Waldtiere in den Boden graben und Wanderwege anlegen.
Dabei standen uns ein Jeep, ein Motorboot und Pferde zur Verfügung.
Ein Demolition-Derby, ein echtes Rodeo, Indianerkultur in Form von
alten Felsmalereien° und historische Ausgrabungen an einem alten
Schlachtfeld spiegelten die Höhepunkte im Leben einer
40 amerikanischen Kleinstadt wider.

*knuckle down / Holzzäune ... build
wooden fences / watering*

rock paintings

Der berühmte Arches Naturpark im Bundesstaat Utah

Nach vier Wochen in Utah führte mich der Weg nach California, wo
ich den Rest meines Aufenthaltes verbrachte. Noch in Deutschland
hatte ich Amerikaner kennen gelernt, die ich nun besuchte. Und so flog
ich nach San Francisco. Die Gastfreundschaft ging soweit, dass ich das
45 Auto benutzen konnte, was mir so manchen Ausflug auf den Highway
No. 1 und nach Napa Valley möglich machte.

Als Clou° für mein Studium konnte ich in den Bibliotheken von
Berkeley und Stanford University so manches Schnäppchen° für meine
anstehende Hausarbeit erstöbern°, wenngleich es mich nach einem
50 Besuch an einer amerikanischen Uni gar nicht mehr zum Studium nach
Hause zog.

„ ... erreichen wir in Kürze Frankfurt am Main. Wir bitten Sie, die
Gurte° anzulegen und hoffen, Sie hatten einen guten Flug und einen
angenehmen Aufenthalt." Die Stimme der Stewardess weckt mich, und
55 erst nach Beginn des Semesters an einer deutschen Hochschule wurde
mir so richtig bewusst°, dass mein „American Dream" wahr gewesen ist.

*(coll.) side benefit
find, bargain
uncover*

seat belts

wurde ... I truly realized

—Quelle: Bernd Maresch; adaptiert aus: "The American Dream," *UNICUM,*
April 2006

Zum Text

A. Beantworten Sie die folgenden Fragen über Bernds Aufenthalt in den USA.

1. Warum wollte er in die USA kommen?
2. Was war Bernds erster Auftrag in New York?
3. Welche Erlebnisse und Erfahrungen hat Bernd in seinem Tagebuch niedergeschrieben?
4. Wo hat Bernd nach seinem Aufenthalt in New York gearbeitet? Was hat er dort erlebt? Was für Arbeit hat er dort gemacht?
5. Welche amerikanischen Sehenswürdigkeiten hat Bernd in Utah gesehen?
6. Wen hat Bernd in Kalifornien besucht? Was hat er in den Bibliotheken dort gefunden?

B. Bernd hat viele Höhepunkte seines Aufenthaltes in Amerika beschrieben aber nur wenige Details gegeben. Was möchten Sie zusätzlich noch gern wissen? Formulieren Sie drei Fragen für Bernd, wo Sie ihn nach mehr Details fragen.

1. _____
2. _____
3. _____

C. Bernd benutzt drei Arten von „Englisch" in seinem Reisebericht: (1) eingedeutschte (*Germanized*) Wörter, (2) Namen auf Englisch für Sehenswürdigkeiten in Amerika und (3) andere englische Wörter.

1. Suchen Sie diese Wörter und sortieren Sie sie in drei Kategorien.

(1) EINGEDEUTSCHTE WÖRTER	(2) NAMEN AUF ENGLISCH	(3) ANDERE ENGLISCHE WÖRTER
jobben	*Napa Valley*	*American Dream*

2. Suchen Sie deutsche Wörter oder Äquivalente für die Wörter, die Sie in Kategorie 3 gefunden haben.
3. Warum benutzt Bernd wohl diese drei Kategorien von Wörtern?

D. Bernds Reisebericht kurz und bündig (*in a nutshell*). Erzählen Sie Bernds Reisebericht mit Hilfe des folgenden Rasters (*template*) nach.

1. Bernds Aufenthalt begann _____.
2. Dort arbeitete er als _____.
3. Für seinen ersten Auftrag musste er _____.
4. In New York erlebte er _____.
5. Nach seinem Aufenthalt in New York _____.
6. Dort musste er schwere Arbeit machen, z.B. _____.
7. Danach _____.
8. Dort _____.
9. Für Bernd war die Reise nach Amerika _____.

Zu guter Letzt

Ein Reisebericht

Haben Sie je eine interessante Reise gemacht? allein? mit Freunden oder mit Familie? Schreiben Sie einen Bericht darüber – so kreativ wie möglich. Wenn Sie wollen, können Sie einen fiktiven Reisebericht oder im Stil von Bernd Maresch schreiben.

Schritt 1: Beginnen Sie mit einem Zitat (*quote*), das den Ton und die Stimmung Ihres Berichts angibt, z.B. aus einem Roman, einer Geschichte oder einem Lied. Das Zitat kann auf Englisch oder auf Deutsch sein. Erklären Sie dann, warum Sie die Reise gemacht haben.

- Freunde oder Familie besuchen?
- etwas Exotisches erleben?
- ein neues Land oder eine neue Stadt kennen lernen?
- einen Ferienjob finden?
- ??

Schritt 2: Schreiben Sie über zwei oder drei spezifische, interessante Erlebnisse auf der Reise. Geben Sie möglichst viele Details. Haben Sie interessante Leute kennen gelernt oder ungewöhnliche Dinge gesehen oder erlebt? (Benutzen Sie bitte drei Adjektive in der Komparativform und drei in der Superlativform. Gebrauchen Sie auch mindestens zehn Verben im Imperfekt.)

Schritt 3: Beenden Sie Ihren Reisebericht mit einer Überraschung (*surprise*) oder einer interessanten Bemerkung (*comment*) für den Hörer oder den Leser. Seien Sie hier so kreativ wie möglich.

Schritt 4: In kleinen Gruppen zu viert lesen Sie Ihre Reiseberichte Ihren Mitstudenten und Mitstudentinnen vor. Sie sollen Ihnen Fragen über den Reisebericht stellen und raten, ob Ihre Geschichte wahr ist oder nicht.

Wortschatz

Beginning with this chapter, the vocabulary section at the end of each chapter will list strong or irregular verbs with their principal parts as follows: **bringen, brachte, gebracht** or **fahren (fährt), fuhr, ist gefahren.**

Verkehrsmittel / Means of Transportation

die **Bahn, -en**	railway; train
der **Bus,** *pl.* **Busse**	bus
das **Fahrrad, ̈er**	bicycle
das **Flugzeug, -e**	airplane
das **Schiff, -e**	ship
das **Taxi, -s**	taxicab
der **Zug, ̈e**	train

Im Reisebüro / At the Travel Agency

das **Angebot, -e**	(special) offer; selection
die **Fahrkarte, -n**	ticket
die **Reise, -n**	trip
das **Reisebüro, -s**	travel agency
der **Reiseprospekt, -e**	travel brochure

Unterwegs / En Route

die **Abfahrt, -en**	departure
die **Ankunft, ̈e**	arrival
der **Anschluss, ̈e**	connection
die **Auskunft, ̈e**	information
der **Bahnsteig, -e**	(train) platform
das **Ding, -e**	thing
der **Fahrkarten-schalter, -**	ticket window
der **Fahrplan, ̈e**	schedule
die **Fahrt, -en**	trip; ride
die **Gepäckaufbe-wahrung**	baggage check
das **Gleis, -e**	track
die **Hütte, -n**	cabin
die **Möglichkeit, -en**	possibility, opportunity
die **Natur**	nature
die **Platzkarte, -n**	seat reservation card
der **Reiseführer, -**	travel guide (book)
der **Strand, ̈e**	beach

Zum Mitnehmen auf Reisen / Things to Take Along on a Trip

das **Bargeld**	cash
das **Handgepäck**	carry-on luggage
der **Handschuh, -e**	glove
die **Kamera, -s**	camera
der **Personalausweis, -e**	ID card
der **Reisescheck, -s**	traveler's check
das **Sonnenschutzmittel**	suntan lotion, sunscreen
das **Zelt, -e**	tent

Verben / Verbs

ab•**fahren (fährt ab), fuhr ab, ist abgefahren**	to depart, leave
beginnen, begann, begonnen	to begin, start
buchen	to book (a trip)
ein•**steigen, stieg ein, ist eingestiegen**	to board, get into (*a vehicle*)
erleben	to experience
hoffen (auf)	to hope (for)
packen	to pack
sich überlegen, überlegt	to think over
um•**steigen, stieg um, ist umgestiegen**	to transfer, change (trains)
unternehmen (unter-nimmt), unternahm, unternommen	to undertake
vergessen (vergisst), vergaß, vergessen	to forget
verreisen, ist verreist	to go on a trip
vor•**schlagen (schlägt vor), schlug vor, vorgeschlagen**	to suggest, propose

Adjektive und Adverbien / Adjectives and Adverbs

aktiv	active(ly)
gefährlich	dangerous(ly)
insgesamt	altogether, total
jung	young
langsam	slow(ly)
laut	loud(ly)
schnell	quick(ly), fast
sicher	safe(ly)

Sonstiges / Other

alles	everything
als (*subord. conj.*)	when
bevor (*subord. conj.*)	before

einfach	one-way (ticket); simple	per Autostop reisen	to hitchhike
einverstanden	to agree (with), be in	pro Person	per person
sein (mit)	agreement (with)	sonst noch	otherwise
erster/zweiter Klasse	to travel first/second	Sonst noch etwas?	Anything else?
fahren	class	sportlich aktiv	active in sports
hin und zurück	round-trip	zu zweit, zu dritt,	as a twosome threesome,
nachdem (*subord. conj.*)	after	zu viert, ...	foursome, . . .

DAS KANN ICH NUN!

1. Sagen Sie, wie Sie am liebsten reisen.

2. Sagen Sie, was Sie am liebsten im Urlaub machen.

3. Sie sind mit Freunden unterwegs in Deutschland und gehen in ein Reisebüro. Sie suchen Information über Wandertouren in den Alpen. Sagen Sie etwas über:

    a. was Sie mochten   **b.** wie lange, wie viele Leute (kleine/große Gruppe)   **c.** die Kosten

4. Sie stehen am Fahrkartenschalter am Kölner Hauptbahnhof. Sie wollen eine Tagesreise von Köln nach Düsseldorf machen. Was sagen Sie?

5. Sie packen Ihren Koffer für eine Reise in die Schweiz im August. Sagen Sie, was Sie mitnehmen.

6. Sie kommen von der Reise zurück und berichten in Ihrem Deutschkurs auf Deutsch:

    a. *The food tasted best in smaller restaurants.*   **b.** *Staying overnight in a youth hostel was the the best deal* (**günstig**).
    c. *The most beautiful and best-known mountain is called* **das Matterhorn.**

7. Sie berichten über eine Reise. Schreiben Sie mit Hilfe der folgenden Notizen einen Bericht im Imporfokt.

    Reise in Frankfurt beginnen / in einem kleinen Hotel günstig übernachten / am nächsten Morgen mit dem Zug von Frankfurt nach Berlin fahren / am späten Nachmittag in Berlin ankommen / sehr lange auf ein Taxi warten / essen in einem gemütlichen Restaurant im Hotel

Der Start in die Zukunft

KAPITEL

11

Gemeinsam lernen in einem
Lehrgang für Zahntechnik

In diesem Kapitel

- **Themen:** Career expectations, world of work, professions, job applications
- **Grammatik:** Future tense, relative clauses, **was für (ein),** negating sentences with **nicht** and **kein**
- **Kultur:** Help-wanted ads, applying for a job, the German school system, civilian service
- **Lesen:** „Karriere beim Film"

Videoclips
Mein Beruf – mein Leben

Alles klar?

A. Was wollen junge Deutsche vom Beruf? Die Informationen finden Sie im Schaubild.

Wünsche an den zukünftigen Beruf

Von je 100 Schülern nennen als sehr wichtig für ihren späteren Beruf

junge Frauen:

gesichertes¹ Einkommen	86
mit Menschen in Kontakt kommen	79
mit anderen zusammenarbeiten	78
nebenbei genug Zeit für Hobbys	75
gute Arbeitsmarktchancen	73
Kenntnisse und Fähigkeiten weiterentwickeln	70
eigene geistige³ Kräfte voll einsetzen⁴ können	67
eigene Ideen verwirklichen⁵	67
neue Herausforderungen⁶	65
sich bei der Arbeit bewegen können	64

junge Männer:

gesichertes Einkommen	86
Kenntnisse und Fähigkeiten weiterentwickeln²	76
nebenbei genug Zeit für Hobbys	75
viel Geld verdienen	73
gute Arbeitsmarktchancen	73
Karrierechancen	70
am Wochenende frei haben	64
eigene Ideen verwirklichen	62
mit anderen zusammenarbeiten	62
abwechslungsreiche Tätigkeit	58

Mehrfachnennungen
Umfrage 2003/2004
G 0038 © Globus
Quelle: BIBB

¹*secure*   ²Kenntnisse ... *continue to develop knowledge and skills*   ³*intellectual*   ⁴*apply*
⁵*realize*   ⁶*challenges*

- Das Wichtigste für den Beruf junger Frauen und junger Männer ist

  _____.

- _____ ist wichtiger für junge Frauen als für junge Männer.

- _____ und _____ sind genau so wichtig im Beruf für junge Frauen und junge Männer.

- Welche Berufswünsche haben junge Frauen, die junge Männer nicht haben und umgekehrt (*vice versa*)? Suchen Sie fünf Unterschiede.

B. Sie hören Gabriele Sommer über ihre Berufspläne sprechen.

- Wie ist sie auf ihre Berufswahl gekommen?
- Wo studiert sie?
- Was studiert sie?
- Was hat sie in ihrem späteren Berufsleben vor?

Wörter im Kontext

wishes

expectations

THEMA 1: Meine Interessen, Wünsche° und Erwartungen°

Wie **stellen** Sie **sich** Ihr **Berufsleben vor?** Was erwarten Sie vom Beruf? Kreuzen Sie an.

Ich möchte gern:	WICHTIG	UNWICHTIG
■ **selbständig** arbeiten	☐	☐
■ einen sicheren **Arbeitsplatz** haben	☐	☐
■ **mich** mit Finanzen **beschäftigen**	☐	☐
■ **im Freien** arbeiten	☐	☐
■ **Gelegenheit** zum Reisen haben	☐	☐
■ **im Ausland** arbeiten	☐	☐
■ ein gutes **Gehalt** haben (viel Geld **verdienen**)	☐	☐
■ eine **abwechslungsreiche Tätigkeit** haben	☐	☐
■ ohne viel Arbeit **erfolgreich** sein	☐	☐
■ einen **Chef** / eine **Chefin** haben, der/die meine Arbeit anerkennt (*appreciates*)	☐	☐
■ sympathische **Mitarbeiter/Mitarbeiterinnen** haben	☐	☐
■ mit Menschen zu tun haben	☐	☐
■ mit Computer **Technik**/Elektronik arbeiten	☐	☐
■ eine kurze **Ausbildung** szeit haben	☐	☐
■ Prestige/**Ansehen** haben	☐	☐
■ im **Büro** arbeiten	☐	☐
■ eine **verantwortliche** Position bei einer großen **Firma** haben	☐	☐
■ einen Beruf haben, der mich **herausfordert**	☐	☐

Vergleichen Sie Ihre Antworten untereinander. Suchen Sie jemand im Kurs, mit dem Sie mehr als fünf Antworten gemeinsam haben.

Neue Wörter

stellen sich vor (sich vorstellen) imagine
das Berufsleben professional life
selbständig independent(ly)
der Arbeitsplatz position, workplace
mich ... beschäftigen (sich beschäftigen) occupy myself
im Freien outdoors
die Gelegenheit opportunity
im Ausland abroad
das Gehalt salary
verdienen earn
abwechslungsreich varied
die Tätigkeit position; activity
erfolgreich successful
der Chef / die Chefin manager, boss
der Mitarbeiter (Mitarbeiter, *pl.*)/die Mitarbeiterin (Mitarbeiterinnen, *pl.*) co-worker, colleague
die Technik technology
die Ausbildung training
das Ansehen prestige
das Büro office
verantwortlich responsible
die Firma firm, company
herausfordert (herausfordern) challenges

Ein Schornsteinfeger arbeitet meistens im Freien.

Aktivität 1 Drei junge Leute

Sie hören drei junge Leute über ihre Interessen, Wünsche und Erwartungen sprechen. Was tun sie gern oder nicht gern? Was ist ihnen wichtig oder nicht wichtig?

PERSON	WAS ER/SIE (NICHT) GERN TUT	WAS IHM/IHR (NICHT) WICHTIG IST
Tina		
Markus		
Andrea		

Erste Adresse für Ihren Karrierestart

Kreativ? Flexibel? Verantwortlich?
Wir fordern Sie heraus! WestLB

Aktivität 2 Hin und her: Wer macht was, und warum?

Ergänzen Sie die Informationen.

BEISPIEL: s1: Was macht Corinna Eichhorn?
          s2: Sie ist Sozialarbeiterin.
          s1: Warum macht sie das?
          s2: Weil ...

NAME	BERUF	WARUM?
Corinna Eichhorn	Sozialarbeiterin	Menschen helfen
Karsten Becker		
Erika Lentz	Filmschauspielerin	mit Menschen zu tun haben
Alex Böhmer		

Aktivität 3   Berufswünsche

Fragen Sie einen Partner / eine Partnerin: „Was erwartest du von deinem Beruf? Was ist dir nicht so wichtig?" Verwenden Sie einige der folgenden Redemittel.

BEISPIEL: s1: Mir ist ein sicherer Arbeitsplatz wichtig.
s2: Ein sicherer Arbeitsplatz ist mir nicht so wichtig, aber ich erwarte, dass ich Gelegenheit zum Reisen habe.

REDEMITTEL	ERWARTUNGEN
Mir ist _____ (nicht) wichtig.	ein gutes Gehalt (haben)
Ich erwarte, dass _____.	viel Kontakt mit Menschen (haben)
Ich möchte gern _____.	Menschen helfen
An erster Stelle kommt _____.	Spaß an der Arbeit (haben)
_____ interessiert mich (nicht).	nette Mitarbeiter/Mitarbeiterinnen (haben)
	Gelegenheit zum Reisen (haben)
	selbständig arbeiten
	im Freien arbeiten
	im Ausland arbeiten
	Ansehen (haben)
	einen sicheren Arbeitsplatz (haben)
	kreativ arbeiten
	flexible Arbeitszeit (haben)
	??

THEMA 2: Berufe

BERUFE

Gesundheitswesen
Arzt/Ärztin
Krankenpfleger/Krankenschwester
Psychologe/Psychologin
Sozialarbeiter/Sozialarbeiterin
Tierarzt/Tierärztin
Zahnarzt/Zahnärztin

Technischer Bereich
Elektroinstallateur/Elektroinstallateurin
Ingenieur/Ingenieurin
Mechaniker/Mechanikerin
Radio- oder Fernsehtechniker/
  Radio- oder Fernsehtechnikerin

Verwaltung
Rechtsanwalt/Rechtsanwältin
Diplomat/Diplomatin
Finanzbeamter/Finanzbeamtin
Personalchef/Personalchefin

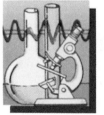

Naturwissenschaften
Biotechnologe/Biotechnologin
Chemiker/Chemikerin
Laborant/Laborantin
Meteorologe/Meteorologin
Physiker/Physikerin

Wirtschaft und Handel
Geschäftsmann/Geschäftsfrau
Informatiker/Informatikerin
Kaufmann/Kauffrau
Sekretär/Sekretärin

Verkehrswesen
Flugbegleiter/Flugbegleiterin
Flugingenieur/Flugingenieurin
Pilot/Pilotin
Reisebüroleiter/Reisebüroleiterin

Kommunikationswesen
Bibliothekar/Bibliothekarin
Dolmetscher/Dolmetscherin
Journalist/Journalistin
Nachrichtensprecher/Nachrichtensprecherin

Kreativer Bereich
Architekt/Architektin
Designer/Designerin
Fotograf/Fotografin
Künstler/Künstlerin
Musiker/Musikerin
Schauspieler/Schauspielerin
Zeichner/Zeichnerin

Welcher Beruf passt zu welcher Beschreibung?

BEISPIEL: Eine Architektin entwirft Häuser.

1. _____ spielt im Film oder auf der Bühne (*stage*).
2. _____ spielt in einem Orchester.
3. _____ **untersucht** Patienten.
4. _____ **entwirft** Gebäude, Häuser und Wohnungen.
5. _____ verkauft Produkte einer Firma.
6. _____ hat mit Computern zu tun.
7. _____ malt Bilder.
8. _____ arbeitet in einer Bibliothek.
9. _____ **übersetzt** Texte mündlich (*orally*).
10. _____ repariert Autos.

a. Arzt/Ärztin
b. Informatiker/Informatikerin
c. Schauspieler/Schauspielerin
d. Bibliothekar/Bibliothekarin
e. Automechaniker/Automechanikerin
f. Musiker/Musikerin
g. Architekt/Architektin
h. Kaufmann/Kauffrau
i. Dolmetscher/Dolmetscherin
j. Künstler/Künstlerin

Aktivität 4 Was meinen Sie?

Suchen Sie Ihre Antworten auf die folgenden Fragen in der Liste von Berufen im **Thema 2.**

1. Wer hat die gefährlichste Arbeit?
2. Welcher Beruf hat das meiste Prestige?
3. Wer hat mit Tieren zu tun?
4. Wer arbeitet meistens in einem Büro?
5. Wer verdient das meiste Geld?
6. Für welche Berufe muss man studieren?
7. Welche Arbeit bringt den meisten Stress mit sich?
8. Wer hat die längsten Arbeitsstunden?
9. Wer hat die langweiligste Arbeit?

Neue Wörter

der Zahnarzt / die Zahnärztin dentist
der Rechtsanwalt / die Rechtsanwältin lawyer, attorney
der Handel sales, trade
der Geschäftsmann / die Geschäftsfrau businessman/businesswoman
der Informatiker / die Informatikerin computer scientist
der Kaufmann / die Kauffrau salesman/saleswoman
der Bibliothekar / die Bibliothekarin librarian
der Dolmetscher / die Dolmetscherin interpreter
der Künstler / die Künstlerin artist
der Schauspieler / die Schauspielerin actor
der Zeichner / die Zeichnerin graphic artist
untersucht (untersuchen) examines
entwirft (entwerfen) designs
übersetzt (übersetzen) translates

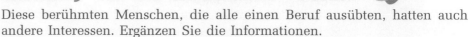

famous **Aktivität 5   Hin und her: Berühmte° Personen**

Diese berühmten Menschen, die alle einen Beruf ausübten, hatten auch andere Interessen. Ergänzen Sie die Informationen.

Siehe *The Interrogative Pronoun **was für (ein)**,* S. 339.

BEISPIEL: S1: Was war Martin Luther von Beruf?
S2: Er war Priester.
S1: Was für andere Interessen hatte er?
S2: Er interessierte sich für Literatur, Musik und die deutsche Sprache.

NAME	BERUF	INTERESSEN
Martin Luther		
Käthe Kollwitz	Künstlerin	Politik
Bertha von Suttner		
Rainer Werner Fassbinder	Filmregisseur	Literatur, Theater
Marlene Dietrich		
Willi Brandt	Politiker	Ski fahren, Lesen

Aktivität 6   Welcher Beruf ist der richtige?

Machen Sie eine Liste von den Kriterien, die Ihnen im Beruf wichtig sind. Benutzen Sie die Vokabeln vom **Thema 1.** Fragen Sie dann jemand im Kurs, was für einen Beruf er/sie Ihnen empfehlen würde.

BEISPIEL: S1: Ich möchte eine abwechslungsreiche Tätigkeit haben, vielleicht im Büro arbeiten und viel Kontakt mit Menschen haben. Was empfiehlst du mir?
S2: Ich empfehle dir, Kaufmann/Kauffrau zu werden.

THEMA 3: Stellenangebote und Bewerbungen

Ein Stellenangebot

Sehen Sie sich das Stellenangebot auf der folgenden Seite an und beantworten Sie die Fragen.

- Was für eine Person sucht die Firma?
- Was für ein Studium braucht man für diesen Job?
- Welche Qualifikationen und Eigenschaften sind der Firma wichtig?
- Wie viele Mitarbeiter und Mitarbeiterinnen hat die Firma?
- In wie vielen Ländern ist die Firma vertreten?

Neue Wörter

das Stellenangebot help-wanted ad
die Zukunft future
der Hersteller producer, manufacturer
die Stärke (Stärken, *pl.***)** strength
das Unternehmen company
beschäftigen employ
der Leiter director
engagiert committed
übernehmen take over
die Beratung advising
die Unterstützung support
die Erfahrung (Erfahrungen, *pl.***)** experience
die Fähigkeit (Fähigkeiten, *pl.***)** skill, ability
die Kenntnis (Kenntnisse, *pl.***)** knowledge
der Vorteil advantage
die Bewerbung application
das Personal personnel

testo

Zeichen setzen[1] für die Zukunft

Wir sind der führende Hersteller tragbarer elektronischer Messgeräte.

Wir verbinden die Stärken eines Konzerns mit der Flexibilität eines mittelständischen Unternehmens.

Wir beschäftigen insgesamt 1200 Mitarbeiter(innen) und sind mit 25 Tochterunternehmen in 23 Ländern weltweit vertreten.

Mein Name ist Michael Thurn. Ich bin Leiter Unternehmenskommunikation. Wir suchen für unser Team einen engagierten

Web-Master/Project Manager

als Motor und Promotor für unsere Web-Sites weltweit. Sie erkennen neue Trends im Online-Marketing und verbessern kontinuierlich die Usability der Sites. Sie übernehmen die Beratung und Unterstützung interner (internationaler) Interessensträger und verantworten die Koordination von Prozessen, die Erstellung[2] und Abstimmung von Inhalten[3] und die Führung externer Dienstleister.[4] Sie analysieren, reporten und leiten Empfehlungen ab. Sie bringen auf Basis eines IT-technischen oder betriebswirtschaftlichen Studiums bereits einschlägige[5] Erfahrungen im Management von Web-Projekten mit.

Engagement, Eigeninitiative, Teamgeist und kommunikative Fähigkeiten – auch in Englisch – sind sehr wichtig. Programmierkenntnisse (HTML, XML, J2EE, SQL) und sehr gute Kenntnisse in Internettechnologien sind von Vorteil.

Arbeiten Sie mit in unserem Team mit vielen internationalen Kontakten.

Wir freuen uns auf Ihre Bewerbung.

Testo AG, Frau Frieda Ebner
Testo-Str. 1, 79853 Lenzkirch
Tel. 07653/681-203
personal@testo.de

www.testo.de

[1]Zeichen ... *pointing the way* [2]*creation* [3]*content* [4]*service providers* [5]*relevant*

Eine Bewerbung

Wie **bewirbt** man **sich um** eine **Stelle**? Bringen Sie folgende Schritte in eine logische Reihenfolge.

_____ einen tabellarischen **Lebenslauf** schreiben

_____ ein **Bewerbungsformular** ausfüllen

_1_ Interessen, Wünsche und Erwartungen mit Familie und Freunden besprechen

_____ **Unterlagen** (**Abiturzeugnis** oder anderen **Abschluss** und **Zeugnisse** von früheren **Arbeitgebern**) sammeln

_____ **sich auf** das **Vorstellungsgespräch vorbereiten**

_____ die Stellenangebote in der Zeitung durchlesen

_____ Informationen über verschiedene Karrieren und Berufe sammeln

_____ zum **Arbeitsamt** an der Uni gehen und mit **Berufsberatern** sprechen

Neue Wörter

bewirbt sich (sich bewerben) um applies for
die Stelle position, job
der Lebenslauf résumé
das Bewerbungsformular application form
die Unterlagen (*pl.*) documentation
das Abitur exam at the end of Gymnasium
der Abschluss completion, degree
das Zeugnis (Zeugnisse, *pl.*) report card, recommendation
der Arbeitgeber employer
sich vorbereiten auf prepare for
das Vorstellungsgespräch job interview
das Arbeitsamt employment office
der Berufsberater employment counselor

Aktivität 7 Ein Stellenangebot

Lesen Sie das Angebot der Firma „testo" auf Seite 329 und wählen Sie passende Wörter aus dem Kasten, um die Sätze zu ergänzen.

> Eigeninitiative   Engagement   Fähigkeit   Kenntnisse   Kontakten
>
> Teamgeist   Vorteil   Web-Master   Websites

Hier klicken!

Weiteres zum Thema Stellenanzeigen finden Sie bei **Deutsch: Na klar!** im World-Wide-Web unter www.mhhe.com/dnk5.

1. Die Firma „testo" sucht einen _____ für ihre _____ weltweit.
2. Drei wichtige Eigenschaften sind _____, _____ und _____.
3. Kommunikative _____ in englischer Sprache ist auch sehr wichtig.
4. Sehr gute _____ in Internettechnologien und Programmieren sind von _____.
5. Die Person, die die Stelle bekommt, wird in dem „testo" Team mit vielen internationalen _____ arbeiten.

Aktivität 8 Ein Gespräch unter Freunden

Was stimmt? Was stimmt nicht? Korrigieren Sie die falschen Aussagen.

	DAS STIMMT	DAS STIMMT NICHT
1. Petra sucht einen Ausbildungsplatz.	☐	☐
2. Petra ist noch nicht zum Arbeitsamt gegangen.	☐	☐
3. Petra hat ein interessantes Stellenangebot in der Zeitung gefunden.	☐	☐
4. Petra hat sich um eine Ausbildungsstelle beworben.	☐	☐
5. Petra hat die Firma sofort angerufen.	☐	☐
6. Petra ist sehr enthusiastisch, weil sie die Firma gut kennt.	☐	☐
7. Die Firma verlangt, dass Bewerber Biologie studiert haben.	☐	☐

Aktivität 9 Ein Gespräch über eine Stellensuche

Führen Sie mit einem Partner / einer Partnerin ein Gespräch über eine Stellensuche. Sie können die Anzeigen in diesem Kapitel oder Anzeigen aus einer Zeitung oder dem Internet zur Information benutzen.

S1	S2
1. Was wirst du ＿＿ machen? 　■ nach dem Studium 　■ in den Semesterferien 　■ ??	2. Ich werde eine Stelle ＿＿ suchen. 　■ in einem Büro 　■ bei einer Firma 　■ in einer Fabrik 　■ ??
3. Wie findet man ＿＿?	4. Man muss mindestens ＿＿ (2/3/4/5/?) Dinge machen: ＿＿. 　■ Informationen über verschiedene Berufe sammeln 　■ Stellenangebote in der Zeitung / im Internet durcharbeiten 　■ zur Arbeitsvermittlung an der Uni gehen 　■ Freunde/Familie/Bekannte fragen 　■ zum Arbeitsamt / zur Berufsberatung gehen 　■ ??
5. Was braucht man für eine Bewerbung?	6. Man muss gewöhnlich ＿＿.
7. Wie lange dauert es, bis ＿＿?	8. ■ ＿＿ geht schnell. 　■ Manchmal dauert es ＿＿. 　■ Meistens dauert es ＿＿ Monate.
9. Na, dann viel Glück!	10. Vielen Dank!

Aktivität 10　Ein Lebenslauf

Hier sehen Sie einen typischen tabellarischen Lebenslauf.

Schritt 1: Beantworten Sie die Fragen:

- Welche Schulen hat Birgit in Bonn besucht?
- Welche Ausbildung hat sie gemacht?
- Was ist ihr jetziger Beruf?
- Welche anderen Interessen hat Birgit?

Schritt 2: Nun erzählen Sie Birgits Lebenslauf in vollständigen Sätzen. Benutzen Sie folgendes Format.

BEISPIEL: Birgit ist am 22. Dezember 1984 in Bonn geboren.
Von ＿＿ bis ＿＿ …
Seit …
Danach …

Grundschule besucht

Realschule besucht

Ausbildung als Bürokauffrau gemacht

als Reisebürokauffrau in Bonn gearbeitet

Lebenslauf

Name	Birgit Hermsen
Geburtsdatum	22. Dezember 1984
Geburtsort	Bonn
Eltern	Friedrich Hermsen Elsbeth Hermsen, geb. Marx
Ausbildungsgang	
1990–1994	Grundschule: Elisabethschule, Bonn
1994–2001	Realschule, Bonn
1999–2000	Austauschschülerin in USA (Experiment in International Living) Redwood City, Kalifornien
2001	Realschulabschluss: Mittlere Reife
2001–2003	Ausbildung als Bürokauffrau, Bonn Reisebüro Wilmers
Seit 2003	Reisebürokauffrau, Bonn Reisebüro am Markt
Familienstand	ledig
Interessen	Reisen (USA, Nepal, Australien und Neuseeland) Sport (Tennis, Reiten) Lesen und Musik

Mit sechs Jahren beginnt für Kinder in Deutschland die Schule. Alle Kinder gehen zuerst vier bis sechs Jahre lang gemeinsam auf **die Grundschule.** Danach trennen sich die Wege.

Ein Teil der Schüler und Schülerinnen geht dann auf **die Hauptschule,** die nach dem neunten oder zehnten Schuljahr mit dem Hauptschulabschluss endet. Danach suchen sich die meisten Schulabgänger eine Ausbildungsstelle für einen praktischen Beruf. Zweimal die Woche müssen die „Azubis" (Auszubildende oder Lehrlinge) auf **die Berufsschule** gehen. Dort lernen sie vor allem praktische Fächer, die für den künftigen Beruf wichtig sind.

Ein anderer Teil der Schüler und Schülerinnen geht von der Grundschule auf **die Realschule.** Sie endet nach dem zehnten Schuljahr mit dem **Abschluss** der **mittleren Reife.** Danach geht man auf eine **Fachschule** oder auch auf eine **Berufsschule.**

Als dritte Möglichkeit gibt es **das Gymnasium,** das als Vorbereitung auf ein Universitätsstudium dient. Das traditionelle Gymnasium umfasst neun Klassen, vom fünften bis zum dreizehnten Schuljahr. Neuerdings (*Recently*) wird die Zeit auf dem Gymnasium auf acht Jahre reduziert. Immer mehr Gymnasien gehen nur bis zum zwölften Schuljahr. Am Ende des Gymnasiums machen Schüler **das Abitur.** Ohne Abitur kann man nicht studieren.

Als Alternative für die drei verschiedenen Schultypen gibt es in Deutschland heutzutage **die Gesamtschule.** Ähnlich wie in nordamerikanischen Schulen gehen alle Schüler zur selben Schule bis zum Abschluss; daher der Name Gesamtschule.

Der erste Schultag: Der Ernst des Lebens beginnt.

Vom Kindergarten zur Universität

	Berufsqualifizierender Studienabschluß
Berufsqualifizierender Abschluß / Allgemeine Hochschulreife	**Universität/Technische Universität, Pädagogische Hochschule, Fachhochschule, Verwaltungsfachhochschule, Kunsthochschule, Gesamthochschule**
Fachschule / **Abendgymnasium/ Kolleg**	

	Berufsbildender Abschluß		Fachhochschulreife	Allgemeine Hochschulreife	
13	Mittlerer Bildungsabschluß			**Gymnasiale Oberstufe**	13
12	Berufsausbildung in Betrieb u.	Berufs-aufbau-Schule	Berufs-fach-Schule / Fach-ober-Schule	(Gymnasium, Berufliches Gymnasium, Fachgymnasium, Gesamtschule)	12
11	Berufsschule (Duales System)				11
10	Berufsgrundbildungsjahr				10

Abschlüsse an Hauptschulen nach 9 oder 10 Jahren / Realschulabschluß

10	10. Schuljahr				10
9					9
8	Sonder-schule	**Hauptschule**	**Realschule**	**Gymnasium**	**Gesamt-schule**	8
7						7
6		Orientierungs-Stufe				6
5		(schulformabhängig oder schulformunabhängig)				5

4			4
3	Sonder-schule	**Grundschule**	3
2			2
1			1

Schuljahr	Sonder-kinder-garten	**Kindergarten**	

Grammatik im Kontext

Future Tense°

Das Futur

You recall that in German the present tense can also refer to future action, particularly when an adverb of time is present.

Nächstes Jahr macht Sabine ein Praktikum in den USA.	*Next year Sabine is going to do an internship in the USA.*
Morgen schickt sie mehrere Bewerbungen ab.	*Tomorrow she will send off several applications.*

In German, the future tense is used most frequently to express future time when the context provides no other explicit reference to the future.

Eines Tages **werde** ich Erfolg **haben.**	*Someday I will be successful.*
Millionen **werden** meine Bücher **kaufen.**	*Millions will buy my books.*
Wir **werden** mal **sehen.**	*We shall see (if that's the case).*

kaufen			
ich	werde kaufen	wir	werden kaufen
du	wirst kaufen	ihr	werdet kaufen
er sie es	wird kaufen	sie	werden kaufen
Sie werden kaufen			

Note:

- The future tense is formed with the auxiliary verb **werden** and the infinitive of the main verb.
- The auxiliary **werden** and the infinitive at the end of the sentence form a sentence bracket (**Satzklammer**).

Eines Tages **werden** Millionen meine Bücher **kaufen.**

Some day, millions will buy my books.

Ich **werde** in einer großen Villa **wohnen.**

I will live in a large villa.

Übung 1 Wunschträume

Was ist Ihr Wunschtraum? Was werden Sie eines Tages sein? Wo werden Sie wohnen?

BEISPIEL: Ich werde Millionär sein.
Ich werde in einem Schloss wohnen.

WAS?	WO?
Akrobat/Akrobatin beim Zirkus	auf dem Mars
Präsident/Präsidentin von ...	in einem Schloss
Astronaut/Astronautin	in einer Grashütte auf Tahiti
Fußballspieler/Fußballspielerin	in einer netten kleinen Villa
Milliardär/Milliardärin	in einem Wohnwagen
berühmte/r Schauspieler/ Schauspielerin	im Weißen Haus
berühmte/r Sänger/Sängerin	in einer Kommune
??	in einer großen Villa
	??

Was möchtest du werden?

ANALYSE

Lesen Sie den Cartoon „Poesie" (*Poetry*).

Poesie von Erich Rauschenbach

- Identify the verbs in each sentence. Which verbs clearly refer to the present?
- How does the poet express his wishful thinking?
- For each sentence expressing the poet's hopes for the future, state the unspoken reality of his present life.

BEISPIEL: Er hat keinen Erfolg mit seinen Gedichten.

[1] *poems*
[2] *Erfolg ... be successful*
[3] *in den ... praise me to the skies*
[4] *famous*
[5] *afterward*
[6] *mache ... continue*
[7] *wie ... as before*
[8] *ausgewählte ... select readership*

Expressing Probability

The future tense is also used in German to express probability, often with the adverb **wohl** or **wahrscheinlich** (*probably*).

Consider the following hypothetical scenario concerning the unsuccessful poet of the cartoon "*Poesie.*"

> Zehn Jahre später: Der Dichter, Anselmus Himmelblau, fährt jetzt einen tollen BMW mit Autotelefon und Navi (GPS) und wohnt in einer Villa in Spanien. Auf seiner Luxusjacht in Monte Carlo trifft sich die Prominenz der ganzen Welt ...

What is probably true about Anselmus?

Er **wird wohl** endlich Erfolg haben.	*He is probably finally successful.*
Millionen **werden** jetzt **wahrscheinlich** seine Bücher **kaufen.**	*Millions are probably buying his books now.*
Er **wird wohl** sehr reich **sein.**	*He is probably very rich.*

Übung 2 Wahrscheinlich

Führen Sie ein Gespräch. Reden Sie mit mindestens zwei Leuten. Jemand hat gerade eine Million Dollar in der Lotterie gewonnen. Was wird er/sie wahrscheinlich mit dem Geld machen?

BEISPIEL: s1: Meine Mutter hat eine Million Dollar gewonnen.
s2: Was wird sie mit dem Geld machen?
s1: Sie wird sich wahrscheinlich einen tollen Ferrari kaufen.

WER?	WAS?
Mutter	das Geld auf die Bank bringen
Vater	(sich) einen tollen Ferrari kaufen
Eltern	nach Florida ziehen
Freundin	(sich) ein Schloss in Frankreich kaufen
Freund	vielen Leuten helfen
ich	(sich) ein tolles Motorrad kaufen
??	auf eine Insel in der Karibik ziehen
	eine Weltreise machen
	??

Describing People or Things: Relative Clauses° Relativsätze

A relative clause provides additional information about a person or an object named in the main clause.

XYZ Company is looking for bright and energetic trainees *who are interested in a career in communications technology.*

XYZ Company is looking for trainees *whose background includes a degree in computer science.*

XYZ Company is looking for trainees *for whom the sky is the limit.*

The Relative Pronoun°

In German, a relative clause is always introduced by a relative pronoun. The forms of the relative pronoun are identical to those of the definite article, except in the genitive singular and the genitive and dative plural.

	SINGULAR			PLURAL
	Masculine	*Neuter*	*Feminine*	*All Genders*
Nominative	der	das	die	die
Accusative	den	das	die	die
Dative	dem	dem	der	**denen**
Genitive	**dessen**	**dessen**	**deren**	**deren**

NOMINATIVE SUBJECT

Ich wünsche mir einen Job, **der** Spaß macht.

*I want a job **that** is fun.*

ACCUSATIVE OBJECT

Wie heißt der junge Mann, **den** du gestern kennen gelernt hast?

*What is the name of the young man (**whom**) you met yesterday?*

DATIVE OBJECT

Sind Sie einer von den Menschen, **denen** ein sicherer Arbeitsplatz wichtig ist?

*Are you one of those people **to whom** a secure position is important?*

GENITIVE OBJECT

Wir sind eine Firma, **deren** Produkte weltbekannt sind.

*We are a company **whose** products are known worldwide.*

PREPOSITIONAL OBJECT

Informatikerin ist ein Beruf, **für den** ich mich interessiere.

*Being a computer scientist is an occupation **in which** I am interested.*

Note:

- Relative pronouns correspond in gender and number to their antecedent—that is, to the noun to which they refer.
- The case of the relative pronoun is determined by its function within the relative clause. It can be the subject, an object, or a prepositional object.
- The conjugated verb is placed at the end of the relative clause.
- A relative clause in German is always set off from the rest of the sentence by a comma.
- The relative pronoun must always be expressed in German; it cannot be omitted as it sometimes can in English.

Der Personalchef, **den** ich kürzlich kennen lernte, ...

The personnel director I met recently . . . (The personnel director whom I met recently . . .)

Die Berufsberaterin, **mit der** ich sprach, ...

The career adviser I spoke with . . . (The career adviser with whom I spoke . . .)

KONSTRUKTEURE,
denen Ihr Radius zu eng ist...

Malte Fischer
Beratung
und Management
für Unternehmen
Schlehenweg 2
D-5063 Overath
Tel. 02206/2231

Ich will einen Job, der zu mir passt.

Wir suchen einen qualifizierten **Mitarbeiter** der mindestens ein Jahr Erfahrung mit Airlines vorweisen kann.

Wir suchen noch Hausfrauen, Rentner, Studenten oder Berufstätige, die es frühmorgens in ihren Betten nicht mehr aushalten.

Lesen Sie, was Leute lesen, die Karriere machen wollen.

- Identify the main clause and the relative clause(s) in each of the four ads.
- About whom or what do the relative clauses provide information?
- Where is the conjugated verb placed in each relative clause?

Übung 3 Attribute

Ergänzen Sie die Relativpronomen. Wie heißen die Sätze auf Englisch?

A. Nominativ

1. Gabriele ist eine Frau, _____ selbständig arbeiten möchte.
2. Nicholas ist ein Mann, _____ selbständig arbeiten möchte.
3. Das sind junge Leute, _____ selbständig arbeiten möchten.
4. Dies ist eine Firma, _____ junge Leute mit Verkaufstalent sucht.
5. ABC ist ein Unternehmen, _____ Azubis sucht.

B. Akkusativ

1. Wie heißt der Arzt, _____ du gestern kennen gelernt hast?
2. Wie heißt die Ärztin, _____ du gestern kennen gelernt hast?
3. Wie heißt der Schauspieler, _____ du gern kennen lernen möchtest?
4. Wie heißen die Musiker, _____ du gern hören möchtest?
5. Wie heißt das Buch, _____ du zum Geburtstag bekommen hast?

C. Dativ

1. Wir suchen eine Studentin, _____ Reisen Spaß macht.
2. Wir suchen einen Studenten, _____ Auto fahren Spaß macht.
3. Wir suchen Leute, _____ Technik Spaß macht.
4. Er ist ein Mensch, _____ Prestige sehr wichtig ist.
5. Plus ist eine Firma, _____ motivierte Manager wichtig sind.

D. Genitiv

1. Dies ist eine Firma, _____ Produkte überall bekannt sind.
2. Dies ist ein Unternehmen, _____ Produkte überall bekannt sind.
3. Das sind Schulen, _____ Schüler eine gute Ausbildung bekommen.

Übung 4 So bin ich.

Schritt 1: Kreuzen Sie drei Dinge an, die auf Sie zutreffen (*apply*).

Ich bin ein Mensch, … der Gruppenarbeit nicht mag. ☐
der gut zuhören kann. ☐
dem man vertrauen (*trust*) kann. ☐
dem Lernen Spaß macht. ☐
den alle Leute mögen. ☐
dem kreative Arbeit gefällt. ☐
der gut organisieren kann. ☐
der am liebsten für sich allein ist. ☐
der weiß, was er will. ☐

Schritt 2: Arbeiten Sie nun zu viert und machen Sie eine Liste mit den Qualitäten, die in Ihrer Gruppe vorkommen (*are found*).

BEISPIELE: Es gibt drei Leute, die Gruppenarbeit nicht mögen.
Es gibt einen Studenten, dem kreative Arbeit gefällt.
Es gibt eine Studentin, die gut organisieren kann.

Übung 5 Qualifikationen

Die folgenden Sätze sind aus Stellenangeboten in deutschen Zeitungen. Setzen Sie die passenden Relativpronomen ein.

1. Unsere Firma sucht Abiturienten, _____ Kreativität und Flexibilität besitzen.

2. Wenn Sie eine junge Dame sind, _____ sich für technische Berufe interessiert, schicken Sie uns Ihre Bewerbung.

3. Wir suchen einen Auszubildenden (Azubi), _____ das Bäckerhandwerk lernen möchte.

4. Elektroniker ist ein Beruf, für _____ sich viele junge Leute interessieren.

5. Wir sind eine Firma, mit _____ Sie über Ihre Zukunft reden sollten.

6. Ist Ihnen die Umwelt, in _____ Sie leben, wichtig? Dann werden Sie doch Umwelt-Techniker, ein Beruf für engagierte Menschen, _____ unsere Umwelt wichtig ist.

7. Wir suchen junge Leute, _____ ein gesundes Selbstbewusstsein (*self-confidence*) haben.

8. Wir suchen junge Leute, _____ einen sicheren Arbeitsplatz suchen und _____ bei der Post Karriere machen wollen.

Übung 6 Ein gefährlicher Beruf

Herr Grimmig, Briefträger von Beruf, hat – wie Sie sehen – mal wieder einen schlechten Tag. Schauen Sie sich zuerst die zwei Bilder an.

Schritt 1: Lesen Sie die folgenden Tatsachen (*facts*).

- Fritz, der Hund, hasst Briefträger. Er hat den Briefträger, Herrn Grimmig, ins Bein gebissen.
- Fritz ist Nikos Hund.
- Herr Sauer ist Nikos Vater. Er ist sehr böse und irritiert.
- Frau Kluge, die Nachbarin, hat alles genau gesehen.
- Herr Grimmig, der Briefträger, hat die Polizei geholt.
- Der Polizist, Herr Gründlich, schreibt alles genau auf.

NÜTZLICHE WÖRTER	
hassen	*to hate*
beißen, gebissen	*to bite*
böse	*angry*
holen	*to fetch, get*
auf•schreiben, aufgeschrieben	*to write down*

Schritt 2: Sagen Sie nun mit Hilfe der Tatsachen etwas über diese Situation.

BEISPIEL: Fritz ist der Hund. Er hasst Briefträger. →
Fritz ist der Hund, der Briefträger hasst.

1. Fritz ist der Hund, …
2. Niko ist …,
3. Herr Grimmig ist …,
4. Frau Kluge ist …,
5. Herr Sauer ist …,
6. Herr Gründlich ist …,

The Interrogative Pronoun° was für (ein)

Das Interrogativpronomen

NOMINATIVE

Was für ein Beruf ist das?   *What kind of a profession is that?*

Was für eine Firma ist das?   *What kind of a firm is that?*

ACCUSATIVE

Was für einen Chef hast du?   *What kind of a boss do you have?*

Was für eine Chefin hast du?   *What kind of a boss do you have?*

Was für Arbeit machst du dort?   *What kind of work do you do there?*

In **was für einer** Firma arbeitest du?	*What kind of a firm do you work for?*
Mit **was für einem** Kollegen arbeitest du?	*What kind of a colleague do you work with?*
Mit **was für** Kollegen arbeitest du?	*What kind of colleagues do you work with?*

Note:

- The interrogative pronoun **was für (ein)** is always followed by a noun.
- The case of the noun that follows **was für (ein)** depends on its function in the sentence. **Für** does not function as a preposition and, therefore, does not determine the case of the noun.
- The expression is always **was für** (without **ein**) when the noun is plural.

Übung 7　Ein unkonventioneller Klub

Hören Sie zu und markieren Sie die richtige(n) Antwort(en).

1. Der eine Sprecher …

   a. liest ein Buch.　**b.** sieht fern.　**c.** schreibt ein Buch.

2. *Das literarische Oktett* ist …

   a. ein Gedicht.　**b.** der Titel eines Buches.　**c.** der Titel einer Erzählung.　**d.** der Name eines Klubs.

3. Die Autoren sind …

   a. fünf Studentinnen.　**b.** acht Studenten.　**c.** acht Hausfrauen.

4. Im Buch stehen …

   a. nur Geschichten.　**b.** nur Gedichte.
   c. hauptsächlich (*mainly*) Geschichten und ein paar Gedichte.

5. Die Themen, über die die Autoren schreiben, beziehen sich auf …

   a. Politik.　**b.** Sex.　**c.** Liebe.　**d.** Deutschland.

6. Der Leser des Buches findet das Buch …

   a. merkwürdig.　**b.** originell.　**c.** dumm.　**d.** provozierend.

Übung 8　Ein Interview

Fragen Sie!

BEISPIEL:　s1: Was für Filme siehst du am liebsten?
　　　　　　s2: Am liebsten sehe ich Dokumentarfilme.

1. Was für Filme siehst du am liebsten? (z.B. Abenteuerfilme, Dokumentarfilme, Liebesfilme, Horrorfilme)
2. Was für einen Wagen fährst du?
3. Was für Musik hörst du gern?
4. Was für Kleidung trägst du am liebsten?
5. Was für Getränke trinkst du am liebsten?
6. Was für einen Job hast du? (z.B. interessant, langweilig, …)
7. In was für einer Stadt möchtest du gern leben? (z.B. Kleinstadt, Großstadt, in überhaupt keiner Stadt)
8. Was für eine Stadt ist ＿＿? (z.B. New York, Toronto, …)

Negating Sentences

Summary: The Position of **nicht**

You recall that **nicht** is used in negation when the negative article **kein** cannot be used. The position of **nicht** varies according to the structure of the sentence.

When **nicht** negates a specific sentence element, it precedes this sentence element.

> Ich komme **nicht heute,** sondern morgen.

> Wir haben **nicht viel Geld.**

When **nicht** negates an entire statement, it generally stands at the end of the sentence.

> Petra kommt morgen leider **nicht.**

> Sie gibt mir das Buch **nicht.**

However, **nicht** precedes:

- *predicate adjectives*   Petras Bewerbungsbrief ist **nicht lang.**
- *predicate nouns*   Das ist **nicht Petras Brief.**
- *verbal complements at the end of the sentence*
  - a. *separable prefixes*   Sie schickt den Brief **nicht ab.**
  - b. *past participles*   Sie hat sich **nicht beworben.**
  - c. *infinitives*   Sie will sich **nicht bewerben.**
- *prepositional phrases*   Sie hat sich **nicht um die Stelle** beworben.

Übung 9   Schwierige° Zeiten

difficult

Beantworten Sie alle Fragen negativ mit **nicht.**

BEISPIEL: Hat Hans die Prüfung bestanden (*passed*)? →
     Nein, er hat die Prüfung **nicht** bestanden.

1. Hat er sich um die Stelle bei der Zeitung beworben?
2. Kennt er den Personalchef der Zeitung?
3. Hat er seine Bewerbung zur Post gebracht?
4. Hat der Personalchef ihn gestern angerufen?
5. Hat der Personalchef ihn zum Gespräch eingeladen?
6. War der Personalchef sehr beeindruckt von (*impressed by*) Hans?
7. Hat Hans die Stelle bekommen?
8. War er traurig?
9. Wird er sich noch einmal bewerben?

Negation: **noch nicht / noch kein(e);**
nicht mehr / kein(e) ... mehr

To respond negatively to a question that includes the adverb **schon** (*already, yet*), use either **noch nicht** (*not yet*), **noch kein** (*no . . . yet*), or **noch nie** (*never yet*) in your answer.

> Geht Ute **schon** zur Schule?   Nein, sie geht **noch nicht** zur Schule.

> Hat Dieter **schon** eine Stelle?   Nein, er hat **noch keine** Stelle.

To respond negatively to a question that includes the adverb **noch** or **immer noch** (*still*), use either **nicht mehr** (*no longer*) or **kein ... mehr** (*no . . . any longer*) in your answer.

Ist Sabine **immer noch** arbeitslos?	Nein, sie ist **nicht mehr** arbeitslos.
Hat Dieter **noch** Arbeit?	Nein, er hat **keine** Arbeit **mehr**.

Übung 10   Leider, noch nicht

Arbeiten Sie zu zweit und stellen Sie Fragen.

BEISPIEL: s1: Weißt du schon, was du mal werden willst?
s2: Nein, das weiß ich noch nicht.

1. Weißt du schon, wo du arbeiten möchtest?
2. Ist dein Bruder / deine Schwester schon mit der Ausbildung fertig?
3. Hast du schon eine Stelle für den Sommer?
4. Hast du heute schon die Zeitung gelesen?
5. Hast du dich schon um eine Stelle beworben?
6. Hast du den Personalchef der Firma schon angerufen?
7. Hast du schon ein Angebot von der Firma bekommen?

Übung 11   Nein, nicht mehr

Beantworten Sie die Fragen mit **ja** und dann mit **nein**. Arbeiten Sie zu dritt und wechseln Sie sich ab.

BEISPIEL: s1: Studiert Barbara noch?
s2: Ja, sie studiert immer noch.
s3: Nein, sie studiert nicht mehr.

1. Wohnt Barbara noch in Heidelberg?
2. Arbeitet Andreas immer noch als Reiseführer?
3. Hat Anna noch Arbeit?
4. Hat Klaus noch ein Motorrad?
5. Macht Astrid die Arbeit als Journalistin noch Spaß?
6. Spricht sie immer noch so enthusiastisch über ihre Arbeit?

Sprache im Kontext

Videoclips

A. Schauen Sie sich die Interviews mit Oliver, Jasmin und Alex an. Wie sind sie zu ihrem Beruf gekommen? Ergänzen Sie die Sätze.

1. Oliver ist selbständig, er ist _____. Er hat eine _____ in neuen Medien wie Fernsehen und Computeranimation gemacht. An seinem Beruf gefällt ihm die _____. Sein Beruf ist aber sehr _____.

2. Jasmin ist _____ bei der Deutschen Bank. Wie hat sie ihre Stelle bekommen? Sie hat die _____ in der Zeitung gelesen und hat sich _____. Sie hat ihren _____ mit Passfoto an die Bank geschickt und hat ein _____ erhalten.

3. Alex ist _____ von Beruf. Wie hat er seine Stelle bekommen? Von einer Freundin hat er erfahren, dass eine _____ frei war. Er hat sich _____. Er arbeitet seit _____ Jahren in diesem Beruf.

B. Was für Schulen haben Peter und Jasmin besucht? Kreuzen Sie an.

	PETER	JASMIN
Grundschule	☐	☐
Gesamtschule	☐	☐
Gymnasium	☐	☐
Realoberschule	☐	☐
Universität	☐	☐

C. Was wollten Oliver, Jasmin und Alex als Kinder werden? Und Sie? Was wollten Sie als Kind werden?

D. Was werden Peter, Jasmin und Alex in zwanzig Jahren tun?

E. Und Sie? Was werden Sie in zwanzig Jahren tun?

Lesen

Zum Thema

Was sind Berufe, von denen junge Leute manchmal träumen? Zu dritt, listen Sie drei Traumberufe. Nennen Sie für jeden Beruf einen Grund (*reason*), warum viele junge Leute sich dafür interessieren. Machen Sie dann eine Umfrage (*survey*) in der Klasse. Was sind Traumberufe für die meisten Leute? Warum?

Auf den ersten Blick

A. Schauen Sie sich den Titel „Karriere beim Film" und alle Bilder (S. 344–346) an. Lesen Sie die ersten drei Zeilen (*lines*). Welche Informationen erwarten Sie von diesen Texten?

B. Überfliegen Sie beide Texte kurz und suchen Sie Informationen über Franka Potente und Daniel Brühl.

	FRANKA POTENTE	DANIEL BRÜHL
Geburtsort		_____
Alter	_____	_____
Familie	_____	_____
Anfang der Karriere	_____	_____

C. Raten im Kontext. Was bedeuten die folgenden Sätze?

1. Die Schauspielschülerin wurde in einer Münchner Kneipe von einer Filmagentin angesprochen.

   a. Die Schauspielschülerin lernte in einer Münchner Kneipe eine Filmagentin kennen.

   b. Die Schauspielschülerin spielte in einem Film in einer Münchner Kneipe.

   c. Die Filmagentin hatte sich mit der Schauspielschülerin in einer Münchner Kneipe verabredet.

2. 1996 brach Franka Potente die Ausbildung ab.

   a. Franka ging weiter zur Schauspielschule.

   b. Sie ging nicht mehr zur Schauspielschule.

   c. Sie fing eine Ausbildung als Schauspielerin an.

3. Sie bekam viele Angebote.

   a. Viele Leute wollten sie in ihren Filmen haben.

   b. Sie nahm viele Rollen nicht an.

   c. Sie spielte in sehr wenigen Filmen.

4. Daniel Brühl gilt als das neue deutsche Schauspielwunder.

   a. Es ist ein Wunder, dass Daniel Brühl Schauspieler geworden ist.

   b. Daniel Brühl findet neue deutsche Filme wunderbar.

   c. Daniel Brühl ist der neue, große deutsche Filmstar.

5. Daniel folgte dem Rat seines Vaters und machte zunächst sein Abitur.

   a. Er handelte gegen den Rat seines Vaters und machte kein Abitur.

   b. Es hat getan, was sein Vater ihm empfohlen hat.

   c. Er brach die Schule ab gegen den Rat seines Vaters.

6. 2002 erhielt Daniel Brühl den Bayrischen Filmpreis als bester Nachwuchsdarsteller.

   a. Daniel Brühl bekam einen Preis als bester bayrischer Filmschauspielschüler.

   b. Daniel Brühl bekam einen Preis als bester Schauspieler in ganz Deutschland.

   c. Daniel Brühl bekam einen Preis als bester Schauspieler der neuen Generation von Filmschauspielern.

KARRIERE BEIM FILM

Spätestens seit *Lola rennt!* und *Good Bye, Lenin!* ist deutsches Kino wieder international erfolgreich. Mit den jungen Filmen sind auch neue Gesichter auf die Leinwand° gekommen. JUMA stellt zwei von ihnen vor.　*silver screen*

Franka Potente

Franka ist die Tochter eines Lehrers. Als 19-jährige
5 Abiturientin zog sie nach München und besuchte
eine Schauspielschule. Ihre Karriere begann in
einer Münchner Kneipe. Dort wurde die
Schauspielschülerin von einer Filmagentin
angesprochen. Als Ferienjob bekam sie eine Rolle
10 in der Komödie *Nach fünf im Urwald* (Bayrischer
Filmpreis 1996). 1996 brach sie die Ausbildung
ab und hatte danach viele Angebote, meistens
schlechte. Doch mit dem Kinostart von Tom Tykwers *Lola rennt* im
Jahre 1998 wurde Franka Potente überall bekannt. Die Geschichte: Lola
15 und Manni sind Anfang 20 und ein Liebespaar. Manni jobbt als Geld-
kurier° und verliert 100 000 Mark, die seinem Chef gehören. Manni ruft　*money courier*
Lola an. Die hat eine Idee – und rennt los.

Franka Potente
Geburtstag: 22.7.1974

Der Film Lola rennt *mit Franka Potente hatte auch außerhalb Deutschlands Erfolg.*

1998 sah man Franka auch in Doris Dörries Tragikomödie *Bin ich schön?* neben Iris Berben, Senta Berger, Joachim Król und Uwe
20 Ochsenknecht. 1999 folgte ihr erster Thriller *Anatomie* 2000 drehte sie mit Johnny Depp das Drama *Blow.* Weitere Filme mit Franka Potente; *Coming In; Rennlauf* (beide 1997); *Downhill City* (1998); *Schlaraffen-land; Südsee, eigene Insel* (beide 1999); *Der Krieger und die Kaiserin* (2000); *Die Bourne Identität* (2002) mit Matt Damon; *Blueprint;*
25 *Anatomie 1* (beide 2003); *Die Bourne Verschwörung* und *Creep* (beide 2004).

Daniel Brühl

Seit dem großen Erfolg der Komödie *Good bye, Lenin!* gilt Daniel Brühl als das neue deutsche Schauspielwunder. Daniel wurde in Barcelona
30 geboren und ist in Köln aufgewachsen. Sein Onkel war Hörspielregisseur° beim Radio. Er besorgte ihm im Alter von acht Jahren einen Job hinter dem Mikrofon. Bereits kurze Zeit später synchronisierte Daniel Spielfilme
35 und versuchte sich im Schultheater als Schauspieler. Im Alter von 16 Jahren stand er zum ersten Mal vor der Kamera und übernahm in Roland Suso Richters TV-Film *Svens Geheimnis*° eine Rolle.

director of radio plays

Daniel Brühl
Geburtstag: 16. Juni 1978

secret

Daniel Brühl folgte dem Rat seines Vaters und machte trotz erster
40 Erfolge zunächst sein Abitur. Während seines Zivildienstes° arbeitete er wieder fürs Fernsehen. Eine Schauspielschule hat er nie besucht.

community service

Sein Debüt auf der Kinoleinwand° feierte Daniel Brühl mit knapp 20 Jahren in dem Film *Schlaraffenland.* Im Jahre 2000 war er in der Erfolgskomödie *Schule* zu sehen. Darin spielte er einen Schüler in der
45 Zeit vor dem Abitur. 2002 erhielt er für die Darstellung eines Schizophrenen in *Das weiße Rauschen* den Bayerischen Filmpreis als bester Nachwuchsdarsteller. Für seine Leistung in der melancholischen Liebesgeschichte *Nichts bereuen* bekam er den Deutschen Filmpreis.

movie screen

Kann man die DDR weiterleben lassen? Daniel Brühl
versucht es in dem Film Good bye, Lenin!

Mit dem Erfolg von *Good bye, Lenin!* wurde Daniel Brühl auch
50 international bekannt. In dieser Komödie spielte er einen jungen
Ostberliner, dessen Mutter während der Öffnung der Mauer im Koma
liegt. Der Sohn will die treue DDR-Bürgerin° nach ihrem Aufwachen
vor einem Schock bewahren. Darum lässt er die DDR in ihrer
Umgebung weiterleben. Der Film war ein riesiger Erfolg und brachte
55 allen Beteiligten zahlreiche Preise ein. Daniel Brühl selbst wurde beim
Deutschen und beim Europäischen Filmpreis als bester Darsteller
ausgezeichnet.

Im Jahre 2004 war er in dem Drama *Was nützt die Liebe in Gedanken*
zu sehen. In *Die fetten Jahre sind vorbei* spielte er eine Hauptrolle. Der
60 Film von Hans Weingartner erhielt 2004 den Preis der deutschen
Filmkritik in der Kategorie bester Spielfilm.

citizen of the GDR (Deutsche Demokratische Republik = German Democratic Republic)

Aus: *JUMA* 4/2005, www.juma.de.

Zum Text

A. Lesen Sie die Kurzbiografien von Franka Potente und Daniel Brühl nun etwas genauer.

1. Wie begann Franka Potentes Karriere?

2. Wie wissen wir, dass sie nicht über Nacht berühmt wurde?

3. Was für eine Rolle hat Franka Potente berühmt gemacht? Um welches Problem geht es in diesem Film?

4. Daniel Brühls Karriere hat mehrere Stationen (*stages*) durchlaufen. Was erfahren wir über den Anfang seiner Karriere?

5. Welche Beweise stehen im Text, dass Daniel Brühl ein sehr talentierter Schauspieler ist?

6. Welche Rolle hat ihn international berühmt gemacht?

B. Stellen Sie sich vor: Die beiden Schauspieler kommen zu Besuch. Welche Fragen möchten Sie den beiden stellen? Was möchten Sie gern über sie wissen?

In Deutschland ist ein Jahr Militärdienst Pflicht (*required*) für deutsche Männer. Im Allgemeinen geht der junge Deutsche mit 18 Jahren oder direkt nach der Ausbildung zum Militär. Viele sind Kriegsdienstverweigerer (*conscientious objectors*) und machen stattdessen Zivildienst. Das bedeutet, dass sie während dieser Zeit in einem Krankenhaus, Altenheim oder einem anderen sozialen oder auch ökologischen Bereich arbeiten. Oft helfen die sogenannten „Zivis" älteren Menschen zu Hause oder auch im Pflegeheim. So helfen sie z.B. morgens beim Anziehen, besorgen Mahlzeiten und helfen in der Wohnung.

Zu guter Letzt

Berufswünsche

Was sind Ihre eigenen Berufswünsche? Wie sehen Sie Ihren zukünftigen Beruf? Machen Sie eine Umfrage in der Klasse und analysieren Sie die Ergebnisse.

Schritt 1: Was würden (*would*) Sie über Ihre eigenen Berufswünsche sagen? Schreiben Sie drei Möglichkeiten für jede der vier Kategorien.

BEISPIEL: Das würde mir gefallen. →
- im Labor experimentieren
- alten Leuten helfen
- Baupläne entwerfen

1. Das würde mir gefallen.

_____

2. Dort würde ich gern arbeiten.

_____

3. Das würde ich gern machen.

_____

4. Für eine gute Stelle würde ich …

_____

Schritt 2: Machen Sie aus jeder Kategorie eine Frage.

1. *Was würde Ihnen am Beruf gefallen?*

2. _____

3. _____

4. _____

Schritt 3: Interviewen Sie fünf Studenten/Studentinnen in der Klasse. Stellen Sie ihnen die vier Fragen und schreiben Sie die Antworten auf.

Schritt 4: Arbeiten Sie in Gruppen und stellen Sie eine Liste von allen Antworten auf die vier Fragen zusammen.

Schritt 5: Analysieren Sie die Antworten. Gibt es Ähnlichkeiten in den Antworten der Studenten/Studentinnen?

Wortschatz

Arbeitswelt — World of Work

das **Ansehen**	prestige
der **Arbeitsplatz, ̈e**	workplace; position
die **Ausbildung**	(career) training
das **Ausland** *(no pl.)*	foreign countries
im Ausland	abroad
das **Berufsleben**	professional life
das **Büro, -s**	office
der **Chef, -s** / die **Chefin, -nen**	manager, boss, head
das **Einkommen**	income
die **Entwicklung, -en**	development
der **Erfolg, -e**	success
Erfolg haben	to be successful
die **Firma,** *pl.* **Firmen**	firm, company
das **Gehalt, ̈er**	salary
die **Gelegenheit, -en**	opportunity
das **Leben** *(no pl.)*	life
der **Mitarbeiter, -** / die **Mitarbeiterin, -nen**	co-worker, colleague; employee
die **Tätigkeit, -en**	activity; position
die **Technik, -en**	technique; technology

Berufe — Professions

der **Bibliothekar, -e** / die **Bibliothekarin, -nen**	librarian
der **Dolmetscher, -** / die **Dolmetscherin, -nen**	interpreter
der **Geschäftsmann,** *pl.* **Geschäftsleute** / die **Geschäftsfrau, -en**	businessman/businesswoman
der **Handel**	sales, trade
der **Informatiker, -** / die **Informatikerin, -nen**	computer scientist
der **Kaufmann,** *pl.* **Kaufleute** / die **Kauffrau, -en**	salesman/saleswoman
der **Künstler, -** / die **Künstlerin, -nen**	artist
der **Mechaniker, -** / die **Mechanikerin, -nen**	mechanic
der **Psychologe (-n** *masc.*)**, -n** / die **Psychologin, -nen**	psychologist
der **Rechtsanwalt, ̈e** / die **Rechtsanwältin, -nen**	lawyer, attorney
der **Schauspieler, -** / die **Schauspielerin, -nen**	actor
der **Zahnarzt, ̈e** / die **Zahnärztin, -nen**	dentist
der **Zeichner, -** / die **Zeichnerin, -nen**	graphic artist

Stellensuche — Job Search

das **Abitur, -e**	*examination at the end of* Gymnasium
der **Abschluss, ̈e**	completion; degree
der **Arbeitgeber, -** / die **Arbeitgeberin, -nen**	employer
das **Arbeitsamt, ̈er**	employment office
die **Beratung**	advising
der **Berufsberater, -** / die **Berufsberaterin, -nen**	employment counselor
die **Bewerbung, -en**	application
das **Bewerbungsformular, -e**	application form
die **Erfahrung, -en**	experience
die **Fähigkeit, -en**	ability, skill
die **Grundschule, -n**	primary school
das **Gymnasium,** *pl.* **Gymnasien**	secondary school
der **Hersteller, -**	manufacturer, producer
die **Kenntnis, -se**	knowledge
der **Kontakt, -e**	contact
der **Lebenslauf**	résumé
der **Leiter, -** / die **Leiterin, -nen**	director
das **Personal**	personnel
die **Stärke, -n**	strength
die **Stelle, -n**	position, job
das **Stellenangebot, -e**	job offer; help-wanted ad
die **Unterlagen** (*pl.*)	documentation, papers
das **Unternehmen, -**	company, enterprise
die **Unterstützung**	support
das **Vorstellungsgespräch, -e**	job interview
der **Vorteil, -e**	advantage
die **Website, -s**	website
das **Zeugnis, -se**	report card; transcript; recommendation (from a former employer)
die **Zukunft**	future

Verben / Verbs

Verben	Verbs
sich beschäftigen (mit)	to occupy oneself (with)
besitzen, besaß, besessen	to own, possess
sich bewerben (um) (bewirbt), bewarb, beworben	to apply (for)
entwerfen (entwirft), entwarf, entworfen	to design
heraus•fordern	to challenge
her•stellen	to produce, manufacture
sich interessieren für (+ acc.)	to be interested in
nach•denken (über + acc.), dachte nach, nachgedacht	to think (about)
übernehmen (übernimmt), übernahm, übernommen	to take over
übersetzen, übersetzt	to translate
untersuchen, untersucht	to examine
verdienen	to earn; to deserve
sich vor•bereiten (auf + acc.)	to prepare (for)
sich (dat.) vor•stellen	to imagine
sich (acc.) vor•stellen	to introduce

Adjektive und Adverbien / Adjectives and Adverbs

Adjektive und Adverbien	Adjectives and Adverbs
abwechslungsreich	varied, diverse
engagiert	committed
erfolgreich	successful(ly)
selbständig	independent(ly)
verantwortlich	responsible
wahrscheinlich	probably
wohl	probably

Sonstiges / Other

Sonstiges	Other
im Freien	outdoors
was für (ein)	what kind of (a)

DAS KANN ICH NUN!

1. Beschreiben Sie in drei Sätzen, was Ihnen für Ihren zukünftigen Beruf wichtig ist.

2. Welche Berufe sind gemeint?

   a. Man arbeitet auf der Bühne. **b.** Man untersucht Patienten. **c.** Man repariert Autos. **d.** Man entwirft Gebäude und Häuser. **e.** Man verkauft Produkte einer Firma.

3. Wenn man sich um eine Stelle bewirbt, muss man oft einen tabellarischen _____ schreiben. Sehr wichtig für eine erfolgreiche Bewerbung sind die _____ von früheren Arbeitgebern.

4. In Deutschland gibt es mehrere Schultypen. Nennen Sie drei.

5. Wenn ein Deutscher / eine Deutsche studieren will, muss er / sie am Ende des Gymnasiums _____ machen.

6. Wie sagt man das auf Deutsch? Benutzen Sie **werden.**

   a. *Someday I will be rich and famous.*
   b. *My brother is going to be a pilot.*
   c. *Niels is probably at home now.*

7. Ergänzen Sie die Sätze mit Relativpronomen.

   a. Ich bin ein Mensch, _____ weiß, was er will. **b.** Meine Mutter ist eine Frau, _____ man vertrauen kann. **c.** Niko ist der Junge, _____ Hund den Briefträger gebissen hat.

8. Wie heißen die Fragen? Wie heißen die Antworten?

   a. _____ ? —Das ist ein BMW Sportkabriolett. **b.** _____ ? —Ich habe sehr nette Kollegen. **c.** _____ ? —Er hat noch nicht von der Firma gehört. **d.** Hast du noch Arbeit? —Nein, _____. **e.** Studierst du immer noch? —Nein, _____.

Haus und Haushalt

Das neue Haus und
seine Bewohner

In diesem Kapitel

- **Themen:** Money matters, housing, the home, renting, household appliances
- **Grammatik:** Verbs with fixed prepositions, **da-** and **wo-**compounds, subjunctive II, **würde**
- **Kultur:** The Swiss franc, BAföG, paying for college, store hours
- **Lesen:** „Fahrkarte bitte" (Helga M. Novak)

Videoclips
Beatrice, Dennis und Jan
sprechen über ihre Finanzen

Alles klar?

A. Die Deutschen sparen aus verschiedenen Gründen. Die Grafik zeigt, wofür sie sparen.

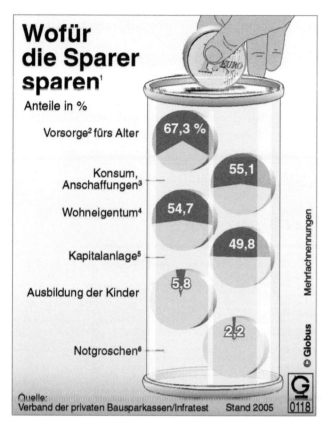

Wofür die Sparer sparen¹

Anteile in %

Vorsorge² fürs Alter	67,3 %
Konsum, Anschaffungen³	55,1
Wohneigentum⁴	54,7
Kapitalanlage⁵	49,8
Ausbildung der Kinder	5,8
Notgroschen⁶	2,2

Mehrfachnennungen

© Globus

Quelle:
Verband der privaten Bausparkassen/Infratest   Stand 2005

G
0118

¹*save* ²*planning ahead* ³Konsum ... *consumer goods, major purchases* ⁴*home ownership* ⁵*investments* ⁶der Notgroschen *emergency fund for a rainy day*

- Die Deutschen sparen am meisten für _____.

- Mehr als die Hälfte der Deutschen sparen für _____ und _____.

- Weniger als 6% der Deutschen sparen für die _____ der Kinder.

- Am wenigsten sparen die Deutschen für einen _____.

B. „Was bedeutet euch Geld?" Diese Frage haben wir Jens, Lucia und Elke gestellt. Hören Sie ihre Antworten. Schreiben Sie J (Jens), L (Lucia) oder E (Elke) neben die zutreffenden Aussagen.

1. _____ lange Urlaub machen und dann wieder arbeiten

2. _____ Armen (*poor people*) helfen

3. _____ Geld für medizinische Forschung spenden (*donate*)

4. _____ ein eigenes Geschäft aufmachen

5. _____ ein neues Auto oder eine neue Wohnung kaufen

6. _____ investieren

7. _____ weiter studieren – vielleicht im Ausland

8. _____ Geld für Welthungerorganisationen spenden

Wörter im Kontext

geben ... aus (ausgeben)
  spend
durchschnittlich on
  average
die Ausgabe (Ausgaben, *pl.***)**
  expense

Siehe *Asking
Questions:*
wo-Compounds, S. 364.

THEMA 1: Finanzen der Studenten

A. Wie **geben** Studenten in der Schweiz ihr Geld **aus**? Schauen Sie sich das Schaubild an.

■ Wie viel Geld brauchen Studenten in der Schweiz **durchschnittlich** pro Monat?

■ Wofür geben sie das meiste Geld aus? das wenigste Geld?

■ Welche **Ausgaben** sind mit „Kommunikation" gemeint?

■ Das Budget ist nur für Studenten, die nicht bei den Eltern wohnen. Wofür würden Studenten, die bei den Eltern wohnen, wahrscheinlich weniger Geld ausgeben?

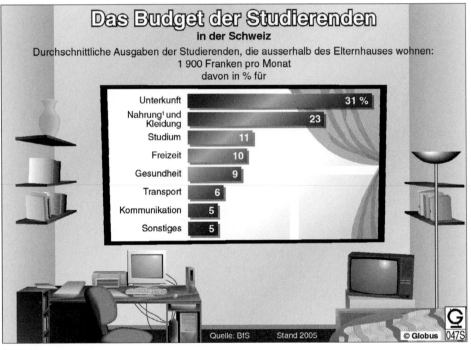

Das Budget der Studierenden
in der Schweiz
Durchschnittliche Ausgaben der Studierenden, die ausserhalb des Elternhauses wohnen:
1 900 Franken pro Monat
davon in % für

Unterkunft	31 %
Nahrung[1] und Kleidung	23
Studium	11
Freizeit	10
Gesundheit	9
Transport	6
Kommunikation	5
Sonstiges	5

Quelle: BfS   Stand 2005   © Globus 047S

[1]*food*

KULTURTIPP

Die Schweiz ist eines der Länder, die kein Mitglied der Europäischen Union (EU) sind und deswegen ihr eigenes Geld beibehalten haben. In der Schweiz zahlt man mit dem Schweizer Franken (CHF). Der Franken ist in 100 Rappen unterteilt.

B. Wie leben deutsche Studenten? Antworten Sie mit Informationen aus der Grafik rechts.

- Wie viel Geld braucht der deutsche „Normalstudent" **monatlich** für Essen? für Kleidung? für die Gesundheit?
- Wofür geben deutsche Studenten das meiste Geld aus?
- Wofür geben sie das wenigste Geld aus?
- Was gehört alles in die Rubrik „Lernmittel"?

C. Ihr monatliches Budget:

- Wofür geben Sie monatlich Geld aus und durchschnittlich ungefähr wie viel?
- Wofür geben Sie das meiste Geld aus? das wenigste?
- Wofür geben Sie nur ab und zu oder gar kein Geld aus?

D. Prozent Ihrer monatlichen Ausgaben:

_____ Miete

_____ **Nebenkosten** im **Haushalt** (**Strom, Heizung,** eigenes Telefon, Handy, Wasser)

_____ Auto (**Benzin, Reparaturen**)

_____ Fahrtkosten (öffentliche Verkehrsmittel, z.B. Bus, Flugzeug, Fahrten nach Hause)

_____ **Ernährung** (Essen, Trinken, Mensa, Restaurants)

_____ **Studiengebühren** (pro Semester, pro Quartal)

_____ Lernmittel (Bücher, **Hefte, Bleistifte, Kugelschreiber, Papier, Computerdisketten,** Sonstiges)

_____ Freizeit (Kino, Theater, Partys, Hobbys)

_____ **sparen** (**Sparkonto,** Sparschwein)

_____ **Versicherungen,** Arztkosten, Medikamente

_____ INSGESAMT (*total*)

- Haben Sie genügend (*enough*) **Einnahmen**? Haben Sie am Ende des Monats etwas Geld **übrig,** oder sind Sie **pleite**? Müssen Sie sich manchmal Geld von Freunden oder Ihrer Familie leihen? **Unterstützen** Ihre Eltern Sie finanziell? Sind Sie **sparsam**? Müssen Sie nebenbei **jobben**?

- **Vergleichen** Sie Ihre monatlichen Ausgaben mit denen eines Mitstudenten / einer Mitstudentin. Wer hat höhere monatliche Ausgaben?

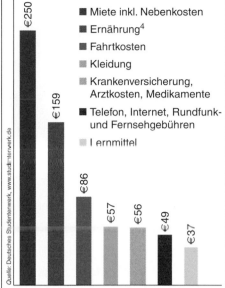

Monatliche Ausgaben der Studierenden in Deutschland

Bezugsgruppe[1] "Normalstudent", arith. Mittel[2] ausgewählte Ausgabenpositionen[3] (2003)

- ■ Miete inkl. Nebenkosten
- ■ Ernährung[4]
- ■ Fahrtkosten
- ■ Kleidung
- ■ Krankenversicherung, Arztkosten, Medikamente
- ■ Telefon, Internet, Rundfunk- und Fernsehgebühren
- ■ Lernmittel

€250 €159 €86 €57 €56 €49 €37

Quelle: Deutsches Studentenwerk, www.studentenwerk.de

[1]*reference group* [2]*arith. ... arithmetic mean (= average)* [3]*ausgewählte ... selected expenditures* [4]*food*

KULTURTIPP

Wie finanziert man das Studium in Deutschland?

- Eltern: Nach dem Gesetz (*law*) müssen Eltern für die Ausbildung ihrer Kinder zahlen, und zwar bis zum Abschluss einer Berufsausbildung, oder für Abiturient/innen bis zum Abschluss eines Studiums.

- Stipendien oder Darlehen (*loans*): Das **BAföG** (= Bundesausbildungsförderungsgesetz) ist ein deutsches Gesetz, das die staatliche Unterstützung von Schüler/innen und Student/innen regelt. BAföG besteht aus Darlehen und Zuschüssen (*grants*).

- Jobben: Studierende können während des Studiums nebenbei jobben.

Neue Wörter

Nebenkosten (*pl.*) utilities
der Strom electricity
die Heizung heat
das Benzin gasoline
die Ernährung food
Studiengebühren (*pl.*) tuition
das Heft (Hefte, *pl.*) notebook
der Bleistift (Bleistifte, *pl.*) pencil
der Kugelschreiber (Kugelschreiber, *pl.*) ballpoint pen
sparen to save
das Sparkonto savings account
die Versicherung (Versicherungen, *pl.*) insurance
Einnahmen (*pl.*) income
übrig left over
pleite broke
unterstützen support
sparsam thrifty
jobben work (at a temporary job)
vergleichen compare

Aktivität 1 Pleite oder nicht?

Schauen Sie sich Ihr monatliches Budget im **Thema 1** an. Vergleichen Sie jetzt Ihre Ausgaben mit den Ausgaben eines Partners / einer Partnerin und berichten Sie darüber. Gebrauchen Sie folgende Redemittel.

Ich gebe das meiste Geld für _____ aus.

Das wenigste Geld gebe ich für _____ aus.

Ich gebe nur ab und zu oder gar kein Geld für _____ aus.

Für _____ und _____ gebe ich mehr/weniger Geld aus als mein Partner / meine Partnerin.

Aktivität 2 Andreas Dilemma

Lesen Sie oder hören Sie sich den Dialog an, und ergänzen Sie die Sätze unten.

ANDREA: Sag mal, könntest du mir einen Gefallen (*favor*) tun?

STEFAN: Was denn?

ANDREA: Würdest du mir bis Ende der Woche 50 Euro leihen? Ich bin total pleite.

STEFAN: Fünfzig Euro? Das ist viel Geld.

ANDREA: Ich musste 100 Euro für Bücher ausgeben. Und jetzt habe ich keinen Cent mehr übrig. Ich warte auf Geld von meinen Eltern.

STEFAN: Hm, ich würde es dir gern leihen. Aber 50 Euro habe ich selber nicht mehr. Ich kann dir höchstens 20 Euro leihen.

ANDREA: Ich zahle es dir bis Ende des Monats bestimmt zurück.

STEFAN: Eben hast du gesagt, bis Ende der Woche.

ANDREA: Ja, ja. Das Geld von meinen Eltern kann jeden Tag kommen.

STEFAN: Na gut. Hier ist ein Zwanziger.

ANDREA: Vielen Dank.

Andrea hat kein _____[1] mehr; sie ist total _____.[2] Sie möchte sich von Stefan _____.[3] Sie hat nämlich ihr ganzes Geld für _____[4] ausgegeben. Deshalb hat sie jetzt nichts mehr für Essen und Trinken _____.[5] Stefan kann ihr aber _____[6] leihen. Andrea hofft, dass sie Stefan das Geld bis _____[7] zurückzahlen kann. Sie wartet auf _____.[8]

Siehe The Subjunctive, S. 364.

Aktivität 3 Drei Studentenbudgets

Vergleichen Sie die Ausgaben der drei Studenten auf der nächsten Seite und beantworten Sie die Fragen.

1. Wie viel Geld geben Marion, Wolfgang und Claudia insgesamt monatlich aus?
2. Wofür geben sie das meiste Geld aus?
3. Wer bezahlt die höchste Miete? Wo ist die Miete billiger?
4. Warum bezahlt Marion weniger als die zwei anderen fürs Telefon?
5. Wer hat die höchsten Kosten für Bücher und Arbeitsmittel?
6. Was ist – außer Miete – günstig, wenn man im Studentenwohnheim wohnt?
7. Wer unterstützt die drei Studenten finanziell?
8. Warum hat Marion keine Ausgaben für Verkehrsmittel?
9. Wer lebt am sparsamsten?

	MARION	WOLFGANG	CLAUDIA
Studienfach	Übersetzer (*translator*)/ Dolmetscher	Medizin	Romanistik/Politik
Studiengebühren pro Semester	keine	keine	500 Euro
Unterhalt (*support*)	Eltern	BAföG	jobben
Miete	200 Euro (1 Zi, Studenten- wohnheim)	300 Euro (1 Zi, Küche, Bad außerhalb)	400 Euro (1 Zi, Küche, Bad)
Verkehrsmittel	keine (alles mit dem Fahrrad erreichbar)	60 Euro	50 Euro
Lebensmittel und Mensa	200 Euro	250 Euro	200 Euro
Bücher/Arbeitsmittel	30 Euro	70 Euro	40 Euro
Telefon, Handy, Internet	20 Euro (kein Internet)	60 Euro (eigenes Telefon)	80 Euro
Freizeit	70 Euro	80 Euro	100 Euro
Fahrt nach Hause	20 Euro (Mitfahrgelegenheit) 40 Euro (mit der Bahn)	—	20 Euro
sonstiges	40 Euro	35 Euro	40 Euro

Aktivität 4 Einnahmen und Ausgaben

Vier Studenten sprechen über ihre monatlichen Einnahmen und Ausgaben. Kreuzen Sie das Zutreffende (*the items that apply*) an. Notieren Sie unter „Ausgaben", wie viel die Studenten für ihre Miete ausgeben.

	STEFANIE	GERT	SUSANNE	MARTIN
1. Einnahmen von:				
a. Job während des Semesters	☐	☐	☐	☐
b. Job während der Semesterferien	☐	☐	☐	☐
c. Eltern	☐	☐	☐	☐
d. Stipendium/BAföG	☐	☐	☐	☐
2. Ausgaben für:				
a. Zimmer (privat)	_____	_____	_____	_____
b. Studentenwohnheim	_____	_____	_____	_____
c. eigene Wohnung	_____	_____	_____	_____
d. Wohngemeinschaft	_____	_____	_____	_____

THEMA 2: Unsere eigenen vier Wände°

DACHGESCHOSS

DACH

ELTERN 13,5

BAD

FLUR 2,5

KIND 2 11,5   KIND 1 11,5

BALKON

ERDGESCHOSS

GAST 11   GARD 3,5   ESSEN

EINGANG

DIELE 7,5   WOHNEN 40

KÜCHE 15

FRÜHSTÜCKSNISCHE

Liebe Martina, lieber Jürgen!

Wir wohnen jetzt endlich in unseren eigenen vier Wänden. Vor einem Monat sind wir in unser neues Haus eingezogen. Wir schicken Euch ein Bild und eine Zeichnung des Grundrisses[1]. Wir sind sehr glücklich. Kommt uns bald mal besuchen.

Viele Grüße
Gitti und Christoph

[1]des … *of the floorplan*

Schauen Sie sich die **Zeichnung** von Gittis und Christophs neuem Haus an. Ergänzen Sie dann die folgenden Sätze durch ein passendes Wort aus der Liste:

Bad	Esszimmer	Schlafzimmer
Dachgeschoss	**Frühstücksnische**	Terrasse
Diele	**Gästezimmer**	**Treppe**
Erdgeschoss	Küche	Wohnzimmer

1. Das Haus hat zwei Stockwerke: ein _____ und ein _____.
2. Vom **Eingang** kommt man zuerst in die _____.
3. Links neben der Diele ist eine **Garderobe** und ein _____.
4. Von der Diele geht man rechts in die _____ und eine kleine _____.
5. **Unten** liegen noch zwei Zimmer: ein _____ und ein _____.
6. Das Wohnzimmer führt auf die _____ und in den Garten.
7. In der Diele führt eine _____ nach **oben** ins Dachgeschoss.
8. Im Dachgeschoss sind drei _____ und ein _____.

Neue Wörter

eigen own
eingezogen (einziehen) moved in
die Zeichnung drawing
bald soon
das Dachgeschoss attic, top floor
der Eingang entrance
die Garderobe closet
die Diele entry, foyer
die Treppe staircase
unten below, downstairs
oben above; upstairs

Aktivität 5   Die ideale Wohnung

Drei Leute (Frau Heine, Herr Zumwald und Thomas) berichten, was für eine Wohnung sie suchen, und was ihnen in der Wohnung wichtig oder unwichtig ist. Stellen Sie zuerst fest, wer welchen Wohnungstyp sucht. Dann notieren Sie in der Tabelle, was jedem wichtig (w) oder unwichtig (u) ist.

Wer sucht:

ein älteres Haus außerhalb der Stadt? _____

eine Neubauwohnung in der Innenstadt? _____

eine gemütliche Altbauwohnung in der Stadt? _____

WICHTIG/UNWICHTIG	FRAU HEINE	HERR ZUMWALD	THOMAS
Lage			
Zentralheizung			
Balkon			
Garage			
Garten			
Teppichboden (carpeting)			
Waschmaschine			

Aktivität 6   Hin und her: Eine neue Wohnung

Diese Leute haben entweder eine neue Wohnung oder ein neues Haus gekauft. Wer hat was gekauft? Wie viele Stockwerke gibt es? Wie groß ist das Wohnzimmer? Wie viele WCs oder Badezimmer gibt es?

BEISPIEL: s1: Was für eine Wohnung hat Bettina Neuendorf gekauft?
  s2: Eine Eigentumswohnung.
  s1: Wie viele Stockwerke hat die Wohnung?
  s2: Eins.
  s1: Und wie viele Schlafzimmer? ...

PERSON	TYP	STOCKWERKE	SCHLAFZIMMER	WOHNZIMMER	WC/BAD
Bettina Neuendorf	Eigentums- wohnung	eins	eins, aber auch ein kleines Gästezimmer	mit Esszimmer kombiniert 30 Quadratmeter	eins
Uwe und Marion Baumgärtner					
Sven Kersten	Eigentums- wohnung	zwei	zwei, eins als Gästezimmer benutzt	mit Esszimmer zusammen 35 Quadratmeter, Balkon vom Wohnzimmer	zwei, ein WC und ein Bad
Carola Schubärth					

Siehe *Prepositional Objects: da-Compounds*, S. 362.

Aktivität 7 Der Grundriss

Schritt 1: Sie sehen hier unten einen Grundriss. Identifizieren Sie, wo das Wohnzimmer, das Esszimmer, die Küche, das Schlafzimmer und andere Räume sind. Beschreiben Sie dann, wo die Zimmer liegen.

Zuerst kommt man in _____.

Rechts von _____ ist _____.

Von der _____ führt eine Tür ins _____.

Links neben der _____ ist ein _____ und daneben ein _____.

Vom Wohnzimmer geht man auf _____.

Unsere Eigentumswohnungen: Ideal— für das Leben zu zweit.

Terrasse / Abstellschrank / W / Eingang

Schritt 2: Zeichnen Sie nun den Grundriss Ihrer Wohnung / Ihres Hauses. (Wenn Sie in einem Studentenheim wohnen, zeichnen Sie eine Phantasiewohnung.) Geben Sie jemandem die Zeichnung und beschreiben Sie ihm/ihr, wo die Zimmer liegen. Ihr Partner / Ihre Partnerin setzt die Zimmernamen in den Grundriss. Schauen Sie sich dann die Zeichnung an, um zu sehen, ob alles richtig identifiziert ist.

Beginnen Sie so: Zuerst kommt man in _____.

THEMA 3: Unser Zuhause

Mieten und Vermieten

Neue Wörter	
mieten	to rent (from someone)
vermieten	to rent out (to someone)
die Umgebung	vicinity

Wir (Brigitte Heyden, Mathias Elsner u. Hündin „Sarah") suchen günstige Wohnung, kleines Haus oder Zimmer in netter WG auf dem Lande[1] (bis ~ 12 km von Gö.[2]) Am liebsten Gemeinde[3] Obichen oder Groß Schneen u. nähere Umgebung! Wer etwas für uns hat oder weiß, rufe bitte mögl. bald an, da[4] wir bis spätestens Ende April etwas gefunden haben müssen. Wir freuen uns über jeden Hinweis[5].

[1]auf ... *in the country*
[2]Gö = Göttingen *university town in north central Germany*
[3]*community* [4]*since*
[5]*lead*

1.

> ### Land-WG sucht Mitbewohner(in)!
>
> Wir, Bruno (26) und Britta (21), Hund und Katze, vermieten eine ganze obere Etage in einem älteren Bauernhaus 1 1/2 Zimmer, ca 38 qm[1]. Benutzbar[2] sind Küche, Bad, großer Garten. Die Miete beträgt monatlich €300,— plus €30,— Nebenkosten. 20 km von Göttingen. Ab 1. Juni.

2.

> Mieter gesucht für große, helle 3 Zimmer in Neubau, ab 1. August, ca. 70 qm. Balkon, eingerichtete Küche (Spülmaschine, Kühlschrank, Mikrowellenherd), Waschraum mit Waschmaschine, Zentralheizung, Teppichboden, Bad und WC, Garage. Zu Fuß ca. 15 Minuten von der Universität, 5 vom Bahnhof, 10 Minuten vom Zentrum. Tiere nicht erwünscht. Miete €400,— Nebenkosten €60,—.

[1]qm = Quadratmeter *square meters*   [2]*available for use*

Neue Wörter

die Katze   cat
die Etage   floor
das Bauernhaus   farm house
ab 1. Juni = ab erstem Juni   as of June 1st
der Neubau   modern building
die Spülmaschine   dishwasher
die Waschmaschine   washing machine
der Teppichboden   wall-to-wall carpeting
das Tier (Tiere, *pl.*)   animal
das Gerät (Geräte, *pl.*)   appliance, device

A. Lesen Sie zuerst das Mietgesuch (*rental flyer*). Wer sucht was und wo?

B. Lesen Sie dann die zwei Mietangebote (*rental ads*). Welches Angebot empfehlen Sie Brigitte und Matthias?

1. Ich finde Angebot Nummer ＿＿ ideal für Brigitte und Matthias, denn es gibt dort ＿＿.

2. Ich empfehle Brigitte und Matthias Angebot Nummer ＿＿, denn ＿＿. Es gibt jedoch ein Problem: ＿＿

Geräte im Haushalt

C. Zum modernen Haushalt gehören immer mehr Elektrogeräte.

- Welche von diesen **Geräten** haben Sie in Ihrem Arbeitszimmer oder Schlafzimmer? Kreuzen Sie an.
- Welche sind für Sie **unbedingt notwendig**?
- Welche sind **nützlich** aber nicht absolut notwendig?
- **Auf** welche könnten Sie **verzichten**?

Elektrogeräte . . .

...im Arbeitszimmer		...im Schlafzimmer
Telefon	Lautsprecher-Boxen (2-4 Dosen)	Telefon
Anrufbeantworter[1]	Kopierer	Fernsehgerät
Telefax-Gerät	Rechen-maschine[2]	Videogerät
Fernsehgerät	Computer	Radio
Videogerät	Drucker[3]	Radiowecker
Radio	Uhr	Alarmanlage
CD-Player	Aquarium (3-5 Dosen)	Staubsauger
DVD-Spieler	Staubsauger	Fernsehgerät

[1]*answering machine*   [2]*calculator*   [3]*printer*

D. Was passt zusammen?

1. ＿＿ Damit macht man den Teppichboden sauber.
2. ＿＿ Dieses Gerät wäscht die Wäsche.
3. ＿＿ Man kann damit das Essen schnell zubereiten.
4. ＿＿ Damit trocknet man die Wäsche.
5. ＿＿ Dieses Gerät spült das **schmutzige** Geschirr.
6. ＿＿ Das ist ein Haus auf dem Land.
7. ＿＿ Das ist ein modernes Haus.
8. ＿＿ Ein anderes Wort für „Region".

a. das **Bauernhaus**
b. der **Mikrowellenherd**
c. der **Staubsauger**
d. der **Wäschetrockner**
e. der **Neubau**
f. die **Spülmaschine**
g. die **Waschmaschine**
h. die **Umgebung**

Neue Wörter

der Staubsauger   vacuum cleaner
unbedingt   absolutely
notwendig   necessary
nützlich   useful
auf ... verzichten (verzichten auf)   do without
der Wäschetrockner   clothes dryer
schmutzig   dirty

Aktivität 8 Ist die Wohnung noch frei?

Frau Krenz hat eine große, helle Dreizimmerwohnung zu vermieten. Die Anzeige stand in der Zeitung. Herr Brunner hat auf die Anzeige hin angerufen. Er weiß, wie groß die Wohnung ist und wie hoch die Miete ist. Was möchte er noch von der Vermieterin wissen? Kreuzen Sie alles Zutreffende an.

Hier klicken!

Weiteres zum Thema Wohnungsangebote finden Sie bei **Deutsch: Na klar!** im World-Wide-Web unter www.mhhe.com/dnk5.

1. Herr Brunner möchte wissen,
   - ☐ ob die Heizung in den Nebenkosten einbegriffen ist.
   - ☐ ob die Küche einen Mikrowellenherd hat.
   - ☐ wie er vom Haus in die Innenstadt kommt.
   - ☐ wo die Wohnung liegt.
   - ☐ ob es einen Aufzug gibt.
   - ☐ wo man parken kann.
   - ☐ ob Hund und Katze willkommen sind.

2. Frau Krenz möchte von Herrn Brunner wissen,
   - ☐ wie viele Kinder er hat.
   - ☐ ob er verheiratet ist.
   - ☐ ob er Arbeit hat.
   - ☐ wann er vorbeikommen kann.
   - ☐ wann er einziehen möchte.

Aktivität 9 Ein interessantes Angebot

Sie interessieren sich für ein Mietangebot, das Sie in der Zeitung gesehen haben und rufen deshalb den Vermieter / die Vermieterin an. Benutzen Sie die Konversationstipps.

S1 VERMIETER/VERMIETERIN	S2 ANRUFER/ANRUFERIN
1. State your last name.	2. Greet the person, state your last name, and ask whether the apartment is still available.
3. Say it is still available.	4. Ask how much the rent is.
5. State a price.	6. Ask whether this price includes all household bills.
7. State that everything is included (**inklusive**) except the heat.	8. Tell the landlord/landlady that you have a cat or dog.
9. Say that it's all right.	10. Find out where the apartment is located.
11. Give the address and location. Suggest to the caller a time when he/she can come to see it.	12. Say that the time is suitable.
13. Say good-bye.	14. Say good-bye.

Grammatik im Kontext

Verbs with Fixed Prepositions

Many German verbs require the use of fixed prepositions; these verb-preposition combinations are usually different from their English equivalents.

Ich **interessiere mich für** schnelle Autos.	*I'm interested in fast cars.*
Wir **warten auf** den Bus.	*We are waiting for the bus.*
Die Studenten **ärgern sich über** die hohen Studienkosten.	*The students are annoyed about the high cost of tuition.*

The following verbs take fixed prepositions:

Angst haben vor (+ *dat.*)	*to be afraid of*
sich ärgern über (+ *acc.*)	*to be annoyed about*
sich beschäftigen mit	*to occupy oneself with*
sich bewerben um	*to apply for*
bitten um	*to ask for; to request*
denken an (+ *acc.*)	*to think of*
sich freuen auf (+ *acc.*)	*to look forward to*
sich freuen über (+ *acc.*)	*to be happy about*
sich interessieren für	*to be interested in*
nach•denken über (+ *acc.*)	*to think about*
verzichten auf (+ *acc.*)	*to do without*
sich vor•bereiten auf (+ *acc.*)	*to prepare for*
warten auf (+ *acc.*)	*to wait for*

Übung 1 So ist das Studentenleben

Was passt zusammen?

1. Die Studenten warten ...
2. Sie haben Angst ...
3. Der Professor ärgert sich ...
4. Die Studenten freuen sich ...
5. Der Professor beschäftigt sich ...
6. Die Studenten bitten ...
7. Sie interessieren sich ...
8. Sie bewerben sich ...

a. mit seiner Forschung (*research*) im Labor.
b. auf das Ende des Semesters.
c. für die Arbeit im Labor.
d. auf den Professor.
e. um ein Praktikum.
f. über die Studenten.
g. vor der Prüfung (*exam*).
h. um mehr Zeit für die Semesterarbeit.

Prepositional Objects: **da**-Compounds°

In German, a personal pronoun following a preposition generally refers to a person or another living being.

Der Student wartet auf **die Professorin.**	*The student is waiting for the professor.*
Er wartet schon lange **auf sie.**	*He has been waiting for her for a long time.*

When the object of a preposition refers to a thing or an idea, this is represented by a **da**-compound consisting of the adverb **da** and a preposition.

Wer ist **für eine Erhöhung der Studiengebühren?**	*Who is for a tuition increase?*
Nicht viele Leute sind **dafür.**	*Not many people are for it.*
Die Studenten sind **dagegen.**	*The students are against it.*

Note:

- **Da-** becomes **dar-** when the preposition begins with a vowel.

Marion wartet auf Geld von ihrem Vater.	*Marion is waiting for money from her father.*
Sie wartet schon eine Woche **darauf.**	*She has been waiting for it for a week.*

- **Da-/Dar-** can combine with most accusative, dative, and two-way prepositions.
- The preposition **ohne** does not form a **da**-compound; it is always used with an accusative pronoun.

Christian hat **einen neuen Porsche.**	*Christian owns a new Porsche.*
Ohne ihn kann er nicht leben.	*He can't live without it.*

ANALYSE

- Identify all **da**-compounds in the following text.
- What nouns do these **da**-compounds refer to?
- Restate all **da**-compounds as prepositional objects using the nouns to which they refer.

BEISPIEL: dafür → Sabines Zimmer → für Sabines Zimmer

Sabines Zimmer im Studentenwohnheim

Sie zahlt nur 150 Euro im Monat dafür. Links an der Wand ist ein Waschbecken. Darüber hängt ein Spiegel. Daneben hängt ein Haken mit einem Handtuch. Rechts an der Wand steht ein Schreibtisch. Darauf liegen viele Bücher und Papiere. Hinten an der Wand steht ein Bett. Darunter stehen Sabines Schuhe und rechts daneben steht ein kleines Bücherregal. Dahinter ist ein Fenster. Davor steht ein Vogelkäfig. Sabines Kanarienvogel, Caruso, wohnt darin und singt pausenlos.

The adverbs **dahin** ([*going*] *there*) and **daher** ([*coming*] *from there*) are commonly used with verbs of motion.

Wann fliegt Martina **nach Spanien**?	—Sie fliegt morgen **dahin.**
Ich war heute **auf der Bank.**	—Ich komme gerade **daher.**

In informal spoken German, **dahin** is often abbreviated to **hin.**

Hans muss noch zur Bank.	Er geht später **hin.**

In conversational German, **da** may be placed at the beginning of a sentence and **hin** at the end.

Gehst du oft ins Museum?	**Da** gehe ich nur selten **hin.**

Übung 2 Gemeinsames und Kontraste

Sabine und ihr Freund Jürgen haben einiges, aber nicht alles gemein (*in common*).

BEISPIEL: Sie interessiert sich für klassische Musik. →
        Er interessiert sich nicht *dafür*.

1. Jürgen gibt viel Geld für sein Auto aus.
   Sabine gibt nichts _____ aus.
2. Er spricht nicht über seine Finanzen.
   Sie spricht oft _____.
3. Er hat nur wenig Geld für Essen und Trinken übrig.
   Sie hat auch wenig _____ übrig.
4. Sie freut sich immer über kleine Geschenke.
   Er freut sich auch _____.
5. Sie denkt immer an alle Geburtstage.
   Er denkt nie _____.
6. Er kommt immer pünktlich zur Vorlesung.
   Sie kommt nie pünktlich _____.
7. Er ärgert sich über die laute Musik im Wohnheim.
   Sie ärgert sich überhaupt nicht _____.
8. Sie freut sich auf das Ende des Studiums.
   Er freut sich auch _____.

Übung 3 Beschreibungen und Situationen

Setzen Sie passende Pronominaladverbien in die Lücken ein.

1. In meinem Zimmer steht ein Sofa. *Daneben* steht eine Stehlampe. _____ steht ein kleiner Tisch. _____ liegen tausend Dinge.
2. —Wir wollen heute ins Kino.
   —Wann geht ihr _____?
3. Im Sommer fahre ich nach Rom. Ich freue mich schon _____.
4. Letztes Jahr hat Robert in Göttingen studiert und viel Spaß gehabt.
   Er denkt noch oft _____.
5. Gestern kam endlich ein Brief von Jürgen. Melanie hat sich sehr _____ gefreut. Sie hat lange _____ gewartet.
6. Morgen hat Thomas eine große Prüfung (*test*). Er hat keine Angst _____. Aber er muss schon um acht Uhr da sein. Er ärgert sich _____, weil er nämlich so früh noch nicht denken kann.

Übung 4 Eine Umfrage im Deutschkurs

Stellen Sie einander Fragen in kleinen Gruppen oder im Plenum.

BEISPIEL: Wie viele Leute haben Angst vor Prüfungen? →
Sechs Leute haben Angst davor.

1. Wie viele Leute interessieren sich für Politik? für Sport? für Yoga?
2. Wer hat Angst vor Prüfungen?
3. Wer denkt (oft, nie, manchmal) an das Leben nach dem Studium?
4. Wie viele Leute sind für oder gegen eine nationale Krankenversicherung? Wer soll dafür zahlen: Arbeitgeber? Arbeitnehmer? der Staat?
5. Wer freut sich auf das Ende des Studiums? auf eine Reise im Sommer?
6. Wer ärgert sich über die hohen Preise für Bücher?

Pronominaladverbien mit **wo**

Asking Questions: **wo**-Compounds°

There are two ways to formulate questions with prepositions when asking about things or ideas. One way is to use a preposition with the interrogative pronoun **was.**

Für was interessiert er sich?	*What is he interested in?*
An was denkst du?	*What are you thinking of?*
Auf was warten Sie?	*What are you waiting for?*

Another way is to combine **wo-** with a preposition to form a **wo**-compound. **Wo-** becomes **wor-** when the preposition begins with a vowel.

Wofür interessiert er sich?	*What is he interested in?*
Woran denkst du?	*What are you thinking of?*
Worauf warten Sie?	*What are you waiting for?*

Übung 5 Das möchte ich wissen!

Formulieren Sie zuerst Fragen. Arbeiten Sie dann zu zweit und beantworten Sie die Fragen abwechselnd (*taking turns*).

Wofür …	freust du dich?
Womit …	denkst du oft?
Woran …	gibst du viel Geld aus?
Worauf …	interessierst du dich?
Worüber …	wartest du?
Wovor …	hast du Angst?
	ärgerst du dich?
	beschäftigst du dich am liebsten?

Der Konjunktiv

The Subjunctive°

The most important function of the subjunctive mood is to express polite requests and convey wishful thinking, conjectures, and conditions that are contrary to fact. You are already familiar with one frequently used subjunctive form: **möchte.**

Expressing Requests Politely

Ich **möchte** gern bezahlen.	*I would like to pay.*
Ich **hätte** gern eine Tasse Kaffee.	*I would like a cup of coffee.*
Könntest du mir einen Gefallen tun?	*Could you do me a favor?*
Würdest du mir 50 Euro leihen?	*Would you lend me 50 Euro?*
Dürfte ich mal Ihren Pass sehen?	*May I see your passport?*

The forms **möchte, hätte, könntest, würdest,** and **dürfte** are subjunctive forms of the verbs **mögen, haben, können, werden,** and **dürfen.** They are frequently used in polite requests.

Forms of the Present Subjunctive II°

Konjunktiv II Präsens

haben	sein	können	mögen	werden	wissen
ich hätte	wäre	könnte	möchte	würde	wüsste
du hättest	wär(e)st	könntest	möchtest	würdest	wüsstest
er sie es hätte	wäre	könnte	möchte	würde	wüsste
wir hätten	wären	könnten	möchten	würden	wüssten
ihr hättet	wär(e)t	könntet	möchtet	würdet	wüsstet
sie hätten	wären	könnten	möchten	würden	wüssten
Sie hätten	wären	könnten	möchten	würden	wüssten

The Present Subjunctive II is based on the simple past forms. Some verbs with an **-a-, -o-,** or **-u-** in the simple past form require an umlaut to be added to the vowel.

Note:

- Modals with an umlaut in the infinitive retain this umlaut in the subjunctive.

INFINITIVE	SIMPLE PAST	PRES. SUBJ.		INFINITIVE	SIMPLE PAST	PRES. SUBJ.
können →	konnte →	**könnte**	*but:* sollen →		sollte →	**sollte**
mögen →	mochte →	**möchte**				

- Strong and irregular weak verbs with an **-a-, -o-,** or **-u-** in the simple past form add an umlaut to the vowel.

sein →	war →	**wäre**		werden →	wurde →	**würde**
haben →	hatte →	**hätte**		wissen →	wusste →	**wüsste**
geben →	gab →	**gäbe**				

- Weak verbs remain unchanged.

kaufen →	kaufte →	**kaufte**
wünschen →	wünschte →	**wünschte**

¹*dig up*   *Uli Stein 2006, www.miceandmoreusa.com*

Übung 6   Im Café: Was hätten Sie gern?

BEISPIEL: Ich *hätte gern* ein Stück Käsekuchen.

1. Wir _____ einen Platz am Fenster.

2. Ich _____ einen Espresso.

3. Kerstin _____ einen Eiskaffee.

4. Herr und Frau Haese _____ einen Platz in der Nichtraucherecke.

5. Wir _____ zwei Eisbecher mit Vanilleeis und Sahne.

6. _____ ihr _____ einen Platz draußen?

Übung 7   Wünsche im Restaurant

Formulieren Sie die Wünsche und Fragen sehr höflich.

BEISPIEL: Ich will ein Bier. →
        Ich hätte gern ein Bier.
  [*oder*] Ich möchte gern ein Bier.

1. Wir wollen die Speisekarte.

2. Ich will eine Tasse Kaffee.

3. Mein Freund will ein Bier.

4. Und was wollen Sie?

5. Willst du ein Stück Kuchen?

6. Wollen Sie sonst noch etwas?

7. Wir wollen die Rechnung.

The Use of **würde** with an Infinitive

In spoken German, one of the most commonly used forms of the subjunctive is **würde** plus infinitive. Like English *would,* the **würde** form can be used with almost any infinitive to express polite requests or wishes, or to give advice.

Würdest du mir **helfen**?	*Would you help me?*
Ich **würde** gerne **mitkommen**.	*I would like to come along.*

Note:

- Verbs that are generally not used with **würde** include **sein, haben, wissen,** and the modals.

Wenn die Studienkosten nur nicht so hoch **wären**.	*If only the cost of studying weren't so high.*
Wenn ich nur **wüsste**, wo meine Schlüssel sind.	*If I only knew where my keys were.*

Übung 8 Etwas höflicher, bitte!

Drücken Sie die folgenden Wünsche höflicher aus.

BEISPIEL: Leih mir bitte 50 Euro. →
  Würdest du mir bitte 50 Euro leihen?
  [*oder*] Könntest du mir bitte 50 Euro leihen?

1. Tu mir bitte einen Gefallen.
2. Tut mir bitte einen Gefallen.
3. Leih mir bitte 100 Euro bis zum Monatsende.
4. Wechseln Sie mir bitte 200 Euro.
5. Geben Sie mir auch etwas Kleingeld.
6. Hilf mir bitte!
7. Helft mir bitte!
8. Unterschreiben Sie die Reiseschecks, bitte.
9. Zeigen Sie mir bitte Ihren Pass.

Übung 9 Wie würden Sie darauf reagieren?

BEISPIEL: Sie haben eine Reise nach Österreich gewonnen. →
  Das wäre toll.

1. Sie sollen mit Freunden Bungeejumping gehen.
2. Ein Freund / Eine Freundin hat eine Million Dollar gewonnen.
3. Sie haben ein Praktikum bei einer deutschen Firma bekommen.
4. Sie sind im Supermarkt und haben Geld und Kreditkarte zu Hause gelassen.
5. Sie haben Ihre Autoschlüssel verloren.
6. Ihre Freunde machen ohne Sie eine Reise in die Karibik.
7. Sie haben eine Reise nach Las Vegas gewonnen.

Das wäre toll.

Das wäre nichts für mich.

Ich wäre sehr ärgerlich darüber.

Ich hätte Angst davor.

Ich wäre neidisch (*envious*).

Ich würde mich darüber freuen.

Expressing Wishes and Hypothetical Situations

Wishes introduced with **wenn** require the subjunctive. The particles **doch, nur,** and **doch nur** are frequently added to conversational **wenn-**clauses for emphasis.

Wenn ich **doch** mehr Geld **hätte.**	*If only I had more money.*
Wenn ich **doch nur** mehr sparen **könnte.**	*If only I could save more money.*
Wenn Benzin nicht so teuer **wäre.**	*If only gasoline weren't so expensive.*
Wenn ich **nur wüsste,** wo meine Autoschlüssel sind.	*If I only knew where my car keys were.*
Wenn Stefan **doch** nicht so viel Geld für seinen Wagen **ausgeben würde.**	*If only Stefan didn't spend so much money on his car.*

Note:

- The conjugated verb in the **wenn-**clause stands at the end of the clause.

Ich wünschte and **ich wollte** (*I wish*) are fixed expressions in the subjunctive when expressing a wish that is counter to reality. They are always followed by a verb in the subjunctive or **würde** + infinitive.

Ich wollte, die Geschäfte in Deutschland **wären** länger geöffnet.	*I wish (that) the stores in Germany were open longer.*
Frau Schiff **wünschte,** sie **könnte** auch sonntags einkaufen.	*Ms. Schiff wishes she could go shopping on Sundays, too.*

The expression **an deiner Stelle** (*if I were you / in your place*) is always used with a verb in the subjunctive. The possessive adjective changes depending on the person in question.

An deiner Stelle würde ich alles bar bezahlen.	*If I were you, I would pay cash for everything.*
An seiner Stelle würde ich nicht mit Kreditkarte bezahlen.	*If I were in his place, I would not pay with a credit card.*

Übung 10   Was sind die Tatsachen hier?

Folgen Sie dem Beispiel.

BEISPIEL: Ich wünschte, ich könnte dir Geld leihen. →
Ich habe aber kein Geld. Ich kann dir nichts leihen.

1. Ich wünschte, ich hätte keine Kreditkarte. Dann hätte ich keine Schulden.
2. Ich wollte, die Kosten für das Studium wären nicht so hoch.
3. Ich wünschte, ich könnte genug Geld für eine Weltreise sparen.
4. Klaus wünschte, er würde nicht so viel Geld für Telefonieren ausgeben.
5. Wir wünschten, wir könnten eine preiswerte Wohnung in München finden.
6. Ich wollte, ich hätte mehr Zeit für Sport.
7. Mein Freund wollte, er könnte sich einen BMW kaufen.
8. Ich wünschte, das Semester wäre zu Ende.
9. Die Studenten wünschten, sie müssten nicht so schwer arbeiten.

Übung 11   Wenn doch nur ...

Was wünscht Helga sich?

BEISPIEL: Helgas Katze ist weg. →
Wenn die Katze doch nur wieder da wäre!

1. Helga kann ihre Autoschlüssel nicht finden.
2. Sie weiß nicht, wo die Schlüssel sind.
3. Ihre Zimmerkollegin kommt sehr spät nach Hause.
4. Sie ist ganz allein.
5. Sie kann nicht zu Hause bleiben.
6. Sie muss um drei zu einer Vorlesung gehen.

Wenn sie doch nur wüsste ...

Übung 12   Wer wünscht sich was?

Drücken Sie aus, was sich diese Leute wünschen. Benutzen Sie dabei Konjunktivformen.

BEISPIEL: Gerhard hat nie Zeit. Was wünscht er sich? →
Er wünschte sich, er hätte mehr Zeit.
[oder] Wenn er doch mehr Zeit hätte!

1. Frau Schmidt fährt viel zu schnell auf der Autobahn. Was wünscht sich Herr Schmidt?
2. Herr Schmidt kann nicht gut Auto fahren. Was wünscht sich Frau Schmidt?
3. Es gibt nichts Interessantes im Fernsehen. Was wünsche ich mir?
4. Max ist total pleite. Was wünscht er sich?
5. Die Gäste bleiben viel zu lange, es ist schon nach Mitternacht. Was wünscht sich der Gastgeber?
6. Morgen fliegt mein Freund nach Tahiti. Ich muss leider zu Hause bleiben. Was wünsche ich mir?

7. Alex und Tanja besuchen Berlin, aber sie können leider kein Deutsch sprechen. Was wünschen sie sich?

8. Petra kann keine Wohnung finden. Was wünscht sie sich?

9. Die Kosten für Bücher sind zu hoch. Was wünschen die Studenten sich?

Übung 13   Heikle Situationen

Beschreiben Sie zuerst die Situation auf jedem Bild. Suchen Sie einen passenden Ausdruck aus der Liste. Überlegen Sie sich dann, was Sie an seiner oder ihrer Stelle tun würden.

BEISPIEL: An ihrer Stelle würde ich weggehen.

1.   2.   3.

1. weggehen; „Guten Tag" sagen; freundlich sein; nichts sagen; böse (*angry*) sein; nicht mit ihm reden; ??

2. eine Reparaturwerkstatt anrufen; sich ins Auto setzen und warten, bis der Regen aufhört; Hilfe anbieten (*offer*); um Hilfe bitten; zu Fuß weitergehen; den Reifen wechseln (*change the tire*); ??

3. nicht länger warten; allein ins Kino gehen; ungeduldig (*impatient*) sein; bei … anrufen; ??

Talking about Contrary-to-Fact Conditions

Compare the following sentences:

Wenn ich Geld **brauche, gehe** ich zur Bank.	*When I need money, I go to the bank.*
Wenn ich Geld **hätte, würde** ich mir einen neuen Wagen **kaufen.**	*If I had money, I would buy a new car.*

The first example states a condition of fact. The second example states a condition that is contrary to fact. The implication is that the speaker does not have enough money to buy a new car. In such cases, the subjunctive II is used.

Die Schnecke in diesem Cartoon singt ein bekanntes deutsches Volkslied (*folk song*).

- Circle the verbs that express the snail's wishful thinking. Note that these verb forms differ from those you have learned: they have no **-e** ending. What could be the reason for this?

- State the three things the snail wishes to be, to have, or to do. (Note that the suffix **-lein**, when added to a noun, makes a diminutive of this noun.)

> der Vogel (*bird*) › das Vöglein
>
> der Flügel (*wing*) → das Flüglein

Sie möchte …

- Was sind die Tatsachen (*facts*) ihres Lebens?

Eine Schnecke ist kein Vöglein; sie hat …
und …

- Interessiert sich die zweite Schnecke für die Sängerin? Was würden Sie als Beweise (*evidence*) dafür anführen?

[1]Unglückliche … *Unhappy conditions*
[2]*little bird*
[3]*little wings*
[4]Diese … *This lame snail gets on my nerves.*

Übung 14 Was würden Sie machen, wenn … ?

Sagen Sie, was Sie machen würden, wenn alles anders wäre.

BEISPIEL: Wenn ich Talent hätte, würde ich Opernsängerin werden.

Wenn ich Zeit hätte,
  Geld
  Talent
  mehr Freizeit
  Präsident/Präsidentin
    wäre,
  ??

ein berühmter / eine berühmte ___??___ (z.B. Sänger/Sängerin) werden.

interessante Leute kennen lernen.

öfter ins Kino gehen.

eine Insel im Pazifik kaufen.

jeden Tag die Zeitung lesen.

??

Übung 15   Rat geben

Stellen Sie sich vor, ein Freund / eine Freundin hat ein Problem. Was raten Sie?

BEISPIEL: s1: Ich bin total pleite. Was soll ich nur machen?
s2: Du solltest dir eine Arbeit suchen.
[*oder*] Ich würde mir eine Arbeit suchen.

PROBLEM	RAT
habe Zahnschmerzen	Arbeit suchen
kann nicht schlafen	Geld von jemand leihen
esse zu viele Süßigkeiten	sofort zum Zahnarzt gehen
bin immer müde und schlapp	keine Süßigkeiten mehr kaufen
habe kein Geld	Vitamintabletten einnehmen
??	nicht so spät schlafen gehen
	??

The Past Subjunctive II°   Der Konjunktiv II der Vergangenheit

The Past Subjunctive II is used to express wishes and conjectures concerning events in the past.

Wenn ich in der Lotterie **gewonnen hätte, wäre** ich überglücklich **gewesen.**

If I had won the lottery, I would have been ecstatic.

The conjecture (*If I had . . .*) speculates about an event in the past: The speaker did not win the lottery. Both English and German require the past subjunctive in this case.

The past subjunctive II forms are derived from the past perfect tense. Use the subjunctive II form **hätte** or **wäre** plus the past participle of the main verb.

INFINITIVE	PAST PERFECT	PAST SUBJUNCTIVE II
kaufen	ich hatte gekauft	ich hätte gekauft
sein	ich war gewesen	ich wäre gewesen

Ich wünschte, ich **hätte** den neuen Porsche nicht **gekauft.**

I wish I had not bought the new Porsche.

Ein gebrauchter Wagen **wäre** billiger **gewesen.**

A used car would have been cheaper.

Note:

■ Use **hätte** or **wäre** according to the same rules that determine the use of **haben** or **sein** in the perfect tense (see **Kapitel 7**).

Ich **habe** die Miete **bezahlt.**

Lars **hätte** die Miete nicht **bezahlt.**

Er **ist** in die Stadt **gefahren.**

Ich **wäre** nicht in die Stadt **gefahren.**

A clause stating a hypothetical situation usually begins with the conjunction **wenn.** As in English, the conjunction can be omitted, in which case the conjugated verb is placed at the beginning.

Wenn wir das nur gewusst hätten!	*If we had only known that!*
Hätten wir das nur gewusst!	*Had we only known that!*

ANALYSE

Schauen Sie sich den Cartoon an.

- Find the verb forms in the past subjunctive and give their infinitives.
- What is the woman speculating about?
- What stereotype does the cartoon allude to? Formulate a conclusion to the hypothesis "**Wenn ich als Blondine geboren wär(e) …**"
- What is the reality of her life?

Übung 16   Andreas ist total pleite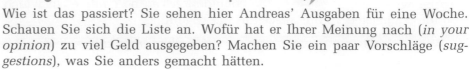

Wie ist das passiert? Sie sehen hier Andreas' Ausgaben für eine Woche. Schauen Sie sich die Liste an. Wofür hat er Ihrer Meinung nach (*in your opinion*) zu viel Geld ausgegeben? Machen Sie ein paar Vorschläge (*suggestions*), was Sie anders gemacht hätten.

	AUSGABEN
Geburtstagsgeschenk, Buch und Blumen für Freundin	€ 65,00
drei Sporthemden	120,00
Karte für „Phantom der Oper"	80,00
zweimal im Kino	22,00
Briefmarken	6,50
zweimal mit Freunden in der Kneipe	25,00
Bücher für Biologie und Computerwissenschaften (*computer science*)	125,00
Benzin fürs Auto	90,00
Zigaretten	48,00
dreimal zum Essen ausgegangen	59,00
Spende für Amnesty International	25,00
Telefon	<u>120,00</u>

REDEMITTEL

An seiner Stelle hätte ich nicht so viel für … ausgegeben.

Das wäre wirklich nicht nötig gewesen.

Braucht er wirklich … ? Ich hätte …

Zweimal … ? Einmal wäre genug (*enough*) gewesen.

Sprache im Kontext

Videoclips

A. Beatrice, Dennis und Jan sprechen über Geld und ihre monatlichen Ausgaben.

1. Alle drei beantworten diese Frage anders: „Was würdest du tun, wenn du eine Million Euro gewinnen würdest?". Was sagt Beatrice? Was sagt Dennis? Und Jan?

2. Wenn Sie eine Million in der Lotterie gewinnen würden, würden Sie dasselbe wie die drei machen oder etwas ganz anderes? Was?

B. Ergänzen Sie die Informationen in der Tabelle. Wenn es keine Information gibt, schreiben Sie „keine Information".

Wie viel Geld gibt er/sie aus für …	BEATRICE	DENNIS	JAN
Miete?	_____	_____	_____
Telefon?	_____	_____	_____
Lebensmittel?	_____	_____	_____
Sonstiges?	_____	_____	_____
Woher bekommt er/sie sein/ihr Geld?	_____	_____	_____

C. Schauen Sie sich alle drei Interviews noch einmal an. Wen beschreiben diese Sätze? Schreiben Sie **B** für Beatrice, **D** für Dennis und **J** für Jan.

1. _____ kann nicht sehr gut mit Geld umgehen.

2. _____ will in der Zukunft Lehrer werden und kleine Kinder unterrichten.

3. _____ wohnt mit einer Freundin zusammen und teilt die Kosten.

4. _____ wohnt allein in einer Wohnung mit Kochnische.

5. _____ macht ein Magisterstudium in Kulturwissenschaften und studiert noch Politik dazu.

6. _____ lebt relativ sparsam.

Lesen

Zum Thema

Fragen zum Thema Geld. Beantworten Sie die folgenden Fragen erst selber, und interviewen Sie dann einige Personen im Kurs.

1. Haben Sie als Kind Taschengeld erhalten? Wie viel? Wie oft und wann?

2. Was war Ihr erster bezahlter Job? Was haben Sie mit dem Geld gemacht?

3. Können Sie gut sparen, oder geben Sie Ihr Geld impulsiv aus?

Auf den ersten Blick

A. Überlegen Sie sich, was Sie in den folgenden Situationen machen würden.

1. Sie sind im Restaurant und gerade mit dem Essen fertig. Da bemerken Sie, dass Sie weder Geld noch Kreditkarten bei sich haben. Was würden Sie machen?

2. Sie fahren durch Europa. Gewöhnlich übernachten Sie in Jugendherbergen, aber an einem Ort gibt es nur Hotels. Dafür haben Sie aber nicht genug Geld. Was würden Sie machen?

B. Lesen Sie die ersten zehn Zeilen der Geschichte „Fahrkarte bitte", und beantworten Sie die folgenden Fragen.

1. Wer sind die Hauptpersonen?

2. Wo findet die Geschichte statt? („Kiel" allein genügt nicht [*is not sufficient*] als Antwort.)

3. Zu welcher Tageszeit beginnt die Erzählung?

4. Was ist das Hauptproblem oder der Konflikt?

von Helga M. Novak

Kiel sieht neu aus. Es ist dunkel. Ich gehe zum Hafen. Mein Schiff ist
nicht da. Es fährt morgen. Es kommt morgen vormittag an und fährt um
dreizehn Uhr wieder ab. Ich sehe ein Hotel. Im Eingang steht ein junger
Mann. Er trägt einen weinroten Rollkragenpullover°.   *turtleneck sweater*

5   Ich sage, haben Sie ein Einzelzimmer?
Er sagt, ja.
Ich sage, ich habe nur eine Handtasche bei mir, mein ganzes Gepäck ist
auf dem Bahnhof in Schließfächern°.   *lockers*
Er sagt, Zimmer einundvierzig. Wollen Sie gleich bezahlen? Ich sage, ach
10 nein, ich bezahle morgen.
Ich schlafe gut. Ich wache auf. Es regnet in Strömen°. Ich gehe hinunter.   *Es ... It's pouring.*
Der junge Mann hat eine geschwollene Lippe.
Ich sage, darf ich mal telefonieren?
Er sagt, naja.
15 Ich rufe an.
Ich sage, du, ja, hier bin ich, heute noch, um eins, ja, ich komme gleich,
doch ich muß, ich habe kein Geld, mein Hotel, ach fein, ich gebe es dir
zurück, sofort, schön.
Der junge Mann steht neben mir. Er hat zugehört.
20 Ich sage, jetzt hole ich Geld. Dann bezahle ich.
Er sagt, zuerst bezahlen.
Ich sage, ich habe kein Geld, meine Freundin.
Er sagt, das kann ich mir nicht leisten.
Ich sage, aber ich muß nachher weiter.
25 Er sagt, da könnte ja jeder kommen°.   *da ... anyone could say that*
Ich sage, meine Freundin kann nicht aus dem Geschäft weg.
Er lacht.
Ich sage, ich bin gleich wieder da.
Er sagt, so sehen Sie aus°.   *idiom: so ... I bet you are (sarcastic)*
30 Ich sage, lassen Sie mich doch gehen. Was haben Sie denn von mir?
Er sagt, ich will Sie ja gar nicht.
Ich sage, manch einer wäre froh°.   *manch ... many a man would be glad*
Er sagt, den zeigen° Sie mir mal.   *show*
Ich sage, Sie kennen mich noch nicht.
35 Er sagt, abwarten und Tee trinken°.   *idiom: abwarten ... let's wait and see*
Es kommen neue Gäste.
Er sagt, gehen Sie solange° in die Gaststube.   *for the time being*
Er kommt nach.
Ich sage, mein Schiff geht um eins.
40 Er sagt, zeigen Sie mir bitte Ihre Fahrkarte.
Er verschließt° sie in einer Kassette°.   *locks / box*
Ich sitze in der Gaststube und schreibe einen Brief.
Liebe Charlotte, seit einer Woche bin ich im „Weißen Ahornblatt"
Serviererin. Nähe Hafen. Wenn Du hier vorbeikommst, sieh doch zu
45 mir herein. Sonst geht
es mir glänzend. Deine Maria.

Zum Text

A. Beantworten Sie die folgenden Fragen.

1. Wer erzählt die Geschichte, ein Mann oder eine Frau? Welchen Beweis (*evidence*) können Sie dafür bringen?

2. Suchen Sie nach Wörtern und Äußerungen, die weitere Informationen über die Hauptpersonen geben. Was können Sie aus diesen Details schließen (*conclude*)? Es steht z.B. im Text, dass der junge Mann „eine geschwollene Lippe" hat.

3. Wann erfahren die Leser, dass eine der Hauptpersonen ein großes Problem hat? Wie würden Sie in dieser Situation handeln (*act*)? Welche Rolle spielt die Fahrkarte?

4. Sie hören nur eine Seite des Telefongesprächs. Was könnte die Person am anderen Ende sagen?

5. Lesen Sie die Geschichte ein zweites Mal. Glauben Sie dieser Frau? Wenn nicht, was für Beweise haben Sie, dass sie lügt (*is lying*)?

6. Die Geschichte endet mit einem Brief. Was sagt uns der Brief über die Erzählerin? Ist Charlotte eventuell (*possibly*) dieselbe Person, mit der die Erzählerin am Telefon gesprochen hat? Welchen Beweis haben Sie dafür oder dagegen?

B. Ein Monat ist vergangen. Was ist aus der Frau geworden? Schreiben Sie eine Fortsetzung (*continuation*) der Geschichte. Was macht die Frau jetzt? Ist sie noch in Kiel? Ist sie abgereist? Hat sie Geld? Ist sie glücklich?

Zu guter Letzt

Vom Lesestück zum Theaterstück

Die Kurzgeschichte „Fahrkarte bitte" von Helga M. Novak ist zum großen Teil in Form eines Dialogs geschrieben. Aus der Geschichte kann man ein interessantes Theaterstück machen. Erstellen Sie einen Bühnentext (*stage text*) und spielen Sie das Stück der Klasse vor.

Schritt 1: Schreiben Sie alle direkten Reden in Form eines Bühnentextes um:

■ Schreiben Sie die „Ich sage"-Sätze als Marias Reden neu:

BEISPIEL: Ich sage, ich habe nur eine Handtasche bei mir, mein ganzes Gepäck ist auf dem Bahnhof in Schließfächern. →
    MARIA: „Ich habe nur eine Handtasche bei mir, mein ganzes Gepäck ist auf dem Bahnhof in Schließfächern."

■ Schreiben Sie die „Er sagt"-Sätze als Reden des jungen Mannes:

BEISPIEL: Er sagt, zuerst bezahlen. →
    JUNGER MANN: „Zuerst bezahlen."
oder JUNGER MANN: „Bezahlen Sie zuerst."

■ Gewisse Sätze können von einem Erzähler / einer Erzählerin gesagt werden:

BEISPIEL: Ich schlafe gut. Ich wache auf. Es regnet in Strömen. →
    ERZÄHLER(IN): „Sie schläft gut. Sie wacht auf. Es regnet in Strömen."

■ Wenn Sie wollen, können Sie zusätzlich Text dazu schreiben. Zum Beispiel könnte der junge Mann Maria fragen, wie viele Tage sie bleiben möchte.

Schritt 2: Schreiben Sie nun einige Bühnenanweisungen (*stage directions*) in den Text. Wo findet die Handlung statt? Was sieht man auf der Bühne? Wie sehen die Hauptpersonen aus? Was für Requisiten (*props*) werden gebraucht, z.B. Handtasche, Telefon? Die Erzählung gibt Ihnen Auskunft, aber Sie können auch eigene Ideen entwickeln.

Schritt 3: Eine Skizze (*sketch*) zum Bühnenbild (*stage set*) gibt die Atmosphäre und den Ton eines Theaterstücks an. Sie zeigt, wie die Szenen aussehen und was die Personen machen. Zeichnen Sie ein oder mehrere Bilder zu den Szenen. Sie können auch Fotos oder Poster benutzen.

Schritt 4: Bestimmen Sie nun:

- wer den Erzähler / die Erzählerin spielt
- wer die junge Frau Maria spielt
- wer den jungen Mann spielt
- wer der Regisseur / die Regisseurin ist

Schritt 5: Üben Sie die Rollen und spielen Sie das Theaterstück anschließend der Klasse vor.

Wortschatz

Geldangelegenheiten / Money Matters

die **Ausgabe, -n**	expense
das **Benzin**	gasoline
der **Bleistift, -e**	pencil
die **Computerdiskette, -n**	computer diskette
die **Einnahmen** (*pl.*)	income
die **Ernährung**	food, nutrition
der **Haushalt, -e**	household
das **Heft, -e**	notebook
die **Heizung**	heat, heating system
der **Kugelschreiber, -**	ballpoint pen
der **Müll**	trash, garbage
die **Nebenkosten**	utilities; extra costs
das **Papier, -e**	paper
die **Reparatur, -en**	repair
das **Sparkonto,** *pl.* **Sparkonten**	savings account
der **Strom**	electricity
die **Studiengebühren** (*pl.*)	tuition, fees
die **Versicherung, -en**	insurance

Das Haus / The House

das **Bauernhaus, ⸚er**	farmhouse
das **Dach, ⸚er**	roof
das **Dachgeschoss, -e**	top floor, attic
die **Diele, -n**	front hall
der **Eingang, ⸚e**	entrance
die **Etage, -n**	floor, story
der **Flur, -e**	hallway
die **Frühstücksnische, -n**	breakfast nook
die **Garderobe, -n**	wardrobe; closet
das **Gästezimmer, -**	guest room
das **Gerät, -e**	appliance, device
der **Mikrowellenherd, -e**	microwave oven
der **Neubau, -ten**	modern building
die **Spülmaschine, -n**	dishwasher
der **Staubsauger**	vacuum cleaner
der **Teppichboden, ⸚**	wall-to-wall carpeting
die **Treppe, -n**	staircase
die **Umgebung, -en**	area, neighborhood, vicinity
die **Waschmaschine, -n**	washing machine
der **Wäschetrockner, -n**	clothes dryer

Verben / Verbs

sich ärgern über (+ *acc.*)	to be annoyed about
aus•geben (gibt aus), gab aus, ausgegeben	to spend (*money*)
bauen	to build
bitten um, bat, gebeten	to ask for, request
denken an (+ *acc.*), **dachte, gedacht**	to think about, of
ein•richten	to furnish, equip
ein•ziehen in (+ *acc.*), **zog ein, ist eingezogen**	to move in

sich freuen auf (+ *acc.*)	to look forward to
sich freuen über (+ *acc.*)	to be glad about
jobben	to work (*at a temporary job*)
mieten	to rent (*from someone*)
sparen	to save
unterstützen, unterstützt	to support
vergleichen, verglich, verglichen	to compare
vermieten	to rent out (*to someone*)
verzichten auf (+ *acc.*)	to do without

Adjektive und Adverbien

Adjectives and Adverbs

ab	from, as of
ab 1. Juni (ab erstem Juni)	as of June 1st
bald	soon
deswegen	because of that
durchschnittlich	on average
eigen	own
ganz	complete(ly), total(ly), entire(ly)
monatlich	monthly
notwendig	necessary

nützlich	useful
oben	above; upstairs
nach oben	above; upstairs (*directional*)
pleite	broke, out of money
schmutzig	dirty
sparsam	thrifty
spätestens	at the latest
übrig	left over
unbedingt	absolutely, by all means
unten	below; downstairs
nach unten	below; downstairs (*directional*)

Sonstiges

Other

an deiner Stelle	if I were you, (if I were) in your place
die **Angst, ⸚e**	fear
Angst haben vor (+ *dat.*)	to be afraid of
der **Gruß, ⸚e**	greeting
viele Grüße	best wishes
die **Katze, -n**	cat
das **Tier, -e**	animal
die **Zeichnung, -en**	drawing

DAS KANN ICH NUN!

1. Machen Sie eine Liste mit den fünf größten Ausgaben, die Sie monatlich haben.

2. Beschreiben Sie das Haus, in dem Sie wohnen, das Haus Ihrer Eltern oder das Haus von Freunden. Wie viele Zimmer gibt es? Was für Zimmer? Wo liegen sie? Was für Geräte gibt es?

3. Beschreiben Sie Ihr Zimmer oder Ihr Klassenzimmer. Benutzen Sie dabei Wörter wie: **daneben, dazwischen, darauf, darunter,** usw.

4. Formulieren Sie passende Fragen zu folgenden Antworten. (Use a **wo**-compound.)

    a. _____? —Das Kind hat Angst vor Gewitter.
    b. _____? —Die Studenten beschäftigen sich mit Politik.   **c.** _____? —Wir warten auf die Post.

5. Wie sagt man dies sehr höflich auf Deutsch?

    a. *You are at a restaurant and would like a table by the window.* (*two ways*)   **b.** *You would like to see the menu.*   **c.** *You would like to pay by credit card.*

6. Sie haben viele Wünsche. Wie drückt man sie auf Deutsch aus?

    a. *You wish you had more time and money.*
    b. *You wish you could stay home today.*
    c. *You are asking someone, very politely, to help you.*

7. Schreiben Sie die Sätze zu Ende.

    a. Wenn ich das Geld für eine Reise hätte, _____.   **b.** Wenn ich gewusst hätte, dass es ein Gewitter gibt, _____.   **c.** Du hast eine Erkältung? An deiner Stelle _____.

Viertes Zwischenspiel

Deutsche Einwanderung[1] nach Nordamerika

Laut US-Census aus dem Jahre 2000 gibt es ca. 43 Millionen Amerikaner deutscher Abstammung[2] in den USA. Die ersten Deutschen kamen schon 1608 nach Jamestown in Virginia. Die Menschen verließen ihre Heimat hauptsächlich aus drei Gründen: aus religiösen, politischen oder wirtschaftlichen Motiven.

Im Jahre 1683 wanderten zum Beispiel achtzehn Familien aus Krefeld mit Franz Daniel Pastorius (1651–1719) nach Pennsylvanien aus, wo sie die erste deutsche Siedlung[3], Germantown, gründeten. Die Beziehung zwischen Krefeld und Germantown wird bis heute aktiv gepflegt.

Die Vorfahren der Amischen wurden in Europa wegen ihrer Religion verfolgt[4] und getötet. (Der Name „Amisch" kommt von dem Begründer der Sekte, dem Prediger Jakob Amman.) Noch heute leben viele Amische in den USA und Kanada. Die größten Siedlungen findet man in Ohio, Pennsylvanien und Indiana. Viele Amische sind dreisprachig: zu Hause sprechen sie ihren deutschen Dialekt und in der Kirche sprechen sie Hochdeutsch. Außerhalb der Gemeinschaft sprechen sie Englisch.

Im Jahre 1848 gab es in den deutschen Staaten eine demokratische Revolution. Deutschland existierte noch nicht als vereinigte Nation. Die Revolution scheiterte[5] allerdings und viele der Revolutionäre mussten flüchten[6]. Einer dieser revolutionären Generation war Carl Schurz (1829–1906), der später in der amerikanischen Regierung eine prominente Rolle spielte.

In den 30er Jahren des 20. Jahrhunderts flohen viele prominente deutsche und österreichische, jüdische sowie nicht-jüdische Intellektuelle vor politischer und rassistischer Verfolgung durch die Hitler-Diktatur nach Nordamerika, unter anderem Albert Einstein, Thomas Mann, Paul Tillich und Billy Wilder.

Im 19. Jahrhundert gab es eine steigende Massenemigration Deutscher aus wirtschaftlichen Gründen. Sie wollten der Armut[7] entfliehen und suchten im Land der „unbegrenzten[8] Möglichkeiten" einen Neuanfang. So verließ Johann Jakob Astor 1784 seine Heimat in Walldorf bei Heidelberg. Mit 25 Dollar in der Tasche landete er

Amische in Lancaster County, Pennsylvanien

in New York. Er brachte es zu einem Vermögen[9] im Immobilienhandel[10] und Pelzhandel[11].

Im Alter von nur 14 Jahren wanderte Levi Strauss (1829–1902) im Jahre 1847 von Bayern in die USA aus. 1853 kam er nach Kalifornien, wo er den Goldgräbern[12] stabile Hosen aus einem Material mit dem französichen Namen „serge de Nîmes" verkaufte. Danach wurde das Material „Denim" benannt.

Levi Strauss

[1]*immigration* [2]*heritage* [3]*settlement* [4]*persecuted* [5]*failed* [6]*flee* [7]*poverty* [8]*unlimited* [9]*fortune* [10]*real estate* [11]*fur trade* [12]*gold-diggers*

Chronologie deutscher Einwanderung nach Amerika

1608   Deutsche Glasmacher kommen nach Jamestown in Virginia.

1683   Mennoniten und Quäker gründen Germantown, Pennsylvanien.

1709   Massenauswanderung aus der Pfalz beginnt.

1732   Erste deutschsprachige Zeitung in Nordamerika, *Die Philadelphische Zeitung*, erscheint.

1741   Die Herrnhuter Brüdergemeinde (*Moravian Brethren*) siedelt im Bundesstaat Pennsylvanien an.

1743   Christoph Sauer druckt die erste deutsche Bibel in Amerika.

1750   Die erste große Welle deutscher Einwanderer kommen nach Neuschottland.

1777   Deutsche spielen eine große Rolle im amerikanischen Revolutionskrieg.

1845   Deutsche gründen Neu Braunfels in Texas.

1850–60   Fast 1.000.000 Deutsche kommen nach Amerika.

1880–90   1.500.000 Deutsche wandern nach Amerika aus, davon 250.000 allein im Jahr 1882.

1894   Es gibt mehr als 800 deutschsprachige Zeitungen und Zeitschriften in Amerika.

1917   Erster Weltkrieg; antideutsche Hysterie bricht aus; die deutsche Sprache wird verboten.

1933   Hitler kommt an die Macht; jüdische Intellektuelle und Künstler verlassen Deutschland.

1950   Über 120.000 Deutsche kommen nach Amerika.

Quelle: Adams, Willi Paul: *The German Americans: An Ethnic Experience* (1993).

Aktivität 1   Fragen zur Einwanderung

1. Warum kamen Deutsche nach Nordamerika?

2. Wie viele Amerikaner waren im Jahre 2000 deutscher Abstammung?

3. Wo leben die meisten Amischen heute?

4. Was für eine Sprache sprechen die Amischen?

5. Warum musste Carl Schurz sein Land verlassen?

6. Welche politischen Ereignisse verursachten (*caused*) die deutsche Auswanderung (*emigration*) im 19. und 20. Jahrhundert?

7. Welcher deutscher Einwanderer wurde durch Immobilienhandel reich? Welcher wurde durch seine Jeans-Hosen bekannt?

8. In welchem Bundesstaat ließen sich (*settled*) viele frühe deutsche Einwanderer nieder?

Aktivität 2   Menschen und Momente

Es gibt viele wichtige Personen und Momente in der Geschichte der deutschen Einwanderung nach Nordamerika. Treiben Sie etwas Forschung und suchen Sie Informationen zu den folgenden Namen. Warum sind sie von Bedeutung?

1. Nikolaus de Meyer

2. Barbara Heck

3. Hessische Truppen

4. Joseph Heister

5. J. A. Sutter

6. *Illinois Staatsanzeiger*

7. Frederick Pabst

8. Mary McCauley

Barbara Heck

Aktivität 3   Mini-Forschungsprojekte

1. Schreiben Sie eine Kurzbiographie eines Einwanderers / einer Einwanderin mit Bildern als Posterpräsentation.

2. Erforschen Sie die deutschen Wurzeln (*roots*) Ihrer Stadt oder Ihrer Region und schreiben Sie einen Bericht darüber.

3. Berichten Sie über eines der folgenden Themen:

   a. eine deutschsprachige Zeitung in den USA/Kanada

   b. Nordamerikanische Firmen, die von Deutsch-Amerikanern gegründet wurden

4. Erstellen Sie eine Grafik über deutsche Einwanderung nach Nordamerika bzw. in die USA oder nach Kanada.

Medien und Technik

Gibt's was Neues in der Zeitung?

In diesem Kapitel

- **Themen:** Television, newspapers, and other media; technology, computers
- **Grammatik:** Infinitive clauses with **zu,** verbs **brauchen** and **scheinen,** infinitive clauses with **um ... zu** and **ohne ... zu,** indirect discourse
- **Kultur:** Radio and television, inventions
- **Lesen:** „Gute Freunde im Netz" (Kerstin Kohlenberg)

Videoclips
In der Zeitung steht ...

Alles klar?

A. Hier sehen Sie verschiedene deutschsprachige Zeitungen.

- Finden Sie drei Zeitungen, die deutsche Städtenamen tragen.
- Welche Zeitung ist für das Rheinland?
- Welche Zeitung erscheint wöchentlich (*weekly*)?
- Zwei Zeitungen sind sehr bunt (*colorful*) und bringen sensationelle Nachrichten. Wie heißen sie?

B. Sie hören vier kurze Berichte aus dem Radio. Welche Schlagzeile passt zu welchem Bericht? Schreiben Sie die passende Zahl (1–4) vor die Schlagzeile.

_____ Kluges (*smart*) Köpfchen vorm Mittagessen

_____ Spender (*donor*) der Woche

_____ Unbekanntes Dorf im Iran entdeckt

_____ Autodieb (*car thief*) auf Surfbrett gefangen

Wörter im Kontext

THEMA 1: Medien

Was gibt's im Fernsehen?

THOMAS: Was gibt's denn heute Abend im Fernsehen?

BARBARA: Nach den **Nachrichten** um 19 Uhr kommt im zweiten **Programm** ein Krimi, „Die Rosenheim-Cops".

THOMAS: Ein Krimi, nein danke! Das ist nichts für mich. **Das ist mir zu blöd.** Was gibt's denn bei RTL?

BARBARA: Eine Seifenoper, „Gute Zeiten, schlechte Zeiten" und eine Quiz-Show, „Wer wird Millionär?".

THOMAS: Auch **nichts Gescheites.**

BARBARA: Was für eine **Sendung** möchtest du denn sehen?

THOMAS: Na, vielleicht Sport … oder einen **Dokumentarfilm.** Ich kann **mich** noch nicht **entschließen.**

Neue Wörter

die Nachrichten (*pl.*) news
das Programm program, channel
Das ist mir zu blöd. I think that's really stupid.
nichts Gescheites nothing decent
die Sendung TV program
mich … entschließen (sich entschließen) decide
der Bericht report
der Spielfilm movie, feature film
ansehen watch
Such dir was aus! (sich etwas aussuchen) Choose something!
Wie wäre es mit … ? How about . . . ?
Na und? So what?
auf jeden Fall in any case
Wovon handelt sie? (handeln von) What's it about?

ZDF **2**

17.15 **hallo deutschland** 31-546
17.45 **Leute heute** 767-701
Journal mit Karen Webb
18.00 **SOKO Köln** 29-527
Krimiserie, Deutschland 2005
Die Spur des Jägers
Die SOKO feiert Alexandras
Dienstjubiläum in einem Lokal
am Waldrand und schlittert in
einen Mordfall. Jagdpächter
Werner König wurde erschossen.
Mit G. Rapsch, Tim Grabowski,
Krystian Martinek, Andrea Lüdke
19.00 **heute** 94-237
19.20 **Wetter** 2-805-614
19.25 **Die Rosenheim-Cops**
Deutschland 2005 8-684-607
Die verschwundene Leiche

KRIMISERIE

**Martha Huber (Lisa Kreuzer) läßt
Hofer (J. Hannesschläger) abblitzen**

Rast im Berghütte. Kommissar Lind glaubt, eine Leiche zu sehen, und wird niedergeschlagen.
Als er wieder zu sich kommt, läßt
kaum etwas auf ein Verbrechen
schließen. Lind und Kollege Hofer
nehmen Gastwirt Weinberger,
seine Verlobte Angelika Huber
und ihre Eltern unter die Lupe.
Schließlich entdecken sie eine
Tote: die Barfrau Rita Pohlberg.
Mit Tom Mikulla, Stephanie
Kellner, Sebastian Bezzel

20.15 **Fußball: DFB-Pokal** 9-755-237
SPORT TIP
Halbfinale: Eintr. Frankfurt – Arminia Bielefeld

FUSSBALL

Live Bundesliga-Duell im November: Bielefeld
(Pinto, I.) strauchelte gegen Frankfurt (Köhler) 0:3
Aus der Commerzbank Arena **Anstoß: 20.30**
Weltfußballerin Birgit Prinz zog das Los – und
die Bielefelder verspürten Zuversicht. Auf
der Website der Westfalen wird die Partie in
Frankfurt als „lösbare Aufgabe" gewertet.
Wenn's stimmt, würde die Arminia erstmals
in der Vereinsgeschichte das DFB-Pokalfinale
erreichen. Die Eintracht kann da mehr
aufweisen: Viermal holten die Hessen die
Trophäe. Der letzte Triumph liegt aber lange
zurück. 1988 bezwang man Bochum 1:0.
Reporter: Thomas Wark. Moderation:
Johannes B. Kerner. In der Halbzeitpause:
ca. **21.15 heute-journal** und **21.25 Wetter**
Verlängerung und Elfmeterschießen möglich!
2. Halbfinale: FC St. Pauli – Bayern München,
morgen ab 20.15 Uhr live in der ARD

22.40 **37°: Meinen Job gibt's billiger** 3-651-053
i TIP
Wenn Arbeit verlagert wird. Von Tine Kugler
Stichwort Globalisierung. Wie fühlen sich
Arbeitnehmer, wenn der Job ins Ausland
verlagert wird und sich das (Berufs-)Leben
komplett verändert? Vier Betroffene schildern
ihre persönlichen Erfahrungen.

RTL — **RTL**

18.00	**Guten Abend RTL**	3-923
	Oder Regionalprogramme	
18.30	**Exclusiv** Starmagazin	28-010
18.45	**RTL aktuell**	450-126
	Anschließend: **19.03 Uhr Wetter**	
19.05	**Explosiv** Mit Markus Lanz	567-381
19.40	**Gute Zeiten,**	
	schlechte Zeiten	8-381-720
	Deutschland 2006 (3460)	

SERIE

Wollen Freunde sein: Franzi (Jasmin Weber) und Philip (Jörn Schlönvoigt) Durch eine auffallend heftige Reaktion gegenüber Schüttler lenkt Paula ihren Freund John auf die richtige Fährte. In einer Aussprache versuchen Franzi und Philip ihr Verhältnis zueinander zu klären, so daß einem freundschaftlichen Miteinander künftig nichts im Wege steht. Doch bei der Theaterprobe sieht die Sache dann wieder ganz anders aus.

20.15 Wer wird Millionär? 114-297
Moderation: Günther Jauch

QUIZSHOW

Die Web-Mutti ist die Beste: Jauch sucht bei Problemen im Haushalt weltweit weibliche Hilfe

Es geschah an einem Montag im März, da schnellte die Anzahl der Zugriffe auf eine Internetseite explosionsartig in die Höhe. Was außer Sex, Geld und Tierbabys besitzt solche Anziehungskraft? Ganz einfach: Hausmittel gegen „Stinkeschuhe" und Rotweinflecken. Für die Aufregung war allein Quizmaster Günther Jauch verantwortlich. Der hatte – ganz Hausfrauen unter sich – im Plausch mit einer Kandidatin vor einem Millionenpublikum für die Ratgeberseite www.frag-mutti.de bekennende Werbung gemacht. Fans wird es gefreut haben, wieder etwas über den kauzigen Medienstar erfahren – und von ihm gelernt zu haben.

WEITERE SPIELFILME

11.30 NDR **Rache ist süß** Ⓢ📺
KOMÖDIE Starreporter Jeff soll für seinen rachsüchtigen Boss einen dunklen Fleck auf der weißen Weste einer attraktiven Richterin finden... Nette Unterhaltung. SV 5-187-268
USA 1941 D Walter Pidgeon, Rosalind Russell, Edward Arnold R Norman Taurog **80 Min. →12.50** ➡

20.15 PRO 7 **Borderline – Unter Mordverdacht**
NEU: THRILLER Gefängnispsychologin Lila wird verdächtigt nach einem Sorgerechtsstreit um die beiden Kinder, ihren Ex-Mann und dessen Freundin ermordet zu haben. Sie glaubt, den wahren Täter aus ihrem Umfeld zu kennen... Spannend. SV 83-341
USA 2002 D Gina Gershon, Sean Patrick Flanery, Eddie Driscoll R Evelyn Purcell **105/07 Min. •22.00** ↘

21.45 BR **Bella Martha**
LIEBESKOMÖDIE Martha kann gut kochen, aber vom Genießen versteht sie nichts. Ein temperamentvoller Italiener und ein kleines Mädchen tauen das Herz der verschlossenen Köchin auf... Garniert mit feinem Humor. SV 7-202-744
Dtl./Ital. 2001 D Martina Gedeck, Sergio Castellitto B+R Sandra Nettelbeck **100 Min. →23.25** ↗

22.05 MDR **Tatort: Das Phantom**
TV-KRIMI Schenk erkennt, daß er vor Jahren einen Unschuldigen hinter Gitter gebracht hat. Bevor er den Fehler wieder gutmachen kann, bricht der junge Mann aus und tötet einen Polizisten... Melancholische Story. SV 3-728-812
Dtl. 2003 D Klaus J. Behrendt, Dietmar Bär, Roman Knizka R Kaspar Heidelbach **90 Min. →23.35** ↗

23.20 SWR **Virus im Paradies (1)**
TV-THRILLER Der Tod eines bretonischen Hühnerzüchters alarmiert Ärzte und Politiker. Die Hühner werden getötet, es beginnt die Jagd auf das Virus... 2. Teil: am Mi. SV 9-844-687
Frkr./Schw./Island/Belg. 2003 D Richard Bohringer R Olivier Langlois **90 Min. →0.50** ↗

0.45 DAS VIERTE **Cocktail für eine Leiche** Ⓢ📺
THRILLER Um ihrem Professor zu beweisen, daß ein perfekter Mord möglich ist, töten zwei Studenten einen Kommilitonen und geben am Tatort eine Party... Von nur einem Kamerastandpunkt aus gedrehter Klassiker. SV 41-952-850
USA 1948 D James Stewart, Farley Granger, John Dall R Alfred Hitchcock FSK 12 **90/76 Min. →2.15** ↗

SYMBOLE: ⬆ Großartig ↗ Gelungen ↘ Annehmbar ⬇ Schwach

BARBARA: Um 20.15 Uhr gibt es ein Fußballspiel ... und später um 22.40 Uhr kommt ein **Bericht** über die Arbeitslage in Deutschland. Aber keine Dokumentarfilme. Ich möchte mir mal einen guten **Spielfilm ansehen.**

THOMAS: Du hast ja das Programm für heute Abend. **Such dir was aus!**

BARBARA: **Wie wäre es mit** „Cocktail für eine Leiche" von Hitchcock?

THOMAS: So ein alter Schinken (*old hat*).

BARBARA: **Na und?** Das ist **auf jeden Fall** ein guter, alter Klassiker. Ach, nein, Moment, der kommt erst um 0.45 Uhr.

THOMAS: Lass mal sehen ... Um 22.05 Uhr läuft im MDR „Tatort: Das Phantom."

BARBARA: Das ist mir auch zu spät.

THOMAS: Wie wäre es mit einer Liebeskomödie, „Bella Martha" um 21.45 Uhr?

BARBARA: Klingt gut. **Wovon handelt** sie denn?

Ergänzen Sie die folgenden Sätze. Die Informationen finden Sie im Gespräch zwischen Barbara und Thomas.

1. Die „Rosenheim-Cops" läuft im zweiten _____.
2. Thomas möchte vielleicht Sport oder einen _____ sehen.
3. Barbara möchte gern einen _____ sehen.
4. Thomas meint, Serien wie „Gute Zeiten, schlechte Zeiten" sind nichts _____.
5. Um 22.40 kommt im Zweiten Programm ein _____ über die Arbeitslage in Deutschland.
6. Barbara fragt Thomas, wovon der Film „Bella Martha" _____.

Was steht in der Zeitung?

Hier sind einige typische Rubriken (*sections*) aus der Zeitung, bzw. der **Zeitschrift.**

A. Welche Rubriken …

- lesen Sie immer? nie? manchmal?
- finden Sie am interessantesten?

B. Finden Sie nun eine passende **Schlagzeile** für die Rubriken.

RUBRIKEN

Lokalnachrichten	**Aktuelles**	Sport
Inland	**Wirtschaft** und **Börse**	Reisen
Ausland	Arbeit und Karriere	**Horoskop**
Politik	Wissen und **Forschen**	Kultur

SCHLAGZEILEN

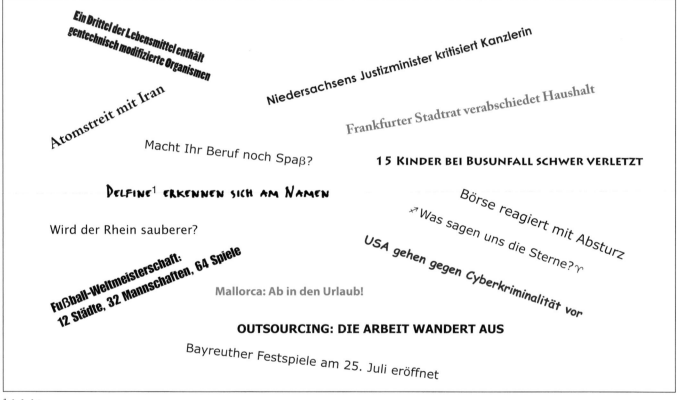

Ein Drittel der Lebensmittel enthält gentechnisch modifizierte Organismen

Atomstreit mit Iran

Niedersachsens Justizminister kritisiert Kanzlerin

Frankfurter Stadtrat verabschiedet Haushalt

Macht Ihr Beruf noch Spaß?

15 KINDER BEI BUSUNFALL SCHWER VERLETZT

DELFINE[1] ERKENNEN SICH AM NAMEN

Wird der Rhein sauberer?

Börse reagiert mit Absturz

Was sagen uns die Sterne?

USA gehen gegen Cyberkriminalität vor

Fußball-Weltmeisterschaft: 12 Städte, 32 Mannschaften, 64 Spiele

Mallorca: Ab in den Urlaub!

OUTSOURCING: DIE ARBEIT WANDERT AUS

Bayreuther Festspiele am 25. Juli eröffnet

[1]dolphins

Aktivität 1   Das Fernsehprogramm

Suchen Sie im Fernsehprogramm auf der nächsten Seite eine Sendung, die zu jeder der folgenden Kategorien passt.

BEISPIEL: Spielfilm →
    Um 0.20 Uhr kommt der Spielfilm „Kansas" im ersten Programm.

1. Nachrichten
2. Komödie (*f.*)
3. Talk-Show (*f.*)
4. Krimi (*m.*)

5. Reportage (*f.*)
6. Dokumentarfilm
7. Sportsendung

DAS ERSTE

20.15 Schmunzelkrimiserie

Adelheid und Eugen finden ein aufschlußreiches Video: **Adelheid und ihre Mörder**

5.30 Morgenmagazin 98-487-688 **9.05** Ein Haus in der Toskana. Familienserie 2-727-441 **10.03 Brisant.** Boulevardmagazin 302-279-441 **10.40** Himmel auf Erden ▣ Lustspiel, A 1935 4-507-422 **12.00** Tagesschau 05-000 **12.15** ARD-Buffet 6-892-354 **13.00** ARD-Mittagsmagazin 78-170 **14.00** Tagesschau 79-489 **14.15** In aller Freundschaft. Arztserie ▨ 57-083

15.00 Fliege 52-118
16.00 Tagesschau ▨ 84-373
16.15 Abenteuer Wildnis Tierdoku. Grizzlys – Riesenbären in Amerika 3-070-809
17.00 Tagesschau ▨ 35-083
17.15 Brisant 690-809 Boulevardmagazin
17.50 Verbotene Liebe 43-083
18.20 Marienhof 95-422
18.50 Plötzlich erwachsen! Familienserie, D 2001/05 „Geplatzte Träume" 16-915
19.20 Das Quiz mit Jörg Pilawa 494-977
19.55 Börse 4-314-286

20.00 Tagesschau ▨ 33-441
20.15 Adelheid und ihre Mörder ▢ ▨ 9-567-460 Schmunzelkrimiserie, D '03 „Botschaft aus dem Grab": Als ein Verleger sein Testament zu Gunsten eines Tierschutzvereins ändert, gibt es Tote
21.05 In aller Freundschaft Arztserie, D 2005 „Geschwisterliebe" 2-775-199
21.55 Plusminus 3-788-460 Wirtschaftsmagazin, moderiert von Jörg Boecker
22.30 Tagesthemen 731
23.00 Frau Thomas Mann Porträt, D 2005 87-880
0.00 Nachtmagazin 95-774
0.20 Kansas 2-305-126 Thriller, USA 1988 Regie: David Stevens. Auf Tramptour verstrickt Ex-Knacki Doyle (Matt Dillon) seine Zufallsbekanntschaft Wade (Andrew McCarthy) in einen Banküberfall...
2.05 Tagesschau 25-457-887
2.10 Fliege 2-534-316
3.10 ARD-Ratgeber: Reise New York – Sightseeing für Filmfreaks (Wh.) 2-381-403
3.40 Weltreisen 4-898-316 Alaska (Wh.)

ZDF

1.05 TV-Thriller

Anwalt Gavin (Tom Berenger) trifft auf blondes Gift (Heidi Schanz). **Body-Language**

5.05 hallo Deutschland 4-984-731 **5.30 Morgenmagazin** 15-953-970 **9.05** Volle Kanne 4-756-147 **10.30** Leichtathletik-WM live. Wettbewerbe der Männer: Zehnkampf (1.Tag mit 100 m-Lauf und Weitsprung): Qualifikationen: Speerwurf, Stabhochsprung sowie 200 m und 400 m Vorläufe 86-993-828 **14.00** heute 60-731 **14.15** Wunderbare Welt ▢ 55-625

15.00 heute – Sport 65-903
15.15 Frauenarzt Dr. Markus Merthin 6-050-712
16.00 heute – in Europa 82-915
16.15 Bianca 3-061-151
17.15 hallo Deutschland Boulevardmagazin 516-712
17.35 Leichtathletik: WM Live. Männer: Hochsprung im Zehnkampf; Frauen: Diskuswurf-Finale; 100-m-Hürden-Vorläufe 3-319-248
19.00 heute ▨ 90-712
19.25 Leichtathletik: WM Live. Finals: 3000-m-Hindernis (M), 800 m (F) 6-823-373

20.15 Familie Hitler ▢ ▨ **TEXT** Im Schatten des Diktators 630-151 (VPS 20.14) 409-575-489
21.00 Frontal 21 45-083 Politmagazin mit Theo Koll
21.45 heute-journal ▨ 104-977
22.15 37°: Teure Liebe 743-880 **TEXT** Gesellschaftsreportage, D 2005. Frauen in der Schuldenfalle. Über bürgschaftsgeschädigte Frauen
22.45 Wo steht Deutschland? (3) 6-428-712 **TEXT** Wahl 2005. Ernstfall für die Bundeswehr
23.15 Die Affäre 6-750-373 **TEXT** Semmeling (1) ▢ TV-Familiensaga, D/A 2002 Regie: Dieter Wedel Mit Fritz Lichtenhahn, Antje Hagen und Stefan Kurt Die letzte Küche (2. Teil am 11. August)
0.45 heute nacht 5-967-403 Nachrichtenmagazin
1.05 Body Language – Verführung in der Nacht TV-Thriller, USA 1995 ▨ Regie: George Case Mit Tom Berenger, Nancy Travis, Heidi Schanz 7-094-584
2.45 37°: Teure Liebe Reportage (Wh.) 7-908-652

RTL

20.15 Krimiserie

Horatio (l.) und Bernstein vom **CSI: Miami** stehen fassungslos vor der aufgehängten Leiche

5.10 EXTRA (Wh.) 7-596-625 **6.00** Punkt 6 61-828 **7.00** Unter uns 4-489 **7.30** GZSZ 8-169-083 **8.05** RTL-Shop 5-158-688 **9.00** Punkt 9 5-199 **9.30** Mein Baby 8-286 **10.00** Dr. Stefan Frank 73-402 **11.00** Einsatz in 4 Wänden 5-335 **11.30** Unsere Klinik 8-422 **12.00** Punkt 12 85-460 **13.00** Die Oliver Geissen Show. Daily Talk 61-880 **14.00** Das Strafgericht 72-996

15.00 Das Familiengericht Gerichtsshow 45-828
16.00 Das Jugendgericht Gerichtsshow 49-644
17.00 Einsatz in 4 Wänden Mit Tine Wittler 3-557
17.30 Unter uns 6-644 Daily Soap, D 2005
18.00 Guten Abend RTL 7-373
18.30 EXCLUSIV – Das Star-Magazin 51-422
18.45 RTL Aktuell 986-557
19.10 Explosiv – Das Magazin Boulevardmagazin 496-335
19.40 Gute Zeiten, schlechte Zeiten Daily Soap 7-294-267

20.15 CSI: Miami ▣▣ 143-606 Krimiserie, USA 2002 „Der Tote am Baum": Professor Metzger, zu dessen Forschungsfeld Gewalt und Folter gehören, wird grausam verstümmelt aufgefunden...
21.15 Im Namen des Gesetzes 8-691-828 Polizeiserie, D 2002 „Das zweite Gesicht"
22.15 Monk 4-718-538 Krimiserie, USA 2002 „Mr. Monk im Flugzeug": Als Monk in einem Flieger einen Mörder zu erkennen glaubt, vergisst er seine panische Flugangst
23.10 Law & Order 8-141-002 Krimiserie, USA 2000 „Im Namen der Liebe"
0.00 RTL-Nachtjournal 8-045 Nachrichtenmagazin
0.30 Golden Girls 2-452-300 Comedy, USA 1988 „Das aufregende Leben der Sophia Petrillo"
1.00 Susan 2-533-229 Comedyserie, USA 1999
1.30 Das Familiengericht Gerichtsshow 5-406-942
2.20 Die Oliver Geissen Show (Wh.) 6-470-478

SAT.1

20.15 TV-Komödie

Ein ganzer Kerl für Mama: Scheidungsanwältin und Supermacho kommen sich näher

5.10 blitz 4-476-977 **5.30** Frühstücksfernsehen 16-715-083 **9.00** HSE24 99-199 **10.00** Lenßen & Partner 4-118 **10.30** Verliebt in Berlin. Telenovela 9-809 **11.00** Stefanie – Eine Frau startet durch 66-047 **12.00** Verrückt Mittag 37-335 **13.00** Britt – Der Talk um Eins. Profi-Hure – „Warum gibst du dich für sowas her?" 46-083 **14.00** Zwei bei Kallwass 57-199

15.00 Richterin Barbara Salesch 13-731
16.00 Richter Alexander Hold 24-847
17.00 Niedrig und Kuhnt – Kommissare ermitteln Ermittler Soap 5-422
17.30 17:30 Live 5-809
18.00 Lenßen & Partner 6-538 Ermittler-Soap
18.30 SAT.1 News 44-644
18.50 blitz 9-713-199
19.15 Verliebt in Berlin Telenovela, D 2005 796-847
19.45 K 11 – Kommissare im Einsatz 328-460

20.15 Ein ganzer Kerl für Mama 2-733-977 TV-Komödie, D 2002 Regie: Zoltan Spirandelli „Du bist eine frustrierte, streitsüchtige Zicke!" Paul Wackernagel (Jörg Schüttauf) hat rasch ein Urteil über jene Frau gefällt, die sein Ferienhaus besetzt. Der Autor von Ratgebern wie „Keine Mark für die Ex" hat einen gültigen Mietvertrag und pocht auf sein Wohnrecht. So wie Tanja (Nina Kronjäger) auf das ihre: Die Villa wurde ihr als Ersatz angeboten, weil das eigentlich geplante Urlaubsdomizil ausgebrannt ist
22.15 alphateam – 5-351-354 **Die Lebensretter im OP** Krankenhausserie, D 2005 „Kaltes Land": Das Personal muss sich mit Skinheads und niederträchtigen Zuhältern rumschlagen. Danach: „Falsche Liebe" ('99)
0.15 Sat.1 News 26-768
0.45 Quiz Night 5-573-010
2.05 blitz 8-603-381
3.05 Richterin Barbara Salesch 1-652-720
3.55 Richter Hold 1-677-039

PRO SIEBEN

19.25 Wissensmagazin

Aiman Abdallah erklärt bei **Galileo** anschaulich Tageserereignisse und Zeitphänomene

5.25 Do it Yourself – S.O.S. 9-121-625 **5.55 taff** (Wh.) 2-950-625 **6.50** Galileo 56-392-793 **7.25** Scrubs – Die Anfänger 4-456-002 **7.50** ClipMix 5-448-460 **8.50** Eure letzte Chance 9-906-557 **10.00** talk talk talk 91-557 **11.00** S.O.S. Style & Home 64-489 **12.00** AVENZIO – Schöner leben! 35-977 **13.00** SAM 44-625 **14.00** Das Geständnis – Heute sage ich alles 48-441

15.00 Freunde – Das Leben geht weiter! 11-373
16.00 Eure letzte Chance Ratgeber-Show 22-489
17.00 taff 70-369
18.00 Die Simpsons 7-880 Zeichentrickserie, USA '93 „Am Kap der Angst"
18.30 Futurama 14-489 Zeichentrickserie, USA '02 „Der letzte Trekki"
18.55 Scrubs – Die Anfänger Comedyserie, USA '02 74-441 „Mein Ticket nach Reno"
19.25 Galileo 626-199 Windkraftwerk

20.00 Newstime 18-644
20.15 Sex and the City 303-151 Comedyserie, USA 1999 „Mädchen gegen Frauen": Die Freundinnen machen Urlaub auf Long Island und müssen sehr bald feststellen, dass sie sehr unterschiedliche Auffassungen von Entspannung haben
20.45 Friends 968-002 Comedyserie, USA 2004 „Was mein ist, ist nicht dein": Joeys Date mit Sarah verläuft anders als geplant
21.15 Desperate Housewives Satireserie, USA 2004 „Schlachtfelder": Gabrielle schleppt ihre ehemals spielsüchtige Schwiegermutter zum Zocken 5-566-557
22.20 Sarah & Marc in Love – Die Hochzeit des Jahres Doku-Soap 9-667-625
23.10 BIZZ 145-373 Unter dem Motto: „BIZZ motzt auf" findet „das große Tuning-Event" statt
23.55 „taff" Spezial 3-397-712 Das Familienhotel – Hinter den Kulissen des „Schwarzen Adlers" in Innsbruck (4+5)
1.00 Sex and the... 1-415-132

▣▣ Zweikanalton ▣▣ Dolby-Surround ▣ schwarzweiß ▢ Breitbild ▨ Untertitel für Hörgeschädigte (OmU) Original mit Untertiteln **TEXT** siehe Spielfilm- und TV-Auswahl

Lange Zeit gab es in Deutschland nur drei Programme. Die ARD (Arbeitsgemeinschaft der Rundfunkanstalten Deutschlands) – auch „Erstes Programm" genannt – und das ZDF (Zweites Deutsches Fernsehen) senden auch heute noch das erste und zweite Programm. Das „Dritte Programm" besteht aus regionalen Sendern aus ganz Deutschland. In diesen drei Programmen werden die meisten Sendungen nicht durch Werbung unterbrochen. Alle Werbespots werden blockweise zu einem bestimmten Zeitpunkt gezeigt. Jeder Haushalt muss für Radio und Fernsehen eine Gebühr, die sogenannte Rundfunkgebühr, bezahlen. Man zahlt die Gebühr an die GEZ (Gebühreneinzugszentrale).

Heutzutage gibt es in deutschsprachigen Ländern eine Vielfalt an Fernsehprogrammen. Kabelfernsehen und Satellitenprogramme, z.B. PRO 7, NBC Super-Channel und CNN, sind sehr beliebt und zeigen viele Sendungen im amerikanischen Stil. Kabelfernsehen muss man abonnieren. Für Sender wie Premiere (sogenannte Pay TV) muss man weitere Gebühren bezahlen.

Ich zahl. Die Rundfunkgebühren

WDR N1/97121

☐ Ich bin noch nicht bei der GEZ angemeldet
☐ Ich bin schon angemeldet unter der Nr. _____

Name/Vorname   Geburtsdatum

Straße/Hausnummer

Postleitzahl   Ort

Ich melde an   ☐ Radio   ☐ Fernsehgerät   ab _____

Ich zahle   ☐ jährlich im Voraus   ☐ vierteljährlich im Voraus
              zum 1. Januar   zum 1. Januar, April, Juli, Oktober
            ☐ halbjährlich im Voraus   ☐ in der Mitte eines Dreimonats-
              zum 1. Januar, Juli   zeitraumes jeweils zum 15.

Ich zahle   ☐ per Überweisung/mit Zahlschein   ☐ Lastschrift (s.u.)

Kontonummer   Bankleitzahl

Bank/Sparkasse   Kontoinhaber

Datum   Unterschrift

Bitte informieren Sie die GEZ, wenn Sie umziehen oder einen Umzug planen. Formulare zur **Änderungsmeldung** liegen bei Banken und Sparkassen aus. Auch telefonisch, per Fax oder im Internet können Sie (unter Angabe Ihrer Teilnehmer-Nummer) Ihre Anschrift korrigieren lassen. Bitte melden Sie sich nicht ab und unter neuer Anschrift wieder an. **www.gez.de**

GEZ Service-Hotline 0180 501 65 65 · Faxline 0180 582 10 10 (12 Cent/Min) · www.gez.de

Übrigens: Für Radio und TV zahlen Sie nur 53 Cent am Tag

Antwort

GEZ

50656 Köln

Hier klicken!

Weiteres zum Thema Medien finden Sie bei **Deutsch: Na klar!** im World-Wide-Web unter www.mhhe.com/dnk5.

Aktivität 2   Hin und her: Wie informieren sie sich?

Wie informieren sich diese Personen? Was lesen sie zur Unterhaltung? Stellen Sie Fragen an Ihren Partner / Ihre Partnerin.

BEISPIEL: s1: Was sieht Martin gern im Fernsehen? Was liest er oft?
           s2: Er _____.

PERSON	FERNSEHSHOWS	ZEITUNGEN UND ZEITSCHRIFTEN
Martin	Talk-Shows und Dokumentarfilme	*die Zeit*
Stephanie		
Patrick	Quizsendungen wie „Der Preis ist heiß", die Nachrichten	*die Frankfurter Allgemeine* und *Stern*
Kristin		
Mein Partner / Meine Partnerin		

Aktivität 3 Das sehe ich gern!

Was mögen Sie im Fernsehen? Warum? Was finden Sie nicht besonders gut im Fernsehen? Geben Sie Beispiele.

BEISPIEL: Ich mag Serien, zum Beispiel „Tatort". Die finde ich spannend. Aber Quizsendungen finde ich schrecklich langweilig.

Krimis	gewöhnlich	aktuell
Nachrichten	immer	interessant
Dokumentarfilme	meistens	komisch
Quizsendungen	schrecklich	langweilig
Talk-Shows	sehr	schlecht
Seifenopern		spannend
Sport		unterhaltsam
Serien		
Musik		
Komödien		
Musicals		
Dramen		

Aktivität 4 Eine Sendung auswählen

Besprechen Sie mit einem Partner / einer Partnerin, was Sie heute Abend sehen möchten. Wählen Sie eine Sendung aus dem Fernsehprogramm in **Aktivität 1** aus.

S1	S2
1. Was gibt es heute Abend im Fernsehen?	2. Um ____ gibt es ____.
3. Was ist denn das?	4a. Das ist eine Sendung über ____. b. Keine Ahnung, klingt aber interessant.
5. Wer spielt mit?	6. Hier steht ____.
7. Wie lange dauert das?	8a. ____ Stunden/Minuten b. Von ____ Uhr bis ____ Uhr.
9. Was gibt es sonst noch?	10a. Magst du ____ ? b. Wie wäre es mit ____ ?
11a. Ja, das finde ich ____. b. Nein, ich sehe lieber ____. c. Ich lese heute Abend lieber.	12. Na gut.

Neue Wörter

der Kabelanschluss cable TV connection
der Anrufbeantworter answering machine
die Sat-Empfangsanlage satellite receiver
erfunden (erfinden) invented
die Erfindung (Erfindungen, *pl.***)** invention
der Drucker printer
speichern store, save
empfangen receive
hinterlassen leave (behind)
drucken print
aufnehmen record

Blick in Deutschlands Haushalte

Von je 100 Haushalten besitzen:

Kühlschrank	99
Telefon (Festnetz)[1]	95
Fernsehgerät	94
Waschmaschine	94
Radiorecorder[2]	84
Fotoapparat, Digitalkamera	83
Fahrrad	79
Pkw[3]	77
Handy	73
Videorecorder	68
Hi-Fi-Anlage	66
Gefrierschrank[4]	66
CD-Player	64
Mikrowellengerät	63
PC	58
Geschirrspülmaschine	57
Kabelanschluss	53
Anrufbeantworter	46
Internet	46
Sat-Empfangsanlage	37
Wäschetrockner	37
DVD-Player	27
Hometrainer[5]	24
CD-Recorder (auch im PC)	24
ISDN[6]	23
Camcorder	22
Telefaxgerät	21
Laptop, Notebook	11
Mini-Disc-Player/-Recorder	11

Stand 2003   Quelle: Stat. Bundesamt   © Globus 9414

[1]*conventional fixed-line network*   [2]*boom box*   [3]= P̲ersonenk̲raf̲tw̲agen *automobile*   [4]*freezer*   [5]*home exercise equipment*   [6][*type of communications link; here:*] *high-speed Internet*

A. Schauen Sie sich das Schaubild an und beantworten Sie die Fragen.

- Wie viel Prozent der Haushalte haben einen Fernseher? einen Pkw? eine **Digitalkamera**? einen PC? **Internet**? ein **Notebook**?
- Haben Deutsche öfter **Kabelanschluss** oder eine **Sat-Empfangsanlage**?
- Welche Geräte im Schaubild hat man in den letzten dreißig Jahren **erfunden**? Was sind **Erfindungen** der letzten fünfzig Jahre?
- Welche von diesen Geräten besitzen Sie?

Siehe *Infinitive Clauses with* **um ... zu** *and* **ohne ... zu**, S. 395.

B. Wozu benutzt man die folgenden Geräte? Verbinden Sie die Satzteile. Für manche Geräte sind mehrere Anworten möglich!

BEISPIEL: Man benutzt eine Digitalkamera, um Fotos zu machen.

Man benutzt ...

1. eine Digitalkamera
2. einen PC / einen Heimcomputer
3. einen Kabelanschluss / eine Sat-Empfangsanlage
4. ein **(Tele-)Faxgerät**
5. einen Laptop / ein Notebook
6. einen Mini-Disc-Player / einen MP3-Player
7. einen **Anrufbeantworter**
8. einen **Drucker**
9. einen **Camcorder**

a. um unterwegs am Computer zu arbeiten
b. um Musik digital zu **speichern** und abzuspielen
c. um mehr Programme im Fernsehen zu **empfangen**
d. um **Dokumente** über das Telefonnetz zu schicken
e. um telefonische Nachrichten zu **hinterlassen**
f. um Dokumente und Bilder zu **drucken**
g. um **E-Mails** zu schicken
h. um Videos **aufzunehmen**
i. um Fotos zu machen

Aktivität 5 Am Computer

Die Sprache der modernen Technologie kommt zum großen Teil aus dem Englischen. Die moderne Computertechnologie verwendet auch viele Symbole.

Schritt 1: Verbinden Sie Symbole mit ihren üblichen (*conventional*) Bedeutungen.

1. ____ ✉   **a.** Audio/Video vorspulen (*fast forward*)
2. ____ 💾   **b.** das Dokument drucken
3. ____ 🗑   **c.** das Dokument speichern
4. ____ 👆   **d.** den Text ausschneiden (*cut*)
5. ____ 🔊   **e.** das Dokument löschen (*delete*)
6. ____ ▶▶   **f.** eine E-Mail lesen
7. ____ ✂   **g.** Hier kann man etwas hören.
8. ____ 🖥   **h.** Hier kann man klicken

Schritt 2: Suchen Sie passende Verben zu den Substantiven. (Manchmal ist mehr als eine Antwort richtig.)

BEISPIEL: Am Computer kann man E-Mails bekommen.

Am Computer kann man …

1. E-Mails ____.
2. Softwareprogramme ____.
3. ein Thema oder ein Wort ____.
4. eine Zeitung im Internet ____.
5. über viele Themen ____.
6. Dokumente ____.

> bloggen   herunterladen/downloaden
>
> googeln   lesen   schicken
>
> speichern
>
> bekommen   kaufen   schreiben

ANALYSE

Schauen Sie sich das Schaubild an und beantworten Sie dann die folgenden Fragen.

- Welche Firma hatte 2004 die meisten Patentanmeldungen in Deutschland?
- Welche Firma auf dieser Liste hatte die wenigsten?
- Aus welchen Ländern sind diese Firmen?
- Nennen Sie mindestens zwei Erfindungen aus Ihrem Land.

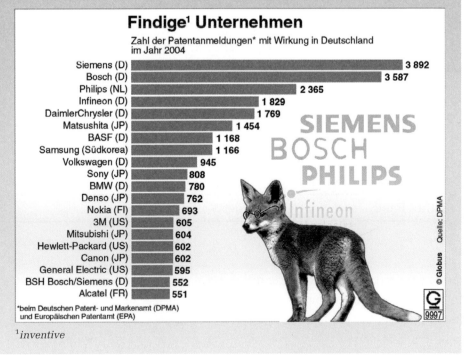

Findige[1] Unternehmen

Zahl der Patentanmeldungen* mit Wirkung in Deutschland im Jahr 2004

Siemens (D)	3 892
Bosch (D)	3 587
Philips (NL)	2 365
Infineon (D)	1 829
DaimlerChrysler (D)	1 769
Matsushita (JP)	1 454
BASF (D)	1 168
Samsung (Südkorea)	1 166
Volkswagen (D)	945
Sony (JP)	808
BMW (D)	780
Denso (JP)	762
Nokia (FI)	693
3M (US)	605
Mitsubishi (JP)	604
Hewlett-Packard (US)	602
Canon (JP)	602
General Electric (US)	595
BSH Bosch/Siemens (D)	552
Alcatel (FR)	551

*beim Deutschen Patent- und Markenamt (DPMA) und Europäischen Patentamt (EPA)

© Globus   Quelle: DPMA   9997

[1]*inventive*

Aktivität 6 Ein findiger Kopf

Wie erfinderisch sind Sie? Beschreiben Sie eine nützliche Erfindung.

BEISPIEL: Medizin →
Ein Hustenbonbon, das wie Schokolade schmeckt.

BEREICHE

1. Medizin
2. Technik
3. Verkehr
4. Haushalt
5. Tiere
6. Stadtplanung
7. Umwelt
8. Häuser

Aktivität 7 Hin und her: Erfindungen durch die Jahrhunderte

Sie möchten erfahren, wer was und wann erfunden hat. Arbeiten Sie zu zweit.

BEISPIELE: s1: Wer hat _____ erfunden?
s2: _____.
s1: Wann hat er/sie es erfunden?
s2: (Im Jahre) _____.

[oder:] s1: Was hat _____ erfunden?
s2: Er/Sie hat _____ erfunden.
s1: In welchem Jahr?
s2: (Im Jahre) _____.

ERFINDER	ERFINDUNG	JAHR
	der Buchdruck mit beweglichen Lettern (*movable type*)	
	das Alkoholthermometer	
Karl von Drais	das Fahrrad (Draisine)	1817
Herta Heuwer		
Gottlieb Daimler	das Motorrad	1885
Rudolf Diesel	der Dieselmotor	1893
Wilhelm Conrad Röntgen		
Melitta Bentz	der Kaffeefilter	1908

Grammatik im Kontext

Infinitive Clauses with zu°

Der Infinitivsatz

Infinitive clauses may be complements of verbs, nouns, or adjectives. When used this way, the infinitive is always preceded by **zu.**

> Familie Baier **hat vor,** einen neuen Computer **zu kaufen.**
>
> *The Baier family is planning to buy a new computer.*

> Es macht mir **Spaß,** E-Mail aus der ganzen Welt **zu bekommen.**
>
> *I enjoy receiving e-mail from all over the world.*

> Es ist **leicht,** einen Brief per E-Mail **zu schicken.**
>
> *It is easy to send a letter via e-mail.*

Note:

- The infinitive with **zu** is always the last element of the sentence.
- With separable-prefix verbs, **zu** is placed between the prefix and the main verb.

> Ich habe versucht, dich gestern **anzurufen.**
>
> *I tried to call you yesterday.*

> Du hast versprochen **vorbeizukommen.**
>
> *You promised to come by.*

- A comma generally sets off an infinitive clause that includes more than just the infinitive with **zu.** No comma is used otherwise.

Übung 1 Felix

Felix studiert Medien an der Hochschule für Technik in Dresden. Er ist ein Erstsemester und es gibt viel Neues für ihn. Bilden Sie Sätze.

BEISPIEL: er hat vor: einen neuen Computer kaufen →
Er hat vor, einen neuen Computer zu kaufen.

1. er findet es nicht leicht: ein Zimmer in einer WG finden
2. er hat versprochen: seine Familie regelmäßig anrufen
3. es macht ihm Spaß: jeden Mittwoch zum Kickboxen gehen
4. er hat keine Zeit: jeden Abend ausgehen
5. er hat sich entschlossen: etwas Geld mit Jobben verdienen
6. er versucht: im Inter-Treff Club andere Studenten kennen lernen
7. er findet es interessant: in Dresden studieren

Übung 2 Meiner Meinung nach ...

Drücken Sie Ihre Meinung aus.

BEISPIEL: Es macht mir Spaß, Seifenopern anzusehen.

Ich habe keine Zeit	stundenlang am Computer sitzen
Es macht mir (keinen) Spaß	im Internet surfen
Ich finde es langweilig	Computerspiele/Videospiele spielen
wichtig	Kriegsfilme/Sportsendungen im Fernsehen ansehen
schwierig	
interessant	eine Fremdsprache lernen
spannend	über Politik diskutieren
schwer	per E-Mail korrespondieren
	mein Horoskop in der Zeitung lesen
	jeden Tag die Zeitung lesen
	Nachrichten im Fernsehen ansehen
	Radio hören
	einen guten Job finden
	studieren und nebenbei jobben

Übung 3 Aus dem Kalender

Schauen Sie sich Cornelias Kalender an. Was hat sie vor? Was darf sie nicht vergessen?

BEISPIEL: Sie hat vor, Sonntag mit Klaus ins Kino zu gehen.
Sie darf nicht vergessen, Montag ...

Sonntag	19.30 mit Klaus ins Kino gehen
Montag	nicht vergessen: Videogerät zur Reparatur bringen Reise nach Spanien buchen
Dienstag	nicht vergessen: Radio und Fernsehen anmelden 14.30 Prof. Hauser: Seminararbeit besprechen
Mittwoch	Job für den Sommer suchen
Donnerstag	nicht vergessen: Mutter anrufen, Geburtstag!
Freitag	Seminararbeit fertig schreiben 20.00 Vera treffen: Café Kadenz
Samstag	14.00 mit Klaus Tennis spielen 20.30 „Casablanca" im Fernsehen ansehen

resolutions ## Übung 4 Gute Vorsätze° für die Zukunft

Schritt 1: Sie haben vor, in Zukunft alles besser zu machen. Was haben Sie sich versprochen? Was haben Sie vor? Überlegen Sie sich zwei gute Vorsätze.

BEISPIELE: Ich habe vor, weniger Geld für CDs auszugeben.
Ich habe mir versprochen, meine Eltern regelmäßig anzurufen.

Schritt 2: Vergleichen Sie Ihre Vorsätze mit den Vorsätzen eines Partners / einer Partnerin. Haben Sie gemeinsame Vorsätze? Wenn ja, welche? Was sind die häufigsten guten Vorsätze Ihrer Kursmitglieder?

The Verbs brauchen and scheinen

The verbs **brauchen** (*to need*) and **scheinen** (*to seem*) are often used with a dependent infinitive preceded by **zu. Brauchen** is used instead of the modal **müssen** when the sentence has a negative meaning.

Heute muss ich arbeiten, aber morgen **brauche** ich **nicht zu arbeiten.**	*Today I have to work, but tomorrow I don't have to work.*
Ich **brauche keinen** neuen Computer **zu kaufen,** der alte ist noch gut genug.	*I don't have to buy a new computer; the old one is still good enough.*
Das Faxgerät **scheint** kaputt **zu sein.**	*The fax machine seems to be broken.*

Übung 5 Nichts scheint zu funktionieren

Was scheint hier los zu sein? Folgen Sie dem Beispiel.

BEISPIEL: Das Telefon klingelt nicht. (Es ist kaputt.) →
  Es scheint kaputt zu sein.

1. Der Computer funktioniert mal wieder nicht. (Er ist kaputt.)
2. Hast du meine Nachricht nicht bekommen? Ich habe eine Nachricht auf deinem Anrufbeantworter hinterlassen. (Er funktioniert nicht.)
3. Meine Kamera funktioniert nicht. (Sie braucht eine neue Batterie.)
4. Bei Firma Bär meldet sich niemand am Apparat. (Niemand ist im Büro.)
5. Drei von meinen Kollegen sind heute nicht zur Arbeit gekommen. (Sie sind alle krank.)

Übung 6 Nein, heute nicht

Fragen Sie einen Partner / eine Partnerin: Was musst du heute noch machen? Folgen Sie dem Beispiel.

BEISPIEL: s1: Musst du heute arbeiten?
  s2: Nein, heute brauche ich nicht zu arbeiten.
  s2: Musst du heute zur Uni gehen? usw.

1. im Labor arbeiten	4. den Computer benutzen	7. zum Arzt gehen
2. Hausaufgaben machen	5. ein Fax schicken	8. kochen
3. in die Vorlesung gehen	6. Rechnungen bezahlen	9. früh ins Bett gehen

Infinitive Clauses
with um ... zu and ohne ... zu

German uses many different ways to explain the reasons for an action. You have already learned a number of them. Compare the following sentences.

Warum spart Stefan?

1. Stefan spart **für einen neuen Computer.**   ← Prepositional phrase

2. Stefan will einen neuen Computer kaufen. **Deswegen** muss er jetzt sparen.   ← Adverb: **deswegen** = *therefore*

3. Stefan spart. Er will **nämlich** einen Computer kaufen. ← Adverb: **nämlich** [*no English equivalent*]

4. Stefan spart, **denn** er will einen Computer kaufen. ← Coordinating conjunction: **denn** = *because*

5. Stefan spart, **weil** er einen Computer kaufen möchte. ← Subordinating conjunction: **weil** = *because*

Yet another way to explain one's reasons for an action is with an infinitive clause with **um ... zu.**

Stefan spart, **um** einen neuen Computer **zu kaufen.**	*Stefan is saving money in order to buy a new computer.*
Manche Leute leben, **um zu arbeiten.**	*Some people live in order to work.*
Ich arbeite schwer, **um** mich auf das Examen **vorzubereiten.**	*I am working hard to prepare for the exam.*

Sie müssen kein Fisch sein, um Meerwasser[1] trinken zu können.

[1]*sea water*

Bessere Dinge für ein besseres Leben **DUPONT**

reasons

Übung 7 Was sind die Gründe° dafür?

Geben Sie die Gründe an. Benutzen Sie dabei **um ... zu, weil, nämlich, denn** oder **deswegen.**

BEISPIEL: Ich muss sparen. Ich möchte mir einen Plasmamonitor kaufen. →
Ich muss sparen, um mir einen Plasmamonitor zu kaufen.
[*oder:*] Ich will mir einen Plasmamonitor kaufen. Deswegen muss ich sparen.

1. Barbara macht den Fernseher an. Sie will die Nachrichten sehen.
2. Thomas setzt sich in den Sessel. Er will die Tageszeitung lesen.
3. Barbara schaut sich das Filmprogramm an. Sie sucht sich einen Spielfilm aus.
4. Thomas programmiert den digitalen Videorecorder. Er möchte die Fußballweltmeisterschaft im Fernsehen aufnehmen.
5. Stephanie füllt ein Formular aus. Sie meldet ihr Radio und ihren Fernseher an.
6. Oliver überfliegt nur die Schlagzeilen in der Zeitung. Er will Zeit sparen.
7. Andreas hört sich die Tagesschau an. Er informiert sich.

To express that you do one thing without doing another, use **ohne ... zu.**

Hubers wollen ein Haus bauen, **ohne** große Schulden **zu machen.**	*The Hubers want to build a house without going heavily into debt.*
Er ist an mir vorbeigegangen, **ohne** mich **zu erkennen.**	*He went past me without recognizing me.*

Übung 8   Man sollte daran denken.

Kombinieren Sie mit **ohne ... zu.**

BEISPIEL: Oliver kauft einen Computer über das Internet. Er sieht ihn vorher nicht. →
Oliver kauft einen Computer über das Internet, ohne ihn vorher zu sehen.

1. Erika kauft eine Digitalkamera. Sie fragt nicht nach dem Preis.
2. Der Radfahrer fährt um die Ecke. Er sieht die Kinder auf der Straße nicht.
3. Jemand hat eine Nachricht auf meinem Anrufbeantworter hinterlassen. Er nennt seinen Namen nicht.
4. Herr Wunderlich hat eine Wohnung gemietet. Er fragt nicht nach den Nebenkosten.
5. Patrick ist heute Morgen zur Arbeit gegangen. Er frühstückt nicht.
6. Silvia sitzt wie hypnotisiert am Computer. Sie hört das Telefon nicht.
7. Meine Freunde kommen oft vorbei. Sie rufen vorher nicht an.

Indirect Discourse°

Die indirekte Rede

When you report what another person has said, you can quote that person verbatim, using direct discourse. In writing, this is indicated by the use of quotation marks. Note that in German, opening quotation marks are placed just below the line.

DIRECT DISCOURSE

Der Autofahrer behauptete: „Ich habe den Radfahrer nicht gesehen."	*The automobile driver claimed, "I did not see the bicyclist."*

Another way of reporting what someone said uses indirect discourse— a style commonly found in newspapers. In this case, German often uses subjunctive verb forms, especially the indirect discourse subjunctive, also called Subjunctive I.

INDIRECT DISCOURSE

Der Autofahrer behauptete, er **habe** den Radfahrer nicht **gesehen.**	*The driver claimed he did not see the bicyclist.*

In using the indirect discourse subjunctive, a speaker or writer signals that the information reported does not necessarily reflect the speaker's own knowledge or views. The indirect discourse subjunctive establishes distance between the reporter and the topic. This is useful when people want to be objective or neutral.

Subjunctive I: Present Tense°

The present tense of the indirect discourse subjunctive, Subjunctive I, is derived from the stem of the infinitive. Only the verb **sein** has a complete set of forms that are used in modern German. For all other verbs, Subjunctive I forms are limited to the third-person singular plus a few verbs in the first-person singular.

Forms Commonly Used in Subjunctive I						
Infinitive	sein	haben	wissen	tun	werden	können
ich	sei	—	wisse	—	—	könne
du	sei(e)st	—	—	—	—	—
er/sie/es	sei	habe	wisse	tue	werde	könne
wir	seien	—	—	—	—	—
ihr	sei(e)t	—	—	—	—	—
sie/Sie	seien	—	—	—	—	—

Note:

- All verbs add **-e** to the infinitive stem to form the third-person singular except for **sein**.
- The verb **wissen** and all modals add **-e** to the infinitive stem to form the first-person singular.

If indirect discourse requires the use of any other verb forms, then Subjunctive II is used as an alternate for Subjunctive I. In spoken or informal German, it is quite common to use exclusively Subjunctive II or **würde** + infinitive for all indirect discourse. In the following examples, the forms in parentheses are more informal.

Der Student sagte, er **sei (wäre)** krank und **habe (hätte)** keine Zeit.	*The student said he is sick and has no time.*
Es **tue (täte)** ihm leid, dass er nicht zur Vorlesung kommen **könne (könnte).**	*He is sorry that he cannot come to the lecture.*
Er **gebe** seine Hausarbeit morgen **ab. (würde ... abgeben)**	*He will turn in his homework tomorrow.*
Die Wähler meinten, sie **wüssten** nicht, wem man glauben **könne (könnte).**	*The voters said they don't know whom to believe* (lit. *whom one can believe).*
Politiker behaupten, sie **würden** immer die Wahrheit **sagen.**	*Politicians claim they always tell the truth.*

Note:

- Weak verbs such as **sagen** use **würde** + infinitive in indirect discourse, except for the third-person singular.

Der Präsident behauptet, er **sage** nur die Wahrheit. (**würde ... sagen**)	*The president claims he's stating only the truth.*

Lesen Sie die folgenden Texte und markieren Sie alle Verben in indirekter Rede. Was sind die Infinitive der Verben? Wie würden Sie diese Sätze auf English ausdrücken?

Im Fernsehen hat man berichtet, das Land sei in einer großen Krise. Niemand wisse, wie es enden soll. Niemand habe eine Lösung.[1]

Technikstress: Telefonieren, Fernsehen, Internet surfen; der moderne Mensch sei zwar immer bestens informiert, aber manchmal ziemlich gestresst von zu viel Technik.

Ein Kriminologe und Jugendforscher schreibt, der durchschnittliche männliche Schüler bringe es auf 5 Stunden Medienkonsum am Tage. Das sei ein krankes Leben. Je mehr Zeit Kinder am Fernseher und Computer verbrächten, desto[3] schlechter seien sie in der Schule. In einigen Computerspielen könne man eine Erklärung für die erhöhte Gewaltbereitschaft finden.

[1]*solution* [2]*to close down* [3]je mehr ... desto schlechter *the more . . . the worse*

Übung 9 Was man über Fernsehen gesagt hat

Ergänzen Sie die Sätze mit dem Konjunktiv I von **sein.**

1. Herr Schwarz hat gesagt, ohne Fernsehen _____ sein Leben schöner.

2. Frau Schwarz meinte, für Kinder _____ Programme wie „Die Sendung mit der Maus" etwas Besonderes.

3. Man hat mir gesagt, ohne Fernsehen _____ ich nicht gut informiert. So ein Quatsch.

4. Die Frau von der Marktforschung fragte, warum wir nicht am Fernsehen interessiert _____.

5. Man hat mir berichtet, dass du jetzt ganz ohne Fernseher _____.

6. Frau Schmidt meinte, ohne ihre tägliche Telenovela _____ sie nicht glücklich.

7. Familie Schulte hat gesagt, die Sportprogramme _____ immer ausgezeichnet.

Übung 10 Das stand in der Zeitung

Berichten Sie in indirekter Rede, was Sie in der Zeitung gelesen haben.

BEISPIEL: Der Mensch denkt am schnellsten vor dem Mittagessen. →
In der Zeitung stand, der Mensch denke am schnellsten vor dem Mittagessen.

1. Man soll also schwierige Probleme zwischen 11 and 12 Uhr lösen.

2. Die Sinne (*senses*) funktionieren dagegen besser abends.

3. Das Abendessen schmeckt deshalb besser als das Frühstück.

4. Wir sind deshalb abends für Theater, Musik und auch für die Liebe am empfänglichsten (*most receptive*).

5. Für den Sport ist der Spätnachmittag ideal.

6. Man wird spätnachmittags nicht so schnell müde.

Übung 11 Immer diese Ausreden°

Sie hören drei Dialoge. Machen Sie sich zuerst Notizen. Erzählen Sie dann mit Hilfe Ihrer Notizen, was das Problem ist und was für Ausreden (*excuses*) die Personen in den Dialogen haben.

BEISPIEL: Peter hat gesagt, er könne nicht mit ins Kino …

SPRECHER/IN	PROBLEM	AUSREDE
1. Peter		
2. Jens		
3. Ursula		

Subjunctive I: Past Tense

To express the past tense in indirect discourse, use the Subjunctive I of the auxiliary verb **sein** or **haben** and the past participle of the main verb.

Die Autofahrerin behauptete, der Motorradfahrer **sei** bei Rot **gefahren.**	*The driver claimed the motorcyclist ran a red light.*
Sie **habe** ihn nicht rechtzeitig **gesehen.**	*She did not see him in time.*

Note:

- Whether to use **sein** or **haben** depends on the main verb. The choice is identical to which auxiliary the verb would use in the perfect tenses.

  Er **ist** gefahren. → Er **sei** gefahren.

  Sie **hat** gesehen. → Sie **habe** gesehen.

- With **haben,** only the third-person singular Subjunctive I, **habe,** is used; Subjunctive II is used for the remaining forms.

Der Motorradfahrer berichtete, seine Bremsen **hätten** nicht funktioniert.	*The motorcyclist reported that his brakes weren't functioning.*

- In informal German, Subjunctive II is increasingly used for all forms in past-tense indirect discourse.

The following table shows examples of the more commonly used third-person forms.

INDIRECT DISCOURSE PAST TENSE: FORMS COMMONLY USED		
INFINITIVE	THIRD-PERSON SINGULAR	THIRD-PERSON PLURAL
sein werden fahren haben wissen tun	er, sie, es { sei/wäre gewesen sei/wäre geworden sei/wäre gefahren habe/hätte gehabt habe/hätte gewusst habe/hätte getan	sie { seien/wären gewesen seien/wären geworden seien/wären gefahren hätten gehabt hätten gewusst hätten getan

Übung 12   Ungewöhnliches° aus den Nachrichten

Unusual happenings

Schreiben Sie die folgenden Sätze in indirekter Rede der Vergangenheit um. Benutzen Sie dabei Konjunktiv I oder Konjunktiv II.

Heute habe ich im Radio gehört:

1. Im Südwesten Irans hat man ein unbekanntes Dorf entdeckt.
2. Ein Mann im Gorillakostüm hat in den Straßen von Dallas 50-Dollar-Scheine an Fußgänger verteilt (*distributed*).
3. Im Jahre 1875 haben die Leute noch 65 Stunden pro Woche gearbeitet. Heutzutage arbeiten die meisten nur noch 39 Stunden pro Woche im Durchschnitt.
4. Bei einer Verkehrskontrolle in Cocoa Beach ist ein Autodieb ins Meer gesprungen. Er ist immer weiter raus geschwommen. Ein Polizist in voller Uniform hat sich auf ein Surfbrett geschwungen und hat den Dieb nach zehn Minuten eingeholt.
5. Gestern ist auf einem Spielplatz in Russland ein UFO gelandet. Die Leute, die aus dem UFO gestiegen sind, sind sehr freundlich gewesen. Nach kurzer Zeit sind sie wieder abgeflogen.

Übung 13   Sensationelles aus der Presse

Lesen Sie zuerst die zwei kurze Berichte aus einer Zeitung und unterstreichen Sie die Verben in indirekter Rede. Wiederholen Sie dann die Sätze als Bericht in direkter Rede.

A. In der Zeitung stand, gestern Abend sei bei einer Geburtstagsfeier in einem Restaurant ein Geburtstagskuchen explodiert. Der Kellner habe zu viel Cognac über den Kuchen gegossen. Die Gäste und der Kellner seien, Gott sei Dank, unverletzt gewesen.

B. In einem Kölner Kiosk habe ein Mann seine Zigaretten mit einem 600-Euro-Schein bezahlt. Der Verkäufer habe geglaubt, es handele sich um einen neuen, noch nicht bekannten Schein. Er habe dem „Kunden" über 500 Euro Wechselgeld zurückgegeben. Erst ein Bekannter des Verkäufers habe die blaue Banknote als Fälschung erkannt und habe die Polizei gerufen. Der Mann mit den Zigaretten sei spurlos verschwunden.

Sprache im Kontext

Videoclips

Jasmin, Peter und Maria sprechen über ihre Lese- und Fernsehgewohnheiten.

A. Schauen Sie sich die Interviews mit Jasmin und Maria an und füllen Sie die Tabelle aus. Wenn die Person keine Information zu dem Thema gibt, schreiben Sie „keine Information."

	PETER	JASMIN	MARIA
Welche Zeitung liest du?			
Was liest du zuerst?			
Welchen Teil liest du ganz genau?			
Was überfliegst du?			
Was siehst du im Fernsehen?			
Welche Filme siehst du gern im Kino?			

B. Schauen Sie sich das Interview mit Peter an und beantworten Sie die Fragen.

1. Welche Tageszeitungen liest er?
2. Peter vergleicht drei verschiedene Zeitungen, den *Tagesspiegel,* die *Welt* und die *Süddeutsche Zeitung.* Wie beschreibt er jede Zeitung?

   a. den *Tagesspiegel*: ———————————————.

   b. die *Welt*: ———————————————.

   c. die *Süddeutsche Zeitung*: ———————————————.
3. Welche Zeitung liest er nie? Warum?
4. Was liest Peter ganz genau? Was überfliegt er?

C. Ein Interview. Benutzen Sie die Tabelle in **Teil A,** um zwei andere Personen zu interviewen. Machen Sie Notizen zu jedem Interview und berichten Sie der Klasse darüber.

Lesen

Zum Thema

A. Wie wichtig sind die folgenden Sachen in Ihrem Leben? Kreuzen Sie zuerst an, was sehr wichtig und was nicht so wichtig ist. Geben Sie an, wie viele Stunden pro Woche Sie damit verbringen. Ordnen Sie sie dann in eine Reihenfolge (1–6) ein: 1 = das wichtigste.

	SEHR WICHTIG	NICHT SO WICHTIG	STUNDEN PRO WOCHE	REIHENFOLGE
Fernsehen	☐	☐	———	———
Radio hören	☐	☐	———	———
Zeitung lesen	☐	☐	———	———
am Computer arbeiten	☐	☐	———	———
im Internet surfen	☐	☐	———	———
Bücher lesen	☐	☐	———	———
Videos, Filme sehen	☐	☐	———	———
Musik hören	☐	☐	———	———

B. Was liegt an erster Stelle unter Ihren Klassenmitgliedern? Wie viel Zeit verbringen sie damit?

C. Womit beschäftigen Sie sich, wenn Sie am Computer sitzen? Kreuzen Sie alles an, was Sie machen.

☐ bloggen
☐ chatten
☐ Filme/Fotos herunterladen
☐ forschen, Information für Kurse und Referate sammeln
☐ Fotos bearbeiten
☐ Hausaufgaben machen
☐ im Internet surfen
☐ Instant-Messaging betreiben
☐ mailen
☐ Musik hören und herunterladen
☐ Nachrichten lesen
☐ Sonstiges: _____

D. Berichten Sie kurz über die drei wichtigsten Dinge, die Sie am Computer machen.

Auf den ersten Blick

A. Schauen Sie sich den Titel des Lesetexts an und lesen Sie die zwei ersten Sätze. Was erwarten Sie von diesem Text?

☐ Informationen über die Freunde junger Deutscher
☐ einen Bericht über den negativen Einfluss von Computer und Fernsehen
☐ Informationen über die Rolle vom Computer im Leben junger Deutscher

B. Überfliegen Sie den Artikel und suchen Sie im Text Wörter, die etwas mit Computer und Internet zu tun haben. Machen Sie eine Liste. Woher stammt das Vokabular zum größten Teil?

C. Was passt zusammen?

1. Man schaltet _____.
2. Man klickt _____.
3. Man checkt _____.
4. Man lädt _____.
5. Man googelt _____.
6. Man bearbeitet _____.
7. Man surft _____.

> auf den Internet-Button   den Computer an
> die E-Mail
> einen Namen   im Internet
> Fotos am Computer   Musik herunter

GUTE FREUNDE IM NETZ

von Kerstin Kohlenberg

Wer heute 17 ist, kennt ein Leben ohne Internet nicht. Für die meisten ist der Computer wichtiger als Fernsehen.

5 Seit einigen Wochen sind die Ferien vorbei. Mel geht wieder zur Schule. Sie kommt aus der Schule nach Hause, schmeißt den Rucksack auf den Sessel in ihrem Zimmer, zieht die Turnschuhe aus und schaltet den Computer im Wohnzimmer an. Sie ist allein in der Wohnung.

10 Heute gehört ihr der Familiencomputer ganz allein.

Eine junge Deutsche am Computer

Sie geht in die Küche, macht sich ein Stück Pizza warm und trägt es zurück zum Computer. Ihr tägliches Ritual beginnt. Mel klickt auf den

15 Internet-Button, schaltet den MSN-Messenger an, ein Programm, das ihr sagt, dass Lisa online ist und der Rest ihrer Freunde noch offline. Sie checkt ihre E-Mail bei Hotmail — nur ein Kettenbrief°, den sie weiterschickt — sie checkt ihre E-Mail bei Yahoo — ihre Mutter aus Paris. Dann betritt° sie ihr Leben: Skyblog.com. Das

20 tägliche Ritual geht weiter. Mel surft, guckt sich die Top 40 Lieder an, und wenn ihr ein neues Lied gefällt, dann lädt sie es herunter. Musik und ihre Freunde, das ist es, was Mel interessiert. Dass sie gestern Spinoza° gegoogelt hat, liegt daran, dass sie über ihn ein Referat° in der Schule halten muss.

chain letter

enters

Baruch Spinoza (philospher) / report

25 Ihre Internet-Seite berichtet über Mel: Sie ist 17 Jahre alt, hat viele Freunde, und fährt oft nach Paris. Ihre Mutter lebt nämlich jetzt wieder in Paris. Die Eltern sind geschieden. Mel lebt mit ihrem Vater und ihrem Bruder in Berlin. Mel hat vier Freundinnen und auch einen Freund und geht auf ein französisches Gymnasium in Berlin. Mel hat zu Hause

30 eine Flatrate, für rund 30 Euro im Monat kann sie ständig° online sein.

constantly

Valentin geht mit Mel in eine Klassenstufe am französischen Gymnasium. Er besitzt einen eigenen Computer — ein Geschenk von seinem Vater zum 17. Geburtstag — und einen eigenen Internet-Zugang. Valentin sitzt jetzt auf einem Schreibtischstuhl am Computer. Der

35 Bildschirmschoner auf seinem Computerdisplay zeigt Fotos seiner Freunde. An den Wänden seines Zimmers sind Poster von Musikern und Breakdancern, und auch Graffiti.

In Valentins Zimmer sieht man zuerst den Computer (Apple), einen Fernseher, Videorecorder, DVD Spieler, ein Handy, einen Walkman,

40 einen Discman, einen MP3-Player, Mini-Disc-Player, Plattenspieler, Mischpult° und eine Digitalkamera. Valentin benutzt den Computer hauptsächlich zum Surfen und Mailen, für die Schule, zum Herunterladen von Filmen und Musik und um seine Fotos und Musik zu bearbeiten. Valentin ist nebenbei DJ.

mixer

45 Mels und Valentins Generation ist mit dem Computer aufgewachsen. Der war vor ein paar Jahren noch vor allem ein Spielzeug der Jungen. Doch inzwischen ist er auch für Mädchen wie Mel ein wichtiger Teil des Lebens. Von den Jugendlichen in Deutschland zwischen 12 und 19 haben so gut wie alle, nämlich 96 Prozent, mindestens einen Computer

50 zu Hause. 85 Prozent haben Internet-Zugang, ein Drittel surft vom eigenen Zimmer aus. Mehr als die Hälfte dieser Internet-Nutzer ist über 10 Stunden pro Woche online. Eine Stuttgarter-Studie berichtet, dass

für Mädchen der Computer noch hinter Fernsehen, Radio und Büchern
rangiert. Für Jungen dagegen ist der Computer der wichtigste
55 Zeitvertreib°.

    Was an Valentin, Mel und ihren Freunden auffällt°, ist ihre fehlende°
Angst vor Menschen. Die Sicherheit, mit der sie auf Fremde° zugehen,
die Offenheit°, mit der sie von ihren Leben erzählen, wirken überraschend
erwachsen. Wie Kinder, die in einem Hotel aufgewachsen sind und
60 jeden Tag mit anderen Leuten am Speisetisch gesessen und geredet
haben. Und die darüber nicht vergessen haben, dass das eigentliche
Leben außerhalb des Hotels stattfindet.

Adaptiert aus: Kerstin Kohlenberg, *Die Zeit,* Nr. 41, 6 Oktober 2005, S. 68

pastime

is striking / lack of

strangers

candor

Zum Text

A. Lesen Sie nun den Text genauer und suchen Sie Information über die
beiden Hauptpersonen: Mel und Valentin. Was erfahren wir über die
folgenden Themen?

	MELS	VALENTINS
Familie	_____	_____
Freunde	_____	_____
Schule	_____	_____
Interessen	_____	_____

B. Die Rolle des Computers

1. Was erfahren wir über die jungen Deutschen und die Rolle des
Computers in ihrem Leben?

2. Gibt es einen Unterschied zwischen Jungen und Mädchen?

3. Glauben Sie, dass es einen Unterschied zwischen jungen US-
Amerikanern/Kanadiern und jungen Deutschen im Gebrauch des
Computers gibt?

C. Im letzten Abschnitt des Artikels sagt die Autorin des Artikels, was
ihr bei diesen jungen Berlinern aufgefallen ist:

- die fehlende Angst vor Menschen
- die Sicherheit, mit der sie auf Fremde zugehen
- die Offenheit, mit der sie von ihren Leben erzählen
- sie wirken überraschend erwachsen

1. Sehen Sie diese Qualitäten als etwas Positives oder haben sie auch
eine negative Seite?

2. Können Sie sich damit identifizieren?

D. Die Autorin schließt mit einem Vergleich (*comparison*). Mit wem
vergleicht sie die junge Generation, die mit dem Computer
aufgewachsen ist? Finden Sie diesen Vergleich passend (*fitting*)?

Zu guter Letzt

Eine neue Erfindung

Sind Sie kreativ und erfinderisch? Benutzen Sie Ihr Talent, um eine neue Erfindung auf den Markt zu bringen.

Schritt 1: In Gruppen zu dritt überlegen Sie sich eine Kategorie für die Erfindung, z.B. Kommunikation, Auto/Transport, Computertechnologie oder Haushalt. Was ist der Zweck (*purpose*) der Erfindung?

Schritt 2: Jede Gruppe arbeitet nun die Einzelheiten (*details*) ihrer Erfindung aus. Wie sieht sie aus? Wie funktioniert sie? Welche Materialien braucht man, um die Erfindung zu bauen?

Schritt 3: Zeichnen Sie die Erfindung als Poster. Die Zeichnung muss etwas detailliert sein, braucht aber nicht total akkurat zu sein.

Schritt 4: Präsentieren Sie der Klasse die Erfindung. Beschreiben Sie Ihre Erfindung mit Hilfe der Zeichnung.

Schritt 5: Die Klasse entscheidet durch Applaus, welche Gruppe die beste Erfindung hat.

Wortschatz

Im Fernsehen / On Television

der **Bericht, -e**	report
der **Dokumentarfilm, -e**	documentary (film)
das **Programm, -e**	station, TV channel; program
die **Sendung, -en**	TV or radio program
der **Spielfilm, -e**	feature film, movie
die **Unterhaltung**	entertainment
zur **Unterhaltung**	for entertainment

Die Presse / The Press

das **Abo(nnement), -s**	subscription
die **Börse, -n**	stock market
das **Horoskop, -e**	horoscope
das **Inland**	at home, domestic, national
im **Inland und Ausland**	at home and abroad
die **Nachrichten** (*pl.*)	news
die **Lokalnachrichten**	local news
die **Politik**	politics
die **Schlagzeile, -n**	headline
die **Wirtschaft**	economy
die **Zeitschrift, -en**	magazine; periodical

Technik / Technology

der **Anrufbeantworter, -**	answering machine
der **Camcorder, -**	camcorder
die **Digitalkamera, -s**	digital camera
das **Dokument, -e**	document
der **Drucker, -**	printer
die **E-Mail, -s**	e-mail
die **Erfindung, -en**	invention
das **Faxgerät, -e**	fax machine
das **Internet**	Internet
der **Kabelanschluss, ¨e**	cable TV connection
das **Notebook, -s**	notebook computer
die **Sat-Empfangsanlage, -n**	satellite receiver

Verben / Verbs

abonnieren	to subscribe
sich (*dat.*) **etwas an•schauen**	to watch, look at
sich (*dat.*) **etwas an•sehen (sieht an), sah an, angesehen**	to look at, watch
auf•nehmen (nimmt auf), nahm auf, aufgenommen	to record (e.g., on video)

sich (et)was aus•suchen	to select, find, choose something	überfliegen, überflog, überflogen	to skim (a text), read quickly
behaupten	to claim, assert	sich unterhalten (unterhält), unterhielt, unterhalten	to entertain (oneself); to converse
berichten	to report, narrate		
drucken	to print		
empfangen (empfängt), empfing, empfangen	to receive		

sich (et)was aus•suchen — to select, find, choose something
behaupten — to claim, assert
berichten — to report, narrate
drucken — to print
empfangen (empfängt), empfing, empfangen — to receive
sich entschließen, entschloss, entschlossen — to decide
erfinden, erfand, erfunden — to invent
forschen — to do research
handeln (von) — to deal with, be about
   Wovon handelt es? — What's it about?
hinter lassen (hinterlässt), hinterließ, hinterlassen — to leave (behind) (e.g., a message)
sich melden — to answer (phone)
   Niemand meldet sich. — No one is answering.
scheinen, schien, geschienen — to seem, appear
speichern — to save, store

überfliegen, überflog, überflogen — to skim (a text), read quickly
sich unterhalten (unterhält), unterhielt, unterhalten — to entertain (oneself); to converse

Adjektive und Adverbien — Adjectives and Adverbs

aktuell — current, topical
   Aktuelles — current events
blöd — stupid
gescheit — intelligent, bright; sensible, decent
   nichts Gescheites — nothing decent
unterhaltsam — entertaining

Ausdrücke — Expressions

auf jeden Fall — in any case
Das ist mir zu blöd. — I think that's really stupid.
Na und? — So what?
Wie wäre es mit … ? — How about … ?

DAS KANN ICH NUN!

1. Sie reden mit Freunden über Fernsehen und Zeitung. Füllen Sie die Lücken mit einem passenden Ausdruck aus dem Kasten.

> ansehen   Dokumentarfilm   Fernsehen
> gibt es   handelt   Nachrichten
> Schlagzeilen   such   aus   wäre es

  a. Na, was _____ denn heute Abend im _____? **b.** Um 20.00 Uhr kommen die _____. **c.** Wie _____ mit einem _____ über die Sahara? **d.** Ich möchte mir lieber einen guten Spielfilm _____. **e.** Na gut, _____ dir was _____. **f.** Wovon _____ der Film übrigens? **g.** Die _____ in der *Bild* Zeitung zeigen immer nur Sensationelles.

2. Was sehen Sie gerne im Fernsehen? Wofür interessieren Sie sich nicht?

3. Nennen Sie zwei deutschsprachige Zeitungen (aus Deutschland, Österreich oder der Schweiz). Was lesen Sie gewöhnlich in der Zeitung? Was nie?

4. Nennen Sie drei technologische Geräte und erklären Sie, wozu sie nützlich sind.

5. Schreiben Sie die folgenden Sätze zu Ende.

  a. Ich habe heute vor, _____. (*to go to the movies*) **b.** Kai hat versucht, _____. (*to call me yesterday*) **c.** Er hat während des Semesters gejobbt, _____. (*in order to pay his rent*) **d.** Er hat das Buch gelesen, _____. (*without understanding it*)

6. Berichten Sie folgende Information in indirekter Rede.

  a. Der Junge sagte: „Ich habe das Comic-Heft nicht genommen." **b.** Er sagte: „Das Geld dafür ist in meiner Tasche." **c.** Inge behauptet: „Ich sehe nicht gern Seifenopern im Fernsehen." **d.** Der Reporter fragte: „Worum handelt es sich?" **e.** In der Zeitung steht: „Immer mehr Berliner wandern aus. Sie suchen bessere Arbeit und wärmeres Klima." **f.** Der Reporter berichtet: „Der Autofahrer ist bei Rot gefahren und hat den Radfahrer nicht gesehen."

Die öffentliche Meinung

Junge Deutsche protestieren gegen die neuen Studiengebühren an der Universität.

Videoclips
Globale Probleme

408

In diesem Kapitel

- **Themen:** Global problems, public opinion, environment, discussion strategies
- **Grammatik:** Passive voice, the present participle
- **Kultur:** The environment, speed limits in Europe, recycling
- **Lesen:** „Was in der Zeitung steht" (Reinhard Mai)

Alles klar?

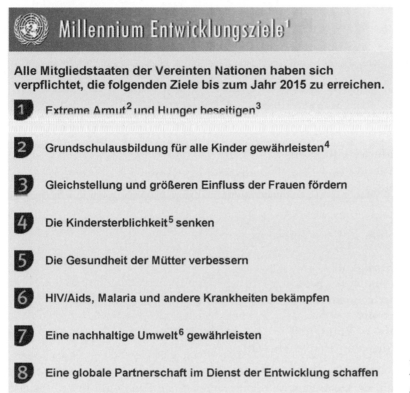

Millennium Entwicklungsziele[1]

Alle Mitgliedstaaten der Vereinten Nationen haben sich verpflichtet, die folgenden Ziele bis zum Jahr 2015 zu erreichen.

1 Extreme Armut[2] und Hunger beseitigen[3]

2 Grundschulausbildung für alle Kinder gewährleisten[4]

3 Gleichstellung und größeren Einfluss der Frauen fördern

4 Die Kindersterblichkeit[5] senken

5 Die Gesundheit der Mütter verbessern

6 HIV/Aids, Malaria und andere Krankheiten bekämpfen

7 Eine nachhaltige Umwelt[6] gewährleisten

8 Eine globale Partnerschaft im Dienst der Entwicklung schaffen

[1]*development goals* [2]*poverty* [3]*eliminate* [4]*ensure* [5]*child mortality* [6]*nachhaltige … sustainable environment*

A. Deutschland ist seit 1973 Mitglied der Vereinten Nationen (UNO). Diese Organisation sucht Lösungen (*solutions*) für globale Probleme. Im Jahr 2000 stellte die UNO acht Entwicklungsziele vor. Schauen Sie sich die acht Entwicklungsziele an. Lesen Sie dann die folgenden Probleme. Welches Ziel richtet sich auf welches Problem?

a. __5__ Jeden Tag sterben (*die*) irgendwo auf der Welt 1.400 Frauen während der Schwangerschaft (*pregnancy*) oder bei der Entbindung (*giving birth*).

b. _____ Mehr als 6 Millionen Kinder sterben jedes Jahr an vermeidbaren (*avoidable*) Ursachen (*causes*).

c. _____ Jeden Tag sterben 6.000 Menschen an HIV/Aids.

d. _____ Alle 3,6 Sekunden verhungert (*dies of starvation*) ein Mensch irgendwo auf der Welt.

e. _____ 584 Millionen Frauen auf der Welt können nicht lesen und schreiben.

f. _____ 114 Millionen Kinder besuchen keine Grundschule.

g. _____ Viele Entwicklungsländer haben finanzielle Probleme und brauchen internationale Hilfe.

h. _____ Mehr als eine Milliarde Menschen haben keinen Zugang zu sauberem Trinkwasser.

B. Sie hören jetzt eine Beschreibung von vier verschiedenen Seminaren über Probleme in der Welt. Welche Themen behandeln diese Seminare? Schreiben Sie die entsprechende Nummer vor jedes Thema.

_____ Kriminalität/Gewalt   _____ Menschenrechte

_____ Umweltverschmutzung   _____ Medizin/Umwelt

Wörter im Kontext

Neue Wörter

die Welt world
sich Sorgen machen um
  worry about
die Krankheit (Krankheiten,
  pl.) disease, illness
die Arbeitslosigkeit
  unemployment
die Armut poverty
die Ausländerfeindlichkeit
  hatred of foreigners
die Drogensucht drug
  addiction
die Gewalttätigkeit
  violence
die Erwärmung warming
die Regierung government
der Krieg war
die Obdachlosigkeit
  homelessness
die Umweltverschmutzung
  environmental pollution
die Verletzung violation
das Menschenrecht
  (Menschenrechte, *pl.*)
  human right
möglich possible
die Lösung (Lösungen, *pl.*)
  solution
lösen solve
der Fortschritt (Fortschritte,
  pl.) progress
teilnehmen (an) participate
  (in)
die Forschung research
entwickeln develop
vermindern lessen
verbieten forbid
die Gefahr (Gefahren, *pl.*)
  danger
verbreiten spread
erziehen raise
das Gefängnis (Gefängnisse,
  pl.) prison
einführen introduce
Obdachlose homeless
  persons
der Lärm noise
fördern promote
schaffen create
umschulen retrain
wählen elect

THEMA 1: Globale Probleme

A. Was sind Ihrer Meinung nach die drei größten Probleme in der **Welt**, in Ihrem Staat und in Ihrer Heimatstadt? Wor**um machen** Sie **sich Sorgen?**

	WELT	STAAT	STADT
Aids und andere sexuell übertragbare **Krankheiten**	☐	☐	☐
Arbeitslosigkeit	☐	☐	☐
Armut	☐	☐	☐
Ausländerfeindlichkeit	☐	☐	☐
Drogensucht	☐	☐	☐
Gewalttätigkeit	☐	☐	☐
globale Erwärmung	☐	☐	☐
Hunger	☐	☐	☐
Korruption in der **Regierung**	☐	☐	☐
Krieg	☐	☐	☐
Obdachlosigkeit	☐	☐	☐
Rassismus	☐	☐	☐
Rechtsextremismus	☐	☐	☐
Terrorismus	☐	☐	☐
Umweltverschmutzung	☐	☐	☐
Verletzung der Menschenrechte	☐	☐	☐
??	☐	☐	☐

B. Mögliche Lösungen. Wie kann man diese Probleme **lösen?** Wie können **Fortschritte** gemacht werden? Suchen Sie aus der folgenden Liste passende Ausdrücke (*expressions*), um Ihre Meinung auszudrücken.

BEISPIEL: In meiner Heimatstadt ist Obdachlosigkeit ein großes Problem. Man sollte mehr Sozialbauwohnungen bauen.

- **an Demonstrationen teilnehmen**
- mehr Fußgängerzonen einrichten
- mehr Geld für **Forschung** ausgeben
- Alternativenergie **entwickeln**
- Giftstoffe (*toxics*) **vermindern** oder **verbieten**
- Hilfsorganisationen mit Geld unterstützen
- Informationen über die **Gefahren** von Alkohol und **Drogen verbreiten**
- Kinder besser **erziehen**
- mehr **Gefängnisse** bauen
- Recyclingprogramme **einführen**
- Safer Sex praktizieren
- Sozialbauwohnungen für **Obdachlose** bauen
- Stressfaktoren (z.B. **Lärm**) reduzieren
- Umschulungsprogramme **fördern**
- Arbeitsplätze **schaffen** und Arbeiter **umschulen**
- verantwortungsbewusste **Politiker/Politikerinnen wählen**

- **sich** politisch **engagieren**
- **öffentliche Verkehrsmittel** fördern
- Umwelt **schützen**
- Luftverschmutzung **streng** kontrollieren
- ??

Die Kunst der Diskussion

DISKUSSIONSREDEMITTEL

Achten Sie auf die Redemittel in der folgenden Diskussion:

ich bin der Meinung	I am of the opinion
So ein Unsinn!	Such nonsense!
ich halte ... für ...	I think ... is/are
ich stimme (dir/Alexandra) zu	I agree (with you/Alexandra)
(ich bin) dafür	(I am) for that
(ich bin) dagegen	(I am) against that
meiner Meinung nach	in my opinion

Fünf Studenten und Studentinnen sollen in Team-Arbeit einen Vortrag über ein globales oder lokales Problem für ihr Hauptseminar in Soziologie vorbereiten. Sie sitzen im Uni-Café und diskutieren.

CHRISTIAN: Also, was **meint** ihr? Sollen wir ein globales Thema wie Terrorismus **behandeln**?

CORNELIA: Aktuell ist es schon, aber ich würde lieber ein Problem behandeln, das uns hier in Deutschland täglich **betrifft**, z.B. Arbeitslosigkeit oder Umweltverschmutzung.

ERMAN: ... oder auch Ausländerfeindlichkeit.

NIELS: **Im Grunde genommen** sind ja all diese Probleme global.

ALEXANDRA: **Ich bin der Meinung, Umweltschutz** ist besonders wichtig, gerade jetzt, wo wir mehr alternative Energie produzieren müssen.

NIELS: Ja, Solarenergie und Windenergie. Könnt ihr euch das vorstellen: hinter jedem Haus ein **Windrad** im Garten? (*Gelächter*) Es gibt sogar schon **Bürgerinitiativen,** die das fördern.

CORNELIA: **So ein Unsinn!** Ich **halte** das **für übertrieben.**

ERMAN: Das ist deine Meinung, nicht unbedingt meine.

CORNELIA: Also, ich **stimme** Alexandra **zu,** Umweltschutz ist relevant und allen irgendwie **vertraut.** Es betrifft uns alle. Und **außerdem** gibt es viel darüber zu sagen.

CHRISTIAN: **Stimmen** wir **ab:** Wer ist **dafür** und wer **dagegen?**

ALLE ANDEREN: Dafür.

CHRISTIAN: Nun gut. Ich mache auch mit. Wie sollen wir das Thema behandeln?

ERMAN: Jeder soll sich einen Aspekt des Themas aussuchen. Ich würde z.B. gern mehr über alternative Energie erfahren.

CORNELIA: Und ich möchte mich mit Bürgerinitiativen zum Umweltschutz beschäftigen.

Windräder erzeugen saubere Energie

CHRISTIAN:	Neulich habe ich von einer Bürgerinitiative gelesen, die gegen Handys in Bussen und Bahn demonstriert. **Meiner Meinung nach** ist das auch Umweltschutz.
ALEXANDRA:	Also, ich schlage vor, wir machen jetzt gleich einen konkreten Plan, wer welchen Aspekt des Themas behandelt.
NIELS:	Tut mir leid, dass ich **unterbrechen** muss. Ich muss jetzt leider weg. Ich habe eine Vorlesung. Wann treffen wir uns wieder?
ALEXANDRA:	Ich schicke dir eine Mail mit allen Informationen.
ALLE:	Tschüss.

Ergänzen Sie die folgenden Sätze mit Informationen aus dem Dialog oben.

1. Cornelia möchte ein Thema _____, das sie in Deutschland täglich _____.
2. Alexandra ist der _____, dass _____ besonders wichtig ist. Cornelia _____ ihr zu.
3. Cornelia hält die Bürgerinitiativen für Windenergie für _____.
4. Niels muss _____, denn er hat eine Vorlesung.

Aktivität 1   Hin und her: Probleme und Lösungen

Stellen Sie Ihrem Partner / Ihrer Partnerin Fragen zu den folgenden Problemen, um herauszufinden, welche möglichen Lösungen es gibt.

BEISPIEL: s1: Was kann man gegen Krieg tun?
          s2: Man kann an Antikriegsdemonstrationen teilnehmen.

PROBLEME	MÖGLICHE LÖSUNGEN
Krieg	an Antikriegsdemonstrationen teilnehmen
Inflation	
Drogensucht	Informationen über die Gefahren von Drogen verbreiten
Umweltverschmutzung	
Verletzung der Menschenrechte	Organisationen wie Amnesty International unterstützen
Obdachlosigkeit	
Arbeitslosigkeit	Arbeiter umschulen

Aktivität 2   Probleme in der Stadt

Vier Leute sprechen über Probleme in ihrer Stadt und wie man sie lösen könnte. Setzen Sie die passende Nummer (1–4) vor das Problem, über das der Sprecher / die Sprecherin redet, und markieren Sie auch die Lösung, die er/sie vorschlägt.

SPRECHER	PROBLEM	LÖSUNG	
_____	Atomkraft (*nuclear power*)	**a.** Solarenergie	**b.** Windenergie
_____	Giftstoffe in Nahrungsmitteln	**a.** strenge Staatskontrolle	**b.** weniger Gemüse essen
_____	Verkehr	**a.** Tempolimit	**b.** Wagen am Stadtrand parken
_____	Lärm	**a.** weniger Flugzeuge	**b.** Autos verbieten

Aktivität 3 Um welche Probleme geht es hier?

Buttons, Aufkleber (*stickers*) und Poster sind beliebte Formen, die Meinung zu äußern (*express*).

Schritt 1: Schauen Sie sich die Buttons und Poster an und stellen Sie fest, wofür oder wogegen sie sind. Schreiben Sie dann die passenden Zahlen in die Liste.

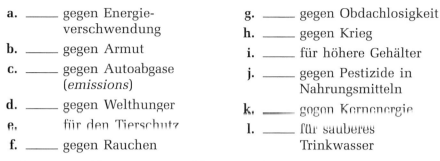

a. _____ gegen Energie-
verschwendung

b. _____ gegen Armut

c. _____ gegen Autoabgase
(*emissions*)

d. _____ gegen Welthunger

e. _____ für den Tierschutz

f. _____ gegen Rauchen

g. _____ gegen Obdachlosigkeit

h. _____ gegen Krieg

i. _____ für höhere Gehälter

j. _____ gegen Pestizide in
Nahrungsmitteln

k. _____ gegen Kernenergie

l. _____ für sauberes
Trinkwasser

Schritt 2: Wählen Sie ein Problem aus **Thema 1** und entwerfen Sie einen Button, einen Aufkleber oder ein Poster.

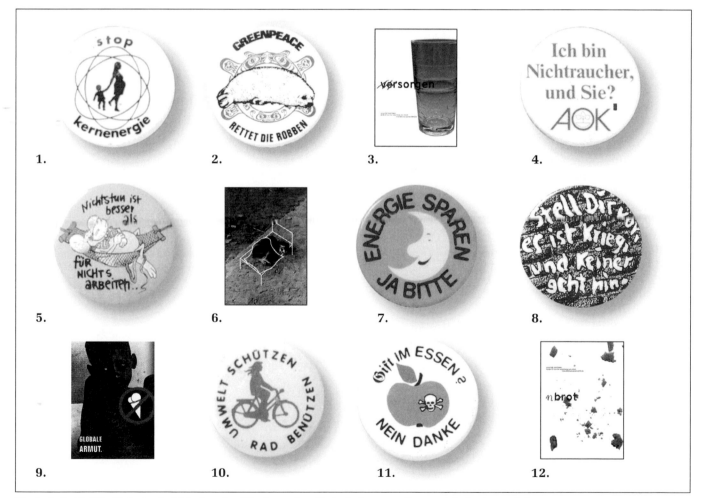

Nr. 3, 6, 9, 12: Die Plakate sind Motive des Wettbewerbs „Farbe bekennen. Gegen globale Armut" des deutschen Bundesministeriums für wirtschaftliche Zusammenarbeit und Entwicklung (BMZ) zum Aktionsprogramm 2015. Weitere Informationen erhalten Sie unter www.ap2015.de.

Aktivität 4 Nehmen Sie Stellung!°

In Vierergruppen, äußern Sie sich zu einigen Problemen im **Thema 1**. Benutzen Sie dabei die Redemittel im **Thema 1**. Jemand nennt das Gesprächsthema; die anderen sagen ihre Meinung.

BEISPIEL: s1: Verkehrsbelästigung (*traffic disturbances*)
s2: Ich bin der Meinung, man sollte Autos in der Innenstadt verbieten.
s3: Meiner Meinung nach sollte man mehr Fußgängerzonen haben.
s4: Ich finde es schade, dass Leute immer ihren Wagen benutzen. Sie sollten öfter zu Fuß gehen.

THEMA 2: Umwelt

Was kann man für die Umwelt tun?

Die Zeitschrift „Natur" fragte ihre Leser, „Bei welchen dieser Punkte auf der Liste glauben Sie, dass Sie mehr für die Umwelt tun könnten?" Hier sind die Antworten.

Keine Wegwerfflaschen oder Getränkedosen kaufen	35
Beim Einkauf auf Artikel mit umweltfreundlicher Verpackung achten	29
Öffentliche Verkehrsmittel dem Auto vorziehen	29
Aluminium getrennt vom Hausmüll sammeln	26
Beim Einkauf keine Plastiktüten verwenden	25
Weniger Strom verbrauchen	24
Alte Arzneimittel in der Apotheke abgeben	24
Energiesparende Haushaltsgeräte anschaffen	22
Heizwärme sparen, die Wohnung besser isolieren	21
Alte Batterien bei den Sammelstellen abgeben	20
Sonderabfälle[1] (z.B. Altöl) zur Deponie[2] bringen	18
Organische Abfälle kompostieren	16
Alte Kleider in die Sammlung geben	15
Auto mit Katalysator fahren	14
Altpapier in die Sammlung geben	13
Glas zum Container bringen	12
Nichts davon	18

[1]*special types of garbage* [2]*garbage dump*

Was tun Sie persönlich für die Umwelt?

Neue Wörter

die Wegwerfflasche (Wegwerfflaschen, *pl.*) nonrecyclable bottle
die Getränkedose (Getränkedosen, *pl.*) beverage can
mit umweltfreundlicher Verpackung with environmentally friendly packaging
vorziehen (+ *dat.*) give preference to . . . (over . . .)
die Plastiktüte (Plastiktüten, *pl.*) plastic bag
verwenden use, apply
verbrauchen use; consume
das Arzneimittel (Arzneimittel, *pl.*) medication
anschaffen buy, acquire
isolieren insulate; isolate
die Sammelstelle (Sammelstellen, *pl.*) recycling center
der Abfall (Abfälle, *pl.*) waste

Tempolimits in Europa

Erlaubte Höchstgeschwindigkeiten für Pkw in km/h

auf Autobahnen	40	60	80	100	120	140
Norwegen			90			
Dänemark						
Estland			110			
Lettland						
Litauen						
Schweden						
Großbritannien				112		
Irland						
Belgien						
Bulgarien						
Finnland						
Griechenland						
Mazedonien				120		
Niederlande						
Portugal						
Rumänien						
Schweiz						
Serbien/Monten.						
Türkei						
Deutschland*						
Frankreich						
Italien						
Kroatien						
Luxemburg				130		
Österreich						
Polen						
Slowakei						
Slowenien						
Spanien						
Tschechien						
Ungarn						

9238 © Globus *empfohlene Richtgeschwindigkeit

Aktivität 5 Langsamer, bitte!

Sie hören zuerst ein Gespräch zwischen Andreas, einem deutschen Autofahrer, und Jennifer, seinem Gast aus den USA. Hören Sie zuerst den Dialog, und lesen Sie die Sätze unten. Bringen Sie dann die Sätze in die richtige Reihenfolge.

_____ Bei uns ist die Höchstgeschwindigkeit (*speed limit*) 110 km pro Stunde.

_____ Wahrscheinlich eine Baustelle (*construction zone*) in der Nähe.

_____ Also doch ein Tempolimit. Gott sei Dank. Bei 100 km pro Stunde fühle ich mich direkt wie zu Hause.

_____ Keine Angst. Der Wagen schafft das spielend.

_____ Dann kann man gleich zu Fuß gehen.

_____ Schau mal. Dort ist ein Schild. Höchstgeschwindigkeit 100 km pro Stunde.

__*1*_ Fliegen wir eigentlich oder fahren wir?

Hier klicken!

Weiteres zum Thema Umwelt finden Sie bei **Deutsch: Na klar!** im World-Wide-Web unter www.mhhe.com/dnk5.

Aktivität 6   Ein Natur-Quiz

Wie gut kennen Sie Ihre Umwelt? Beantworten Sie die Fragen und vergleichen Sie dann Ihre Antworten mit denen eines Partners / einer Partnerin.

1. Was ist am sparsamsten im Energieverbrauch?

   a. das Motorrad   **b.** das Auto
   c. das Fahrrad   **d.** die Bahn

2. In welchem Jahr und wo wurden erstmals Mülleimer (*garbage cans*) benutzt?

   a. 1213 in Rom   **b.** 1473 in Amsterdam
   c. 1621 in Hamburg   **d.** 1872 in Chicago

3. Wann und wo wurde die Konservendose erfunden?

   a. 1746 in Norwegen   **b.** 1810 in England
   c. 1899 in Deutschland   **d.** 1902 in der Schweiz

4. Wie viel Wasser verbrauchen Deutsche pro Person im Durchschnitt am Tag?

   a. 14 Liter   **b.** 130 Liter
   c. 295 Liter   **d.** 320 Liter

5. In welchem Land wird 69% des Stroms aus Wasserkraft gewonnen?

   a. in den Niederlanden   **b.** in Deutschland
   c. in der Schweiz   **d.** in Österreich

Siehe *The Passive Voice*, S. 417.

ANALYSE

Seit über dreißig Jahren wächst das Umweltbewusstsein der Deutschen. Daher werden Berufe im Umweltbereich immer beliebter. Hier sind drei neue Berufe.

Beate Lehmkuhl, 41, ist Fachärztin für Umweltmedizin in Hamburg. Sie studierte Humanmedizin in Freiburg. „Ich beschäftige mich hauptsächlich mit Schadstoffen und ihrer Wirkung auf den Menschen. Diese Schadstoffe sind in Boden, Wasser, Luft, Lebensmitteln und in Dingen, die wir jeden Tag benutzen."

Dr. Ralph Hantschel, 34, zählt zu den ersten Studienabgängern der Geoökologie: „Die Ausbildung in Bayreuth war intensiv und gut." Heute sucht er Wege zu einer umweltverträglichen Landwirtschaft und ist beim Forschungszentrum für Umwelt und Gesundheit (GSF) tätig.

Siegfried Müller vom Amt für Abfallwirtschaft der Stadt München: „Es macht Spaß. Aber die Verwaltungswege erscheinen mir mitunter zu lang." Der 32jährige studierte Physik. Er arbeitet in der Entsorgungsplanung.

- Dr. Beate Lehmkuhl. Fachärztin für Umweltmedizin. Was hat sie studiert? Wo arbeitet sie jetzt?
- Dr. Ralph Hantschel. Geoökologe. Wo hat er studiert? Wo arbeitet er jetzt?
- Siegfried Müller. Entsorger (*waste management engineer*). Was hat er studiert? Wo arbeitet er jetzt?

Gibt es diese oder ähnliche (*similar*) Berufe in Ihrem Land? Wer befasst sich mit dem Folgenden? Schreiben Sie **F** (für Facharzt/Fachärztin), **G** (für Geoökologe/Geoökologin) oder **E** (für Entsorger/Entsorgerin).

1. _____ Altöl, Altbatterien und ihre Wirkung (*effect*) auf die Umwelt
2. _____ Kontrolle der Verpackungsflut (*glut of packaging*)
3. _____ Messung des sauren Regens
4. _____ organische Abfälle und Kompost
5. _____ Bakterien oder Gift in Lebensmitteln
6. _____ Verschmutzung der Seen, Flüsse
7. _____ Einfluss auf den Menschen durch Schadstoffe (*toxins*)

Grammatik im Kontext

The Passive Voice°

Das Passiv

So far you have learned to express sentences in German in the active voice. In the active voice, the subject of a sentence performs the action expressed by the verb. In the passive voice, the subject is acted on by an agent, the person or thing performing the action. This agent is not always named, because it is either understood, unimportant, or unknown. Compare the following sentences

ACTIVE VOICE

Viele Leute lesen täglich eine Zeitung.	*Many people read a newspaper daily.*
Welche Zeitung lesen die Deutschen am meisten?	*Which paper do Germans read the most?*

PASSIVE VOICE

In Deutschland werden viele Zeitungen verkauft.	*Many newspapers are sold in Germany.*
Welche Zeitung wird am meisten gelesen?	*Which newspaper is read the most?*

The active voice emphasizes the subject that carries out an activity; in the passive voice the emphasis shifts to the activity itself. For this reason, the passive voice tends to be more impersonal. It is commonly used in newspapers, scientific writing, and descriptions of procedures and activities.

Formation of the Passive Voice

The passive voice is formed with the auxiliary verb **werden** and the past participle of the main verb. (English uses *to be* and the past participle.) Although it can be used in all personal forms, the passive occurs most frequently in the third-person singular or plural. Following are the commonly used tenses of the passive.

PRESENT

Die Zeitung **wird verkauft.**	*The newspaper is (being) sold.*
Die Zeitungen **werden verkauft.**	*The newspapers are (being) sold.*

SIMPLE PAST

Die Zeitung **wurde verkauft.**	*The newspaper was (being) sold.*
Die Zeitungen **wurden verkauft.**	*The newspapers were (being) sold.*

PRESENT PERFECT

Die Zeitung **ist verkauft worden.**	*The newspaper has been sold.*
Die Zeitungen **sind verkauft worden.**	*The newspapers have been sold.*

Die Zeitung **war verkauft worden.**   *The newspaper had been sold.*

Die Zeitungen **waren verkauft worden.**   *The newspapers had been sold.*

Note:

- In the perfect tenses of the passive, the past participle **geworden** is shortened to **worden.**
- The presence of **worden** in any sentence is a clear signal that the sentence is in the passive voice.

ANALYSE

You now know three ways in which the verb **werden** can function.

1. **werden** as independent verb (*to become*)
2. **werden** + infinitive (future tense)
3. **werden** + past participle (passive voice)

Read the headlines and captions and determine . . .

- how the verb **werden** is used in each case (independent verb, future tense, passive)
- the position of the past participle in

   a. a main clause in the passive voice
   b. a dependent clause in the passive voice

Muß unser Dorf so häßlich werden?

In jeder Minute werden 21 Hektar[1] Regenwald vernichtet[2]
Schon in wenigen Jahren wird es die „Grünen Lungen[3] der Erde" nicht mehr geben

GREENPEACE

Wie konnten Sie es zulassen[4], daß unsere Erde[5] in so kurzer Zeit vergiftet[6] wurde?

Du meinst, Fleisch essen und Umweltschutz vertragen sich?

Denk mal genau nach!

Wenn dir wirklich was an diesem Planeten liegt, werde Vegetarier!

[1]Hektar = *2.47 acres*   [2]*destroyed*   [3]*lungs*   [4]*allow*   [5]*earth*   [6]*poisoned*

Expressing the Agent

As already noted, the agent causing the action in a passive voice sentence is often not stated. However, when it is stated, the agent is expressed with the preposition **von** (+ *dat.*).

In einer Stunde werden 1,5 Millionen Briefe **von Deutschen** geschrieben.

*In one hour 1.5 million letters are written **by Germans.***

When the action is caused by an impersonal force, the preposition **durch** (+ *acc.*) is used.

Die Ozonschicht wird **durch Luftverschmutzung** zerstört.

*The ozone layer is being destroyed **by air pollution.***

Sentences in the passive voice that state the agent can also be expressed in the active voice. There is no difference in meaning, only in emphasis.

PASSIVE: In einer Stunde werden 1,5 Millionen Briefe [SUBJECT] von Deutschen [PREPOSITIONAL OBJECT (AGENT)] geschrieben.

ACTIVE: Die Deutschen [SUBJECT (AGENT)] schreiben in einer Stunde 1,5 Millionen Briefe [DIRECT OBJECT].

Note that the subject in the passive voice sentence becomes the direct object in the active voice sentence, and the subject in the active voice sentence becomes the prepositional object (**von**) in the passive voice sentence.

Übung 1   Was passiert alles in 60 Minuten in Deutschland?

Schritt 1: Bilden Sie Sätze im Passiv Präsens.

BEISPIEL: 1,5 Millionen Briefe werden geschrieben.

1. 1,5 Millionen Briefe	exportiert
2. mehr als eine Million Liter Bier	geboren
3. weniger als 80 Kinder	gegessen
4. 434 Autos	gekauft
5. 639 Fernsehgeräte	geschrieben
6. über eine Million Zeitungen	getrunken
7. 57 Menschen / in Unfällen auf der Straße	produziert
8. 786 Tonnen Brot	verletzt

Schritt 2: Drücken Sie die Sätze aus **Schritt 1** im Passiv Perfekt aus.

BEISPIEL: In einer Stunde sind weniger als 80 Kinder geboren worden.

Übung 2   Wer handelt hier?

Ergänzen Sie die folgenden Sätze im Passiv mit **von** order **durch.**

1. In den 80er Jahren ist das Ozonloch _____ Wissenschaftlern entdeckt worden.
2. Die Umwelt wird _____ Luftverschmutzung zerstört.
3. Die Aktion „Saubere Luft" wird _____ vielen Bürgern unterstützt.
4. Bei der Initiative „Gegen Atomkraft" sind einige Studenten _____ der Polizei verhaftet (*arrested*) worden.

5. Die Bürgerinitiative „Kein Handy in Bus und Bahn" ist _____ Zeitung und Fernsehen verbreitet worden.

6. Manche Leute glauben, in Bus und Bahn werden Sitznachbarn von Handytelefonierern _____ Strahlen belastet (*contaminated by radiation*). Deswegen soll es verboten werden.

Übung 3   In der Schweiz

Ergänzen Sie die folgenden Sätze mit Verben im Passiv Präsenz.

1. In der Schweiz _____ vier Sprachen _____: deutsch, französisch, italienisch und rätoromanisch. (sprechen)

2. In 17 Kantonen _____ Deutsch _____. (sprechen)

3. Jährlich _____ rund drei Milliarden Franken für Umweltschutz _____. (ausgeben)

4. 237 Liter Wasser _____ per Person pro Tag _____. (verbrauchen)

5. Im Durchschnitt _____ mehr Kaffee von den Schweizern als von den Deutschen _____. (trinken)

6. Die Bahn _____ zweimal so oft von den Schweizern _____ wie von den Deutschen. (benutzen)

Übung 4   Achtung, Uhren umstellen!

Lesen Sie folgende Nachricht über die Sommerzeit (*daylight saving time*).

1. Identifizieren Sie alle Sätze im Passiv.

2. Was sind die Tatsachen?
   - a. Die Uhren ...
   - b. Die Nacht ...
   - c. Die Sommerzeit ...
   - d. Das Ziel (*goal*) ...

NÜTZLICHE WÖRTER

die Uhr umstellen *to change the clock*

die Uhr vorstellen *to set the clock ahead*

verkürzen *to shorten*

einführen *to introduce*

erreichen *to reach*

Achtung, Uhren umstellen: Die Sommerzeit beginnt

BM/dpa Hamburg, 26. März

Der Osterhase[1] bringt in diesem Jahr auch die Sommerzeit: In der Nacht zum Sonntag um 2 Uhr werden die Uhren auf 3 Uhr vorgestellt; die Nacht wird um eine Stunde verkürzt. Die Sommerzeit endet am 24. September – traditionsgemäß wieder eine Sonntag-Nacht.

Die Sommerzeit war in der Bundesrepublik Deutschland – nach 30 Jahren Unterbrechung[2] – erstmals 1980 wieder eingeführt worden. Das eigentliche[3] Ziel, Energie einzusparen, wurde jedoch nicht erreicht. Dafür genießen[4] viele ihre Freizeit an den langen hellen Abenden.

In der Nacht zum Sonntag...

...Uhr 1 Stunde vorstellen

[1]*Easter Bunny* [2]*interruption* [3]*real* [4]*enjoy*

Expressing a General Activity

Sometimes a sentence in the passive voice expresses a general activity without stating a subject at all. In such cases, the "impersonal" **es** is generally understood to be the subject, and therefore the conjugated verb always appears in the third-person singular. This grammatical feature has no equivalent in English.

Hier wird gerudert.	*People are rowing here.*
Im Fernsehen wird viel über Terrorismus gesprochen.	*There's a lot of talk about terrorism on television.*
Hier wird Deutsch gesprochen.	*German (is) spoken here.*

Eins – und eins – und eins . . .

Hier wird mächtig gerudert! **Jochen** sitzt zwischen **Peter** und **Stefan, Armin** sitzt zwischen **Martin** und **Thomas.** Vorn in einem Boot sitzt **Peter,** während **Martin** hinten sitzt. **Kalli** und **Stefan** rudern nicht in demselben Boot. Wer ist wer?

Lösung: 1. Stefan, 2. Jochen, 3. Peter, 4. Martin, 5. Armin, 6. Thomas, 7. Kalli

Übung 5 Was ist hier los?

Beschreiben Sie, was die Leute auf diesen Bildern machen. Gebrauchen Sie die Verben:

debattieren	feiern	reden
demonstrieren	lachen	tanzen
diskutieren	Musik machen	trinken
essen		

BEISPIEL: Bild 1: Da wird gefeiert und …

1.

2.

3.

Übung 6　Hin und her: Zwei umweltbewusste Städte

In zwei Städten, Altstadt und Neustadt, wird für eine bessere Umwelt gesorgt.

BEISPIEL:　s1: Was ist zuerst in Altstadt gemacht worden?
　　　　　　s2: Zuerst sind Autos aus der Innenstadt verbannt worden. Und in Neustadt?
　　　　　　s1: Zuerst sind naturnahe Gärten angelegt worden.

	ALTSTADT	**NEUSTADT**
zuerst		naturnahe Gärten anlegen
dann		Kinderspielplätze verbessern
danach		Park im Zentrum säubern
schließlich		keine Wegwerfartikel in Geschäften verkaufen
zuletzt		nach Alternativenergie suchen

KULTURTIPP

In einigen Orten Deutschlands können alte Medikamente in die Apotheke zurückgebracht werden, damit sie nicht in den Abfall geworfen werden und als Giftstoffe die Umwelt gefährden. Andere potentiell gefährliche Substanzen wie alte Batterien und Farben werden von "Umweltbussen" abgeholt.

Beispiele für Gefahrensymbole

Gifte　　　　Leicht entzündlich　　　　Ätzend　　　　Gesundheitsschädlich

The Passive with Modal Verbs

Modal verbs used with a passive infinitive convey something that should, must, or can be done. Only the present tense, the simple past tense, and the present subjunctive of modals are commonly used in the passive.

Die Umwelt **muss geschützt werden.**	*The environment must be protected.*
Die Natur **darf** nicht **zerstört werden.**	*Nature must not be destroyed.*
Recyclingprogramme **sollten gefördert werden.**	*Recycling programs ought to be promoted.*
Alte Medikamente **konnten** in die Apotheke **zurückgebracht werden.**	*Old medications could be returned to the pharmacy.*

Note:

- The passive infinitive consists of the past participle of the main verb and **werden**:

ACTIVE INFINITIVE	PASSIVE INFINITIVE
schützen *to protect*	geschützt werden *to be protected*
zerstören *to destroy*	zerstört werden *to be destroyed*
fördern *to promote*	gefördert werden *to be promoted*
zurückbringen *to return*	zurückgebracht werden *to be returned*

Übung 7   Aus Liebe zur Umwelt

Was kann und muss gemacht werden? Folgen Sie dem Beispiel.

BEISPIEL: die Umwelt schonen / müssen →
  Die Umwelt muss geschont werden.

1. alle Menschen über Umweltschutz informieren / müssen
2. mehr Energie sparen / sollen
3. Recyclingprogramme fördern / sollen
4. Altglas sammeln / können
5. Wälder und Flüsse schützen / müssen
6. Alternativenergie entwickeln / müssen
7. Luftverschmutzung vermindern / müssen
8. globale Erwärmung verhindern / können
9. Abfälle wie Plastiktüten und Einwegflaschen vermeiden / müssen
10. Altbatterien nicht in den Müll werfen / dürfen
11. Wegwerfprodukte (wie z.B. Einmal-Rasierer, Einmal-Fotoapparate) nicht kaufen / sollen
12. Verpackungen (wie die Mehrweg-Eierbox) wieder ins Geschäft bringen / können

Übung 8   Was ist das Problem?

Was soll, kann oder darf damit (nicht) gemacht werden?

BEISPIEL: Digitaluhren können nicht repariert werden.

1. Billiguhren (Digitaluhren)
2. Einmal-Fotoapparate
3. alte Batterien
4. Einwegflaschen
5. alte Medikamente
6. Giftstoffe

a. vom Umweltbus abholen
b. in fast alle Apotheken zurückbringen
c. nur für einen Film gebrauchen
d. nicht in den Müll werfen
e. nicht wieder füllen
f. nicht reparieren

Use of **man** as an Alternative to the Passive

Generally, the passive voice is used whenever the agent of an action is unknown. One alternative to the passive is to use the pronoun **man** in the active voice.

PASSIVE VOICE	ACTIVE-VOICE ALTERNATIVE
Die Gefahr ist nicht erkannt worden.	**Man hat** die Gefahr nicht **erkannt.**
The danger was not recognized.	*People (One) did not recognize the danger.*
Die Zerstörung der Altstadt muss verhindert werden.	**Man muss** die Zerstörung der Altstadt **verhindern.**
The destruction of the old city must be prevented.	*People (One) must prevent the destruction of the old city.*

Übung 9   Was kann man für die Umwelt tun?

Bilden Sie neue Sätze mit **man**.

BEISPIEL: Wegwerfprodukte sollen vermieden werden. →
    Man soll Wegwerfprodukte vermeiden.

1. Die Umwelt darf nicht weiter zerstört werden.
2. Altpapier und Glas sollten zum Recycling gebracht werden.
3. In Göttingen ist Geld für den Umweltschutz gesammelt worden.
4. Mehr Recycling-Container sind aufgestellt worden.
5. Chemikalien im Haushalt sollen vermieden werden.
6. Batterien sollen nicht in den Hausmüll geworfen werden.
7. Der Wald muss besonders geschützt werden.

Übung 10   Lebensqualität

Was kann man tun, um die Lebensqualität zu verbessern? Bilden Sie zwei Sätze je mit **man** und Passiv.

BEISPIEL: alte Zeitungen →
    Man kann alte Zeitungen zum Recycling bringen.
    Alte Zeitungen können zum Recycling gebracht werden.

alte Zeitungen	bauen
Plastiktüten	fördern
Windenergie	vermeiden
Kinderspielplätze	sammeln
Altpapier	schützen
öffentliche Verkehrsmittel	benutzen
Wälder	zum Recycling bringen

Das Partizip Präsens

The Present Participle°

The present participle (ending in -*ing* in English) is used in a more limited way in German than it is in English. In German it functions primarily as an adjective or an adverb. As an attributive adjective (preceding a noun), the participle takes appropriate adjective endings. The present participle of a German verb is formed by adding **-d** to the infinitive.

INFINITIVE	PRESENT PARTICIPLE
kommen	kommend (*coming*)
steigen	steigend (*climbing, increasing*)

PRESENT PARTICIPLE AS ATTRIBUTIVE ADJECTIVE

im **kommenden** Sommer	*in the coming (next) summer*
die **steigende** Arbeitslosigkeit	*increasing unemployment*

PRESENT PARTICIPLE AS ADVERB

Jennifer spricht **fließend** Deutsch.	*Jennifer speaks German fluently.*

Übung 11   In der Zeitung

Worüber liest man fast täglich? Ergänzen Sie die Sätze mit einem Partizip Präsens.

Man liest oft über …

1. ___*wachsende*___ Obdachlosigkeit. (wachsen)
2. die _____ Preise. (steigen)
3. _____ Studenten. (demonstrieren)
4. _____ Arbeitslosigkeit. (wachsen)
5. die _____ Luftverschmutzung. (steigen)
6. die _____ Arbeiter. (streiken)
7. die _____ Menschen. (hungern)

Sprache im Kontext

Videoclips

A. Claudia, Harald und Wiebke sprechen über die Probleme in der Welt.

1. Was sind für sie die drei größten Probleme heute?

2. Und für Sie? Was sind für Sie die drei größten Probleme heute in der Welt?

B. Harald spricht über ein ganz spezifisches Problem in Berlin. Erklären Sie das Problem.

C. Wiebke spricht über Aids und was dagegen gemacht wird. Was sagt sie? Ergänzen Sie ihre Worte.

„Ich verfolge in der Zeitung ab und zu die Entwicklung von Aids. Ich sehe, dass es in Afrika sehr stark _____ hat, dass auch die _____ Versorgung für Aids noch nicht das _____, was es bringen könnte. Man arbeitet an Wirkstoffen und _____, aber die Versorgung zum Beispiel für _____ Leute in Afrika oder für Leute in den Ostblockländern ist nicht so gut. Und Medikamente sind auch nicht so verfügbar, wie man sich das _____.“

D. Was tun Claudia und Wiebke für die Umwelt? Schauen Sie sich die Interviews an und schreiben Sie vor jede Aussage entweder **C** für Claudia oder **W** für Wiebke.

_____ sammelt Zeitungen

_____ benutzt öffentliche Verkehrsmittel oder Fahrrad

_____ bringt leere Flaschen zurück

_____ benutzt Stoffbeutel statt Plastikbeutel

_____ lässt das Wasser beim Zähneputzen nicht laufen

_____ badet und duscht weniger und wäscht sich mehr, denn es ist gesünder für die Haut

_____ gebraucht so wenig Strom wie möglich

E. Und Sie? Was machen Sie für die Umwelt?

Lesen

Zum Thema

Die Skandalpresse. In den meisten Ländern gibt es Zeitschriften, die von den jüngsten Sensationen und Skandalen berichten. Auch im Fernsehen wird oft von sensationellen und skandalösen Ereignissen (*events*) berichtet, die aber oft erfunden sind.

Machen Sie eine Umfrage im Kurs.

1. Wie heißen die Zeitungen und Zeitschriften, die sich auf Sensationen und Skandale spezialisieren?
2. Wer liest sie regelmäßig? Welche? Warum?

Auf den ersten Blick

Lesen Sie den Text, eine Ballade von Reinhard Mai, kurz durch.

1. Wovon handelt diese Ballade?
2. Wer sind die Hauptfiguren?
3. Wo spielt sich das Ereignis ab?

WAS IN DER ZEITUNG STEHT

von Reinhard Mai

Wie jeden Morgen war er pünktlich dran, seine
Kollegen sahen ihn fragend an, „Sag' mal,
hast du noch nicht gesehen, was in der
Zeitung steht?"
5 Er schloß die Türe hinter sich,
hängte Hut und Mantel in den Schrank fein säuberlich°,   *neatly*
setzte sich, „da wollen wir erst mal sehen,
was in der Zeitung steht."

Und da stand es fett auf Seite zwei
10 „Finanzskandal", sein Bild dabei
und die Schlagzeile „Wie lang das wohl so weitergeht?"
Er las den Text,
und ihm war sofort klar,
eine Verwechslung°, nein, da war kein Wort von wahr,   *mistake, mix-up*
15 aber wie kann so etwas verlogen° sein,   *fabricated*
was in der Zeitung steht?

Er starrte auf das Blatt°,   *paper*
das vor ihm lag,
es traf ihn wie ein heimtückischer° Schlag°,   *malicious / blow*
20 wie ist das möglich, daß so etwas in der Zeitung steht?
Das Zimmer ringsherum begann sich zu drehen°,   *sich … to turn*
die Zeilen konnte er nur noch verschwommen° sehen.   *as blurred*
Wie wehrt man sich° nur gegen das,   *wehrt … does one defend oneself*
was in der Zeitung steht?

25 Die Kollegen sagten, „stell dich einfach stur"°,   *stell … be stolid*
er taumelte° zu seinem Chef über den Flur,   *staggered*
„aber selbstverständlich,
daß jeder hier zu Ihnen steht,
ich glaube, das Beste ist, Sie spannen erst mal aus,
30 ein paar Tage Urlaub, bleiben Sie zu Haus,
Sie wissen ja, die Leute glauben gleich alles,
nur weil es in der Zeitung steht."

Er holte Hut und Mantel, wankte° aus dem Raum,   *swayed*
nein, das war wirklich kalt, das war kein böser Traum,
35 wer denkt sich sowas aus, wie das,
was in der Zeitung steht?
Er rief den Fahrstuhl°, stieg ein und gleich wieder aus,   *elevator*
nein, er ging doch wohl besser durch das Treppenhaus°.   *stairwell*
Da würde ihn keiner sehen, der wüßte,
40 was in der Zeitung steht.
Er würde durch die Tiefgarage gehen, er war zu Fuß.
Der Pförtner° würde ihn nicht sehen,   *custodian*
der wußte immer ganz genau,
was in der Zeitung steht.
45 Er stolperte° die Wagenauffahrt° rauf,   *stumbled / driveway*
sah den Rücken des Pförtners,
das Tor war auf,
das klebt wie Pech° an dir,   *klebt wie … sticks like tar*
das wirst du nie mehr los°,   *wirst … you will never get rid of*
50 was in der Zeitung steht,
was in der Zeitung steht,
was in der Zeitung steht,
was in der Zeitung steht.

Er eilte° zur U-Bahnstation,   *hurried*
55 jetzt wüßten es die Nachbarn schon,
jetzt war es im ganzen Ort herum,
was in der Zeitung steht.
Solange die Kinder in der Schule waren,
solange würden sie es vielleicht nicht erfahren°,   *find out*
60 aber irgendwer hat ihnen längst erzählt,
was in der Zeitung steht.

Er wich den Leuten auf dem Bahnsteig aus°,   wich ... aus *avoided*
im schien, die Blicke, alle richteten sich nur auf ihn,
der Mann im Kiosk da, der wußte Wort für Wort,
65 was in der Zeitung steht.
Wie eine Welle° war es, die über ihm zusammenschlug°,   *wave / crashed down*
wie die Erlösung° kam der Vorortszug°,   *deliverance / suburban train*
du wirst nie mehr ganz frei, das hängt dir ewig an,
was in der Zeitung steht.

70 „Was wollen Sie eigentlich?" fragte der Redakteur°,   *editor*
„Verantwortung°, Mann, wenn ich das schon hör',   *responsibility*
die Leute müssen halt nicht gleich alles glauben,
nur weil es in der Zeitung steht."
„Na, schön, so eine Verwechslung kann schon mal passieren,
75 da kannst du noch so sorgfältig° recherchieren°.   *carefully / research*
Mann, was glauben Sie, was Tag für Tag für ein Unfug°   *nonsense*
in der Zeitung steht?"

„Ja", sagte der Chef vom Dienst, „das ist wirklich zu dumm,
aber ehrlich°, man bringt sich doch nicht gleich um°,   *honestly / bringt ... one doesn't kill oneself*
80 nur weil mal aus Versehen°   *aus ... by mistake*
was in der Zeitung steht."
Die Gegendarstellung° erschien am Abend schon,   *retraction, corrected version*
fünf Zeilen mit dem Bedauern° der Redaktion,   *regret*
aber Hand aufs Herz, wer liest, was so klein
85 in der Zeitung steht?

Zum Text

A. Lesen Sie die folgenden Sätze, und setzen Sie sie in die richtige Reihenfolge.

_____ Er eilte zur U-Bahnstation, um nach Hause zu fahren.

_____ Es war ganz klein gedruckt.

_____ Der Chef vom Dienst fand, dass sein Selbstmord (*suicide*) übertrieben war.

_____ Kein Wort war wahr. Es war eine Verwechslung.

_____ Er verließ das Gebäude durch die Parkgarage, um die Leute zu vermeiden.

_*1*_ Ein Mann ging ins Büro zur Arbeit und las zuerst die Zeitung.

_____ Er sah sein Bild neben der Schlagzeile „Finanzskandal" in der Zeitung.

_____ Er ging zu seinen Kollegen und zu seinem Chef.

_____ Er warf sich vor den Zug.

_____ In der Zeitung stand später, dass der Bericht ein Irrtum (*mistake*) war.

_____ Sein Chef schickte ihn nach Hause.

_____ Der Redakteur der Zeitung meinte, dass er keine Verantwortung trage.

B. Beantworten Sie die folgenden Fragen.

1. Wie reagieren die Personen in der Ballade auf die falsche Information in der Zeitung?

2. Wie steht der Liedermacher zu der Presse?

3. „Was in der Zeitung steht" ist eine Ballade. Was ist charakteristisch für eine Ballade? Was macht diesen Text zu einer Ballade?

C. Was finden Sie über die deutschsprachigen Länder in den Nachrichten und Zeitungen? Suchen Sie sich mehrere Zeitungen oder Zeitschriften aus. Schauen Sie nach, was in den letzten zwei Monaten über die deutschsprachigen Länder berichtet wurde. Welche Themen über die deutschsprachigen Länder kommen vor? Warum sind diese Themen wichtig? Wählen Sie ein Thema und geben Sie einen kurzen Bericht in der Klasse.

D. Schreiben Sie einen kurzen Artikel über die Fakten in der Ballade von Reinhard Mai. Nehmen Sie dazu Stellung. Benutzen Sie dabei die indirekte Rede.

Zu guter Letzt

Diskussion im Plenum

Diskutieren Sie im Plenum einen Vorschlag zur Lösung eines globalen oder lokalen Problems.

Schritt 1: Das Thema. Wählen Sie ein Thema oder Problem aus der Liste mit globalen Problemen auf S. 410 oder ein aktuelles Thema an Ihrer Universität oder in Ihrer Stadt.

BEISPIELE: Armut
Verkehr in der Innenstadt
Umweltverschmutzung

Schritt 2: Die Lösung. Formulieren Sie eine mögliche Lösung des Problems. Sie brauchen nicht unbedingt alle mit dieser Lösung einverstanden zu sein.

BEISPIEL: Umweltverschmutzung → Die Benzinsteuern sollen drastisch erhöht werden.

Schritt 3: Dafür oder dagegen? Entscheiden Sie sich, ob Sie dafür oder dagegen sind. Schreiben Sie drei Argumente, um Ihre Meinung auszudrücken.

Schritt 4: Redemittel. Wie führen Sie Ihre Argumente ein? Wählen Sie mindestens drei Redemittel aus der Liste auf S. 411, um Ihre Argumente einzuleiten.

Schritt 5: Die Klasse wählt eine/n Diskussionsmoderator/in, um die Diskussion zu leiten. Zwei Klassenmitglieder führen Protokoll (*take notes*).

Schritt 6: Diskutieren Sie über die vorgeschlagene Lösung im Plenum. Hier sind einige Redemittel, die dem/der Moderator/in behilflich sein können.

Wir sind hier, um das Thema _____ zu besprechen.	*We are here to discuss the topic _____.*
Wer möchte etwas dazu sagen?	*Who would like to say something about that?*
Einer nach dem anderen bitte!	*Please take turns!*
Wir müssen die Diskussion jetzt zu Ende führen.	*We have to bring the discussion to a close now.*

Schritt 7: Jeder bekommt eine Kopie des Protokolls, um damit eine Zusammenfassung der Diskussion zu schreiben.

Wortschatz

Weltweite Probleme / World Problems

die **Arbeitslosigkeit**	unemployment
die **Armut**	poverty
die **Ausländer-feindlichkeit**	xenophobia, hatred directed toward foreigners
die **Drogensucht**	drug addiction
die **Gewalttätigkeit, -en**	(act of) violence
der **Hunger**	hunger, famine
die **Korruption**	corruption
die **Krankheit, -en**	illness, disease, ailment
der **Krieg, -e**	war
das **Menschenrecht, -e**	human right (*usu. plural*)
der/die **Obdachlose** (*decl. adj.*)	homeless (person)
die **Obdachlosigkeit**	homelessness
der **Rassismus**	racism
der **Rechtsextremismus**	right-wing extremism
der **Terrorismus**	terrorism
die **Umwelt-verschmutzung**	environmental pollution
die **Verletzung, -en**	injury, violation
die **Welt**	world, earth

Umwelt / Environment

der **Abfall, ̈e**	waste, garbage, trash, litter
die **Dose, -n**	(tin or aluminum) can; jar
die **Erwärmung**	warming
die **Flasche, -n**	bottle
die **Wegwerfflasche, -n**	nonrecyclable bottle
die **Getränkedose, -n**	beverage can
der **Lärm**	noise
die **Plastiktüte, -n**	plastic bag
die **Sammelstelle, -n**	recycling center
der **Umweltschutz**	environmental protection
das **Verkehrsmittel, -**	vehicle, means of transportation
die **Verpackung, -en**	packaging, wrapping
das **Windrad, ̈er**	wind power generator

Sonstige Substantive / Other Nouns

das **Arzneimittel, -**	medication
der **Ausländer, -** / die **Ausländerin, -nen**	foreigner
der **Bürger, -** / die **Bürgerin, -nen**	citizen
die **Demonstration, -en**	demonstration
die **Droge, -n**	drug; medicine
die **Forschung, -en**	research
der **Fortschritt, -e**	progress
Fortschritte machen	to make progress
die **Gefahr, -en**	danger
das **Gefängnis, -se**	prison, jail
die **Lösung, -en**	solution
die **Meinung, -en**	opinion
ich bin der Meinung ...	I'm of the opinion . . .
meiner Meinung nach ...	in my opinion . . .
der **Politiker, -** / die **Politikerin, -nen**	politician
die **Regierung, -en**	government
die **Steuer, -n**	tax

Verben / Verbs

ab•stimmen	to take a vote
sich etwas an•schaffen	to purchase or acquire something
behandeln	to deal with
betreffen (betrifft), betraf, betroffen	to affect
ein•führen	to introduce
sich engagieren	to get involved
entwickeln	to develop
erziehen, erzog, erzogen	to raise, bring up
fördern	to promote
halten für (hält), hielt, gehalten	to consider, think
isolieren	to isolate; to insulate
lösen	to solve
sich Sorgen machen um (etwas)	to worry about (something)
meinen	to think, be of the opinion
schaffen, schuf, geschaffen	to create
schützen	to protect
teil•nehmen an (+ *dat.*) (nimmt teil), nahm teil, teilgenommen	to participate (in)
(sich) trennen	to separate
um•schulen	to retrain

unterbrechen (unterbricht), unterbrach, unterbrochen	to interrupt	sauber	clean
		streng	strict(ly)
		übertrieben	exaggerated
verbieten, verbot, verboten	to prohibit, forbid	umweltfreundlich	environmentally friendly
		vertraut	familiar
verbrauchen	to consume		
verbreiten	to spread, disseminate		
vermeiden, vermied, vermieden	to avoid		

Andere Ausdrücke **Other Expressions**

verbrauchen	to consume
verbreiten	to spread, disseminate

vermindern	to decrease, lessen
verwenden	to use, apply
vor•ziehen, zog vor, vorgezogen	to prefer
~~wählen~~	~~to vote, elect; to choose~~

Andere Ausdrücke / **Other Expressions**

außerdem	besides, in addition
Ich bin dafür.	I'm in favor of it.
Ich bin dagegen.	I'm against it.
im Grunde genommen	basically
So ein Unsinn!	Nonsense!

Adjektive und Adverbien / Adjectives and Adverbs

global	global
möglich	possible, possibly
öffentlich	public

DAS KANN ICH NUN!

1. Nennen Sie fünf globale Probleme.

2. Welche Verben assoziieren Sie mit den Substantiven? (Mehrere Antworten sind möglich.)

   a. an Demonstrationen ____ entwickeln
   b. die Umwelt ____ einführen
   c. Plastiktüten ____ schützen
   d. Obdachlosigkeit ____ fördern
   e. Fußgängerzonen ____ vermindern
   f. Recylingprogramme ____ verbieten
   g. Umweltschutz ____ teilnehmen
   h. Alternativenergie ____ einrichten

3. Nennen Sie zwei oder drei Sachen, die man in Ihrer Stadt tut oder die Sie persönlich machen, um die Umweltz zu schützen.

4. Sie diskutieren mit einem Bekannten über globale Klimaerwärmung. Wie sagt man folgende Ausdrücke auf Deutsch?

   a. *In my opinion . . .* b. *I think it is exaggerated . . .* c. *I agree with you that . . .* d. *I am against that.*

5. Bilden Sie nun vier Sätze mit den Ausdrücken aus Übung **4**, in denen Sie etwas über globale Erwärmung aussagen.

6. Drücken Sie die folgenden Sätze im Passiv aus.

   a. Man muss die Umwelt schützen. b. Kann man globale Klimaerwärmung verhindern? c. Man darf Altbatterien nicht in den Abfall werfen.

7. Ergänzen Sie die folgenden Sätze im Passiv.

   a. In Deutschland ____ viele Zeitungen gelesen. b. Letztes Jahr ____ Millionen Digitalkameras gekauft ____. c. In der Schweiz ____ in 17 Kantonen Deutsch gesprochen. d. Handytelefonieren in Bus and Bahn soll verboten ____. e. Mozart ____ in Salzburg geboren.

8. Ergänzen Sie die fehlenden Partizipial- adjektive.

   a. Im kommen____ Sommer mache ich ein Praktikum im Umweltschutz. b. Die steigen____ Klimaerwärmung ist ein globales Problem. c. Die Studenten demonstrierten wegen wachsen____ Arbeitslosigkeit nach dem Studium.

Gestern und heute

Die Skulptur "Berlin" mit Blick auf die Kaiser Wilhelm-Gedächtniskirche im Zentrum Berlins

In diesem Kapitel

■ Short history of modern Germany, remembrances of war and survival, Berlin—the capital, European Union, looking to the future

Videoclips
Berlin: Damals und heute

Kleine Chronik deutscher Geschichte

1. September 1939	Der Zweite Weltkrieg beginnt mit der Invasion Polens durch deutsche Truppen.
9. Mai 1945	Um null Uhr eins endet der Zweite Weltkrieg in Europa offiziell mit der Kapitulation der Deutschen Wehrmacht°. Durch diesen Krieg verloren insgesamt 55 Millionen Menschen ihr Leben.

armed forces

Das zerbombte Reichstagsgebäude, Berlin 1945

Trümmerfrauen bei der Arbeit

5. Juni 1945	Die vier Alliierten (die Vereinigten Staaten, die Sowjetunion, Großbritannien und Frankreich) übernehmen die oberste Regierungsgewalt in Deutschland. Deutschland wird in vier Besatzungszonen° aufgeteilt. Berlin, die ehemalige Hauptstadt, wird separat in vier Besatzungszonen aufgeteilt.
5. Juni 1947	Der Marshallplan wird für Deutschland die Grundlage° für das kommende Wirtschaftswunder°.

occupation zones

foundation
economic miracle

Menschenschlangen stehen 1946 nach Lebensmitteln an.

*Die „Luftbrücke": Ein „Rosinenbomber" kurz vor der
Landung in Berlin*

20. Juni 1948	Es gibt neues Geld: die Deutsche Mark. Jeder Bürger der Westzonen und West-Berlins bekommt zu Anfang 40 Mark.
24. Juni 1948	Beginn der Berliner Blockade. Die Sowjetunion blockiert alle Wege nach West-Berlin außer den Luftwegen. Elf Monate lang werden die Berliner durch die „Luftbrücke" versorgt.
23. Mai 1949	Gründung der Bundesrepublik Deutschland (BRD).

7. Oktober 1949	Gründung der Deutschen Demokratischen Republik (DDR).	
17. Juni 1953	Volksaufstand° in Ost-Berlin und der DDR gegen das kommunistische Regime.	*popular uprising*
13. August 1961	Bau der Mauer° in Berlin.	*wall*
26. Juni 1963	Besuch Präsident John F. Kennedys in Berlin. Seine Erklärung der Solidarität mit Berlinern endet mit den oft zitierten Worten: „Ich bin ein Berliner."	
9. November 1989	Die Grenzen zwischen der DDR und der BRD werden geöffnet.	
3. Oktober 1990	Tag der offiziellen deutschen Einigung. Fünf neue Bundesländer (Brandenburg, Mecklenburg-Vorpommern, Sachsen, Sachsen-Anhalt und Thüringen) treten der Bundesrepublik bei.°	*treten … bei join*
20. Juni 1991	Der deutsche Bundestag wählt Berlin zum Regierungssitz° des vereinigten Deutschlands.	*seat of government*
1. Januar 1993	Der Vertrag über die Europäische Union tritt in Kraft.°	*tritt … Kraft comes into force*
8. September 1994	Offizieller Abschied der Besatzungstruppen von Berlin.	
19. April 1999	Der Bundestag tagt zum ersten Mal im neuen Reichstagsgebäude in Berlin.	
1. Januar 2002	Der Euro ersetzt die Deutsche Mark als Währung im täglichen Gebrauch.	
2003–2004	Die Bundesrepublik wird zwei Jahre lang Mitglied des UNO-Sicherheitsrates.	
22. November 2005	Deutschland bekommt seine erste Bundeskanzlerin, Angela Merkel, eine ehemalige Bürgerin der DDR.	

Die Kaiser-Wilhelm-Gedächtniskirche liegt am Kudamm (Kurfürstendamm), dem großen Einkaufsboulevard Berlins. Die Kirche lag am Ende des Zweiten Weltkriegs in Trümmern (*ruins*). Man baute eine neue, moderne Kirche auf, ließ aber die schwarze Ruine des Turms als Mahnmal (*memorial*) an die dunklen Jahre des Krieges stehen.

Die Kaiser-Wilhelm-Gedächtniskirche in Berlin

Aktivität 1   Aus der deutschen Geschichte

Ordnen Sie zuerst die Daten und die Satzteile einander zu. Welches Bild passt zu welchem Satz?

a. Am 9. Mai 1945

b. Am 13. August 1961

c. Am 9. November 1989

d. Am 19. April 1999

—— wurde die Grenze zwischen Ost- und West-Berlin durch den Bau der Mauer geschlossen. BILD ——.

—— feierte ganz Deutschland die Öffnung der Grenze zwischen Ost- und West-Berlin und zwischen der DDR und der BRD. BILD ——.

—— tagte der Bundestag zum ersten Mal im neuen Reichstagsgebäude. BILD ——.

—— als der Zweite Weltkrieg in Europa endete, lag ganz Deutschland in Trümmern. BILD ——.

1.

2.

3.

4.

Aktivität 2   Faktum oder nicht?

Stimmt das oder stimmt es nicht? Korrigieren Sie die falschen Aussagen.

	DAS STIMMT	DAS STIMMT NICHT
1. Der Zweite Weltkrieg begann mit der Invasion der Sowjetunion durch deutsche Truppen im September 1939.	☐	☐
2. Der Zweite Weltkrieg kostete 55 Millionen Menschen das Leben.	☐	☐
3. Deutschland wurde nach dem Zweiten Weltkrieg in vier Besatzungszonen geteilt.	☐	☐
4. Berlin gehörte ganz zur russischen Besatzungszone.	☐	☐
5. Die BRD und die DDR wurden 1945 gegründet.	☐	☐
6. Der Marshallplan spielte eine wichtige Rolle beim Wiederaufbau Europas.	☐	☐
7. Im Juni 1948 blockierte die Sowjetunion alle Transportwege nach Berlin.	☐	☐
8. Im Jahre 1990 wurden die DDR und die BRD vereinigt.	☐	☐
9. Im Jahre 1992 trat der Vertrag über die Europäische Union in Kraft.	☐	☐
10. 2005 wurde Angela Merkel, ehemalige Bürgerin der DDR, die erste Bundeskanzlerin Deutschlands.	☐	☐

Aktivität 3   Ein kleines Quiz

Bilden Sie mehrere Gruppen. Machen Sie mit Hilfe der kleinen Chronik deutscher Geschichte ein Quiz. Das Format bleibt jeder Gruppe überlassen. Es könnte z.B. in Form einer Quizshow sein: Wer bin ich?; es könnte eine Serie von Fragen sein, die Sie gemeinsam entwickeln; oder es könnte ein Wortratespiel sein. Die anderen im Kurs übernehmen die Rolle der Teilnehmer (*participants*).

Große Freude nach der Öffnung der Grenzen: Eine Westberlinerin begrüßt eine DDR-Bürgerin.

Das neue Regierungsviertel in Berlin

Das moderne Sony Center am Potsdamer Platz

Berlin: Hauptstadt im Wandel

Im Juni 1991 wählte der deutsche Bundestag die Stadt Berlin zum offiziellen Regierungssitz. Mit etwa 3,4 Millionen Einwohnern ist Berlin die größte Stadt des vereinigten Deutschlands und dazu ein eigenständiger Staat der Bundesrepublik.

Von der Mauer, die von 1961 bis 1989 West-Berlin von Ost-Berlin trennte, ist kaum eine Spur geblieben. Stattdessen sieht man überall moderne Bürohäuser, Einkaufszentren und Wohnhäuser, sowohl wie renovierte und neue Regierungsgebäude. Das Stadtbild Berlin hat sich sehr verändert, vor allem am Potsdamer Platz und im früheren östlichen Teil. Die Stadt Berlin ist stolz auf ihre Rolle als Metropole.

Beiträge° zur deutschen Geschichte

Contributions

Wie berührt (*touches*) Geschichte unser Leben? In diesem Teil des Kapitels erleben Sie Geschichte, indem Sie persönliche Dokumente, Auszüge aus einer Autobiographie und Briefe lesen. Diese persönlichen Dokumente bringen uns historische Ereignisse auf ungewöhnliche Weise näher.

Auf den ersten Blick ı

Der folgende Text, ein kurzer Ausschnitt aus der Autobiographie der Zigeunerin (*Gypsy*) Ceja Stojka, *Wir leben im Verborgenen: Erinnerungen einer Rom-Zigeunerin,* ist im Jahre 1989 erschienen. Ceja Stojka wurde 1933 in einem Gasthaus in der Steiermark in Österreich geboren. Während des Dritten Reiches wurde sie als Zigeunerin – sie gehörte zu der Rom Gruppe – aus rassistischen Gründen verfolgt (*persecuted*). Sie kam zusammen mit ihrer Mutter und ihren Schwestern in die Konzentrationslager Auschwitz und Ravensbrück.

Überfliegen Sie den ersten Abschnitt des Textes. Welche der folgenden Namen und Wörter stehen im Text?

☐ Auschwitz   ☐ SS-Soldaten
☐ Hitler   ☐ sterilisieren
☐ experimentieren   ☐ Ravensbrück
☐ nach Hause gehen   ☐ SS-Frauen
☐ Berlin   ☐ Konzentrationslager

KULTURTIPP

Die Aufseherinnen (*female guards*) in den Konzentrationslagern wurden automatisch zu Mitgliedern der SS. Daher die Bezeichnung SS-Frauen, die Ceja Stojka benutzt.

Für „arische" Frauen waren Verhütungsmittel (*birth control*), Abtreibungen (*abortions*) und Sterilisation gegen das Gesetz; aber für andere Frauen, die nicht der Norm entsprachen, gab es Zwangssterilisation (*forced sterilization*). In den Konzentrationslagern wurden Zwangssterilisationen an vielen Frauen vorgenommen, um mit neuen Methoden der Sterilisation zu experimentieren.

WIR LEBEN IM VERBORGENEN

von Ceja Stojka

Ja, es war nicht einfach in diesem Frauenlager Ravensbrück. Die SS-Frauen waren schlechter als jeder Satan. Eines Tages kamen zwei von ihnen und sagten zu uns: „Hört alle gut zu, was wir euch sagen. Es ist ein Schreiben aus Berlin gekommen und das sagt, alle Frauen und
5   Kinder, die sich sterilisieren lassen, können bald nach Hause gehen."
Und weiter sagten sie: „Na, ihr braucht ja keine Kinder mehr, also kommt morgen und unterschreibt°, daß ihr freiwillig dazu bereit seid.   *sign*
Der Oberarzt wird euch diesen Eingriff° machen. In ein paar Tagen   *operation*
könnt ihr dann das Lager verlassen." (Das war alles eine Lüge°. Ja,   *lie*
10   es war eine Lüge, denn wir standen alle schon auf der Liste.)
Die SS-Frauen wurden immer böser. So verging° ein Tag um den   *passed*
anderen. Täglich warf man Frauen in den Bunker, und sie kamen nicht
mehr zurück. So ging es wochenlang.
Die Tage wurden nun schon länger und manchesmal war es nicht
15   mehr so kalt. Ich, Mama, Kathi, Chiwe mit Burli und Rupa mußten in
die Waschküche. Wir machten dort unsere Arbeit und als wir zurück-
kamen, sahen wir, wie zwei Häftlinge° einen Bretterwagen° vor unsere   *inmates / wooden wagon*
Baracke zogen. Viele Frauen waren darauf, wie Schweine lagen sie
übereinander. Ganz oben lag unsere kleine liebe Resi. Sie waren
20   sterilisiert worden, alle hatten große Schmerzen, sie konnten nicht einmal
ein einziges Wort sagen. Die kleine Resi starb° gleich, auch die anderen   *died*

kamen nicht mehr durch. Alle waren tot. Die SS-Frauen sagten dann zu
uns: „Ihr braucht keine Angst zu haben, der Oberarzt hat ein neues
Gerät bekommen, das alte hatte einen Kurzschluß°, also ein Versehen°." *short circuit / accident*
25 Wir wußten ganz genau, daß sie uns nur besänftigen° wollten, aber wir *quiet*
wußten auch, daß wir ihnen nicht entkommen°. Eines Tages kamen *escape*
Binz und Rabl und holten Mama, Kathi und mich ab. Sie sprachen
nicht viel und sagten nur: „Marsch, Marsch". Wir gingen sehr schnell.
In diesem Moment war uns alles egal. Wir kamen zu einem richtigen
30 Haus. Es ging stockaufwärts. Die SS-Frauen machten im Vorraum dem
Oberarzt ihre Meldung°. Nun warteten wir. Mama zeigte uns mit ihren *report*
blauen Augen, daß wir mutig° sein sollten, sprechen durften wir ja *brave*
nicht. Die Zeit verging und es geschah nichts. Plötzlich kam der
Oberarzt und sagte: „Heute ist nichts mehr, wir haben leider keinen
35 Strom." Er schaute uns mit großen Augen an und machte seine Tür zu.
Zwei SS-Frauen brachten uns wieder in das Lager zurück. Unterwegs
sahen wir eine Baracke. Drinnen waren viele Frauen mit Schreibma-
schinen. Das war die Schreibstube. Nun waren wir wieder in unserer
Baracke. Alle fragten, was geschehen war, und alle Frauen weinten
40 vor Freude.
   Mama sagte: „*O swundo Dell gamel awer wariso de gerel amenza.*"
(Der liebe Gott hat was anderes mit uns vor.)

Zum Text ı

A. Wie wurden Ceja und ihre Familie durch die Rassenpolitik der Nazis
betroffen?

B. Welche Erfahrungen beschreibt die Autorin?

1. Die SS-Frauen versprachen den Häftlingen, wenn sie sich freiwillig
sterilisieren lassen, …

   a. bekommen sie besseres Essen.

   b. brauchen sie eine Woche nicht zu arbeiten.

   c. werden sie bald freigelassen.

2. Der Sterilisationsprozess im Lager war …

   a. freiwillig.

   b. ein medizinisches Experiment.

   c. eine Gesundheitsmaßnahme (*health precaution*).

3. Die Autorin erinnert sich daran, dass sie im Konzentrationslager …

   a. zur Schule ging.

   b. in der Waschküche arbeitete.

   c. auf der Schreibstube arbeitete.

4. Die ersten Frauen, die sterilisiert wurden …

   a. starben an den Folgen der Sterilisation.

   b. kamen nie in die Baracken zurück.

   c. durften nach Hause gehen.

5. Die Autorin wurde nicht sterilisiert, weil …

   a. der Oberarzt Mitleid (*sympathy*) mit ihr hatte.

   b. man sie in der Waschküche brauchte.

   c. es keine Elektrizität gab.

Auf den ersten Blick 2

Im Frühjahr 1947 reiste der ehemalige Präsident Herbert Hoover nach Deutschland und Österreich, um die katastrophale Ernährungssituation zu untersuchen (*investigate*). Das Resultat war die Hoover-Speisung für Schulkinder in beiden Ländern. Kinder schickten Hoover Hunderte von Briefen, um ihm für seine Hilfe zu danken. Sie lesen hier zwei dieser Briefe, die jetzt in den Archiven des Hoover Instituts in Stanford, Kalifornien, gesammelt sind.

Überfliegen Sie die zwei Briefe kurz.

A. Wer hat die Briefe geschrieben? (Namen und ungefähres Alter)

B. Aus welchem Jahr stammen die Briefe?

C. Wie reden (*address*) die Kinder Herbert Hoover an? Wie enden ihre Briefe?

DANK
FÜR ALLE SPENDEN
AUS AMERIKA!
DIE DANKBAREN
KINDER AUS
WIEN.

BRIEFE AN HERBERT HOOVER

THE HERBERT HOOVER ARCHIVES

Eckernförde, den 26.3.47.
Lieber Onkel Hoover!
Ich habe Dich neulich im Kino gesehen und da Du so lieb und gut aussiehst, will ich Dir heute schreiben. Wir sind aus Oberschlesien hierher gekommen und haben dort unsre schönen Sachen lassen müssen.

Giebt es in Amerika schon Puppen mit langen Haaren zu kaufen? Wir sind so oft allein, weil unsre Mutti nach Brot anstehen muß. Werden bei euch alle Leute satt? Nun willst Du uns ja hier helfen in Deutschland. Viele Grüße, von Heike Leopold.

Margot Fränkel

Bayreuth, den 28.5. 1947.

Sehr geehrter Herr Hoover!

Wir freuten uns sehr, als uns ver-
kündet[1] wurde, daß alle die Auslandsspeisen bekommen. Denn es wurde
durch Wiegen und Messen festgestellt,[2]
daß viele unterernährt[3] sind. Wir
sind schon immer auf die Minute
gespannt,[4] wenn es läutet[5] und wir
unser Essen bekommen. Heute gibt
es Teigwaren[6] mit Obsttunke.[7] Wenn
manchmal ein Rest übrig bleibt,
freuen wir uns am meisten, wenn
wir es bekommen. Es gibt jetzt schon
2½ Wochen Essen. Am meisten aber
freuen wir uns, wenn es am Ende
der Wochen Eiscremepaste gibt. Als es
das erstemal die Auslandsspeisen gab,

bekamen wir am Ende der Woche
eine Tafel Schokolade. Wir mußten
sie gleich anbeißen,[8] damit wir nicht
Schwarzhandel trieben.[9] Jeder geht es jetzt
gerne in die Schule.

Ich danke Ihnen nochmals dafür,
für die guten Gaben.[10]

Mit dankbarem Gruß
eine ergebene Schülerin

Margot Fränkel

[1]announced [2]es ... it was found by weighing and measuring [3]malnourished [4]eager [5]the bell rings [6]noodles [7]fruit syrup [8]bite into it [9]Schwarzhandel ... deal on the black market [10]gifts

Zum Text 2

1. Was erfahren wir über die Folgen (*consequences*) des Krieges für die Kinder?

2. Welche Probleme erwähnen die Kinder? Wer schreibt davon, dass

- die meisten Kinder unterernährt sind?
- die Kinder wissen, wie man Schwarzhandel treibt?
- die Familie aus ihrer Heimat geflüchtet (*fled*) ist?
- sie oft allein ist, weil die Mutter nach Brot anstehen muss?

Der Weg nach Europa

Nach dem Zweiten Weltkrieg beschlossen einige europäische Länder, internationale Konflikte in Zukunft durch Zusammenarbeit und Gemeinschaft zu lösen anstatt durch Gewalt. Dies begann mit der wirtschaftlichen Zusammenarbeit von sechs Staaten, die 1957 die Europäische Wirtschaftsgemeinschaft (EWG) gründeten. Die Europäische Union (EU) wurde dann 1993 durch den Maastrichter Vertrag gegründet. Dieser Vertrag bahnte den Weg zur weiteren europäischen Integration.

Die Mitgliedstaaten planten in vielen Bereichen zusammenzuarbeiten, z.B. in Sicherheitspolitik, Justiz und Wirtschaft. Eine gemeinsame Währung, der Euro, wurde am 1. Januar 1999 eingeführt. Allerdings begannen die Länder erst am 1. Januar 2002, den Euro im täglichen Gebrauch zu benutzen.

Belgien, Dänemark, Deutschland, Frankreich, Griechenland, Großbritannien, Irland, Italien, Luxemburg, die Niederlande, Portugal und Spanien waren die ersten Länder der EU. Finnland, Österreich und Schweden wurden 1995 Mitgliedstaaten. Im Jahr 2004 traten noch mehr Länder der EU bei: Estland, Lettland, Litauen, Malta, Polen, die Slowakei, Slowenien, die Tschechische Republik, Ungarn und Zypern.

Wie sieht die Zukunft der EU aus? Wie viele andere Länder wollen der EU noch beitreten? Wird die Integration der europäischen Länder erfolgreich sein? Das sind Fragen, die die Zukunft beantworten wird.

Europa Europa

Suchen Sie die Informationen im Text und beantworten Sie die Fragen:

1. Warum wurde die EU gegründet?

2. Welcher Vertrag signalisierte die Gründung der EU?

3. Wann wurde der Euro im täglichen Gebrauch in den Ländern der EU eingeführt?

Zu guter Letzt

Die Welt im Jahre 2050

Wie wird die Welt im Jahre 2050 aussehen? Wie wird sich Ihr Leben ändern?

Schritt 1: Was sind Ihre Hoffnungen für die Zunkuft? Ihre Erwartungen, Phantasien und auch Ihre Ängste? Zwei Studenten/Studentinnen sammeln die Ideen aller Kursmitglieder und schreiben sie an die Tafel oder auf eine Folie (*transparency*).

Schritt 2: Arbeiten Sie zu dritt, um Ihre Vorstellung von der Welt im Jahre 2050 zu präsentieren. Wählen Sie aus den Erwartungen, Phantasien und eventuell auch Ängsten Ihrer Mitstudenten/Mitstudentinnen ein Thema und machen Sie Ihre Vorstellung so kreativ wie möglich, z.B. mit Bildern, Postern oder als PowerPoint Präsentation.

Schritt 3: Präsentieren Sie Ihre Ideen der Klasse. Die anderen machen sich Notizen und stellen drei Fragen.

Schritt 4: Wie wird die Welt im Jahre 2050 persönlich auf Sie wirken? Schreiben Sie einen Aufsatz mit dem Titel: „1. Januar 2050 – Ein Tag in meinem Leben".

Sprache im Kontext

Videoclips

Berlin: Eine persönliche Geschichte

Hören Sie das Interview mit Herrn Borowsky und schauen Sie sich gleichzeitig die Bilder an. Er spricht über die Kriegszeit, Berlin in Trümmern, den Bau der Mauer, den Fall der Mauer und die Wiedervereinigung.

A. Die Kriegszeit. Beantworten Sie die Fragen.

1. Wann ist Herr Borowsky geboren?
2. Wann musste er Soldat werden?
3. In welchen Ländern war er stationiert?
4. Wann ist er dann zurückgekommen?

B. Berlin in Trümmern. Schauen Sie sich diesen Teil noch einmal an und ergänzen Sie diese kurze Zusammenfassung.

Herr Borowsky kannte Berlin, wie es in _____ lag. 1943 war das meiste _____. Durch die Endkämpfe war noch mehr _____. Er war erschüttert aber darauf _____. Er hat Arbeit in seinem erlernten Beruf als _____ bekommen. Damals gab es die _____ von Westberlin und es gab wenig _____ und die _____ haben nicht gearbeitet. Daher ist er zur _____ gegangen und war _____ Jahre Polizeibeamter.

C. Als die Mauer gebaut wurde. Warum war Herr Borowsky von dem Bau der Mauer nicht so betroffen?

D. Als die Mauer fiel. Bringen Sie die Aussagen von Herrn Borowsky in die richtige chronologische Reihenfolge.

1. _____ Er sagte seiner Frau, „Du, die Mauer ist auf."
2. _____ Er ist mit der U-Bahn in den Osten gefahren. An der Grenze waren die Volkspolizisten überfreundlich und sehr behilflich.
3. _____ Er war zu Hause und hat alles im Fernsehen verfolgt.
4. _____ Herr Borowsky hat gesehen, wie viele vom Osten in den Westen mit ihren Trabbis gefahren sind.

E. Die Wiedervereinigung und Berlin. Beantworten Sie die Fragen.

1. Wie beantwortet Herr Borowsky die Frage des Interviewers: „Glauben Sie, dass Ost und West gut wieder zusammengefunden haben?"
2. Was für ein Gefühl hat Herr Borowsky, wenn er heute durch Berlin geht?

Appendix A: Hin und her, Part 2

Einführung

Aktivität 13 Hin und her°: Wie ist die Postleitzahl?   *back and forth*

This is the first of many activities in which you will exchange information
with a partner. Take turns asking each other for the postal codes missing
from your charts.

BEISPIEL: s1: Wie ist die Postleitzahl von Bitburg?
s2: D-54634. Wie ist die Postleitzahl von Salzburg?
s1: A-5020.

D-54634	Bitburg
	Salzburg
CH-3800	Interlaken
	Straubing
D-06217	Merseburg
	Buxtehude
FL-9490	Vaduz
	Eisenach

Kapitel 2

Aktivität 8　Hin und her: Machen sie das gern?

Find out what the following people like to do or don't like to do by asking your partner.

BEISPIEL: s1: Was macht Denise gern?
　　　　　s2: Sie reist gern. Was macht Thomas nicht gern?
　　　　　s1: Er fährt nicht gern Auto.

	GERN	NICHT GERN
Thomas		
Denise	reisen	kochen
Niko		
Anja	laufen	Bier trinken
Sie		
Ihr Partner / Ihre Partnerin		

Kapitel 3

relationships

Aktivität 8　Hin und her: Verwandtschaften°

Ask a partner questions about Bernd's family. How is each person related to Bernd?

BEISPIEL: s1: Wie ist Gisela mit Bernd verwandt?
　　　　　s2: Gisela ist Bernds Tante.
　　　　　s1: Wie alt ist sie denn?
　　　　　s2: Sie ist 53.
　　　　　s1: Wann hat sie Geburtstag?
　　　　　s2: Im Februar.

PERSON	VERWANDTSCHAFT	ALTER	GEBURTSTAG
Gisela	Tante	53	Februar
Alexandra			
Christoph	Schwager	36	Dezember
Andreas			
Sabine	Kusine	19	August

Kapitel 4

Aktivität 5   Hin und her: Zwei Stundenpläne

Schritt 1: Sven und Frank sind 18 Jahre alt und gehen aufs Gymnasium (*secondary school*). Vergleichen Sie ihre Stundenpläne. Welche Kurse haben sie zusammen (*together*)?

BEISPIEL: s1: Welchen Kurs hat Frank montags um acht?
s2: Montags um acht hat Frank Informatik. Welchen Kurs hat Sven montags um acht?
s1: Montags um acht hat Sven Englisch.

Schritt 2: Sven und Frank möchten Tennis spielen. Wann ist die beste Zeit? Wann haben sie beide frei?

Zeit	Montag	Dienstag	Mittwoch	Donnerstag	Freitag	Samstag
8 – 8⁴⁵	Informatik	Physik	Kunst	Englisch	frei	Deutsch
8⁴⁵ – 9³⁰	Informatik	Physik	Kunst	Englisch	frei	Deutsch
9³⁵ – 10²⁰	Religion	Deutsch	Mathematik	Geschichte	Sozialkunde	
10⁴⁰ – 11²⁵	Religion	Mathematik	Deutsch	Mathematik	Deutsch	
11³⁰ – 12¹⁵	Erdkunde	frei	Sozialkunde	Erdkunde	Geschichte	
12¹⁵ – 13⁰⁰	Mathematik	Englisch	Physik	Informatik	frei	
13¹⁵ – 14⁰⁰			Sport			
14⁰⁰ – 14⁴⁵			Sport			

Franks Stundenplan

Kapitel 6

Übung 16 Hin und her: Warum nicht?

Fragen Sie Ihren Partner / Ihre Partnerin, warum die folgenden Leute nicht da waren.

BEISPIEL: s1: Warum war Andreas gestern Vormittag nicht in der Vorlesung?
s2: Er hatte keine Lust.

PERSON	WANN	WO	WARUM
Andreas	gestern Vormittag	in der Vorlesung	keine Lust haben
Anke			arbeiten müssen
Frank	gestern Abend	auf der Party	
Yeliz			schlafen wollen
Mario	Samstag	im Café	
Ihr Partner / Ihre Partnerin			

Kapitel 7

Übung 9 Hin und her: Wochenende und Freizeit

Wer hat was gemacht? Arbeiten Sie zu zweit.

BEISPIEL: s1: Was hat Dagmar gemacht?
s2: Sie ist ins Alte Land gefahren.

WER	WAS
Dagmar	ins Alte Land fahren
Thomas	
Jürgen	zu Hause bleiben
Stefanie	
Susanne	bis 11 Uhr schlafen
Felix und Sabine	
die Kinder	Schlittschuh laufen

Kapitel 8

Aktivität 8   Hin und her: Meine Routine — deine Routine

Jeder hat eine andere Routine. Was machen diese Leute und in welcher Reihenfolge? Machen Sie es auch so?

BEISPIEL: s1: Was macht Alexander morgens?
s2: Zuerst rasiert er sich und putzt sich die Zähne. Dann kämmt er sich. Danach setzt er sich an den Tisch und frühstückt.

WER	WAS ER/SIE MORGENS MACHT
Alexander	zuerst / sich rasieren / sich die Zähne putzen dann / sich kämmen danach / sich an den Tisch setzen / frühstücken
Elke	zuerst / sich anziehen dann / sich die Zähne putzen danach / sich kämmen
Tilo	
Kamal	zuerst / sich das Gesicht waschen dann / frühstücken danach / sich rasieren / sich anziehen
Sie	zuerst / ? dann / ? danach / ?
Ihr Partner / Ihre Partnerin	zuerst / ? dann / ? danach / ?

Kapitel 9

unfamiliar

Aktivität 6   Hin und her: In einer fremden° Stadt

Sie sind in einer fremden Stadt. Fragen Sie nach dem Weg. Benutzen Sie die Tabelle unten.

BEISPIEL: s1: Ist das Landesmuseum weit von hier?
s2: Es ist sechs Kilometer von hier, bei der Universität.
s1: Wie komme ich am besten dahin?
s2: Nehmen Sie die Buslinie 7, am Rathaus.

WOHIN?	WIE WEIT?	WO?	WIE?
Landesmuseum	6 km	bei der Universität	Buslinie 7, am Rathaus
Bahnhof			
Post	nicht weit	in der Nähe vom Bahnhof	zu Fuß
Schloss			
Opernhaus	ganz in der Nähe	rechts um die Ecke	zu Fuß, die Poststraße entlang

Übung 15   Hin und her: Was gibt es hier?

Fragen Sie einen Partner / eine Partnerin nach den fehlenden Informationen.

BEISPIEL: s1: Was gibt es beim Gasthof zum Bären?
s2: Warme Küche.
s1: Was gibt es sonst noch?
s2: Bayerische Spezialitäten.

WO?	WAS?	WAS SONST NOCH?
Gasthof zum Bären	Küche / warm	Spezialitäten / bayerisch
Gasthof Adlersberg		
Gasthaus Schneiderwirt	Hausmusik / originell	Gästezimmer / rustikal
Hotel Luitpold		
Restaurant Ökogarten	Gerichte / vegetarisch	Bier / alkoholfrei

Kapitel 10

Aktivität 3 Hin und her: Was nehmen sie mit?

Wohin fahren diese Leute im Urlaub? Was nehmen sie mit? Und warum?
Ergänzen Sie die Informationen.

BEISPIEL: s1: Wohin fährt Angelika Meier in Urlaub?
s2: Sie fährt in die Türkei.
s1: Warum fährt sie in die Türkei?
s2: Weil ...
s1: Was nimmt sie mit?
s2: Sie nimmt ...

PERSONEN	WOHIN?	WARUM?	WAS NIMMT ER/SIE MIT?
Angelika Meier	in die Türkei	sich am Strand erholen	Buch, Sonnenbrille, Badesachen
Peter Bayer	auf die Insel Rügen	Windsurfen gehen	Sonnenschutzmittel, Badehose
Roland Metz			
Sabine Graf	nach Griechenland	eine Studienreise machen	Reiseführer, Wörterbuch, Kamera

Übung 3 Hin und her: Wie war der Urlaub?

Herr Ignaz Huber aus München war drei Wochen im Urlaub in Norddeutschland. Er war zwei Tage in Hamburg, eine Woche in Cuxhaven und nicht ganz zwei Wochen auf der Insel Sylt. Stellen Sie Ihrem Partner / Ihrer Partnerin Fragen über seinen Urlaub. Benutzen Sie den Superlativ.

BEISPIEL: s1: Wo war es am wärmsten?
s2: Am wärmsten war es in Cuxhaven.

	IN HAMBURG	IN CUXHAVEN	AUF DER INSEL SYLT
1. *Wo war es (kalt/warm)?*	20°C	25°C	15°C
2. *Wo waren die Hotelpreise (günstig/teuer)?*			
3. *Wo hat es (viel) geregnet?*	zwei Tage	einen Tag	fünf Tage
4. *Wo war das Hotelpersonal (freundlich)?*			
5. *Wo war der Strand (schön)?*	kein Strand	sehr sauber, angenehm	zu windig
6. *Wo hat das Essen (gut) geschmeckt?*			

Kapitel 11

Aktivität 2　Hin und her: Wer macht was, und warum?

Ergänzen Sie die Informationen.

BEISPIEL: s1: Was macht Corinna Eichhorn?
　　　　　s2: Sie ist Sozialarbeiterin.
　　　　　s1: Warum macht sie das?
　　　　　s2: Weil ...

NAME	BERUF	WARUM?
Corinna Eichhorn	Sozialarbeiterin	Menschen helfen
Karsten Becker	Bibliothekar	sich für Bücher interessieren
Erika Lentz		
Alex Böhmer	Informatiker	mit Computern arbeiten

famous

Aktivität 5　Hin und her: Berühmte° Personen

Diese berühmten Menschen, die alle einen Beruf ausübten, hatten auch andere Interessen. Ergänzen Sie die Informationen.

BEISPIEL: s1: Was war Martin Luther von Beruf?
　　　　　s2: Er war Priester.
　　　　　s1: Was für andere Interessen hatte er?
　　　　　s2: Er interessierte sich für Literatur, Musik und die deutsche Sprache.

NAME	BERUF	INTERESSEN
Martin Luther	Priester	Literatur, Musik, die deutsche Sprache
Käthe Kollwitz		
Bertha von Suttner	Schriftstellerin	die europäische Friedensbewegung (*peace movement*)
Rainer Werner Fassbinder		
Marlene Dietrich	Schauspielerin	Ski fahren
Willi Brandt		

Kapitel 12

Aktivität 6 Hin und her: Eine neue Wohnung

Diese Leute haben entweder eine neue Wohnung oder ein neues Haus gekauft. Wer hat was gekauft? Wie viele Stockwerke gibt es? Wie groß ist das Wohnzimmer? Wie viele WCs oder Badezimmer gibt es?

BEISPIEL: s1: Was für eine Wohnung hat Bettina Neuendorf gekauft?
        s2: Eine Eigentumswohnung.
        s1: Wie viele Stockwerke hat die Wohnung?
        s2: Eins.
        s1: Und wie viele Schlafzimmer? ...

PERSON	TYP	STOCKWERKE	SCHLAFZIMMER	WOHNZIMMER	WC/BAD
Bettina Neuendorf	Eigentums- wohnung	eins	eins, aber auch ein kleines Gästezimmer	mit Esszimmer kombiniert 30 Quadratmeter	eins
Uwe und Marion Baumgärtner	Haus	zwei	drei: Elternschlaf- zimmer, Kinder- schlafzimmer, Gästezimmer	sehr groß mit Balkon 37 Quadratmeter	zwei Badezim- mer: eins im Dachgeschoss und eins im Erdgeschoss
Sven Kersten					
Carola Schubärth	Haus	eins	zwei: ein Schlaf- zimmer ist Arbeitszimmer	klein 25 Quadratmeter	ein Bad

Kapitel 13

Aktivität 2 Hin und her: Wie informieren sie sich?

Wie informieren sich diese Personen? Was lesen sie zur Unterhaltung? Stellen Sie Fragen an Ihren Partner / Ihre Partnerin.

BEISPIEL: s1: Was sieht Martin gern im Fernsehen? Was liest er oft?
s2: Er _____.

PERSON	FERNSEHSHOWS	ZEITUNGEN UND ZEITSCHRIFTEN
Martin	Talkshows und Dokumentarfilme	*die Zeit*
Stephanie	klassische Spielfilme und Komödien	*der Spiegel*
Patrick		
Kristin	Sportsendungen, Krimi-Serien wie „Die Rosenheim-Cops"	die *Süddeutsche Zeitung* und *Brigitte*
Mein Partner / Meine Partnerin		

Aktivität 7 Hin und her: Erfindungen durch die Jahrhunderte

Sie möchten erfahren, wer was und wann erfunden hat. Arbeiten Sie zu zweit.

BEISPIELE: s1: Wer hat _____ erfunden?
s2: _____.
s1: Wann hat er / sie es erfunden?
s2: (Im Jahre) _____.

[*oder:*] s1: Was hat _____ erfunden?
s2: Er / Sie hat _____ erfunden.
s1: In welchem Jahr?
s2: (Im Jahre) _____.

PERSON	ERFINDUNG	DATUM
Johannes Gutenberg	der Buchdruck mit beweglichen Lettern (*movable type*)	um 1450
Daniel Gabriel Fahrenheit	das Alkoholthermometer	1709
	das Fahrrad (Draisine)	
Herta Heuwer	Currywurst	1949
Gottlieb Daimler		
	der Dieselmotor	
Wilhelm Conrad Röntgen	Röntgenstrahlen (*X rays*)	1895
Melitta Bentz		1908

Kapitel 14

Aktivität 1 Hin und her: Probleme und Lösungen

Stellen Sie Ihrem Partner / Ihrer Partnerin Fragen zu den folgenden Problemen, um herauszufinden, welche möglichen Lösungen es gibt.

BEISPIEL: s1: Was kann man gegen Krieg tun?
s2: Man kann an Antikriegsdemonstrationen teilnehmen.

PROBLEME	MÖGLICHE LÖSUNGEN
Krieg	an Antikriegsdemonstrationen teilnehmen
Inflation	die Ausgaben der Regierung kontrollieren
Drogensucht	
Umweltverschmutzung	alternative Energiequellen (*energy sources*) entwickeln
Verletzung der Menschenrechte	
Obdachlosigkeit	neue Wohnungen bauen
Arbeitslosigkeit	

Übung 6 Hin und her: Zwei umweltbewusste Städte

In zwei Städten, Altstadt und Neustadt, wird für eine bessere Umwelt gesorgt.

BEISPIEL: s1: Was ist zuerst in Altstadt gemacht worden?
s2: Zuerst sind Autos aus der Innenstadt verbannt worden. Und in Neustadt?
s1: Zuerst sind naturnahe Gärten angelegt worden.

	ALTSTADT	NEUSTADT
zuerst	Autos aus der Innenstadt verbannen	
dann	neue Siedlungen am Stadtrand bauen	
danach	Bürger über Umweltschutz informieren	
schließlich	neue, moderne Busse kaufen	
zuletzt	ein großes Umweltfest in der Innenstadt feiern	

Appendix B

Studienfächer

Anthropologie	anthropology
Architektur	architecture
Astronomie	astronomy
Bauingenieurwesen	structural engineering
Betriebswirtschaftslehre	business administration
Bibliothekswissenschaft	library science
Biochemie	biochemistry
Biologie	biology
Chemie	chemistry
Elektrotechnik	electrical engineering
Ernährungswissenschaft	nutritional science
Forstwissenschaft	forestry
Geographie/Erdkunde	geography
Geologie	geology
Geophysik	geophysics
Germanistik	German Studies
Geschichte/Geschichtswissenschaft	history
Informatik	computer science
Journalistik/Publizistik	journalism
Kerntechnik/Reaktortechnik	nuclear engineering
Kunstgeschichte	art history
Maschinenbau	mechanical engineering
Mathematik	mathematics
Medizin	medicine
Musik	music
Pädagogik	education
Pharmakologie/Pharmazie	pharmacology
Philosophie	philosophy
Physik	physics
Politikwissenschaft	political science
Psychologie	psychology
Rechtswissenschaft/Jura	law
Sport	physical education
Sprachwissenschaft/Linguistik	linguistics
Städtebau/Stadtplanung	urban planning
Statistik	statistics
Theaterwissenschaft	dramatic arts
Theologie	theology
Tiermedizin	veterinary science
Volkswirtschaftslehre	economics
Zahnmedizin	dentistry

Appendix C

Grammar Tables

1. Personal Pronouns

	SINGULAR					PLURAL		
Nominative	ich	du / Sie	er	sie	es	wir	ihr / Sie	sie
Accusative	mich	dich / Sie	ihn	sie	es	uns	euch / Sie	sie
Dative	mir	dir / Ihnen	ihm	ihr	ihm	uns	euch / Ihnen	ihnen

2. Definite Articles

	SINGULAR			PLURAL
	Masculine	*Neuter*	*Feminine*	*All genders*
Nominative	der	das	die	die
Accusative	den	das	die	die
Dative	dem	dem	der	den
Genitive	des	des	der	der

Words declined like the definite article: **jeder, dieser, welcher**

3. Indefinite Articles and the Negative Article kein

	SINGULAR			PLURAL
	Masculine	*Neuter*	*Feminine*	*All genders*
Nominative	(k)ein	(k)ein	(k)eine	keine
Accusative	(k)einen	(k)ein	(k)eine	keine
Dative	(k)einem	(k)einem	(k)einer	keinen
Genitive	(k)eines	(k)eines	(k)einer	keiner

Words declined like the indefinite article: all possessive adjectives (**mein, dein, sein, ihr, unser, euer, Ihr**)

4. Relative and Demonstrative Pronouns

	SINGULAR			PLURAL
	Masculine	*Neuter*	*Feminine*	*All genders*
Nominative	der	das	die	die
Accusative	den	das	die	die
Dative	dem	dem	der	denen
Genitive	dessen	dessen	deren	deren

5. Principal Parts of Strong and Mixed Verbs

The following is a list of the most important strong and mixed verbs that are used in this book. Included in this list are the modal auxiliaries. Since the principal parts of compound verbs follow the forms of the base verb, compound verbs are generally not included, except for a few high-frequency compound verbs whose base verb is not commonly used. Thus you will find **anfangen** and **einladen** listed, but not **zurückkommen** or **ausgehen**.

INFINITIVE	(3RD PERS. SG. PRESENT)	SIMPLE PAST	PAST PARTICIPLE	MEANING
anbieten		bot an	angeboten	*to offer*
anfangen	(fängt an)	fing an	angefangen	*to begin*
backen		backte	gebacken	*to bake*
beginnen		begann	begonnen	*to begin*
begreifen		begriff	begriffen	*to comprehend*
beißen		biss	gebissen	*to bite*
bitten		bat	gebeten	*to ask, beg*
bleiben		blieb	(ist) geblieben	*to stay*
bringen		brachte	gebracht	*to bring*
denken		dachte	gedacht	*to think*
dürfen	(darf)	durfte	gedurft	*to be allowed to*
einladen	(lädt ein)	lud ein	eingeladen	*to invite*
empfehlen	(empfiehlt)	empfahl	empfohlen	*to recommend*
entscheiden		entschied	entschieden	*to decide*
essen	(isst)	aß	gegessen	*to eat*
fahren	(fährt)	fuhr	(ist) gefahren	*to drive*
fallen	(fällt)	fiel	(ist) gefallen	*to fall*
finden		fand	gefunden	*to find*
fliegen		flog	(ist) geflogen	*to fly*
geben	(gibt)	gab	gegeben	*to give*
gefallen	(gefällt)	gefiel	gefallen	*to like; to please*
gehen		ging	(ist) gegangen	*to go*
genießen		genoss	genossen	*to enjoy*
geschehen	(geschieht)	geschah	(ist) geschehen	*to happen*
gewinnen		gewann	gewonnen	*to win*

INFINITIVE	(3RD PERS. SG. PRESENT)	SIMPLE PAST	PAST PARTICIPLE	MEANING
haben	(hat)	hatte	gehabt	*to have*
halten	(hält)	hielt	gehalten	*to hold; to stop*
hängen		hing	gehangen	*to hang*
heißen		hieß	geheißen	*to be called*
helfen	(hilft)	half	geholfen	*to help*
kennen		kannte	gekannt	*to know*
kommen		kam	(ist) gekommen	*to come*
können	(kann)	konnte	gekonnt	*can; to be able to*
lassen	(lässt)	ließ	gelassen	*to let; to allow (to)*
laufen	(läuft)	lief	(ist) gelaufen	*to run*
leihen		lieh	geliehen	*to lend; to borrow*
lesen	(liest)	las	gelesen	*to read*
liegen		lag	gelegen	*to lie*
mögen	(mag)	mochte	gemocht	*to like (to)*
müssen	(muss)	musste	gemusst	*must; to have to*
nehmen	(nimmt)	nahm	genommen	*to take*
nennen		nannte	genannt	*to name*
raten	(rät)	riet	geraten	*to advise*
reiten		ritt	(ist) geritten	*to ride*
scheinen		schien	geschienen	*to seem; to shine*
schlafen	(schläft)	schlief	geschlafen	*to sleep*
schließen		schloss	geschlossen	*to close*
schreiben		schrieb	geschrieben	*to write*
schwimmen		schwamm	(ist) geschwommen	*to swim*
sehen	(sieht)	sah	gesehen	*to see*
sein	(ist)	war	(ist) gewesen	*to be*
singen		sang	gesungen	*to sing*
sitzen		saß	gesessen	*to sit*
sollen	(soll)	sollte	gesollt	*should, ought to; to be supposed to*
sprechen	(spricht)	sprach	gesprochen	*to speak*
stehen		stand	gestanden	*to stand*
steigen		stieg	ist gestiegen	*to rise; to climb*
sterben	(stirbt)	starb	(ist) gestorben	*to die*
tragen	(trägt)	trug	getragen	*to carry; to wear*
treffen	(trifft)	traf	getroffen	*to meet*
trinken		trank	getrunken	*to drink*
tun		tat	getan	*to do*
umsteigen		stieg um	(ist) umgestiegen	*to change; to transfer*
vergessen	(vergisst)	vergaß	vergessen	*to forget*
vergleichen		verglich	verglichen	*to compare*
verlieren		verlor	verloren	*to lose*
wachsen	(wächst)	wuchs	(ist) gewachsen	*to grow*
waschen	(wäscht)	wusch	gewaschen	*to wash*
werden	(wird)	wurde	(ist) geworden	*to become*
wissen	(weiß)	wusste	gewusst	*to know*
wollen	(will)	wollte	gewollt	*to want (to)*
ziehen		zog	(ist/hat) gezogen	*to move; to pull*

6. Conjugation of Verbs

In the charts that follow, the pronoun **Sie** (*you*) is listed with the third-person plural **sie** (*they*).

Present Tense

Auxiliary Verbs

	sein	haben	werden
ich	bin	habe	werde
du	bist	hast	wirst
er/sie/es	ist	hat	wird
wir	sind	haben	werden
ihr	seid	habt	werdet
sie/Sie	sind	haben	werden

Regular Verbs, Verbs with Vowel Changes, Irregular Verbs

	REGULAR		VOWEL CHANGE		IRREGULAR
	fragen	finden	geben	fahren	wissen
ich	frage	finde	gebe	fahre	weiß
du	fragst	findest	gibst	fährst	weißt
er/sie/es	fragt	findet	gibt	fährt	weiß
wir	fragen	finden	geben	fahren	wissen
ihr	fragt	findet	gebt	fahrt	wisst
sie/Sie	fragen	finden	geben	fahren	wissen

Simple Past Tense

Auxiliary Verbs

	sein	haben	werden
ich	war	hatte	wurde
du	warst	hattest	wurdest
er/sie/es	war	hatte	wurde
wir	waren	hatten	wurden
ihr	wart	hattet	wurdet
sie/Sie	waren	hatten	wurden

	WEAK	STRONG		MIXED
	fragen	**geben**	**fahren**	**wissen**
ich	fragte	gab	fuhr	wusste
du	fragtest	gabst	fuhrst	wusstest
er/sie/es	fragte	gab	fuhr	wusste
wir	fragten	gaben	fuhren	wussten
ihr	fragtet	gabt	fuhrt	wusstet
sie/Sie	fragten	gaben	fuhren	wussten

Present Perfect Tense

	sein	haben	geben	fahren
ich	bin	habe	habe	bin
du	bist	hast	hast	bist
er/sie/es	ist } gewesen	hat } gehabt	hat } gegeben	ist } gefahren
wir	sind	haben	haben	sind
ihr	seid	habt	habt	seid
sie/Sie	sind	haben	haben	sind

Past Perfect Tense

	sein	haben	geben	fahren
ich	war	hatte	hatte	war
du	warst	hattest	hattest	warst
er/sie/es	war } gewesen	hatte } gehabt	hatte } gegeben	war } gefahren
wir	waren	hatten	hatten	waren
ihr	wart	hattet	hattet	wart
sie/Sie	waren	hatten	hatten	waren

Future Tense

	geben
ich	werde
du	wirst
er/sie/es	wird } geben
wir	werden
ihr	werdet
sie/Sie	werden

Subjunctive

Present Tense: Subjunctive I (Indirect Discourse Subjunctive)

	sein	haben	werden	fahren	wissen
ich	sei	—	—	—	wisse
du	sei(e)st	habest	—	—	—
er/sie/es	sei	habe	werde	fahre	wisse
wir	seien	—	—	—	—
ihr	sei(e)t	habet	—	—	—
sie/Sie	seien	—	—	—	—

For those forms left blank in the chart above, the subjunctive II forms are preferred in indirect discourse.

Present Tense: Subjunctive II

	fragen	sein	haben	werden	fahren	wissen
ich	fragte	wäre	hätte	würde	führe	wüsste
du	fragtest	wär(e)st	hättest	würdest	führ(e)st	wüsstest
er/sie/es	fragte	wäre	hätte	würde	führe	wüsste
wir	fragten	wären	hätten	würden	führen	wüssten
ihr	fragtet	wär(e)t	hättet	würdet	führ(e)t	wüsstet
sie/Sie	fragten	wären	hätten	würden	führen	wüssten

Past Tense: Subjunctive I (Indirect Discourse)

	fahren	wissen
ich	sei	—
du	sei(e)st	habest
er/sie/es	sei ⎱ gefahren	habe ⎱ gewusst
wir	seien	—
ihr	sei(e)t	habet
sie/Sie	sei(e)n ⎰	— ⎰

Past Tense: Subjunctive II

	sein	geben	fahren
ich	wäre	hätte	wäre
du	wär(e)st	hättest	wär(e)st
er/sie/es	wäre ⎱ gewesen	hätte ⎱ gegeben	wäre ⎱ gefahren
wir	wären	hätten	wären
ihr	wär(e)t	hättet	wär(e)t
sie/Sie	wären ⎰	hätten ⎰	wären ⎰

Passive Voice

einladen			
	Present	*Simple Past*	*Present Perfect*
ich	werde ⎫	wurde ⎫	bin ⎫
du	wirst	wurdest	bist
er/sie/es	wird ⎬ eingeladen	wurde ⎬ eingeladen	ist ⎬ eingeladen worden
wir	werden	wurden	sind
ihr	werdet	wurdet	seid
sie/Sie	werden ⎭	wurden ⎭	sind ⎭

Imperative

	sein	**geben**	**fahren**	**arbeiten**
Familiar Singular	sei	gib	fahr	arbeite
Familiar Plural	seid	gebt	fahrt	arbeitet
Formal	seien Sie	geben Sie	fahren Sie	arbeiten Sie

Appendix D

Alternate Spelling and Capitalization

As a result of the recent German spelling reform, some words now have an alternate, old spelling along with a new one. In some realia and literature selections, you may see alternate spellings. The vocabulary lists at the end of each chapter in this text present the new spelling. Listed here are words appearing in the end of chapter vocabulary lists that are affected by the spelling reform, along with their traditional alternate spellings. This list is not a complete list of words affected by the spelling reform.

NEW	ALTERNATE
Abschluss (¨e)	Abschluß (Abschlüsse)
Anschluss (¨e)	Anschluß (Anschlüsse)
auf Deutsch	auf deutsch
Dachgeschoss (-e)	Dachgeschoß (Dachgeschosse)
dass	daß
Erdgeschoss (-e)	Erdgeschoß (Erdgeschosse)
essen (isst), aß, gegessen	essen (ißt), aß, gegessen
Esszimmer (-)	Eßzimmer (-)
Fass (¨er)	Faß (Fässer)
Fitness	Fitneß
Fluss (¨e)	Fluß (Flüsse)
heute Abend / … Mittag / … Morgen / … Nachmittag / … Vormittag	heute abend /… mittag / … morgen / … nachmittag / … vormittag
Imbiss (-e)	Imbiß (Imbisse)
kennen lernen, kennen gelernt	kennenlernen, kennengelernt
lassen (lässt), ließ, gelassen Lass uns doch …	lassen (läßt), ließ, gelassen Laß uns doch …
leidtun, leidgetan	Leid tun, Leid getan
morgen Abend / … Mittag / … Nachmittag / … Vormittag	morgen abend / … mittag / … nachmittag / … vormittag
müssen (muss), musste, gemusst	müssen (muß), mußte, gemußt
passen (passt), gepasst	passen (paßt), gepaßt
Rad fahren (fährt Rad), fuhr Rad, ist Rad gefahren	radfahren (fährt Rad), fuhr Rad, ist radgefahren
Reisepass (¨e)	Reisepaß (Reisepässe)
Samstagabend / -mittag / -morgen / -nachmittag / -vormittag	Samstag abend / … mittag / … morgen / … nachmittag / … vormittag
Schloss (¨er)	Schloß (Schlösser)
spazieren gehen (geht spazieren), ging spazieren, ist spazieren gegangen	spazierengehen (geht spazieren), ging spazieren, ist spazierengegangen
Stress	Streß
vergessen (vergisst), vergaß, vergessen	vergessen (vergißt), vergaß, vergessen
wie viel	wieviel

Vocabulary

German–English

This vocabulary contains the German words as used in various contexts in this text, with the following exceptions: (1) compound words whose meaning can be easily guessed from their component parts; (2) most identical or very close cognates that are not part of the active vocabulary. (Frequently used cognates are, however, included so students can verify their gender.)

Active vocabulary in the end-of-chapter **Wortschatz** lists is indicated by the number of the chapter in which it first appears. The letter E refers to the introductory chapter, **Einführung.**

The following abbreviations are used:

acc.	accusative	*indef. pron.*	indefinite pronoun
adj.	adjective	*inform.*	informal
adv.	adverb	**-(e)n** *masc.*	masculine noun ending in **-n** or **-en** in all cases but the nominative singular
coll.	colloquial		
coord. conj.	coordinating conjunction		
dat.	dative	*pl.*	plural
decl. adj.	declined adjective	*sg.*	singular
form.	formal	*subord. conj.*	subordinating conjunction
gen.	genitive		

A

ab (+ *dat.*) from; as of (12); **ab 1. Juni (ab erstem Juni)** as of June 1st (12)

ab und zu now and then, occasionally (8)

abblitzen (blitzt ab) to be rebuffed

abbrechen (bricht ab), brach ab, abgebrochen to break off, cut short

der Abend (-e) evening (4); **am Abend** in the evening, at night; **gestern Abend** last night; **guten Abend** good evening (E); **der Heilige Abend** Christmas Eve (3); **heute Abend** this evening (1); **jeden Abend** every evening; **morgen Abend** tomorrow evening (4)

das Abendessen (-) evening meal (5); dinner, supper; **zum Abendessen** for dinner, supper

das Abendkleid (-er) evening gown

abends in the evening, evenings (4)

das Abenteuer (-) adventure

der Abenteuerfilm (-e) adventure film

aber (*coord. conj.*) but (1); however

abfahren (fährt ab), fuhr ab, ist abgefahren to depart, leave (10)

die Abfahrt (-en) departure (10)

der Abfall (-̈e) waste, garbage, trash, litter (14)

die Abfallwirtschaft waste management

abfliegen (fliegt ab), flog ab, ist abgeflogen to depart, leave (by plane)

abgeben (gibt ab), gab ab, abgegeben to drop off, turn in (8)

abgucken (guckt ab) to copy (someone else's work)

abhängig dependent

abholen (holt ab) to pick up (*from a place*) (4)

das Abitur (-e) *examination at the end of Gymnasium* (11)

der Abiturient (-en *masc.***) (-en) / die Abiturientin (-nen)** *graduate of the Gymnasium, person who has passed the Abitur*

die Abkürzung (-en) abbreviation

ablehnen (lehnt ab) to decline

ableiten (leitet ab) to derive

ablenken (lenkt ab) to distract

abnehmen (nimmt ab), nahm ab, abgenommen to lose weight

das Abo(nnement) (-s) subscription (13)

abonnieren to subscribe (13)

die Abrechnung (-en) final account

abreisen (reist ab), ist abgereist to depart, leave (on a trip) (9)

der Absatz (-̈e) paragraph

abschalten (schaltet ab) to shut down, turn off

abschicken (schickt ab) to send off, mail

der Abschied (-e) farewell

der Abschluss (-̈e) completion; degree (11)

der Abschnitt (-e) section; phase

der Absender (-) sender

absetzen (setzt ab) to take off

absolut absolute(ly)

sich abspielen (spielt ab) to take place, proceed

die Abstammung origin, heritage

absteigen (steigt ab), stieg ab, ist abgestiegen to dismount, get off

abstellen (stellt ab) to turn off

abstimmen (stimmt ab) to take a vote (14)

die Abstimmung vote; coordination

der Absturz (-̈e) fall; crash

das Abteil (-e) compartment

die Abtreibung (-en) abortion

abwarten (wartet ab) to wait; **abwarten und Tee trinken** wait and see

abwechseln (wechselt ab) to alternate, take turns

abwechslungsreich varied, diverse (11)

das Accessoire (-s) accessory

ach oh; **Ach so!** I see!

acht eight (E)

achte eighth (3)

achten auf (+ *acc.*) to pay attention to, watch (8)

die Achtung attention

achtzehn eighteen (E)

achtzehnte eighteenth

achtzig eighty (E)

der ADAC = Allgemeiner Deutscher Automobilclub *German automobile club*

das Adjektiv (-e) adjective

die Adjektivendung (-en) adjective ending

der Adler, - eagle

das Adrenalin adrenaline

die **Adresse** (-n) address (E)
das **Adverb** (-ien) adverb
das **Aerobic** aerobics
afghanisch Afghan
(das) **Afghanistan** Afghanistan
(das) **Afrika** Africa
afrikanisch African
(die) **AG** = **Aktiengesellschaft**
  corporation
der **Agent** (-en *masc.*) (-en) / die **Agentin**
  (-nen) agent
das **Aggregat** (-e) set; setting
aggressiv aggressive
agieren to play one's part
(das) **Ägypten** Egypt
ah ah; **Ah so!** I see! I get it!
ähnlich similar(ly)
die **Ähnlichkeit** (-en) similarity
die **Ahnung: Keine Ahnung!** (I have) no
  idea!
das **Ahornblatt** (-̈er) maple leaf
das **Aids** AIDS
akkurat precise(ly), exact(ly)
der **Akkusativ** accusative case
das **Akkusativobjekt** (-e) accusative object
die **Akkusativpräposition** (-en) preposition governing the accusative case
das **Akkusativpronomen** (-) pronoun in
  the accusative case
der **Akrobat** (-en *masc.*) (-en) / die
  Akrobatin (-nen) acrobat
die **Aktion** (-en) (political) action
aktiv active(ly) (10); **sportlich aktiv** active
  in sports (10)
die **Aktivität** (-en) activity
aktuell current, topical (13); **Aktuelles**
  current events (13)
akzentuieren to accentuate; **deutsch-**
  akzentuiert German-accented
die **Alarmanlage** (-n) alarm system
alarmieren to alarm
der **Alkohol** alcohol (8)
alkoholfrei nonalcoholic (6)
all all; **vor allem** above all
alle (*pl.*) all; every (5); **alle zwei Jahre**
  every two years; **aller** of all
die **Allee, -n** avenue
allein(e) alone
allerdings however; to be sure
allerlei all kinds of; **Leipziger Allerlei**
  Leipzig-style mixed vegetables
alles everything (10); **Alles Gute!** All the
  best! (3); **Alles klar.** I get it., Everything is clear. (E); **das ist alles**
  that is all
allgemein general; **im Allgemeinen** in
  general
die **Alliierten** (*pl.*) the Allies, the Allied
  Forces
der **Alltag** everyday routine; workday
alltäglich everyday, ordinary
die **Alpen** (*pl.*) the Alps
alphabetisch alphabetical(ly)
als (*subord. conj.*) as; when (10); than (7);
  als Kind as a child
also thus, therefore; so; well
alt (**älter, ältest-**) old (1); **Alt-** used
die **Altbatterie** (-n) used-up battery

die **Altbauwohnung** (-en) apartment in a
  pre-World-War-II building
das **Altenheim** (-e) old people's home
das **Alter** (-) age
alternativ alternative(ly)
das **Altglas** used glass
die **Altkleidung** used clothing
das **Altöl** used oil
das **Altpapier** used paper
die **Altstadt** (-̈e) old part of town
das **Aluminium** aluminum
am = **an dem**; **am ersten Mai** on May first
  (3); **am Montag** on Monday (3); **möchte**
  am liebsten would like to (do) most (4)
der **Amateurfunker** (-) / die **Amateurfun-**
  kerin (-nen) amateur radio operator
(das) **Amerika** America
der **Amerikaner** (-) / die **Amerikanerin**
  (-nen) American (*person*) (1)
amerikanisch American
die **Amischen** (*pl.*) Amish (*people*)
die **Ampel** (-n) traffic light (9)
das **Amt** (-̈er) bureau, agency
amüsant amusing, entertaining
an (+ *acc./dat.*) at; near; on; onto; to (6);
  an deiner Stelle if I were you, (if I
  were) in your place (12); **an der Ecke**
  at the corner (9)
der **Analphabet** (-en *masc.*) (-en) illiterate
  person
die **Analyse** (-n) analysis
analysieren to analyze
die **Anatomie** (-n) anatomy
anbeißen (**beißt an**), **biss an, angebissen**
  to take a bite (out of)
anbieten (**bietet an**), **bot an, angeboten** to
  offer
anbrennen (**brennt an**), **brannte an,**
  angebrannt to burn
anbringen (**bringt an**), **brachte an,**
  angebracht to put up, install
ander- different, other; **am anderen**
  Morgen the next morning; **der/die/das**
  andere (*decl. adj.*) the other one,
  different one; **(et)was anderes**
  something else
(**sich**) **ändern** to change
anders different(ly), in another way;
  jemand anders somebody else
anderswo elsewhere, somewhere/
  anywhere else
die **Änderung** (-en) change
anerkennen, erkannte an, anerkannt to
  recognize, acknowledge
der **Anfang** (-̈e) beginning, start; **am**
  Anfang in the beginning
anfangen (**fängt an**), **fing an, angefangen**
  to begin, start (4)
der **Anfänger** (-) / die **Anfängerin** (-nen)
  beginner
anfordern (**fordert an**) to request, order
anführen (**führt an**) to lead; to give,
  quote
die **Angabe** (-n) statement, information;
  persönliche Angaben personal
  information
angeben (**gibt an**), **gab an, angegeben** to
  state, declare, give

das **Angebot** (-e) (special) offer;
  selection (10)
die **Angelegenheit** (-en) matter, issue,
  affair
angeln to fish (7)
die **Angelrute** (-n) fishing rod
angenehm pleasant(ly) (7)
der/die **Angestellte** (*decl. adj.*) employee
die **Anglistik** (study of) English language
  and literature
die **Angst** (-̈e) fear (12); **Angst haben** (**vor**
  + *dat.*) to be afraid (of) (12); **keine**
  Angst don't be afraid
angucken (**guckt an**) (*coll.*) to look at; **sich**
  (*dat.*) **etwas angucken** (*coll.*) to look at
  something
der **Anhang** (-̈e) appendix; attachment
sich anhören (**hört an**) to listen to
der **Ankauf** purchase; **An- und Verkauf**
  buying and selling
ankommen (**kommt an**), **kam an, ist**
  angekommen to arrive (9)
ankreuzen (**kreuzt an**) to mark; to check off
die **Ankunft** (-̈e) arrival (10)
anlegen (**legt an**) to put on; to put down,
  lay out
das **Anmeldeformular** (-e) registration
  form (9)
(**sich**) **anmelden** (**meldet an**) to check in,
  register (9)
anmieten (**mietet an**) to rent
annehmbar acceptable
annehmen (**nimmt an**), **nahm an,**
  angenommen to accept, take
anno: pro anno per year, annual(ly)
anprobieren (**probiert an**), **anprobiert** to
  try on (5)
anreden (**redet an**) to address
anregen (**regt an**) to prompt, stimulate
die **Anreise** (-n) journey to a place; arrival
der **Anruf** (-e) (telephone) call
der **Anrufbeantworter** (-) answering
  machine (13)
anrufen (**ruft an**), **rief an, angerufen** to
  call up (on the phone) (4); **sich**
  anrufen to call one another
der **Anrufer** (-) / die **Anruferin** (-nen)
  caller
ans = **an das**
die **Ansage** (-n) announcement
der **Ansager** (-) / die **Ansagerin** (-nen)
  announcer
(**sich**) **etwas anschaffen** (**schafft an**) to
  purchase something, acquire
  something (14)
die **Anschaffung** (-en) purchase,
  acquisition
anschalten (**schaltet an**) to turn on
anschauen (**schaut an**) to look at; **sich**
  (*dat.*) **etwas anschauen** to look at,
  watch (13)
der **Anschlagzettel** (-) notice, bulletin
anschließend afterward
der **Anschluss** (-̈e) connection (10)
die **Anschrift** (-en) address
ansehen (**sieht an**), **sah an, angesehen** to
  watch; **sich** (*dat.*) **etwas ansehen** to
  watch, look at (13)

das Ansehen prestige (11)
die Ansicht (-en) view
ansprechen (spricht an), sprach an, ange-sprochen to talk to
(an)statt (+ *gen.*) instead of
anstehen (nach + *dat.***) (steht an), stand an, angestanden** to stand in line (for)
anstehend upcoming, waiting to be done
anstrengend tiring, strenuous (8)
der Anteil (-e) share
die Antikriegsdemonstration (-en) anti-war demonstration
das Antiquariat secondhand bookshop; **modernes Antiquariat** *shop or department selling remaindered books*
der Antrag (-̈e) application, request
die Antwort (-en) answer
antworten (auf + *acc.***)** to answer (to)
die Anzahl amount, number
die Anzeige (-n) (newspaper) advertisement
die Anzeigenannahme (-n) classified ad department
anziehen (zieht an), zog an, angezogen to put on; **sich anziehen** to get dressed (8)
die Anziehungskraft (-̈e) force of attraction; allure
der Anzug (-̈e) suit (5)
der Apfel (-̈) apple (5)
das Apfelmus applesauce (6)
der Apfelrotkohl *dish containing apples and red cabbage*
der Apfelstrudel (-) apple strudel, apple pastry (6)
die Apotheke (-n) pharmacy (5)
der Apparat (-e) set, appliance (*such as TV or telephone*) (9); **sich am Apparat melden** to answer the telephone
das Appartement (-s) one-room apartment
der Applaus (-e) applause
die Aprikose (-n) apricot
(der) April April (9)
das Aquarium (Aquarien) aquarium
das Äquivalent (-e) equivalent
(das) Arabien Arabia
die Arbeit (-en) work; job; assignment; paper (8)
arbeiten to work (1)
der Arbeiter (-) / die Arbeiterin (-nen) worker, laborer
der Arbeitgeber (-) / die Arbeitgeberin (-nen) employer (11)
der Arbeitnehmer (-) / die Arbeitnehmerin (-nen) employee
das Arbeitsamt (-̈er) employment office (11)
die Arbeitserfahrung (-en) work experience
arbeitsfrei off from work
die Arbeitsgemeinschaft (-en) work group, team
die Arbeitslage (-n) employment situation
der Arbeitslohn (-̈e) wage(s)
arbeitslos unemployed
die Arbeitslosigkeit unemployment (14)
der Arbeitsmarkt job market
das Arbeitsmittel (-) material(s); tool

der Arbeitsplatz (-̈e) workplace; position (11)
die Arbeitsstunde (-n) working hour
die Arbeitssuche (-n) job search
die Arbeitsvermittlung (-en) employment agency
die Arbeitszeit (-en) working hours
das Arbeitszimmer (-) workroom, study (2)
der Architekt (-en *masc.***) (-en) / die Architektin (-nen)** architect
die Architektur (-en) architecture
das Archiv (-e) archive
die ARD = Arbeitsgemeinschaft der Rundfunkanstalten Deutschlands (*German radio and television network*)
die Arena (Arenen) arena
(das) Argentinien Argentina
der Ärger annoyance, trouble
ärgerlich annoyed, angry; annoying, vexing
ärgern to annoy; **sich ärgern (über** + *acc.***)** to be annoyed (about) (12)
das Argument (-e) argument
arisch Aryan
arith. = arithmetisch arithmetical(ly)
arm poor
der Arm (-e) arm (8)
die Armee (-n) armed forces
die Armen (*pl.*) poor people
die Armut poverty (14)
arrangieren to arrange
arrogant arrogant(ly)
die Art (-en) kind, type; manner
der Artikel (-) article; item
das Arzneimittel (-) medication (14)
der Arzt (-̈e) / die Ärztin (-nen) physician, doctor (8)
die Arztkosten (*pl.*) medical costs
der Asbesthut (-̈e) asbestos hat
der Aspekt (-e) aspect
das Aspirin aspirin
die Assoziation (-en) association
assoziieren to associate
der AStA = Allgemeiner Studentenaus-schuss students' union
der Astronaut (-en *masc.***) (-en) / die Astronautin (-nen)** astronaut
die Atmosphäre (-n) atmosphere
die Atomkraft nuclear power
der Atomstreit nuclear conflict
attraktiv attractive(ly)
ätzend corrosive; caustic
au ouch
die Aubergine (-n) eggplant
auch also, too (1); **ich auch** me too
die Aue (-n) meadow
auf (+ *acc./dat.*) on, upon; on top of; at (6); onto; to; **auf Deutsch** in German (E); **auf jeden Fall** in any case (13); **auf welchen Namen?** under what name? (9); **auf Wiederhören** good-bye (*on the phone*) (9); **auf Wiedersehen** good-bye (E)
der Aufenthalt (-e) stay; layover (9)
auffallen (fällt auf), fiel auf, ist aufgefallen to stand out, be conspicuous

auffallend conspicuous(ly)
die Aufforderung (-en) request
die Aufgabe (-n) task; exercise
aufgeben (gibt auf), gab auf, aufgegeben to give up; to hand in
aufhören (mit + *dat.***) (hört auf)** to end, quit, stop (doing something) (4)
aufklären (über + *acc.***) (klärt auf)** to inform (about)
der Aufkleber (-) sticker
der Auflauf (-̈e) casserole (6)
auflisten (listet auf) to list
(sich) auflockern (lockert auf) to loosen up
aufmachen (macht auf) to open
aufnehmen (nimmt auf), nahm auf, aufgenommen to record (*on tape, video, etc.*) (13)
aufräumen (räumt auf) to clean up, straighten up (*a room*) (4)
aufregend exciting
die Aufregung (-en) excitement
aufs = auf das
der Aufsatz (-̈e) essay
der Aufschnitt cold cuts (5)
aufschreiben (schreibt auf), schrieb auf, aufgeschrieben to write down
der Aufseher (-) / die Aufseherin (-nen) guard, overseer
aufsetzen (setzt auf) to put on
der Aufstand (-̈e) rebellion, uprising
aufstehen (steht auf), stand auf, ist aufgestanden to get up; to stand up (4)
auftauen (taut auf) to thaw (out)
aufteilen (teilt auf) to divide
der Auftrag (-̈e) task, assignment
der Auftritt (-e) appearance (*on stage*)
aufwachen (wacht auf), ist aufgewacht to wake up (4)
aufwachsen (wächst auf), wuchs auf, ist aufgewachsen to grow up
aufweisen (weist auf), wies auf, aufgewiesen to demonstrate, show
der Aufzug (-̈e) elevator (9)
das Auge (-n) eye (8)
der Augenarzt (-̈e) / die Augenärztin (-nen) eye doctor, optometrist
die Augenfarbe (-n) eye color
(der) August August (3)
aus (+ *dat.*) from; out of; (made) of (5); **aus Baumwolle** made of cotton; **Ich komme aus ...** I'm from . . . (E)
ausarbeiten (arbeitet aus) to work out, develop
ausbauen (baut aus) to convert (*a room or building*)
die Ausbildung (-en) (career) training (11)
der Ausbildungsgang (-̈e) training course
der Ausbildungsplatz (-̈e) training position
die Ausbildungsstelle (-n) training position
die Ausbildungszeit (-en) training period
ausbrechen (bricht aus), brach aus, ausgebrochen to break out
der Ausdruck (-̈e) expression
ausdrücken (drückt aus) to express

auseinandernehmen (nimmt auseinander), nahm auseinander, auseinandergenommen to take apart

der Ausflug (¨e) excursion

die Ausflugsfahrt (-en) excursion (*by car, bus, etc.*)

ausfüllen (füllt aus) to fill out (9)

die Ausgabe (-n) expense (12)

ausgeben (gibt aus), gab aus, ausgegeben to spend (*money*) (12)

ausgehen (geht aus), ging aus, ist ausgegangen to go out (4)

ausgerechnet of all things

ausgesucht chosen, choice, select

ausgezeichnet excellent (E)

ausgleiten (gleitet aus), glitt aus, ist ausgeglitten to slip and fall

die Ausgrabung (-en) excavation

aushalten (hält aus), hielt aus, ausgehalten to endure

auskommen (kommt aus), kam aus, ist ausgekommen to make ends meet, get by with (*money*)

die Auskunft (¨e) information (10)

auslachen (lacht aus) to laugh at

das Ausland (*sg. only*) foreign countries (11); **im Ausland** abroad (11)

der Ausländer (-) / die Ausländerin (-nen) foreigner (14)

die Ausländerfeindlichkeit xenophobia, hatred toward foreigners (14)

die Auslandsspeise (-n) foreign food

die Ausnahme (-n) exception

ausprobieren (probiert aus), ausprobiert to try out

die Ausrede (-n) excuse

ausreichend sufficient(ly), enough

sich ausruhen (ruht aus) to rest

die Ausrüstung (-en) equipment

die Aussage (-n) statement

ausscheiden (scheidet aus), schied aus, ist ausgeschieden to be eliminated

ausschneiden (schneidet aus), schnitt aus, ausgeschnitten to cut out

der Ausschnitt (-e) excerpt

aussehen (sieht aus), sah aus, ausgesehen to look, appear

außer (+ *dat.*) except for, besides

äußer- outer

außerdem besides, in addition (14)

außerhalb (+ *gen.*) outside of (9)

(sich) äußern to express (oneself); **die Meinung äußern** to voice an opinion

die Äußerung (-en) statement

die Aussicht (-en) view, prospect

die Aussichtsseite (-n) side with a view

ausspannen (spannt aus) to rest, relax, take a break

die Aussprache (-n) pronunciation; discussion, talk

ausstatten (stattet aus) to equip, furnish

ausstellen (stellt aus) to put out; to display, exhibit

ausstreichen (streicht aus), strich aus, ausgestrichen to cross out, strike through

sich (*dat.*) **(et)was aussuchen (sucht aus)** to select, find, choose something (13)

austauschen (tauscht aus) to trade, exchange

der Austauschschüler (-) / die Austauschschülerin (-nen) exchange student (*high school*)

(das) Australien Australia

ausüben (übt aus) to practice, exercise, do

auswählen (wählt aus) to choose, select

auswandern (wandert aus), ist ausgewandert to emigrate

ausweichen (+ *dat.*) **(weicht aus), wich aus, ist ausgewichen** to get out of the way of, make way for

der Ausweis (-e) ID card

ausziehen (zieht aus), zog aus, ist ausgezogen to move out; **sich** (*acc.*) **ausziehen** to get undressed (8); **sich** (*dat.*) **etwas ausziehen** to take something off (*clothing etc.*)

der/die Auszubildende (*decl. adj.*) trainee, apprentice

der Auszug (¨e) excerpt, extract

das Auto (-s) car, auto (2)

die Autoabgase (*pl.*) exhaust fumes

die Autobahn (-en) highway

der Autodieb (-e) car thief

der Autofahrer (-) / die Autofahrerin (-nen) (automobile) driver

automatisch automatic(ally)

der Automechaniker (-) / die Automechanikerin (-nen) car mechanic

das Automobil (-e) automobile, car

der Autor (-en) / die Autorin (-nen) author

die Autoschlange (-n) long line of cars

Autostop: per Autostop reisen to hitch-hike (10)

das Autotelefon (-e) car telephone

der/die Azubi (-s) = **der/die Auszubildende**

B

die Babywäsche baby clothes

der Bäcker (-) / die Bäckerin (-nen) baker

die Bäckerei (-en) bakery (5)

das Bäckerhandwerk bakery trade

die Backwaren (*pl.*) baked goods

das Bad (¨er) bath; bathroom (2); spa

der Badeanzug (¨e) bathing suit (5)

die Badehose (-n) bathing trunks

der Bademantel (¨) bathrobe

die Bademoden (*pl.*) beachwear

baden to bathe

die Badesachen (*pl.*) beach accessories

das Badezimmer (-) bathroom (2)

das BAföG = **Bundesausbildungsförderungsgesetz** government financial aid for students

die Bahn (-en) train; railway (10); **mit der Bahn** by train; **die U-Bahn (-en)** subway

bahnen: den Weg bahnen to pave the way

der Bahnhof (¨e) train station (9)

der Bahnsteig (-e) (train) platform (10)

die Bakterie (-n) bacterium

bald soon (12); **möglichst bald** as soon as possible

der Baldrian (-e) valerian

der Balkon (-e) balcony (2)

der Ball (¨e) ball

die Ballade (-n) ballad

das Ballett (-e) ballet (4)

die Banane (-n) banana (5)

die Bande (-n) gang, mob

die Bank (¨e) bench

die Bank (-en) bank (*financial institution*) (9)

die Bankkauffrau (-en) (female) bank administrator

der Bankkaufmann (Bankkaufleute) (male) bank administrator

die Banknote (-n) banknote

bar in cash

die Bar (-s) bar

der Bär (-en *masc.***) (-en)** bear

die Baracke (-n) hut, shack

die Barfrau (-en) barmaid

das Bargeld cash (10)

der Baron (-e) / die Baronin (-nen) baron / baroness

der Baseball baseball

Baseler (*adj.*) of/from Basel (Switzerland)

das Basilikum basil

die Basis (Basen) basis

die Batterie (-n) battery

der Bau (Bauten) building; construction

der Bauch (¨e) belly, abdomen, stomach (8)

der Bauchredner (-) / die Bauchrednerin (-nen) ventriloquist

die Bauchschmerzen (*pl.*) bellyache, stomachache

bauen to build (12)

der Bauer (-n *masc.***) (-n) / die Bäuerin (-nen)** farmer

das Bauernhaus (¨er) farmhouse (12)

der Bauernhof (¨e) farm

der Baum (¨e) tree

der Baumast (¨e) tree branch, bough

die Baumwolle cotton

der Bauplan (¨e) building plan

die Baustelle (-n) building site

bayerisch (*adj.*) Bavarian

(das) Bayern Bavaria

Bayreuther (*adj.*) of/from Bayreuth (*a town in Bavaria*)

bayrisch (*adj.*) Bavarian

der Beamte (*decl. adj.*) **/ die Beamtin (-nen)** agent; government employee

beantworten to answer

bearbeiten to work on, deal with

das Bedauern regret

bedeuten to mean, signify; **Was bedeutet … ?** What does . . . mean? (E)

die Bedeutung (-en) meaning, significance

bedienen to serve

die Bedienung service (6)

das Bedienungsgeld service charge

sich beeilen to hurry (up) (8)

beeindrucken to impress

beenden to complete, finish, end

sich befassen mit (+ *dat.*) to occupy oneself with

befehlen (befiehlt), befahl, befohlen to order, command

das Befinden health, well-being

befragen to question

beginnen, begann, begonnen to begin, start (10)

die Begegnung (-en) meeting, encounter

begeistert enthusiastic(ally)

begreifen, begriff, begriffen to understand, comprehend

der Begründer (-) / die Begründerin (-nen) founder

begrüßen to greet, welcome

die Begrüßung (-en) greeting

behandeln to treat, deal with (14)

behaupten to claim, assert (13)

die Behauptung (-en) claim, assertion

behilflich helpful

bei (+ *dat.*) at; near; with (5); at the place of

beibehalten (behält bei), behielt bei, beibehalten to keep, retain

beide (*pl.*) both

der Beifahrer (-) / die Beifahrerin (-nen) (front-seat) passenger

der Beifahrersitz (-e) passenger seat

beifügen (fügt bei) to add; to enclose

beige beige (5)

die Beilage (-n) side dish (6)

beim = bei dem

das Bein (-e) leg (8)

das Beispiel (-e) example; **zum Beispiel** for example

beißen, biss, gebissen to bite

der Beitrag (-̈e) contribution

beitreten (+ *dat.*) **(tritt bei), trat bei, ist beigetreten** to join

bekämpfen to combat, fight against

bekannt acquainted, known; well-known; **bekannt werden** to get acquainted

der/die Bekannte (*decl. adj.*) acquaintance

bekennen, bekannte, bekannt to admit, confess

die Bekleidung clothing, attire

bekommen, bekam, bekommen to receive, get (6); **Was bekommen Sie?** What will you have? (6)

belasten to burden

beleben to animate, liven up

(das) Belgien Belgium (E)

der Belgier (-) / die Belgierin (-nen) Belgian (*person*)

beliebt popular (7)

die Belohnung (-en) reward

bemerken to observe, notice

die Bemerkung (-en) remark, comment

benutzbar usable

benutzen to use

der Benutzerausweis (-e) user ID

die Benutzung use

das Benzin gasoline (12)

die Benzinsteuer (-n) gasoline tax

bequem comfortable, comfortably (2)

die Beratung (-en) advising (11); consultation

berechenbar predictable

der Bereich (-e) area, field

bereit sein to be ready, be willing

bereits already

bereuen to regret

der Berg (-e) mountain (7)

die Bergseite (-n) side facing the mountain(s)

das Bergsteigen mountain climbing

die Bergwanderung (-en) hike in the mountains

der Bericht (-e) report (13)

berichten to report, narrate (13)

Berliner (*adj.*) of/from Berlin; **der Berliner Pfannkuchen (-)** jelly doughnut

der Berliner (-) / die Berlinerin (-nen) person from Berlin

der Beruf (-e) profession, occupation (1); **Was sind Sie von Beruf?** What do you do for a living? (1)

beruflich professional(ly), on business

die Berufsaufbauschule (-n) *(night) school toward a vocational college degree*

die Berufsausbildung vocational training

der Berufsberater (-) / die Berufsberaterin (-nen) employment counselor (11)

die Berufsberatung job counseling, vocational guidance

berufsbildender Abschluss trade school degree

die Berufsfachschule (-n) vocational college

das Berufsgrundbildungsjahr (-e) year of basic vocational training

das Berufsleben professional life, working life (11)

der Berufsplan (-̈e) career plan

berufsqualifizierend providing qualifications for a profession

die Berufsschule (-n) vocational school

der/die Berufstätige (*decl. adj.*) working person

die Berufswahl (-en) career choice

berühmt famous

berühren to touch; to affect

besänftigen to appease, placate

die Besatzungstruppen (*pl.*) occupation troops

die Besatzungszone (-n) occupied zone

beschäftigen to employ (11); **sich beschäftigen mit** (+ *dat.*) to occupy oneself with (11)

beschließen, beschloss, beschlossen to decide

beschreiben, beschrieb, beschrieben to describe

die Beschreibung (-en) description

die Beschwerde (-n) complaint

sich beschweren (über + *acc.*) to complain (about) (9)

beseitigen to remove, get rid of

der Besen (-) broom

der Besenstiel (-e) broomstick

besetzen to occupy; **besetzt** occupied, taken (6); **Hier ist besetzt.** This place is taken. (6)

besichtigen to view, see

besitzen, besaß, besessen to own, possess (11)

der Besitzer (-) / die Besitzerin (-nen) owner

besonder- special, particular; **etwas/nichts Besonderes** something/nothing special

besonders especially, particularly (8); **nicht besonders gut** not especially well (E)

besorgen to purchase, procure, get

besprechen (bespricht), besprach, besprochen to discuss, talk about

die Besprechung (-en) discussion; conference

besser better

die Besserung: Gute Besserung! Get well soon! (8)

best- best; **am besten** (the) best; **Wie komme ich am besten dahin?** What's the best way to get there? (9)

beständig continous(ly)

bestehen, bestand, bestanden to pass (an exam); **bestehen aus** (+ *dat.*) to consist of

bestellen to order (6); to reserve

der Bestellservice order service

die Bestellung (-en) order; reservation

bestens excellently, to the highest level

bestimmen to determine, decide

bestimmt (*adj.*) particular, certain; (*adv.*) no doubt; definitely (1)

der Besuch (-e) visit; visitors; **zu Besuch kommen** to come for a visit (1)

besuchen to visit (1)

der Besucher (-) / die Besucherin (-nen) visitor, guest

der/die Beteiligte (*decl. adj.*) person involved

betragen (beträgt), betrug, betragen to amount to, come to; **die Miete beträgt …** the rent comes to . . .

betreffen (betrifft), betraf, betroffen to concern; to affect (14)

betreiben, betrieb, betrieben to drive; to run

der Betrieb (-e) business, firm; operation

die Betriebswirtschaft business management

das Bett (-en) bed (2)

die Bettwäsche linens (9)

bevor (*subord. conj.*) before (10)

bewahren vor (+ *dat.*) to protect from

(sich) bewegen to move, move about

beweglich movable

der Beweis (-e) proof, evidence

beweisen, bewies, bewiesen to prove

sich bewerben (um + *acc.*) **(bewirbt), bewarb, beworben** to apply (for) (11)

der Bewerber (-) / die Bewerberin (-nen) applicant

die Bewerbung (-en) application (11)

das Bewerbungsformular (-e) application form (11)

bewerten to evaluate

die Bewertung (-en) evaluation, assessment

bewirken to cause, bring about

der Bewohner (-) / die Bewohnerin (-nen) resident, tenant

bewölkt cloudy, overcast (7)

bewundern to admire

bewusst conscious, aware

bezahlen to pay

bezeichnen als to call, describe as

die Bezeichnung (-en) label, term
sich beziehen auf (+ *acc.*), bezog, bezogen to refer to
die Beziehung (-en) relationship; affair
die Beziehungskiste (-n) (*coll.*) difficult relationship
der Bezug: mit Bezug auf (+ *acc.*) with reference to
die Bezugsgruppe (-n) reference group
bezweifeln to doubt
bezwingen, bezwang, bezwungen to conquer
die Bibliothek (-en) library (4)
der Bibliothekar (-e) / die Bibliothekarin (-nen) librarian (11)
der Bielefelder (-) / die Bielefelderin (-nen) person from Bielefeld (*town in northern Germany*)
das Bier (-e) beer (5)
der Bierdeckel (-) beer coaster
der Biergarten (⁻) beer garden (*restaurant*) (6)
der Bierkeller (-) *type of restaurant where beer is served*
der Bierkrug (⁻e) beer stein, beer mug
bieten, bot, geboten to offer, present
das Biken (motor)biking
der Bikini (-s) bikini, two-piece bathing suit
das Bild (-er) picture
bilden to form
der Bildschirmschoner (-) screen saver
das Bildsymbol (-e) pictogram
der Bildungsabschluss (⁻e) educational diploma
die Bildungswissenschaft (-en) science/field of education
das Billard (-e) billiards
billig inexpensive(ly), cheap(ly) (2)
die Billiguhr (-en) cheap watch
bin am; Ich bin ... I am . . . (E)
binden, band, gebunden to tie (up)
die Biographie (-n) biography
die Biokost organic food
der Bioladen (⁻) natural foods store (5)
das Biolebensmittel (-) organic food (8)
die Biologie biology
biologisch biological(ly)
der Biotechnologe (-n *masc.*) (-n) / die Biotechnologin (-nen) biotechnician
bis (+ *acc.*) until (6); to, up to; bis (um) fünf Uhr until five o'clock (6); bis zum/zur (+ *dat.*) to, as far as (9); von zwei bis drei Uhr from two to three o'clock (6)
bisher so far, up to now
bisherig previous
ein bisschen a little (bit); somewhat
bissig biting; cutting, caustic
bist are (*2nd person inform. sg.*); du bist you are
das Bistro (-s) bistro
bitte please; you're welcome (E); bitte schön you're welcome; please; bitte sehr you're welcome; please; Wie bitte? Pardon? What did you say? (E); Würden Sie bitte ... ? Would you please . . . ? (9)

bitten, bat, gebeten to ask; bitten um (+ *acc.*) to ask for, request (12)
blasen (bläst), blies, geblasen to blow
das Blatt (⁻er) leaf; sheet (of paper)
blau blue (5); in Blau in blue
blauweiß blue and white
das Blei (-e) lead
bleiben, blieb, ist geblieben to stay, remain (1)
der Bleigurt (-e) lead belt
der Bleistift (-e) pencil (12)
der Blick (-e) look, glance; view;
blitzen to flash (7); Es blitzt. There's lightning. (7)
die Blockade (-n) blockade
blockieren to block; to blockade
blockweise in blocks
blöd stupid (13); Das ist mir zu blöd. I think that's really stupid. (13)
bloggen to blog, keep an online journal (7)
die Blondine (-n) blonde woman
bloß merely; only
blühen to blossom
die Blume (-n) flower
das Blumengeschäft (-e) flower shop
der Blumenkohl cauliflower (5)
die Bluse (-n) blouse (5)
die Blusengröße (-n) blouse size
der BMW (-s) (Bayerische Motoren Werke) BMW automobile
die Bockwurst (⁻e) *type of German sausage*
der Boden (⁻) floor of a room; ground
das Bodybuilding bodybuilding; Bodybuilding machen to do bodybuilding, do weight training (7)
das Bogenschießen archery
die Bohne (-n) bean (6); grüne Bohne green bean, string bean
böig gusty; squally
(das) Bolivien Bolivia
das Boot (-e) boat
der Bootsführer (-) / die Bootsführerin (-nen) boat guide
die Börse (-n) stock exchange (13)
böse angry, mad; angrily; mean; bad
(das) Bosnien Bosnia
der Boss (-e) (*coll.*) boss
die Boutique (-n) boutique, trendy shop
das Bowling bowling
die Box (-en) stereo speaker
der Brandstifter (-) arsonist
(das) Brasilien Brazil
braten (brät), briet, gebraten to fry; to roast
die Bratkartoffeln (*pl.*) fried potatoes (6)
die Bratwurst (⁻e) *type of German sausage*
brauchen to need (2)
das Brauhaus (⁻er) brewery
braun brown (5)
bräunen to tan
das Braunglas brown glass
die BRD = Bundesrepublik Deutschland
das Breakdancen break dancing
brechen (bricht), brach, gebrochen to break

Bremer (*adj.*) of/from Bremen; die Bremer Stadtmusikanten the Bremen Town Musicians
die Bremse (-n) brake
brennen, brannte, gebrannt to burn
bretonisch (*adj.*) Breton
das Brett (-er) board; das Schwarze Brett bulletin board
der Bretterwagen (-) wagon/truck for hauling lumber
das Brevier (-e) breviary
die Brezel (-n) pretzel (6)
der Brief (-e) letter (7)
der Brieffreund (-e) / die Brieffreundin (-nen) pen pal
die Briefmarke (-n) postage stamp (7)
der Briefträger (-) / die Briefträgerin (-nen) mail carrier
die Brille (-n) (pair of) eyeglasses (5)
bringen, brachte, gebracht to bring (7)
der Brite (-n *masc.*) (-n) / die Britin (-nen) Briton, British person
britisch (*adj.*) British
der Brokkoli broccoli (5)
die Broschüre (-n) brochure, pamphlet
das Brot (-e) (loaf of) bread (5)
das Brötchen (-) bread roll (5)
die Brücke (-n) bridge
der Bruder (⁻) brother (3)
der Brunch (-[e]s) brunch
der Brunnen (-) spring, well; fountain
die Brust (⁻e) breast; chest (8)
das Buch (⁻er) book (1)
der Buchdruck letterpress printing
buchen to book (*a trip*) (10)
das Bücherregal (-e) bookcase, bookshelf (2)
die Büchertasche (-n) bookbag
die Buchhandlung (-en) bookshop
der Buchstabe (-n *masc.*) (-n) letter (of the alphabet)
buchstabieren to spell
die Buchung (-en) booking, reservation
das Budget (-s) budget
das Büffet (-s) buffet
die Bühne (-n) stage
die Bühnenanweisung (-en) stage direction
das Bühnenbild (-er) stage decoration
der Bühnentext (-e) script (for a stage play)
das Bundesausbildungsförderungsgesetz (BAföG) *government financial aid for students*
die Bundesbank (-en) federal bank
der Bundeskanzler (-) / die Bundeskanzlerin (-nen) (German or Austrian) chancellor
das Bundesland (⁻er) German state
die Bundesliga federal division, federal league
das Bundesministerium (Bundesministerien) federal ministry
die Bundesrepublik federal republic; die Bundesrepublik Deutschland (BRD) Federal Republic of Germany
der Bundesstaat (-en) federal state; state (of the USA)

der **Bundestag** federal German parliament

das **Bundestagsgebäude** federal German parliament building

bündig concise, succinct

das **Bungeejumping** bungee jumping

der **Bunker** (-) bunker

bunt colorful

die **Burg** (-en) fortress, castle

der **Bürger** (-) / die **Bürgerin** (-nen) citizen (14)

das **Bürgerhaus** (¨er) (bourgeois) town house

die **Bürgerinitiative** (-n) citizens' group; grassroots movement

der **Bürgermeister** (-) / die **Bürgermeisterin** (-nen) mayor

das **Büro** (-s) office (11)

das **Bürohaus** (¨er) office building

die **Bürokauffrau** (-en) (female) office administrator

der **Bürokaufmann** (¨er) (male) office administrator

der **Bus** (-se) bus (10)

die **Bushaltestelle** (-n) bus stop

die **Buslinie** (-n) bus line

der **Busunfall** (¨e) bus accident

die **Butter** butter (5)

der **Button** (-s) button

bzw. = **beziehungsweise** respectively; or

C

ca. = **circa, zirka** approximately, about

das **Café** (-s) café (6)

die **Cafeteria** (Cafeterien) cafeteria

der **Camcorder** (-) camcorder, handheld video camera (13)

das **Camp** (-s) camp

campen to camp

das **Camping** camping

die **Campingausrüstung** camping equipment

der **Campingplatz** (¨e) campground

der **Campus** (-) (school) campus

der **Cappuccino** (-s) cappuccino

der **Cartoon** (-s) cartoon

das **Casino** (-s) casino

das **Cassettendeck** (-s) cassette deck, tape deck

die **CD** (-s) CD, compact disc

der **CD-Spieler** (-) CD player (2)

das **Cello** (-s) cello

Celsius centigrade

der **Cent** (-[s]) cent

die **Cerealien** (pl.) cereal

CH (= **Confoederatio Helvetica**) official name of Switzerland

der **Champignon** (-s) mushroom

die **Chance** (-n) chance; opportunity

der **Chaot** (-en masc.) (-en) scatterbrain; anarchist

chaotisch chaotic

der **Charakter** (-e) character, personality

charakterisieren to characterize

die **Charakterisierung** (-en) characterization

charakteristisch characteristic

chatten to chat (online)

die **Checkliste** (-n) checklist

checken to check

der **Chef** (-s) / die **Chefin** (-nen) manager, boss, head (11)

die **Chemie** chemistry

die **Chemieprüfung** (-en) chemistry test

die **Chemikalie** (-n) chemical

der **Chemiker** (-) / die **Chemikerin** (-nen) chemist

chemisch chemical

CHF = der **Schweizer Franken** Swiss Franc

(das) **China** China

chinesisch (adj.) Chinese

der **Chor** (¨e) choir, chorus

die **Chronik** (-en) chronicle

chronisch chronic(ally)

chronologisch chronological(ly)

circa = **zirka** approximately, about

der **Clou** (-s) (coll.) main point, highlight

der **Clown** (-s) / die **Clownin** (-nen) clown

der **Club** = der **Klub**

der **Cocktail** (-s) cocktail

der **Cognac** (-s) cognac

die **Cola** (-s) cola

das **Comicheft** (-e) comic book

der **Computer** (-) computer (2)

der **Computeranschluss** (¨e) computer connection (2)

die **Computerdiskette** (-n) computer diskette (12)

das **Computerspiel** (-e) computer game; **Computerspiele spielen** to play computer games (1)

die **Computertechnik** computer technology

die **Computertechnologie** (-n) computer technology

die **Computerwissenschaft** (-en) computer science

der **Container** (-) recycling bin

die **Cornflakes** (pl.) cornflakes

der **Couchtisch** (-e) coffee table (2)

die **Couleur** (-s) shade, persuasion; sort

der **Coupon** (-s) coupon

der **Cousin** (-s) male cousin

die **Cousine** (-n) = **Kusine** female cousin

der **Cowboy** (-s) cowboy

die **Crew** (-s) crew, team

die **Currywurst** (¨e) sausage served with curry powder and ketchup

die **Cyberkriminalität** cybercrime

D

da there (2); here; (subord. conj.) since; **da drüben** over there (6); **hie und da** here and there

dabei with that; in that context

dabeihaben (hat dabei) to have with one

das **Dach** (¨er) roof (12)

das **Dachgeschoss** (-e) top floor, attic (12)

die **Dachwohnung** (-en) attic apartment

dafür for that; **Ich bin dafür.** I'm in favor of it. (14)

dagegen against that; on the other hand; **Ich bin dagegen.** I'm against it. (14)

daher from there; for that reason, therefore

dahin there (to that place); **Wie komme ich am besten dahin?** What's the best way to get there? (9)

dahinter behind that

damals formerly; at that time, (back) then

die **Dame** (-n) lady; **meine Damen und Herren** ladies and gentlemen

der **Damenhut** (¨e) ladies' hat

die **Damenkonfektion** (-en) ladies' wear

der **Damenschuh** (-e) ladies' shoe

die **Damenwäsche** lingerie, ladies' undergarments

damit with that; (subord. conj.) so that

danach after that; afterward

daneben next to that

(das) **Dänemark** Denmark (E)

der **Dank** thanks; **Gott sei Dank** thank God; **Vielen Dank!** Many thanks! (6)

dankbar grateful, thankful

danke thanks (E); **danke, gut** fine, thanks (E); **danke schön** thank you very much (E); **danke sehr** thanks a lot (1); **nein danke** no, thank you

danken (+ dat.) to thank (5); **Nichts zu danken.** No thanks necessary; Don't mention it. (8)

dann then

daran on that; at that; to that; **es liegt daran, dass** ... it is because . . .

darauf on that; for that; to that

darin in that; in there

das **Darlehen** (-) loan

darstellen (stellt dar) to portray, depict

der **Darsteller** (-) / die **Darstellerin** (-nen) actor/actress

die **Darstellung** (-en) portrayal

darüber above that; about that

darum therefore

darunter under that; among them

das that, this; **Das ist** ... This is . . . (E); the

dass (subord. conj.) that (8)

dasselbe the same

die **Datei** (-en) data file

die **Daten** (pl.) data

der **Dativ** dative case

das **Dativobjekt** (-e) dative object

die **Dativpräposition** (-en) preposition governing the dative case

das **Dativpronomen** (-) pronoun in the dative case

das **Datum** (Daten) date; **Welches Datum ist heute/morgen?** What is today's/tomorrow's date? (3)

dauerhaft durable

dauern to last; to take (time) (7)

davon of that; about that; of them

davor before that; in front of that

dazu to that; for that; in addition to that

dazugeben (gibt dazu), gab dazu, dazugegeben to add

dazugehören (gehört dazu) to belong to that/them

dazwischen between them; during that

die **DDR** = **Deutsche Demokratische Republik** German Democratic Republic

debattieren to debate

das **Debüt** (-s) debut

die **Decke** (-n) ceiling; blanket, cover

decken to cover; **den Tisch decken** to set the table

dein your (*inform. sg.*) (3)

die Delikatesse (-n) delicacy

demokratisch democratic(ally)

die Demonstration (-en) demonstration, rally (14)

demonstrieren to demonstrate

denken, dachte, gedacht to think; **denken an** (*+ acc.*) to think about/of (12)

das Denkmal (-er) monument

denn (*coord. conj.*) for, because (7); then; (*particle used in questions to express interest*); **Was ist denn los?** What's the matter? (2)

die Deponie (-n) garbage dump

deprimiert depressed (8)

der, die, das the; that one; who, which

derselbe the same

deshalb therefore, for that reason (8)

der Designer (-) / die Designerin (-nen) designer

das Dessin (-s) design, pattern

desto: je ... desto ... the ... the ...

deswegen because of that (12)

das Detail (-s) detail

detailliert detailed

der Detektiv (-e) / die Detektivin (-nen) (private) detective

der Detektivroman (-e) detective novel

deutsch (*adj.*) German; **deutsch-akzentuiert** German-accented

(das) Deutsch German (language) (1); **auf Deutsch** in German (E)

der/die Deutsche (*decl. adj.*) German (person)

die Deutsche Demokratische Republik (DDR) German Democratic Republic (GDR)

die Deutsche Mark (DM) (-) German mark

der Deutschkurs (-e) German course

(das) Deutschland Germany (E); **die Bundesrepublik Deutschland (BRD)** Federal Republic of Germany (FRG)

der Deutschlehrer (-) / die Deutschlehrerin (-nen) German teacher

deutschsprachig German-speaking

deutschstämmig of German heritage

der Deutschunterricht German class

(der) Dezember December (3)

dezent discreet(ly), unostentatious(ly)

der DFB-Pokal DFB Cup (*championship trophy of the **Deutscher Fußball-Bund***)

d.h. = das heißt that is, i.e. (8)

der Dialekt (-e) dialect

die Dialektik dialectics

der Dialog (-e) dialogue

dich you (*inform. sg. acc.*) (3); **grüß dich** hello, hi (*among friends and family*) (E)

der Dichter (-) / die Dichterin (-nen) poet

dichtmachen (macht dicht) (*coll.*) to close, shut (down)

dick fat; **dick machen** to be fattening

die the

der Dieb (-e) / die Diebin (-nen) thief

die Diele (-n) front hall (12)

dienen to serve, be in service

der Dienst (-e) service; duty

(der) Dienstag Tuesday (3)

dienstags Tuesdays, on Tuesday(s) (4)

das Dienstjubiläum (Dienstjubiläen) anniversary of service

der Dienstleister (-) / die Dienstleisterin (-nen) worker

dieselbe the same

der Dieselmotor (-en) diesel engine

dieser, diese, dies(es) this (2)

diesmal this time

digital digital(ly)

die Digitalkamera (-s) digital camera (13)

die Digitaluhr (-en) digital watch

die Diktatur (-en) dictatorship

das Dilemma (-s) dilemma

der Dilettant (-en *masc.*) (-en) / die Dilettantin (-nen) dilettante

dilettantisch amateurish(ly)

der Dill dill (*herb*)

das Ding (-e) thing, object (10)

die Diplomarbeit (-en) dissertation (*for an academic degree*)

der Diplomat (-en *masc.*) (-en) / die Diplomatin (-nen) diplomat

dir (to/for) you (*inform. sg. dat.*) (5); **Was fehlt dir?** What's the matter? (8); **Wie geht's dir?** How are you? (*inform.*) (E)

direkt direct(ly); (*coll.*) really

das Direktwahltelefon (-e) direct-dial telephone

der Dirigent (-en *masc.*) (-en) / die Dirigentin (-nen) (orchestra) conductor

der Discman (-s) Discman, portable CD player

die Disko (-s) disco, dance club (4); **in die Disko gehen** to go to a disco, go clubbing (4)

die Diskussion (-en) discussion

diskutieren über (*+ acc.*) to discuss (1); to debate

die D-Mark = die Deutsche Mark

doch still, nevertheless; (*intensifying particle used with imperatives*) (4)

das Dokument (-e) document (13)

der Dokumentarfilm (-e) documentary film (13)

der Dollar (-[s]) dollar

der Dollarschein (-e) dollar bill

der Dolmetscher (-) / die Dolmetscherin (-nen) interpreter (11)

die Dolomiten (*pl.*) the Dolomites

der Dom (-e) cathedral

die Donau Danube (*river*)

donnern to thunder (7); **Es donnert.** It's thundering. (7)

(der) Donnerstag Thursday (3)

donnerstags Thursdays, on Thursday(s) (4)

das Donnerwetter: (zum) Donnerwetter! (*exclamation of anger or annoyance*)

das Doppelzimmer (-) double room, room with two beds (9)

das Dorf (-er) village

der Dorfkrug (-e) village inn, village pub

dort there

die Dose (-n) (tin or aluminum) can; jar (14); box

downloaden (downloadet), downgeloadet to download

dpa = Deutsche Presse-Agentur German Press Agency

Dr. = Doktor doctor

der Draht (-e) wire; thread

die Draisine (-n) dandy-horse (*predecessor of the bicycle*)

das Drama (Dramen) drama

dran = daran; dran sein to have (one's) turn

drastisch drastic(ally)

draußen outside (7)

die Dreharbeiten (*pl.*) shooting of a film

(sich) drehen to turn, spin; **einen Film drehen** to shoot a film

drei three (E)

dreihundert three hundred (E)

dreimal three times (7)

dreisprachig trilingual

dreißig thirty (E)

dreißigjährig: der Dreißigjährige Krieg the Thirty Years' War

dreitägig lasting three days

dreitausend three thousand (E)

dreizehn thirteen (E)

dreizehnte thirteenth (3)

die Dreizimmerwohnung (-en) three-room apartment

Dresdner (*adj.*) of/from Dresden (*city in eastern Germany*)

drin = darin (*coll.*) inside

dringend urgent(ly) (2)

drinnen inside (7)

dritt: zu dritt as a threesome (10)

dritte third (3)

ein Drittel a third

die Droge (-n) drug; medicine (14)

die Drogensucht drug addiction (14)

die Drogerie (-n) drugstore (*toiletries and sundries*) (5)

drohen to threaten

drüben, da drüben over there (6); on the other side

drucken to print (13)

das Drücken pressure

der Drucker (-) printer (13)

drum = darum (*coll.*) therefore

der Dschungel (-) jungle

du you (*inform. sg.*) (1)

dual (*adj.*) dual

dudeln to toot

der Duft (-e) aroma, fragrance

dumm dumb, stupid

die Dummheit (-en) stupidity

dunkel dark (2)

dunkelblau dark blue

dünn thin; slender, skinny

durch (*+ acc.*) through (3); by, by means of

durcharbeiten (arbeitet durch) to work through

das Durcheinander confusion; commotion

durchkommen (kommt durch), kam durch, ist durchgekommen to come through, get through

durchlaufen (läuft durch), lief durch, ist durchgelaufen to run through, go through

durchlesen (liest durch), las durch, durchgelesen to read through

durchs = durch das

der Durchschnitt (-e) average; im Durchschnitt on average

durchschnittlich on average (12)

durchstreichen (streicht durch), strich durch, durchgestrichen to cross out, strike through

dürfen (darf), durfte, gedurft to be permitted to; may (4); Hier darf man nicht parken. You may not park here. (4); Was darf's sein? What will you have?

der Durst thirst; Durst haben to be thirsty (2)

die Dusche (-n) shower, shower bath (9)

(sich) duschen to take a shower (8)

duzen to address with du (informally)

die DVD (-s) DVD

der DVD-Spieler (-) DVD player (2)

dynamisch dynamic(ally)

E

eben just; simply

die Ebene (-n) plain; plane, level

echt genuine(ly); (coll.) really (1)

die Ecke (-n) corner (9); an der Ecke at the corner (9)

egal: Das ist mir egal. I don't care. (5)

ehemalig former

eher rather, sooner

die Ehre (-n) honor

ehrlich honest

das Ei (-er) egg (5)

die Eierbox (-en) egg carton

der Eierlikör egg liqueur

eigen own (12)

die Eigeninitiative (-n) one's own initiative

die Eigenregie one's own control

die Eigenschaft (-en) characteristic; trait

eigenständig independent(ly)

eigentlich actual(ly), real(ly)

die Eigentumswohnung (-en) condominium

eilen to hurry

ein, eine a(n); one; Es ist eins. / Es ist ein Uhr. It's one o'clock. (4); was für ein … what kind of a . . . (11)

einander one another, each other

einbegriffen included

einbiegen (biegt ein), bog ein, ist eingebogen to turn, make a turn (9)

einbringen (bringt ein), brachte ein, eingebracht to bring in, yield

einer, eine, eines one (of several)

einfach simple; simply; one-way (ticket) (10)

einfallen (fällt ein), fiel ein, ist eingefallen: etwas fällt mir ein something occurs to me

der Einfluss (-e) influence

einführen (führt ein) to introduce (14)

die Einführung (-en) introduction

der Eingang (-e) entrance, entryway (12)

eingedeutscht Germanized

der Eingriff (-e) small (surgical) operation

einheimisch native; local

die Einheit (-en) unity; unit

einholen (holt ein) to catch up with

einhundert one hundred (E)

einig united; in agreement

einige (pl.) several, some

einiges several things

die Einigung (-en) unification

der Einkauf (-e) purchase

einkaufen (kauft ein) to shop (4); einkaufen gehen to go shopping (4)

der Einkaufsboulevard (-s) street for shopping

der Einkaufstag (-e) day for shopping

das Einkaufszentrum (Einkaufszentren) shopping center

der Einkaufszettel (-) shopping list

das Einkommen income (11)

einladen (lädt ein), lud ein, eingeladen to invite (4)

die Einladung (-en) invitation

einleiten (leitet ein) to introduce

die Einleitung (-en) introduction

einmal once (7); einmal die Woche once a week (7); einmal im Monat/ Jahr once a month/year (7)

der Einmal-Fotoapparat (-e) disposable camera

einmalig unique

der Einmalrasierer (-) disposable razor

die Einnahmen (pl.) income (12)

einnehmen (nimmt ein), nahm ein, eingenommen to take (medicine)

einordnen (ordnet ein) to put in order; to classify, categorize

einrichten (richtet ein) to furnish, equip (12)

die Einrichtung (-en) furnishings

eins (numeral) one (E); Es ist eins. It's one (o'clock). (4)

einschlafen (schläft ein), schlief ein, ist eingeschlafen to fall asleep (4)

einschlägig specialist, relevant

einsenden, sandte ein, eingesandt to send in

einsetzen (setzt ein) to insert

der Einsetzer (-) / die Einsetzerin (-nen) risk taker

einsparen (spart ein) to save, conserve

einsteigen (steigt ein), stieg ein, ist eingestiegen to board, get into (a vehicle) (10)

eintausend one thousand (E)

die Eintracht harmony

eintragen (trägt ein), trug ein, eingetragen to register; eingetragener Verein (e.V.) registered organization

einverstanden sein (mit + dat.) to agree (with), be in agreement (with) (10)

der Einwanderer (-) / die Einwanderin (-nen) immigrant

einwandern (wandert ein), ist eingewandert to immigrate

die Einwanderung (-en) immigration

die Einwanderungsbehörde (-n) department of immigration

die Einwegflasche (-n) nonreturnable bottle

einwöchig lasting one week

der Einwohner (-) / die Einwohnerin (-nen) resident, inhabitant

das Einwohnermeldeamt (-er) government office for registration of residents

die Einzelheit (-en) detail, particular

einzeln individual; scattered

der Einzelunterricht (-e) one-on-one teaching

das Einzelzimmer (-) single room, room with one bed (9)

einziehen in (+ acc.) (zieht ein), zog ein, ist eingezogen to move in(to) (12)

einzig only, sole; nicht ein einziges Wort not a single word

das Eis ice cream; ice (5)

der Eisbecher (-) dish of ice cream (6)

die Eiscreme ice cream

die Eiscrempaste ice cream paste

der Eiskaffee (-s) iced coffee (mixed with ice cream and topped with whipped cream)

der Eissalat (-e) iceberg lettuce

das Eisstadion (Eisstadien) ice-skating rink (7)

die Elbe Elbe (River)

die Elblandschaft (-en) landscape of the Elbe River region

das Elbufer (-) bank of the Elbe

der Elefant (-en masc.) (-en) elephant

elegant elegant(ly)

die Elektrizität electricity

das Elektrogerät (-e) electrical appliance

der Elektroinstallateur (-e) / die Elektroinstallateurin (-nen) electrician

die Elektronik electronics

der Elektroniker (-) / die Elektronikerin (-nen) electronics engineer

elektronisch electronic(ally)

das Element (-e) element

elf eleven (E)

elfmal eleven times

das Elfmeterschießen penalty kick

elfte eleventh (3)

der Ell(en)bogen (-) elbow (8)

(das) Elsass Alsace

die Eltern (pl.) parents (3)

das Elternschlafzimmer (-) parents' bedroom

die E-Mail (-s) e-mail (13)

der Emmentaler Käse Emmental cheese

der Empfang (-e) reception

empfangen (empfängt), empfing, empfangen to receive (13)

der Empfänger (-) / die Empfängerin (-nen) recipient

empfänglich receptive, susceptible

die Empfangsanlage (-n) receiver

empfehlen (empfiehlt), empfahl, empfohlen to recommend (5)

die Empfehlung (-en) recommendation

Emser (adj.) of/from Bad Ems (town in western Germany)

das Ende (-n) end; am Ende at the end, in the end; Ende April at the end of April; zu Ende to completion

enden to end

der Endkampf ("-e) final battle; final (game)

endlich finally, at last

die Endung (-en) ending

die Energie (-n) energy

die Energiequelle (-n) source of energy

energiesparend energy-saving

die Energiesparlampe (-n) energy-saving lamp

der Energieverbrauch energy consumption

die Energieverschwendung waste of energy

eng narrow, tight

das Engagement involvement

sich engagieren (für + acc.) to get involved (with), become committed (to) (14)

engagiert committed (11)

(das) England England

(das) Englisch English (language); auf Englisch in English

englisch (adj.) English

englischsprechend English-speaking

der Enkel (-) grandson (3)

die Enkelin (-nen) granddaughter (3)

das Enkelkind (-er) grandchild

das Ensemble (-s) ensemble

die Entbindung (-en) birth, delivery of a child

entdecken to discover

entfernt von (+ dat.) away from

entfliehen (+ dat.), entfloh, ist entflohen to escape

enthalten (enthält), enthielt, enthalten to contain, include; im Preis enthalten included in the price (9)

enthusiastisch enthusiastic(ally)

entlanggehen (geht entlang), ging entlang, ist entlanggegangen to go along, walk along (9)

entlaufen (entläuft), entlief, ist entlaufen to run away

entnervt unnerved

(sich) entscheiden, entschied, entschieden to decide

sich entschließen, entschloss, entschlossen to decide (13)

entschuldigen to excuse (6); Entschuldigen Sie! Excuse me! (6)

die Entschuldigung (-en) apology, excuse; Entschuldigung. Excuse me. (9)

der Entsorger (-) / die Entsorgerin (-nen) (toxic) waste disposal worker

die Entsorgungsplanung waste disposal planning

sich entspannen to relax, take a rest (8)

entsprechen (+ dat.) (entspricht), entsprach, entsprochen to correspond to

entsprechend corresponding

entweder ... oder either . . . or (8)

entwerfen (entwirft), entwarf, entworfen to design, draw up (11)

entwickeln to develop (14)

die Entwicklung (-en) development (11)

das Entwicklungsland ("-er) developing country

das Entwicklungsziel (-e) developmental goal

entzündlich flammable

er he; it (1)

die Erdbeere (-n) strawberry (5)

die Erdbeermarmelade (-n) strawberry jam

die Erde Earth

das Erdgeschoss (-e) ground floor (9)

die Erdkunde geography

das Ereignis (-se) event

erfahren (erfährt), erfuhr, erfahren to find out, learn; to experience

die Erfahrung (-en) experience (11)

erfinden, erfand, erfunden to invent (13)

der Erfinder (-) / die Erfinderin (-nen) inventor

erfinderisch inventive

die Erfindung (-en) invention (13)

der Erfolg (-e) success (11); Erfolg haben to be successful (11)

erfolgreich successful(ly) (11)

die Erfolgskomödie (-n) hit comedy

erfragen to inquire, ask for; to ascertain

das Erfrischungstuch ("-er) towelette

erfüllen to fulfill

ergänzen to complete; to add to

die Ergänzung (-en) completion; addition

ergeben (adj.) devoted

das Ergebnis (-se) result

erhalten (erhält), erhielt, erhalten to get, receive

erhöhen to raise, increase

die Erhöhung (-en) raising, increase

sich erholen to get well, recover (8)

die Erholung rest and recuperation

erinnern an (+ acc.) to remind of; sich erinnern an (+ acc.) to remember

die Erinnerung (-en) memory; remembrance

sich erkälten to catch a cold (8)

die Erkältung (-en) cold (8)

erkennen, erkannte, erkannt to recognize

erklären to explain

die Erklärung (-en) explanation

sich erkundigen to seek information, inquire

die Erkundigung (-en) inquiry

erlauben to allow, permit (9)

erleben to experience (10)

das Erlebnis (-se) experience, event

erleiden, erlitt, erlitten to suffer

erlernbar learnable

erlernen to learn

die Erlösung (-en) redemption, salvation

ermorden to murder

die Ernährung food; nutrition (12)

ernst serious(ly) (1)

der Ernst seriousness

erobern to conquer

eröffnen to open

die Eröffnung (-en) opening

erraten (errät), erriet, erraten to guess

erreichbar reachable

erreichen to reach

errichten to build, put up

erscheinen, erschien, ist erschienen to appear

erschießen, erschoss, erschossen to shoot dead

erschüttern to shake

ersetzen to replace

erst only, not until

erste first (3); ab erstem Juni as of June 1st (12); am ersten Mai on May first (3); der erste Mai May first (3); der erste Stock second floor; erster Klasse fahren to travel first class (10); zum ersten Mal for the first time

erstellen to build; to draw up

die Erstellung construction; drawing up

erstmals (adv.) for the first time

erstöbern to browse

erstrahlen, ist erstrahlt to shine

das Erstsemester (-) first-semester student; freshman

ertönen, ist ertönt to sound, ring out

erwachsen (adj.) grown-up

erwähnen to mention

die Erwähnung (-en) mention

die Erwärmung warming, increase in temperature (14)

erwarten to expect; to wait for

die Erwartung (-en) expectation

erwerben (erwirbt), erwarb, erworben to acquire, buy

erwünscht desired; desirable

erzählen to tell, narrate

der Erzähler (-) / die Erzählerin (-nen) narrator

die Erzählung (-en) story; narration

erziehen, erzog, erzogen to raise, bring up (14)

es it (1, 3); es gibt ... (+ acc.) there is/are . . . (3); Es ist eins. / Es ist ein Uhr. It's one o'clock. (4); Es regnet. It's raining. (7) Es tut mir leid. I'm sorry; Wie geht es dir? / Wie geht's dir? How are you? (inform.) (E); Wie geht es Ihnen? How are you? (form.) (E); Wie wäre es mit ... ? How about . . . ? (13)

der Espresso (-s) espresso (coffee)

essen (isst), aß, gegessen to eat (1)

das Essen (-) food; meal; eating (1); Essen und Trinken food and drinks; zum Essen for dinner

der Essig vinegar

der Esstisch (-e) dining room table

das Esszimmer (-) dining room (2)

(das) Estland Estonia

die Etage (-n) floor, story (12)

etwa approximately, about

etwas something; (adv.) somewhat, a little (2); etwas anderes something different; etwas Neues something new; Hast du etwas Geld? Do you have some money?; Sonst noch etwas? Anything else? (10)

die EU (= die Europäische Union) European Union

euch you (inform. pl. acc.) (3); (to/for) you (inform. pl. dat.) (5)

euer, eure your (*inform. pl.*) (3)
der Euro (-[s]) euro (*monetary unit*) (2)
der Euro-Schein (-e) euro banknote, bill
(das) Europa Europe
europäisch (*adj.*) European; **die Europäische Union (EU)** European Union
der Euroscheck (-s) *type of personal check used in Europe*
die Eurostats (*pl.*) European statistics
e.V. = eingetragener Verein registered organization
eventuell possible; possibly, perhaps
ewig eternal(ly); constant(ly)
das Examen (-) examination
die Ex-Frau (-en) ex-wife
existieren to exist
exklusiv exclusive(ly)
der Ex-Mann (-er) ex-husband
exotisch exotic(ally)
das Experiment (-e) experiment
experimentieren to experiment
der Experte (-n *masc.*) **(-n) / die Expertin (-nen)** expert
explodieren to explode
explosionsartig like an explosion
explosiv explosive(ly)
exportieren to export
extern external(ly)
extra extra
extrem extreme(ly)
exzellent excellent(ly)
exzentrisch excentric(ally) (1)

F

die Fabrik (-en) factory
die Facette (-n) facet
das Fach (-er) subject, field of study
der Facharzt (-e) / die Fachärztin (-nen) specialist (*physician*)
das Fachgeschäft (-e) specialty store
das Fachgymnasium (Fachgymnasien) technical high school
die Fachhochschule (-n) technical college
die Fachhochschulreife technical college degree
die Fachoberschule (-n) trade school
die Fachschule (-n) technical school
die Fähigkeit (-en) ability, skill (11)
fahren (fährt), fuhr, ist gefahren to drive, ride; **erster/zweiter Klasse fahren** to travel first/second class (10); **Fahrrad/Rad fahren** to ride a bicycle (1, 7); **Ski fahren** to ski
die Fahrkarte (-n) ticket (*for train or bus*) (10)
der Fahrkartenschalter (-) ticket window (10)
der Fahrplan (-e) (train or bus) schedule (10)
das Fahrrad (-er) bicycle (10); **Fahrrad fahren** to ride a bicycle (1)
der Fahrradverleih (-e) bicycle rental company
der Fahrstuhl (-e) elevator
die Fahrt (-en) trip; ride (10)
die Fährte (*pl.*) trail, tracks
die Fahrtkosten (*pl.*) traveling expenses
der Faktor (-en) factor

das Faktum (Fakten) fact
der Fall (-e) case; **auf jeden Fall** in any case (13)
fallen (fällt), fiel, ist gefallen to fall (7)
falls (*subord. conj.*) if; in case
falsch false(ly), wrong(ly), incorrect(ly)
die Fälschung (-en) fake, counterfeit
die Familie (-n) family (3)
das Familienessen (-) family meal
das Familienfest (-e) family celebration (3)
das Familienmitglied (-er) family member
der Familienname (-n *masc.*) **(-n)** family name, last name
der Familienstand marital status
der Fan (-s) fan, enthusiast
fangen (fängt), fing, gefangen to catch
die Fantasie (-n) fantasy
fantastisch fantastic(ally) (1)
die Farbe (-n) color (5)
farblos colorless
(der) Fasching Mardi Gras (*southern Germany and Austria*) (3)
das Fass (-er) barrel, vat; **vom Fass** on tap, draft (6)
die Fasson (-s) style
fast almost (8)
faszinierend fascinating
faul lazy, lazily (1)
faulenzen to be lazy, lie around (7)
das Fax (-e) fax
das Faxgerät (-e) fax machine (13)
die FAZ (= Frankfurter Allgemeine Zeitung) *major German newspaper*
der FC = Fußballclub
(der) Februar February (3)
fehlen to be missing; to lack; to need; **Was fehlt Ihnen/dir?** What's the matter? (8)
fehlend missing
der Fehler (-) mistake, error
der Feierabend (-e) end of the workday; **am Feierabend** after work
feiern to celebrate (3)
der Feiertag (-e) holiday
fein fine, delicate; all right; **fein säuberlich** nice(ly) and neat(ly)
die Felsmalerei (-en) rock painting
das Fenster (-) window (2)
die Fensterbank (-e) windowsill
die Ferien (*pl.*) vacation
der Ferienjob (-s) job during the vacation
der Ferientraum (-e) dream vacation
das Fernglas (-er) binoculars
fernsehen (sieht fern), sah fern, ferngesehen to watch television (4)
das Fernsehen television; watching television (4); **im Fernsehen** on television
der Fernseher (-) TV set (2)
die Fernsehgebühr (-en) television license fee
das Fernsehgerät (-e) television set
das Fernsehprogramm (-e) TV program, TV schedule
die Fernsehshow (-s) TV show
der Ferrari Ferrari (automobile)
fertig finished, done; ready
das Fest (-e) festival; party, feast
sich festlegen (legt fest) to commit oneself

das Festnetz (-e) conventional fixed-line network
das Festspiel (-e) festival production
feststellen (stellt fest) to establish
die Fete (-n) (*coll.*) party
fett fat; greasy; **fett gedruckt** printed in boldface
feucht damp
das Feuer (-) fire
feuergefährlich flammable
die Feuerwehr (-en) fire department
das Feuerwerk (-e) fireworks
das Fieber fever (8)
fiktiv fictitious
die Filiale (-n) branch office
das Filet (-s) filet
der Film (-e) film, movie (1)
filmen to film
die Filmkritik film criticism
der Filmkritiker (-) / die Filmkritikerin (-nen) movie critic
der Filmpreis (-e) film prize
das Filmprogramm (-e) movie program
der Filmschauspieler (-) / die Filmschauspielerin (-nen) movie actor/actress
der Filmstar (-s) movie star
der Filter (-) filter
der Filz felt (*material*)
der Filzhut (-e) felt hat
der Finanzbeamte (*decl. adj.*) **/ die Finanzbeamtin (-nen)** tax official
die Finanzen (*pl.*) finance(s)
finanziell financial(ly)
finanzieren to finance
der Finanzskandal (-e) financial scandal
finden, fand, gefunden to find; to think (1); **Ich finde … I think . . . ; Wie findest du … ?** How do you like . . . ? What do you think of . . . ? (1)
der Finderlohn (-e) finder's reward
findig resourceful
der Finger (-) finger (8)
(das) Finnland Finland
die Firma (Firmen) firm, company (11)
der Fisch (-e) fish
der Fischer (-) / die Fischerin (-nen) fisherman/fisherwoman
fit fit, in shape (8); **sich fit halten (hält), hielt, gehalten** to keep fit, stay in shape (8)
die Fitness fitness (8)
die Fitnessaktivität (-en) fitness activity
der Fitnessberater (-) / die Fitnessberaterin (-nen) fitness consultant, personal trainer
das Fitnesscenter (-) fitness center; gym (4)
der Fitnessplan (-e) fitness plan
die Fitnessroutine (-n) fitness routine
das Fitnessstudio (-s) fitness studio
das Fitnesszentrum (Fitnesszentren) fitness center; gym
die Flasche (-n) bottle (14)
die Flaschenpost (-en) message in a bottle
die Flatrate flat rate
der Fleck (-e) *also* **der Flecken (-)** stain, spot

das Fleisch meat (5)
fleißig industrious(ly), diligent(ly), hardworking (1)
flexibel flexible, flexibly
die Flexibilität flexibility
fliegen, flog, ist geflogen to fly (7)
fliehen, floh, ist geflohen to flee
fließend fluent(ly)
der Flitzer (-) (*coll.*) sporty car
der Flohmarkt (-̈e) flea market
die Flöte (-n) flute
flüchten, ist geflüchtet to flee
der Flug (-̈e) flight
der Flugbegleiter (-) / die Flugbegleiterin (-nen) flight attendant
der Flügel (-) wing
der Flughafen (-̈) airport
das Flüglein (-) little wing
das Flugzeug (-e) airplane (10)
der Flur (-e) hallway (12); **für den ganzen Flur** for the whole floor
der Fluss (-̈e) river (7)
flüstern to whisper
der Föhn (-e) hair dryer (9)
die Folge (-n) consequence, result
folgen (+ *dat.*), **ist gefolgt** to follow; **folgend** following
die Folie (-n) foil; sheet; film
fordern to demand
fördern to promote (14)
die Form (-en) form, shape
das Format (-e) format
das Formular (-e) form (*paper to be filled out*)
formulieren to formulate
forschen to do research (13)
der Forscher (-) / die Forscherin (-nen) researcher
die Forschung (-en) research (14)
das Forsthaus (-̈er) forester's house
der Fortschritt (-e) progress (14); **Fortschritte machen** to make progress (14)
die Fortsetzung (-en) continuation
(die) Fortuna Fortune; **Glücksrad Fortuna** *Wheel of Fortune* (*quiz show*)
das Foto (-s) photograph (2)
das Fotoalbum (Fotoalben) photo album
der Fotoapparat (-e) camera
der Fotograf (-en *masc.*) (-en) / die Fotografin (-nen) photographer
fotografieren to photograph
das Fotografieren taking photographs
die Fotokopie (-n) photocopy
das Fotomodell (-e) photo model
das Foyer (-s) foyer
die Frage (-n) question; **eine Frage stellen** to ask a question; **Ich habe eine Frage.** I have a question. (E)
der Fragebogen (-) questionnaire
fragen to ask (2); **fragen nach** (+ *dat.*) to ask about; **nach dem Weg fragen** to ask for directions (9)
der (Schweizer) Franken (-) (Swiss) franc
Frankfurter (*adj.*) of/from Frankfurt
(das) Frankreich France (E)
der Franzose (-n *masc.*) (-n) / die Französin (-nen) French person
französisch (*adj.*) French

(das) Französisch French (language)
(die) Frau (-en) Mrs., Ms.; woman (E); wife (3)
frei free(ly) (2); vacant, available, unoccupied; **Ist hier noch frei?** Is this seat available? (6)
das Freibad (-̈er) outdoor swimming pool (7)
Freien: im Freien outdoors (11)
freihaben (hat frei), hatte frei, freigehabt (*coll.*) to have free, have off
die Freiheit (-en) freedom
freilassen (lässt frei), ließ frei, freigelassen to set free, release
freilich admittedly; of course
(der) Freitag Friday (3)
freitags Fridays, on Friday(s) (4)
freiwillig voluntary, voluntarily
die Freizeit free time (7)
die Freizeitaktivität (-en) leisure activity
die Freizeitbeschäftigung (-en) leisure activity
die Freizeitpläne (*pl.*) plans for leisure time
fremd strange; unknown; foreign
der/die Fremde (*decl. adj.*) stranger
der Fremdenführer (-) / die Fremdenführerin (-nen) tour guide
der Fremdenverkehrsverein (-e) tourist association
die Fremdsprache (-n) foreign language
die Freude (-n) joy; **vor Freude** with joy
freuen to please; **sich freuen auf** (+ *acc.*) to look forward to (12); **sich freuen über** (+ *acc.*) to be glad about (12); **Freut mich.** Pleased to meet you. (E)
der Freund (-e) / die Freundin (-nen) friend (1); boyfriend/girlfriend
freundlich friendly (1)
freundschaftlich friendly
der Friede (-n *masc.*) (*also* **der Frieden**) peace
die Friedensbewegung (-en) peace movement
friedlich peaceful(ly)
frieren, fror, gefroren to freeze
das Frisbee (-s) Frisbee
frisch fresh(ly) (5)
frittieren to deep-fry
froh glad, happy
fröhlich cheerful(ly)
frönen (+ *dat.*) to indulge in
der Frosch (-̈e) frog
die Frucht (-̈e) fruit
früh early (4); **morgen früh** tomorrow morning (4)
früher earlier; once; used to (*do, be, etc.*) (7)
das Frühjahr (-e) spring (*season*) (7)
der Frühling (-e) spring (*season*) (7)
frühmorgens early in the morning
das Frühstück (-e) breakfast (5); **zum Frühstück** for breakfast
frühstücken to eat breakfast (4)
die Frühstücksnische (-n) breakfast nook (12)
der Frühstücksraum (-̈e) breakfast room (9)

der Frühstückstisch (-e) breakfast table
die FU = Freie Universität (Berlin) Free University (of Berlin)
(sich) fühlen to feel (8); **sich wohl fühlen** to feel well (8)
führen to lead, guide, conduct; to carry (*merchandise*); **führend** leading; **ein Gespräch führen** to have a conversation; **Protokoll führen** to make a transcript, keep the minutes
der Führerschein (-e) driver's license
die Führung (-en) management; guide, lead; tour
füllen to fill; to fill in
fünf five (E)
fünfmonatig lasting five months
fünfte fifth (3)
fünfzehn fifteen (E)
das Fünfzeilenformat (-e) five-line format
fünfzig fifty (E)
funktionieren to work, function (9)
für (+ *acc.*) for (3); **was für (ein)** what kind of (a) (11)
fürchterlich horrible, horribly
fürs = für das
der Fuß (-̈e) foot (8); **zu Fuß gehen, ging, ist gegangen** to walk, go on foot (8)
der Fußball (-̈e) soccer; soccer ball (7); **Fußball spielen** to play soccer (7)
der Fußballplatz (-̈e) soccer field
der Fußballspieler (-) / die Fußballspielerin (-nen) soccer player
der Fußballtrainer (-) / die Fußballtrainerin (-nen) soccer coach
die Fußballweltmeisterschaft (-en) world soccer championship, World Cup
der Fußgänger (-) / die Fußgängerin (-nen) pedestrian
die Fußgängerzone (-n) pedestrian zone (9)

G

die Gabe (-n) gift
die Gabel (-n) fork (6)
der Gang (-̈e) course (*of a meal*)
ganz complete(ly), total(ly), entire(ly) (12); quite, very, really (1); **ganz gut** quite good; **ganz toll** really great
gar even; **gar kein(e)** not any; **gar nicht** not at all; **gar nichts** nothing at all
die Garage (-n) garage (2)
garantieren to guarantee
die Garderobe (-n) wardrobe; closet (12)
die Gardine (-n) curtain, drapes
garnieren to garnish
der Garten (-̈) garden; yard (2)
die Gartenarbeit (-en) gardening; yard work
die Gartenlaube (-n) garden house
das Gartenlokal (-e) garden restaurant
der Gärtner (-) / die Gärtnerin (-nen) gardener
die Gasse (-n) lane, narrow street
der Gast (-̈e) guest
das Gästehaus (-̈er) guesthouse
das Gästezimmer (-) guest room (12)
die Gastfamilie (-n) host family
gastfreundlich hospitable

die Gastfreundschaft hospitality
der Gastgeber (-) / die Gastgeberin (-nen) host/hostess
das Gasthaus (¨-er) restaurant; inn
der Gasthof (¨-e) hotel; restaurant; inn
die Gastronomie gastronomy
die Gaststätte (-n) full-service restaurant (6)
die Gaststube (-n) (hotel) dining room, lounge
der Gastwirt (-e) / die Gastwirtin (-nen) restaurant owner; restaurant manager
geb. = geboren(e)
das Gebäck (-e) baked goods; cakes and pastries
das Gebäude (-) building
geben (gibt), gab, gegeben to give (3); to put; **es gibt** there is/are (6); **eine Party geben** to have a party, throw a party; **Rat geben** to advise
geboren born; **geboren werden** to be born; **geborene** née (*maiden name*); **ich bin geboren** I was born (1)
der Gebrauch use
gebrauchen to use
gebraucht used
die Gebühr (-en) fee
das Geburtsdatum (Geburtdaten) date of birth
der Geburtsort (-e) birthplace (1)
der Geburtstag (-e) birthday, date of birth (1); **Herzlichen Glückwunsch zum Geburtstag!** Happy birthday! (3); **Wann hast du Geburtstag?** When is your birthday? (3)
die Geburtstagsfeier (-n) birthday celebration
die Gedächtniskirche *famous church in Berlin*
der Gedanke (-n *masc.*) (-n) thought; **sich über etwas (*acc.*) Gedanken machen** to think about something, to ponder something
das Gedicht (-e) poem
geehrt: sehr geehrter/geehrte (+ *proper name*) *formal letter address form*
geeignet suitable, appropriate
die Gefahr (-en) danger (14)
gefährden to endanger
gefährlich dangerous(ly) (10)
gefallen (+ *dat.*) (gefällt), gefiel, gefallen to be pleasing (5); **Wie gefällt Ihnen … ?** How do you like … ? (5)
der Gefallen (-) favor; **einen Gefallen tun** to do a favor
das Gefängnis (-se) prison, jail (14)
das Geflügel poultry
der Gefrierpunkt (-e) freezing point
der Gefrierschrank (¨-e) (upright) freezer
gefroren frozen (5)
das Gefühl (-e) feeling; emotion
gegen (+ *acc.*) against; around, about (+ *time*) (3, 6); **(so) gegen fünf Uhr** around five o'clock (6)
die Gegend (-en) area, region
die Gegendarstellung (-en) opposing view
der Gegensatz (¨-e) contrast
gegenseitig mutual(ly); reciprocal(ly)
das Gegenteil (-e) opposite

gegenüber von (+ *dat.*) across from (9)
gegenwärtig present(ly), current(ly)
das Gehalt (¨-er) salary (11)
das Geheimnis (-se) secret
gehen, ging, ist gegangen to go (1); **einkaufen gehen** to go shopping (4); **Geht's gut?** Are you doing well? (E); **Na, wie geht's?** How are you? (*casual*) (E); **spazieren gehen** to go for a walk (4); **Wie geht es Ihnen?** How are you? (*form.*) (E); **Wie geht's (dir)?** How are you? (*inform.*) (E); **zu Fuß gehen** to walk, go on foot (8)
gehoben upper; elevated
gehören (+ *dat.*) to belong to (*a person*) (5); **gehören zu (+ *dat.*)** to be a part of
die Geige (-n) violin
geistig mental, intellectual
das Gelächter (-) laughter
gelb yellow (5)
das Geld money (2)
der Geldkurier (-e) money courier
gelegen situated, located; **zentral gelegen** centrally located (2)
die Gelegenheit (-en) opportunity (11); occasion
gelegentlich occasional(ly)
gelten (+ *dat.*) (gilt), galt, gegolten to be valid; **gelten als** to be considered as
gelungen inspired; priceless
das Gemälde (-) painting
gemein common; **gemein haben** to have in common
die Gemeinde (-n) community
gemeinsam common; in common; together
die Gemeinschaft (-en) community
gemischt mixed
das Gemüse vegetable(s) (5)
der Gemüsestand (¨-e) vegetable stand
gemütlich cozy, cozily (4); comfortable, comfortably; leisurely
die Gemütlichkeit comfort; informality
genau exact(ly) (2); meticulous(ly)
genauso just/exactly as (7); **genauso … wie** just/exactly as . . . as
die Generation (-en) generation
das Genie (-s) genius
genießen, genoss, genossen to enjoy, savor, relish
der Genießer (-) / die Genießerin (-nen) connoisseur
der Genitiv (-e) genitive case
das Genitivobjekt (-e) genitive object
die Genitivpräposition (-en) preposition governing the genitive case
gentechnisch modifiert genetically modified
genug enough, sufficient(ly)
genügen to suffice
genügend enough, sufficient(ly)
geöffnet open(ed)
die Geographie geography
geographisch geographical(ly)
der Geoökologe (-n *masc.*) (-n) / die Geoökologin (-nen) geo-ecologist
die Geoökologie geo-ecology
das Gepäck luggage (9)

die Gepäckaufbewahrung baggage check (10)
gerade just, exactly (2); straight
geradeaus straight ahead (9); **immer geradeaus** (keep on going) straight ahead (9)
das Gerät (-e) appliance, device (12)
geräuchert smoked
das Gericht (-e) dish (*of prepared food*) (6)
germanisch Germanic, Teutonic
die Germanistik German studies
gern(e) (lieber, liebst-) gladly (2); **gern (+ *verb*)** to like to (*do something*) (2); **gern haben** to like (*a person or thing*) (2); **ich hätte gern** I would like to have
das Gesamtbild (-er) overall view, big picture
die Gesamthochschule (-n) *combined scientific and pedagogical university*
die Gesamtschule (-n) German secondary school (*grades 6 to 12*)
der Gesangsverein (-e) choral society
das Geschäft (-e) store, shop; business
die Geschäftsfrau (-en) businesswoman (11)
die Geschäftsleute (*pl.*) businesspeople
der Geschäftsmann (Geschäftsleute) businessman (11)
geschehen (geschieht), geschah, ist geschehen to happen
gescheit intelligent, bright; sensible, decent (13); **nichts Gescheites** nothing decent (13)
das Geschenk (-e) present, gift (3)
die Geschichte (-n) story; history
das Geschirr dishes
die Geschirrspülmaschine (-n) dishwasher
geschlossen closed (6)
der Geschmack (¨-e) taste
geschützt protected
geschweige denn … let alone . . .
die Geschwindigkeit (-en) speed
die Geschwindigkeitsbegrenzung (-en) speed limit
die Geschwister (*pl.*) brothers and sisters, siblings (3)
geschwollen swollen
die Geselligkeit good company
die Gesellschaft (-en) society
das Gesetz (-e) law
das Gesicht (-er) face (8)
gespannt eager(ly), expectant(ly)
das Gespräch (-e) conversation
gestern yesterday (7); **gestern Abend** yesterday evening; **gestern Vormittag** yesterday morning
gestreift striped (5)
gestresst (*adj.*) under stress
gesund healthy, healthful; well (8)
die Gesundheit health (8)
gesundheitsbewusst health-conscious(ly)
gesundheitsschädlich unhealthy, unhealthily
das Gesundheitswesen health-care system
das Getränk (-e) beverage, drink (5)
die Getränkedose (-n) beverage can (14)
der Getränkeladen (¨-) beverage store (5)
das Getreide (-) cereal, grain

getrennt separate(ly) (6)
gewährleisten to guarantee, ensure
die Gewalt violence, force; power, dominion
die Gewaltbereitschaft readiness for violence
die Gewalttätigkeit (-en) (act of) violence (14)
das Gewicht (-e) weight
gewinnen, gewann, gewonnen to win
gewiss certain(ly)
das Gewitter (-) thunderstorm (7)
die Gewohnheit (-en) habit
der Gewohnheitsmensch (-en *masc.*) (-en) creature of habit
gewöhnlich usual(ly) (4)
gewöhnt an (+ *acc.*) accustomed to
die Gewürzgurke (-n) pickle, pickled gherkin
gießen, goss, gegossen to pour
das Gift (-e) poison
giftfrei nontoxic
der Giftstoff (-e) toxic substance
die Gitarre (-n) guitar
das Gitter (-) bars; hinter Gitter(n) (*coll.*) behind bars
glänzend shiny; excellent(ly)
das Glas (¨er) glass
glauben to believe (5); Ich glaube dir nicht. I don't believe you.
gleich right away, immediately (8); same; gleich da drüben right over there
gleichfalls likewise (E)
die Gleichstellung equality, equal rights
gleichzeitig simultaneous(ly)
das Gleis (-e) track (10); platform
global global(ly) (14)
die Globalisierung globalization
der Globus (Globen) globe
das Glöckchen (-) little bell
das Glockenspiel (-e) chimes, glockenspiel
das Glück fortune, luck; happiness; Viel Glück! Good luck! (1)
glücklich happy, happily
das Glücksrad (¨er) wheel of fortune
der Glückwunsch (¨e) congratulations; Herzlichen Glückwunsch zum Geburtstag! Happy birthday! (3)
die Glühbirne (-n) lightbulb
die Glühlampe (-n) lightbulb
GmbH = Gesellschaft mit beschränkter Haftung corporation
das Gold gold
golden golden
der Goldgräber (-) gold digger
die Goldmedaille (-n) gold medal
(das) Golf golf
googeln to Google, use the Google search engine
der Gott (¨er) God; god; Gott sei Dank thank God; grüß Gott hello (*in southern Germany and Austria*)
der Gourmet (-s) gourmet
Gr. = Größe
graben (gräbt), grub, gegraben to dig
der Grad (-e) degree (7); 35 Grad 35 degrees (7)

die Graffiti (*pl.*) graffiti
die Grafik (-en) drawing
das Gramm (-e) gram
die Grammatik (-en) grammar; grammar book
grandios magnificent(ly)
das Gras (¨er) grass
gratulieren (+ *dat.*) to congratulate (3); Ich gratuliere! Congratulations!
grau gray (5)
graugetigert with gray stripes
die Grenze (-n) border, boundary
(das) Griechenland Greece
griechisch (*adj.*) Greek
der Grill (-s) grill, barbeque (6)
grillen to grill, barbeque
der Grillteller (-) grill platter
die Grippe flu (8)
groß big, large (2); tall (1); great
großartig magnificent(ly)
(das) Großbritannien Great Britain
die Größe (-n) size (5); height
die Großeltern (*pl.*) grandparents (3)
die Großmutter (¨) grandmother (3)
der Großraumwagen (-) rail car without compartments
die Großstadt (¨e) big city, metropolis
größtenteils for the most part
der Großvater (¨) grandfather (3)
großzügig generous(ly)
grün green (5)
der Grund (¨e) reason; ground; im Grunde genommen basically (14)
gründen to found, establish
die Grundform (-en) basic form
die Grundgangart (-en) basic pace
die Grundlage (-n) basis, foundation
der Grundlsee *lake in Austria*
der Grundriss (-e) outline; layout; blueprint
die Grundschule (-n) primary school (11)
die Gründung (-en) founding, establishment
das Grüne (*decl. adj.*) green, greenery; im Grünen in the country; ins Grüne fahren to drive out to the country
die Gruppe (-n) group
der Gruß (¨e) greeting (12); herzliche Grüße kind regards; viele Grüße best wishes (12)
(sich) grüßen to say hello (to one another); grüß dich hello, hi (*among friends and family*) (E); grüß Gott hello (*in southern Germany and Austria*)
die Grütze: rote Grütze *dessert made of red berries*
(das) Guatemala Guatemala
gucken (*coll.*) to look
das Gulasch (-e) goulash
gültig valid
günstig convenient(ly); favorable, favorably (9); reasonable (in price); günstig liegen to be conveniently located (9)
die Gurke (-n) cucumber (5)
der Gurt (-e) strap; seatbelt
der Gürtel (-) belt (5)
gut (besser, best-) good, well (1); Alles Gute! All the best! (3); danke, gut fine,

thanks (E); Er tanzt gut. He dances well. (1); Es geht mir gut. I am fine; Geht's gut? Are you doing well? (E); Gute Besserung! Get well soon! (8); gute Nacht good night (E); guten Abend good evening (E); guten Morgen good morning (E); guten Tag hello, good day (E); Mach's gut. Take care, so long. (*inform.*) (E); nicht besonders gut not particularly well (E); sehr gut very well; fine; good (E); zu guter Letzt in the end, at long last
gutmachen (macht gut) to make good
gymnasial pertaining to secondary school
der Gymnasiast (-en *masc.*) (-en) / die Gymnasiastin (-nen) secondary school student
das Gymnasium (Gymnasien) secondary school (*leading to university*) (11)

H

das Haar (-e) hair (8)
haben (hat), hatte, gehabt to have (2); Angst haben (vor + *dat.*) to be afraid (of) (12); Durst haben to be thirsty (2); Erfolg haben to be successful (11); gern haben to like (*a person or thing*) (2); Hunger haben to be hungry (2); Ich habe eine Frage. I have a question. (E) Ich hätte gern … I would like to have … ; Lust haben to feel like (*doing something*) (2); Recht haben to be correct (2); Wann hast du Geburtstag? When is your birthday? (3); Zeit haben to have time (2)
der Hackbraten (-) meatloaf
der Hafen (¨) harbor, port (9)
der Häftling (-e) prisoner
der Hagel hail (7)
das Hähnchen (-) chicken (5)
der Haken (-) hook
halb half (4); halb zwei half past one, one-thirty (4)
das Halbfinale semifinal
die Halbpension *accommodation with two meals per day included*
die Hälfte (-n) half
der Halfter (-) halter
das Hallenbad (¨er) indoor swimming pool (7)
hallo hello (*among friends and family*) (E)
der Hals (¨e) neck; throat (8)
das Halsband (¨er) (animal) collar
die Halsschmerzen (*pl.*) sore throat (8)
halt (*particle*) just
halten (hält), hielt, gehalten to hold, keep; to stop; sich fit halten to keep fit, stay in shape (8); halten für (+ *acc.*) to hold; to consider, think (14); halten von (+ *dat.*) to think of; ein Referat halten to give a paper; eine Vorlesung halten to deliver a lecture
die Haltestelle (-n) (bus or streetcar) stop (9)
die Haltung (-en) posture, stance; attitude
Hamburger (*adj.*) of/from Hamburg
der Hamburger (-) hamburger
Hamelner (*adj.*) of/from Hamelin

der Hamster (-) hamster
die Hand (¨e) hand (8)
der Handel sales, trade (11)
handeln to act; **sich handeln um** (+ *acc.*) to be about; **handeln von** (+ *dat.*) to deal with, be about (13); **Wovon handelt es?** What's it about? (13)
das Handgepäck carry-on luggage (10)
die Handlung (-en) plot, action
der Handschuh (-e) glove (10)
die Handtasche (-n) handbag
das Handtuch (¨er) towel
das Handy (-s) cell phone (2)
hängen, hängte, gehängt to hang (up), put up (6)
hängen, hing, gehangen to hang, be hanging (6)
hart hard; severe(ly)
das Häschen (-) bunny, little rabbit (*term of endearment*)
hassen to hate
hässlich ugly (2)
der Hauch (-e) breath; wind; whiff
hauen, haute, gehauen to beat
häufig frequent(ly), often
Haupt- main, major, central (*used in compound words*)
das Hauptfach (¨er) major subject
die Hauptfigur (-en) main character, protagonist
das Hauptgericht (-e) main dish, entrée (6)
hauptsächlich mainly, mostly
die Hauptschule (-n) junior high school (*grades 5–9/10*)
das Hauptseminar (-e) advanced seminar
die Hauptstadt (¨e) capital (city)
die Hauptstraße (-n) main street
das Haus (¨er) house (2); **nach Haus(e) gehen** to go home (5); **zu Haus(e)** at home (5)
die Hausarbeit (-en) housework; homework
die Hausaufgabe (-n) homework
der Hausbewohner (-) / die Hausbewohnerin (-nen) tenant
die Hausfrau (-en) homemaker, housewife
die Hausfrauensauce (-n) homemade sauce
hausgemacht homemade
der Haushalt (-e) household (12)
die Haushaltswaren (*pl.*) household utensils
der Hausmanager (-) / die Hausmanagerin (-nen) building manager
der Hausmann (¨er) house husband, stay-at-home husband
das Hausmittel (-) household remedy
die Hausmusik music performed at home
die Hausnummer (-n) street address (number) (E)
der Hausschuh (-e) slipper (5)
das Haustier (-e) pet
die Haustür (-en) front door
die Haut (¨e) skin
die Hautcreme (-s) skin cream
Hbf. = Hauptbahnhof main train station
heben, hob, gehoben to lift
das Hefeweizen *unfiltered wheat beer*

das Heft (-e) notebook (12); **das Comic-Heft (-e)** comic book
heftig heavy, heavily; violent(ly)
heikel awkward, delicate
das Heilbad (¨er) spa
der Heilige Abend Christmas Eve (3); **am Heiligen Abend** on Christmas Eve
das Heilmittel (-) remedy
die Heimat (-en) homeland, hometown
der Heimatverein (-e) local history society
der Heimcomputer home computer
heimtückisch treacherous
heiraten to marry, get married (3)
heiß hot (7)
heißen, hieß, geheißen to be called, be named (1); **das heißt (d.h.)** that is, i.e. (1); **Ich heiße ...** My name is ... (E); **Wie heißen Sie?** What's your name? (*form.*) (E); **Wie heißt ... ?** What's the name of . . . ? (E); **Wie heißt du?** What's your name? (*inform.*) (E)
der Heißluftballon (-s) hot air balloon
heiter pleasant, fair, bright (7)
die Heizung (-en) heating (12)
die Heizwärme warmth from a heater
das Hektar (-e) hectare (= 2.471 acres)
hektisch hectic(ally)
helfen (+ *dat.*) **(hilft), half, geholfen** to help (5)
hell light, bright(ly) (2)
hellblau light blue
hellgelb light yellow
das Hemd (-e) shirt (5)
her this way; here; **hin und her** back and forth
herausfinden (findet heraus), fand heraus, herausgefunden to find out
herausfordern (fordert heraus) to challenge (11)
die Herausforderung (-en) challenge
der Herbst (-e) autumn, fall (7)
hereinkommen (kommt herein), kam herein, ist hereingekommen to come inside
hereinsehen (sieht herein), sah herein, hereingesehen to look in (on somebody)
herhaben (hat her), hatte her, hergehabt (*coll.*): **Wo hast du die gute Wurst her?** Where did you get the good sausage?
herkommen (kommt her), kam her, ist hergekommen to come here; to come from
herkömmlich conventional, traditional
der Herr (-n *masc.*) **(-en)** Mr.; gentleman (E); **meine Damen und Herren** ladies and gentlemen
der Herrenartikel (-) men's accessory
die Herrenkonfektion men's ready-to-wear clothing
herrlich wonderful(ly), magnificent(ly)
herstellen (stellt her) to produce, manufacture (11)
der Hersteller (-) producer, manufacturer (11)
herum: um ... herum around (*a place*)
herumfahren (um + *acc.*) **(fährt herum), fuhr herum, ist herumgefahren** to drive around

herumtönen (tönt herum) to resound
herunter down
herunterladen (lädt herunter), lud herunter, heruntergeladen to download
das Herz (*gen.* **-ens,** *dat.* **-en) (-en)** heart
die Herzensdame (-n) woman in one's heart
herzlich cordial(ly); **herzlich willkommen** welcome (E); **Herzlichen Glückwunsch zum Geburtstag!** Happy birthday! (3)
(das) Hessen Hesse (*a German state*)
heute today (1); **heute Abend** this evening (1); **heute Morgen** this morning (4); **heute Nachmittag** this afternoon (4); **heute Nacht** last night; tonight **Welches Datum ist heute?** What is today's date? (3)
heutzutage nowadays
hi (*coll.*) hi (E)
hie und da here and there
hier here (1); **Ist hier noch frei?** Is this seat available? (6)
hierher (to) here, hither
die Hi-Fi-Anlage (-n) hi-fi system
die Hilfe help, assistance; **um Hilfe bitten** to ask for help
die Hilfsorganisation (-en) aid organization
das Hilfsverb (-en) helping verb, auxiliary verb
der Himmel (-) sky (7); heaven
hin (to) there, thither; **hin und her** back and forth; **hin und zurück** round-trip (10); **vor sich hin** to oneself
hinaufgehen (geht hinauf), ging hinauf, ist hinaufgegangen to go up
hinausschieben (schiebt hinaus), schob hinaus, hinausgeschoben to put off, postpone
hinfahren (fährt hin), fuhr hin, ist hingefahren to go there, drive there, ride there
hingehen (geht hin), ging hin, ist hingegangen to go there
hinlegen (legt hin) to lay down; **sich hinlegen** to lie down (8)
sich hinsetzen (setzt hin) to sit down (8)
hinstecken (steckt hin) to stick (in), put (in)
hinten in the back
hinter (+ *acc./dat.*) behind, in back of (6)
hinterher afterward
hinterlassen (hinterlässt), hinterließ, hinterlassen to leave behind; leave (*e.g., a message*) (13)
hinuntergehen (geht hinunter), ging hinunter, ist hinuntergegangen to go down
hinunterstürzen (stürzt hinunter) to throw down; to gulp down
der Hinweis (-e) tip, clue
historisch historical(ly)
der Hit (-s) hit
das HIV (= humanes Immundefizienzvirus) HIV
hm (*interjection*) hmm
das Hobby (-s) hobby (1)

hoch (hoh-) (höher, höchst-) high(ly) (2); tall

hochgemut cheerful(ly)

die Hochschule (-n) university, college

der Hochschullehrer (-) / die Hochschullehrerin (-nen) university instructor (1)

die Hochschulreife college qualification

die Höchstgeschwindigkeit (-en) maximum speed, speed limit

die Hochzeit (-en) wedding (3)

der Hof (¨e) farm; court

das Hofbräuhaus *famous beer hall in Munich*

hoffen (auf + *acc.*) to hope (for) (10)

hoffentlich hopefully; I/we/let's hope (6)

die Hoffnung (-en) hope

höflich polite(ly)

die Höhe (-n) height; **in die Höhe** upward

der Höhepunkt (-e) climax, peak; highlight

holen to get, fetch

(das) Holland Holland

holländisch (*adj.*) Dutch

der Höllenlärm hellish noise

das Holz wood

der Holzhammer (-) (wooden) mallet

der Holzpantoffel (-n) wooden shoe, clog

der Holzzaun (¨e) wooden fence

der Hometrainer (-) home exercise equipment

der Honig honey

die Honigmelone (-n) honeydew melon

hören to hear, listen to (1)

das Horoskop (-e) horoscope (13)

das Hörspiel (-e) radio play

der Hörtext (-e) listening text

die Hose (-n) (pair of) pants, trousers (5)

das Hotel (-s) hotel (9)

das Hotelpersonal hotel personnel

das Huhn (¨er) chicken

der Humor (-e) humor, sense of humor

der Humorist (-en *masc.*) **(-en) / die Humoristin (-nen)** humorist; comedian

humorvoll full of humor, humorous(ly)

der Hund (-e) dog (3) **/ die Hündin (-nen)** female dog

hundert one hundred (E)

hundsmiserabel (*coll.*) sick as a dog (8)

der Hunger hunger; famine (14) **Hunger haben** to be hungry (2)

husten to cough

der Husten (-) cough, coughing (8)

das Hustenbonbon (-s) cough drop

der Hut (¨e) hat (5)

die Hütte (-n) hut, cabin (10)

hypnotisieren to hypnotize

I

der ICE (= Intercityexpresszug) intercity express train

ich I (1); **ich auch** me too (1); **ich bin ... geboren** I was born . . . (1)

ideal ideal(ly)

die Idee (-n) idea

identifizieren to identify

die Identität (-en) identity

das Idyll (-e) idyllic setting

idyllisch idyllic(ally)

ihm (to/for) him/it (*dat.*) (5)

ihn him; it (*acc.*) (3)

Ihnen (to/for) you (*dat., form.*); **Was fehlt Ihnen?** What's the matter? (8); **Wie gefällt Ihnen . . . ?** How do you like . . . ? (5); **Wie geht es Ihnen?** How are you? (*form.*) (E)

ihnen (to/for) them (*dat.*) (5)

Ihr your (*form.*) (3)

ihr you (*inform. pl.*) (1); her, its; their (3); (to/for) her/it (*dat.*) (5)

illegal illegal(ly)

im = **in dem**; **im Freien** outdoors (11); **im Grunde genommen** basically (14); **im Januar** in January (3); **im Kaufhaus** at the department store

der Imbiss (-e) fast-food stand (6)

immer always (1); **immer geradeaus** (keep on going) straight ahead (9) **immer noch** still

die Immobilien (*pl.*) real estate

der Imperativ (-e) imperative verb form

der Imperativsatz (¨e) imperative clause

das Imperfekt (-e) imperfect tense, simple past

impulsiv impulsive(ly)

in (+ *acc./dat.*) in/into; inside; to (*a place*) (6); **in der Mitte (der Stadt)** in the center (of the city) (9); **in der Nähe (des Bahnhofs)** near (the train station) (9); **in die Disko gehen** to go to a disco, go clubbing (4); **in die Oper gehen** to go to the opera (4); **in zwei Tagen** in two days (6)

incl. = **inkl.**

indem (*subord. conj.*) while, as

der Indianer (-) / die Indianerin (-nen) American Indian (*person*)

indirekt indirect(ly)

indisch (*adj.*) Indian, of/from/pertaining to India

individuell individual(ly)

die Industrie (-n) industry

der Infinitiv (-e) infinitive verb form

die Inflation (-en) inflation

das Info (-s) (*coll.*) info(rmation)

die Informatik computer science

der Informatiker (-) / die Informatikerin (-nen) computer scientist (11)

die Information (-en) information

(sich) informieren (über + *acc.*) to inform (oneself) (about) (8)

der Ingenieur (-e) / die Ingenieurin (-nen) engineer

Inh. = **Inhaber(in)**

der Inhaber (-) / die Inhaberin (-nen) proprietor

der Inhalt (-e) content(s)

die Initiative (-n) initiative

inkl. = **inklusive**

inklusive inclusive; included

das Inland (*sg. only*) home country (13); **im Inland und Ausland** at home and abroad (13)

das Inlineskaten inline skating

inmitten (+ *gen.*) in the midst of

die Innenstadt (¨e) downtown, city center (9)

innerhalb (+ *gen.*) within, inside of (9)

ins = **in das**; **ins Kino gehen** to go to the movies (4); **ins Theater gehen** to go to the theater (4)

das Insekt (-en) insect

die Insel (-n) island

insgesamt altogether, in total (10)

das Institut (-e) institute

das Instrument (-e) instrument

die Integration (-en) integration

intelligent intelligent(ly)

intensiv intense(ly); intensive(ly)

die Interaktion (-en) interaction

interessant interesting (1); **nichts Interessantes** nothing interesting

das Interesse (-n) interest (1)

der Interessensträger (-) / die Interessensträgerin (-nen) stakeholder

interessieren to interest; **sich interessieren für** (+ *acc.*) to be interested in (11)

interessiert (an + *dat.*) interested (in)

intern internal(ly)

international international(ly)

das Internet Internet (13)

die Internetsuche (-n) Internet search

der Internetzugang Internet access (9)

das Interrogativpronomen (-) interrogative pronoun

der Inter-Treff-Club (-s) club for meeting one another

das Interview (-s) interview

interviewen to interview

der Interviewer (-) / die Interviewerin (-nen) interviewer

investieren to invest

inzwischen in the meantime, meanwhile

der Iran Iran

irgendwer (*coll.*) somebody

irgendwie somehow

irgendwo somewhere

(das) Irland Ireland

irritieren to irritate

der Irrtum (¨er) error

das Isartal Isar Valley

isolieren to isolate; to insulate (14)

(das) Israel Israel

ist is; **Das ist ...** This is . . . (E)

(das) Italien Italy (E)

der Italiener (-) / die Italienerin (-nen) Italian (*person*)

italienisch (*adj.*) Italian

(das) Italienisch Italian (language)

J

ja yes (E); of course

die Jacke (-n) jacket (5)

die Jagd (-en) hunt

der Jagdpächter (-) / die Jagdpächterin (-nen) game tenant

der Jäger (-) / die Jägerin (-nen) hunter

das Jahr (-e) year (1); **dieses Jahr** this year; **einmal im Jahr** once a year (7); **im Jahr(e) ...** in the year . . . ; **jedes Jahr** every year; **letztes Jahr** last year; **mit 10 Jahren** at age 10; **nächstes Jahr** next

year (1); **die 90er Jahre** the nineties;
seit zwei Jahren for two years (6)
die Jahreszeit (-en) season
das Jahrhundert (-e) century
-jährig: 12-jährig (*adj.*) twelve-year(-old),
twelve years old; **der/die 12-Jährige**
(*decl. adj.*) twelve-year-old (person)
jährlich annual(ly)
(das) Jamaika Jamaica
(der) Jänner January (*Austrian*)
(der) Januar January (3); **im Januar** in
January (3)
der Jazz jazz
je ever; every, each **je** (+ *comparative*) …
desto (+ *comparative*) … the … the …
je nachdem depending on
je (*interjection*); **oh je** oh dear
die Jeans (*pl.*) jeans (5)
jeder, jede, jedes each, every (5);
everybody; **auf jeden Fall** in any case
(13); **jeden Abend** every evening; **jeden
Morgen** every morning; **jeden Tag**
every day (7); **jedes Jahr** every year
jedesmal every time
jedoch however, but
der Jeep (-s) jeep
jemand somebody, someone
Jenaer (*adj.*) of/from Jena (*a town in
central Germany*)
jetzig current, present
jetzt now (1)
jeweils each time, in each case
der Job (-s) (temporary) job
jobben to work (at a temporary job) (12)
jobbenderweise with respect to working at
a temporary job
die Jobbörse (-n) job-finding agency
joggen to jog (7)
der Joghurt yogurt (5)
der Joghurtbecher (-) carton of yogurt
das Journal (-e) journal
der Journalist (-en *masc.*) **(-en) / die
Journalistin (-nen)** journalist (1)
das Jubiläum (Jubiläen) anniversary
die Jugend youth; young people
das Jugendgästehaus (¨er) (type of) youth
hostel
die Jugendherberge (-n) youth hostel (9)
der/die Jugendliche (*decl. adj.*) young
person; teenager
(das) Jugoslawien Yugoslavia
(der) Juli July (3)
jung young (10)
der Junge (-n *masc.*) **(-n)** boy (2)
(der) Juni June (3)
(die) Jura (*pl.*) law (*as a subject of
study*)
die Justiz justice

K

das Kabel (-) cable
der Kabelanschluss (¨e) cable TV
connection (13)
der Käfer (-) beetle (*also Volkswagen
Beetle*)
der Kaffee (-s) coffee
der Kaffeebecher (-) coffee cup
die Kaffeemaschine (-n) coffeemaker

der Käfig (-e) cage
(das) Kairo Cairo
der Kaiser (-) / die Kaiserin (-nen)
emperor/empress
der Kaiserschmarren *broken-up pancake
sprinkled with powdered sugar and
raisins*
der Kajak (-s) kayak
die Kalbsleberwurst (¨e) veal liver sausage
der Kalender (-) calendar (3)
(das) Kalifornien California
die Kalorie (-n) calorie
kalt (kälter, kältest-) cold (7)
die Kamera (-s) camera (10)
der Kamerastandpunkt (-e) camera's
point of view
der Kamillentee chamomile tea
der Kamin (-e) fireplace, hearth
(sich) kämmen to comb (one's hair) (8)
die Kammermusik chamber music
das Kammerspiel (-e) chamber drama
(das) Kanada Canada
der Kanadier (-) / die Kanadierin (-nen)
Canadian (person)
der Kanarienvogel (¨) canary
die Kanarischen Inseln (*pl.*) Canary
Islands
der Kandidat (-en *masc.*) **(-en) / die
Kandidatin (-nen)** candidate
der Kanton (-e) canton (*division of
Switzerland*)
die Kanu (-s) canoe
der Kanzler (-) / die Kanzlerin (-nen)
chancellor
**der Kapellmeister (-) / die
Kapellmeisterin (-nen)** bandleader;
conductor
die Kapitalanlage (-n) investment of
capital
der Kapitän (-e) captain
das Kapitel (-) chapter
die Kapitulation (-en) capitulation
kaputt broken (9)
die Karibik the Caribbean
kariert checkered, plaid (5)
Karlsruher (*adj.*) of/from Karlsruhe (*city
in southwestern Germany*)
(der) Karneval Mardi Gras (*Rhineland*) (3)
die Karotte (-n) carrot (5)
die Karriere (-n) career; **Karriere machen**
to be successful in a career
die Karte (-n) card (7); ticket; chart; map;
Karten spielen to play cards (1)
die Kartoffel (-n) potato (5)
die Kartoffelchips (*pl.*) potato chips
der Kartoffelkloß (¨e) potato dumpling
das Kartoffelpüree mashed potatoes
der Kartoffelspieß (-e) *potatoes (and other
ingredients) roasted on a spit*
der Käse (-) cheese (5)
das Käsesortiment (-e) range of cheeses
die Kasse (-n) cash register; check-out (5);
vorne an der Kasse up front at the
cash register
die Kassette (-n) cash box; cassette (tape)
der Kasten (¨) box
das Kastenweißbrot (-e) *white bread
baked in a square loaf pan*

der Katalysator (-en) catalytic converter
der Katamaran (-e) catamaran
katastrophal catastrophic(ally)
die Kategorie (-n) category
der Kater (-) tomcat, male cat
katholisch Catholic
die Katze (-n) cat (12)
der Kauf (¨e) purchase; buying,
purchasing
kaufen to buy (2)
die Kauffrau (-en) saleswoman (11)
das Kaufhaus (¨er) department store (2);
im Kaufhaus at the department store
die Kaufleute (*pl.*) salespeople (11)
der Kaufmann (Kaufleute) salesman (11)
kaum hardly, scarcely (8)
kauzig (*coll.*) odd, weird
der Kaviar (-e) caviar
das KDW (= Kaufhaus des Westens) *large
department store in Berlin*
kegeln to bowl
der Kegler (-) / die Keglerin (-nen) bowler
kein, keine no, none, not any (2);
kein(e) … mehr no more … ; **noch
kein(e)** no … yet
der Keks (-e) cookie (5)
der Keller (-) cellar, basement
der Kellner (-) / die Kellnerin (-nen)
waiter, waitress; server (6)
kennen, kannte, gekannt to know, be
acquainted with (*person or thing*) (3);
kennen lernen (lernt kennen) to meet,
get to know
die Kenntnis (-se) knowledge (11)
der Kern (-e) core; nucleus
die Kernenergie nuclear energy
die Kerze (-n) candle
der Ketchup (-s) ketchup
der Kettenbrief (-e) chain letter
der Kick (-s) kick
das Kickboxen kickboxing
das Kilo (-s) = Kilogramm (-e) kilogram
der Kilometer (-) kilometer
das Kind (-er) child; **als Kind** as a child
der Kindergarten (¨) nursery school,
preschool
die Kinderkonfektion (-en) children's
wear
die Kindersterblichkeit child mortality
die Kindheit childhood
kindisch childish(ly)
das Kinn (-e) chin (8)
das Kino (-s) cinema, (movie) theater (4);
ins Kino gehen to go to the movies (4)
die Kinoleinwand (¨e) movie screen
der Kiosk (-e) kiosk
die Kirche (-n) church (9)
der Kirchhof (¨e) churchyard; graveyard,
cemetery
kitschig kitschy
die Kiwi (-s) kiwi (fruit)
die Klammer (-) parenthesis
die Klamotte (-n) duds, rags (*slang for
clothes*)
klar clear; of course; **Alles klar.**
Everything is clear., I get it. (E); **na klar**
absolutely (E); but of course, you bet
klären to clarify

die **Klasse** (-n) class; classroom; **erster/zweiter Klasse fahren (fährt), fuhr, ist gefahren** to travel first/second class (10)
der **Klassiker** (-) classic
klassisch classic; classical(ly)
das **Klavier** (-e) piano
kleben to stick, adhere
das **Kleid** (-er) dress (5)
die **Kleider** (*pl.*) clothes
der **Kleiderschrank** (-̈e) wardrobe; clothes closet (2)
die **Kleidung** clothing, clothes
klein small, little (2)
die **Kleinanzeige** (-n) classified ad
das **Kleingeld** (small) change
die **Kleinkinderbetreuung** child care
die **Kleinstadt** (-̈e) small city, town
der **Klettergarten** (-̈) climbing garden
klettern, ist geklettert to climb
klicken to click
der **Klient** (-en *masc.*) (-en) / die **Klientin** (-nen) client
das **Klima** climate
klingeln to ring
klingen, klang, geklungen to sound (8); **Du klingst so deprimiert.** You sound so depressed. (8)
die **Klinik** (-en) hospital; clinic
klopfen to knock
der **Klub** (-s) club
klug smart, intelligent(ly)
km = Kilometer
die **Knackwurst** (-̈e) *type of German sausage*
knallen to slam, bang
knapp just about, barely
die **Kneipe** (-n) pub, bar (6)
der **Kneipenbummel** (-) pub-crawl, bar-hopping
das **Knie** (-) knee (8)
der **Knoblauch** garlic
die **Knolle** (-n) tuber
knurren to growl
die **Kobra** (-s) cobra
der **Koch** (-̈e) / die **Köchin** (-nen) cook, chef
kochen to cook (1); to boil; **gekochtes Ei** boiled egg
die **Kochnische** (-n) kitchen nook
der **Kochschinken** (-) boiled ham
der **Koffer** (-) suitcase (5)
das **Kolleg** (-s) lecture
der **Kollege** (-n *masc.*) (-n) / die **Kollegin** (-nen) colleague, co-worker
(das) **Köln** Cologne (*city in western Germany*)
Kölner (*adj.*) of/from Cologne
das **Koma** (-s) coma
kombinieren to combine
der **Komfort** (-s) comfort
komisch funny, funnily; strange(ly)
kommen, kam, ist gekommen to come (1); **Ich komme aus ...** I'm from . . . (E); **Wie komme ich am besten dahin?** What's the best way to get there? (9); **Woher kommen Sie?** (*form.*) / **Woher kommst du?** (*inform.*) Where are you from? (E)

der **Kommentar** (-e) commentary
der **Kommilitone** (-n *masc.*) (-n) / die **Kommilitonin** (-nen) fellow student
der **Kommissar** (-e) detective inspector; commissioner
die **Kommode** (-n) dresser (2)
die **Kommune** (-n) commune
die **Kommunikation** (-en) communication
das **Kommunikationswesen** communications
kommunikativ communicative(ly)
kommunistisch communist
die **Komödie** (-n) comedy (4)
der **Komparativ** (-e) comparative
die **Komparativform** (-en) comparative form (of adjective)
komplett complete(ly)
komplex complex
kompliziert complicated (1)
komponieren to compose
der **Komponist** (-en *masc.*) (-en) / die **Komponistin** (-nen) composer
das **Kompositum** (**Komposita**) compound word
der **Kompost** (-e) compost
kompostieren to compost
die **Kondition** (-en) condition
die **Konditorei** (-en) pastry shop (5)
die **Konferenz** (-en) conference
der **Konflikt** (-e) conflict
der **Kongress** (-e) congress, convention
der **König** (-e) / die **Königin** (-nen) king/queen
die **Konjunktion** (-en) conjunction
der **Konjunktiv** (-e) subjunctive
die **Konjunktivform** (-en) subjunctive form (of verb)
konkret concrete(ly)
können (kann), konnte, gekonnt to be able to; can (4); to know how to
der **Könner** (-) / die **Könnerin** (-nen) one who can, expert
konservativ conservative(ly) (1)
die **Konservendose** (-n) can
der **Konstrukteur** (-e) / die **Konstrukteurin** (-nen) technical designer
der **Konsum** consumption
der **Kontakt** (-e) contact (11)
der **Kontext** (-e) context
kontinuierlich continuous(ly)
der **Kontrast** (-e) contrast
die **Kontrolle** (-n) control
kontrollieren to control
die **Konversation** (-en) conversation
das **Konzentrationslager** (-) concentration camp
der **Konzern** (-e) concern, group of companies
das **Konzert** (-e) concert (4); **ins Konzert gehen** to go to a concert (4)
die **Koordination** (-en) coordination
der **Kopf** (-̈e) head (8)
das **Köpfchen** (-): **kluges Köpfchen** clever little person
der **Kopfsalat** (-e) lettuce
die **Kopfschmerzen** (*pl.*) headache (8)
die **Kopie** (-n) copy

der **Kopierer** (-) copying machine
(das) **Korea** Korea
(das) **Korfu** Corfu
das **Korn** (-̈er) grain, kernel
der **Körper** (-) body
körperlich physical(ly)
der **Körperteil** (-e) body part (8)
die **Korrektur** (-en) correction, revision
korrespondieren to correspond
korrigieren to correct
die **Korruption** (-en) corruption (14)
(das) **Korsika** Corsica
die **Kosmetik** cosmetics
die **Kost** food
kosten to cost (2)
die **Kosten** (*pl.*) cost, expense
kostenlos free of charge
das **Kostüm** (-e) costume; fancy dress
der **Krach** loud noise
die **Kraft** (-̈e) power, strength; **in Kraft treten (tritt), trat, ist getreten** to come to power
kräftig strong(ly), powerful(ly)
krank sick, ill (8)
das **Krankenhaus** (-̈er) hospital
der **Krankenpfleger** (-) / die **Krankenschwester** (-n) nurse (8)
die **Krankenversicherung** (-en) health insurance
die **Krankheit** (-en) illness, disease, ailment (14)
krass blatant(ly), crass(ly)
das **Kraut** (-̈er) herb
die **Kräuterbutter** herb butter
der **Kräutertee** herbal tea (8)
die **Krawatte** (-n) necktie (5)
kreativ creative(ly)
die **Kreativität** creativity
die **Kreditkarte** (-n) credit card (9)
die **Kreuzung** (-en) intersection (9)
das **Kreuzworträtsel** (-) crossword puzzle; **Kreuzworträtsel machen** to do crossword puzzles (1)
der **Krieg** (-e) war (14)
kriegen (*coll.*) to get, receive
der **Krieger** (-) / die **Kriegerin** (-nen) warrior
der **Kriegsdienstverweigerer** (-) conscientious objector
der **Krimi** (-s) crime/detective/mystery story, film, or TV show (4)
die **Kriminalität** criminality
der **Kriminologe** (-n *masc.*) (-n) / die **Kriminologin** (-nen) criminologist
die **Krimiserie** (-n) detective series
die **Krise** (-n) crisis
das **Kriterium** (**Kriterien**) criterion
der **Kritiker** (-) / die **Kritikerin** (-nen) critic
kritisch critical(ly)
kritisieren to criticize
die **Krönungsmesse** (-n) coronation mass
(das) **Kuba** Cuba
die **Küche** (-n) kitchen (2); cuisine, food (6)
der **Kuchen** (-) cake (5)
der **Kuckuck** (-e) cuckoo
die **Kuckucksuhr** (-en) cuckoo clock

der Ku'damm = Kurfürstendamm *famous shopping street in Berlin*

der Kugelschreiber (-) ballpoint pen (12)

kühl cool(ly) (7)

der Kühlschrank (-̈e) refrigerator (9)

kulinarisch culinary

die Kultur (-en) culture

der Kulturtipp (-s) cultural tip

die Kulturwissenschaften (*pl.*) cultural sciences, arts and humanities

kümmern to concern

der Kunde (-n *masc.*) (-n) / die Kundin (-nen) customer (2)

künftig future; in the future

die Kunst (-̈e) art

der Kunstbetrachter (-) / die Kunstbetrachterin (-nen) art viewer

das Kunstgebilde (-) art object

die Kunsthalle (-n) art museum, exhibition hall

der Künstler (-) / die Künstlerin (-nen) artist (11)

das Kunstwerk (-e) work of art

die Kur (-en) health cure, treatment (at a spa)

der Kurfürstendamm *famous shopping street in Berlin*

der Kurort (-e) health spa, resort

der Kurs (-e) course

kurz (kürzer, kürzest-) short, brief(ly), for a short time (7)

die Kürze: in Kürze soon, shortly

die Kurzgeschichte (-n) short story

kürzlich recently

der Kurzschluss (-̈e) short circuit

die Kusine (-n) female cousin (3)

das Küsschen (-): ein dickes Küsschen a big kiss

die Küste (-n) coast

L

das Labor (-s) laboratory

der Laborant (-en *masc.*) (-en) / die Laborantin (-nen) laboratory technician

das Labskaus *type of beef stew eaten with a fried egg*

lächeln to smile

das Lächeln smile

lachen to laugh

der Lachs (-e) salmon

laden (lädt), lud, geladen to load

der Laden (-̈) store, shop (5)

das Ladenschlussgesetz (-e) law regulating store-closing times

die Lage (-n) location (9); situation

das Lager (-) camp

lala: so lala (*coll.*) OK, so-so (E)

das Lamm (-̈er) lamb

die Lampe (-n) lamp (2)

das Land (-̈er) country; nation, land; auf dem Land(e) in the countryside

das Landei (-er) farm egg

landen, hat/ist gelandet to land

die Landkarte (-n) map

das Landkind (-er) rural person

die Landschaft (-en) landscape, scenery

die Landung (-en) landing

die Landwirtschaft agriculture

lang (länger, längst-) long (7)

lange long (*temporal*); wie lange (for) how long

langsam slow(ly) (10); Langsamer, bitte. Slower, please. (E)

längst (*adv.*) long since, a long time ago

langweilig boring (1)

der Laptop (-s) laptop (computer)

der Lärm noise (14)

das Laserspektakel (-) laser show, laser spectacular

lassen (lässt), ließ, gelassen to leave (behind); to let (6); to have something done; Lass uns (doch) ... Let's . . . (6)

(das) Lateinamerika Latin America

der Lauch (-e) look

der Lauf (-e) course; im Laufe der Zeit over the course of time

laufen (läuft), lief, ist gelaufen to run, jog (2); to walk; der Film läuft im ... the film is playing at . . . ; Schlittschuh laufen to ice skate (7)

der Laufschritt (-e): im Laufschritt at a running pace

laut loud(ly) (10); according to

läuten: es läutet the bell is ringing

die Lautsprecherbox (-en) (stereo) speaker

leben to live

das Leben life (11)

der Lebenslauf (-̈e) résumé (11); tabellarischer Lebenslauf résumé in outline form

das Lebensmittel (-) food, groceries

das Lebensmittelgeschäft (-e) grocery store

der Lebensraum (-̈e) habitat

der Leberkäs *Bavarian-style meatloaf* (6)

der Lebkuchen (-) gingerbread

lecker tasty, delicious

das Leder (-) leather

die Lederhose (-n) leather pants (*mostly worn in southern Germany*)

die Lederwaren (*pl.*) leather goods

ledig unmarried, single

leer empty

legen to lay, put (*in a lying position*) (6); sich legen to lie down (8)

der Lehrer (-) / die Lehrerin (-nen) teacher (E)

der Lehrling (-e) apprentice, trainee

die Leibesübungen (*pl.*) physical education

die Leiche (-n) corpse

leicht easy, easily; light(ly)

das Leid sorrow, grief

leidtun (+*dat.*) (tut leid), tat leid, leidgetan (*impersonal*) to be sorry Das tut mir leid. I'm sorry. (9)

leider unfortunately (3)

leihen, lieh, geliehen to lend; to borrow (5)

Leipziger (*adj.*) of/from Leipzig

leise quiet(ly); softly

sich (*dat.*) etwas leisten to afford something

die Leistung (-en) accomplishment

leiten to lead

der Leiter (-) / die Leiterin (-nen) leader, director (11)

die Lektüre (-n) reading (material)

lernen to learn; to study (1); kennen lernen (lernt kennen) to meet, get to know

die Lernmittel (*pl.*) school supplies

das Leseexemplar (-e) copy of a book

lesen (liest), las, gelesen to read (1, 2)

der Leser (-) / die Leserin (-nen) reader

die Leserschaft readers, readership

das Lesestück (-e) reading selection

die Letter (-n) piece of type (used in printing)

(das) Lettland Latvia

letzt- last, letzte Nacht last night, letzte Woche last week; letztes Jahr last year; zum letzten Mal for the last time

Letzt: zu guter Letzt in the end

leuchten to shine, glow

die Leute (*pl.*) people (2)

liberal liberal(ly)

lieb kind; dear alles Liebe all my love (*at end of letter*)

die Liebe (-n) love

lieben to love

lieber (+ *verb*) rather, preferably; möchte lieber would rather (4)

das Liebespaar (-e) couple, pair of lovers

der Liebling (-e) darling; Lieblings- favorite (*first component of compound nouns*)

am liebsten (+ *verb*) the best, the most; möchte am liebsten would like to (do) most (4)

(das) Liechtenstein Liechtenstein (E)

das Lied (-er) song

der Liedermacher (-) / die Liedermacherin (-nen) (folk) songwriter

liegen, lag, gelegen to lie; to be located (6); es liegt daran, dass ... it is because . . . ; günstig liegen to be conveniently located (9)

liegen bleiben (bleibt liegen), blieb liegen, ist liegen geblieben to stay down

lila purple, violet (5)

die Limonade (-n) lemonade; any flavored soda, soft drink

die Linguistik linguistics

die Linie (-n) line; in erster Linie first and foremost

link- left, left-hand; auf der linken Seite on the left side

links (on the) left (9); nach links to the left (9)

Linzer (*adj.*) of/from Linz (*city in Austria*)

die Lippe (-n) lip

die Liste (-n) list

(das) Litauen Lithuania

der Liter (-) liter

literarisch literary

die Literatur (-en) literature

locker loose(ly); relaxed

sich lockern to relax, loosen

der Löffel (-) spoon (6)

logisch logical(ly)

lokal local(ly)

das Lokal (-e) restaurant, pub, bar (6)

die Lokalität (-en) locality

die Lokalnachrichten (*pl.*) local news (13)

die Lokomotive (-n) locomotive

los loose; off; **Was ist denn los?** What's the matter? (2)

lösbar solvable

löschen to delete

lösen to solve (14)

losgehen (geht los), ging los, ist losgegangen to start

loslegen (legt los) (*coll.*) to start, let rip

losrennen (rennt los), rannte los, ist losgerannt to run off

die Lösung (-en) solution (14)

loswerden (wird los), wurde los, ist losgeworden (*coll.*) to get rid of

losziehen (zieht los), zog los, losgezogen (*coll.*) to take off, leave

die Lotterie (-n) lottery

das Lotto (-s) lottery

die Lücke (-n) gap, space, blank

das Lückendiktat (-e) fill-in-the-blank dictation

die Luft (¨e) air (8)

die Luftbrücke "air bridge," Berlin airlift (1948–49)

das Luftschloss (¨er) castle in the air, pipe dream

die Luftverschmutzung air pollution

der Luftweg (-e) air route

die Lüge (-n) lie, falsehood

der Lügebaron lying baron (*Münchhausen*)

lügen, log, gelogen to lie, tell a falsehood

die Lunge (-n) lung

die Lupe (-n) magnifying glass

Lust haben to feel like (*doing something*) (2)

lustig cheerful(ly); fun-loving (1); funny, funnily

das Lustspiel (-e) comedy

(das) Luxemburg Luxembourg (E)

die Luxusjacht (-en) luxury yacht

(das) Luzern Lucerne (*in Switzerland*)

M

der Maastrichter Vertrag the Maastricht Treaty (*which formed the European Union*)

machen to make; to do (1); **Das macht nichts.** That doesn't matter. (8); **Das macht Spaß.** That's fun. (1); **das macht zusammen ...** all together, that comes to . . . (5) **Fortschritte machen** to make progress (14); **Kreuzworträtsel machen** to do crossword puzzles (1); **Mach schnell!** Hurry up!; **Mach's gut.** Take care, so long (*inform.*) (E); **ein Praktikum machen** to do an internship (1); **sich Sorgen machen um** (+ *acc.*) to worry about (14); **Urlaub machen** to go on vacation (8); **Was machst du gern?** What do you like to do?

mächtig powerful(ly)

das Mädchen (-) girl

der Magen (¨) stomach

die Magermilch skim milk

das Magisterstudium study toward a master's degree

die Mahlzeit (-en) meal

das Mahnmal (¨er) memorial

(der) Mai May (3); **der erste Mai** May first (3); **am ersten Mai** on May first (3)

die Mail (-s) e-mail

mailen to e-mail

der Main Main (*river, tributary of the Rhine*)

der Mais corn, maize (6)

mal = **einmal** once; just; (*softening particle used with imperatives*) (4); **-mal** time(s); **ich möchte lieber mal** I would rather; **noch mal** again, once again; **sag mal** tell me (1); **schau mal** look

die Malaria malaria

die Malediven (*pl.*) the Maldives

malen to paint (7)

der Maler (-) / die Malerin (-nen) painter

(das) Mallorca Majorca

(das) Malta Malta

die Mama (-s) mom, mommy

man (*indef. pron.*) one; you; they; people (4); **Hier darf man nicht parken.** You may not park here. (4); **Wie sagt man ... auf Deutsch?** How do you say . . . in German? (E)

das Management (-s) management

der Manager (-) / die Managerin (-nen) manager

mancher, manche, manches some; **manch ein(e)** many a; **manches Mal** many a time

manchmal sometimes (8)

der Mann (¨er) man (1); husband (3)

männlich masculine, male

die Mannschaft (-en) team

der Mantel (¨) (over)coat (5)

das Marathon (-s) marathon

das Märchen (-) fairy tale

marineblau navy blue

die Mark (-) mark (*former German currency*); **die D-Mark (Deutsche Mark)** German mark

das Marketing marketing

markieren to mark

der Markt (¨e) (open-air) market, marketplace (5); **auf dem Markt** at the market

der Marktplatz (¨e) market square

die Marmelade (-n) jam

(das) Marokko Morocco

der Mars Mars

marschieren to march; **marsch!** march!

der Marshallplan Marshall Plan (*American recovery program for Europe after World War II*)

(der) März March (3)

die Masche (-n) (*coll.*) trick

die Maschine (-n) machine

der Maschinenbau mechanical engineering

die Massage (-n) massage

mäßig moderate(ly)

die Maßnahme (-n) measure, action

das Material (-ien) material

die Mathematik mathematics

die Matheprüfung (-en) math test

das Matjesfilet (-s) herring filet

der Matjeshering (-e) young, *slightly salted herring*

das Matterhorn (*mountain in the Swiss Alps*)

die Mauer (-n) wall

die Maus (¨e) mouse (*also as term of endearment*)

maximal maximum

der MDR = Mitteldeutscher Rundfunk *broadcasting company in Germany*

der Mechaniker (-) / die Mechanikerin (-nen) mechanic (11)

(das) Mecklenburg-Vorpommern *one of the German states*

die Medien (*pl.*) media

die Medienwissenschaft (-en) media science

das Medikament (-e) medicine, medication (5)

die Meditation (-en) meditation

meditieren to meditate

die Medizin (field of) medicine

medizinisch medical(ly)

das Meer (-e) sea; ocean (7); **am Meer** at the seaside

die Meeresfrüchte (*pl.*) seafood

mehr more; **immer mehr** more and more; **kein(e) ... mehr** no more; **nicht mehr** not anymore; **nie mehr** never again

das Mehrbettzimmer (-) room with several beds

mehrere (*pl.*) several

die Mehrfachnennungen (*pl.*) multiple mentions

mehrmals often, several times, on several occasions

die Mehrweg-Eierbox (-en) recyclable egg carton

die Mehrwertsteuer (-n) value-added tax; national sales tax

die Mehrzweckhalle (-n) multipurpose hall

mein my (3)

meinen to mean; to think, be of the opinion (14); **Was meinen Sie?** (*form.*) / **Was meinst du?** (*inform.*) What do you think?

die Meinung (-en) opinion (14); **ich bin der Meinung ...** I'm of the opinion . . . (14); **meiner Meinung nach ...** in my opinion . . . (14)

meist mostly

meist- most; **am meisten** (the) most

meistens mostly (8)

der Meister (-) / die Meisterin (-nen) master; champion

melancholisch melancholic(ally)

die Melange (-n) blend; coffee with milk

sich melden to answer (*phone*) (13); **Niemand meldet sich.** No one is answering. (13)

die Meldung (-en) message, announcement

das Memo (-s) memo

die Mensa (-s) student cafeteria (1)

der Mensch (-en *masc.***) (-en)** human being, person (2)

das **Menschenrecht (-e)** human right (*usually pl.*) (14)
die **Menschenschlange (-n)** (long) line of people
menschlich human
der **Mercedes (-)** Mercedes (*automobile*)
merken to notice, observe
das **Merkmal (-e)** feature, characteristic
merkwürdig strange(ly); remarkable, remarkably
messen (misst), maß, gemessen to measure
das **Messer (-)** knife (6)
das **Messgerät (-e)** measuring device
die **Messung (-en)** measurement
der **Meteorologe (-n** *masc.*) **(-n) /** die **Meteorologin (-nen)** meteorologist
der/das **Motor ( )** motor
die **Methode (-n)** method
die **Metropole (-n)** metropolis, large city
der **Metzger (-) /** die **Metzgerin (-nen)** butcher
die **Metzgerei (-en)** butcher shop (5)
(das) Mexiko Mexico
mich me (*acc.*) (3); **Freut mich.** Pleased to meet you. (E)
das **Mietangebot (-e)** rental offer
die **Miete (-n)** rent (2)
mieten to rent (*from someone*) (12)
der **Mieter (-) /** die **Mieterin (-nen)** renter
das **Mietgesuch (-e)** rental request
das **Mietshaus (¨er)** apartment building
der **Mietwagen (-)** rental car
das **Mikrofon (-e)** microphone
das **Mikrowellengerät (-e)** microwave oven
der **Mikrowellenherd (-e)** microwave oven (12)
die **Milch** milk (5)
das **Militär** armed forces, military
das **Millennium (Millennien)** millennium
der **Milliardär (-e) /** die **Milliardärin (-nen)** billionaire
die **Milliarde (-n)** billion (1,000,000,000)
der **Milliliter (-)** milliliter, one thousandth of a liter
die **Million (-en)** million
der **Millionär (-e) /** die **Millionärin (-nen)** millionaire
das **Millionenpublikum** audience of millions
die **Mindestbestellung (-en)** minimum order
mindestens at least (8)
die **Mineralstofftablette (-n)** mineral salt tablet
das **Mineralwasser** mineral water
der **Minidialog (-e)** mini-dialogue
das **Minigolf** miniature golf (game)
minimalistisch minimalistic(ally)
der **Minister (-) /** die **Ministerin (-nen)** (government) minister
die **Minute (-n)** minute (4)
mir (to/for) me (*dat.*) (5); **Das ist mir zu blöd.** I think that's really stupid. (13); **Mir ist schlecht.** I'm sick to my stomach (8)
mischen to mix

das **Mischpult (-e)** mixing desk, mixing console
die **Mischung (-en)** mixture
mit (+ *dat.*) with; by means of (5); **Wie wäre es mit … ?** How about . . . ? (13); **Willst du mit?** (*coll.*) Do you want to come along?
der **Mitarbeiter (-) /** die **Mitarbeiterin (-nen)** co-worker, colleague; employee (11)
mitbekommen (bekommt mit), bekam mit, mitbekommen to get to take along; to notice
mitbestimmen (bestimmt mit) to have an influence on
der **Mitbewohner (-) /** die **Mitbewohnerin (-nen)** roommate (?)
mitbringen (bringt mit), brachte mit, mitgebracht to bring along
miteinander together, with one another
die **Mitfahrgelegenheit (-en)** ride-sharing opportunity
mitgehen (geht mit), ging mit, ist mitgegangen to come along, go along
das **Mitglied (-er)** member
mithelfen (hilft mit), half mit, mitgeholfen to help, lend a hand
mitkommen (kommt mit), kam mit, ist mitgekommen to come along (4)
das **Mitleid** compassion, pity
mitmachen (macht mit) to join in
mitnehmen (nimmt mit), nahm mit, mitgenommen to take along (4); **zum Mitnehmen** (food) to go; take-out (6)
mitspielen (spielt mit) to play along
der **Mitstudent (-en** *masc.*) **(-en) /** die **Mitstudentin (-nen)** fellow student
der **Mittag (-e)** noon (4); **heute Mittag** today at noon
das **Mittagessen (-)** midday meal; lunch (5)
mittags at noon (4)
die **Mitte (-n)** middle, center (9); **in der Mitte (der Stadt)** in the center (of the city) (9)
das **Mittel (-)** means, method
das **Mittelalter** Middle Ages
mittelalterlich medieval
die **Mittelklasse (-n)** middle class
mittelmäßig mediocre, indifferent(ly)
der **Mittelpunkt (-e)** center
mittelständisch middle-class
der **Mittelwesten** Midwest (USA)
mitten in the midst; **mitten im Dorf** in the middle of the village
die **Mitternacht** midnight; **um Mitternacht** at midnight (3)
mittler- middle; **die mittlere Reife** high school diploma (*not sufficient for university studies*)
(der) Mittwoch Wednesday (3)
mittwochs Wednesdays, on Wednesday(s) (4)
mitunter sometimes
die **Mitwohnzentrale (-n)** shared housing agency
der **Mix (-e)** mix
ml = Milliliter

die **Möbel** (*pl.*) furniture (2)
möbliert furnished (2)
möchte would like to (4); **ich möchte (gern)** I would like; **möchte am liebsten** would like to (do) most (4); **möchte lieber** would rather (4)
das **Modalverb (-en)** modal verb
die **Mode (-n)** fashion
das **Modell (-e)** example, model
der/das **Modem (-s)** modem
die **Moderation (-en)** presentation; presenter, moderator
der **Moderator (-en) /** die **Moderatorin (-nen)** presenter, moderator
modern modern, in a modern manner
modernisieren to modernize
modifizieren to modify
modisch fashionable, fashionably (5)
mögen (mag), mochte, gemocht to care for; to like (4); **ich möchte (gern)** I would like; **Wo mag das sein?** Where can that be?
möglich possible, possibly (14)
die **Möglichkeit (-en)** possibility, opportunity (10)
möglichst as . . . as possible
die **Möhre (-n)** carrot
der **Moment (-e)** moment; **im Moment** at the moment; **Moment (mal)** just a moment
der **Monat (-e)** month; **einmal im Monat** once a month (7)
-monatig lasting . . . months
monatlich monthly (12)
die **Mongolei** Mongolia
(der) Montag Monday (3); **am Montag** on Monday (3)
montags Mondays, on Monday(s) (4)
der **Mord (-e)** murder
der **Mörder (-) /** die **Mörderin (-nen)** murderer
der **Mordverdacht** suspicion of murder
morgen tomorrow (3); **morgen Abend** tomorrow evening (4); **morgen früh** tomorrow morning (4); **morgen Nachmittag** tomorrow afternoon; **morgen Vormittag** tomorrow morning; **Welches Datum ist morgen?** What is tomorrow's date? (3)
der **Morgen (-)** morning (4); **am Morgen** in the morning; **(guten) Morgen** good morning (E); **heute Morgen** this morning (4); **jeden Morgen** every morning
morgendlich (*adj.*) morning
die **Morgenpost (-en)** morning mail
die **Morgenroutine (-n)** morning routine
morgens in the morning, mornings (4)
das **Motel (-s)** motel
das **Motiv (-e)** motive; motif
motivieren to motivate
der **Motor (-en)** motor, engine
das **Motorrad (¨er)** motorcycle (2); **Motorrad fahren** to ride a motorcycle
das **Mountainbike (-s)** mountain bike
das **Mountainbiking** mountain biking
der **Mozzarella** mozzarella (cheese)
müde tired (8)

die **Mühe (-n)** trouble
die **Mühle (-n)** mill
der **Müll** trash, garbage (12)
der **Mülleimer (-)** garbage can
der **Multivitaminsaft (⸚e)** multivitamin
juice
(das) München Munich
Münchner (*adj.*) of/from Munich
der **Mund (⸚er)** mouth (8)
mündlich oral(ly), verbal(ly)
das **Museum (Museen)** museum (9)
das **Musical (-s)** musical
die **Musik** music (1)
der **Musikant (-en** *masc.*) **(-en)** / die
Musikantin (-nen) musician, music
maker
der **Musiker (-)** / die **Musikerin (-nen)**
(professional) musician
der **Musikfreund (-e)** / die **Musikfreundin**
(-nen) music lover
musizieren to make music, play an
instrument
der **Muskel (-n)** muscle (8)
das **Müsli (-)** granola; cereal (5)
müssen (muss), musste, gemusst to have
to; must (4)
das **Muster (-)** pattern, model, example;
nach dem Muster according to the
example
mutig brave(ly)
die **Mutter (⸚)** mother (3)
die **Muttersprache (-n)** mother tongue,
native language
der **Muttertag** Mother's Day (3)
die **Mutti (-s)** mommy, mom
die **Mütze (-n)** cap (5)
Mwst. = Mehrwertsteuer
der **Mythos (Mythen)** myth

N

na well; so; **na ja** oh well; **na klar** absolutely (E); but of course; you bet; **Na
und?** So what? (13); **Na, wie geht's?**
How are you? (*casual*) (E)
nach (+ *dat.*) after (4, 6); to (*place name*)
(5); according to; **Es ist Viertel nach
zwei.** It's a quarter after two. (4); **fünf
nach zwei** five after two (4); **meiner
Meinung nach …** in my opinion …
(14); **nach dem Befinden fragen** to ask
about someone's well-being; **nach dem
Weg fragen** to ask for directions (9);
nach Dienstag after Tuesday (6); **nach
links/rechts** to the left/right (9); **nach
Hause** (to) home (5); **nach oben** above,
upstairs (*directional*) (12); **nach unten**
below, downstairs (*directional*) (12)
der **Nachbar (-n** *masc.*) **(-n)** / die
Nachbarin (-nen) neighbor
nachdem (*subord. conj.*) after (10); **je
nachdem** it all depends
nachdenken (über + *acc.*) **(denkt nach),
dachte nach, nachgedacht** to think
(about), ponder (over) (11)
nachhaltig lasting; for a long time
nachher afterward
**nachkommen (kommt nach), kam nach,
ist nachgekommen** to come later, follow

der **Nachmittag (-e)** afternoon (4); **am
Nachmittag** in the afternoon; **heute
Nachmittag** this afternoon (4); **morgen
Nachmittag** tomorrow afternoon
nachmittags in the afternoon,
afternoons (4)
der **Nachname (***gen.* **-ns,** *acc./dat.* **-n) (-n)**
family name, surname (1)
die **Nachricht (-en)** message; die
Nachrichten (*pl.*) news (13)
der **Nachrichtensprecher (-)** / die
Nachrichtensprecherin (-nen) news
anchor
nachschauen (schaut nach) to check,
look up
die **Nachspeise (-n)** dessert (6)
nächst- next, following; closest, nearest;
am nächsten Tag on the next day;
nächstes Jahr next year
die **Nacht (⸚e)** night (4); **gute Nacht** good
night (E); **letzte Nacht** last night; **über
Nacht** overnight
der **Nachteil (-e)** disadvantage
der **Nachtisch (-e)** dessert (6)
nächtlich nocturnal, during the night
nachts at night, nights (4)
der **Nachttisch (-e)** nightstand (2)
der **Nachwuchsdarsteller (-)** / die
Nachwuchsdarstellerin (-nen)
up-and-coming actor/actress
das **Nackensteak (-s)** neck steak
nah (näher, nächst-) close by, near
die **Nähe** vicinity (9); **in der Nähe (des
Bahnhofs)** near (the train station) (9)
die **Naherholung (-en)** vacationing nearby
die **Nahrung** nutrition; food
das **Nahrungsmittel (-)** food
der **Name (***gen.* **-ns,** *acc./dat.* **-n) (-n)** name
(1); **auf den Namen … hören** to answer
to the name … ; **Auf welchen Namen?**
Under what name? (9); **Mein Name
ist …** My name is … (E); **Wie ist
Ihr/dein Name?** What is your name?
(*form./inform.*) (E)
nämlich namely, that is to say (3)
nanu now what
die **Nase (-n)** nose (8)
die **Nation (-en)** nation; die **Vereinten
Nationen** United Nations
national national(ly)
die **Natur (-en)** nature (10)
das **Naturbett (-en)** natural bed
die **Naturkraft (⸚e)** natural energy
die **Naturkunde** nature study
natürlich natural(ly); of course (1)
naturnah close to nature
die **Naturwissenschaft (-en)** natural
science
das **Navi (-s)** navigation system
der **Nazi (-s)** (*abbreviation for*) member of
the German National Socialist Party
'ne = eine
das **Neandertal** *valley near Düsseldorf*
der **Nebel** fog (7)
neben (+ *acc./dat.*) next to, beside (6)
die **Nebenarbeit (-en)** side job
nebenbei on the side
nebeneinander next to each other

die **Nebenkosten** (*pl.*) utilities; extra
costs (12)
die **Nebensache (-n)** something of
secondary importance
der **Nebentisch (-e)** adjacent table
neblig foggy (7)
der **Neffe (-n** *masc.*) **(-n)** nephew (3)
negativ negative(ly)
nehmen (nimmt), nahm, genommen to
take (2); **im Grunde genommen**
basically (14); **Platz nehmen** to take a
seat; **zu etwas** (*dat.*) **Stellung nehmen**
to take a stand on something
neidisch envious(ly)
nein no (E)
nennen, nannte, genannt to name, call
(das) Nepal Nepal
der **Nerv (-en)** nerve
nerven (*coll.*) to irritate, get on one's
nerves
nervös nervous(ly)
nett nice(ly) (1); pleasant(ly)
das **Netz (-e)** net; network
neu new(ly) (3); **nichts Neues** nothing new
neuartig new kind of
der **Neubau (Neubauten)** modern
building (12)
neuerdings recently
neugierig curious, nosy, inquisitive(ly)
das **Neujahr** New Year's Day (3)
neulich recently, the other day
neun nine (E)
neunte ninth (3)
neunzehn nineteen (E)
neunzig ninety (E)
(das) Neuseeland New Zealand
die **Neustadt (⸚e)** new part of town
nicht not (1); **Das weiß ich nicht.** I don't
know. (E); **Ich verstehe das nicht.** I
don't understand. (E); **nicht besonders
gut** not particularly well (E); **nicht
mehr** no longer; **noch nicht** not yet;
nicht wahr? isn't that so?
die **Nichte (-n)** niece (3)
der **Nichtraucher (-)** / die **Nichtraucherin
(-nen)** nonsmoker (2)
nichts nothing (2); **Das macht nichts.** That
doesn't matter. (8); **gar nichts** nothing
at all; **nichts Gescheites** nothing
decent (13); **nichts Neues** nothing new;
Nichts zu danken. No thanks
necessary; Don't mention it. (8)
der **Nichtskönner (-)** incompetent person
das **Nichtstun** inactivity, doing nothing
nie never (1); **nie mehr** never again
die **Niederlande** (*pl.*) the Netherlands (E)
der **Niederländer (-)** / die **Niederländerin
(-nen)** Dutch person
**sich niederlassen (lässt nieder), ließ
nieder, niedergelassen** to settle down
(das) Niedersachsen Lower Saxony
(*German state*)
**niederschlagen (schlägt nieder), schlug
nieder, niedergeschlagen** to strike
down
**niederschreiben (schreibt nieder), schrieb
nieder, niedergeschrieben** to write
down

niedlich sweet(ly), cute(ly)

niedrig low (2)

niemals never

niemand nobody; **Niemand meldet sich.** No one is answering. (13)

das Niveau (-s) level; standard

der Nobelpreis (-e) Nobel prize

noch still; yet (2); **Ist hier noch frei?** Is this seat available? (6); **noch (ein)mal** once more; **noch mehr** even more; **noch nicht** not yet; **Sonst noch (et)was?** Anything else? (10)

nochmals again, once again

das Nomen (-) noun

der Nominativ (-e) nominative case

nordamerikanisch (*adj.*) North American

(das) Norddeutschland northern Germany

der Norden north; **im Norden** in the north

nördlich (von + *dat.***)** north (of)

Nordost (*without article*) northeast

(das) Nordrhein-Westfalen North Rhine-Westphalia (*German state*)

die Nordsee North Sea

Nordwest (*without article*) northwest

die Norm (-en) norm

normal normal(ly)

normalerweise normally, usually

der Normalstudent (-en *masc.***) (-en) / die Normalstudentin (-nen)** average student

(das) Norwegen Norway

das Notebook (-s) notebook computer (13)

der Notgroschen (-) savings for a rainy day

notieren to write down

nötig necessary (5); urgent(ly)

die Notiz (-en) note; **sich Notizen machen** to take notes

notwendig necessary, necessarily (12)

(der) November November (3)

die Nudel (-n) noodle (6)

null zero (E)

nummerieren to number

die Nummer (-n) number

das Nummernschild (-er) license plate

nun now

nur only (2); **nicht nur** not only

(das) Nürnberg Nuremberg

Nürnberger (*adj.*) of/from Nuremberg

der Nutzer (-) / die Nutzerin (-nen) user

nützen to be of use

nützlich useful(ly) (12)

O

die Oase (-n) oasis

ob (*subord. conj.*) if, whether (or not) (8)

der/die Obdachlose (*decl. adj.*) homeless person (14)

die Obdachlosigkeit homelessness (14)

oben at the top; above; upstairs (12); **nach oben** above, upstairs (*directional*) (12)

ober upper

der Ober (-) waiter (6)

der Oberarzt (¨e) / die Oberärztin (-nen) chief physician

(das) Oberschlesien Upper Silesia

die Oberschule (-n) secondary school

die Oberstufe (-n) upper level

das Objekt (-e) object

das Obst fruit (5)

die Obsttunke (-n) fruit sauce

der Obst- und Gemüsestand (¨e) fruit and vegetable stand (5)

obwohl (*subord. conj.*) although, even though

oder (*coord. conj.*) or (7); **entweder … oder** either . . . or (8)

offen open

die Offenheit openness, candor

öffentlich public(ly) (14); **öffentliche Verkehrsmittel** (*pl.*) means of public transportation

offiziell official(ly)

der Offizier (-e) / die Offizierin (-nen) officer

öffnen to open

die Öffnung (-en) opening

oft often (1)

oh oh; **oh je!** oh, dear!

ohne (+ *acc.*) without (3)

das Ohr (-en) ear (8)

der Ökogarten (¨) organic garden

die Ökologie ecology

ökologisch ecological(ly)

das Oktett (-e) octet

(der) Oktober October (3)

die Olive (-n) olive (6)

die Oma (-s) (*coll.*) grandma (3)

die Omi (-s) (*coll.*) granny

der Onkel (-) uncle (3)

der Opa (-s) (*coll.*) grandpa (3)

die Oper (-n) opera (4); **in die Oper gehen** to go to the opera (4)

die Optik optics

optimal optimal(ly)

orange (*adj.*) orange (color) (5)

die Orange (-n) orange

die Orangenmarmelade (-n) orange marmelade

das Orchester (-) orchester

die Ordinalzahl (-en) ordinal number

die Ordnung order

die Organisation (-en) organization

organisch organic(ally)

organisieren to organize

der Organismus (Organismen) organism

die Orientierungsstufe (-n) orientation level (*in German school system*)

der Orientteppich (-e) oriental rug

originell original, in an original fashion; inventive(ly), unique(ly)

der Ort (-e) place; locality; location

Ost (*without article*) east

(das) Ostberlin East Berlin

der Ostberliner (-) / die Ostberlinerin (-nen) person from East Berlin

das Ostblockland (¨er) country in the Eastern Bloc

der Osten east; **im Osten** in the east

der Osterhase (-n *masc.***) (-n)** Easter bunny

(das) Ostern Easter (3)

(das) Österreich Austria (E)

österreichisch (*adj.*) Austrian

östlich (von + *dat.***)** east (of)

die Ostsee Baltic Sea

das Outsourcing outsourcing

oxydieren to oxidize

der Ozean (-e) ocean

das Ozonloch (¨er) hole in the ozone layer

die Ozonschicht (-en) ozone layer

P

das Paar (-e) pair

ein paar a few, a couple of; **ein paar Mal** a couple of times

packen to pack (10)

die Packung (-en) package; box

die Pädagogik pedagogy

pädagogisch pedagogical(ly)

das Paket (-e) package, packet

der Papa (-s) dad, daddy

das Papier (-e) paper (12)

die Papierlaterne (-n) paper lantern

die Paprika bell pepper (6)

das Paradies (-e) paradise

das Paragliding paragliding

das Parfüm (-s) perfume

die Parfümerie (-n) perfumery

der Park (-s) park

parken to park; **Hier darf man nicht parken.** You may not park here. (4)

der Parkplatz (¨e) parking space; parking lot (9)

das Parkverbot: hier ist Parkverbot no parking here

die Partei (-en) (political) party

die Partie (-n) game, round

das Partizip (-ien) participle; **das Partizip Perfekt** past participle; **das Partizip Präsens** present participle

das Partizipialadjektiv (-e) participial adjective

der Partner (-) / die Partnerin (-nen) partner

die Partnerschaft (-en) partnership

die Party (-s) party (3); **eine Party geben** to throw a party, have a party

der Pass (¨e) passport; pass

der Passant (-en *masc.***) (-en) / die Passantin (-nen)** passerby (9)

passen (+ *dat.*) to match; to fit (5); **passen zu** (+ *dat.*) to be suitable for

passend fitting, suitable

das Passfoto (-s) passport photo

passieren, ist passiert to happen (7)

das Passiv (-e) passive voice (of the verb)

die Pasta pasta

die Pastille (-n) pastille

die Patentanmeldung (-en) patent application

der Patient (-en *masc.***) (-en) / die Patientin (-nen)** patient

die Pauke (-n) kettle drum

das Pauschalangebot (-e) package tour offer

die Pause (-n) pause, break

pausenlos continuous(ly), without interruption

der Pazifik Pacific Ocean

der PC = Personalcomputer (-) personal computer

das Pech pitch; bad luck; **So ein Pech!** What a shame! What bad luck! (8)

der Pelz (-e) fur

die Pension (-en) small family-run hotel; bed and breakfast (9)

per via; by way of; **per Autostop reisen** to hitchhike (10)

perfekt perfect

das Perfekt present perfect tense; **das Partizip Perfekt** past participle

die Person (-en) person; **pro Person** per person (10)

das Personal personnel, staff (11)

der Personalausweis (-e) (personal) ID card (10)

das Personalpronomen (-) personal pronoun

der Personenkraftwagen (Pkw) (-) automobile, car

persönlich personal(ly)

die Persönlichkeit (-en) personality

die Perspektive (-n) perspective

das Pestizid (-e) pesticide

der Pfad (-e) path; **der Trimm-Pfad (-e)** parcourse, jogging path

die Pfanne (-n) pan (6)

der Pfannkuchen (-) pancake; **der Berliner Pfannkuchen (-)** jelly doughnut

der Pfeffer pepper (5)

der Pfennig (-e) penny (*former German monetary unit*)

das Pferd (-e) horse

das Pferderennen (-) horse race

das Pfifferling chanterelle mushroom

pfiffig clever(ly); stylish(ly)

die Pflanze (-n) plant

pflanzen to plant

pflanzlich (*adj.*) plant, vegetable

das Pflegeheim (-e) nursing home

pflegen to look after, care for; maintain

die Pflicht (-en) duty

der Pförtner (-) / die Pförtnerin (-nen) porter, doorkeeper

das Pfund (-e) pound; 500 grams

phantasievoll imaginative(ly)

das Phantom (-e) phantom

die Philharmonie (-n) philharmonic (orchestra)

die Philosophie philosophy

die Physik physics

der Physiker (-) / die Physikerin (-nen) physicist

das Picknick (-s) picnic

der Picknickkorb (¨e) picnic basket

der Pilot (-en *masc.*) (-en) / die Pilotin (-nen) pilot

(das) Pilsen Plzeň (*town in the Czech Republic*)

das Pilsener (-) Pilsner beer (6)

der Pilz (-e) mushroom

die Pipeline (-s) pipeline

die Pistole (-n) pistol, revolver

die Pizza (-s) pizza

die Pizzeria (-s) pizzeria

der Pkw = Personenkraftwagen

der Plan (¨e) plan (4)

planen to plan (3)

das Plasmamonitor (-en) plasma screen

das Plastik plastic

der Plastikbeutel (-) plastic bag

die Plastiktüte (-n) plastic bag (14)

der Plattenspieler (-) record player

der Platz (¨e) place; seat (6); room, space; plaza, square; **Platz nehmen** to take a seat

die Platzkarte (-n) place card, seat reservation card (10)

der Plausch (-e) chat

pleite (*coll.*) broke, out of money (12)

das Plenum: im Plenum all together

plötzlich sudden(ly); unexpected(ly)

die Pluralform (-en) plural form

plus plus

das Plusquamperfekt (-e) past perfect tense, pluperfect tense

die Poesie poetry

der Pokal (-e) trophy, cup

das Pokalfinale (-) cup final(s)

(das) Polen Poland (E)

die Politik politics (13)

der Politiker (-) / die Politikerin (-nen) politician (14)

politisch political(ly)

politisieren to politicize

die Politologie political science

die Polizei police; police station (9)

der Polizist (-en *masc.*) (-en) / die Polizistin (-nen) police officer

der Polyester polyester

die Pommes (frites) (*pl.*) French fries (6)

die Popmusik pop music

populär popular(ly)

der Porree (-s) leek

der Porsche (-) Porsche (*automobile*)

die Portion (-en) portion; helping, serving

das Porträt (-s) portrait

(das) Portugal Portugal

(das) Portugiesisch Portuguese (language)

das Porzellan porcelain, china

die Posaune (-n) trombone

die Position (-en) position

positiv positive(ly)

das Possessivadjektiv (-e) possessive adjective

die Post mail; postal system; (*pl.* **Postämter**) post office (9)

das Postamt (¨er) post office (9)

das Poster (-) poster (2)

das Postfach (¨er) post office box

die Postleitzahl (-en) postal code (E)

potentiell potential(ly)

das Präfix (-e) prefix

(das) Prag Prague

das Praktikum (Praktika) internship (1); **ein Praktikum machen** to do an internship (1)

praktisch practical(ly) (1)

praktizieren to practice

prall full(y); intense(ly)

die Präposition (-en) preposition

das Präsens (Präsentia) present tense; **das Partizip Präsens** present participle

präsentieren to present

die Präsentierung (-en) presentation

der Präsident (-en *masc.*) (-en) / die Präsidentin (-nen) president

das Präteritum (Präterita) preterit tense, simple past tense

präzis precise(ly)

der Prediger (-) / die Predigerin (-nen) preacher

der Preis (-e) price, cost (9); prize; **im Preis enthalten** included in the price (9)

preiswert inexpensive(ly), bargain (2); **recht preiswert** quite inexpensive, reasonable (2)

die Presse press (*newspapers, etc.*)

pressen to press, squeeze

das Prestige prestige

der Priester (-) / die Priesterin (-nen) priest

prima great, super (E)

der Prinz (-en *masc.*) (-en) / die Prinzessin (-nen) prince/princess

das Prinzip (-ien) principle; **im Prinzip** in principle

privat private(ly)

pro per; **pro Person** per person (10); **pro Woche** per week (4)

die Probe (-n) rehearsal

das Problem (-e) problem (2); **ein Problem lösen** to solve a problem

problemlos without any problem

das Produkt (-e) product

produzieren to produce

der Professor (-en) / die Professorin (-nen) professor (1)

das Profil (-e) profile

das Programm (-e) program; TV station, channel (13); **im ersten Programm** on channel 1

programmieren to program

die Programmierkenntnis (-se) knowledge of programming

progressiv progressive(ly)

das Projekt (-e) project

promenieren to promenade

die Prominenz prominent people, socialites

das Pronomen (-) pronoun

das Pronominaladverb (Pronominaladverbien) pronominal adverb

der Prospekt (-e) brochure

das Protokoll (-e) transcript, minutes; **Protokoll führen** to make a transcript, take the minutes

provozieren to provoke

provozierend provocative(ly)

das Prozent (-e) percent

der Prozess (-e) process; legal case

die Prüfung (-en) test, exam

PS = Postskript postscript

der Psychologe (-n *masc.*) (-n) / die Psychologin (-nen) psychologist (11)

die Psychologie psychology

der Psychothriller (-) psycho-thriller (*movie, etc.*)

der Pudding (-e) pudding

der Pudel (-) poodle

der Pulli (-s) (*coll.*) sweater, pullover

der Pullover (-) pullover sweater (5)

der Pumpernickel pumpernickel (bread)

der Punkt (-e) point

pünktlich punctual(ly), on time

die Puppe (-n) doll

die Pute (-n) turkey (hen)
das Putenmedaillon (-s) turkey medallion, small slice of turkey
der Putenspieß (-e) turkey kebab, turkey on a skewer
putzen to polish, clean; sich (dat.) die Zähne putzen to brush one's teeth (8)
der Pyjama (-s) pajamas

Q

qm = Quadratmeter
der/das Quadratmeter (-) square meter
die Qualifikation (-en) qualification
qualifizieren to qualify
die Qualität (-en) quality
der Quark curd cheese (German-style yogurt cheese)
das Quartal (-e) (academic) quarter
der Quatsch (coll.) nonsense; So ein Quatsch! Nonsense!
die Quelle (-n) source
das Quiz (-) quiz
der Quizmaster (-) quizmaster, host of a quiz show
die Quizsendung (-en) quiz show
die Quizshow (-s) quiz show

R

der Rabatt (-e) discount
rachsüchtig vengeful(ly)
das Rad (-̈er) wheel; bicycle; Rad fahren (fährt Rad), fuhr Rad, ist Rad gefahren to bicycle, ride a bike (7)
der Radfahrer (-) / die Radfahrerin (-nen) bicyclist
radikal radical(ly)
das Radio (-s) radio (2); im Radio on the radio
der Radiorecorder (-) boom box
der Radiowecker (-) clock radio
der Radius (Radien) radius
das Rafting rafting
die Rakete (-n) rocket
der Rand (-̈er) edge, border
die Rapmusik rap music
rappelvoll (coll.) crazily full
der Rappen (-) (Swiss) centime
rar rare, scarce
die Rasiercreme (-s) shaving cream (5)
sich rasieren to shave (8)
die Rassenpolitik politics of race
der Rassismus racism (14)
rassistisch (adj.) racist
die Rast (-en) rest
der Raster (-) grid
der Rat advice (8); Rat geben to give advice
raten (rät), riet, geraten to guess; to advise
das Ratespiel (-e) guessing game
die Ratgeberseite (-n) advice page
das Rathaus (-̈er) city hall (9)
(das) Rätoromanisch Rhaeto-Romance (language)
der Ratschlag (-̈e) piece of advice
der Rattenfänger (-) ratcatcher; der Rattenfänger von Hameln the Pied Piper of Hamelin
rauchen to smoke (8)

räuchern to smoke (meat)
rauf = herauf: raufstolpern (stolpert rauf), ist raufgestolpert (coll.) to stumble up
der Raum (-̈e) room; space
raus = heraus (adv.) out
das Rauschen rush, roar; das weiße Rauschen white noise
reagieren to react
die Reaktion (-en) reaction
das Reaktionsvermögen (-) ability to react
die Realität (-en) reality
die Realoberschule (-n) secondary school with a curriculum emphasizing mathematics and science
die Realschule (-n) secondary school with a commercially oriented curriculum
das Rebland (-̈er) wine country
die Rechenmaschine (-n) calculator
recherchieren to research, investigate
die Rechnung (-en) bill (6)
recht quite, rather (2); recht preiswert quite inexpensive, reasonable (2)
recht- right, right-hand; auf der rechten Seite on the right-hand side
das Recht (-e) right; law; Recht haben to be correct (2)
rechts (on the) right (9); nach rechts to the right (9)
der Rechtsanwalt (-̈e) / die Rechtsanwältin (-nen) attorney, lawyer (11)
der Rechtsextremismus right-wing extremism (14)
rechtzeitig in time, on time
das Recycling recycling
der Redakteur (-e) / die Redakteurin (-nen) chief editor
die Redaktion (-en) editorial staff
die Rede (-n) speech; indirekte Rede indirect discourse
das Redemittel (-) speaking resources
reden to talk (about)
reduzieren to reduce
das Referat (-e) paper, report; ein Referat halten (hält), hielt, gehalten to give a paper/report
der Referent (-en masc.) (-en) / die Referentin (-nen) speaker; advisor, expert
reflexiv reflexive(ly)
das Reflexivpronomen (-) reflexive pronoun
die Reformation Reformation
das Regal (-e) shelf (2)
regelmäßig regular(ly) (8)
regeln to regulate, control
der Regen rain (7)
der Regenschauer (-) rain shower (7)
der Regenschirm (-e) umbrella (7)
die Regierung (-en) government (14); administration
die Regierungsgewalt (-en) governmental power
der Regierungssitz (-e) seat of government
das Regime (-) regime
die Region (-en) region
regional regional(ly)

der Regisseur (-e) / die Regisseurin (-nen) (film) director
regnen to rain (7); Es regnet. It's raining. (7)
regnerisch rainy (7)
der Reibekuchen (-) pancake made of grated potatoes
reich rich(ly)
das Reich (-e) empire, realm; das Dritte Reich the Third Reich, Nazi Germany (1933–1945)
reichhaltig extensive; abundant
das Reichstagsgebäude German Parliament Building
die Reife: mittlere Reife diploma attained at the end of the Realschule
der Reifen (-) tire
die Reihenfolge (-n) sequence, order
rein = herein (adv.) in
der Reis rice (6)
die Reise (-n) trip, journey (10)
die Reiseapotheke (-n) portable first-aid kit
der Reisebericht (-e) travel report, travelogue
das Reisebüro (-s) travel agency (10)
die Reisecheckliste (-n) travel checklist
der Reiseführer (-) travel guide (book) (10)
das Reisejournal (-e) travel journal
der Reiseleiter (-) / die Reiseleiterin (-nen) tour guide
die Reiselektüre vacation reading material
reisen, ist gereist to travel (1); per Autostop reisen to hitchhike (10)
das Reisen traveling
der Reisepass (-̈e) passport (9)
der Reiseprospekt (-e) travel brochure (10)
der Reisescheck (-s) traveler's check (10)
der Reisetermin (-e) date of travel
die Reiseverbindung (-en) travel connection
reiten, ritt, ist geritten to ride (on horseback) (7)
die Reitführung riding instruction
die Reitschule (-n) riding school
relativ relative(ly)
die Relativitätstheorie theory of relativity
das Relativpronomen (-) relative pronoun
relevant relevant
die Religion (-en) religion
religiös religious(ly)
die Renaissance Renaissance (period)
die Rendite (-n) yield on an investment
rennen, rannte, ist gerannt to run, race
renommiert renowned
renovieren to renovate
der Rentner (-) / die Rentnerin (-nen) retiree
die Reparatur (-en) repair (12)
die Reparaturwerkstatt (-̈e) repair shop
reparieren to repair (9)
der Report (-e) report
die Reportage (-n) report
der Reporter (-) / die Reporterin (-nen) reporter
die Reproduktion (-en) reproduction
die Republik (-en) republic
das Requiem (-s) requiem
das Requisit (-en) prop

reservieren to book, reserve (7)
die Reservierung (-en) reservation
die Residenzstadt (¨e) royal capital
der Rest (-e) remainder
das Restaurant (-s) restaurant (6)
restlich remaining
das Resultat (-e) result
retten to save, rescue
die Rettungsleitstelle (-n) control room for rescue operations
revidieren to revise
das Revier (-e) province, region; preserve
das Rezept (-e) recipe; prescription
die Rezeption reception desk (9)
der Rhein Rhine (River)
rheinisch Rhenish, of the Rhine River
(die) Rheinland-Pfalz Rhineland-Palatinate (*German state*)
der Rhythmus (Rhythmen) rhythm
sich richten auf (+ *acc.*) to be directed at
die Richtgeschwindigkeit (-en) recommended maximum speed
richtig correct(ly), right(ly)
die Richtigkeit correctness, accuracy
die Richtung (-en) direction
der Riese (-n *masc.***) (-n)** giant
riesig enormous, gigantic
das Riff (-e) reef
das Rind (-er) cow, bull, head of cattle
das Rinderfilet (-s) beef filet
die Rinderroulade (-n) beef roulade
das Rindfleisch beef (5)
der Ring (-e) ring
rings: rings um (+ *acc.*) all around
ringsherum all around
ringsum all around
der Risotto (-s) risotto
das Ritual (-e) ritual
die Robbe (-n) seal
der Rock (¨e) skirt (5)
das Rodeo (-s) rodeo
die Rolle (-n) role
das Rollenspiel (-e) role-play
das Rollerbladen rollerblading
der Rollkragenpullover (-) turtleneck sweater
(das) Rom Rome
der Rom (-a) non-German Romany (gypsy)
der Roman (-e) novel
die Romanistik (study of) Romance languages and literatures
romantisch romantic(ally) (1)
die Römerzeit Roman era
die Röntgenstrahlen (*pl.*) X-rays
der Rosinenbomber (-) raisin bomber (*supply plane in the Berlin Airlift*)
die Rösti (Swiss) thinly sliced fried potatoes
rot red (5); **rote Grütze** *dessert made of red berries*
der Rotwein (-e) red wine
rotweiß red and white
die Routine (-n) routine
RTL *radio and television broadcasting company based in Luxembourg*
die Rubrik (-en) category, section; column
der Rücken (-) back (8)
die Rückenschmerzen (*pl.*) backache

der Rucksack (¨e) backpack (5)
die Rückseite (-n) back, back side
rudern, ist gerudert to row
rufen, rief, gerufen to call (out), shout
die Ruhe quiet; calm(ness); rest; **in Ruhe** in peace and quiet
der Ruhetag (-e) *day that a business is closed* (6)
ruhig quiet(ly) (1); calm(ly)
das Rührei (-er) scrambled egg
die Ruine (-n) ruin
der Rum (-s) rum
(das) Rumänien Romania
rund round; around; **rund um** (+ *acc.*) all around
die Rundfahrt (-en) (circular) tour
der Rundfunk radio; broadcasting
die Rundfunkanstalt (-en) broadcasting corporation; radio station
die Rundschau (-en) panorama
rundum all around
russisch (*adj.*) Russian
(das) Russland Russia
rustikal rustic

S

die Sache (-n) thing, object; matter
die Sachertorte (-n) *type of rich chocolate torte from Vienna*
(das) Sachsen Saxony (*German state*)
(das) Sachsen-Anhalt Saxony-Anhalt (*German state*)
sächsisch (*adj.*) Saxon
die Safari (-s) safari
der Safer Sex safe sex
der Saft (¨e) juice (5)
sagen to say, tell (1); **sag mal** tell me (1); **Wie sagt man ... auf Deutsch?** How do you say . . . in German? (E)
die Sahara Sahara (Desert)
die Sahne cream; whipped cream (6)
das Sakko (-s) man's jacket, sport coat (5)
der Salat (-e) salad; lettuce (6)
das Salz salt (5)
salzen, salzte, gesalzen to salt
salzig salty
sammeln to collect (7); to gather **sich sammeln** to gather, come together
die Sammelstelle (-n) recycling center (14)
die Sammlung (-en) collection
(der) Samstag Saturday (3)
samstags Saturdays, on Saturday(s) (4)
der Sand (-e) sand
die Sandale (-n) sandal
der Sänger (-) / die Sängerin (-nen) singer
der Satan (-e) Satan, devil
die Sat-Empfangsanlage (-n) satellite receiver (13)
satt full, having had enough to eat
der Satz (¨e) sentence
die Satzklammer (-n) sentence frame
der Satzteil (-e) part of a sentence, clause
sauber clean(ly) (14)
säuberlich neat(ly)
säubern to clean (up)
die Sauce = die Soße
sauer sour; **saurer Regen** acid rain

das Sauerkraut sauerkraut, pickled cabbage (6)
die Sauna (-s) sauna
säuseln to murmur
(das) Schach chess; **Schach spielen** to play chess (7)
schade too bad
schaden to harm
der Schaden (¨) damage, injury
der Schadstoff (-e) harmful substance
schaffen, schuf, geschaffen to create (14)
schaffen, schaffte, geschafft to manage to do; **sich schaffen** to busy oneself
der Schafskäse sheep's milk cheese
der Schal (-s) scarf (5)
die Schallplatte (-n) (phonograph) record
schalten to switch
der Schalter (-) counter; window
scharf sharp; spicy
der Schatz (¨e) treasure; **mein Schatz** my darling
das Schaubild (-er) diagram
schauen (auf + *acc.*) to look (at/to); **Fernsehen schauen** to watch TV; **Schau mal!** Look!
der Schauer (-) (rain) shower
das Schaufenster (-) store window
der Schauplatz (¨e) scene
der Schauspieler (-) / die Schauspielerin (-nen) actor/actress (11)
der Scheck (-s) check
scheiden, schied, geschieden to separate
der Schein (-e) banknote, bill, piece of paper money; **der Dollar-Schein** dollar bill; **der Euro-Schein** euro note/bill
scheinen, schien, geschienen to shine; to seem, appear (13); **Die Sonne scheint.** The sun is shining. (7)
scheitern, ist gescheitert to fail
schenken to give (as a gift) (5)
die Scheu shyness
schick stylish(ly)
schicken to send (1); **SMS schicken** to send text messages
schießen, schoss, geschossen to shoot
das Schiff (-e) ship (10)
das Schild (-er) sign, road sign
schildern to describe, portray
schimpfen to scold; to grumble, curse
der Schinken (-) ham (5)
der Schirm (-e) umbrella
der/die Schizophrene (*decl. adj.*) schizophrenic (person)
das Schlachtfeld (-er) battlefield
der Schlaf sleep
schlafen (schläft), schlief, geschlafen to sleep (2)
der Schlafsack (¨e) sleeping bag
das Schlafzimmer (-) bedroom (2)
der Schlag (¨e) blow, punch, slap; whipped cream
die Schlagcreme whipped cream
schlagen (schlägt), schlug, geschlagen to beat, strike
schlagkräftig powerful(ly)
die Schlagzeile (-n) headline (13)
das Schlagzeug (-e) (set of) drums; percussion instruments

schlank slender

schlapp weak, worn out (8)

das Schlaraffenland fool's paradise

schlecht bad(ly), poor(ly) (E); **Mir ist schlecht.** I feel bad; I'm sick to my stomach. (8)

der Schlegel (-) mallet

(das) Schleswig-Holstein *one of the German states*

schließen, schloss, geschlossen to close; **schließen (aus** + *dat.)* to conclude (from)

das Schließfach (¨er) locker

schließlich finally, in the end

die Schließung (-en) closing

schlimm bad

der Schlips (-e) necktie (5)

~~schlittern, ist geschlittert to slip, slide~~

der Schlittschuh (-e) ice skate; **Schlittschuh laufen (läuft), lief, ist gelaufen** to ice skate (7)

das Schloss (¨er) castle, palace (9)

der Schluckauf (-) hiccup(s)

schlucken to swallow (8)

der Schlüssel (-) key (9)

schmecken (+ *dat.)* to taste (good) (5); **schmecken nach (+** *dat.)* to taste of

schmeißen, schmiss, geschmissen to hurl, fling

schmelzen (schmilzt), schmolz, geschmolzen to melt

der Schmerz (-en) pain (8)

der Schmuck jewelry

schmutzig dirty (12)

das Schnäppchen (-) *(coll.)* bargain

die Schnecke (-n) snail

der Schnee snow (7)

der Schneefall (¨e) snowfall

schneiden, schnitt, geschnitten to cut

schneien to snow (7); **Es schneit.** It's snowing. (7)

schnell fast, quick(ly) (10); **Machen Sie schnell!** *(form.)* / **Mach schnell!** *(inform.)* Hurry up!

schnellen, ist geschnellt to shoot (upward)

der Schnittlauch chives

das Schnitzel (-) cutlet; **das Wiener Schnitzel** breaded veal cutlet

der Schnupfen nasal congestion; head cold (8)

der Schnupperkurs (-e) introductory course

der Schock (-s) shock

der Schokoeisbecher (-) dish of chocolate ice cream

die Schokolade (-n) chocolate

schon already (2); yet

schön nice(ly), beautiful(ly) (2); **bitte schön** please; you're welcome; **danke schön** thank you very much (E)

schonen to protect

der Schornsteinfeger (-) / die Schornsteinfegerin (-nen) chimney sweep

(das) Schottland Scotland

der Schrank (¨e) cupboard; closet; wardrobe

schrecklich horrible, horribly

schreiben, schrieb, geschrieben to write (2); **Wie schreibt man … ?** How do you write … ? (E)

die Schreibmaschine (-n) typewriter

der Schreibtisch (-e) desk (2)

die Schreibwaren *(pl.)* stationery goods

der Schriftsteller (-) / die Schriftstellerin (-nen) writer, author

der Schritt (-e) step

die Schublade (-n) drawer

der Schuh (-e) shoe (5)

das Schuhwerk footwear

der Schulabgänger (-) / die Schulabgängerin (-nen) school graduate

die Schuld guilt

die Schulden *(pl.)* debts; **Schulden machen** to go into debt

die Schule (-n) school; **in die Schule gehen, ging, ist gegangen** to go to school; **zur Schule gehen, ging, ist gegangen** to go to school

der Schüler (-) / die Schülerin (-nen) pupil, student in primary or secondary school

die Schulter (-n) shoulder (8)

die Schupfnudeln *(pl.)* potato noodles

der Schuss (¨e) shot; **eine (Berliner) Weiße mit Schuss** *light, fizzy beer served with raspberry syrup*

schützen to protect (14)

(das) Schwaben Swabia *(region in southwestern Germany)*

schwäbisch *(adj.)* Swabian

schwach weak(ly); gentle, gently

der Schwager (¨) / die Schwägerin (-nen) brother-in-law (3) / sister-in-law (3)

die Schwangerschaft (-en) pregnancy

der Schwank (¨e) comic tale, farce

der Schwarm (¨e) swarm; heartthrob, idol

schwarz black (5); **das Schwarze Brett** bulletin board

schwarzhaarig dark-haired

der Schwarzhandel black market

der Schwarzwald Black Forest

(das) Schweden Sweden

das Schwein (-e) pig

der Schweinebraten (-) pork roast (6)

das Schweinefleisch pork (5)

das Schweinemedaillon (-s) pork medallion, small slice of pork

die Schweinshaxe (-n) pork knuckle

das Schweinskotelett (-s) pork cutlet

die Schweiz Switzerland (E); **aus der Schweiz** from Switzerland; **in die Schweiz** to Switzerland

Schweizer *(adj.)* of/from Switzerland; **der Schweizer Franken (-)** Swiss franc

der Schweizer (-) / die Schweizerin (-nen) Swiss person

schwer heavy, heavily; difficult, with difficulty

die Schwester (-n) sister (3)

die Schwiegermutter (¨) mother-in-law

der Schwiegervater (¨) father-in-law

schwierig difficult, with difficulty

das Schwimmbad (¨er) swimming pool (7)

schwimmen, schwamm, ist geschwommen to swim (2)

die Schwimmflosse (-n) flipper

sich schwingen, schwang, geschwungen to swing oneself, jump

schwitzen to sweat

schwül muggy, humid (7)

der Schwung: voll Schwung full of zest

sechs six (E)

sechsmal six times

sechste sixth (3)

sechzehn sixteen (E)

sechzig sixty (E)

der See (-n) lake (7)

die See (-n) sea, ocean

das Seemannspfännchen (-) *fried seafood dish*

die Segelboote (-n) fleet of sailboats

segeln to sail (7)

sehen (sieht), sah, gesehen to see (2)

die Sehenswürdigkeit (-en) (tourist) attraction

sehr very (1); very much; **bitte sehr** you're welcome; **danke sehr** thanks a lot (1); **sehr gut** very well; fine; good (E)

seid (you [*inform. pl.*]) are

die Seidenbluse (-n) silk blouse

die Seife (-n) soap

das Seil (-e) rope; cable

sein (ist), war, gewesen to be (1)

sein his, its (3)

seit (+ *dat.)* since; (+ *time*) for (5, 6); *(subord. conj.)* since; **seit zwei Jahren** for two years (6)

die Seite (-n) side; page; **die Internet-Seite (-n)** web page

der Sekretär (-e) / die Sekretärin (-nen) secretary

die Sekte (-n) sect

die Sekunde (-n) second (4)

selb *(adj.)* same

selber self (my-, your-, him-, her-, *etc.*)

selbst self (my-, your-, him-, her-, *etc.*)

selbständig independent(ly) (11)

das Selbstbewusstsein self-confidence

das Selbstbildnis (-se) self-portrait

das Selbstgespräch (-e) conversation with oneself

der Selbstmord (-e) suicide

selbstversorgend self-sufficient

die Selbstversorgung self-sufficiency

selbstverständlich natural(ly), of course

selten rare(ly) (2), seldom

seltsam strange(ly)

das Semester (-) semester (1)

das Seminar (-e) seminar

senden, sandte, gesandt to send

senden, sendete, gesendet to broadcast

der Sender (-) broadcaster

die Sendung (-en) broadcast, TV or radio program (13)

der Senf mustard (6)

senken to sink, drop

die Sensation (-en) sensation

sensationell sensational(ly)

sensitiv sensitive

separat separate(ly)

(der) September September (3)

die Serie (-n) series; **die Krimi-Serie (-n)** detective series
der Service service; service department
servieren to serve
der Servierer (-) / die Serviererin (-nen) server
die Serviette (-n) napkin (6)
der Sessel (-) armchair (2)
setzen to set; to put (*in a sitting position*) (6); **sich setzen** to sit down (8)
der Sex sex; **der Safer Sex** safer sex
sexuell sexual(ly)
das Shampoo (-s) shampoo
der Sheriff (-s) sheriff
die Show (-s) show
der Shrimp (-s) shrimp
sich oneself, yourself (*form.*), himself, herself, itself, themselves
sicher safe(ly) (10); sure(ly), certain(ly)
die Sicherheit security, safety
die Sicherheitspolitik security policy; politics of security
der Sicherheitsrat (-̈e) security council
sichern to make secure
Sie you (*form. sg./pl.*) (1, 3)
sie she; it; they (1); her; it; them (*acc.*) (3)
sieben seven (E)
sieb(en)te seventh (3)
siebenjährig seven-year-(old), seven years old
siebzehn seventeen (E)
siebzehnjährig seventeen-year-(old), seventeen years old
siebzig seventy (E)
der Siedepunkt (-e) boiling point
die Siedlung (-en) settlement; housing development
signalisieren to signal, indicate
der Silbershop (-s) silver shop
(das) Silvester New Year's Eve (3)
sind (we/they/you [*form.*]) are
singen, sang, gesungen to sing
der Sinn (-e) sense
sinnvoll sensible, sensibly
die Sitte (-n) custom, tradition
die Situation (-en) situation
sitzen, saß, gesessen to sit, be (sitting) (6)
der Sitznachbar (-n *masc.*) (-n) / die Sitznachbarin (-nen) person seated nearby
(das) Sizilien Sicily
der Skandal (-e) scandal
skandalös scandalous(ly)
der Skater (-) / die Skaterin (-nen) skater
das Skeetschießen skeet shooting
skeptisch skeptical(ly)
Ski fahren (fährt), fuhr, ist gefahren to ski
der Skifahrer (-) / die Skifahrerin (-nen) skier
die Skizze (-n) sketch
die Slowakei Slovakia (E)
(das) Slowenien Slovenia (E)
SMS schicken to send text messages
so so (2); like that; **so ein(e)** such a; **So ein Pech!** What a shame! What bad luck! (8); **So ein Unsinn!** Nonsense! (14); **(so) gegen fünf Uhr** around five o'clock (6); **so lala** (*coll.*) OK, so-so (E); **so was**

something like that; **so weit** so far; **so ... wie** as . . . as (7)
sobald (*subord. conj.*) as soon as
die Socke (-n) sock (5)
das Sofa (-s) sofa (2)
sofort immediately (9)
die Software (-s) (piece of) software
sofür for that
sogar even (8)
sogenannt so-called
der Sohn (-̈e) son (3)
solange (*subord. conj.*) as long as
die Solarenergie solar energy
solch such
der Soldat (-en *masc.*) (-en) / die Soldatin (-nen) soldier
die Solidarität solidarity
der Solist (-en *masc.*) (-en) / die Solistin (-nen) soloist
sollen (soll), sollte, gesollt to be supposed to; shall; ought to; should (4); to be said to be
somit with that, thus
der Sommer (-) summer (7)
sommerlich summer(y)
die Sommerzeit (-en) daylight savings time
der Sonderabfall (-̈e) toxic waste
die Sonderaktion (-en) special (sales) offer
sonderbar strange(ly)
der Sonderkindergarten (-̈) special preschool
sondern (*coord. conj.*) but, rather (7)
die Sonderschule (-n) special school
(der) Sonnabend Saturday (3)
sonnabends Saturdays, on Saturday(s) (4)
die Sonne (-n) sun (7); **Die Sonne scheint.** The sun is shining. (7)
die Sonnenbrille (-n) (pair of) sunglasses
der Sonnenschein sunshine (7)
das Sonnenschutzmittel (-) suntan lotion, sunscreen (10)
sonnig sunny (7)
(der) Sonntag Sunday (3)
sonntags Sundays, on Sunday(s) (4)
sonst otherwise; else; other than that (10); **Sonst noch (et)was?** Anything else? (10)
sonstig other, additional
Sonstiges other items, miscellaneous
die Sorge (-n) worry; **sich Sorgen machen um** (+ *acc.*) to worry about (14)
sorgen für (+ *acc.*) to take care of, look after
der Sorgerechtsstreit (-e) custody battle
sorgfältig careful(ly)
die Sorte (-n) kind, sort
sortieren to sort
die Soße (-n) sauce; gravy
sowie as well as
die Sowjetunion Soviet Union
sowohl (als/wie) as well (as)
sozial social(ly)
der Sozialarbeiter (-) / die Sozialarbeiterin (-nen) social worker
die Sozialbauwohnung (-en) low-income apartment
die Sozialkunde social studies

der Soziologe (-n *masc.*) (-n) / die Soziologin (-nen) sociologist
die Soziologie sociology
die Spalte (-n) (printed) column
das Spanferkel (-) roasted suckling pig
(das) Spanien Spain
(das) Spanisch Spanish (language)
spannend exciting(ly), suspenseful(ly) (4)
sparen to save, conserve (12)
der Sparer (-) / die Sparerin (-nen) saver
der Spargel (-) asparagus
die Spargelzeit (-en) asparagus season
das Sparkonto (Sparkonten) savings account (12)
der Sparpreis (-e) discount price
sparsam thrifty, economical(ly) (12)
das Sparschwein (-e) piggy bank
der Spaß (-̈e) fun (1); **Das macht Spaß.** That's fun. (1); **Spaß haben** to have fun; **Viel Spaß!** Have fun! (1)
spät late (4); **Wie spät ist es?** What time is it? (4)
spätestens at the latest (12)
die Spätzle, Spätzli (*pl.*) *a kind of noodles*
spazieren gehen (geht spazieren), ging spazieren, ist spazieren gegangen to go for a walk (4)
der Spaziergang (-̈e) walk, stroll
der Speck bacon (6)
die Speckbohnen (*pl.*) beans with bacon
speichern to store, save (13)
die Speise (-n) food; dish (of prepared food) (6)
die Speisekarte (-n) menu (6)
der Speiseplan (-̈e) menu, diet
die Speisung (-en) feeding, supplying
spektakulär spectacular(ly)
die Spende (-n) donation, contribution
spenden to donate, contribute
der Spender (-) / die Spenderin (-nen) donor, contributor
das Spezial (-s) special
spezialisieren to specialize
die Spezialität (-en) specialty
die Spezies (-) species
spezifisch specific(ally)
der Spiegel (-) mirror
das Spiegelbild (-er) reflection
das Spiegelei (-er) fried egg (sunny-side up) (6)
spiegeln to reflect
das Spiel (-e) game; play
spielen to play (1); **Computerspiele spielen** to play computer games (1); **Fußball spielen** to play soccer (7); **Karten spielen** to play cards (1); **Schach spielen** to play chess (7); **Tennis spielen** to play tennis (7)
spielend (*adv.*) without effort, easily
der Spieler (-) / die Spielerin (-nen) player; **der CD-Spieler (-)** CD player
der Spielfilm (-e) feature film, movie (13)
die Spielkarte (-n) playing card (7)
der Spielplatz (-̈e) playground
das Spielzeug (-e) toy
die Spinne (-n) spider
spitze (*coll.*) marvelous(ly)
die Spitze (-n) tip; (pointed) top

spontan spontaneous(ly)

der Sport (*pl.* **Sportarten**) sports, sport (7); **Sport treiben, trieb, getrieben** to play sports (7)

die Sportanlage (-n) sports field

die Sporthalle (-n) gymnasium, sports arena (7)

das Sportkabriolett (-s) sports convertible

sportlich athletic(ally) (1); **sportlich aktiv** active in sports (10)

der Sportplatz (¨e) athletic field (7)

die Sporttasche (-n) athletic bag

der Spot (-s) advertising spot, commercial

die Sprache (-n) language

das Sprachinstitut (-e) institute for language

der Sprachkurs (-e) language course

der Sprachtipp (-s) language tip

der Sprachurlaub (-e) language-learning vacation

sprechen (spricht), sprach, gesprochen to speak (2)

der Sprecher (-) / die Sprecherin (-nen) speaker

das Sprechschema (-s) conversational pattern

die Sprechstunde (-n) office hour (8)

der Springbrunnen (-) fountain

springen, sprang, ist gesprungen to jump

der Sprudel (-) mineral water (6)

spülen to wash, rinse; **das Geschirr spülen** to wash the dishes

die Spülmaschine (-n) dishwasher (12)

die Spur (-en) track, trail; trace

spurlos without a trace

das Squash squash (game)

die SS = Schutzstaffel *elite organization within the Nazi party*

der Staat (-en) state, nation

staatlich governmental(ly), of/by the state

die Staatsangehörigkeit (-en) nationality

das Stadion (Stadien) stadium (7)

die Stadt (¨e) town; city (E)

die Stadtansicht (-en) view of a town

das Stadtbad (¨er) municipal bath/pool

das Stadtbild (-er) townscape; cityscape

das Städtchen (-) little town

die Stadtentwicklung (-en) urban development

der Stadtplan (¨e) city street map

die Stadtplanung urban planning

der Stadtrat (¨e) city council

der Stahlhelm (-e) steel helmet

der Stammbaum (¨e) family tree

stammen aus (+ *dat.*) to come from, originate in

der Standard (-s) standard

ständig constant(ly); permanent(ly)

stark (stärker, stärkst-) strong(ly) (7); heavy, heavily

die Stärke (-n) strength (11)

das Starmagazin *German entertainment magazine*

starren (auf + *acc.*) to stare (at)

der Start (-s) start

starten to start

die Station (-en) station

stationieren to station

statt (+ *gen.*) instead of

stattdessen instead (of that)

stattfinden (findet statt), fand statt, stattgefunden to take place

die Statue (-n) statue

der Stau (-s) traffic jam

der Staubsauger (-) vacuum cleaner (12)

das Steak (-s) steak

der Steckbrief (-e) personal details; wanted poster

stecken to place, put (*inside*); to be (*inside*) (6)

stehen, stand, gestanden to stand; to be located (6); (+ *dat.*) to look good (on a person) (5); **Die Farbe steht mir.** The color looks good on me. (5)

die Stehlampe (-n) floor lamp

die Steiermark Styria (*one of the Austrian states*)

steif stiff(ly)

steigen, stieg, ist gestiegen to climb, go up, rise

steigend increasing

die Stelle (-n) place, position; job (11) **an deiner Stelle** if I were you, (if I were) in your place (12)

stellen to stand up, place, put (*in a standing position*) (6); **eine Frage stellen** to ask a question; **sich stellen** to place oneself

das Stellenangebot (-e) job offer; help-wanted ad (11)

die Stellensuche (-n) job search

die Stellung (-en) position; **Stellung nehmen zu** (+ *dat.*) to state one's opinion on

der Stephansdom St. Stephen's Cathedral

sterben (an + *dat.*) **(stirbt), starb, ist gestorben** to die (of)

die Stereoanlage (-n) stereo (system) (2)

die Sterilisation (-en) sterilization

sterilisieren to sterilize

der Stern (-e) star

das Sternzeichen (-) star sign, sign of the zodiac

die Steuer (-n) tax (14)

der Steward (-s) / die Stewardess (-en) steward/stewardess, flight attendant

das Stichwort (¨er) key word, cue

der Stiefbruder (¨) stepbrother

der Stiefel (-) boot (5)

die Stiefschwester (-n) stepsister

der Stil (-e) style

das Stillleben (-) still life

die Stimme (-n) voice

stimmen to be correct; **(das) stimmt** that is correct

die Stimmung (-en) mood

stinken, stank, gestunken to stink

das Stipendium (Stipendien) scholarship, stipend

der Stock (*pl.* **Stockwerke**) floor, story (9); **im ersten Stock** on the second floor

stockaufwärts up to the next floor

das Stockwerk (-e) floor, story

der Stoffbeutel (-) fabric bag

der Stollen (-) (type of) fruit cake

stolpern, ist gestolpert to stumble

stolz proud(ly)

der Storch (¨e) stork

stören to bother, disturb

stoßen (stößt), stieß, gestoßen to push

der Strafzettel (-) (parking/speeding) ticket

der Strahl (-en) ray, beam

der Strand (¨e) beach (10)

die Straße (-n) street (E)

die Straßenbahn (-en) streetcar

die Strategie (-n) strategy

sich strecken to stretch (8)

streckenweise in places, at times

der Streifen (-) strip; band

streiken to go on strike

streng strict(ly) (14)

der Stress (-e) stress (8)

stressig stressful (1)

der Strohhut (¨e) straw hat

der Strom (¨e) stream; (electrical) current, electricity (12); **Es regnet in Strömen.** It is pouring rain.

der Strumpf (¨e) stocking; sock (5)

die Stube (-n) room

das Stüberl (-) (*Austrian, Bavarian*) small room

das Stück (-e) piece; (theater) play

der Student (-en *masc.*) **(-en) / die Studentin (-nen)** (university) student (1)

die Studentenbude (-n) (*coll.*) student's room

das Studentenheim (-e) dormitory

das Studentenwerk (-e) student service organization

das Studentenwohnheim (-e) dormitory (2)

die Studie (-n) study

der Studienabgänger (-) graduate

das Studienfach (¨er) academic subject

die Studiengebühren (*pl.*) fees, tuition (12)

studieren to study (1); to major in

der/die Studierende (*decl. adj.*) student

das Studio (-s) studio

das Studium (Studien) study, course of studies

die Stufe (-n) step; level

der Stuhl (¨e) chair (2)

die Stunde (-n) hour (4)

stundenlang for hours

der Stundenplan (¨e) hourly class schedule

-stündig lasting . . . hours

stur obstinate(ly)

Stuttgarter (*adj.*) of/from Stuttgart

das Substantiv (-e) noun

die Substanz (-en) substance

subventionieren to subsidize

die Suche (-n) search

suchen to search, look for (2); **nach etwas** (*dat.*) **suchen** to look for something (14)

süddeutsch (*adj.*) southern German

(das) Süddeutschland southern Germany

der Süden south; **im Süden** in the south

südlich (von + *dat.*) south (of)

(das) Südspanien southern Spain

Südwest (*without article*) southwest

der Südwesten southwest; **im Südwesten** in the southwest

die Summe (-n) sum, total
super (*coll.*) super
der Superlativ (-e) superlative
die Superlativform (-en) superlative form
    (of an adjective)
der Supermarkt (ꞏe) supermarket (5)
die Suppe (-n) soup (6)
surfen to surf (1); **im Internet surfen** to
    surf the Internet
das Surfboard (-s) surfboard
das Surfbrett (-er) surfboard
das Sushi sushi
süß sweet(ly)
die Süßigkeiten (*pl.*) sweets
das Sweatshirt (-s) sweatshirt
(das) Sylt *German island in the North Sea*
Sylter (*adj.*) of/from Sylt
das Symbol (-e) symbol
sympathisch likable, pleasant, nice (1)
die Symphonie (-n) symphony
symphonisch symphonic(ally)
das Symptom (-e) symptom
synchronisieren to dub (*film*)
das Synthetik synthetic material
das System (-e) system
die Szene (-n) scene
die Szenekneipe (-n) trendy bar
die Szenekultur (-en) trendy culture

T

der Tabak (-e) tobacco
tabellarisch tabular, in tabular/outline
    form
die Tabelle (-n) table, chart
die Tablette (-n) tablet, pill
die Tafel (-n) (chalk)board; **eine Tafel
    Schokolade** a bar of chocolate
der Tag (-e) day (2); **eines Tages** one day;
    (guten) Tag hello, good day (E); **in zwei
    Tagen** in two days (6); **jeden Tag** every
    day (7); **vor zwei Tagen** two days ago
das Tagebuch (ꞏer) diary
tagen to meet, convene
der Tagesablauf (ꞏe) daily routine
das Tagesangebot (-e) daily special
der Tagesspiegel "daily mirror" (*German
    newspaper*)
die Tagestemperatur (-en) temperature
    during the day
die Tageszeit (-en) time of day
die Tageszeitung (-en) daily newspaper
-tägig lasting … days
täglich daily (6)
die Tagung (-en) convention, meeting
das Tal (ꞏer) valley
das Talent (-e) talent
talentiert talented
der Tango (-s) tango
die Tante (-n) aunt (3)
der Tanz (ꞏe) dance
tanzen to dance (1); **Er tanzt gut.** He dan-
    ces well. (1)
die Tasche (-n) handbag, purse (5); pocket
das Taschengeld (monetary) allowance
die Tasse (-n) cup (4); **eine Tasse Kaffee** a
    cup of coffee (4)
der Täter (-) / die Täterin (-nen) culprit
tätig active, working

die Tätigkeit (-en) activity; position (11)
der Tatort (-e) scene of the crime
die Tatsache (-n) fact
tatsächlich actual(ly); in fact
tauchen to dive (7)
der Tauchgang (ꞏe) dive
tauglich suitable; usable
taumeln, ist getaumelt to stagger
tauschen to exchange
tausend one thousand (E)
das Taxi (-s) taxicab (10)
das Team (-s) team
der Teamgeist team spirit
die Technik technique; technology (11);
    technical engineering
der Techniker (-) / die Technikerin (-nen)
    technician
der Technikstress (-e) technological stress
technisch technical(ly); mechanical(ly)
das/der Techno techno (music)
die Technologie (-n) technology
der Tee tea (5)
die Teigwaren (*pl.*) pasta
der/das Teil (-e) part; share
teilen to divide; to share; **sich** (*dat.*) **etwas
    teilen (mit** + *dat.*) to share something
    (with)
die Teilnahme (-n) participation
teilnehmen (an + *dat.*) (nimmt teil),
    nahm teil, teilgenommen to participate
    (in) (14)
der Teilnehmer (-) / die Teilnehmerin
    (-nen) participant
das Telefaxgerät (-e) fax machine
das Telefon (-e) telephone (2)
telefonieren to telephone, talk on the
    phone (1)
telefonisch by telephone
die Telefonnummer (-n) telephone
    number (E); **Wie ist deine/Ihre
    Telefonnummer?** What is your
    telephone number? (*inform./form.*) (E)
das Telegramm (-e) telegram
die Telekom = Deutsche Telekom AG
    (*German telecommunications
    corporation*)
die Telenovela (-s) type of soap opera
das Telephon (-e) = das Telefon (-e)
das Telex telex
der Teller (-) plate (6)
temperamentvoll spirited, lively
die Temperatur (-en) temperature (7)
das Tempolimit (-s) speed limit
temporal temporal
(das) Tennis tennis; **Tennis spielen** to play
    tennis (7)
die Tennisanlage (-n) tennis court
der Tennisplatz (ꞏe) tennis court (7)
der Tennisschuh (-e) tennis shoe (5)
der Teppich (-e) rug, carpet (2)
der Teppichboden (ꞏ) wall-to-wall
    carpeting (12)
der Termin (-e) appointment (8)
die Terrasse (-n) terrace, patio (2)
der Terrorismus terrorism (14)
der Test (-s) test
teuer expensive(ly) (2)
der Teufel (-) devil

der Text (-e) text
das Theater (-) theater (4); **ins Theater
    gehen** to go to the theater (4)
das Theaterstück (-e) play, (stage) drama (4)
die Theke (-n) bar, counter
das Thema (Themen) theme; topic
die Theologie theology
das Thermalbad (ꞏer) thermal bath
der Thermalbrunnen (-) thermal spring
die Thermalkur (-en) thermal cure
die These (-n) thesis
(das) Thüringen Thuringia (*German state*)
Thüringer (*adj.*) Thuringian
der Tick (-s) tic
das Ticket (-s) ticket
tief deep(ly)
die Tiefgarage (-n) underground garage
das Tier (-e) animal (12)
der Tierarzt (ꞏe) / die Tierärztin (-nen)
    veterinarian
das Tierbaby (-s) baby animal
der Tierpark (-s) zoo (9)
der Tierschutz animal protection
der Tiger (-) tiger
der Tipp (-s) tip, hint
der Tiroler Hut (ꞏe) Tyrolean hat
der Tisch (-e) table (2)
der Titel (-) title
der Toast (-e) toast
die Tochter (ꞏ) daughter (3)
das Tochterunternehmen (-) subsidiary
    company
der Tod (-e) death
der Tofu tofu
die Toilette (-n) toilet
das Toilettenpapier toilet paper (5)
die Toilettensachen (*pl.*) toiletries
(das) Tokio Tokyo
tolerant tolerant(ly)
toll! (*coll.*) super! (1); **ganz toll!** super!
    great! (1)
die Tomate (-n) tomato (5)
der Ton (ꞏe) tone; (musical) note
die Tonne (-n) ton; barrel
das Tor (-e) gate
die Torte (-n) torte, pie, cake
die Toskana Tuscany
tot dead
total total(ly)
töten to kill
die Tour (-en) tour; trip
der Tourist (-en *masc.*) (-en) / die
    Touristin (-nen) tourist (9)
der Trabbi (-s) (*coll.*) Trabant (*automobile
    made in the former GDR*)
die Tradition (-en) tradition (3)
traditionell traditional(ly)
traditionsgemäß traditionally
tragbar portable
tragen (trägt), trug, getragen to wear; to
    carry (5); **die Verantwortung tragen** to
    be responsible
die Tragikomödie (-n) tragicomedy
die Tragödie (-n) tragedy (4)
trainieren to train; to practice
das Training training; practice
der Trainingsanzug (ꞏe) jogging suit
die Tränke (-n) watering hole

der Transfer (-s) transfer
der Transformator (-en) transformer
der Transport (-e) transportation
der Transportweg (-e) transport road
die Traube (-n) grape (5)
der Traum (¨e) dream
träumen (von + dat.) to dream (of)
traurig sad(ly)
treffen (trifft), traf, getroffen to hit; to meet (4); sich treffen mit (+ dat.) to meet with
treiben, trieb, getrieben to drive; Schwarzhandel treiben to trade on the black market; Sport treiben to play sports (7)
das Treibhaus (¨er) greenhouse
der Treibhauseffekt greenhouse effect
der Trend (-s) trend
trennbar separable
(sich) trennen to separate (14)
die Trennung (-en) separation
die Treppe (-n) staircase (12)
das Treppenhaus (¨er) stairwell
treten (tritt), trat, ist getreten to step; in Kraft treten to go into effect
treu loyal(ly) (1); faithful(ly)
der Trimm-Pfad (-e) jogging path
trinken, trank, getrunken to drink (2)
die Trinkkur (-en) mineral water drinking cure
die Trinkmilch low-fat pasteurized milk
das Trinkwasser drinking water
der Triumph (-e) triumph
trocken dry
trocknen to dry
die Trompete (-n) trumpet
der Tropenwald (¨er) tropical forest
die Trophäe (-n) trophy
trotz (+ gen.) in spite of (9)
die Trümmer (pl.) rubble, ruins
die Trümmerfrau (-en) woman who cleared away rubble after World War II
die Truppen (pl.) troops
der Truthahn (¨e) turkey (5)
das T-Shirt (-s) T-shirt (5)
(das) Tschechien Czech Republic (E)
tschechisch (adj.) Czech
tschüss so long, bye (inform.) E
tun (tut), tat, getan to do (8)
die Tür (-en) door (2)
der Türke (-n masc.) (-n) / die Türkin (-nen) Turk, Turkish person
die Türkei Turkey
türkisch (adj.) Turkish
der Turm (¨e) tower; steeple
turnen to do gymnastics (7)
das Turnen gymnastics
die Turnhalle (-n) gymnasium (7)
der Turnschuh (-e) gym shoe, sneaker
der Typ (-en) type, sort
der Typ (-en masc.) (-en) (coll.) guy
typisch typical(ly)

U

über (+ acc./dat.) over, above (6); about
überall everywhere
überbacken: mit Käse überbacken topped with cheese and baked

der Überblick (-e) overview
übereinander on top of one another
überfliegen, überflog, überflogen to skim (a text), read quickly (13)
überfreundlich super-friendly
überglücklich super-happy, overjoyed
übergroß huge; plus-sized
überhaupt at all; überhaupt nicht not at all
die Überholspur (-en) passing lane
überlassen (überlässt), überließ, überlassen to leave up to; Das bleibt dir überlassen. That's up to you.
überleben to survive
sich (dat.) etwas überlegen to consider something, think something over (10)
übernachten to stay overnight (9)
die Übernachtung (-en) overnight stay (9)
übernehmen (übernimmt), übernahm, übernommen to take over (11)
überraschen to surprise; überraschend surprising(ly)
die Überraschung (-en) surprise
überreden to persuade
die Überredungskunst (¨e) persuasiveness, ability to persuade
der Überrest (-e) remnant; ruin
übersetzen to translate (11)
der Übersetzer (-) / die Übersetzerin (-nen) translator
übertragbar transferable, communicable
übertreiben, übertrieb, übertrieben to exaggerate; übertrieben exaggerated (14)
üblich usual
übrig left over, remaining (12)
übrigens by the way (9)
die Übung (-en) exercise
das Ufo (-s) UFO (flying saucer)
die Uhr (-en) clock (2); watch; o'clock; bis (um) fünf Uhr until five o'clock (6); Es ist ein Uhr. It's one o'clock. (4); (so) gegen fünf Uhr around five o'clock (6); um ein Uhr at one o'clock; Um wie viel Uhr? At what time? (4); von zwei bis drei Uhr from two to three o'clock (6); Wie viel Uhr ist es? What time is it? (4); zwischen zwei und drei Uhr between two and three o'clock (6)
die Uhrzeit (-en) time of day
um (+ acc.) at (+ time) (3, 4); around; circa; bis (um) fünf Uhr until five o'clock (6); sich Sorgen machen um to worry about (14); um ein Uhr at one o'clock; um ... herum around (spatial) (3); um Mitternacht at midnight (3); Um wie viel Uhr? At what time? (4); um ... zu in order to; um zwei at two (o'clock) (4)
sich umbringen (bringt um), brachte um, umgebracht to commit suicide
umfassen to contain, include
das Umfeld (-er) milieu, surroundings
die Umfrage (-n) poll, survey
die Umgebung (-en) area, neighborhood, vicinity (12)
umgehen mit (+ dat.), ging um, ist umgegangen to handle, deal with
umgekehrt the other way around

der Umlaut (-e) changed vowel sound represented by ä, ö, or ü
umschulen (schult um) to retrain (14)
die Umschulung (-en) retraining
umsteigen (steigt um), stieg um, ist umgestiegen to transfer, change (trains) (10)
umstellen (stellt um) to reset
die Umwelt environment
umweltbewusst environmentally conscious
das Umweltbewusstsein environmental consciousness
das Umweltbundesamt federal department of the environment
der Umweltbus (-se) ecological bus
umweltfreundlich environmentally friendly (14)
der Umweltschutz environmental protection (14)
die Umweltverschmutzung environmental pollution (14)
umweltverträglich environmentally safe
umziehen (zieht um), zog um, ist umgezogen to move (residence)
unabhängig independent(ly)
unangenehm unpleasant(ly)
unbedingt absolutely, by all means (12)
unbegrenzt unlimited
unbekannt unknown
unbequem uncomfortable, uncomfortably
und (coord. conj.) and (E); Na und? So what? (13)
unerträglich unbearable, unbearably
die UNESCO UNESCO (United Nations Educational, Scientific and Cultural Organization)
unfair unfair(ly)
der Unfall (¨e) accident, mishap
unfreundlich unfriendly (1)
der Unfug nonsense
(das) Ungarn Hungary (E)
ungeduldig impatient(ly)
ungefähr approximately, about (9)
ungemütlich uncomfortable, uncomfortably
ungesund unhealthy, unhealthily
ungewöhnlich unusual(ly)
unglaublich unbelievable, unbelievably
unglücklich unhappy, unhappily
unhöflich impolite(ly)
die Uni (-s) (coll.) = Universität
die Uniform (-en) uniform
uninteressant uninteresting
die Union (-en) union; die Europäische Union European Union
die Universität (-en) university (1); college
unkonventionell unconventional(ly)
unmittelbar direct(ly), immediate(ly)
unmöbliert unfurnished (2)
unmöglich impossible, impossibly
die UNO UN (United Nations)
unordentlich disorderly
unpraktisch impractical (1)
uns us (acc.) (3); (to/for) us (dat.) (5)
unschuldig innocent(ly)
unser our (3)

der Unsinn nonsense; **So ein Unsinn!** (Such) nonsense! (14)
unsympathisch unlikable (1)
unten below; downstairs (12); **nach unten** below; downstairs (directional) (12)
unter (+ acc./dat.) under, below, beneath; among (6)
unterbrechen (unterbricht), unterbrach, unterbrochen to interrupt (14)
die Unterbrechung (-en) interruption
unterdurchschnittlich below average
untereinander amongst ourselves/ yourselves/themselves
unterernährt malnourished
das Untergeschoss (-e) basement
sich unterhalten (unterhält), unterhielt, unterhalten to entertain (oneself); to converse (13)
unterhaltsam entertaining (13)
die Unterhaltung entertainment (13); **zur Unterhaltung** for entertainment (13)
die Unterkunft (ᵈe) accommodation (9)
die Unterlagen (pl.) documentation, papers (11)
unternehmen (unternimmt), unternahm, unternommen to undertake (10)
das Unternehmen (-) business, company, enterprise (11)
die Unternehmenskommunikation (-en) business communication
unterordnend: unterordnende Konjunktion (-en) subordinating conjunction
der Unterricht (-e) instruction, lesson
unterrichten to teach
der Unterschied (-e) difference
unterschiedlich different
unterschreiben, unterschrieb, unterschrieben to sign
die Unterschrift (-en) signature
unterstreichen, unterstrich, unterstrichen to underline
unterstützen to support (12)
die Unterstützung support (11)
untersuchen to examine (11)
unterteilen to divide, subdivide
der Untertitel (-) subtitle
die Unterwäsche underwear
unterwegs on the way, en route
untrennbar inseparable
unverbraucht unused; untouched
unverletzt unharmed, uninjured
unwichtig unimportant
der Urenkel (-) / die Urenkelin (-nen) great-grandson/great-granddaughter
die Urgroßmutter (ᵈ) great-grandmother
der Urgroßvater (ᵈ) great-grandfather
urig natural; cozy
urkundlich documentary, in a document
der Urlaub (-e) vacation; **Urlaub machen** to go on vacation (8)
der Urlauber (-) / die Urlauberin (-nen) person on vacation
der Urlaubsort (-e) vacation resort
die Ursache (-n) cause
ursprünglich original(ly)
der Urwald (ᵈer) primeval forest

die USA (pl.) United States; **aus den USA** from the United States
der US-Amerikaner (-) / die US-Amerikanerin (-nen) American, person from the USA
usw. = und so weiter and so on

V

der Valentinstag Valentine's Day (3)
der Vampir (-e) vampire
das Vanilleeis vanilla ice cream
variieren to vary
der Vater (ᵈ) father (3)
väterlicherseits on the father's side
der Vatertag (-e) Father's Day
der Vati (-s) dad, daddy
der Vegetarier (-) / die Vegetarierin (-nen) vegetarian (person)
vegetarisch vegetarian (6)
(das) Venedig Venice (Italy)
sich verabreden mit (+ dat.) to arrange to meet with
die Verabredung (-en) appointment; date
verabschieden to say goodbye to
verändern to change
die Veränderung (-en) change
die Veranstaltung (-en) event
verantworten to take responsibility for
verantwortlich responsible (11)
die Verantwortung (-en) responsibility
verantwortungsbewusst responsible, conscious of responsibility
verarbeiten to process
das Verb (-en) verb
die Verbalform (-en) verbal form
verbannen to ban; to banish
verbessern to correct; to improve
die Verbform (-en) verb form
verbieten, verbot, verboten to prohibit, forbid (14)
verbinden, verband, verbunden to connect
verborgen: im Verborgenen leben to live in isolation
der Verbrauch consumption
verbrauchen to use; to consume (14)
der Verbraucher (-) consumer
das Verbrechen (-) crime
verbreiten to spread, disseminate (14)
verbringen, verbrachte, verbracht to spend (time) (7)
verdächtigen to suspect
verdienen to earn; to deserve (11) **sich** (dat.) **etwas verdient haben** to have deserved something
verdünnen to dilute
der Verein (-e) club, association (7)
vereinbaren to agree; to arrange
vereinen to unite; **die Vereinten Nationen** (pl.) United Nations
vereinigen to unite; **die Vereinigten Staaten** (pl.) United States
verfehlen to miss
verfolgen to follow, pursue; to persecute
die Verfolgung (-en) persecution
verfügbar available
die Verfügbarkeit availability

die Verfügung: zur Verfügung stehen, stand, gestanden to be available, to be at one's disposal
die Vergangenheit past
vergehen, verging, ist vergangen to pass; **ein Monat ist vergangen** a month has passed
vergessen (vergisst), vergaß, vergessen to forget (10)
vergiften to poison
der Vergleich (-e) comparison
vergleichen, verglich, verglichen to compare (12)
das Vergnügen (-) pleasure; leisure
die Vergnügung (-en) amusement, entertainment
verhaften to arrest
das Verhältnis (-se) relationship
verheiratet married
verhindern to prevent
verhungern, ist verhungert to die of starvation
das Verhütungsmittel (-) contraceptive
der Verkauf (ᵈe) sale
verkaufen to sell
der Verkäufer (-) / die Verkäuferin (-nen) salesperson (2)
der Verkehr traffic
die Verkehrsbelästigung (-en) traffic disturbance
die Verkehrskontrolle (-n) vehicle checkpoint
das Verkehrsmittel (-) vehicle, means of transportation (14)
das Verkehrsmuseum (Verkehrsmuseen) transportation museum
das Verkehrswesen (-) transportation system
verkochen, ist verkocht to boil away
verkraften to handle, cope with
verkünden to announce
verkürzen to shorten
der Verlag (-e) publishing house
verlagern to move, transfer
verlangen to demand
die Verlängerung (-en) lengthening; prolongation
verlassen (verlässt), verließ, verlassen to leave
(sich) verletzen to injure (oneself) (8)
die Verletzung (-en) injury; violation (14)
sich verlieben (in + acc.) to fall in love (with)
verlieren, verlor, verloren to lose (7)
der/die Verlobte (decl. adj.) fiancé/ fiancée
verlocken to tempt, entice
verlogen: verlogen sein to be full of lies
vermeidbar avoidable
vermeiden, vermied, vermieden to avoid (14)
vermieten to rent out (to someone) (12); **zu vermieten** for rent
der Vermieter (-) / die Vermieterin (-nen) landlord/landlady
vermindern to decrease, lessen (14)
das Vermögen (-) fortune; wealth
vernichten to destroy

veröffentlichen to publish

die Verpackung (-en) packaging, wrapping (14)

die Verpackungsflut (-en) excess use of packaging

die Verpflegung (-en) food; **Unterkunft und Verpflegung** room and board

sich verpflichten to commit oneself

verraten (verrät), verriet, verraten to betray, give away

verreisen, ist verreist to go on a trip (10)

verrückt crazy, crazily (8)

der Versandkatalog (-e) mail-order catalogue

verschieden different

verschließen, verschloss, verschlossen to close; to lock

verschlingen, verschlang, verschlungen to devour

verschlossen taciturn; reserved

die Verschmutzung (-en) pollution

verschreiben, verschrieb, verschrieben to prescribe (8)

verschwinden, verschwand, ist verschwunden to disappear

verschwommen blurred

die Verschwörung (-en) conspiracy

das Versehen (-) oversight

die Versicherung (-en) insurance (12)

versorgen to supply

die Versorgung (-en) supplying

verspätet delayed, late

versprechen (verspricht), versprach, versprochen to promise

versprühen to spray

verstehen, verstand, verstanden to understand; **Ich verstehe das nicht.** I don't understand. (E)

versuchen to try, attempt (8)

verteilen to distribute

der Vertrag (-e) contract; treaty

vertrauen (+ dat.) to trust

vertraut familiar (14)

vertreten (vertritt), vertrat, vertreten to represent

vervollständigen to complete

die Verwaltung (-en) administration

die Verwaltungsfachhochschule (-n) *college that provides training for higher-level civil service positions*

der Verwaltungsweg (-e) administrative route

verwandt mit (+ dat.) related to (3)

die Verwandtschaft (-en) relationship

die Verwechslung (-en) confusion, mistake, mix-up

verwenden to utilize, use, apply (14)

verwirklichen to make real

verwöhnen to spoil, pamper

das Verzeichnis (-se) list, directory, schedule

verzichten auf (+ acc.) to do without (12)

der Vetter (-n) male cousin (3)

das Video (-s) video; videotape (2)

das Videogerät (-e) video recorder (VCR)

der Videorecorder (-) video recorder (VCR) (2)

viel (mehr, meist-) a lot, much (1, 2); **Um wie viel Uhr?** At what time? (4); **Viel Glück!** Good luck! (1); **Viel Spaß!** Have fun! (1); **Vielen Dank!** Many thanks! (6); **wie viel** how much; **Wie viel Uhr ist es?** What time is it? (4)

viele (pl.) many (2); **viele Grüße** best wishes (12); **wie viele** how many

die Vielfalt diversity

vielfältig many and diverse

vielleicht maybe, perhaps (1)

vier four (E)

die Vierergruppe (-n) group of four

viermal four times

viert: zu viert as a foursome (10)

viertägig four-day, lasting four days

vierte fourth (3)

das Viertel (-) quarter (-); **Es ist Viertel nach/vor zwei.** It's a quarter after/to two. (4)

vierzehn fourteen (E)

vierzig forty (E)

die Villa (Villen) villa

das Virus (Viren) virus

vis-à-vis (+ dat.) across from

die Visitenkarte (-n) business card

das Vitamin (-e) vitamin

der Vogel (-) bird

das Vög(e)lein (-) little bird

die Vokabeln (pl.) vocabulary

das Vokabular (-e) vocabulary

das Volk (-er) people; nation

die Völkerkunde ethnology

der Volksaufstand (-e) people's revolt

das Volksfest (-e) public festival; fair

das Volkslied (-er) folk song

der Volkspolizist (-en masc.) (-en) / die Volkspolizistin (-nen) officer of the People's Police (GDR)

der Volkswagen (-) Volkswagen (*automobile*)

die Volkswirtschaft economics

voll full; crowded (6); **voller Leben** full of life

die Vollendung (-en) completion

völlig total(ly), complete(ly)

das Vollkornbrot (-e) whole-grain bread

die Vollkornnudeln (pl.) whole-grain pasta

die Vollmilch whole milk

die Vollpension accommodation with three meals per day included

vollständig complete(ly)

vom = von dem; vom Fass on tap; draft (6)

von (+ dat.) of; from; by (5, 6); out of; **gegenüber von** across from (9); **von zwei bis drei Uhr** from two to three o'clock (6); **weit (weg) von** far away from (2)

vor (+ acc./dat.) before; in front of; ago (6); (+ *time*) to, of (4) **Es ist Viertel vor zwei.** It's a quarter to two. (4); **fünf vor zwei** five to/of two (4); **vor allem** above all; **vor zwei Tagen** two days ago (6)

vorbei past, gone, over

vorbeifahren (fährt vorbei), fuhr vorbei, ist vorbeigefahren to drive past

vorbeigehen (geht vorbei), ging vorbei, ist vorbeigegangen to pass by

vorbeikommen (kommt vorbei), kam vorbei, ist vorbeigekommen to drop in, come by (4)

(sich) vorbereiten (auf + acc.) (bereitet vor) to prepare (oneself) (for) (11)

die Vorbereitung (-en) preparation

die Vorderseite (-n) front side

der Vorfahr (-en masc.) (-en) / die Vorfahrin (-nen) ancestor, predecessor

vorgehen (geht vor), ging vor, ist vorgegangen to happen, go on

vorgestern the day before yesterday

vorhaben (hat vor) to plan (*to do*) (4)

vorher before that; before

vorig previous, last

vorkommen (kommt vor), kam vor, ist vorgekommen to occur

vorlesen (liest vor), las vor, vorgelesen to read aloud

die Vorlesung (-en) (university) lecture (4)

die Vorliebe (-n) preference; particular fondness

vorm = vor dem

der Vormittag (-e) morning, before noon (4); **gestern Vormittag** yesterday morning; **heute Vormittag** this morning; **morgen Vormittag** tomorrow morning

vormittags before noon (4)

der Vorname (gen. -ns, acc./dat. -n) (-n) first name, given name (1)

vorne in front

vornehmen (nimmt vor), nahm vor, vorgenommen to plan; to carry out

der Vorort (-e) suburb

der Vorortszug (-e) commuter train

der Vorraum (-e) front hall

der Vorsatz (-e) intention, resolution

der Vorschein: zum Vorschein kommen to appear, come to light

der Vorschlag (-e) suggestion

vorschlagen (schlägt vor), schlug vor, vorgeschlagen to suggest, propose (10)

die Vorsicht care, caution

vorsichtig careful(ly), cautious(ly)

die Vorsorge precautions, provisions

die Vorspeise (-n) appetizer (6)

vorspielen (spielt vor): das Stück der Klasse vorspielen to perform the piece in front of the class

vorspulen (spult vor) to fast forward

vorstellen (stellt vor) to set forward (*clock*); to introduce; **sich (acc.) vorstellen** to introduce oneself (11); **sich (dat.) etwas vorstellen** to imagine something (11)

die Vorstellung (-en) idea, concept; introduction

das Vorstellungsgespräch (-e) job interview (11)

der Vorteil (-e) advantage (11)

der Vortrag (-e) lecture (4)

der Vorverkauf (-e) advance sale

vorwärts kommen (kommt vorwärts), kam vorwärts, ist vorwärts gekommen to get ahead

vorweisen (weist vor), wies vor, vorgewiesen to show, present
vorzeigen (zeigt vor) to show
vorziehen (zieht vor), zog vor, vorgezogen to prefer (14)
der VW (-s) = Volkswagen

W

wachsen (wächst), wuchs, ist gewachsen to grow
der Wachtturm (¨e) watchtower
der Wagen (-) car (7)
die Wagenauffahrt (-en) driveway
wählen to choose; to vote, elect (14)
der Wähler (-) / die Wählerin (-nen) voter
wahllos indiscriminate(ly)
wahr true; real, genuine
während (+ *gen.*) during (9); (*subord. conj.*) while, whereas
die Wahrheit (-en) truth
wahrscheinlich probable, probably (11)
die Währung (-en) currency
der Wald (¨er) forest (7)
der Walkman (-s) Walkman (*portable cassette player*)
der Walzer (-) waltz
die Wand (¨e) wall (2); **die vier Wände** one's own home
der Wandel change; **im Wandel** in transition
wandern, ist gewandert to hike (1)
der Wanderschuh (-e) hiking shoe
der Wanderstab (¨e) hiking staff
der Wanderstock (¨e) hiking staff
der Wandervogel (¨) enthusiastic hiker
der Wanderweg (-e) hiking trail
wanken, ist gewankt to stagger, sway
wann when (1); **seit wann** since when; **Wann hast du Geburtstag?** When is your birthday? (3)
der Wannsee *lake in Berlin*
wäre: Wie wäre es mit ... ? How about . . . ? (13)
warm (wärmer, wärmst-) warm(ly) (7); heated
warnen to warn
die Warte (-n) vantage point, lookout
warten (auf + *acc.*) to wait (for) (6)
warum why (2)
was what (1); something (*colloquial form of etwas*); **na, so was** something like that; **Was bedeutet ... ?** What does . . . mean? (E); **Was fehlt dir/Ihnen?** What's the matter? (8); **was für (ein)** what kind of (a) (11); **Was ist denn los?** What's the matter? (2); **Was sind Sie von Beruf?** What do you do for a living? (1)
das Waschbecken (-) sink
die Wäsche laundry
(sich) waschen (wäscht), wusch, gewaschen to wash (oneself) (8)
der Wäschetrockner (-) clothes dryer (12)
die Waschküche (-n) laundry room
die Waschmaschine (-n) washing machine (12)
das Wasser water (5)
der Wassermann Aquarius (*sign of the Zodiac*)

das Watt (-) watt
die Wattstunde (-n) watts per hour
das WC (-s) toilet; bathroom (9)
das Web (World Wide) Web
die Webseite (-n) webpage
die Website (-s) website (11)
der Wechsel (-) change, alternation
das Wechselgeld change (*money*)
wechseln to change, exchange; **wechselnd bewölkt** with variable cloudiness
die Wechselpräposition (-en) two-way preposition, preposition governing either accusative or dative case
wecken to wake
der Wecker (-) alarm clock (2)
weder ... noch neither . . . nor
weg away, off; **weit weg von** (+ *dat.*) far away from
der Weg (-e) path, trail, way; road (9); **nach dem Weg fragen** to ask for directions (9)
wegen (+ *gen.*) because of, on account of (9)
weggehen (geht weg), ging weg, ist weggegangen to leave, go away
der Wegwerfartikel (-) disposable item
die Wegwerfflasche (-n) nonrecyclable bottle (14)
weh: oh weh alas
wehen to blow
sich wehren (gegen) to defend oneself (against)
die Wehrmacht armed forces (*especially the German army during World War II*)
wehtun (+ *dat.*) **(tut weh), tat weh, wehgetan** to hurt (8); **Das tut mir weh.** That hurts. (8)
weiblich feminine, female
weich soft
das Weihnachten Christmas (3)
der Weihnachtsbaum (¨e) Christmas tree (3)
der Weihnachtstag (-e): der erste Weihnachtstag Christmas Day; **der zweite Weihnachtstag** the day after Christmas, Boxing Day
weil (*subord. conj.*) because (8)
der Wein (-e) wine (6)
weinen to cry
weinrot wine-red
die Weintraube (-n) (wine) grape
die Weise (-n) manner, way
weiß white (5)
die (Berliner) Weiße: eine Weiße mit Schuss *light, fizzy beer served with raspberry syrup*
das Weißglas colorless glass
die Weißwurst (¨e) white sausage (*made from veal*) (6)
weit far (9); **weit (weg) von** (+ *dat.*) far (away) from
weiter further, farther
weiterentwickeln (entwickelt weiter) to continue to develop
weiterfahren (fährt weiter), fuhr weiter, ist weitergefahren to ride on, continue to ride
weitergehen (geht weiter), ging weiter, ist weitergegangen to go on, continue to go

weiterleben (lebt weiter) to go on living
weitermachen (macht weiter) to carry on, continue
weiterreisen (reiste weiter), ist weitergereist to continue to travel
weiterreiten, ritt weiter, ist weitergeritten to ride on, continue to ride (*on horseback*)
weiterschicken (schickt weiter) to forward, send on
weiterspielen (spielt weiter) to play on, continue to play
das Weizenbier (-e) wheat beer
welcher, welche, welches which (2); **Auf welchen Namen?** Under what name? (9); **Welches Datum ist heute/morgen?** What is today's/tomorrow's date? (3)
die Welle (-n) wave
die Welt (-en) world, earth (14)
weltbekannt world-famous
weltberühmt world-famous
der Weltkrieg (-e) world war
das Weltkulturerbe world cultural heritage
die Weltmeisterschaft (-en) world championship
weltstädtisch cosmopolitan
weltweit worldwide
wem (to/for) whom (*dat.*) (5)
wen whom (*acc.*)
wenig little (8); **zu wenig** too little
wenige (*pl.*) few, a few (8)
wenn (*subord. conj.*) if; when (8); whenever
wenngleich (*subord. conj.*) even though, although
wer who (1)
das Werbeplakat (-e) advertising poster
der Werbespot (-s) commercial
die Werbung (-en) advertisement, commercial
werden (wird), wurde, geworden to become (3); (+ *infinitive*) *future tense;* (+ *past participle*) *passive voice;* **Würden Sie bitte ... ?** Would you please . . . ? (9)
werfen (wirft), warf, geworfen to throw
das Werk (-e) work, opus
werten to judge, assess, rate
wessen whose
West (*without article*) west
(das) Westberlin West Berlin
der Westberliner (-) / die Westberlinerin (-nen) person from West Berlin
die Weste (-n) vest
der Westen west; **im Westen** in the west
die Western-Musik country-western music
(das) Westfalen Westphalia (*region of Germany*)
westfälisch (*adj.*) Westphalian
die Westzone (-n) western zone (*the occupation zone that later became the Federal Republic of Germany*)
das Wetter weather
der Wetterbericht (-e) weather report (7)
der Wetterhahn (¨e) weathercock
die WG = Wohngemeinschaft (2)
wichtig important(ly) (3)
widerspiegeln (spiegelt wider) to reflect

wie how (1); as; **so … wie** as . . . as (7); **Um wie viel Uhr?** At what time? (4); **Wie bitte?** Pardon? What did you say? (E); **Wie findest du …?** How do you like . . . ? / What do you think of . . . ? (1); **Wie geht es Ihnen?** How are you (*form.*) (E); **Wie geht's (dir)?** How are you? (*inform.*) (E); **Wie heißen Sie? / Wie heißt du?** What's your name? (*form./inform.*) (E); **Wie heißt die Stadt?** What is the name of the town/city? (E); **Wie ist Ihr/dein Name?** What's your name? (*form./inform.*) (E); **Wie komme ich am besten dahin?** What's the best way to get there? (9); **Wie sagt man … auf Deutsch?** How do you say . . . in German? (E); **Wie spät ist es? / Wie viel Uhr ist es?** What time is it? (4); **wie viel** how much; **wie viele** how many; **Wie wäre es mit …?** How about . . . ? (13)

wieder again (2); back; **schon wieder** yet again (*emphatic*)

der Wiederaufbau reconstruction

wiederholen to repeat; to review

die Wiederholung (-en) review; **zur Wiederholung** as a review

das Wiederhören: (auf) Wiederhören good-bye (*on the phone*) (9)

das Wiedersehen: (auf) Wiedersehen good-bye (E)

die Wiedervereinigung (-en) reunification

die Wiederverwertung recycling

wiegen, wog, gewogen to weigh

(das) Wien Vienna

Wiener (*adj.*) of/from Vienna; **das Wiener Schnitzel** breaded veal cutlet; **das Wiener Würstchen (-)** wiener, frankfurter

die Wiese (-n) meadow (7)

wieso why

das Wildgehege (-) game preserve

wildlebend wild, free

das Wildwasser white water

der Wildwestfilm (-e) Western (*movie*)

willkommen (*adj.*) welcome; **herzlich willkommen** welcome (E)

der Wind (-e) wind (7)

die Windenergie wind energy

windig windy (7)

das Windrad (¨-er) wind power generator (14)

das Windsurfen / das Windsurfing windsurfing

der Winter (-) winter (7)

wir we (1)

wirken (auf + *acc.*) to have an effect (on)

wirklich real(ly) (1)

die Wirklichkeit (-en) reality

der Wirkstoff (-e) active agent

die Wirkung (-en) effect

die Wirtschaft (-en) economy (13)

wirtschaftlich economic(ally)

das Wirtschaftswunder (-) economic miracle

das Wirtshaus (¨-er) pub (6)

wissen (weiß), wusste, gewusst to know (*something as a fact*) (3); **Das weiß ich nicht.** I don't know. (E)

die Wissenschaft (-en) science

der Wissenschaftler (-) / die Wissenschaftlerin (-nen) scientist, scholar

wissenswert worth knowing

Wittenberger (*adj.*) of/from Wittenberg

witzig amusing(ly)

wo where (1)

die Woche (-n) week (4); **einmal die Woche** once a week (7); **pro Woche** per week (4)

das Wochenende (-n) weekend (4); **am Wochenende** on the weekend

wochenlang for weeks

der Wochenplan (¨-e) weekly schedule

der Wochentag (-e) day of the week

-wöchig lasting . . . weeks

wofür for what; why

wogegen against what

woher from where (1); **Woher kommen Sie?** (*form.*) / **Woher kommst du?** (*inform.*) Where are you from? (E)

wohin (to) where (5); **Wohin gehst du?** Where are you going?

wohl well; probably (11); **sich wohl fühlen** to feel well (8)

das Wohlbefinden well-being

das Wohneigentum residential property

wohnen to reside, live (1)

die Wohngemeinschaft (-en) (WG) shared housing (2)

das Wohnheim (-e) dormitory

der Wohnort (-e) place of residence (1)

die Wohnung (-en) apartment (2)

der Wohnwagen (-) camper, trailer

das Wohnzimmer (-) living room (2)

die Wolke (-n) cloud (7)

die Wolkendecke cloud cover

wolkenlos cloudless (7)

wolkig cloudy

wollen (will), wollte, gewollt to want to, to plan to (4)

womit with what

woran on what; about what

worauf on what; for what

Worpsweder (*adj.*) of/from Worpswede

das Wort (¨-er) word; **Worte** (*pl.*) words (*in connected speech*)

das Wörterbuch (¨-er) dictionary

das Wortratespiel (-e) word-guessing game

der Wortschatz vocabulary

worüber about what

worum about what; around what

wovon of what; **Wovon handelt es?** What's it about? (13)

wovor before what; in front of what; of what

wozu for what; why

das Wunder (-) wonder, miracle; **kein Wunder** no wonder

wunderbar wonderful(ly)

der Wunsch (¨-e) wish

wünschen to wish (3)

der Wunschtraum (¨-e) wishful dream

die Wurst (¨-e) sausage (5)

das Würstchen (-) small sausage; hot dog

die Wurzel (-n) root

würzig tasty; spicy

der Wüstenstamm (¨-e) desert tribe

X

das Xylophon (-e) xylophone

Y

der/das Yoga yoga

Z

die Zahl (-en) number; amount

zahlen to pay (5)

zählen to count; **zählen zu (+** *dat.*) to be one of, belong to

das Zahlenlotto (-s) number lottery

zahlreich numerous

die Zahlung (-en) payment

der Zahn (¨-e) tooth **sich** (*dat.*) **die Zähne putzen** to brush one's teeth (8)

der Zahnarzt (¨-e) / die Zahnärztin (-nen) dentist (11)

die Zahnpasta (Zahnpasten) toothpaste (5)

die Zahnschmerzen (*pl.*) toothache

zart tender(ly) (5)

die Zauberflöte *Magic Flute*

(das) ZDF = Zweites Deutsches Fernsehen (*German television network*)

die Zehe (-n) toe (8)

zehn ten (E)

zehnte tenth (3)

das Zeichen (-) sign

zeichnen to draw, sketch (7)

der Zeichner (-) / die Zeichnerin (-nen) graphic artist (11)

die Zeichnung (-en) drawing (12)

zeigen to show (5)

die Zeile (-n) line (*of text*)

die Zeit (-en) time (2); **Zeit haben** to have time (2); **Zeit verbringen, verbrachte, verbracht** to spend time (7)

die Zeitansage (-n) time recording

zeitgenössisch contemporary

der Zeitpunkt (-e) moment, point in time

die Zeitschrift (-en) magazine; periodical (13)

die Zeitung (-en) newspaper (1)

der Zeitvertreib (-e) pastime

das Zelt (-e) tent (10)

der Zentimeter (-) centimeter

zentral central(ly); **zentral gelegen** centrally located (2)

das Zentrum (Zentren) center (of town) (9); **im Zentrum** in the center of town

zerbomben to destroy by bombing

zerschlagen (*adj.*) worn-out, tired out

zerstören to destroy

die Zerstörung (-en) destruction

zeugen to testify

das Zeugnis (-se) report card; transcript; recommendation (from a former employer)

ziehen, zog, gezogen to pull, drag; **ziehen, zog, ist gezogen** to move; to go on

das Ziel (-e) goal, target; destination

ziemlich somewhat, rather (6)

zieren to decorate

die **Zigarette** (-n) cigarette
der **Zigeuner** (-) / die **Zigeunerin** (-nen) gypsy;
das **Zimmer** (-) room (2)
die **Zimmerbestellung** (-en) room reservation
der **Zimmerkollege** (-n *masc.*) (-n) / die **Zimmerkollegin** (-nen) roommate
die **Zimmerpflanze** (-n) houseplant (2)
die **Zimmervermittlung** (-en) room rental agency
zirka approximately, about
der **Zirkus** (-se) circus
das **Zitat** (-e) quotation
zitieren to quote
der **Zivi** (-s) (*coll.*) *person who does Zivildienst*
der **Zivildienst** community service (*as an alternative to military conscription*)
der **Zivilist** (-en *masc.*) (-en) / die **Zivilistin** (-nen) civilian
der **Zoo** (-s) zoo
zu (+ *dat.*) to; at; for (5); (+ *infinitive*) to; (*adv.*) too; **ab und zu** now and then, occasionally (8); **bis zu** until; to, as far as (9); **Das ist mir zu blöd.** I think that's really stupid. (13); **ohne ... zu** without doing; **um ... zu** in order to; **zu Fuß gehen, ging, ist gegangen** to walk, go on foot (8); **zu Hause** at home (5); **zu zweit** in pairs; as a couple, as a twosome (10)
zubereiten (bereitet zu) to prepare
die **Zucchini** (*pl.*) zucchini
der **Züchter** (-) / die **Züchterin** (-nen) breeder, grower
der **Zucker** sugar (5)
zueinander to one another
zuerst first, at first (9)
zufrieden content, satisfied
der **Zug** (-̈e) train (10)
der **Zugang** (-̈e) access
zugehen auf (+ *acc.*) **(geht zu), ging zu, ist zugegangen** to approach
zugehören (+ *dat.*) **(gehört zu)** to belong to
der **Zugriff** (-e) grasp
die **Zugspitze** *name of the highest mountain in Germany*
das **Zuhause** home
zuhören (hört zu) to listen (4)
zukriegen (kriegt zu) (*coll.*) to get shut
die **Zukunft** future (11)

zukünftig in the future
zulassen (lässt zu), ließ zu, zugelassen to allow, permit
zuletzt last(ly), finally
zuliebe (+ *dat.*) for the sake of
zum = zu dem; zum Mitnehmen (food) to go; take-out (6)
zumachen (macht zu) to close
zunächst first, at first; for the time being
zünftig proper(ly)
zupacken (packt zu) to work hard, pitch in
zur = zu der
Zürcher (*adj.*) of/from Zurich
(das) Zürich Zurich
zurück back; **hin und zurück** round-trip (10)
zurückbringen (bringt zurück), brachte zurück, zurückgebracht to bring back
zurückfaxen (faxt zurück) to fax back
zurückgeben (gibt zurück), gab zurück, zurückgegeben to give back
zurückhaltend reserved, restrained
zurückkommen (kommt zurück), kam zurück, ist zurückgekommen to return, come back (4)
zurückliegen (liegt zurück), lag zurück, zurückgelegen to lie behind, be in the past
zurückreichen (reicht zurück) to reach back, extend back
zurückrufen (ruft zurück), rief zurück, zurückgerufen to call back
zurückzahlen (zahlt zurück) to pay back
zusammen together; **das macht zusammen ...** all together, that comes to . . . (5)
die **Zusammenarbeit** teamwork; cooperative effort
zusammenarbeiten (arbeitet zusammen) to work together, collaborate
zusammenfassen (fasst zusammen) to summarize
die **Zusammenfassung** (-en) summary
sich zusammenfinden (findet zusammen), fand zusammen, zusammengefunden to get together
zusammenpassen (passt zusammen) to match, go together
zusammenschlagen über (+ *dat.*) **(schlägt zusammen), schlug zusammen, ist zusammengeschlagen** to engulf

zusammensetzen (setzt zusammen) to put together; **zusammengesetztes Wort** compound word
zusammenstellen (stellt zusammen) to put together
zusammenwohnen (wohnt zusammen) to live together, cohabitate
zusätzlich additional(ly)
zuschneien (schneit zu), ist zugeschneit to snow in
der **Zuschuss** (-̈e) contribution; grant
zustimmen (+ *dat.*) **(stimmt zu)** to agree with
die **Zutat** (-en) ingredient
zutreffen auf (+ *acc.*) **(trifft zu), traf zu, zugetroffen** to apply to
die **Zuversicht** confidence
zu viel too much
zuvor before
zuweilen now and again
die **Zwangssterilisation** (-en) forced sterilization
zwanzig twenty (E)
der **Zwanziger** (-) twenty-euro/mark/ dollar bill
zwanzigste twentieth (3)
zwar admittedly; **und zwar** that is to say
der **Zweck** (-e) purpose
zwei two (E)
das **Zweibettzimmer** (-) double room, room with two beds
zweieinhalb two and a half
zweihundert two hundred (E)
zweimal twice (7)
zweit: zu zweit in pairs; as a couple, as a twosome (10)
zweitausend two thousand (E)
zweite second (3); **zweiter Klasse fahren** to travel second class (10)
zweithöchst- second highest
zweitlängst- second longest
die **Zwiebel** (-n) onion (6)
der **Zwilling** (-e) twin
zwischen (+ *acc./dat.*) between (6); **zwischen zwei und drei Uhr** between two and three o'clock (6)
das **Zwischenspiel** (-e) interlude
zwölf twelve (E)
zwölfjährig twelve-year-(old), twelve years old
zwölfte twelfth (3)
(das) Zypern Cyprus

English–German

This list contains all the words from the end-of-chapter vocabulary sections.

A

a ein, eine

ability die Fähigkeit (-en) (11)

able: to be able to können (kann), konnte, gekonnt (4)

about über (+ acc.); gegen (+ time) (6); ungefähr (9); **to be about** handeln von (+ dat.) (13); **How about . . . ?** Wie wäre es mit … ? (13); **What's it about?** Wovon handelt es? (13)

above über (+ acc./dat.) (6); (adv.) oben; (directional) nach oben (12)

abroad im Ausland (11); **at home and abroad** im Inland und Ausland (13)

absolutely na klar (E); unbedingt (12)

access: Internet access der Internetzugang (9)

accommodation die Unterkunft (¨e) (9)

account: on account of wegen (+ gen.) (9); **savings account** das Sparkonto (Sparkonten) (12)

to acquire something sich (dat.) etwas anschaffen (schafft an) (14)

across from gegenüber von (+ dat.) (9)

act of violence die Gewalttätigkeit (-en) (14)

active(ly) aktiv (10); **active in sports** sportlich aktiv (10)

activity die Tätigkeit (-en) (11)

actor/actress der Schauspieler (-) / die Schauspielerin (-nen) (11)

ad: help-wanted ad das Stellenangebot (-e) (11)

addiction: drug addiction die Drogensucht (14)

addition: in addition außerdem (14)

address die Adresse (-n) (E); **street address** die Hausnummer (-n) (E)

advantage der Vorteil (-e) (11)

advice der Rat (8)

advising die Beratung (11)

to affect betreffen (betrifft), betraf, betroffen (14)

afraid: to be afraid of Angst haben vor (+ dat.) (12)

after nach (+ dat.) (4, 5, 6); (subord. conj.) nachdem (10); **after Tuesday** nach Dienstag (6); **five after two** fünf nach zwei (4); **It's a quarter after two.** Es ist Viertel nach zwei. (4)

afternoon der Nachmittag (-e) (4); **afternoons, in the afternoon** nachmittags (4); **this afternoon** heute Nachmittag (4)

again wieder (2)

against gegen (+ acc.) (3); **I'm against it.** Ich bin dagegen. (14)

agency: travel agency das Reisebüro (-s) (10)

ago vor (+ dat.) (6); **two days ago** vor zwei Tagen (6)

to agree (with), be in agreement (with) einverstanden sein (mit + dat.) (10)

ahead: straight ahead geradeaus (9)

ailment die Krankheit (-en) (14)

air die Luft (¨e) (8)

airplane das Flugzeug (-e) (10)

alarm clock der Wecker (-) (2)

alcohol der Alkohol (8)

all alle (5); **All the best!** Alles Gute! (3); **all together, that comes to** das macht zusammen (5); **by all means** unbedingt (12)

to allow erlauben (9)

almost fast (8)

along: to come along mitkommen (kommt mit), kam mit, ist mitgekommen (4); **to take along** mitnehmen (nimmt mit), nahm mit, mitgenommen (4); **to walk along** entlanggehen (geht entlang), ging entlang, ist entlanggegangen (9)

already schon (2)

also auch (1)

altogether insgesamt (10)

aluminum can die Dose (-n) (14)

always immer (1)

am bin, **I am** Ich bin (E)

American der Amerikaner (-) / die Amerikanerin (-nen) (1)

among unter (+ acc./dat.) (6)

an ein, eine

and (coord. conj.) und (E)

animal das Tier (-e) (12)

annoyed: to be annoyed about sich ärgern über (+ acc.) (12)

to answer (phone) sich melden (13); **No one is answering.** Niemand meldet sich. (13)

answering machine der Anrufbeantworter (-) (13)

any: in any case auf jeden Fall (13); **not any** kein (2)

anything: Anything else? Sonst noch etwas? (10)

apartment die Wohnung (-en) (2)

to appear scheinen, schien, geschienen (13)

appetizer die Vorspeise (-n) (6)

apple der Apfel (¨) (5); **apple strudel** der Apfelstrudel (-) (6)

applesauce das Apfelmus (6)

appliance das Gerät (-e) (12); (TV, telephone, camera, etc.) der Apparat (-e) (9)

application die Bewerbung (-en) (11); **application form** das Bewerbungsformular (-e) (11)

to apply verwenden (14); **to apply (for)** sich bewerben (um + acc.) (bewirbt), bewarb, beworben (11)

appointment der Termin (-e) (8)

approximately ungefähr (9)

April (der) April (3)

are (you sg. inform.) bist; (you pl. inform.) seid; (you sg./pl. form.; we; they) sind; **Are you doing well?** Geht's gut? (E); **there are** es gibt (3)

area die Umgebung (-en) (12)

arena: sports arena die Sporthalle (-n) (7)

arm der Arm (-e) (8)

armchair der Sessel (-) (2)

around (spatial) um… herum (3); gegen (+ time) (3, 6); **around five o'clock** (so) gegen fünf Uhr (6); **to lie around** faulenzen (7)

arrival die Ankunft (¨e) (10)

to arrive ankommen (kommt an), kam an, ist angekommen (9)

article of clothing das Kleidungsstück (-e) (5)

artist der Künstler (-) / die Künstlerin (-nen) (11); **graphic artist** der Zeichner (-) / die Zeichnerin (-nen) (11)

as: as . . . as so … wie (7); **as a twosome/threesome/foursome** zu zweit/dritt/viert (10); **as far as** bis zum/zur (9); **as of** ab (+ dat.) (12); **as of June 1st** ab 1. Juni (ab erstem Juni) (12)

to ask fragen (2); **to ask for** bitten um (+ acc.), bat, gebeten (12); **to ask someone for directions** jemanden nach dem Weg fragen (9)

asleep: to fall asleep einschlafen (schläft ein), schlief ein, ist eingeschlafen (4)

to assert behaupten (13)

assignment die Arbeit (-en) (8)

association der Verein (-e) (7)

at (+ time) um (+ acc.) (3, 4); bei (+ dat.) (5); zu (+ dat.) (5); an (+ acc./dat.) (6); auf (+ acc./dat.) (6); **at first** zuerst (9); **at home** zu Hause (5); **at home and abroad** im Inland und Ausland (13); **at least** mindestens (8); **at midnight** um Mitternacht (3); **at night** nachts (4); **at noon** mittags (4); **at the corner** an der Ecke (9); **at the latest** spätestens (12); **at two** um zwei (4); **At what time?** Um wie viel Uhr? (4)

athletic sportlich (1); **athletic field** der Sportplatz (¨e) (7)

to attempt versuchen (8)
attention: to pay attention to achten auf (+ *acc.*) (8)
attic das Dachgeschoss (-e) (12)
attorney der Rechtsanwalt (ᵉe) / die Rechtsanwältin (-nen) (11)
August (der) August (3)
aunt die Tante (-n) (3)
Austria (das) Österreich (E)
autumn der Herbst (-e) (7)
available: Is this seat available? Ist hier noch frei? (6)
average: on average durchschnittlich (12)
to avoid vermeiden, vermied, vermieden (14)
away: far away from . . . weit weg von . . . (2)

B

back der Rücken (-) (8); **in back of** hinter (+ *acc./dat.*) (6); **to come back** zurückkommen (kommt zurück), kam zurück, ist zurückgekommen (4)
backpack der Rucksack (ᵉe) (5)
bacon der Speck (6)
bad(ly) schlecht (E); **What bad luck!** So ein Pech! (8)
bag: plastic bag die Plastiktüte (-n) (14)
baggage check die Gepäckaufbewahrung (10)
bakery die Bäckerei (-en) (5)
balcony der Balkon (-e) (2)
ball: soccer ball der Fußball (ᵉe) (7)
ballet das Ballett (-e) (4)
ballpoint pen der Kugelschreiber (-) (12)
banana die Banane (-n) (5)
bank die Bank (-en) (9)
bar die Kneipe (-n) (6); das Lokal (-e) (6)
barbeque der Grill (-s) (6)
(a) bargain preiswert (2)
basically im Grunde genommen (14)
bathing suit der Badeanzug (ᵉe) (5)
bathroom das Bad (ᵉer) (2); das Badezimmer (-) (2); das WC (-s) (9)
to be sein (ist), war, ist gewesen (1); (+ *past participle*) werden (wird), wurde, ist geworden (3)
to be able to können (kann), konnte, gekonnt (4)
to be about handeln von (+ *dat.*) (13)
to be afraid of Angst haben vor (+ *dat.*) (12)
to be annoyed about sich ärgern über (+ *acc.*) (12)
to be called heißen, hieß, geheißen (1)
to be correct Recht haben (hat Recht) (2)
to be glad about sich freuen über (+ *acc.*) (12)
to be hanging hängen, hing, gehangen (6)
to be hungry Hunger haben (hat Hunger) (2)
to be inside stecken (6)
to be interested in sich interessieren für (+ *acc.*) (11)
to be lazy faulenzen (7)
to be located liegen, lag, gelegen (6); stehen, stand, gestanden (6)
to be named heißen, hieß, geheißen (1)
to be of the opinion meinen (14)

to be permitted to dürfen (darf), durfte, gedurft (4)
to be pleasing to gefallen (+ *dat.*) (gefällt), gefiel, gefallen (5)
to be successful Erfolg haben (11)
to be supposed to sollen (soll), sollte, gesollt (4)
to be thirsty Durst haben (hat Durst) (2)
beach der Strand (ᵉe) (10)
bean die Bohne (-n) (6)
beautiful(ly) schön (2)
because (*coord. conj.*) denn (7); (*subord. conj.*) weil (8); **because of** wegen (+ *gen.*) (9); **because of that** deswegen (12)
to become werden (wird), wurde, ist geworden (3)
bed das Bett (-en) (2); **bed and breakfast** die Pension (-en) (9); **room with one bed** das Einzelzimmer (-) (9); **room with two beds** das Doppelzimmer (-) (9)
bedroom das Schlafzimmer (-) (2)
beef das Rindfleisch (5)
beer das Bier (-e) (5); **beer garden** der Biergarten (ᵉ) (6); **Pilsner beer** das Pilsener (-) (6)
before vor (+ *acc./dat.*) (6); (*subord. conj.*) bevor (10); **before noon** der Vormittag (-e) (4); (*adv.*) vormittags (4)
to begin anfangen (fängt an), fing an, angefangen (4); beginnen, begann, begonnen (4)
behind hinter (+ *acc./dat.*) (6)
beige beige (5)
Belgium (das) Belgien (E)
to believe glauben (5)
bell pepper die Paprika (6)
belly der Bauch (ᵉe) (8)
to belong to (*a person*) gehören (+ *dat.*) (5)
below unter (+ *acc./dat.*) (6); (*adv.*) unten; (*directional*) nach unten (12)
belt der Gürtel (-) (5)
beneath unter (+ *acc./dat.*) (6)
beside neben (+ *acc./dat.*) (6)
besides außerdem (14)
best best-; **All the best!** Alles Gute! (3); **best wishes** viele Grüße (12); **What's the best way to get there?** Wie komme ich am besten dahin? (9)
better besser
between zwischen (+ *acc./dat.*) (6); **between two and three o'clock** zwischen zwei und drei Uhr (6)
beverage: beverage can die Getränkedose (-n) (14); **beverage store** der Getränkeladen (ᵉ) (5)
bicycle das Fahrrad (ᵉer) (10); **to bicycle, ride a bicycle** Fahrrad/Rad fahren (fährt), fuhr, ist gefahren (1, 7)
big groß (2)
bill die Rechnung (-en) (6)
birth: date of birth der Geburtstag (-e) (1)
birthday der Geburtstag (-e) (1); **Happy birthday!** Herzlichen Glückwunsch zum Geburtstag! (3); **When is your birthday?** Wann hast du Geburtstag? (3)
birthplace der Geburtsort (-e) (1)
black schwarz (5)
to blog bloggen (7)

blouse die Bluse (-n) (5)
blue blau (5)
to board (*a vehicle*) einsteigen (steigt ein), stieg ein, ist eingestiegen (10)
body: part of the body der Körperteil (-e) (8)
bodybuilding: to do bodybuilding Bodybuilding machen (7)
book das Buch (ᵉer) (1)
to book (*a trip*) buchen (10)
bookcase, bookshelf das Bücherregal (-e) (2)
boot der Stiefel (-) (5)
boring langweilig (1)
born: I was born ich bin geboren (1)
to borrow leihen, lieh, geliehen (5)
boss der Chef (-s) / die Chefin (-nen) (11)
bottle die Flasche (-n) (14); **nonrecyclable bottle** die Wegwerfflasche (-n) (14)
boy der Junge (-n *masc.*) (-n) (2)
bread das Brot (-e) (5)
breakfast das Frühstück (-e) (5); **bed and breakfast** die Pension (-en) (9); **breakfast nook** die Frühstücksnische (-n) (12); **breakfast room** der Frühstücksraum (ᵉe) (9); **to eat breakfast** frühstücken (4)
breast die Brust (ᵉe) (8)
bright(ly) hell (2); (*weather*) heiter (7); (*intelligent*) gescheit (13)
to bring bringen, brachte, gebracht (7); **to bring up** (*raise children*) erziehen, erzog, erzogen (14)
broccoli der Brokkoli (5)
brochure: travel brochure der Reiseprospekt (-e) (10)
broke (*coll.*) pleite (12)
broken kaputt (9)
brother der Bruder (ᵉ) (3)
brother-in-law der Schwager (ᵉ) (3)
brown braun (5)
to brush one's teeth sich die Zähne putzen (8)
to build bauen (12)
building: modern building der Neubau (-ten) (12)
bus der Bus (-se) (10); **bus stop** die Haltestelle (-n) (9)
business: day that a business is closed der Ruhetag (-e) (6)
businessman der Geschäftsmann (*pl.* Geschäftsleute) (11)
businesswoman die Geschäftsfrau (-en) (11)
but (*coord. conj.*) aber (1); **but rather** (*coord. conj.*) sondern (7)
butcher shop die Metzgerei (-en) (5)
butter die Butter (5)
to buy kaufen (2)
by von (+ *dat.*) (5); **by all means** unbedingt (12); **by means of** mit (+ *dat.*) (5); **by the way** übrigens (9); **to come by** vorbeikommen (kommt vorbei), kam vorbei, ist vorbeigekommen (4)
bye tschüss (*inform.*) (E)

C

cabin die Hütte (-n) (10)
cable TV connection der Kabelanschluss (ᵉe) (13)

café das Café (-s) (6)

cafeteria: student cafeteria die Mensa (-s) (1)

cake der Kuchen (-) (5)

to call (up) anrufen, rief an, angerufen (4)

called: to be called heißen, hieß, geheißen (1)

camcorder der Camcorder (-) (13)

camera die Kamera (-s) (10); **digital camera** die Digitalkamera (-s) (13)

can (*tin or aluminum*) die Dose (-n) (14); **beverage can** die Getränkedose (-n) (14)

can, to be able to können (kann), konnte, gekonnt (4)

cap die Mütze (-n) (5)

car das Auto (-s) (2); der Wagen (-) (7)

card die Karte (-n) (7); **credit card** die Kreditkarte (-n) (9); **ID card** der Personalausweis (-e) (10); **playing card** die Spielkarte (-n) (7); **report card** das Zeugnis (-se) (11); **seat reservation card** die Platzkarte (-n) (10); **to play cards** Karten spielen (1)

care: I don't care. Das ist mir egal. (5); **Take care.** Mach's gut. (*inform.*) (E)

to care for mögen (mag), mochte, gemocht (4)

career training die Ausbildung (11)

carpet der Teppich (-e) (2)

carpeting (wall-to-wall) der Teppichboden (¨) (12)

carrot die Karotte (-n) (5)

to carry tragen (trägt), trug, getragen (5)

carry-on luggage das Handgepäck (10)

case: in any case auf jeden Fall (13)

cash das Bargeld (10); **cash register** die Kasse (-n) (5)

cashier die Kasse (-n) (5)

casserole der Auflauf (¨e) (6)

castle das Schloss (¨er) (9)

cat die Katze (-n) (12)

to catch a cold sich erkälten (8)

cauliflower der Blumenkohl (5)

CD player der CD-Spieler (-) (2)

to celebrate feiern (3)

cell phone das Handy (-s) (2)

center die Mitte (9); **center (of town)** das Zentrum (Zentren) (9); **in the center (of the city)** in der Mitte (der Stadt) (9); **recycling center** die Sammelstelle (-n) (14)

centrally located zentral gelegen (2)

cereal das Müsli (-) (5)

chair der Stuhl (¨e) (2)

to challenge herausfordern (fordert heraus) (11)

to change (*trains*) umsteigen (steigt um), stieg um, ist umgestiegen (10)

channel (*TV*) das Programm (-e) (13)

cheap(ly) billig (2)

check der Scheck (-s); **baggage check** die Gepäckaufbewahrung (10); **traveler's check** der Reisescheck (-s) (10)

to check in (*hotel*) sich anmelden (meldet an) (9)

check-out die Kasse (-n) (5)

cheerful lustig (1)

cheese der Käse (5)

chess: to play chess Schach spielen (7)

chest die Brust (¨e) (8)

chicken das Hähnchen (-) (5)

chin das Kinn (-e) (8)

to choose wählen (14); **to choose something** sich (*dat.*) etwas aussuchen (sucht aus) (13)

Christmas das Weihnachten (3); **Christmas Eve** der Heilige Abend (3); **Christmas tree** der Weihnachtsbaum (¨e) (3)

church die Kirche (-n) (9)

cinema das Kino (-s) (4)

citizen der Bürger (-) / die Bürgerin (-nen) (14)

city die Stadt (¨e) (E); **city hall** das Rathaus (¨er) (9); **in the center of the city** in der Mitte der Stadt (9)

to claim behaupten (13)

class: to travel first/second class erster/zweiter Klasse fahren (fährt), fuhr, ist gefahren (10)

clean sauber (14)

to clean up aufräumen (räumt auf) (4)

cleaner: vacuum cleaner der Staubsauger (-) (12)

clear: Everything is clear. Alles klar. (E)

clock die Uhr (-en) (2); **alarm clock** der Wecker (-) (2); **It's one o'clock** Es ist eins. / Es ist ein Uhr. (4)

closed geschlossen (6); **day that a business is closed** der Ruhetag (-e) (6)

closet die Garderobe (-n) (12); **clothes closet** der Kleiderschrank (¨e) (2)

clothes dryer der Wäschetrockner (-) (12)

clothing: article of clothing das Kleidungsstück (-e) (5)

cloud die Wolke (-n) (7)

cloudless wolkenlos (7)

cloudy bewölkt (7)

club der Verein (-e) (7)

clubbing: to go clubbing in die Disko gehen, ging, ist gegangen (4)

coat der Mantel (¨) (5); **sport coat** das Sakko (-s) (5)

code: postal code die Postleitzahl (-en) (E)

coffee der Kaffee; **coffee table** der Couchtisch (-e) (2); **a cup of coffee** eine Tasse Kaffee (4)

cold (*adj.*) kalt (kälter, kältest-) (7)

cold die Erkältung (-en) (8); **head cold** der Schnupfen (8); **to catch a cold** sich erkälten (8)

cold cuts der Aufschnitt (5)

colleague der Mitarbeiter (-) / die Mitarbeiterin (-nen) (11)

to collect sammeln (7)

color die Farbe (-n) (5)

to comb (one's hair) sich kämmen (8)

to come kommen, kam, ist gekommen (1); **to come along** mitkommen (kommt mit), kam mit, ist mitgekommen (4); **to come back** zurückkommen (kommt zurück), kam zurück, ist zurückgekommen (4); **to come by** vorbeikommen (kommt vorbei), kam vorbei, ist

vorbeigekommen (4); **that comes to** das macht zusammen (5)

comedy die Komödie (-n) (4)

comfortable, comfortably bequem (2)

committed engagiert (11)

company die Firma (Firmen) (11); das Unternehmen (-) (11)

to compare vergleichen, verglich, verglichen (12)

to complain about sich beschweren über (+ *acc.*) (9)

complete(ly) ganz (12)

completion (*of training or school*) der Abschluss (¨e) (11)

complicated kompliziert (1)

computer der Computer (-) (2); **computer connection** der Computeranschluss (¨e) (2); **computer diskette** die Computerdiskette (-n) (12); **computer scientist** der Informatiker (-) / die Informatikerin (-nen) (11); **notebook computer** das Notebook (-s) (13); **to play computer games** Computerspiele spielen (1)

concert das Konzert (-e) (4); **to go to a concert** ins Konzert gehen (4)

congestion: nasal congestion der Schnupfen (8)

to congratulate gratulieren (+ *dat.*) (3)

connection der Anschluss (¨e) (10); **cable TV connection** der Kabelanschluss (¨e) (13); **computer connection** der Computeranschluss (¨e) (2)

conservative konservativ (1)

to consider halten (für + *acc.*) (hält), hielt, gehalten (14)

to consume verbrauchen (14)

contact der Kontakt (-e) (11)

convenient(ly) günstig (9); **to be conveniently located** günstig liegen, lag, gelegen (9)

to converse sich unterhalten (unterhält), unterhielt, unterhalten (13)

to cook kochen (1)

cookie der Keks (-e) (5)

cool kühl (7)

corn der Mais (6)

corner die Ecke (-n) (9); **at the corner** an der Ecke (9)

correct: to be correct Recht haben (hat Recht) (2)

corruption die Korruption (14)

cost der Preis (-e) (9); **extra costs** die Nebenkosten (*pl.*) (12)

to cost kosten (2)

cough, coughing der Husten (8)

counselor: employment counselor der Berufsberater (-) / die Berufsberaterin (-nen) (11)

country das Land (¨er); **foreign countries** das Ausland (*sg. only*) (11); **home country** das Inland (*sg. only*) (13)

course: of course natürlich (1)

court: tennis court der Tennisplatz (¨e) (7)

cousin (*female*) die Kusine (-n) (3); (*male*) der Vetter (-n) (3)

co-worker der Mitarbeiter (-) / die Mitarbeiterin (-nen) (11)

cozy, cozily gemütlich (4)

crazy verrückt (8)

cream die Sahne (6); **dish of ice cream** der Eisbecher (-) (6); **ice cream** das Eis (5); **shaving cream** die Rasiercreme (-s) (5); **whipped cream** die Sahne (6)

to create schaffen, schuf, geschaffen (14)

credit card die Kreditkarte (-n) (9)

crime film or book der Krimi (-s) (4)

crossword: to do crossword puzzles Kreuzworträtsel machen (1)

crowded voll (6)

cucumber die Gurke (-n) (5)

cuisine die Küche (6)

cup die Tasse (-n) (4); **a cup of coffee** eine Tasse Kaffee (4)

current aktuell (13); **current events** Aktuelles (13)

customer der Kunde (-n *masc.*) (-n) / die Kundin (-nen) (2)

cutlet das Schnitzel (-) (5)

Czech Republic Tschechien (E)

D

daily täglich (6)

to dance tanzen (1); **He dances well.** Er tanzt gut. (1)

dance club die Disko (4)

danger die Gefahr (-en) (14)

dangerous(ly) gefährlich (10)

dark dunkel (2)

date das Datum (Daten); **date of birth** der Geburtstag (-e) (1); **What is today's/tomorrow's date?** Welches Datum ist heute/morgen? (3)

daughter die Tochter (⸚) (3)

day der Tag (-e) (2); **day of the week** der Wochentag (-e) (3); **day that a business is closed** der Ruhetag (-e) (6); **every day** jeden Tag (7); **good day** (guten) Tag (E); **in two days** in zwei Tagen (6); **time of day** die Tageszeit (-en) (4); **two days ago** vor zwei Tagen (6)

to deal with (*be about*) handeln von (+ *dat.*) (13); (*treat, take care of*) behandeln (14)

December (der) Dezember (3)

decent gescheit (13); **nothing decent** nichts Gescheites (13)

to decide sich entschließen, entschloss, entschlossen (13)

to decrease vermindern (14)

definitely bestimmt (1)

degree (*school*) der Abschluss (⸚e) (11); (*temperature*) der Grad (-e) (7); **35 degrees** 35 Grad (7)

demonstration die Demonstration (-en) (14)

Denmark (das) Dänemark (E)

dentist der Zahnarzt (⸚e) / die Zahnärztin (-nen) (11)

to depart abreisen (reist ab), ist abgereist (9); abfahren (fährt ab), fuhr ab, ist abgefahren (10)

department store das Kaufhaus (⸚er) (2)

departure die Abfahrt (-en) (10)

depressed deprimiert (8); **You sound so depressed.** Du klingst so deprimiert. (8)

to deserve verdienen (11)

to design entwerfen (entwirft), entwarf, entworfen (11)

desk der Schreibtisch (-e) (2); **reception desk** die Rezeption (9)

dessert die Nachspeise (-n) (6); der Nachtisch (-e) (6)

detective film or book der Krimi (-s) (4)

to develop entwickeln (14)

development die Entwicklung (-en) (11)

device das Gerät (-e) (12)

digital camera die Digitalkamera (-s) (13)

diligent fleißig (1)

dining room das Esszimmer (-) (2)

directions: to ask someone for directions jemanden nach dem Weg fragen (9)

director der Leiter (-) / die Leiterin (-nen) (11)

dirty schmutzig (12)

disco die Disko (-s) (4); **to go to a disco** in die Disko gehen (4)

to discuss diskutieren (1)

disease die Krankheit (-en) (14)

dish (*of prepared food*) das Gericht (-e) (6); die Speise (-n) (6); **dish of ice cream** der Eisbecher (-) (6); **main dish** das Hauptgericht (-e) (6); **side dish** die Beilage (-n) (6)

dishwasher die Spülmaschine (-n) (12)

diskette: computer diskette die Computerdiskette (-n) (12)

to disseminate verbreiten (14)

to dive tauchen (7)

diverse abwechslungsreich (11)

to do machen (1); tun (tut), tat, getan (8); **to do an internship** ein Praktikum machen (1); **to do body-building** Bodybuilding machen (7); **to do crossword puzzles** Kreuzworträtsel machen (1); **to do gymnastics** turnen (7); **to do research** forschen (13); **to do weight training** Bodybuilding machen (7); **to do without** verzichten auf (+ *acc.*) (12); **Are you doing well?** Geht's gut? (E); **What do you do for a living?** Was sind Sie von Beruf? (1)

doctor der Arzt (⸚e) / die Ärztin (-nen) (8)

document das Dokument (-e) (13)

documentary (film) der Dokumentarfilm (-e) (13)

documentation die Unterlagen (*pl.*) (11)

dog der Hund (-e) (3); **sick as a dog** (*coll.*) hundsmiserabel (8)

door die Tür (-en) (2)

dormitory das Studentenwohnheim (-e) (2)

double room das Doppelzimmer (-) (9)

doubt: no doubt bestimmt (1)

down: to lie down sich (hin)legen (legt hin) (8); **to sit down** sich (hin)setzen (setzt hin) (8)

downstairs unten; (*directional*) nach unten (12)

downtown die Innenstadt (⸚e) (9)

draft vom Fass (6)

drama (*stage*) das Theaterstück (-e) (4)

to draw zeichnen (7)

drawing die Zeichnung (-en) (12)

dress das Kleid (-er) (5)

dressed: to get dressed sich anziehen (zieht an), zog an, angezogen (8)

dresser die Kommode (-n) (2)

drink das Getränk (-e) (5)

to drink trinken, trank, getrunken (2)

to drive fahren (fährt), fuhr, ist gefahren (1)

to drop off abgeben (gibt ab), gab ab, abgegeben (8)

drug die Droge (-n) (14); **drug addiction** die Drogensucht (14)

drugstore (*toiletries and sundries*) die Drogerie (-n) (5)

dryer: clothes dryer der Wäschetrockner (-) (12); **hair dryer** der Föhn (-e) (9)

during während (+ *gen.*) (9)

DVD player der DVD-Spieler (-) (2)

E

each jeder, jede, jedes (5)

ear das Ohr (-en) (8)

early früh (4); **earlier** früher (7)

to earn verdienen (11)

earth die Welt (14)

Easter (das) Ostern (3)

to eat essen (isst), aß, gegessen (1); **to eat breakfast** frühstücken (4)

eating das Essen (1)

eccentric exzentrisch (1)

economy die Wirtschaft (13)

egg das Ei (-er) (5); **fried egg** das Spiegelei (-er) (6)

eight acht (E)

eighteen achtzehn (E)

eighth achte (3)

eighty achtzig (E)

either . . . or entweder … oder (8)

elbow der Ell(en)bogen (-) (8)

to elect wählen (14)

electricity der Strom (12)

elevator der Aufzug (⸚e) (9)

eleven elf (E)

eleventh elfte (3)

else: Anything else? Sonst noch etwas? (10)

e-mail die E-Mail (-s) (13)

to employ beschäftigen (11)

employee der Mitarbeiter (-) / die Mitarbeiterin (-nen) (11)

employer der Arbeitgeber (-) / die Arbeitgeberin (-nen) (11)

employment: employment counselor der Berufsberater (-) / die Berufsberaterin (-nen) (11); **employment office** das Arbeitsamt (⸚er) (11)

enterprise das Unternehmen (-) (11)

to entertain oneself sich unterhalten (unterhält), unterhielt, unterhalten (13)

entertaining unterhaltsam (13)

entertainment die Unterhaltung (13); **for entertainment** zur Unterhaltung (13)

entire(ly) ganz (12)

entrance der Eingang (⸚e) (12)

enivironment die Umwelt (14)

environmental: environmental pollution die Umweltverschmutzung (14); **environmental protection** der Umweltschutz (14); **environmentally friendly** umweltfreundlich (14)

to equip einrichten (richtet ein) (12)

especially besonders (8)
euro das Euro (-[s]) (2)
even sogar (8)
evening der Abend (-e) (4); **evening meal** das Abendessen (-) (5); **good evening** guten Abend (E); **in the evening, evenings** abends (4); **this evening** heute Abend (1); **tomorrow evening** morgen Abend (4)
event: current events Aktuelles (13)
every alle (5); jeder, jede, jedes (5); **every day** jeden Tag (7)
everything alles (10); **Everything is clear.** Alles klar. (E)
exact(ly) genau (2); **exactly** gerade (2); **exactly as . . . as** genauso … wie (7)
exaggerated übertrieben (14)
examination (*at the end of Gymnasium*) das Abitur (-e) (11)
to examine untersuchen, untersucht (11)
excellent ausgezeichnet (E)
exciting spannend (4)
to excuse entschuldigen (6); **Excuse me!** Entschuldigen Sie! (6), Entschuldigung! (9)
expense die Ausgabe (-n) (12)
expensive(ly) teuer (2)
experience die Erfahrung (-en) (11)
to experience erleben (10)
extra costs die Nebenkosten (*pl.*) (12)
extremism: right-wing extremism der Rechtsextremismus (14)
eye das Auge (-n) (8)
eyeglasses die Brille (-n) (5)

F

face das Gesicht (-er) (8)
fair (*weather*) heiter (7)
fall (*autumn*) der Herbst (-e) (7)
to fall fallen (fällt), fiel, ist gefallen (7); **to fall asleep** einschlafen (schläft ein), schlief ein, ist eingeschlafen (4)
familiar vertraut (14)
family die Familie (-n) (3); **family gathering** das Familienfest (-e) (3); **family name** der Nachname (*gen.* -ns, *acc./dat.* -n) (-n) (1); **family tree** der Stammbaum (¨e) (3); **small family-run hotel** die Pension (-en) (9)
famine der Hunger (14)
fantastic fantastisch (1)
far weit (9); **as far as** bis zum/zur (9); **far (away) from . . .** weit (weg) von … (2)
farmhouse das Bauernhaus (¨er) (12)
fashionable, fashionably modisch (5)
fast schnell (10)
fast-food stand der Imbiss (-e) (6)
father der Vater (¨) (3)
favor: I'm in favor of it. Ich bin dafür. (14)
favorable günstig (9)
fax machine das Faxgerät (-e) (13)
fear die Angst (¨e) (12)
feature film der Spielfilm (-e) (13)
February (der) Februar (3)
to feel (well) sich (wohl) fühlen (8); **to feel like** (*doing something*) Lust haben (hat Lust) (2)
fees (*tuition*) die Studiengebühren (*pl.*) (12)

female cousin die Kusine (-n) (3)
fever das Fieber (8)
few wenig (8)
field: athletic field der Sportplatz (¨e) (7)
fifteen fünfzehn (E)
fifth fünfte (3)
fifty fünfzig (E)
to fill out ausfüllen (füllt aus) (9)
film der Film (-e) (4); **feature film** der Spielfilm (-e) (13)
to find finden, fand, gefunden (1); **to find something** sich (*dat.*) etwas aussuchen (sucht aus) (13)
fine sehr gut (E); **fine, thanks** danke, gut (E)
finger der Finger (-) (8)
firm die Firma (Firmen) (11)
first erste (3); (*at first*) zuerst (9); **first name** der Vorname (*gen.* -ns, *acc./dat.* -n) (-n) (1); **May first** der erste Mai (3); **on May first** am ersten Mai (3)
to fish angeln (7)
fit (*adj.*) fit (8); **to keep fit** sich fit halten (hält), hielt, gehalten (8)
to fit passen (+ *dat.*) (5)
fitness die Fitness (8)
five fünf (E)
to flash blitzen (7)
floor der Stock (*pl.* Stockwerke) (9); die Etage (-n) (12); **ground floor** das Erdgeschoss (-e) (9); **top floor** das Dachgeschoss (-e) (12)
flu die Grippe (8)
to fly fliegen, flog, ist geflogen (7)
fog der Nebel (7)
foggy neblig (7)
food das Essen (-) (1); die Küche (6); die Ernährung (12); **food to go** zum Mitnehmen (6); **natural foods store** der Bioladen (¨) (5); **organic foods** die Biolebensmittel (*pl.*) (8)
foot der Fuß (¨e) (8); **to go on foot** zu Fuß gehen, ging, ist gegangen (8)
for für (+ *acc.*) (3); (+ *time*) seit (+ *dat.*) (5, 6); zu (+ *dat.*) (5); (*coord. conj.*) denn (7); **for two years** seit zwei Jahren (6)
to forbid verbieten, verbot, verboten (14)
foreign countries das Ausland (*sg. only*) (11)
foreigner der Ausländer (-) / die Ausländerin (-nen) (14); **hatred directed toward foreigners** die Ausländerfeindlichkeit (14)
forest der Wald (¨er) (7)
to forget vergessen (vergisst), vergaß, vergessen (10)
fork die Gabel (-n) (6)
form das Formular (-e) (11); **application form** das Bewerbungsformular (-e) (11); **registration form** das Anmeldeformular (-e) (9)
forty vierzig (E)
forward: to look forward to sich freuen auf (+ *acc.*) (12)
four vier (E)
foursome: as a foursome zu viert (10)
fourteen vierzehn (E)
fourth vierte (3)

France (das) Frankreich (E)
free(ly) frei (2)
free time die Freizeit (7)
French fries die Pommes frites (*pl.*) (6)
fresh(ly) frisch (5)
Friday (der) Freitag (3); **Fridays, on Friday(s)** freitags (4)
fried: fried egg das Spiegelei (-er) (6); **fried potatoes** die Bratkartoffeln (*pl.*) (6)
friend der Freund (-e) / die Freundin (-nen) (1)
friendly freundlich (1); **environmentally friendly** umweltfreundlich (14)
fries: French fries die Pommes frites (*pl.*) (6)
from aus (+ *dat.*) (5); von (+ *dat.*) (5, 6); ab (+ *dat.*) (12); **across from** gegenüber von (+ *dat.*) (9); **far (away) from . . .** weit (weg) von … (2); **from two to three o'clock** von zwei bis drei Uhr (6); **from where** woher (1); **I'm from . . .** Ich komme aus … (E); **Where are you from?** Woher kommen Sie? (*form.*) / Woher kommst du? (*inform.*) (E)
front: front hall die Diele (-n) (12); **in front of** vor (+ *acc./dat.*) (6)
frozen gefroren (5)
fruit das Obst (5); **fruit and vegetable stand** der Obst- und Gemüsestand (¨e) (5)
full voll (6)
full-service restaurant die Gaststätte (-n) (6)
fun der Spaß (¨e) (1); **have fun!** viel Spaß! (1); **That's fun.** Das macht Spaß. (1)
to function funktionieren (9)
fun-loving lustig (1)
to furnish einrichten (richtet ein) (12)
furnished möbliert (2)
furniture die Möbel (*pl.*) (2)
future die Zukunft (11)

G

game das Spiel (-e); **to play computer games** Computerspiele spielen (1)
garage die Garage (-n) (2)
garbage der Müll (12); der Abfall (¨e) (14)
garden der Garten (¨) (2); **beer garden** der Biergarten (¨) (6)
gasoline das Benzin (12)
gathering: family gathering das Familienfest (-e) (3)
generator: wind power generator das Windrad (¨er) (14)
gentleman der Herr (-n *masc.*) (-en) (E)
German deutsch; (*language*) (das) Deutsch (1); **How do you say . . . in German?** Wie sagt man … auf Deutsch? (E)
Germany (das) Deutschland (E)
to get (*receive*) bekommen, bekam, bekommen (6); **What's the best way to get there?** Wie komme ich am besten dahin? (9)
to get dressed sich anziehen (zieht an), zog an, angezogen (8)
to get into (*a vehicle*) einsteigen (steigt ein), stieg ein, ist eingestiegen (10)
to get involved sich engagieren (14)

to get undressed sich ausziehen (zieht aus), zog aus, ausgezogen (8)

to get up aufstehen (steht auf), stand auf, ist aufgestanden (4)

to get well sich erholen (8); **Get well soon!** Gute Besserung! (8)

gift das Geschenk (-e) (3)

to give geben (gibt), gab, gegeben (3); (*as a gift*) schenken (5); (*drop off, turn in*) abgeben (gibt ab), gab ab, abgegeben (8)

given name der Vorname (*gen.* -ns, *acc./dat.* -n) (-n) (1)

glad: to be glad about sich freuen über (+ *acc.*) (12)

gladly gern (2)

glasses (eyeglasses) die Brille (-n) (5)

global global (14)

glove der Handschuh (-e) (10)

to go gehen, ging, ist gegangen (1); **(food) to go** zum Mitnehmen (6); **to go clubbing** in die Disko gehen (4); **to go for a walk** spazieren gehen (geht spazieren) (4); **to go on a trip** verreisen, ist verreist (10); **to go on foot** zu Fuß gehen (8); **to go on vacation** Urlaub machen (8); **to go out** ausgehen (geht aus), ging aus, ist ausgegangen (4); **to go shopping** einkaufen gehen (geht einkaufen) (4); **to go to a concert** ins Konzert gehen (4); **to go to a disco** in die Disko gehen (4); **to go to the movies** ins Kino gehen (4); **to go to the opera** in die Oper gehen (4); **to go to the theater** ins Theater gehen (4)

good sehr gut (E); gut (1); **good day** (guten) Tag (E); **good evening** guten Abend (E); **good luck!** viel Glück! (1); **good morning** (guten) Morgen (E); **good night** gute Nacht (E); **to look good** (*on a person*) stehen (+ *dat.*), stand, gestanden (5); **to taste good** schmecken (+ *dat.*) (5)

good-bye (auf) Wiedersehen (E); (*on telephone*) auf Wiederhören! (9)

government die Regierung (-en) (14)

granddaughter die Enkelin (-nen) (3)

grandfather der Großvater (¨) (3)

grandma die Oma (-s) (3)

grandmother die Großmutter (¨) (3)

grandpa der Opa (-s) (3)

grandparents die Großeltern (*pl.*) (3)

grandson der Enkel (-) (3)

granola das Müsli (-) (5)

grape die Traube (-n) (5)

graphic artist der Zeichner (-) / die Zeichnerin (-nen) (11)

gray grau (5)

great prima (E); **great!** ganz toll! (1)

green grün (5)

greeting der Gruß (¨e) (12)

grill der Grill (-s) (6)

ground floor das Erdgeschoss (-e) (9)

guest room das Gästezimmer (-) (12)

guide: travel guide (book) der Reiseführer (-) (10)

gym das Fitnesscenter (-) (4)

gymnasium die Turnhalle (-n) (7)

gymnastics: to do gymnastics turnen (7)

H

hail der Hagel (7)

hair das Haar (-e) (8); **hair dryer** der Föhn (-e) (9)

half halb (4); **half past one** halb zwei (4)

hall: city hall das Rathaus (¨er) (9); **front hall** die Diele (-n) (12)

hallway der Flur (-e) (12)

ham der Schinken (-) (5)

hand die Hand (¨e) (8)

handbag die Tasche (-n) (5)

to hang (*something*) hängen (6); **to hang, be hanging** hängen, hing, gehangen (6)

to happen passieren, ist passiert (7)

happy glücklich; **Happy birthday!** Herzlichen Glückwunsch zum Geburtstag! (3)

harbor der Hafen (¨) (9)

hardly kaum (8)

hardworking fleißig (1)

hat der Hut (¨e) (5)

hatred directed toward foreigners die Ausländerfeindlichkeit (14)

to have haben (hat), hatte, gehabt (2); **have fun!** viel Spaß! (1); **to have time** Zeit haben (hat Zeit) (2); **to have to** müssen (muss), musste, gemusst (4); **I have a question.** Ich habe eine Frage. (E); **What will you have?** Was bekommen Sie? (6)

he er (1)

head der Kopf (¨e) (8); (*boss*) der Chef (-s) / die Chefin (-nen) (11); **head cold** der Schnupfen (-) (8)

headache die Kopfschmerzen (*pl.*) (8)

headline die Schlagzeile (-n) (13)

health die Gesundheit (8)

healthful, healthy gesund (8)

to hear hören (1)

heat, heating system die Heizung (12)

hello grüß dich (*inform.*) (E); (guten) Tag (E); hallo (*among friends and family*) (E)

to help helfen (+ *dat.*) (hilft), half, geholfen (5)

help-wanted ad das Stellenangebot (-e) (11)

her ihr (3); sie (*acc.*) (3); **(to/for) her** ihr (*dat.*) (5)

herbal tea der Kräutertee (8)

here hier (1)

hi grüß dich (*inform.*) (E); hi (E)

high(ly) hoch (hoh-) (2)

to hike wandern, ist gewandert (1)

him ihn (*acc.*) (3); **(to/for) him** ihm (*dat.*) (5)

his sein (3)

to hitchhike per Autostop reisen, ist gereist (10)

hobby das Hobby (-s) (1)

to hold halten (hält), hielt, gehalten (14)

home (to home) nach Hause (5); **at home** zu Hause (5); **at home and abroad** im Inland und Ausland (13); **home country** das Inland (*sg. only*) (13)

homeless person der/die Obdachlose (*decl. adj.*) (14)

homelessness die Obdachlosigkeit (14)

to hope (for) hoffen (auf + *acc.*) (10); **I hope** hoffentlich (6)

horoscope das Horoskop (-e) (13)

horseback: to ride on horseback reiten, ritt, ist geritten (7)

hostel: youth hostel die Jugendherberge (-n) (9)

hot heiß (7)

hotel das Hotel (-s) (9); **small family-run hotel** die Pension (-en) (9)

hour die Stunde (-n) (4); **office hour** die Sprechstunde (-n) (8)

house das Haus (¨er) (2)

household der Haushalt (-e) (12)

houseplant die Zimmerpflanze (-n) (2)

housing: shared housing die Wohngemeinschaft (-en) / die WG (-s) (2)

how wie (1); **How about . . . ?** Wie wäre es mit ... ? (13); **How are you?** Na, wie geht's? (*casual*) / Wie geht's (dir)? (*inform.*) / Wie geht es Ihnen? (*form.*) (E); **How do you like . . . ?** Wie findest du ... ? (1); **Wie gefällt Ihnen ... ?** (5); **How do you say . . . in German?** Wie sagt man ... auf Deutsch? (E); **How do you write . . . ?** Wie schreibt man ... ? (E)

human (being) der Mensch (-en *masc.*) (-en) (2); **human right** das Menschenrecht (-e) (14)

humid schwül (7)

hundred (ein)hundert (E)

Hungary Ungarn (E)

hunger der Hunger (14)

hungry: to be hungry Hunger haben (hat Hunger) (2)

to hurry up sich beeilen (8)

to hurt wehtun (+ *dat.*) (tut weh), tat weh, wehgetan (8); **That hurts.** Das tut mir weh. (8)

husband der Mann (¨er) (3)

I

I ich (1); **I am** Ich bin... (E); **I don't care** Das ist mir egal. (5); **I don't know.** Das weiß ich nicht. (E); **I'm from . . .** Ich komme aus ... (E); **I think that's really stupid!** Das ist mir zu blöd. (13); **I was born** ich bin geboren (1)

ice, ice cream das Eis (5); **dish of ice cream** der Eisbecher (-) (6)

to ice skate Schlittschuh laufen (läuft Schlittschuh), lief Schlittschuh, ist Schlittschuh gelaufen (7)

ice-skating rink das Eisstadion (Eisstadien) (7)

ID card der Personalausweis (-e) (10)

i.e. d.h. (= das heißt) (8)

if (*subord. conj.*) wenn (8); **if I were you** an deiner Stelle (12)

ill krank (8)

illness die Krankheit (-en) (14)

to imagine sich (*dat.*) vorstellen (stellt vor) (11)

immediately gleich (8), sofort (9)

important wichtig (3)

impractical unpraktisch (1)

in in (+ *acc./dat.*) (6); **in addition** außerdem (14); **in any case** auf jeden Fall (13); **in back of** hinter (+ *acc./dat.*) (6); **in front of** vor

(+ *acc./dat.*) (6); **in January** im Januar (3); **in shape** fit (8); **in spite of** trotz (+ *gen.*) (9); **in the afternoon** nachmittags (4); **in the evening** abends (4); **in the morning** morgens (4); **in two days** in zwei Tagen (6); **to keep in shape** sich fit halten (hält), hielt, gehalten (8)

included in the price im Preis enthalten (9)

income das Einkommen (11); die Einnahmen (12)

independent(ly) selbständig (11)

indoor swimming pool das Hallenbad (¨er) (7)

inexpensive(ly) billig (2); preiswert (2); **quite inexpensive** recht preiswert (2)

to inform oneself (about) sich informieren (über + *acc.*) (8)

information die Auskunft (¨o) (10)

to injure oneself sich verletzen (8)

injury die Verletzung (-en) (14)

inside drinnen (7); **inside of** innerhalb (+ *gen.*) (9)

instructor: university instructor der Hochschullehrer (-) / die Hochschullehrerin (-nen) (1)

to insulate isolieren (14)

insurance die Versicherung (-en) (12)

intelligent gescheit (13)

interest das Interesse (-n) (1)

interested: to be interested in sich interessieren für (+ *acc.*) (11)

interesting interessant (1)

Internet das Internet (13); **Internet access** der Internetzugang (9)

internship das Praktikum (Praktika) (1); **to do an internship** ein Praktikum machen (1)

interpreter der Dolmetscher (-) / die Dolmetscherin (-nen) (11)

to interrupt unterbrechen (unterbricht), unterbrach, unterbrochen (14)

intersection die Kreuzung (-en) (9)

interview das Interview (-s); **job interview** das Vorstellungsgespräch (-e) (11)

to introduce einführen (führt ein) (14); **to introduce oneself** sich (*acc.*) vorstellen (stellt vor) (11)

to invent erfinden, erfand, erfunden (13)

invention die Erfindung (-en) (13)

to invite einladen (lädt ein), lud ein, eingeladen (4)

involved: to get involved sich engagieren (14)

is ist; **that is** d.h. (= das heißt) (8); **there is** es gibt (3); **This is . . .** Das ist … (E); **What is . . . ?** Wie ist … ? (E)

to isolate isolieren (14)

it es, er, sie (1); es, ihn, sie (*acc.*) (3); **(to/for) it** ihm, ihr (*dat.*) (5); **It's one o'clock** Es ist eins. / Es ist ein Uhr. (4)

Italy (das) Italien (E)

its sein, ihr (3)

J

jacket die Jacke (-n) (5)

jail das Gefängnis (-se) (14)

January (der) Januar (3); **in January** im Januar (3)

jar die Dose (-n) (14)

jeans die Jeans (5)

job die Stelle (-n) (11); **job interview** das Vorstellungsgespräch (-e) (11); **job offer** das Stellenangebot (-e) (11)

to jog joggen (7); laufen (läuft), lief, ist gelaufen (2)

journalist der Journalist (-en *masc.*) (-en) / die Journalistin (-nen) (1)

juice der Saft (¨e) (5)

July (der) Juli (3)

June (der) Juni (3)

just gerade (2); **just as . . . as** genauso … wie (7)

K

to keep fit, in shape sich fit halten (hält), hielt, gehalten (8)

to keep on going straight ahead immer geradeaus (9)

key der Schlüssel (-) (9)

kind: what kind of (a) was für (ein) (11)

kitchen die Küche (-n) (2, 6)

knee das Knie (-) (8)

knife das Messer (-) (6)

to know (*be acquainted with*) kennen, kannte, gekannt (3); **to know** (*something as a fact*) wissen (weiß), wusste, gewusst (3); **I don't know.** Das weiß ich nicht. (E)

knowledge die Kenntnis (-se) (11)

L

lake der See (-n) (7)

lamp die Lampe (-n) (2)

large groß (2)

to last dauern (7)

late spät (4); **at the latest** spätestens (12)

lawyer der Rechtsanwalt (¨e) / die Rechtsanwältin (-nen) (11)

to lay legen (6)

layover der Aufenthalt (-e) (9)

lazy faul (1); **to be lazy** faulenzen (7)

to learn lernen (1)

least: at least mindestens (8)

to leave (*depart*) abfahren (fährt ab), fuhr ab, ist abgefahren (10); (*e.g., a message*) hinterlassen (hinterlässt), hinterließ, hinterlassen (13)

lecture der Vortrag (¨e) (4); **university lecture** die Vorlesung (-en) (4)

left links (9); **to the left** nach links (9)

left over übrig (12)

leg das Bein (-e) (8)

to lend leihen, lieh, geliehen (5)

to lessen vermindern (14)

to let lassen (lässt), ließ, gelassen (6); **Let's . . .** Lass uns (doch) … (6)

letter der Brief (-e) (7)

lettuce der Salat (-e) (6)

librarian der Bibliothekar (-e) / die Bibliothekarin (-nen) (11)

library die Bibliothek (-en) (4)

to lie, be lying down liegen, lag, gelegen (6); **to lie around** faulenzen (7); **to lie down** sich (hin)legen (legt hin) (8)

Liechtenstein (das) Liechtenstein (E)

life das Leben (11); **professional life** das Berufsleben (11)

light (*adj.*) hell (2)

light: traffic light die Ampel (-n) (9)

lightning: There's lightning. Es blitzt. (7)

likable sympathisch (1)

to like mögen (mag), mochte, gemocht (4); **to like** (*a person or thing*) gern haben (hat gern) (2); **to like** (*to do something*) gern (+ *verb*) (2); **to feel like** (*doing something*) Lust haben (hat Lust) (2); **How do you like . . . ?** Wie findest du … ? (1); **Wie gefällt Ihnen … ?** (5); **would like to** möchte (4); **would like to (do) most** möchte am liebsten (4)

likewise gleichfalls (E)

linens die Bettwäsche (9)

to listen hören (1); zuhören (hört zu) (4)

litter der Abfall (¨e) (14)

little wenig (8); **a little** (*adv.*) etwas (2)

to live wohnen (1)

living: What do you do for a living? Was sind Sie von Beruf? (1)

living room das Wohnzimmer (-) (2)

loaf of bread das Brot (-e) (5)

local news die Lokalnachrichten (*pl.*) (13)

located: to be located liegen, lag, gelegen (6); stehen, stand, gestanden (6); **centrally located** zentral gelegen (2); **to be conveniently located** günstig liegen, lag, gelegen (9)

location die Lage (-n) (9)

long lang (länger, längst-) (7); **So long.** Mach's gut. (*inform.*) (E); tschüss (*inform.*) (E)

to look at something sich (*dat.*) etwas anschauen (schaut an) (13); sich (*dat.*) etwas ansehen (sieht an), sah an, angesehen (13)

to look for suchen (2)

to look forward to sich freuen auf (+ *acc.*) (12)

to look good (*on a person*) stehen (+ *dat.*), stand, gestanden (5)

to lose verlieren, verlor, verloren (7)

lot: a lot viel (1); **thanks a lot** danke sehr (1)

lot: parking lot der Parkplatz (¨e) (9)

lotion: suntan lotion das Sonnenschutzmittel (10)

loud(ly) laut (10)

low niedrig (2)

loyal treu (1)

luck: good luck! viel Glück! (1); **What bad luck!** So ein Pech! (8)

luggage das Gepäck (9); **carry-on luggage** das Handgepäck (10)

lunch das Mittagessen (-) (5)

Luxembourg (das) Luxemburg (E)

M

machine die Maschine (-n); **answering machine** der Anrufbeantworter (-) (13); **fax machine** das Faxgerät (-e) (13); **washing machine** die Waschmaschine (-n) (12)

made of aus (+ *dat.*) (5)

magazine die Zeitschrift (-en) (13)

main dish das Hauptgericht (-e) (6)

to make machen (1); **to make a turn** einbiegen (biegt ein), bog ein, ist eingebogen (9); **to make progress** Fortschritte machen (14)

male cousin der Vetter (-n) (3)

man der Mann (¨er) (1)

manager der Chef (-s) / die Chefin (-nen) (11)

to manufacture herstellen (stellt her) (11)

manufacturer der Hersteller (-) (11)

many viele (2); **Many thanks!** Vielen Dank! (6)

March (der) März (3)

Mardi Gras (der) Fasching (*southern Germany, Austria*) (3); (der) Karneval (*Rhineland*) (3)

market, marketplace der Markt (¨e) (5); **stock market** die Börse (-n) (13)

to marry heiraten (3)

to matter: That doesn't matter. Das macht nichts. (8); **What's the matter?** Was ist denn los? (2); Was fehlt Ihnen/dir? (8)

May (der) Mai (3); **May first** der erste Mai (3); **on May first** am ersten Mai (3)

may, to be permitted to dürfen (darf), durfte, gedurft (4); **You may not park here.** Hier darf man nicht parken. (4)

maybe vielleicht (1)

me mich (*acc.*) (3); **(to/for) me** mir (*dat.*) (5); **me too** ich auch (1)

meadow die Wiese (-n) (7)

meal: evening meal das Abendessen (-) (5); **midday meal** das Mittagessen (-) (5)

to mean: What does . . . mean? Was bedeutet . . . ? (E)

means: by all means unbedingt (12); **by means of** mit (+ *dat.*) (5); **means of transportation** das Verkehrsmittel (-) (14)

meat das Fleisch (5)

meatloaf: Bavarian-style meatlofe der Leberkäs (6)

mechanic der Mechaniker (-) / die Mechanikerin (-nen) (11)

medication das Arzneimittel (-) (14)

medicine das Medikament (-e) (5); die Droge (-n) (14)

to meet treffen (trifft), traf, getroffen (4); **Pleased to meet you.** Freut mich. (E)

to mention: Don't mention it. Nichts zu danken. (8)

menu die Speisekarte (-n) (6)

microwave oven der Mikrowellenherd (-e) (12)

midday meal das Mittagessen (-) (5)

middle die Mitte (9)

midnight: at midnight um Mitternacht (3)

milk die Milch (5)

mineral water der Sprudel (6)

minute die Minute (-n) (4)

modern building der Neubau (-ten) (12)

Monday (der) Montag (3); **Mondays, on Monday(s)** montags (4); **on Monday** am Montag (3)

money das Geld (2); **out of money** (*coll.*) pleite (12)

month der Monat (-e) (3); **once a month** einmal im Monat (7)

monthly monatlich (12)

morning der Morgen (-) (4); der Vormittag (-e) (4); **good morning** (guten) Morgen (E); **in the morning, mornings** morgens (4); **this morning** heute Morgen (4); **tomorrow morning** morgen früh (4)

most: would like to (do) most möchte am liebsten (4)

mostly meistens (8)

mother die Mutter (¨) (3)

Mother's Day der Muttertag (3)

motorcycle das Motorrad (¨er) (2)

mountain der Berg (-e) (7)

mouth der Mund (¨er) (8)

to move in einziehen in (+ *acc.*), zog ein, ist eingezogen (12)

movie der Spielfilm (-e) (13); **movie theater** das Kino (-s) (4); **to go to the movies** ins Kino gehen (4)

Mr. Herr (E)

Mrs., Ms. Frau (E)

much viel (1, 2); **thank you very much** danke schön (E)

muggy schwül (7)

muscle der Muskel (-n) (8)

museum das Museum (Museen) (9)

music die Musik (1)

must, to have to müssen (muss), musste, gemusst (4)

mustard der Senf (6)

my mein (3); **My name is . . .** Ich heiße … (E); Mein Name ist… (E)

mystery film or book der Krimi (-s) (4)

N

name der Name (*gen.* -ns, *acc./dat.* -n) (-n) (1); **family name** der Nachname (*gen.* -ns, *acc./dat.* -n) (-n) (1); **first name, given name** der Vorname (*gen.* -ns, *acc./dat.* -n) (-n) (1); **My name is . . .** Ich heiße … (E); Mein Name ist … (E); **Under what name?** Auf welchen Namen? (9); **What is the name of . . . ?** Wie heißt … ? (E); **What's your name?** Wie heißen Sie? (*form.*) / Wie heißt du? (*inform.*) (E); Wie ist Ihr Name? (*form.*) / Wie ist dein Name? (E)

named: to be named heißen, hieß, geheißen (1)

namely nämlich (3)

napkin die Serviette (-n) (6)

to narrate berichten (13)

nasal congestion der Schnupfen (8)

natural(ly) natürlich (1); **natural foods store** der Bioladen (¨) (5)

nature die Natur (10)

near bei (+ *dat.*) (5); **near (the train station)** in der Nähe (des Bahnhofs) (9)

necessary nötig (5); notwendig (12); **No thanks necessary.** Nichts zu danken. (8)

neck der Hals (¨e) (8)

necktie die Krawatte (-n) (5); der Schlips (-e) (5)

to need brauchen (2)

neighborhood die Umgebung (-en) (12)

nephew der Neffe (-n *masc.*) (-n) (3)

Netherlands die Niederlande (*pl.*) (E)

never nie (1)

new neu (3)

New Year's Day das Neujahr (3)

New Year's Eve (das) Silvester (3)

news die Nachrichten (*pl.*) (13); **local news** die Lokalnachrichten (*pl.*) (13)

newspaper die Zeitung (-en) (1)

next nächst-; **next to** neben (+ *acc./ dat.*) (6); **next year** nächstes Jahr (1)

nice(ly) nett (1); schön (2)

niece die Nichte (-n) (3)

night die Nacht (¨e) (4); **at night, nights** nachts (4); **good night** gute Nacht (E)

nightstand der Nachttisch (-e) (2)

nine neun (E)

nineteen neunzehn (E)

ninety neunzig (E)

ninth neunte (3)

no nein (E); **no (not any)** kein (2); **no doubt** bestimmt (1); **No one is answering.** Niemand meldet sich. (13); **No thanks necessary.** Nichts zu danken. (8)

noise der Lärm (14)

nonalcoholic alkoholfrei (6)

none kein (2)

nonrecyclable bottle die Wegwerfflasche (-n) (14)

nonsense: Nonsense! So ein Unsinn! (14)

nonsmoker der Nichtraucher (-) / die Nichtraucherin (-nen) (2)

noodle die Nudel (-n) (6)

nook: breakfast nook die Frühstücksnische (-n) (12)

noon der Mittag (-e) (4); **at noon** mittags (4); **before noon** der Vormittag (-e) (4); (*adv.*) vormittags (4)

nose die Nase (-n) (8)

not nicht (1); **not any** kein (2); **not particularly well** nicht besonders gut (E)

notebook das Heft (-e) (12); **notebook computer** das Notebook (-s) (13)

nothing nichts (2); **nothing decent** nichts Gescheites (13)

November (der) November (3)

now jetzt (1); **now and then** ab und zu (8)

number die Nummer (-n); **telephone number** die Telefonnummer (-n) (E)

nurse der Krankenpfleger (-) / die Krankenschwester (-n) (8)

nutrition die Ernährung (12)

O

occasionally ab und zu (8)

occupation der Beruf (-e) (1)

occupied besetzt (6)

to occupy oneself (with) sich beschäftigen (mit + *dat.*) (11)

ocean das Meer (-e) (7)

o'clock: It's one o'clock Es ist eins. / Es ist ein Uhr. (4)

October (der) Oktober (3)

of von (+ *dat.*) (5); **five of/to two** fünf vor zwei (4); **made of** aus (+ *dat.*) **of course** natürlich (1); (5); **out of** aus (+ *dat.*) (5)

offer das Angebot (-e) (10); **job offer** das Stellenangebot (-e) (11) office das Büro (-s) (11); **employment office** das Arbeitsamt (-er) (11); **office hour** die Sprechstunde (-n) (8); **post office** die Post (*pl.* Postämter) (9)

often oft (1)

OK so lala (E)

old alt (älter, ältest-) (1)

olive die Olive (-n) (6)

on an (+ *acc./dat.*) (6); auf (+ *acc./dat.*) (6); **on account of** wegen (+ *gen.*) (9); **on average** durchschnittlich (12); **on May first** am ersten Mai (3); **on Monday** am Montag (3); **on Monday(s)** montags (4); **on tap** vom Fass (6); **on top of** auf (+ *acc./dat.*) (6)

once einmal (7); früher (7); **once a month/year** einmal im Monat/Jahr (7); **once a week** einmal die Woche (7)

one eins (E); (*indef. pron.*) man (4); **half past one, one-thirty** halb zwei (4); **It's one o'clock** Es ist eins. / Es ist ein Uhr. (4)

one-way (ticket) einfach (10)

onion die Zwiebel (-n) (6)

only nur (2)

open geöffnet (6)

open-air market der Markt (-e) (5)

opera die Oper (-n) (4); **to go to the opera** in die Oper gehen (4)

opinion die Meinung (-en) (14); **to be of the opinion** meinen (14); **I'm of the opinion . . .** ich bin der Meinung … (14); **in my opinion . . .** meiner Meinung nach … (14)

opportunity die Möglichkeit (-en) (10); die Gelegenheit (-en) (11)

or (*coord. conj.*) oder (7); **either . . . or** entweder … oder (8)

orange (*adj.*) orange (5)

to order bestellen (6)

organic foods die Biolebensmittel (*pl.*) (8)

otherwise sonst, sonst noch (10)

ought to sollen (soll), sollte, gesollt (4)

our unser (3)

out of aus (+ *dat.*) (5); **out of money** (*coll.*) pleite (12)

outdoor swimming pool das Freibad (-er) (7)

outdoors im Freien (11)

outside draußen (7); **outside of** außerhalb (+ *gen.*) (9)

oven: microwave oven der Mikrowellenherd (-e) (12)

over über (+ *acc./dat.*) (6); **over there** da drüben (6); **left over** übrig (12)

overcast bewölkt (7)

overnight stay die Übernachtung (-en) (9); **to stay overnight** übernachten (9)

own (*adj.*) eigen (12)

to own besitzen, besaß, besessen (11)

P

to pack packen (10)

packaging die Verpackung (-en) (14)

pains die Schmerzen (*pl.*) (8)

to paint malen (7)

pair of eyeglasses die Brille (-n) (5)

palace das Schloss (-er) (9)

pan die Pfanne (-n) (6)

pants die Hose (-n) (5)

paper das Papier (-e) (12); (*report*) die Arbeit (-en) (8); **papers** (*documents*) die Unterlagen (*pl.*) (11); **toilet paper** das Toilettenpapier (5)

Pardon? Wie bitte? (E)

parents die Eltern (*pl.*) (3)

to park parken; **You may not park here.** Hier darf man nicht parken. (4)

parking lot, parking space der Parkplatz (-e) (9)

part der/das Teil (-e); **part of the body** der Körperteil (-e) (8)

to participate (in) teilnehmen (an + *dat.*) (nimmt teil), nahm teil, teilgenommen (14)

particularly besonders; **not particularly well** nicht besonders gut (E)

party die Party (-s) (3)

passer-by der Passant (-en *masc.*) (-en) / die Passantin (-nen) (9)

passport der Reisepass (-e) (9)

past: half past one halb zwei (4)

pastry shop die Konditorei (-en) (5)

path der Weg (-e) (9)

patio die Terrasse (-n) (2)

to pay zahlen (5); **to pay attention to** achten auf (+ *acc.*) (8)

pedestrian zone die Fußgängerzone (-n) (9)

pen: ballpoint pen der Kugelschreiber (-) (12)

pencil der Bleistift (-e) (12)

people die Leute (*pl.*) (2); (*indef. pron.*) man (4)

pepper der Pfeffer (5); **bell pepper** die Paprika (6)

per pro; **per person** pro Person (10); **per week** pro Woche (4)

perhaps vielleicht (1)

periodical die Zeitschrift (-en) (13)

to permit erlauben (9)

permitted: to be permitted to dürfen (darf), durfte, gedurft (4)

person der Mensch (-en *masc.*) (-en) (2); **per person** pro Person (10)

personnel das Personal (11)

pharmacy die Apotheke (-n) (5)

phone das Telefon (-e) (2); **cell phone** das Handy (-s) (2); **to talk on the phone** telefonieren (1)

photograph das Foto (-s) (2)

physician der Arzt (-e) / die Ärztin (-nen) (5)

to pick up (*from a place*) abholen (holt ab) (4)

Pilsner beer das Pilsener (-) (6)

place der Platz (-e) (6); **place of residence** der Wohnort (-e) (1); **(if I were) in your place** an deiner Stelle (12); **This place is taken.** Hier ist besetzt. (6)

to place (*in a standing position*) stellen (6); **to place inside** stecken (6)

plaid kariert (5)

plan der Plan (-e) (4)

to plan planen (3); **to plan** (*to do*) vorhaben (hat vor), hatte vor, vorgehabt (4); **to plan to** wollen (will), wollte, gewollt (4)

plastic bag die Plastiktüte (-n) (14)

plate der Teller (-) (6)

platform (*train*) der Bahnsteig (-e) (10)

play (*theater*) das Theaterstück (-e) (4)

to play spielen (1); **to play cards** Karten spielen (1); **to play chess** Schach spielen (7); **to play computer games** Computerspiele spielen (1); **to play soccer** Fußball spielen (7); **to play sports** Sport treiben, trieb, getrieben (7); **to play tennis** Tennis spielen (7)

player: CD player der CD-Spieler (-) (2); **DVD player** der DVD-Spieler ( ) (2)

playing card die Spielkarte (-n) (7)

pleasant angenehm (7)

please bitte (E); **Slower, please.** Langsamer, bitte. (E); **Would you please . . . ?** Würden Sie bitte … ? (9)

pleased: Pleased to meet you. Freut mich. (E)

pleasing: to be pleasing to gefallen (+ *dat.*) (gefällt), gefiel, gefallen (5)

Poland (das) Polen (E)

police, police station die Polizei (9)

politician der Politiker (-) / die Politikerin (-nen) (14)

politics die Politik (13)

pollution: environmental pollution die Umweltverschmutzung (14)

pool: swimming pool das Schwimmbad (-er) (7); **indoor swimming pool** das Hallenbad (-er) (7); **outdoor swimming pool** das Freibad (-er) (7)

poor(ly) schlecht (E)

popular beliebt (7)

pork das Schweinefleisch (5); **pork roast** der Schweinebraten (-) (6)

port der Hafen (-) (9)

position der Arbeitsplatz (-e) (11); die Stelle (-n) (11); die Tätigkeit (-en) (11)

to possess besitzen, besaß, besessen (11)

possibility die Möglichkeit (-en) (10)

possible, possibly möglich (14)

post office die Post (*pl.* Postämter) (9)

postage stamp die Briefmarke (-n) (7)

postal code die Postleitzahl (-en) (E)

poster das Poster (-) (2)

potato die Kartoffel (-n) (5); **fried potatoes** die Bratkartoffeln (*pl.*) (6)

poverty die Armut (14)

practical praktisch (1)

to prefer vorziehen (zieht vor), zog vor, vorgezogen (14)

to prepare (for) sich vorbereiten (auf + *acc.*) (bereitet vor) (11)

to prescribe verschreiben, verschrieb, verschrieben (8)

present das Geschenk (-e) (3)

prestige das Ansehen (11)

pretzel die Brezel (-n) (6)

price der Preis (-e) (9); **included in the price** im Preis enthalten (9)

primary school die Grundschule (-n) (11)

to print drucken (13)

printer der Drucker (-) (13)
prison das Gefängnis (-se) (14)
probably wahrscheinlich (11); wohl (11)
problem das Problem (-e) (2)
to produce herstellen (stellt her) (11)
producer der Hersteller (-) (11)
profession der Beruf (-e) (1)
professional life das Berufsleben (11)
professor der Professor (-en) / die Professorin (-nen) (1)
program das Programm (-e) (13); **TV or radio program** die Sendung (-en) (13)
progress der Fortschritt (-e) (14); **to make progress** Fortschritte machen (14)
to prohibit verbieten, verbot, verboten (14)
to promote fördern (14)
to propose vorschlagen (schlägt vor), schlug vor, vorgeschlagen (10)
to protect schützen (14); **environmental protection** der Umweltschutz (14)
psychologist der Psychologe (-n *masc.*) (-n) / die Psychologin (-nen) (11)
pub die Kneipe (-n) (6); das Lokal (-e) (6); das Wirtshaus (¨er) (6)
public öffentlich (14)
pullover sweater der Pullover (-) (5)
to purchase something sich (*dat.*) etwas anschaffen (schafft an) (14)
purple lila (5)
purse die Tasche (-n) (5)
to put (*in a lying position*) legen (6); (*in a sitting position*) setzen (6); (*inside*) stecken (6); (*in a standing position*) stellen (6)
puzzle: to do crossword puzzles Kreuzworträtsel machen (1)

Q

quarter das Viertel (-) (4); **It's a quarter after/to two.** Es ist Viertel nach/vor zwei. (4)
question die Frage (-n); **I have a question.** Ich habe eine Frage. (E)
quick(ly) schnell (10); **to read quickly** überfliegen, überflog, überflogen (13)
quiet ruhig (1)
quite ganz (1); recht (2); **quite inexpensive** recht preiswert (2)

R

racism der Rassismus (14)
radio das Radio (-s) (2); **radio program** die Sendung (-en) (13)
railway die Bahn (-en) (10)
rain der Regen (7)
to rain regnen (7); **It's raining.** Es regnet. (7)
rain shower der Regenschauer (-) (7)
rainy regnerisch (7)
to raise erziehen, erzog, erzogen (14)
rare(ly) selten (2)
rather recht (2); ziemlich (6); (*coord. conj.*) sondern (7); **would rather** möchte lieber (4)
to read lesen (liest), las, gelesen (1, 2); **to read quickly** überfliegen, überflog, überflogen (13)
really echt (*coll.*) (1); ganz (1); wirklich (1)

reasonable (*in price*) preiswert (2)
to receive empfangen (empfängt), empfing, empfangen (13)
receiver: satellite receiver die Sat-Empfangsanlage (-n) (13)
reception desk die Rezeption (9)
to recommend empfehlen (empfiehlt), empfahl, empfohlen (5)
recommendation (*from a former employer*) das Zeugnis (-se) (11)
to record (*e.g., on video*) aufnehmen (nimmt auf), nahm auf, aufgenommen (13)
recorder: video recorder der Videorecorder (-) (2)
to recover sich erholen (8)
recycling center die Sammelstelle (-n) (14)
red rot (5)
refrigerator der Kühlschrank (¨e) (9)
register: cash register die Kasse (-n) (5)
to register sich anmelden (meldet an) (9)
registration form das Anmeldeformular (-e) (9)
regular(ly) regelmäßig (8)
related to verwandt mit (3)
to relax sich entspannen (8)
to remain bleiben, blieb, ist geblieben (1)
rent die Miete (-n) (2)
to rent (*from someone*) mieten (12); **to rent out** (*to someone*) vermieten (12)
repair die Reparatur (-en) (12)
to repair reparieren (9)
report der Bericht (-e) (13); **report card** das Zeugnis (-se) (11); **weather report** der Wetterbericht (-e) (7)
to report berichten (13)
to request bitten um (+ *acc.*), bat, gebeten (12)
research die Forschung (-en) (14)
research: to do research forschen (13)
reservation: seat reservation card die Platzkarte (-n) (10)
to reserve reservieren (7)
to reside wohnen (1)
residence: place of residence der Wohnort (-e) (1)
responsible verantwortlich (11)
restaurant das Restaurant (-s) (6); das Lokal (-e) (6); **full-service restaurant** die Gaststätte (-n) (6)
résumé der Lebenslauf (¨e) (11)
to retrain umschulen (schult um) (14)
to return zurückkommen (kommt zurück), kam zurück, ist zurückgekommen (4)
rice der Reis (6)
ride die Fahrt (-en) (10)
to ride fahren (fährt), fuhr, ist gefahren (1); **to ride a bike** Fahrrad/Rad fahren (fährt Fahrrad/Rad) (1, 7); **to ride on horseback** reiten, ritt, ist geritten (7)
right rechts (9); **to the right** nach rechts (9)
right das Recht (-e); **human right** das Menschenrecht (-e) (14)
right-wing extremism der Rechtsextremismus (14)
rink: ice-skating rink das Eisstadion (Eisstadien) (7)

river der Fluss (¨e) (7)
road der Weg (-e) (9)
roast: pork roast der Schweinebraten (-) (6)
roll das Brötchen (-) (5)
romantic romantisch (1)
roof das Dach (¨er) (12)
room das Zimmer (-) (2); **breakfast room** der Frühstücksraum (¨e) (9); **dining room** das Esszimmer (-) (2); **guest room** das Gästezimmer (-) (12); **living room** das Wohnzimmer (-) (2); **room with one bed** das Einzelzimmer (-) (9); **room with two beds** das Doppelzimmer (-) (9)
roommate der Mitbewohner (-) / die Mitbewohnerin (-nen) (2)
round-trip hin und zurück (10)
rug der Teppich (-e) (2)
to run laufen (läuft), lief, ist gelaufen (2)

S

safe(ly) sicher (10)
to sail segeln (7)
salad der Salat (-e) (6)
salary das Gehalt (¨er) (11)
sales der Handel (11)
salesman der Kaufmann (*pl.* Kaufleute) (11)
salesperson der Verkäufer (-) / die Verkäuferin (-nen) (2)
saleswoman die Kauffrau (-en) (11)
salt das Salz (5)
satellite receiver die Sat-Empfangsanlage (-n) (13)
Saturday (der) Samstag (3); (der) Sonnabend (3); **Saturdays, on Saturday(s)** samstags (4); sonnabends (4)
sauerkraut das Sauerkraut (6)
sausage die Wurst (¨e) (5); **white sausage** die Weißwurst (¨e) (6)
to save (*conserve*) sparen (12); (*store*) speichern (13)
savings account das Sparkonto (Sparkonten) (12)
to say sagen (1); **How do you say . . . in German?** Wie sagt man ... auf Deutsch? (E); **that is to say** nämlich (3); **What did you say?** Wie bitte? (E)
scarcely kaum (8)
scarf der Schal (-s) (5)
schedule der Fahrplan (¨e) (10)
school die Schule (-n); **primary school** die Grundschule (-n) (11); **secondary school** das Gymnasium (Gymnasien) (11)
scientist: computer scientist der Informatiker (-) / die Informatikerin (-nen) (11)
sea das Meer (-e) (7)
season die Jahreszeit (-en) (7)
seat der Platz (¨e) (6); **Is this seat available?** Ist hier noch frei? (6); **seat reservation card** die Platzkarte (-n) (10)
second (*adj.*) zweite (3)
second die Sekunde (-n) (4)
secondary school das Gymnasium (Gymnasien) (11)

to see sehen (sieht), sah, gesehen (2)

to seem scheinen, schien, geschienen (13)

to select something sich (*dat.*) etwas aussuchen (sucht aus) (13)

selection das Angebot (-e) (10)

semester das Semester (-) (1)

to send schicken (1)

sensible gescheit (13)

to separate (sich) trennen (14)

separate(ly) getrennt (6)

September (der) September (3)

serious ernst (1)

server der Kellner (-) / die Kellnerin (-nen) (6)

service die Bedienung (6)

set (*TV, telephone, camera, etc.*) der Apparat (-e) (9)

to set setzen (6)

seven sieben (E)

seventeen siebzehn (E)

seventh sieb(en)te (3)

seventy siebzig (E)

shame: What a shame! So ein Pech! (8)

shape: in shape fit (8); **to keep in shape** sich fit halten (hält), hielt, gehalten (8)

shared housing die Wohngemeinschaft (-en) / die WG (-s) (2)

to shave sich rasieren (8)

shaving cream die Rasiercreme (-s) (5)

she sie (1)

shelf das Regal (-e) (2)

to shine scheinen, schien, geschienen; **The sun is shining.** Die Sonne scheint. (7)

ship das Schiff (-e) (10)

shirt das Hemd (-en) (5); **T-shirt** das T-Shirt (-s) (5)

shoe der Schuh (-e) (5); **tennis shoe** der Tennisschuh (-e) (5)

shop das Geschäft (-e) (5); **butcher shop** die Metzgerei (-en) (5); **pastry shop** die Konditorei (-en) (5)

to shop einkaufen (kauft ein) (4)

shopping: to go shopping einkaufen gehen (geht einkaufen), ging einkaufen, ist einkaufen gegangen (4)

short kurz (kürzer, kürzest-) (7)

should, to be supposed to sollen (soll), sollte, gesollt (4)

shoulder die Schulter (-n) (8)

to show zeigen (5)

shower die Dusche (-n) (9); **rain shower** der Regenschauer (-) (7)

to shower sich duschen (8)

siblings die Geschwister (*pl.*) (3)

sick krank (8); **sick as a dog** (*coll.*) hundsmiserabel (8); **I'm sick to my stomach.** Mir ist schlecht. (8)

side dish die Beilage (-n) (6)

simple einfach (10)

since seit (+ *dat.*) (5, 6)

single room das Einzelzimmer (-) (9)

sister die Schwester (-n) (3)

sister-in-law die Schwägerin (-nen) (3)

to sit sitzen, saß, gesessen (6); **to sit down** sich (hin)setzen (setzt hin) (8)

six sechs (E)

sixteen sechzehn (E)

sixth sechste (3)

sixty sechzig (E)

size die Größe (-n) (5)

to skate: to ice skate Schlittschuh laufen (läuft Schlittschuh), lief Schlittschuh, ist Schlittschuh gelaufen (7)

skill die Fähigkeit (-en) (11)

to skim (a text) überfliegen, überflog, überflogen (13)

skirt der Rock (¨e) (5)

sky der Himmel (7)

to sleep schlafen (schläft), schlief, geschlafen (2)

slipper der Hausschuh (-e) (5)

Slovakia die Slowakei (E)

Slovenia (das) Slowenien (E)

slow(ly) langsam (10); **Slower, please.** Langsamer, bitte. (E)

small klein (2)

to smoke rauchen (8)

snow der Schnee (7)

to snow schneien (7); **It's snowing.** Es schneit. (7)

so so (2); **So long.** Mach's gut. (*inform.*) (E); tschüss (*inform.*) (E); **So what?** Na und? (13)

soccer, soccer ball der Fußball (¨e) (7); **to play soccer** Fußball spielen (7)

sock die Socke (-n) (5); der Strumpf (¨e) (5)

sofa das Sofa (-s) (2)

solution die Lösung (-en) (14)

to solve lösen (14)

something etwas (2)

sometimes manchmal (8)

somewhat etwas (2); ziemlich (6)

son der Sohn (¨e) (3)

soon bald (12); **Get well soon!** Gute Besserung! (8)

sore throat die Halsschmerzen (*pl.*) (8)

sorry: I'm sorry. Das tut mir leid. (9)

so-so so lala (E)

to sound klingen, klang, geklungen (8); **You sound so depressed.** Du klingst so deprimiert. (8)

soup die Suppe (-n) (6)

space: parking space der Parkplatz (¨e) (9)

to speak sprechen (spricht), sprach, gesprochen (2)

special offer das Angebot (-e) (10)

to spend (*money*) ausgeben (gibt aus), gab aus, ausgegeben (12); (*time*) verbringen, verbrachte, verbracht (7)

spite: in spite of trotz (+ *gen.*) (9)

spoon der Löffel (-) (6)

sport, sports der Sport (*pl.* Sportarten) (7); **active in sports** sportlich aktiv (10); **to play sports** Sport treiben, trieb, getrieben (7); **sport coat** der/das Sakko (-s) (5); **sports arena** die Sporthalle (-n) (7)

to spread verbreiten (14)

spring (*season*) das Frühjahr (-e), der Frühling (-e) (7)

stadium das Stadion (Stadien) (7)

staircase die Treppe (-n) (12)

stamp: postage stamp die Briefmarke (-n) (7)

stand der Stand (¨e); **fast-food stand** der Imbiss (-e) (6); **fruit and vegetable stand** der Obst- und Gemüsestand (¨e) (5)

to stand stehen, stand, gestanden (6); **to stand up** (*get up*) aufstehen (steht auf), stand auf, ist aufgestanden (4); **to stand up** (*put in a standing position*) stellen (6)

to start beginnen, begann, begonnen (10)

station (*TV or radio*) das Programm (-e) (13); **police station** die Polizei (9); **train station** der Bahnhof (¨e) (9)

stay der Aufenthalt (-e) (9); **overnight stay** die Übernachtung (-en) (9)

to stay bleiben, blieb, ist geblieben (1); **to stay overnight** übernachten (9)

stereo die Stereoanlage (-n) (2)

still (*yet*) noch (2)

stock market die Börse (-n) (13)

stocking der Strumpf (¨e) (5)

stomach der Bauch (¨e) (8); **I'm sick to my stomach.** Mir ist schlecht. (8)

stop: bus stop die Haltestelle (-n) (9)

to stop (*doing something*) aufhören (mit + *dat.*) (hört auf) (4)

store das Geschäft (-e) (5); der Laden (¨) (5); **beverage store** der Getränkeladen (¨) (5); **department store** das Kaufhaus (¨er) (2); **natural foods store** der Bioladen (¨) (5); **toiletries and sundries store** die Drogerie (-n) (5)

to store speichern (13)

story (*level*) der Stock (*pl.* Stockwerke) (9); die Etage (-n) (12)

straight ahead geradeaus (9)

to straighten up aufräumen (räumt auf) (4)

strawberry die Erdbeere (-n) (E); **street address** die Hausnummer (-n) (E)

street die Straße (-n) (E); **street address** die Hausnummer (-n) (E)

strength die Stärke (-n) (11)

strenuous anstrengend (8)

stress der Stress (8)

stressful stressig (1)

to stretch sich strecken (8)

strict(ly) streng (14)

striped gestreift (5)

strong stark (stärker, stärkst-) (7)

strudel: apple strudel der Apfelstrudel (-) (6)

student der Student (-en *masc.*) (-en) / die Studentin (-nen) (1); **student cafeteria** die Mensa (-s) (1)

study (*room*) das Arbeitszimmer (-) (2)

to study (*at university*) studieren (1); (*for an exam*) lernen (1)

stupid blöd (13); **I think that's really stupid.** Das ist mir zu blöd. (13)

to subscribe abonnieren (13)

subscription das Abo(nnement) (-s) (13)

success der Erfolg (-e) (11)

successful(ly) erfolgreich (11); **to be successful** Erfolg haben (11)

sugar der Zucker (5)

to suggest vorschlagen (schlägt vor), schlug vor, vorgeschlagen (10)

suit der Anzug (¨e) (5); **bathing suit** der Badeanzug (¨e) (5)

suitcase der Koffer (-) (5)

summer der Sommer (-) (7)

sun die Sonne (7); **The sun is shining.** Die Sonne scheint. (7)

Sunday (der) Sonntag (3); **Sundays, on Sunday(s)** sonntags (4)

sunny sonnig (7)

sunscreen das Sonnenschutzmittel (10)

sunshine der Sonnenschein (7)

suntan lotion das Sonnenschutzmittel (10)

super prima (E); **super!** (*coll.*) (ganz) toll! (1)

supermarket der Supermarkt (¨e) (5)

support die Unterstützung (11)

to support unterstützen, unterstützt (12)

supposed: to be supposed to sollen (soll), sollte, gesollt (4)

to surf surfen (1)

surname der Nachname (*gen.* -ns, *acc./dat.* -n) (-n) (1)

suspenseful spannend (4)

to swallow schlucken (8)

sweater: pullover sweater der Pullover (-) (5)

to swim schwimmen, schwamm, ist geschwommen (2)

swimming pool das Schwimmbad (¨er) (7); **indoor swimming pool** das Hallenbad (¨er) (7); **outdoor swimming pool** das Freibad (¨er) (7)

Switzerland die Schweiz (E)

T

table der Tisch (-e) (2)

table: coffee table der Couchtisch (-e) (2)

to take nehmen (nimmt), nahm, genommen (2); **to take** (*time*) dauern (7); **to take a vote** abstimmen (stimmt ab) (14); **to take along** mitnehmen (nimmt mit), nahm mit, mitgenommen (4); **Take care.** Mach's gut. (*inform.*) (E); **to take over** übernehmen (übernimmt), übernahm, übernommen (11); **take-out** zum Mitnehmen (6)

taken besetzt (6); **This place is taken.** Hier ist besetzt. (6)

to talk on the phone telefonieren (1)

tall groß (1)

tap: on tap vom Fass (6)

to taste (good) schmecken (+ *dat.*) (5)

tax die Steuer (-n) (14)

taxicab das Taxi (-s) (10)

tea der Tee (5); **herbal tea** der Kräutertee (8)

teacher der Lehrer (-) / die Lehrerin (-nen) (E)

technique die Technik (-en) (11)

technology die Technik (-en) (11)

telephone das Telefon (-e) (2); **telephone number** die Telefonnummer (-n) (E); **to talk on the telephone** telefonieren (1)

television (set) der Fernseher (-) (2); **to watch television** fernsehen (sieht fern), sah fern, ferngesehen (4); **watching television** das Fernsehen (4)

to tell sagen (1); **tell me** sag mal (1)

temperature die Temperatur (-en) (7)

ten zehn (E)

tender zart (5)

tennis das Tennis; **tennis court** der Tennisplatz (¨e) (7); **tennis shoe** der Tennisschuh (-e) (5); **to play tennis** Tennis spielen (7)

tent das Zelt (-e) (10)

tenth zehnte (3)

terrace die Terrasse (-n) (2)

terrorism der Terrorismus (14)

than als (7)

to thank danken (+ *dat.*) (5); **thank you very much** danke schön (E)

thanks danke (E); **thanks a lot** danke sehr (1); **fine, thanks** danke, gut (E); **Many thanks!** Vielen Dank! (6); **No thanks necessary.** Nichts zu danken. (8)

that das; (*subord. conj.*) dass (8); **that comes to** das macht zusammen (5); **That doesn't matter.** Das macht nichts. (8); **that is** d.h. (= das heißt) (8); **that is to say** nämlich (3); **That's fun.** Das macht Spaß. (1)

the der, die, das

theater das Theater (-) (4); **to go to the theater** ins Theater gehen (4); **movie theater** das Kino (-s) (4)

their ihr (3)

them sie (*acc.*) (3); **(to/for) them** ihnen (*dat.*) (5)

then: now and then ab und zu (8)

there da (2); **there is/are** es gibt (3); **over there** da drüben (6); **What's the best way to get there?** Wie komme ich am besten dahin? (9)

therefore deshalb (8)

they sie (1); (*indef. pron.*) man (4)

thing das Ding (-e) (10)

to think (about/of) denken (an + *acc.*), dachte, gedacht (12); **to think (about)** nachdenken (über + *acc.*) (denkt nach), dachte nach, nachgedacht (11); **to think** (*be of the opinion*) meinen (14); **to think** (*consider*) halten (für + *acc.*) (hält), hielt, gehalten (14); **to think over** sich überlegen, überlegt (10); **I think that's really stupid.** Das ist mir zu blöd. (13); **What do you think of . . . ?** Wie findest du ... ? (1)

third dritte (3)

thirsty: to be thirsty Durst haben (hat Durst) (2)

thirteen dreizehn (E)

thirteenth dreizehnte (3)

thirty dreißig (E)

this dieser, diese, dies(es) (2); **this afternoon** heute Nachmittag (4); **this evening** heute Abend (1); **This is . . .** Das ist ... (E); **this morning** heute Morgen (4)

thousand (ein)tausend (E)

three drei (E); **three times** dreimal (7)

threesome: as a threesome zu dritt (10)

thrifty sparsam (12)

throat der Hals (¨e) (8); **sore throat** die Halsschmerzen (*pl.*) (8)

through durch (+ *acc.*) (3)

to thunder donnern (7); **It's thundering.** Es donnert. (7)

thunderstorm das Gewitter (-) (7)

Thursday (der) Donnerstag (3); **Thursdays, on Thursday(s)** donnerstags (4)

ticket (*bus or train*) die Fahrkarte (-n) (10); **ticket window** der Fahrkartenschalter (-) (10)

time die Zeit (-en) (2); **At what time?** Um wie viel Uhr? (4); **to have time** Zeit haben (hat Zeit) (2); **to spend time** Zeit verbringen, verbrachte, verbracht (7); **three times** dreimal (7); **time of day** die Tageszeit (-en) (4); **What time is it?** Wie spät ist es? / Wie viel Uhr ist es? (4)

tin can die Dose (-n) (14)

tired müde (8)

tiring anstrengend (8)

to nach (+ *dat.*) (5); zu (+ *dat.*) (5); (*a place*) in (+ *acc.*) (6); **five to two** fünf vor zwei (4); **It's a quarter to two.** Es ist Viertel vor zwei. (4); **to (as far as)** bis zum/zur (9); **(to) home** nach Hause (5); **to the left/right** nach links/rechts (9); **to where** wohin (5)

today heute (1); **What is today's date?** Welches Datum ist heute? (3)

toe die Zehe (-n) (8)

together zusammen; **all together, that comes to** das macht zusammen (5)

toilet das WC (-s) (9); **toilet paper** das Toilettenpapier (5)

toiletries and sundries store die Drogerie (-n) (5)

tomato die Tomate (-n) (5)

tomorrow morgen (3); **tomorrow evening** morgen Abend (4); **tomorrow morning** morgen früh (4); **What is tomorrow's date?** Welches Datum ist morgen? (3)

too (*also*) auch; **me too** ich auch (1)

tooth der Zahn (¨e); **to brush one's teeth** sich die Zähne putzen (8)

toothpaste die Zahnpasta (Zahnpasten) (5)

top: on top of auf (+ *acc./dat.*) (6); **top floor** das Dachgeschoss (-e) (12)

topical aktuell (13)

total insgesamt (10); **total(ly)** ganz (12)

tourist der Tourist (-en *masc.*) (-en) / die Touristin (-nen) (9)

town die Stadt (¨e) (E); **center of town** das Zentrum (Zentren) (9)

track das Gleis (-e) (10)

trade der Handel (11)

tradition die Tradition (-en) (3)

traffic light die Ampel (-n) (9)

tragedy die Tragödie (-n) (4)

train der Zug (¨e) (10); (*railway*) die Bahn (-en) (10); **train platform** der Bahnsteig (-e) (10); **train station** der Bahnhof (¨e) (9)

training die Ausbildung (11); **to do weight training** Bodybuilding machen (7)

transcript das Zeugnis (-se) (11)

to transfer (*trains*) umsteigen (steigt um), stieg um, ist umgestiegen (10)

to translate übersetzen, übersetzt (11)

transportation: means of transportation das Verkehrsmittel (-) (14)

trash der Müll (12); der Abfall (¨e) (14)

travel: travel agency das Reisebüro (-s) (10); **travel brochure** der Reiseprospekt (-e) (10); **travel guide (book)** der Reiseführer (-) (10)

to travel reisen, ist gereist (1); **to travel first/second class** erster/zweiter Klasse fahren (fährt), fuhr, ist gefahren (10)

traveler's check der Reisescheck (-s) (10)

tree der Baum (¨e); **Christmas tree** der Weihnachtsbaum (¨e) (3); **family tree** der Stammbaum (¨e) (3)

trip die Fahrt (-en) (10); die Reise (-n) (10); **to go on a trip** verreisen, ist verreist (10)

trousers die Hose (-n) (5)

to try versuchen (8); **to try on** anprobieren (probiert an) (5)

T-shirt das T-Shirt (-s) (5)

Tuesday (der) Dienstag (3); **Tuesdays, on Tuesday(s)** dienstags (4)

tuition die Studiengebühren (pl.) (12)

turkey der Truthahn (¨e) (5)

to turn einbiegen (biegt ein), bog ein, ist eingebogen (9)

TV das Fernsehen; **cable TV connection** der Kabelanschluss (¨e) (13); **TV channel** das Programm (-e) (13); **TV program** die Sendung (-en) (13); **TV set** der Fernseher (-) (2)

twelfth zwölfte (3)

twelve zwölf (E)

twentieth zwanzigste (3)

twenty zwanzig (E)

twice zweimal (7)

two zwei (E)

twosome: as a twosome zu zweit (10)

U

ugly hässlich (2)

umbrella der Regenschirm (-e) (7)

uncle der Onkel (-) (3)

under unter (+ acc./dat.) (6); **Under what name?** Auf welchen Namen? (9)

to understand verstehen, verstand, verstanden; **I don't understand.** Ich verstehe das nicht. (E)

to undertake unternehmen (unternimmt), unternahm, unternommen (1)

undressed: to get undressed sich ausziehen (zieht aus), zog aus, ausgezogen (8)

unemployment die Arbeitslosigkeit (14)

unfortunately leider (3)

unfriendly unfreundlich (1)

unfurnished unmöbliert (2)

university die Universität (-en) (1); **university instructor** der Hochschullehrer (-) / die Hochschullehrerin (-nen) (1); **university lecture** die Vorlesung (-en) (4)

unlikable unsympathisch (1)

until bis (um) (+ acc.) (6); **until five o'clock** bis (um) fünf Uhr (6)

upstairs oben; (directional) nach oben (12)

urgent(ly) dringend (2)

us uns (acc.) (3); **(to/for) us** uns (dat.) (5)

to use verwenden (14)

used to (do, be, etc.) früher (7)

useful nützlich (12)

usual(ly) gewöhnlich (4)

utilities die Nebenkosten (pl.) (12)

V

vacation: to go on vacation Urlaub machen (8)

vacuum cleaner der Staubsauger (-) (12)

Valentine's Day der Valentinstag (3)

varied abwechslungsreich (11)

VCR der Videorecorder (-) (2)

vegetable das Gemüse (5); **fruit and vegetable stand** der Obst- und Gemüsestand (¨e) (5)

vegetarian vegetarisch (6)

vehicle das Verkehrsmittel (-) (14)

very ganz (1); sehr (1); **thank you very much** danke schön (E); **very well** sehr gut (E)

vicinity die Nähe (9); die Umgebung (-en) (12)

video(tape) das Video (-s) (2); **video recorder** der Videorecorder (-) (2)

violation die Verletzung (-en) (14)

violence die Gewalttätigkeit (14)

to visit besuchen (1)

vote: to take a vote abstimmen (stimmt ab) (14)

to vote wählen (14)

W

to wait warten (6)

waiter der Kellner (-) (6); der Ober (-) (6)

waitress die Kellnerin (-nen) (6)

to wake up aufwachen (wacht auf) (4)

to walk zu Fuß gehen, ging, ist gegangen (8); **to go for a walk** spazieren gehen (geht spazieren), ging spazieren, ist spazieren gegangen (4); **to walk along** entlanggehen (geht entlang), ging entlang, ist entlanggegangen (9)

wall die Wand (¨e) (2)

wall-to-wall carpeting der Teppichboden (¨) (12)

to want to wollen (will), wollte, gewollt (4)

war der Krieg (-e) (14)

wardrobe die Garderobe (-n) (12)

warm warm (wärmer, wärmst-) (7)

warming die Erwärmung (14)

to wash (oneself) sich waschen (wäscht), wusch, gewaschen (8)

washing machine die Waschmaschine (-n) (12)

waste der Abfall (¨e) (14)

to watch something sich (dat.) etwas anschauen (schaut an) (13); sich (dat.) etwas ansehen (sieht an), sah an, angesehen; **to watch television** fernsehen (sieht fern), sah fern, ferngesehen (4); **watching television** das Fernsehen (4)

water das Wasser (5); **mineral water** der Sprudel (6)

way der Weg (-e) (9); **by the way** übrigens (9); **What's the best way to get there?** Wie komme ich am besten dahin? (9)

we wir (1)

weak schlapp (8)

to wear tragen (trägt), trug, getragen (5)

weather das Wetter (7); **weather report** der Wetterbericht (-e) (7)

website die Website (-s) (11)

wedding die Hochzeit (-en) (3)

Wednesday (der) Mittwoch (3); **Wednesdays, on Wednesday(s)** mittwochs (4)

week die Woche (-n) (4); **day of the week** der Wochentag (-e) (3); **once a week** einmal die Woche (7); **per week** pro Woche (4)

weekend das Wochenende (-n) (4)

weight training: to do weight training Bodybuilding machen (7)

welcome herzlich willkommen (E); **you're welcome** bitte (E)

well gut (1); (healthy) gesund (8); **Are you doing well?** Geht's gut? (E); **to feel well** sich wohl fühlen (8); **to get well** sich erholen (8) **Get well soon!** Gute Besserung! (8); **He dances well.** Er tanzt gut. (1); **not particularly well** nicht besonders gut (E); **very well** sehr gut (E)

were: if I were you an deiner Stelle (12)

what was (1); **At what time?** Um wie viel Uhr? (4); **So what?** Na und? (13); **Under what name?** Auf welchen Namen? (9); **What a shame! What bad luck!** So ein Pech! (8); **What did you say?** Wie bitte? (E); **What do you do for a living?** Was sind Sie von Beruf? (1); **What do you think of . . . ?** Wie findest du . . . ? (1); **What does . . . mean?** Was bedeutet . . . ? (E); **What is . . . ?** Wie ist . . . ? (E); **What is the name of . . . ?** Wie heißt . . . ? (E); **What is today's/tomorrow's date?** Welches Datum ist heute/morgen? (3); **what kind of (a)** was für (ein) (11); **What's it about?** Wovon handelt es? (13); **What's the best way to get there?** Wie komme ich am besten dahin? (9); **What's the matter?** Was ist denn los? (2); Was fehlt Ihnen/dir? (8); **What's your name?** Wie heißen Sie? (form.) / Wie heißt du? (inform.) (E); Wie ist Ihr Name? (form.) / Wie ist dein Name? (E); **What time is it?** Wie spät ist es? / Wie viel Uhr ist es? (4); **What will you have?** Was bekommen Sie? (6)

when (adv.) wann (1); (subord. conj.) wenn (8); (subord. conj.) als (10); **When is your birthday?** Wann hast du Geburtstag? (3)

where wo (1); **(to) where** wohin (5); **from where** woher (1); **Where are you from?** Woher kommen Sie? (form.) / Woher kommst du? (inform.) (E)

whether (subord. conj.) ob (8)

which welcher, welche, welches (2)

while (subord. conj.) während (9)

whipped cream die Sahne (6)

white weiß (5); **white sausage** die Weißwurst (¨e) (6)

who wer (1)

whom wen (*acc.*); **(to/for) whom** wem (*dat.*) (5)

why warum (2)

wife die Frau (-en) (3)

wind der Wind (-e) (7); **wind power generator** das Windrad (¨er) (14)

window das Fenster (-) (2); **ticket window** der Fahrkartenschalter (-) (10)

windy windig (7)

wine der Wein (-e) (6)

winter der Winter (-) (7)

wish: best wishes viele Grüße (12)

to wish wünschen (3)

with mit (+ *dat.*) (5); bei (+ *dat.*) (5)

within innerhalb (+ *gen.*) (9)

without ohne (+ *acc.*) (3); **to do without** verzichten auf (+ *acc.*) (12)

woman die Frau (-en) (E)

work die Arbeit (-en) (8)

to work arbeiten (1); (*at a temporary job*) jobben (12); (*function*) funktionieren (9)

workplace der Arbeitsplatz (¨e) (11)

workroom das Arbeitszimmer (-) (2)

world die Welt (14)

worn out schlapp (8)

to worry about sich Sorgen machen um (+ *acc.*) (14)

would: would like to möchte (4); **would like to (do) most** möchte am liebsten (4); **would rather** möchte lieber (4); **Would you please . . . ?** Würden Sie bitte … ? (9)

wrapping die Verpackung (-en) (14)

to write schreiben, schrieb, geschrieben (2); **How do you write . . . ?** Wie schreibt man … ? (E)

X

xenophobia die Ausländerfeindlichkeit (14)

Y

yard der Garten (¨) (2)

year das Jahr (-e) (1); **for two years** seit zwei Jahren (6); **next year** nächstes Jahr (1); **once a year** einmal im Jahr (7)

yellow gelb (5)

yes ja (E)

yesterday gestern (7)

yet noch (2)

yogurt der Joghurt (5)

you du (*inform. sg.*), ihr (*inform. pl.*), Sie (*form. sg./pl.*) (1); dich (*inform. sg. acc.*), euch (*inform. pl. acc.*), Sie (*form. sg./pl. acc.*) (3); dir (*inform. sg. dat.*), euch (*inform. pl. dat.*), Ihnen (*form. sg./pl. dat.*) (5); (*indef. pron.*) man (4); **You may not park here.** Hier darf man nicht parken. (4); **you're welcome** bitte (E)

young jung (jünger, jüngst-) (10)

your dein (*inform. sg.*), euer (*inform. pl.*), Ihr (*form. sg./pl.*) (3)

youth hostel die Jugendherberge (-n) (9)

Z

zero null (E)

zone: pedestrian zone die Fußgängerzone (-n) (9)

zoo der Tierpark (-s) (9)

Index

The index is followed by a list of major topics. **Kulturtipp** categories are listed under the heading **Culture;** vocabulary items are grouped by category under **Vocabulary;** reading titles are listed under **Readings;** and Video subjects are listed under **Videoclips.** References to reading strategies are listed in the index under *reading strategies.*

Note: KT = **Kulturtipp;** ST = **Sprachtipp.**

A

aber vs. **sondern,** 216
academic subjects, 29
accusative case
  of definite articles, 57 *ST,* 65 (*chart*)
  of demonstrative pronouns, 74
  of der-words, 67 (*chart*)
  direct object in, 67
  es gibt with, 148 *ST*
  of indefinite articles, 68 (*chart*)
  of interrogative pronouns, 69
  of negative article **kein,** 68 (*chart*)
  of nouns, 64–65
  of personal pronouns, 98 (*chart*)
  of possessive adjectives, 100–101,
    186–187
  prepositions requiring, 97, 186–187, 194
  of reflexive pronouns, 249–250
  of relative pronouns, 336
  of weak masculine nouns, 65
  word order of, 64, 161
active voice, 417
address, forms of, 5–6
  du vs. **Sie,** 3 *KT*
  Herr, Frau, 3
addresses, 10–11
adjectival nouns, 306–307 (*chart*)
adjective endings, 55 *ST,* 274, 306–307.
  See also attributive adjectives
adjectives
  ending in **–a,** 280 *ST*
  attributive, 274, 275 *ST,* 303–304, 305
  comparative form, 225–226, 303–306
  after definite article, 275 (*chart*)
  demonstrative, 165
  after indefinite article, 278 (*chart*)
  possessive, 93–94 (*charts*), 271
  possessive, with dative case, 157
  without preceding article, 279 (*chart*)
  present participles used as, 424–425
  referring to city names, 282
  superlative form, 305
  three forms of, 225
  used as nouns, 306–307
adverbs
  comparative form, 225–226
  dahin, 362
  gern, 59 *ST,* 226
  immer, with comparative, 226
  nämlich, 92 *ST*
  nicht, 341

present participles used as,
  424–425
  superlative form, 301–302
  of time, 119 *ST*
agent
  in passive sentences, 419
  passive without (using **es**), 421
alle, 165
alphabet, German, 4–5
als
  with comparative form, 226
  as subordinating conjunction, 311
alternatives to passive
  with impersonal **es,** 421
  with **man,** 424
an-, 223
antecedent
  personal pronouns agreeing with, 34
  relative pronouns referring to, 336
arbeiten vs. **lernen/studieren,** 27 *ST*
articles. *See* definite articles;
  indefinite articles; **kein**
attributive adjectives
  city names used as, 282
  comparative form, 303–304
  endings of, 55 *ST,* 274
  present participles used as, 424–425
  superlative form, 305
aus, 164
auxiliary verbs, 217, 221, A16 (*chart*). *See also* **haben;** modal auxiliary verbs;
  sein; werden

B

be-, 223
bei, 146 *ST,* 164
besser, 226
Beuys, Joseph, 204
bitte, used with imperative, 134
brauchen, with dependent infinitive plus
  zu, 395
Brecht, Bertolt, 231
Bremer, Claus, 205

C

capitalization, A20
  of adjectival nouns, 306
  of adjectives referring to cities and
    regions, 282
  of nouns, 32
  of pronouns, 34
  of **Sie,** 3, 34

cardinal numbers, 91 *ST*
case. *See* accusative case; dative case;
  genitive case; nominative case
Celsius scale, 215
city names, attributive adjectives
  referring to, 282
clauses
  dependent clauses, 244
  infinitive clauses, 395
  main clauses, 244
  relative clauses, 335–336
clock, 114, 115 *ST,* 116 *ST,* 118, 119 *ST*
cognates, 14
commands. *See* imperative
comparative form, 225–226. *See also*
  superlative form
compound nouns, 33
compounds
  da-, 362
  noun, 33
  wo-, 166, 364
conjugation, verb, A16–A19 (*chart*)
conjunctions
  coordinating, 216
  subordinating, 244 (*chart*)
contractions of prepositions and
  articles, 165
contrary-to-fact conditions, 370. *See also*
  subjunctive mood
conversational phrases, standard, 13, 14,
  26, 27 *ST*
coordinating conjunctions, 216
counting, 8–9
country abbreviations, 11

D

da-compounds, 362
daher, 362
dahin, 362
dann, 154 *ST*
dates, 88 *ST*
dative case, 157–166
  adjectives with, 151 *ST*
  contractions of prepositions in, 165
  of definite and indefinite articles,
    160 (*chart*), A13 (*chart*)
  of **der-**words, 160 (*chart*)
  and indirect objects, 160–161
  of nouns, 157–158
  of personal pronouns, 158 (*chart*)
  of possessive adjectives, 160 (*chart*)

dative case (*Cont.*)
  prepositions requiring, 164–165,
    186–187
  of reflexive pronouns, 250
  of relative pronouns, 336
  verbs requiring, 161–163
  word order, 161
  with **zu,** 151 *ST*
days of week, 108, 141
definite articles, A13 (*chart*). *See also*
    der-words
  accusative case of, 55 *ST*, 57, 65 (*chart*),
    A13 (*chart*)
  dative case of, 160 (*chart*), A13 (*chart*)
  genitive case of, 271 (*chart*), A13 (*chart*)
  nominative case of, 32 (*chart*),
    65 (*chart*), A13 (*chart*)
  plural form, 62
demonstrative adjectives. *See* **dieser**
demonstrative pronouns, 74
denn
  as coordinating conjunction, 216
  as particle in questions, 26 *ST*
dependent clause, 244. *See also*
    main clause; subordinating
    conjunctions
  indirect questions as, 245
  relative clauses as, 335
  word order in, 244
der-words
  accusative case of, 67 (*chart*)
  with attributive adjectives, 275 (*chart*)
  dative case of, 160 (*chart*), A13
  genitive case of, 275 (*chart*)
  nominative case of, 67 (*chart*)
descriptions, personal, 21–23
deshalb, 154 *ST*
dieser, 67
direct discourse, 397
direct object, 57 *ST*, 67
  and **ein,** 53 *ST*
  reflexive pronouns as, 248–249
  word order of, 64, 155, 156
direction (**wohin**) vs. location
    (**wo**), 187
doch, as particle, 134
Döhl, Reinhard, 205
Dokoupil, Georg Jiri, 205
du vs. **Sie,** 3 *KT,* 34
durch, as agent in passive voice, 419
dürfen, 129 (*chart*). *See also* modal
    auxiliary verbs
dürfte, in polite requests, 365

E

ein-words, 53 *ST. See also* indefinite
    articles
  accusative case of, 68 (*chart*)
  dative case of, 278 (*chart*)
  in genitive case, 278 (*chart*)
  nominative case of, 68 (*chart*)
Einstein, Albert, 111
emp-, 223
ent-, 223
er-, 223
es, in impersonal passive
    constructions, 421
es gibt, 148 *ST*

F

fahren, present tense of, 73 (*chart*)
Fahrenheit scale, 215
family, 83, 85 ST, 86 ST
finden, present tense of, 36
formal imperative, 133
future tense, 333 (*chart*), A17 (*chart*)

G

ge-, 223
gefallen (gefällt mir), 151 *ST*, 162
gender
  agreement of pronouns and nouns
    in, 34
  of nouns, 32–33
  and plural nouns, 62–63 (*chart*)
gender-inclusive language, 63 *ST*
genitive case, 271–272 (*chart*), 273
  adjective endings with nouns in,
    271 (*chart*)
  prepositions requiring, 273
  proper names in, 271–272
  of relative pronouns, A13 (*chart*)
  von, replacing, 85 *ST*
German-speaking population, 16, 47
gern, 59 *ST,* 226, 302
gibt: es gibt, 148 *ST*
Glasmeier, Rolf, 204
greetings, 2, 3, 5, 6, 7, 8
Grundform, 225

H

haben
  as auxiliary, 221, 400
  present tense of, 70 (*chart*)
  simple past of, 194 (*chart*)
  subjunctive I of, 398, 400
  subjunctive II of, 365, 372
hängen, 189, 191
hätte, in polite requests, 365, 372
Heck, Barbara, 381
heißen, present tense of, 36
hoch
  comparative form, 296
  superlative form, 302
holidays, 89–90, 91 *ST*
hypothetical situations.
    See subjunctive mood

I

-ieren, verbs ending in, 218
ihr, and **du/Sie,** 34 (*chart*)
immer, comparative form, 226
imperative, 133–134, A19 (*chart*)
  formal imperative, 134
  informal imperative, 135
  particles used with imperative, 134
  of **sein,** 134
Imperfekt, 194, 217
impersonal **es,** 421
indefinite articles, A13 (*chart*). *See also*
    ein-words
  accusative case of, 68 (*chart*)
  dative case of, 160 (*chart*)
  genitive case of, 267 (*chart*)
  nominative case of, 66 (*chart*)
indefinite pronouns. *See* **es, man**
independent clause, 244. *See also*
    dependent clause

indirect discourse, 397–398, 401
  past tense, 401
  subjunctive I in, 398 (*chart*), 401
indirect object, 160–161. *See also*
    dative case
  reflexive pronouns as, 248–251 (*charts*)
  word order of, 161
indirect questions, 245
infinitive, A15 (*chart*)
  form, 36
  as noun, 38 *ST*
  in passive constructions, 417–419,
    421, 423
  with **würde,** 367
  with **zu,** 393
infinitive clauses, 395
informal imperative, 135
inseparable-prefix verbs, 223
  past participles of, 223–224
  simple past of, 309
interrogative words. *See also*
    wo-compounds
  accusative case of, 69
  dative case of, 157, 187
  genitive case of (**wessen**), 271
  in indirect questions, 245
  in information questions, 41
  nominative case of, 69
  as pronouns, 69, 166, 339–340
  was für (ein), 339
  in yes/no questions, 41
introductions, 21–22

J

ja, in affirmative answer to
    questions, 42

K

kein, A13 (*chart*). *See also* **ein**-words;
    negation
  with **... mehr,** 341
  vs. **nicht,** 71 (*chart*)
kennen vs. **wissen,** 103
kommen, present tense of, 36
können. *See* modal auxiliary verbs
könnte, in polite requests, 365

L

lassen, 178 *ST*
legen, 191
lernen vs. **studieren,** 27 *ST*
lieber, 226, 302
liegen, 189
liking to, ways of expressing, 32 *ST,*
    59 *ST. See also* modal auxiliary
    verbs (**mögen, möchte**)
location (**wo**) vs. direction (**wohin**), 187
  placement, 191, 191 *ST*

M

main clauses, 244. *See also*
    coordinating conjunctions;
    dependent clauses
  word order in, 40
mal
  as particle in imperative forms, 134
man, 131 *ST,* 424
metric system, 153 *ST*
mit, 158, 164

mixed verbs, 223, 311
  principal parts of, A14–A15 (*chart*)
  simple past tense, A17 (*chart*)
möchte, 129 (*chart*), 130 (*chart*),
  364, 365
modal auxiliary verbs, 128–130
  (*charts*), 422
  passive infinitive and, 422–423
  simple past of, 196 (*chart*)
  subjunctive forms of, 365, 398
Modersohn-Becker, Paula, 110
mögen, 130 (*chart*). *See also* modal
  auxiliary verbs
months, names of, 108
mood. *See* imperative; subjunctive mood
motion, verbs of, 221
Mozart, Wolfgang Amadeus, 110
mussen, 129 (*chart*). *See also* modal
  auxiliary verbs

N

nach, 164
nämlich, 92 *ST*
negation, 341
  with **kein** vs. **nicht,** 71
  position of **nicht** in, 341
negative article. *See* **kein**
nehmen, 73 (*chart*)
nein, 42
nicht, 341
  vs. **kein,** 71
  with **... mehr,** 341
  with **noch...,** 341
  position of, 341
  so... wie, 227
noch kein, 341
noch nicht, 341
nominative case, 64–65
  of definite articles, 32 (*chart*),
    271 (*chart*), A13 (*chart*)
  of demonstrative pronouns, 74, A13
  of indefinite articles, 66
  of possessive adjectives, 93–94 (*chart*)
  subjects of sentences in, 64
  word order of, 64
nouns, 32–33
  accusative case of, 64–65
  adjectival, 306–307
  capitalization of, 32, 34, 306, A20
  dative case of, 158
  gender of, 32–33
  genitive case of, 271–272, 273
  infinitive used as, 38 *ST*
  plural forms of, 62–63 (*chart*)
  weak masculine, 65
numbers
  cardinal, 8–9
  dates, 88
  ordinal, 91 *ST*
  telephone, 10
nur, as particle in wishes, 366

O

ob, 244
objects. *See* accusative case; **da-**
  compounds; dative case; direct
  object; indirect object
official time, 115 *ST*

ohne... zu, plus infinitive, 395–396
ordinal numbers, 91 *ST*

P

participles. *See* past participles;
  present participles
particles. 134. *See also* **bitte; denn;**
  doch; mal
Partizip Perfekt, 217
parts of body, as object of reflexive verbs,
  250–251
passive voice, 417–419, 421, 424
  and **man,** 424
  and modals, 422
past events, 194. *See also* past perfect
  tense; past subjunctive; present
  perfect tense; simple past tense
past participles, A14–A16. *See also*
  passive voice; past perfect tense; past
  subjunctive; present perfect tense
  of inseparable prefix verbs, 223–224
  of mixed verbs, 223
  of separable-prefix verbs, 223
  of strong verbs, 220
  of weak verbs, 218 (*chart*)
past perfect tense, 313, A17 (*chart*)
  passive voice in, 418
past subjunctive I, 400
past subjunctive II, 372
Perfekt, 194, 217
personal descriptions, 21–23
personal pronouns, 34
  accusative case of, 98 (*chart*), A13 (*chart*)
  capitalization of, A13 (*chart*)
  dative case of, 158 (*chart*), A13 (*chart*)
  nominative case of, 34 (*chart*),
    A13 (*chart*)
placement, 191, 191 *ST*
plural forms of nouns, 62–63 (*chart*)
polite requests. *See* subjunctive mood
possession. *See* genitive case
Postleitzahl, 12
preferences. *See* subjunctive mood
prefixes. *See* inseparable-prefix verbs;
  separable-prefix verbs
prepositions
  contractions of articles with, 165
  in **da-**compounds, 362
  expressing time with, 193–194
  fixed, with verbs, 361
  in passive constructions
    (**von/durch**), 419
  requiring accusative case,
    100–101
  requiring dative case, 164–165
  requiring genitive case, 273
  two-way, 186–187
  in **wo-**compounds, 364
present participles, 424–425
present perfect tense, A17 (*chart*)
  formation of, 217–218
  passive voice in, 417
present subjunctive, 397–398
present tense, 36–37, 40,
  A16 (*chart*)
  of auxiliary verbs, A16 (*chart*)
  of **haben,** 70 (*chart*)
  of **heißen,** 36 (*chart*)

  of **kommen,** 36 (*chart*)
  of modal auxiliary verbs,
    129–130 (*charts*)
  of passive constructions, 417
  of **sein,** 40 (*chart*)
  of separable-prefix verbs, 124–125
  of stem-vowel changing verbs,
    73 (*chart*)
  use of vs. English, 36
  verb endings in, 36 (*chart*), 37
  of **werden,** 102 (*chart*)
  of **wissen,** 102 (*chart*)
principal parts of verbs, A14–A16 (*chart*)
probability
  expressed by future tense, 335
  expressed by **wohl/wahrscheinlich,** 335
pronouns
  dative case, 158 (*chart*)
  demonstrative, 74, A13 (*chart*)
  interrogative, 339–340
  as objects of prepositions, 164–165
  personal, 34 (*chart*), A13 (*chart*)
  possessive, 93 (*chart*)
  reflexive, 248–249, (*charts*)
  relative, 335–336, A13 (*chart*)
proper names, genitive case of, 217–272

Q

questions
  denn, used as particle in, 42
  direct, 245
  indirect, 245
  with interrogative pronouns,
    41, 46 *ST*
  with **wo-**compounds, 364
  word order in, 41–42
  yes/no, 42, 245
quotation marks, 399

R

reading strategies, 45–46, 76, 105–106, 139,
  140, 168, 198–199, 229–230, 253–254,
  283–284, 314–315, 343–344, 375,
  402–403, 426
reflexive
  pronouns, 248–249 (*charts*),
    250–251
  verbs, 248–249, 250–251
relative clauses, 335–336
relative pronouns, 336 (*chart*)
requests. *See* imperative

S

Satzklammer, 125–126, 128
scheinen, with dependent infinitive plus
  zu, 395
schwache Verben, 218
sein
  as auxiliary, 221, 400
  imperative of, 134
  past participle of, 217, A15
  used in present perfect tense, 217
  present tense of, 40 (*chart*)
  simple past of, 194 (*chart*)
  subjunctive I of, 398 (*chart*), 400
  subjunctive II of, 372
seit, 165
sentence bracket, 125–126, 128
separable-prefix verbs, 124–125, 223–224

setzen, 191
  sich setzen, 191 *ST*
sich, 191 *ST*
Sie vs. du, 3, 34
simple past tense, 217, 308, A16 (*chart*)
  of auxiliary verbs (haben, sein,
    werden), 195 (*chart*), A16 (*chart*)
  of modal verbs, 196 (*chart*)
  passive constructions in, 417
  of strong verbs, 310 (*chart*)
  of weak verbs, 308 (*chart*)
  of werden, 311
sitzen, 189
so ... wie (nicht so ... wie), 227
sollen, 129 (*chart*). *See also* modal
    auxiliary verbs
sondern vs. aber, 216
Spaß machen, 30, 32 *ST*, 158
spelling reform, A20
starke Verben, 218
stecken, 191
stehen, 163, 192 *ST*
stellen, 191
stem-vowel changing verbs, 58 *ST*,
    62, 73 (*chart*)
Strauss, Levi, 380
strong verbs, 218, 220, 310
  past participles of, 220 (*chart*)
  principal parts of,
    A14–A15 (*chart*)
  simple past of, 310 (*chart*)
  subjunctive I of, 398
  subjunctive II of, 365
studieren vs. lernen, 27 *ST*
subject in sentence. *See* nominative case
subjunctive, A18 (*charts*)
subjunctive I, 397–398
  past tense, 400–401, A18 (*chart*)
  present tense, 397–398, A18 (*chart*)
  use of in indirect discourse, 397–398
subjunctive II, 364, 365 (*chart*), 372–373
  of haben, 365 (*chart*), 372
  of modal auxiliary verbs, 365
  past tense, A18 (*chart*)
  present tense, A18 (*chart*)
  of sein, 372
  of strong verbs, 365
  of weak verbs, 365
subjunctive mood, 364. *See also*
    subjunctive I; subjunctive II
  with würde plus infinitive, 367
subordinate clause, 244
subordinating conjunctions, 244
superlative form, 301–302, 305

T

telephone numbers, 10
tense
  future, 333 (*chart*), A17 (*chart*)
  past perfect, 313, A17 (*chart*)
  present, 36
  present perfect, 217–218, A17 (*chart*)
  simple past, 195, 196, 217, 308, 310,
    311, A16–A17 (*chart*)
time
  of day, 114, 115 *ST*, 116 *ST*, 118, 119
  expressions of, 116, 119, 141, 193,
    210 *ST*, 297 *ST*

official, 115 *ST*
prepositions for expressing, 193–194
two-part verbs. *See* separable-prefix verbs
two-way prepositions, 186–187

U

um ... herum, 101
um ... zu, plus infinitive, 395–396
umlauts, 4
un-, 66 *ST*

V

ver-, 223
verbs. *See also* tense; haben; modal
    auxiliary verbs; sein; strong verbs;
    weak verbs; werden
  change of condition, 221
  conjugation of, A16–A19 (*charts*)
  with dative objects, 162–163
  ending in -ieren, 218
  finden (present tense), 36
  with fixed prepositions, 361
  heißen (present tense), 36
  with inseparable prefixes, 223
  mixed, 311
  möchte, 364
  motion, 221
  position in sentence, 40
  present participles of, 424–425
  present tense of, 36
  principal parts of, A14–A16 (*chart*)
  reflexive, 248–249, 250–251
  with separable prefixes, 124–125, 223
  simple past tense, A16 (*chart*)
  and stem-vowel changes, 58 *ST*,
    62, 73 (*chart*)
  strong, 220
  weak, 218, 310, A17 (*chart*)
viel/mehr, 226
von, 165
  as agent in passive voice, 419
vowel changes. *See* stem-vowel changing
    verbs

W

wahrscheinlich, 335
wann, as interrogative, 41
wäre, 372
warum, as interrogative, 245
was, as interrogative, 245
was für (ein), 339
weak masculine nouns, 65
weak verbs, 218, 308
  past participles of, 218
  simple past tense of, 308 (*chart*)
  subjunctive I of, 398–400
  subjunctive II of, 365
weil, 244
welcher, 67. *See also* der-words
wem, 157. *See also* interrogative words
wen, 69. *See also* interrogative words
wenn, 244
wenn-clause, 368. *See also*
    subjunctive mood
wer, 69. *See also* interrogative words
werden, 102
  as auxiliary of future tense, 333, 334
  as auxiliary of passive constructions,
    417–418, 423

  with passive infinitive, 423
  present tense of, 102 (*chart*)
  sein as auxiliary with, 221
  simple past tense of, 311
  subjunctive of, 398
  three ways of functioning of, 418
wessen, 271. *See also* interrogative
    words
wishes, 368. *See also* subjunctive
    mood
wissen, 102
  vs. kennen, 103
  present tense of, 102 (*chart*)
  subjunctive I of, 398
  subjunctive II of, 365
wo, 166, 187
wo-compounds, 166, 187, 364
woher, 46 *ST*, 166
wohin, 166, 187, 191
wohl, expressing probability, 335
wollen, 129 (*chart*). *See also* modal
    auxiliary verbs
word order, 40
  of accusative objects, 161
  and connectors, 154 *ST*
  of dative objects, 161
  of direct and indirect object, 161
  fixed position of conjugated verb
    (*chart*), 40
  in main clauses, 40
  in questions, 41–42
würde, in polite requests,
    365, 367

Y

yes/no questions, 41–42

Z

zip codes (Postleitzahl), 10
zu, 151 *ST*, 158, 165, 393, 395
  brauchen/scheinen with, 395
  in infinitive clause with ohne,
    395–396
  in infinitive clause with um,
    395–396
  infinitive with, 393
zuerst, 154 *ST*
zuletzt, 154 *ST*

CULTURE

academic subjects, 29, A12
addresses, 10 *KT*, 11 *KT*
apartments, 52 *KT*, 53 *KT*, 54
Amish, in America, 380
Anschlagzettel, 51
art, 204–205
BAföG (Bundesausbildungsförderungs-
    gesetz), 353 *KT*
Berlin, 438
bicycling, 222 *KT*
birthdays, 106, 107 *KT*
Celsius scale, 215 *KT*
characteristics and interests,
    personal, 30, 32 *KT*
cities, 267, 290–291
clothing sizes, 150 *KT*
country names, 11 *KT*
days of week, 108, 141
drugstore vs. pharmacy, 246 *KT*

du vs. Sie, 3 *KT*
Einwohnermeldeamt, 24 *KT*
environment, 414, 415 *KT,* 422 *KT*
Erfurt, 290
Euro, 54 *KT*
European Union (EU), 352
Fahrenheit scale, 215 *KT*
family relationships, 83, 84, 85 *ST,* 86 *ST*
food specialties, 152, 156, 175–178, 180, 182 *KT,* 254 *KT*
foreigners in Germany, 47 *KT*
forms of address, 3
furniture, 56– 57, 79
German history (1939–2005), 433–435, 439 *KT,* 443
German school system, 332 *KT*
German-speaking areas, 16 *KT,* 47 *KT*
Germany, facts about, 305 *KT*
global problems, 410
greetings, 2–3 *KT,* 6, 8 *KT*
health, 236 *KT*
health spas, 240 *KT*
holidays, 89–90, 91 *ST*
hotels, 260–263
housing, 52–53, 56–57, 80, 390
immigration, German, to America, 381
invitations, 61 *ST*
Kaiser-Wilhelm-Gedächtniskirche, 435 *KT*
Köln, 290
Ladenschlussgesetz, 368 *KT*
Lebenslauf, 331
metric system, 153 *ST*
military service, 347 *KT*
money, 54 *KT,* 352 *KT, 353* KT
music, 121, 122 *ST*
names, 12 *KT*
newspapers, 386
Nürnberg, 290–291
pharmacy vs. drugstore, 246 *KT*
postal abbreviations for European countries, 11 *KT*
recycling, 415 *KT*
restaurants, 177 *KT,* 180, 183 *KT,* 185 *KT*
school, 332 *KT*
seasons, 212
shopping, 57, 79–80, 145, 153 *KT,* 368 *KT*
size (height), 23 *ST*
speed limits in Europe, 415 *KT*
sports, 207, 222 *KT,* 235, 236 *KT*
telephone numbers, 10
television, 384–385, 387, 388 *KT*
theater, 121 *KT,* 122 *ST*

tourist information, 264 *KT*
travel, 294
UNO, 409
vacations, 296 *KT*
weather, 212
Wittenberg, 270 *KT*
zip codes (Postleitzahl), 10, 12, 13

READINGS

"Dialog," Nasrin Siege, 46
"So wohne ich," 77
"Wie feierst du deinen großen Tag?" 106
"Immer das gleiche," Christine Wuttke, 139
"Im Hutladen," Kurt Valentin, 169
"Die Soße," Ekkehard Müller, 199
"Vergnügungen," Bertolt Brecht, 231
"Sage mir, was du isst ... Was das Frühstück über den Charakter verrät," Monika Hillemacher, 255
"Die Gitarre des Herrn Hatunoglu," Heinrich Hannover, 284
"The American Dream," Bernd Maresch, 316
"Karriere beim Film," *JUMA,* 344
"Fahrkarte, bitte," Helga M. Novak, 376
"Gute Freunde im Netz," Kerstin Kohlenberg, 404
"Was in der Zeitung steht," Reinhard Mai, 426
"Wir leben im Verborgenen," Ceja Stojka, 439
"Briefe an Herbert Hoover," 441

VIDEOCLIPS

E 16, 1 45, 2 75, 3 105, 4 137, 5 167, 6 198, 7 229, 8 252, 9 283, 10 313, 11 342, 12 374, 13 402, 14 425, A 444

VOCABULARY

academic subjects, 18
apartments and houses, 52–53, 79–80
body parts, 238, 258
cardinal numbers, 89 *KT*
characteristics (of people), 48
city-related terms, 288
classroom conversation (terms), 17–18
clock times, 142, 420
clothing, 146, 147, 171
colors, 172
days of week, 108, 141
descriptions, personal, 21–23

direction giving, 268, 288–289
discussion, 411–412
employment, 348–349
entertainment terms, 142, 202, 207–209, 232
environment, 414, 430
family terms, 108
fitness and health, 258–259
food, 152, 154, 171, 175–178, 180, 202
furnishings, 56–57, 78
German-speaking countries, 18
global problems, 410–411, 430
greetings and farewells, 3, 5–6, 17–18
health and fitness, 235–236, 241 *ST,* 240 *KT*
holidays, 108
hotels, 263 *ST,* 288
housing (houses), 378
leisure time activities, 207–209
metric system, 153 *ST*
money matters, 351–353, 378
months, names of, 108
musical instruments, 286
newspapers, 386, 406
numbers
  cardinal, 18
  ordinal, 109
occupations and professions, 323, 326–327, 348–349
personal information, terms for, 22–23, 30, 48–49
questions, 49
restaurant terms, 176–177, 180, 181, 202
seasons, 212, 232
shopping, 79–80, 145, 153 *KT,* 171
shops, types of, 171
sports, 207, 208–209, 232, 235
studying, 27 *ST,* 48, A12
technology, 406
television, 384–385, 387, 406
theater terms, 142
time
  of day, 141
  duration, 210 *ST,* 297 *ST*
tourism, 320–321
transportation, 320–321
travel, 294, 320–321
weather, 212, 214, 215 *KT,* 232–233
work, world of, 348–349

Credits

Photos *Page 1* © Ulrike Welsch; *2* (top) © JOKER/Ausserhofer/ullstein bild/The Granger Collection, New York; *2* (bottom) © Paul Vozdic/Getty Images; *3* © Ulrike Welsch; *20* © Grabowsky/ullstein bild/The Granger Collection, New York; *21* © Yavuz Arslan/Peter Arnold, Inc.; *22* (top left) © Kevin Galvin; *22* (right) © Ulrike Welsch; *22* (bottom left) © Owen Franken/Stock Boston; *30* © Beryl Goldberg; *50* © Ullstein bild/The Granger Collection, New York; *60* (left) © Photofusion Picture Library/Alamy; *60* (right) © Robert Harding Picture Library Ltd/Alamy; *66* © Benja Weller/Das Fotoarchiv; *82* © Sylent Press/ullstein bild/The Granger Collection, New York; *83* (camera) © Bartomeu Amengual/Age Fotostock; *83* (inset) © Wolfgang Kaehler; *87* © Koelb Stern; *90* (top) © Schmied-HELGA LADE FOTOAGENTUR/Peter Arnold, Inc.; *90* (bottom) © BAV-HELGA LADE FOTOAGENTUR/Peter Arnold, Inc.; *91* © McGraw-Hill, Inc; *103* © Archive Fur Kunst und Geschichte, Berlin; *106* © Monica Clyde; *107* © Wodicka/ullstein bild/The Granger Collection, New York; *101* (all) © Archive Fur Kunst und Geschichte, Berlin; *111* (top) © Bilderdienst Suddeutscher Verlag, Munchen; *111* (bottom) © Archive Fur Kunst und Geschichte, Berlin; *112* © Peter Hirth/Peter Arnold, Inc.; *121* (left) © Zefa/Damm/Corbis; *121* (right) © Visum/ullstein bild/The Granger Collection, New York; *135* © Monica Clyde; *139* © Eckel/ullstein bild/The Granger Collection, New York; *144, 154, 167* Courtesy of Monica Clyde; *174* © oterhauser/CARO/ullstein bild/The Granger Collection, New York; *177* (top left) © Mahns Techau/ullstein bild/The Granger Collection , New York; *177* (top right) © Fishman/ullstein bild/The Granger Collection, New York; *177* (bottom left) © Ilona Studre/ullstein bild/The Granger Collection, New York; *177* (bottom right) © Lengemann/ullstein bild/The Granger Collection, New York; *179* © Chybiak/ullstein bild/The Granger Collection, New York; *182* (left) © Brinckmann/ullstein bild/The Granger Collection, New York; *182* (middle) © Kujath/ullstein bild/The Granger Collection, New York; *182* (right) © Springer-Pics/ullstein bild/The Granger Collection, New York; *191* Courtesy of Monica Clyde; *204* (top left) © 1995 Artists Rights Society, NY/Bild Kunst, Bonn © AKG London; *204* (middle) © 1995 Artists Rights Society, NY/Bild Kunst, Bonn; *204* (bottom left) © 1995 Artists Rights Society, NY/Bild Kunst, Bonn © AKG London; *205* "Der Leser" by Jiri Georg Dokoupil. Reproduced with permission. *206* © Ric Ergenbright; *212* (top left) © Julie Marcotte/Stock Boston; *212* (top right) © Reichmann; *212* (bottom left) © Fridmar Dann/eStock; *212* (bottom right) © David Ulmer/Stock Boston; *218* © Ulrike Welsch/PhotoEdit; *222* © CARO/Riedmiller/ ullstein bild/The Granger Collection, New York; *231* © Topham/The Image Works; *234* © Oberhäuser/CARO/ullstein bild/The Granger Collection, New York; *236* (top) © Michael P. Gadomski/Photo Researchers; *236* (middle) © Teich/Caroullstein bild/The Granger Collection, New York; *236* (bottom) © Photodisc; *240* © Wodicka/ullstein bild/The Granger Collection, New York; *246* © Ulrike Welsch; *254* © MEDIUM / ullstein bild / The Granger Collection, New York; *260* © Bob Krist/CORBIS; *264* © Keith/ullstein bild/The Granger Collection, New York; *270* (left) Lutherstadt Wittenberg; *270* (right) © Lange/ullstein bild/The Granger Collection, New York; *276* © Monica Clyde; *281* © Shaun Egan/Getty; *282* © Jochen Kallhardt/BlueBox; *290* (both) © Helga Lade/Peter Arnold; *209* (bottom right) © Hartmann/ullstein bild/The Granger Collection, New York; *292* © Theissen/ullstein bild/The Granger Collection, New York; *296* © Werner Otto/AGE Fotostock; *298* © Thomas Rosenthal/ullstein bild/The Granger Collection, New York; *305* © Merlen/The Granger Collection, New York; *309* © Ulrike Welsch/PhotoEdit; *310* © Visum/The Image Works; *316* © Pixtal/age fotostock; *317* © Digital Vision; *322* © Visum/Plus 49/The Image Works; *331* © David Young-Wolff/PhotoEdit, Inc.; *332* © Helga Lade/Peter Arnold; *344* © Scherf/ullstein bild/The Granger Collection, New York; *345* (top) © KPA Honorar & Belege/ullstein bild/The Granger Collection, New York; *345* (bottom) © Stephane Masson/Corbis; *346* © KPA Honorar & Belege/ullstein bild/The Granger Collection, New York; *350* © Visum/Plus 49/The Image Works; *352* (bottom) © Jüschke/ullstein bild/The Granger Collection, New York; *368* © Neuhauser/ullstein bild/The Granger Collection, New York; *382* © CARO Fotoagentur/A. Bastian; *383* (left) © Wodicka/ullstein bild/The Granger Collection, New York; *383* (right) © Joko/ullstein bild/The Granger Collection , New York; *394* © Wodicka/ullstein bild/The Granger Collection, New York; *400* © KPA/ullstein bild/The Granger Collection, New York; *404* © Froese/ullstein bild/The Granger Collection, New York; *408* © Helga Lade/Peter Arnold, Inc.; *411* © Royalty Free/Corbis; *415* (bottom) © David Frazier/The Image Works; *416* (left) © BananaStock/Alamy; *432* © Paul Thompson/ImageState/Heritage Image Partnership; *433* (left) © Topham/The Image Works; *433* (right) © UPI/Bettmann Archive; *434* (top) © Keystone Press/The Image Works; *434* (bottom) © Bettmann Archive; *435* © Dallas and John Heaton/Stock Boston; *436* (top left) © ReutersNewmedia Inc./CORBIS; *436* (top right) © UPI Bettmann Archive; *436* (bottom right) © Topham/The Image Works; *437* © Michael Schwarz/The Image Works; *438* (top) © Rufus F. Folkks/Corbis; *438* (bottom): © Walter Bibikow/AGE; *443* © Kaiser/Caro/ullstein bild/The Granger Collection, New York.

Realia *Page 5* (bottom right) © Eva Heller, from *Vielleicht sind wir eben zu verschieden;* *6* (elephant cartoon) Michel & Co.; *8* (top left) *Funk Uhr;* *9* © *Berliner Morgenpost;* *10* Gebecke Buchandlung & Antiquariat, Quedlinburg; *11* Volkswagen AG; *37* (top left) Courtesy of Universitat Leipzig, Uni-Journal 4/25, photo Randy Kühn; (top right) Photo: PR;

About the Authors

Robert Di Donato is Professor of German and Chair of the Department of German, Russian, and East Asian Languages with Hebrew and Arabic at Miami University in Oxford, Ohio. He received his Ph.D. from The Ohio State University. He is the chief academic and series developer of *Fokus Deutsch,* a telecourse with accompanying texts and materials for teaching and learning German, and coauthor of *The Big Yellow Book of German Verbs.* He has also edited two volumes for the Central States Conference, written articles about language methodology, and has given numerous keynote speeches, workshops, and presentations – both in the United States and abroad – on teaching methods and teacher education. He has won a number of awards for his work in language education, including the Florence Steiner Award for Leadership in Foreign Language Education.

Monica D. Clyde is a native of Düsseldorf. She received her Ph.D. in German literature from the University of California at Berkeley. She has taught German language and literature at Mills College, Cañada College, the Defense Language Institute, and the College of San Mateo. She was Director of Faculty Development and Scholarship at Saint Mary's College of California until her retirement in 2003. She coauthored *Texte und Kontexte* and was a contributor to *Mosaik: Deutsche Kultur und Literatur,* Third Edition, both intermediate college-level German textbooks.

Jacqueline Vansant received her Ph.D. from the University of Texas at Austin. She has taught at Hamilton College and Miami University in Oxford, Ohio, and currently teaches at the University of Michigan Dearborn, where she also heads the German section of the Department of Humanities. Her particular interest in language pedagogy lies in reading and reading strategies. She has written widely on contemporary Austrian literature and culture, served as coeditor of *Modern Austrian Literature* from 2000–05, and is presently working on a book entitled *Austria: Made in Hollywood.*